T.O. 1F-104A-1
F-104A, B, C, & D
U.S.A.F. SERIES AIRCRAFT
FLIGHT
MANUAL
F04606-68-A-0067-0008
This publication replaces T.O. 1F-104A-1-4, dated 15 September 1967, and T.O. 1F-104A-1 and 1F-104C-1, dated 31 October 1964. This publication incorporates Safety Supplements T.O. 1F-104A-1SS-71, -72, -73, -75, -76, -77, -78, T.O. 1F-104C-1SS-77, -79, -80, -81, -82 and Operational Supplements T.O. 1F-104A-1-4S-1 and -2 and T.O. 1F-104A-1S-10, -12, -13, -14, -15, -16, -17, -18, -19, -20, -21, T.O. 1F-104C-1S-15, -17, -18, -19, -20, -21, -22, -23, -24, -25, -26, -27, -28. Refer to T.O. 0-1-1-4A for current status of Flight Manuals, Safety/Operational supplements, and Flight Crew Checklists.
Commanders are responsible for bringing this manual to the attention of all personnel cleared for operation of affected aircraft.
PUBLISHED UNDER AUTHORITY OF THE SECRETARY OF THE AIR FORCE

1 June 1968

Reproduction for non-military use of the information or illustrations contained in this publication is not permitted without specific approval of the issuing service (NASC or USAF). The policy for use of Classified Publications is established for the Air Force in AFR 205-1 and for the Navy in Navy Regulations, Article 1509.

Technical Orders are normally distributed promptly after printing. Date(s) shown on the title page (lower right) are for identification only. This is not a distribution date. Processing time sometimes causes distribution to only appear to have been delayed.

INSERT LATEST CHANGED PAGES. DESTROY SUPERSEDED PAGES.

LIST OF EFFECTIVE PAGES

NOTE: The portion of the text affected by the changes is indicated by a vertical line in the outer margins of the page. Changes to illustrations are indicated by miniature pointing hands. Changes to wiring diagrams are indicated by shaded areas.

Dates of issue for original and changed pages are:
Original . . 0 . . 1 June 1968

Page No.	Change No.
Title	0
A	0
i thru iii	0
iv Blank	0
v	0
vi	0
1-1 thru 1-98	0
2-1 thru 2-28	0
3-1 thru 3-36	0
4-1 thru 4-55	0
4-56 Blank	0
5-1 thru 5-17	0
5-18 Blank	0
6-1 thru 6-27	0
6-28 Blank	0
9-1 thru 9-10	0

CURRENT FLIGHT CREW CHECKLISTS

T.O. 1F-104A-1CL-1 1 June 1968

ISBN 978-1-940453-42-2
WWW.PERISCOPEFILM.COM

Upon receipt of the second and subsequent changes to this technical order, personnel responsible for maintaining this publication in current status will ascertain that all previous changes have been received and incorporated. Action should be taken promptly if the publication is incomplete.

*The asterisk indicates pages changed, added, or deleted by the current change.

ADDITIONAL COPIES OF THIS PUBLICATION MAY BE OBTAINED AS FOLLOWS: **USAF**

USAF ACTIVITIES.—In accordance with T.O. 00-5-2.

NAVY ACTIVITIES.—Use Publications and Forms Order Blank (NAVAIR 140) and submit in accordance with instructions thereon. For listing of available material and details of distribution see Naval Air Systems Command Publications Index NAVAIR 00-500.

TABLE OF CONTENTS

F52-0-1-4

READ THE FINE PRINT !!

SCOPE. This manual contains the information necessary for safe and efficient operation of the F-104A, B, C and D airplane. These instructions provide you with a general knowledge of the airplane, its characteristics, and specific normal and emergency operating procedures. Your flying experience is recognized, and therefore basic flight principles are not discussed.

SOUND JUDGMENT. This manual provides the best possible operating instructions under most circumstances, but it is not a substitute for sound judgment. Multiple emergencies, adverse weather, terrain, etc. may require modification of the procedures.

PERMISSIBLE OPERATIONS. The Flight Manual takes a positive approach and normally states only what you CAN do. Unusual operations or configurations (such as asymmetrical loading) are prohibited unless specifically covered herein. Clearance must be obtained from SMAMA before any questionable operation not specifically permitted in this manual, is attempted.

STANDARDIZATION AND ARRANGEMENTS. Standardization procedures ensure that the scope and arrangement of all flight manuals are identical. The Manual is divided into ten nearly independent sections to simplify using it as a reference manual. The first three sections must be read thoroughly and be understood fully before attempting to fly the airplane. The remaining sections provide important information for safe and efficient mission accomplishment. All airspeeds referenced throughout the manual are knots indicated airspeed unless otherwise specified.

OPERATIONAL AND SAFETY SUPPLEMENTS. Information involving normal operation as well as safety will be promptly forwarded to you by Supplements. Supplements affecting loss of life will get to you in 48 hours by TWX; those concerning serious damage to equipment, within 10 days by mail. Each safety supplement and operational supplement includes a status page which lists the current flight manual, checklist and current safety supplements or operational supplements. Any rescissions or replacements of supplements as of the status page date will be included also. Also, the status of each Supplement affecting your airplane can be determined by referring to the Weekly Numerical Index and Requirement Table, Fighter Aircraft Supplements (T.O. 0-1-1-4A). The Flight Manual title page and the title block of each Supplement should also be checked to determine their effect on existing supplements. You must remain constantly aware of the status of all supplements—current supplements must be complied with but there is no point in restricting your operation by operating in accordance with a replaced or rescinded supplement.

CHECKLISTS. The Flight Manual contains amplified procedures. Abbreviated procedures have been issued as separate technical orders. Refer to the back of the title page for T.O. number and date of your latest checklist. Line items in the Flight Manual and checklists are identical with respect to arrangement and item number. Whenever a supplement affects the abbreviated checklist, a change to the checklist will be issued concurrently with the supplement.

HOW TO GET PERSONAL COPIES. Each flight crew member is entitled to personal copies of the Flight Manual, Supplements, and Checklists. The required quantities should be ordered before you need them to ensure their prompt receipt. Check with your supply personnel; it is their job to fill your technical order requests. Basically, you must order the required quantities on the Numerical Index and Requirement Table (T.O. 0-1-1-4). Technical Orders 00-5-1 and 00-5-2 give detailed information for properly ordering these publications. Make sure a system is established at your base to deliver these publications to the flight crews immediately upon receipt.

FLIGHT MANUAL AND CHECKLIST BINDERS. Looseleaf binders and sectionalized tabs are available for use with your Manual. These are obtained through local purchase procedures and are listed in the Federal Supply Schedule (FSC Group 75, Office Supplies, Part 1). Binders are also available for carrying your abbreviated checklist. These binders contain plastic envelopes into which individual checklist pages are inserted. The binders are obtainable in three capacities through normal Air Force supply channels under the following stock list numbers: 7510-766-4268, -4269, and -4270 for 15, 25, and 40-envelope binders, respectively. Check with your supply personnel for assistance in securing these items.

WARNINGS, CAUTIONS, AND NOTES. The following definitions apply to "Warnings," "Cautions," and "Notes" found throughout the manual.

WARNING — Operating procedures practices, etc., which will result in personal injury or loss of life if not correctly followed.

CAUTION — Operating procedures, practices, etc., which if not strictly observed will result in damage to or destruction of equipment.

Note — An operating procedure, condition, etc., which it is essential to highlight.

YOUR RESPONSIBILITY — TO LET US KNOW. Every effort is made to keep the Flight Manual current. Review conferences with operating personnel and a constant review of accident and flight test reports assure inclusion of the latest data in the manual. However, we cannot correct an error unless we know of its existence. In this regard, it is essential that you do your part. Comments and questions regarding this manual or any phase of the Flight Manual program are welcomed. AF Form 847 will be used for recommending changes to the Flight Manual in accordance with instructions in AFR 60-9 and T.O. 00-5-1. These will be forwarded through command headquarters to SMAMA, McClellan AFB, California, Attn: SMNSTA. AF Forms 847's are routed to SMNSTA for control purposes only. Technical content of the Flight Manual is the responsibility of the Flight Manual Manager (SMNEAH) and all comments and questions transmitted by means other than the AF Form 847 will be submitted directly to the Flight Manual Manager, SMAMA, McClellan AFB, California, ATTN: SMNEAH.

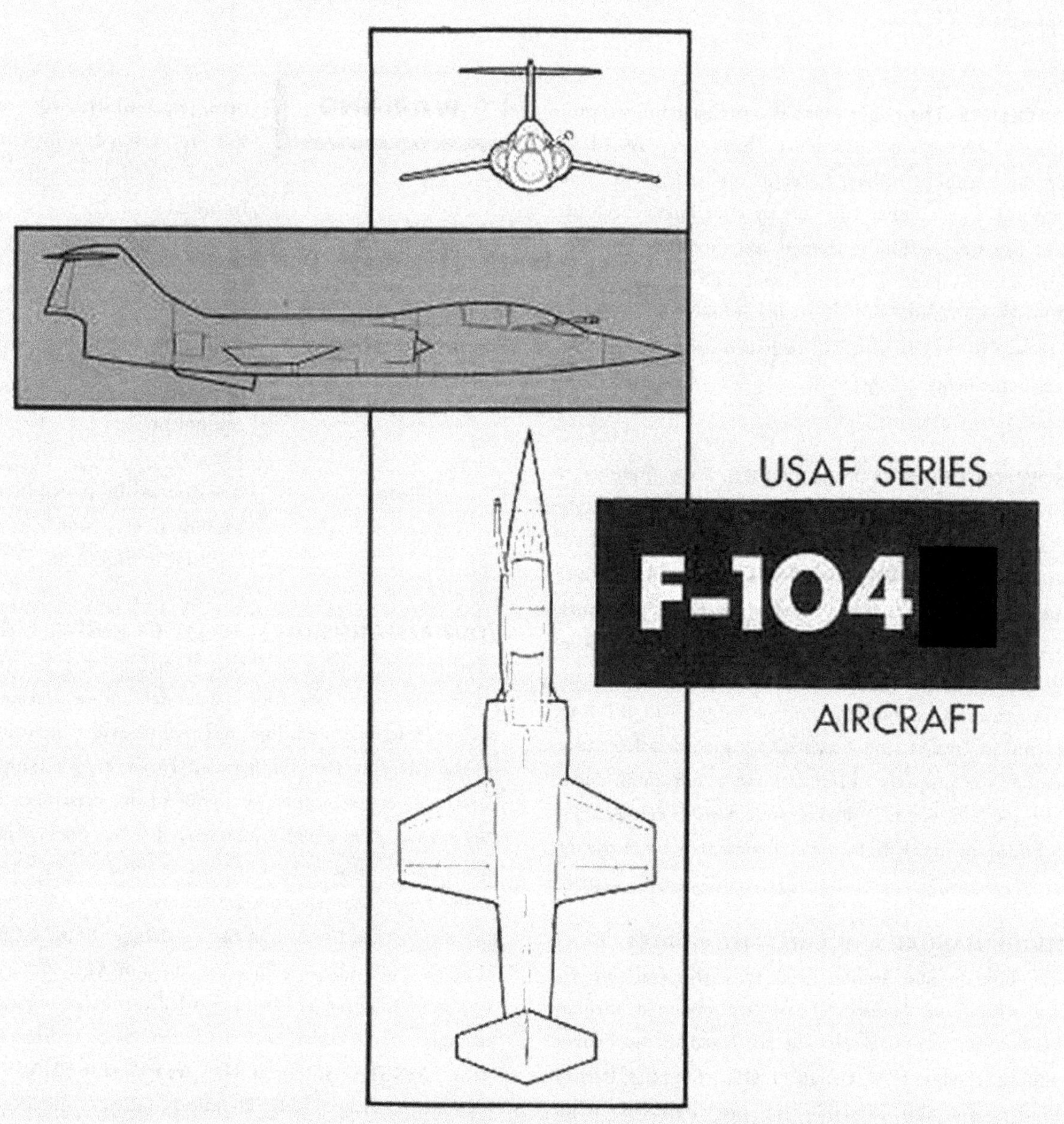

This page intentionally left blank.

CODING

This Flight Manual provides the necessary pilot operating information for F-104A, B, C and D aircraft. A coding system of reversed type letters or numbers in a square or circle is used to identify the data pertaining to an individual aircraft/engine combination.

F-104A and B aircraft have either the J79-GE-3B or J79-GE-19 engine installed. F-104C and D have the J79-GE-7A engine installed. The coding is as follows:

AIRCRAFT	CODE	ENGINE	CODE
F-104A	A	J79-GE-3B	3B
F-104B	B	J79-GE-19	19
F-104C	C	J79-GE-7A	7A
F-104D	D		

Separate appendices are provided for A B aircraft equipped with the 3B engine, A B aircraft equipped with the 19 engine, and for C D aircraft equipped with the 7A engine. Appendices not applicable to the aircraft/engine combination being used may be removed from the flight manual.

When complete paragraphs are affected, the appropriate code letter will appear at the end of the first line or opposite the heading. Notes, cautions, and warnings are treated as individual paragraphs regarding coding.

Coding for individual sentences within the body of the text will appear at the end of the sentence to which it applies.

Steps of procedure have the code following the action item.

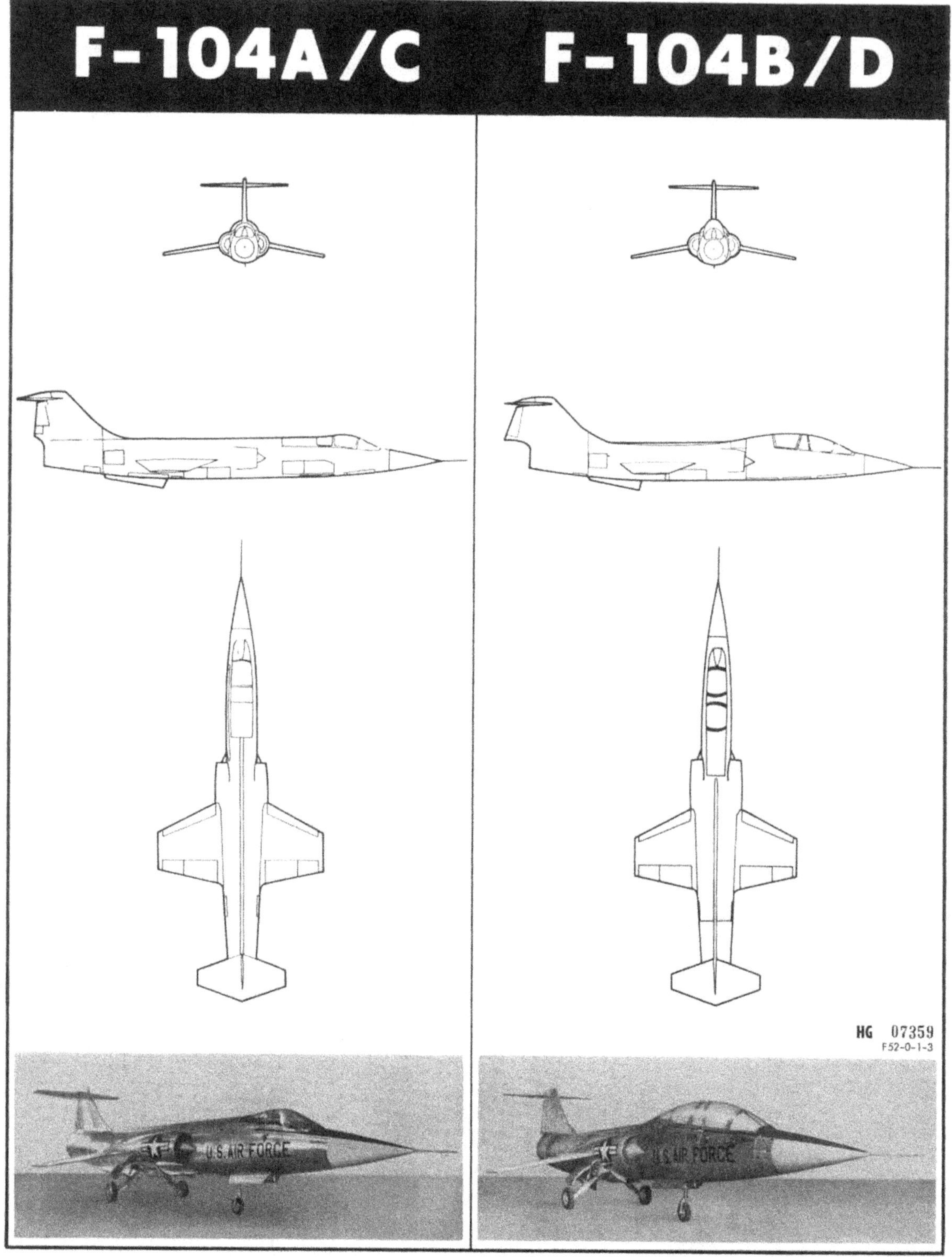

Figure 1-1

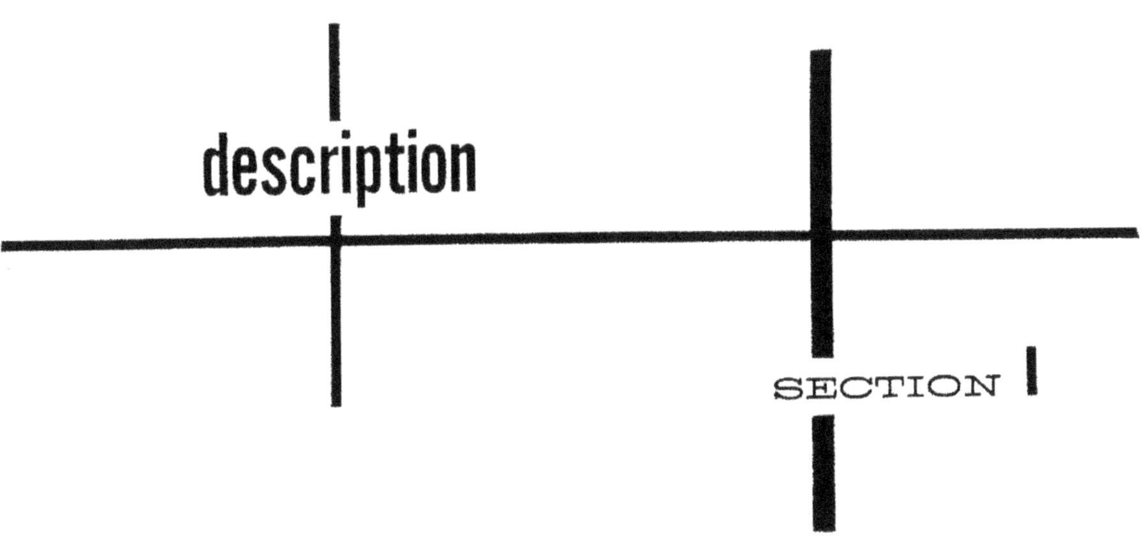

TABLE OF CONTENTS

THE AIRCRAFT. (See figure 1-1)

F-104 aircraft are high-performance day and night fighters powered by an axial-flow, turbojet engine with afterburner. F-104A and C are single place aircraft; F-104B and D are two place aircraft. The aircraft, built by Lockheed Aircraft Corporation, are designed for cruise at high subsonic speeds and combat at high supersonic speeds. Notable features of the aircraft include extremely thin flight surfaces, short straight wings with negative dihedral, irreversible hydraulically powered ailerons, and a controllable horizontal stabilizer mounted at the top of the vertical stabilizer. The wings, with leading and trailing edge flaps, have a boundary layer control system which is used in conjunction with the trailing edge flap to reduce landing speeds. A drag chute is installed to reduce the landing roll. In-flight escape is accomplished by an upward ejection system.

AIRCRAFT DIMENSIONS.

Overall dimensions of the aircraft are as follows:

Wing span	21.94 feet
Length	54.77 feet
Height (to top of vertical stabilizer)	13.49 feet
Tread	8.79 feet

GENERAL ARRANGEMENT A C

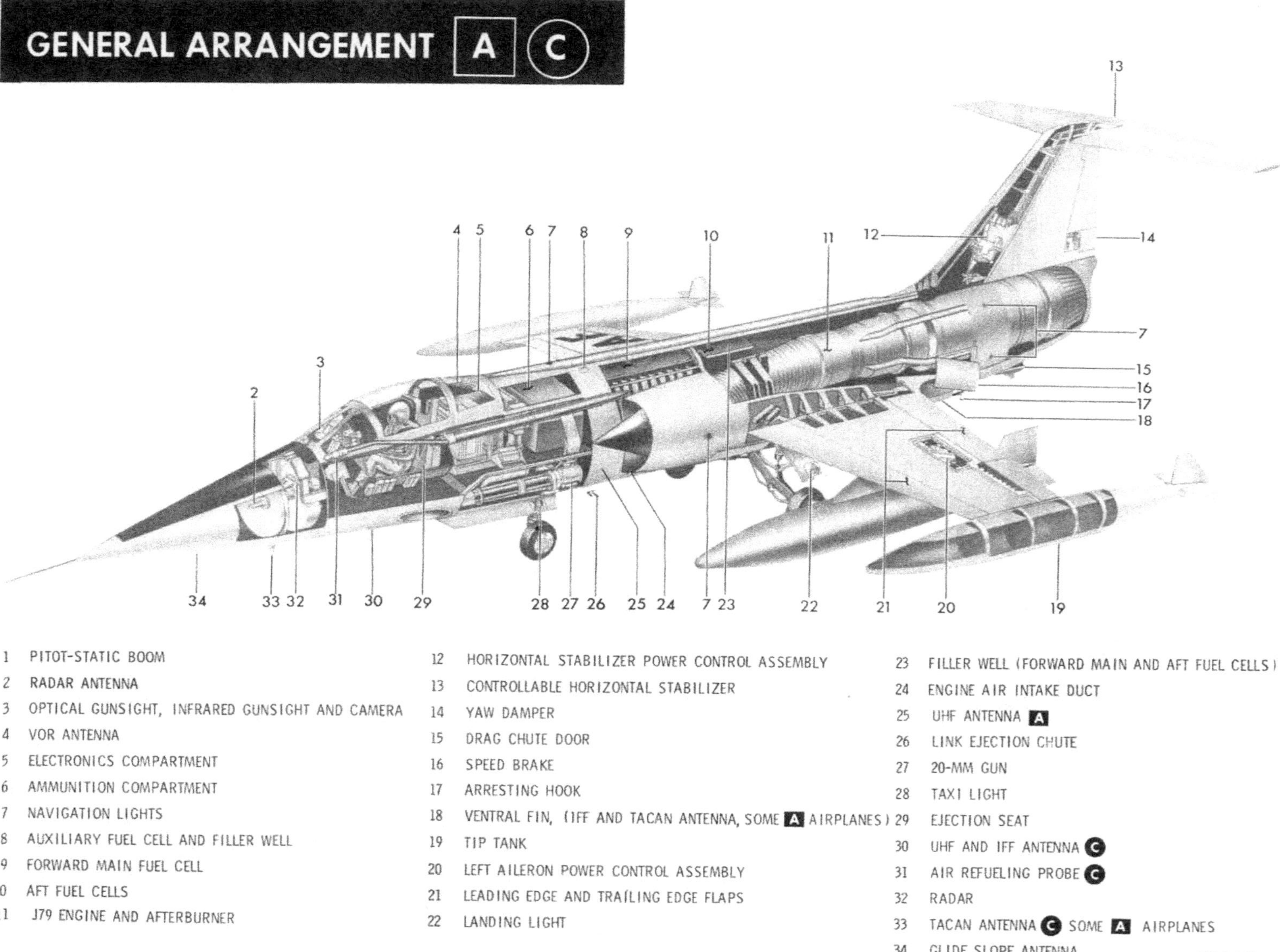
1 PITOT-STATIC BOOM
2 RADAR ANTENNA
3 OPTICAL GUNSIGHT, INFRARED GUNSIGHT AND CAMERA
4 VOR ANTENNA
5 ELECTRONICS COMPARTMENT
6 AMMUNITION COMPARTMENT
7 NAVIGATION LIGHTS
8 AUXILIARY FUEL CELL AND FILLER WELL
9 FORWARD MAIN FUEL CELL
10 AFT FUEL CELLS
11 J79 ENGINE AND AFTERBURNER
12 HORIZONTAL STABILIZER POWER CONTROL ASSEMBLY
13 CONTROLLABLE HORIZONTAL STABILIZER
14 YAW DAMPER
15 DRAG CHUTE DOOR
16 SPEED BRAKE
17 ARRESTING HOOK
18 VENTRAL FIN, (IFF AND TACAN ANTENNA, SOME A AIRPLANES)
19 TIP TANK
20 LEFT AILERON POWER CONTROL ASSEMBLY
21 LEADING EDGE AND TRAILING EDGE FLAPS
22 LANDING LIGHT
23 FILLER WELL (FORWARD MAIN AND AFT FUEL CELLS)
24 ENGINE AIR INTAKE DUCT
25 UHF ANTENNA A
26 LINK EJECTION CHUTE
27 20-MM GUN
28 TAXI LIGHT
29 EJECTION SEAT
30 UHF AND IFF ANTENNA C
31 AIR REFUELING PROBE C
32 RADAR
33 TACAN ANTENNA C SOME A AIRPLANES
34 GLIDE SLOPE ANTENNA
F52-0-1-39

Figure 1-2

TYPICAL GENERAL ARRANGEMENT B D

NOTE

△1 AF SERIALS 57-1320 AND SUBSEQUENT D

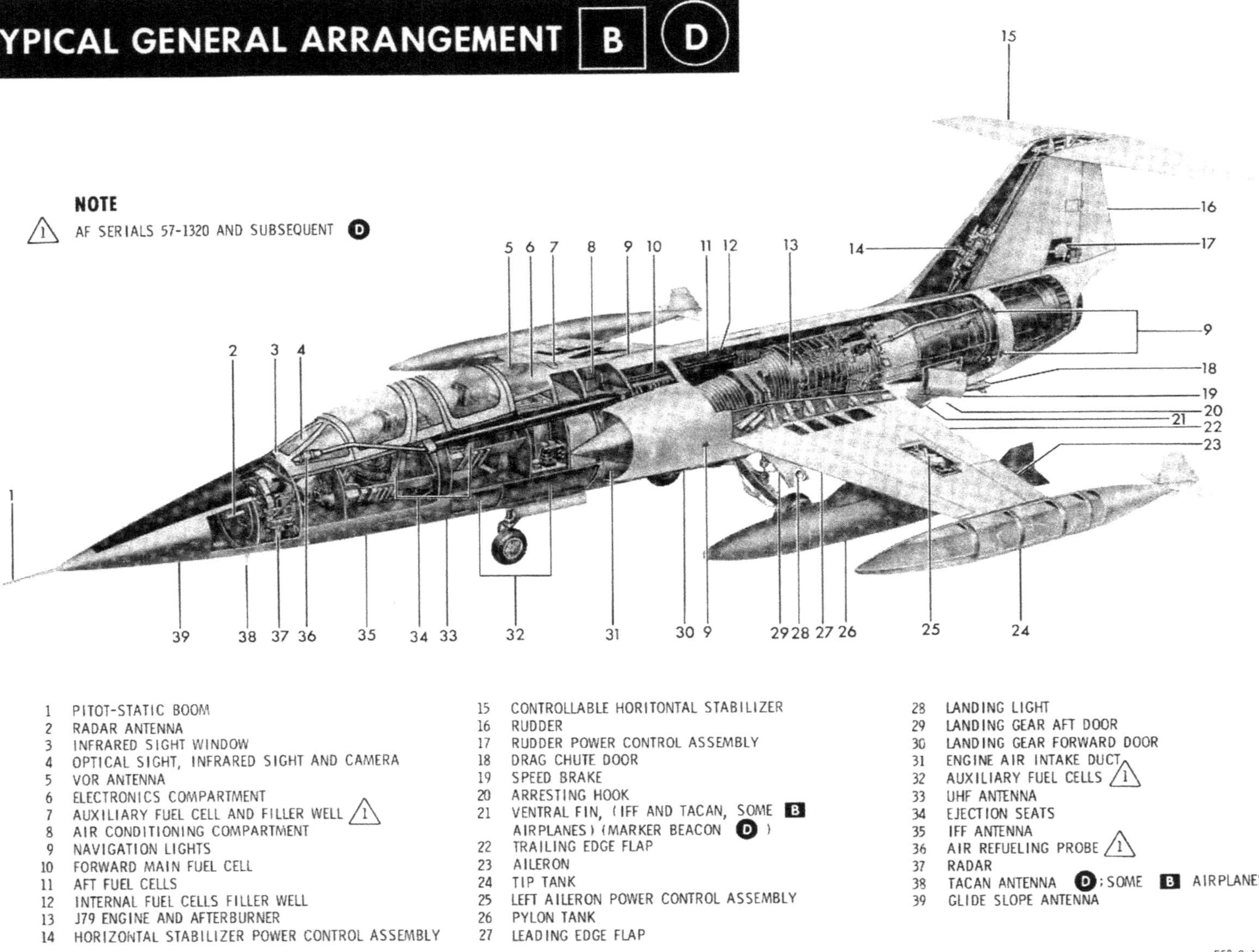

1 PITOT-STATIC BOOM
2 RADAR ANTENNA
3 INFRARED SIGHT WINDOW
4 OPTICAL SIGHT, INFRARED SIGHT AND CAMERA
5 VOR ANTENNA
6 ELECTRONICS COMPARTMENT
7 AUXILIARY FUEL CELL AND FILLER WELL △1
8 AIR CONDITIONING COMPARTMENT
9 NAVIGATION LIGHTS
10 FORWARD MAIN FUEL CELL
11 AFT FUEL CELLS
12 INTERNAL FUEL CELLS FILLER WELL
13 J79 ENGINE AND AFTERBURNER
14 HORIZONTAL STABILIZER POWER CONTROL ASSEMBLY
15 CONTROLLABLE HORITONTAL STABILIZER
16 RUDDER
17 RUDDER POWER CONTROL ASSEMBLY
18 DRAG CHUTE DOOR
19 SPEED BRAKE
20 ARRESTING HOOK
21 VENTRAL FIN, (IFF AND TACAN, SOME B AIRPLANES) (MARKER BEACON D)
22 TRAILING EDGE FLAP
23 AILERON
24 TIP TANK
25 LEFT AILERON POWER CONTROL ASSEMBLY
26 PYLON TANK
27 LEADING EDGE FLAP
28 LANDING LIGHT
29 LANDING GEAR AFT DOOR
30 LANDING GEAR FORWARD DOOR
31 ENGINE AIR INTAKE DUCT
32 AUXILIARY FUEL CELLS △1
33 UHF ANTENNA
34 EJECTION SEATS
35 IFF ANTENNA
36 AIR REFUELING PROBE △1
37 RADAR
38 TACAN ANTENNA D; SOME B AIRPLANES
39 GLIDE SLOPE ANTENNA

F52-0-1-5

Figure 1-3

MAIN DIFFERENCE TABLE

	A	B	C	D
	AF-56-748 THROUGH AF-56-882	AF-56-3720 THROUGH AF-56-3724 AF-57-1294 THROUGH AF-57-1313	AF-56-883 THROUGH AF-57-930	AF-57-1314 THROUGH AF-57-1334
CREW	ONE	TWO	ONE	TWO
ENGINE	J79-GE-3B J79-GE-19 OR J79-GE-11A	J79-GE-3B J79-GE-19 OR J79-GE-11A	J79-GE-7A	J79-GE-7A
POWER RUDDER	NO	YES	NO	YES
NOSE GEAR	RETRACTS FORWARD	RETRACTS AFT	RETRACTS FORWARD	RETRACTS AFT
REFUELING PROVISIONS	GRAVITY FILLING	GRAVITY FILLING	PRESSURE TYPE SINGLE-POINT AND AIR REFUELING	GRAVITY FILLING ON UNMODIFIED AIRCRAFT. PRESSURE TYPE SINGLE-POINT AND AIR REFUELING ON MODIFIED AIRCRAFT (503 C/W)
OXYGEN SYSTEM	5 LITER LIQUID WITH PRESSURE SUIT CONTROL PANEL AND MD-1 PRESSURE DEMAND REGULATOR	10 LITER LIQUID WITH PRESSURE SUIT CONTROL PANEL AND MD-1 PRESSURE DEMAND REGULATOR	5 LITER LIQUID WITH PRESSURE SUIT CONTROL PANEL AND MD-1 PRESSURE DEMAND REGULATOR	10 LITER LIQUID WITH PRESSURE SUIT CONTROL PANEL AND MD-1 PRESSURE DEMAND REGULATOR
ARMAMENT	ONE 20-MM GUN	TWO AIM-93 MISSILES	ONE 20-MM GUN	

F52-0-1-9

Figure 1-4

GROSS WEIGHT. A

The approximate gross weights of the airplane (including full internal fuel, ammunition and pilot) are as follows:

No external load . . . . . 19,600 pounds
AIM-9B missiles . . . . . 20,000 pounds
Tip tanks . . . . . 22,300 pounds
AIM-9B missiles and pylon tanks . . . . . 23,200 pounds
Tip tanks and pylon tanks . . . . . 25,300 pounds

GROSS WEIGHT. B

The approximate gross weights of the airplane (including full internal fuel and two crew members) are as follows:

No external stores . . . . . 18,100 pounds
AIM-9B missiles . . . . . 18,400 pounds
Tip tanks . . . . . 20,700 pounds
AIM-9B missiles and pylon tanks . . . . . 21,600 pounds
Tip tanks and pylon tanks . . . . . 23,900 pounds

Note

Installation of the 19 engine increases the above gross weight approximately 600 pounds.

GROSS WEIGHT. C D

The approximate takeoff gross weight of the aircraft without external stores is tabulated below. C weight includes full internal fuel, 725 rounds of ammunition, and a pilot. D weights include full internal fuel and two crewmembers.

C . . . . . 19,800 lb
D (AF Serials prior to 57-1320) . . . . . 18,000 lb
D (AF Serial 57-1320 and subsequent) . . . . . 18,700 lb

(The increased weight of AF Serials 57-1320 and subsequent aircraft is due to the addition of auxiliary fuel.) The gross weight of various external stores available for carriage is tabulated below. The figures include the weights of the devices used for attachment to the airplane.

Tip tanks (including fuel) . . . . . 2700 lb
Tip AIM-9B missiles . . . . . 400 lb
Fuselage AIM-9B missiles . . . . . 600 lb
Fuselage SUU-21 dispenser . . . . . 700 lb
Pylon tanks (including fuel) . . . . . 3100 lb
Pylon, LAU-3/A launchers and rockets. . . . 1170 lb
Aerial refueling probe . . . . . 100 lb

Note

All the above gross weights are approximate and should not be used for detailed mission planning.

ARMAMENT. A B

The basic armament consists of two AIM-9B air-to-air guided missiles, carried one on each wing tip in place of the tip tanks. A Aircraft also incorporate a 20mm electrically operated gun located in the lower left side of the forward fuselage. Its ammunition supply of 725 rounds is fired at an average rate of 4000 rounds per minute.

ARMAMENT. C D

The basic armament consists of one 20-mm electrically operated gun located in the lower left side of the forward fuselage. Its ammunition supply of 725 rounds is fired at an average rate of 4000 rounds per minute C. The aircraft also incorporates provisions for carrying conventional and special weapons.

ENGINE.

The aircraft is powered by a General Electric J79 turbojet engine. (See figures 1-5, 1-6.) Its sea-level static thrust rating is approximately 15,800 pounds at Maximum thrust (with full afterburning) 3B 7A and 17,500 19 and approximately 10,000 pounds at Military thrust (Maximum thrust without afterburning) 3B 7A and 11,870 19. A 17-stage axial-flow compressor, driven by a three-stage turbine produces a compressor, pressure ratio of 12 to 1 3B 7A and 13.4 to 1 19. An anti-icing system and (a guided expansion) 19 (aerodynamic, variable-area) 3B 7A exhaust nozzles system are provided. The inlet guide vanes and the first six stages of stator blades are variable; they are positioned by engine fuel pressure and are automatically controlled by the engine fuel control unit as a function of engine speed and engine air inlet temperature. By varying vane angle, the volume of air passing through the engine is controlled. This reduces the possibility of compressor stall. Three turbine wheels are bolted together and move as a unit on a common shaft which is splined directly to the compressor rotor. The exhaust gases, after passing through the turbine section, pass into the afterburner. At this point, additional fuel may be injected into the hot gases and burned, thus producing considerable thrust augmentation. The exhaust gases then pass through the variable area exhaust nozzles and are dispersed into the atmosphere.

ENGINE CONTROL SYSTEM. 19

The engine employs the concept of constant corrected speed control of the rotor, rather than a constant physical speed control, to provide maximum compressor operation efficiency. Engine speed is controlled so that the corrected speed, in general, remains at 100% rpm. Physical engine speed, in other words, is increased as the ambient temperature rises, up to 103.5% rpm. Available thrust is a smoothly increasing function of Mach number.

Exhaust gas temperature is controlled as a function of physical engine speed when operating at Military or afterburner power settings.

In summary, during Military and afterburner operation the rpm may not be 100% but will vary with CIT. Likewise, exhaust gas temperature will vary with rpm. See figure 5-2 for rpm and exhaust gas temperature scheduling.

ENGINE FUEL SYSTEM.

The engine fuel system (figures 1-7, 1-8) incorporates a fuel control unit which is supplied fuel from an engine-driven high pressure fuel pump. Fuel is supplied to this pump at aircraft boost pump pressure. Metered fuel from the engine fuel control unit is piped through an oil cooler and then enters the pressurizing and drain valve. The outlet from the pressurizing valve is connected directly to the main fuel manifold. An afterburner fuel system is also provided. Refer to Afterburner System, this Section.

Engine Fuel Pump.

An engine-driven fuel pump, having a centrifugal boost element and two gear-type elements, supplies the high fuel pressure required by the engine fuel system. The centrifugal boost element supplements fuel cell boost pump pressure. Failure of the centrifugal boost element cannot affect engine operation except at high fuel demands required during low altitude – high Mach number conditions. Either of the gear-type elements is capable of supplying a sufficient flow of fuel to the engine fuel control unit if one element should fail.

ENGINE FUEL FILTER.

The engine fuel filter removes contamination from the fuel before it enters the fuel control unit. In the event the filter becomes clogged the bypass valve will permit unfiltered fuel to flow to the fuel control unit.

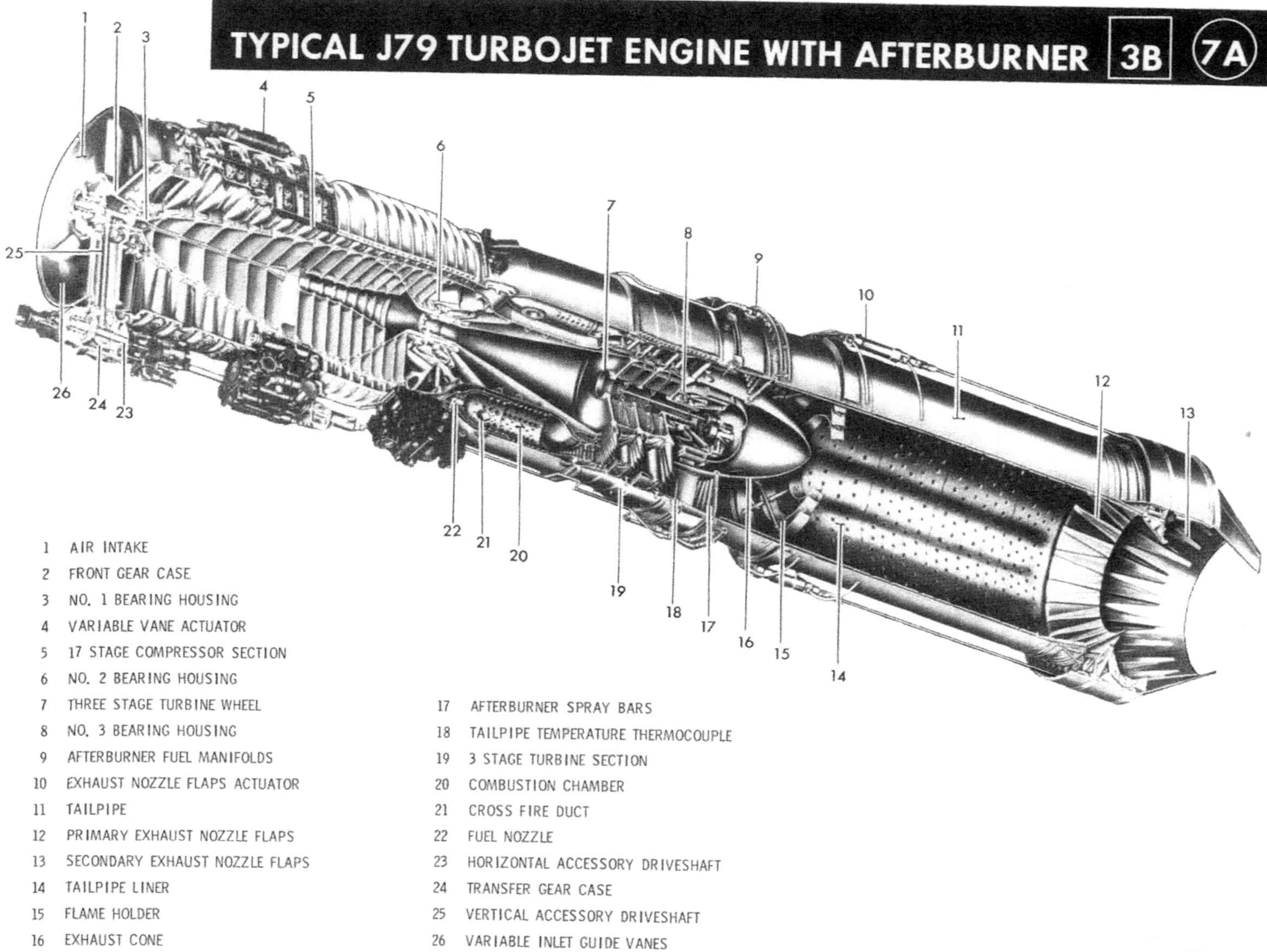
TYPICAL J79 TURBOJET ENGINE WITH AFTERBURNER
3B
7A
1 AIR INTAKE
2 FRONT GEAR CASE
3 NO. 1 BEARING HOUSING
4 VARIABLE VANE ACTUATOR
5 17 STAGE COMPRESSOR SECTION
6 NO. 2 BEARING HOUSING
7 THREE STAGE TURBINE WHEEL
8 NO. 3 BEARING HOUSING
9 AFTERBURNER FUEL MANIFOLDS
10 EXHAUST NOZZLE FLAPS ACTUATOR
11 TAILPIPE
12 PRIMARY EXHAUST NOZZLE FLAPS
13 SECONDARY EXHAUST NOZZLE FLAPS
14 TAILPIPE LINER
15 FLAME HOLDER
16 EXHAUST CONE
17 AFTERBURNER SPRAY BARS
18 TAILPIPE TEMPERATURE THERMOCOUPLE
19 3 STAGE TURBINE SECTION
20 COMBUSTION CHAMBER
21 CROSS FIRE DUCT
22 FUEL NOZZLE
23 HORIZONTAL ACCESSORY DRIVESHAFT
24 TRANSFER GEAR CASE
25 VERTICAL ACCESSORY DRIVESHAFT
26 VARIABLE INLET GUIDE VANES
F52-0-1-6

Figure 1-5

J79 TURBOJET ENGINE WITH AFTERBURNER 19

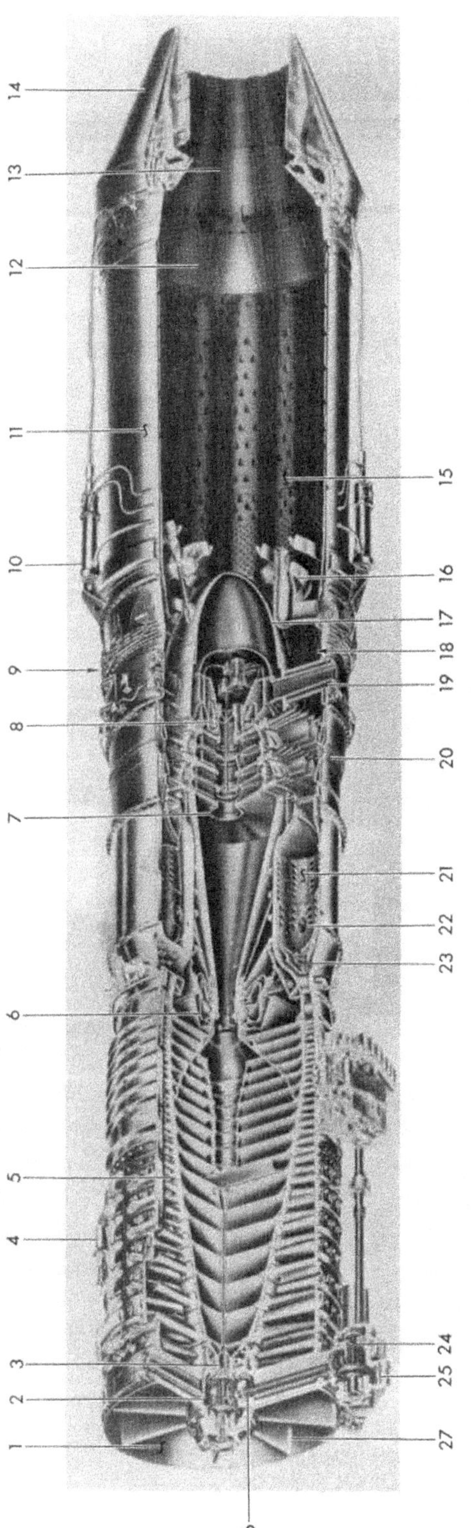

1 AIR INTAKE
2 FRONT GEAR CASE
3 NO. 1 BEARING HOUSING
4 VARIABLE VANE ACTUATOR
5 17 STAGE COMPRESSOR SECTION
6 NO. 2 BEARING HOUSING
7 THREE STAGE TURBINE WHEEL
8 NO. 3 BEARING HOUSING
9 AFTERBURNER FUEL MANIFOLDS
10 EXHAUST NOZZLE FLAPS ACTUATOR
11 TAILPIPE
12 PRIMARY EXHAUST NOZZLE FLAPS
13 DIVERGENT EXHAUST NOZZLE FLAPS
14 SECONDARY OUTER NOZZLE FLAPS
15 TAILPIPE LINER
16 FLAME HOLDER
17 EXHAUST CONE
18 AFTERBURNER SPRAY BARS
19 TAILPIPE TEMPERATURE THERMOCOUPLE
20 3 STAGE TURBINE SECTION
21 COMBUSTION CHAMBER
22 CROSS FIRE DUCT
23 FUEL NOZZLE
24 HORIZONTAL ACCESSORY DRIVESHAFT
25 TRANSFER GEAR CASE
26 VERTICAL ACCESSORY DRIVESHAFT
27 COMPRESSOR FRONT FRAME

HG 07358 F52-0-1-2

Figure 1-6

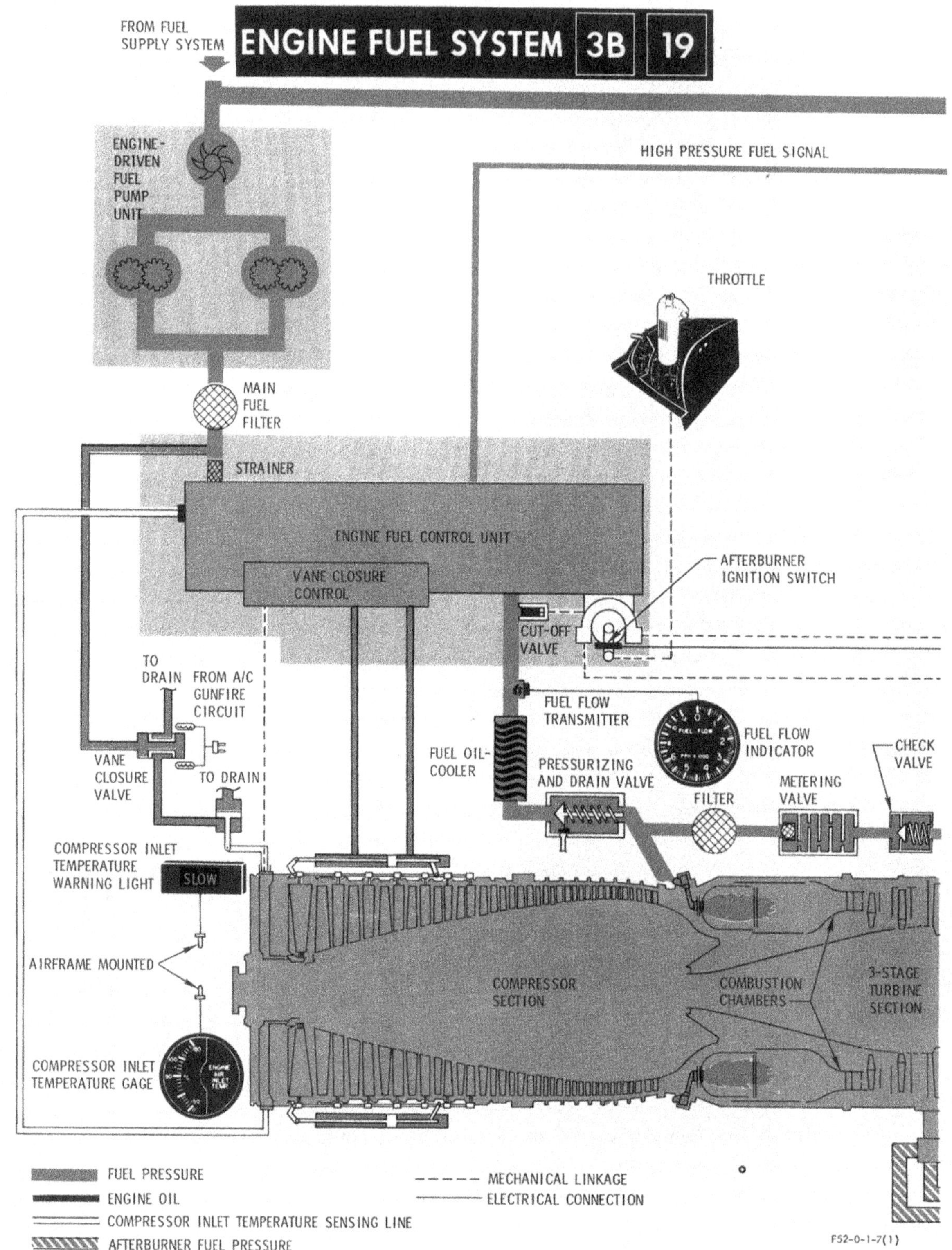
FROM FUEL SUPPLY SYSTEM
ENGINE FUEL SYSTEM 3B 19
ENGINE-DRIVEN FUEL PUMP UNIT
HIGH PRESSURE FUEL SIGNAL
THROTTLE
MAIN FUEL FILTER
STRAINER
ENGINE FUEL CONTROL UNIT
VANE CLOSURE CONTROL
AFTERBURNER IGNITION SWITCH
CUT-OFF VALVE
TO DRAIN
FROM A/C GUNFIRE CIRCUIT
FUEL FLOW TRANSMITTER
FUEL FLOW INDICATOR
CHECK VALVE
VANE CLOSURE VALVE
TO DRAIN
FUEL OIL-COOLER
PRESSURIZING AND DRAIN VALVE
FILTER
METERING VALVE
COMPRESSOR INLET TEMPERATURE WARNING LIGHT
SLOW
AIRFRAME MOUNTED
COMPRESSOR SECTION
COMBUSTION CHAMBERS
3-STAGE TURBINE SECTION
COMPRESSOR INLET TEMPERATURE GAGE
FUEL PRESSURE
ENGINE OIL
COMPRESSOR INLET TEMPERATURE SENSING LINE
AFTERBURNER FUEL PRESSURE
MECHANICAL LINKAGE
ELECTRICAL CONNECTION
F52-0-1-7(1)

Figure 1-7 (Sheet 1 of 2)

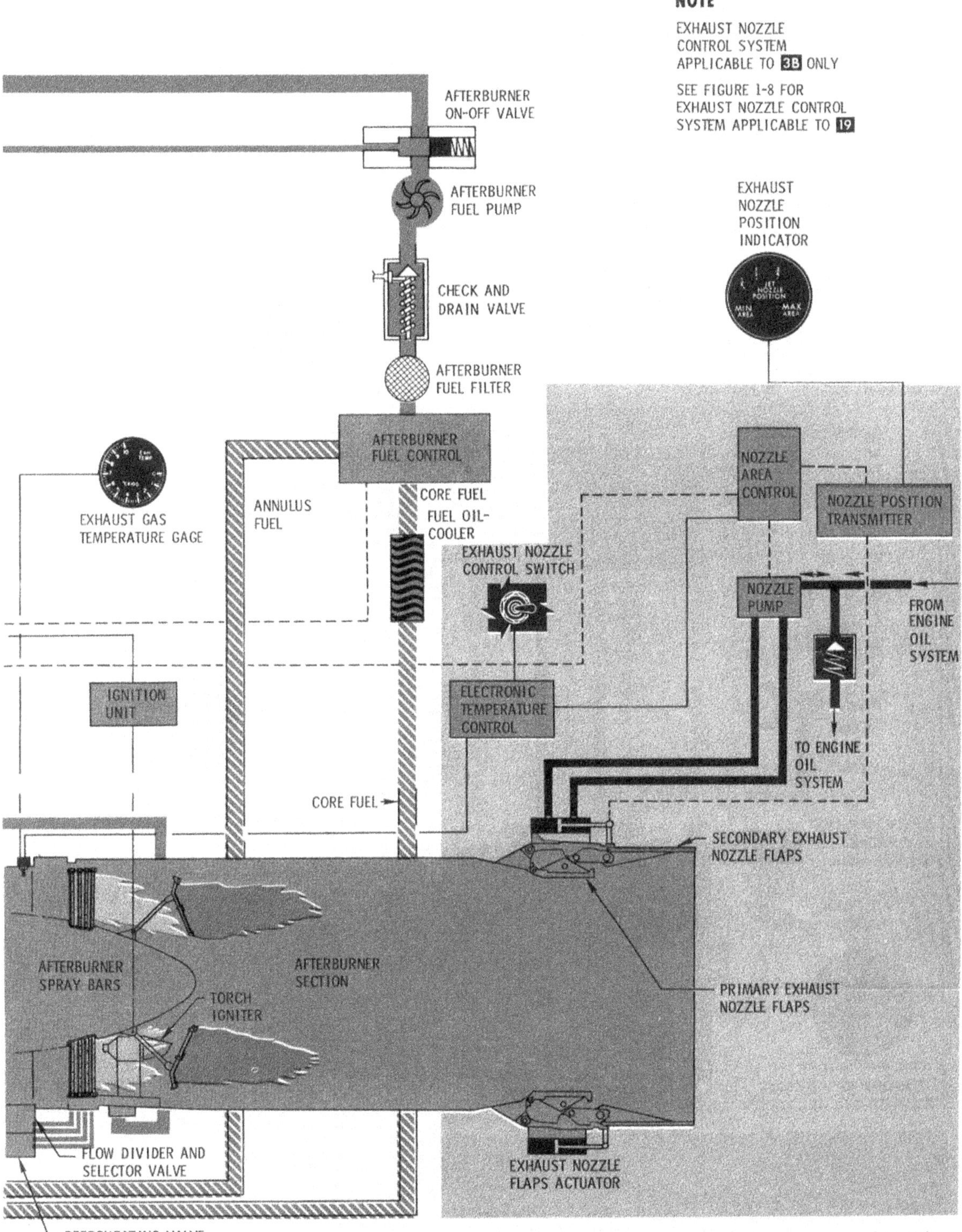
NOTE
EXHAUST NOZZLE CONTROL SYSTEM APPLICABLE TO 3B ONLY
SEE FIGURE 1-8 FOR EXHAUST NOZZLE CONTROL SYSTEM APPLICABLE TO 19
AFTERBURNER ON-OFF VALVE
AFTERBURNER FUEL PUMP
CHECK AND DRAIN VALVE
AFTERBURNER FUEL FILTER
AFTERBURNER FUEL CONTROL
EXHAUST NOZZLE POSITION INDICATOR
NOZZLE AREA CONTROL
NOZZLE POSITION TRANSMITTER
EXHAUST GAS TEMPERATURE GAGE
ANNULUS FUEL
CORE FUEL
FUEL OIL-COOLER
EXHAUST NOZZLE CONTROL SWITCH
NOZZLE PUMP
FROM ENGINE OIL SYSTEM
IGNITION UNIT
ELECTRONIC TEMPERATURE CONTROL
TO ENGINE OIL SYSTEM
CORE FUEL
SECONDARY EXHAUST NOZZLE FLAPS
AFTERBURNER SPRAY BARS
AFTERBURNER SECTION
TORCH IGNITER
PRIMARY EXHAUST NOZZLE FLAPS
FLOW DIVIDER AND SELECTOR VALVE
EXHAUST NOZZLE FLAPS ACTUATOR
PRESSURIZING VALVE
F52-0-1-7(2)

Figure 1-7 (Sheet 2 of 2)

ENGINE FUEL SYSTEM (7A)

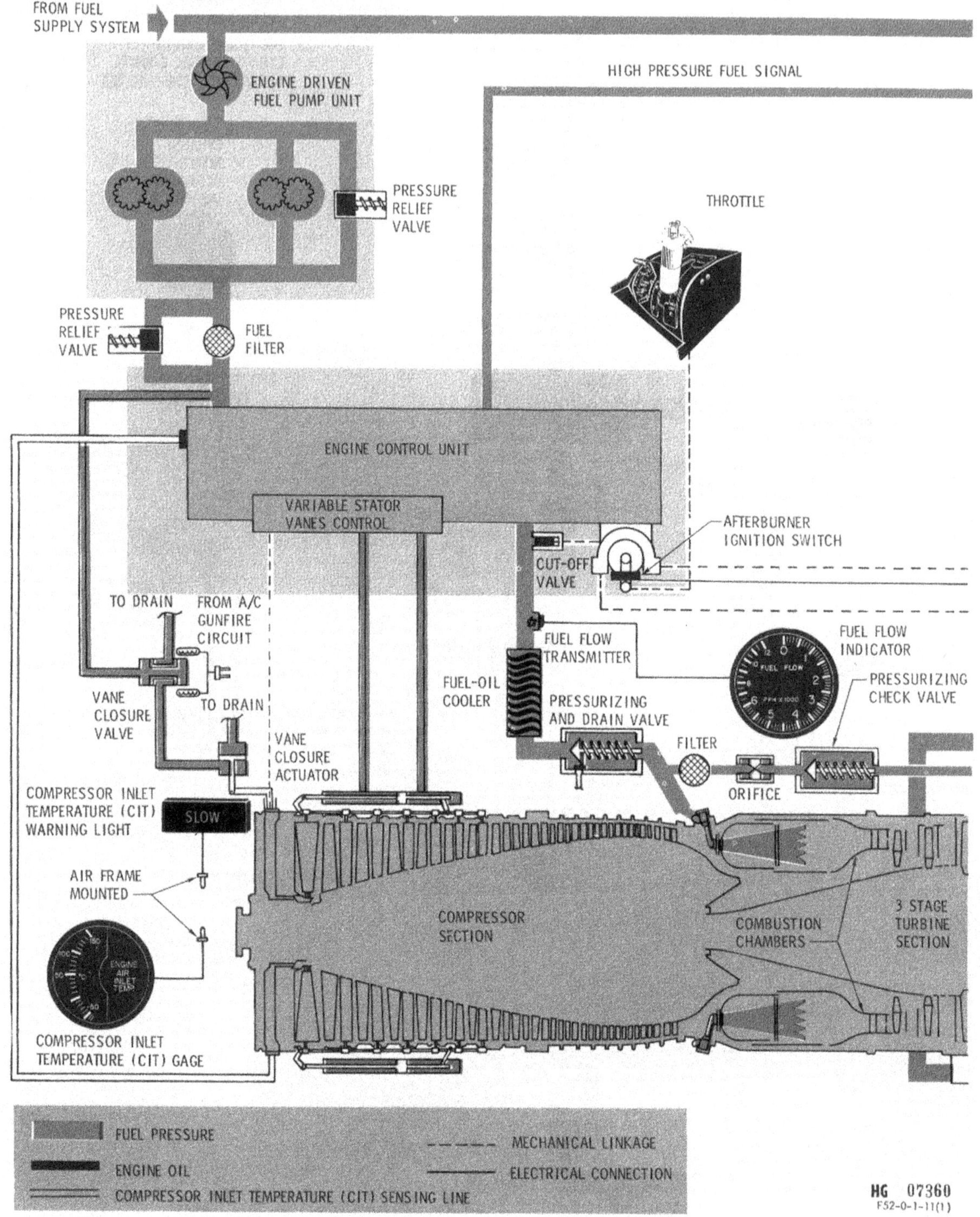

Figure 1-8 (Sheet 1 of 2)

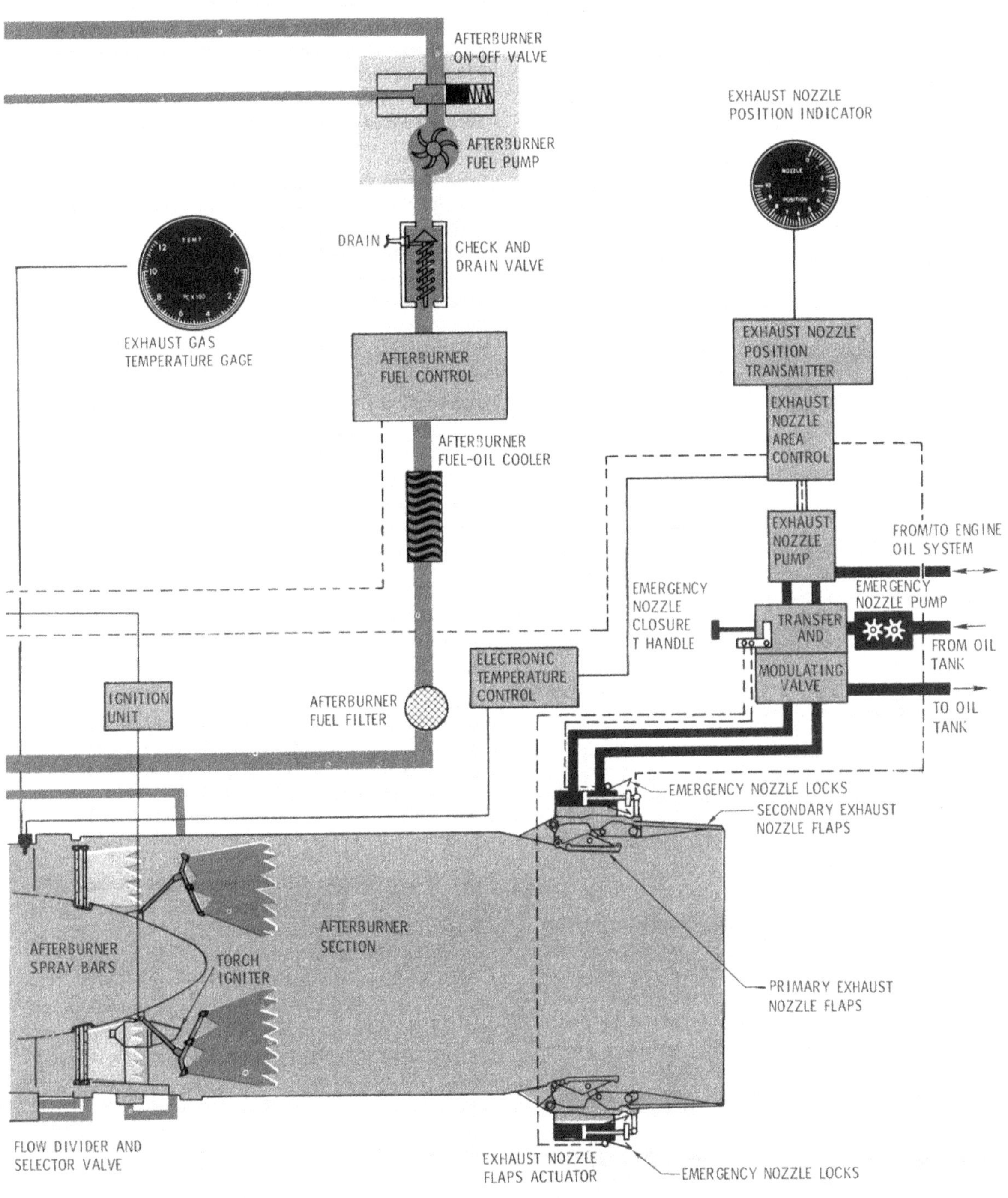
AFTERBURNER ON-OFF VALVE
AFTERBURNER FUEL PUMP
EXHAUST NOZZLE POSITION INDICATOR
DRAIN
CHECK AND DRAIN VALVE
EXHAUST GAS TEMPERATURE GAGE
AFTERBURNER FUEL CONTROL
EXHAUST NOZZLE POSITION TRANSMITTER
EXHAUST NOZZLE AREA CONTROL
AFTERBURNER FUEL-OIL COOLER
EXHAUST NOZZLE PUMP
FROM/TO ENGINE OIL SYSTEM
EMERGENCY NOZZLE CLOSURE T HANDLE
EMERGENCY NOZZLE PUMP
TRANSFER AND
MODULATING VALVE
FROM OIL TANK
ELECTRONIC TEMPERATURE CONTROL
IGNITION UNIT
AFTERBURNER FUEL FILTER
TO OIL TANK
EMERGENCY NOZZLE LOCKS
SECONDARY EXHAUST NOZZLE FLAPS
AFTERBURNER SECTION
AFTERBURNER SPRAY BARS
TORCH IGNITER
PRIMARY EXHAUST NOZZLE FLAPS
FLOW DIVIDER AND SELECTOR VALVE
EXHAUST NOZZLE FLAPS ACTUATOR
EMERGENCY NOZZLE LOCKS
F52-0-1-11(2)

Figure 1-8 (Sheet 2 of 2)

Engine Fuel Control Unit.

The engine fuel control unit is a hydromechanical device which uses engine fuel as the hydraulic controlling medium. Fuel flow to the engine is controlled by the throttle and is delivered and regulated by the engine fuel control unit. Fuel from the engine fuel pump enters the fuel control unit through an inlet strainer. Major basic control elements consist of a metering valve and a bypass valve. The bypass valve maintains a constant pressure head across the metering valve by bypassing excess fuel back to the engine fuel pump inlet. The metering valve is positioned in response to various internal operating signals, and meters fuel to the engine as a function of these integrated signals. A cutoff valve, located in the fuel outlet port of the engine fuel control unit, shuts off the fuel supply to the engine burners when the pilot retards the throttle to OFF. The nozzle area control system is connected to the fuel control unit.

LINKAGE SYSTEM.

Various related signals are transmitted by linkage to provide a single-point control of engine thrust. The linkage consists of throttle linkage, exhaust nozzle control linkage, emergency nozzle closure linkage, and variable stator and inlet guide vane linkage.

Throttle Linkage. The aircraft throttle mechanism rotates the input shaft of the main fuel control unit. The input shaft contains a sheave which converts input shaft rotation into a linear motion of a flexible cable. The flexible cable links the main fuel control unit to the afterburner fuel control and the variable area nozzle control. Thrust selection is provided through rotation of the main fuel control shaft.

Exhaust Nozzle Control Linkage. Signals to control the exhaust nozzle are transmitted to a variable displacement pump through a mechanical linkage. Nozzle position information is transmitted from the exhaust nozzle to the nozzle control and nozzle area sensor by linear motion of a flexible cable 3B 7A and by a pulley feedback system 19 . This motion indicates to the control that the nozzle has reached the required opening.

Emergency Nozzle Closure Linkage 19 , 7A . An emergency nozzle closure linkage transmits a signal representing exhaust nozzle area to the emergency nozzle closure control. Another linkage, connected to the nozzle locks, transmits the signal from the emergency nozzle closure control to the nozzle locks representing proper position of the locking mechanism.

Inlet Guide Vane and Variable Stator Linkage. Information on the position of the inlet guide vanes is transmitted by a linear motion of a flexible cable to the main fuel control unit. This signal indicates when the vanes have become positioned to their scheduled angles. The vane closure valve and actuator act to close the vanes during gunfire to prevent compressor stall.

Inlet Guide Vanes and Variable Stator Vanes Control. The inlet guide vanes and variable stator vanes are mechanically linked and affected by the same control. They are hydraulically positioned as a function of engine air inlet temperature and engine speed to control airflow during the initial stages of compression. The two actuators of this system are supplied with engine fuel pressure from the engine fuel control unit. The mechanical feedback linkage of this system prevents overtravel or vane angle error by transmitting actual vane position to the servo piston in the engine fuel control unit.

Variable Stator Actuators. The variable stator actuators are double-acting hydraulic cylinders which position the inlet guide vanes and variable stator vanes.

Vane Closure Valve. The vane closure valve controls fuel pressure to the variable stator vane closure actuator. The valve is solenoid operated and is activated by a 28-volt dc signal from the gunfire system.

Vane Closure Actuator. The vane closure actuator is a single-acting hydraulic cylinder which mechanically increases the length of the feedback conduit during gunfiring. This causes the main fuel control to close the vanes five degrees.

Inlet Guide Vanes Emergency Reset Switch 3B . An inlet guide vanes emergency reset switch (38, 34, figures 1-12, 1-13) is installed on the lower left portion of the instrument panel. The switch is labeled IGV CONT and has two positions, MAN and AUTO. The switch is placed in the AUTO position for normal ground and inflight operation. The MANUAL position is used for emergency inflight operation. The system is energized through the battery bus.

FUEL OIL-COOLER.

The purpose of the fuel oil-cooler is to remove heat from the engine oil system. This is accomplished by the main flow of fuel acting as a coolant to control the oil temperature. The assembly consists of a fuel oil-cooler, a fuel temperature control valve, and a fuel by-pass valve. The fuel temperature control valve senses oil

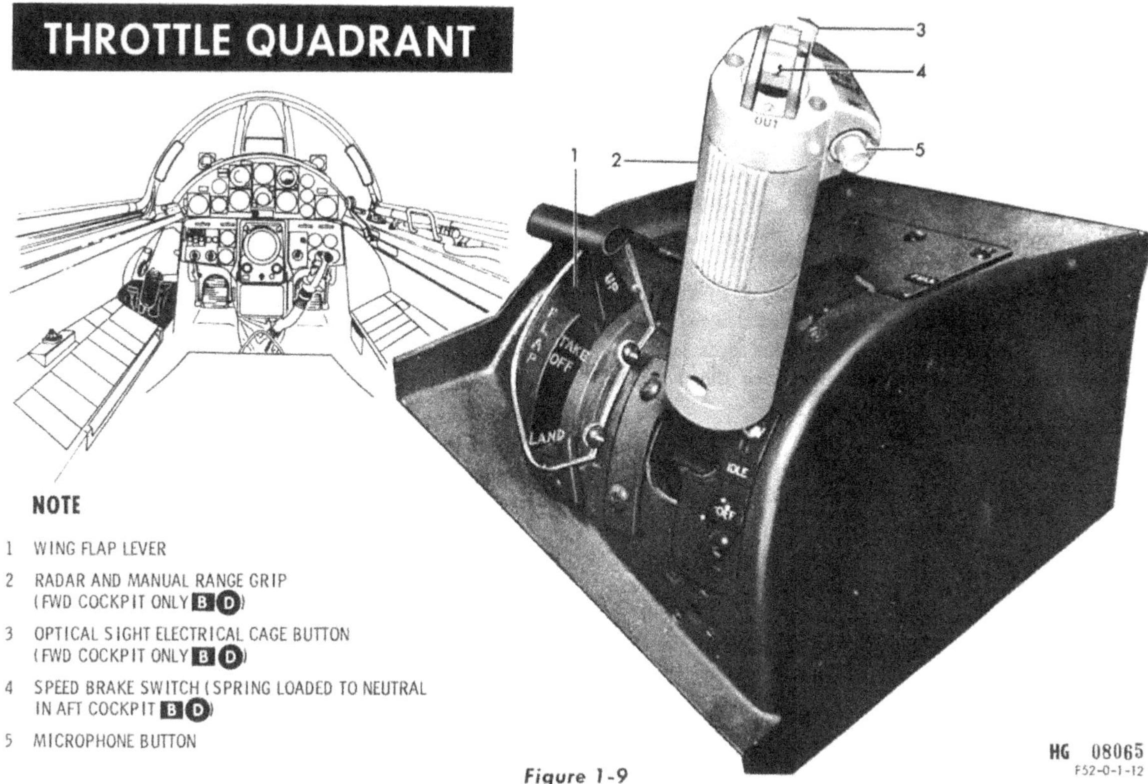

Figure 1-9

outlet temperature and controls routing of the fuel. The bypass valve system is designed so that if the oil is cool it will not go through the cooler; also it allows the fuel to bypass the cooler if the fuel flow becomes high or it will bypass oil if the fuel becomes too hot.

PRESSURIZING AND DRAIN VALVE.

The pressurizing and drain valve maintains back pressure to the engine fuel control unit in order to provide an acceptable fuel pressure level for servo operation. The valve opens to allow fuel to flow to the engine when discharge pressure exceeds a preset value. The drain valve in the unit drains the engine fuel manifold whenever the engine is shut down.

THROTTLE.

The throttle quadrant (figure 1-9) is labeled OFF, IDLE, and FULL. The throttle is spring loaded to the inboard direction so that forward motion from OFF will cause it to drop into IDLE without forcing. Full travel from IDLE to the point where Military thrust is reached is by a straight, forward movement. During engine ground starts the throttle is moved from OFF to IDLE position. This opens the fuel cut-off valve. After the engine has started, advancing the throttle increases engine speed to 100 percent rpm. At this rpm, engine speed is maximum and is governed at this rpm even though the throttle is advanced to maximum afterburner position. Afterburning is initiated by moving the throttle outboard and forward into the afterburner slot. A substantial thrust variation in the afterburner range is possible by moving the throttle in this slot. The throttle linkage is designed to provide the correct amount of friction and to prevent the lever from creeping; therefore, no throttle friction control is provided in the cockpit. A potentiometer with a built-in switch for gunsight manual range control is installed in the grip assembly of the throttle (forward cockpit B D). The throttle also incorporates the speed brake switch and two pushbutton switches, one for the microphone and one for gunsight cage. A throttle-actuated switch for the landing gear warning signal circuit is installed on the throttle quadrant. On B D aircraft the forward and aft throttle quadrants are mechanically interconnected and are identical, except that the aft throttle has no optical sight electrical cage button and the speed brake switch is spring loaded to neutral.

AERODYNAMIC VARIABLE AREA EXHAUST NOZZLE.  

Two sets of flaps, operating together, provide the variable exhaust area. The primary exhaust nozzle flaps, hinged to the aft end of the tailpipe, control the convergent portion of the nozzle while the secondary exhaust nozzle flaps, hinged to a support ring, control the divergent portion of the nozzle. (See figure 1-30.) The two sets of flaps are linked together and maintain an area-and-spacing ratio which is infinitely variable between open and closed. Movement of the flaps is accomplished automatically by four synchronized hydraulic actuators. The exhaust gases leave the primary flaps at sonic velocity, and are accelerated to supersonic velocity by the controlled expansion of the gases. Control of this expansion is provided by the cushioning effect of the secondary airflow through the annular passage between the two sets of flaps.

GUIDED EXPANSION EXHAUST NOZZLE SYSTEM. *(See figure 1-31)* 19

The exhaust nozzle consists of sixteen sets of primary, secondary and divergent nozzle flaps linked to function together. The primary exhaust nozzle flaps, hinged at the aft end of the tailpipe, control the convergent portion of the nozzle. The secondary outer flaps function with the divergent flap to introduce secondary airflow to the primary exhaust stream and control the expansion rate of the exhaust gases. The three sets of flaps maintain a scheduled area and spacing ratio which is determined by a cam schedule on the primary and secondary outer flaps.

The flaps are positioned automatically according to the schedule of the nozzle area control by four synchronized hydraulic actuators. The exhaust gases leave the primary flaps at sonic velocity and are accelerated to a supersonic velocity as they expand through the divergent portion of the nozzle. This expansion is primarily controlled by the divergent flap position.

Secondary Airflow Supply.

Suck-In Doors. Secondary airflow is supplied for engine ground operation through four sets of inward-opening (suck-in) doors (spring-loaded to closed) just aft of the firewall.

Bypass Flaps. During flight, secondary airflow is supplied through automatically operated engine air bypass flaps installed at the joint between the main duct and the engine. Electrically operated valves, actuated by the main landing gear door uplock switches, allow No. 2 hydraulic pressure to open the two lower bypass flaps. When the landing gear is extended, the two lower flaps are closed. Electrical power for operation of the bypass flap valves is derived from the dc monitored bus.

Emergency Blowout Panel. An emergency blowout panel is installed on the bottom of the airplane, forward of the hydraulic panel, to relieve excessively high pressures which could build up in the aft fuselage.

NOZZLE AREA CONTROL SYSTEM.  

The nozzle area control system comprises an electro-hydromechanical computer. The parameters affecting operation of the nozzle area control are throttle angle, nozzle position, electrical overtemperature signal from the temperature amplifier, and an off-speed signal from the engine fuel control unit. Regulated servo fuel is received from the engine fuel control unit to operate the hydraulic force amplifiers in the nozzle area control system. Throttle angle and exhaust gas temperature are the parameters used to determine the correct nozzle area (see figure 1-10). The two parameters are combined within the nozzle area control. During engine operation in the sub-military region, nozzle are is primarily a function of throttle angle. The nozzle is almost fully open at IDLE and the area is decreased as the throttle is advanced to MILITARY; however, during a rapid throttle burst, the engine fuel control unit generates a hydraulic off-speed signal which is delivered to the nozzle area control. The signal overrides the nozzle "mechanical schedule," as established by the throttle angle, permitting a rapid increase in engine rpm. During engine operation in the Military thrust and afterburner region it becomes necessary to limit the nozzle opening as established by throttle angle, to prevent exhaust gas temperature from exceeding limits. Exhaust gas temperature is sensed by 12 dual-loop thermocouples and the resulting signal is transmitted to the temperature amplifier. The amplifier, which receives its power supply from the engine-driven control alternator, compares the thermocouple signal with a preset reference voltage representing desired engine temperature. The difference voltage is amplified and transmitted to the nozzle area control which overrides the mechanical schedule signal and drives the nozzle in the open direction.

NOZZLE AREA CONTROL SYSTEM. 

The nozzle area control system is an electronic-hydraulic-mechanical computer incorporating an exhaust gas temperature sensing amplifier, nozzle area control unit, and an engine-driven control alternator. These units function to position the engine exhaust nozzle to conform with engine operating requirements. This feature is effective throughout the entire engine operating range but is primarily important in the Military thrust and afterburning

VARIATION OF ENGINE SPEED, TEMPERATURE AND NOZZLE AREA WITH THROTTLE POSITION

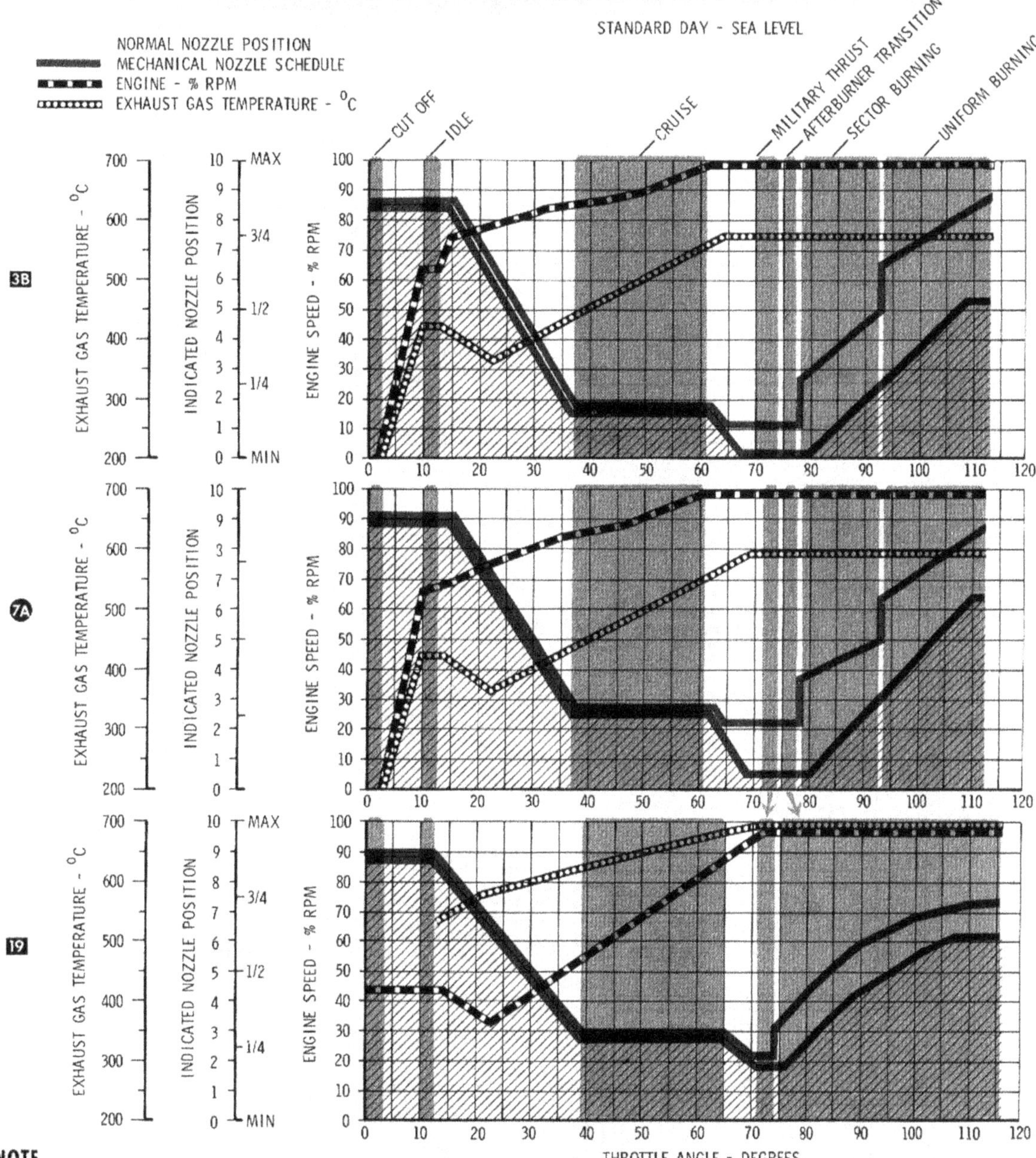

NOTE

NOZZLE AREA NORMALLY FOLLOWS THE MECHANICAL SCHEDULE UNTIL EXHAUST GAS REACHES THE HIGHEST TEMPERATURE DEPICTED; BEYOND THIS POINT, THE TEMPERATURE AMPLIFIER PRODUCES ELECTRONIC SIGNALS REQUIRED FOR NOZZLE AREA VARIATION. AS THROTTLE ANGLE IS INCREASED INTO THE MILITARY AND AFTERBURNER THRUST REGIONS, THE TEMPERATURE AMPLIFIER SIGNALS THE NOZZLE AREA CONTROL WHICH CAUSES THE NOZZLES TO MODULATE AS NECESSARY TO MAINTAIN EXHAUST GAS TEMPERATURE. AT MILITARY THRUST, INDICATED NOZZLE POSITION MAY VARY FROM 1 TO 3.5 TO MAINTAIN EGT. AT MAXIMUM AFTERBURNER, INDICATED NOZZLE POSITION MAY VARY FROM 7.5 TO 9.5 TO MAINTAIN EGT. EXHAUST GAS TEMPERATURE IS THE MOST ACCURATE INDICATION OF PROPER NOZZLE AREA. NOZZLE AREA WILL NOT DECREASE BELOW THOSE VALUES SHOWN FOR THE MECHANICAL SCHEDULE.

F52-0-1-19

Figure 1-10

EXHAUST NOZZLE CLOSURE SYSTEM 19 7A

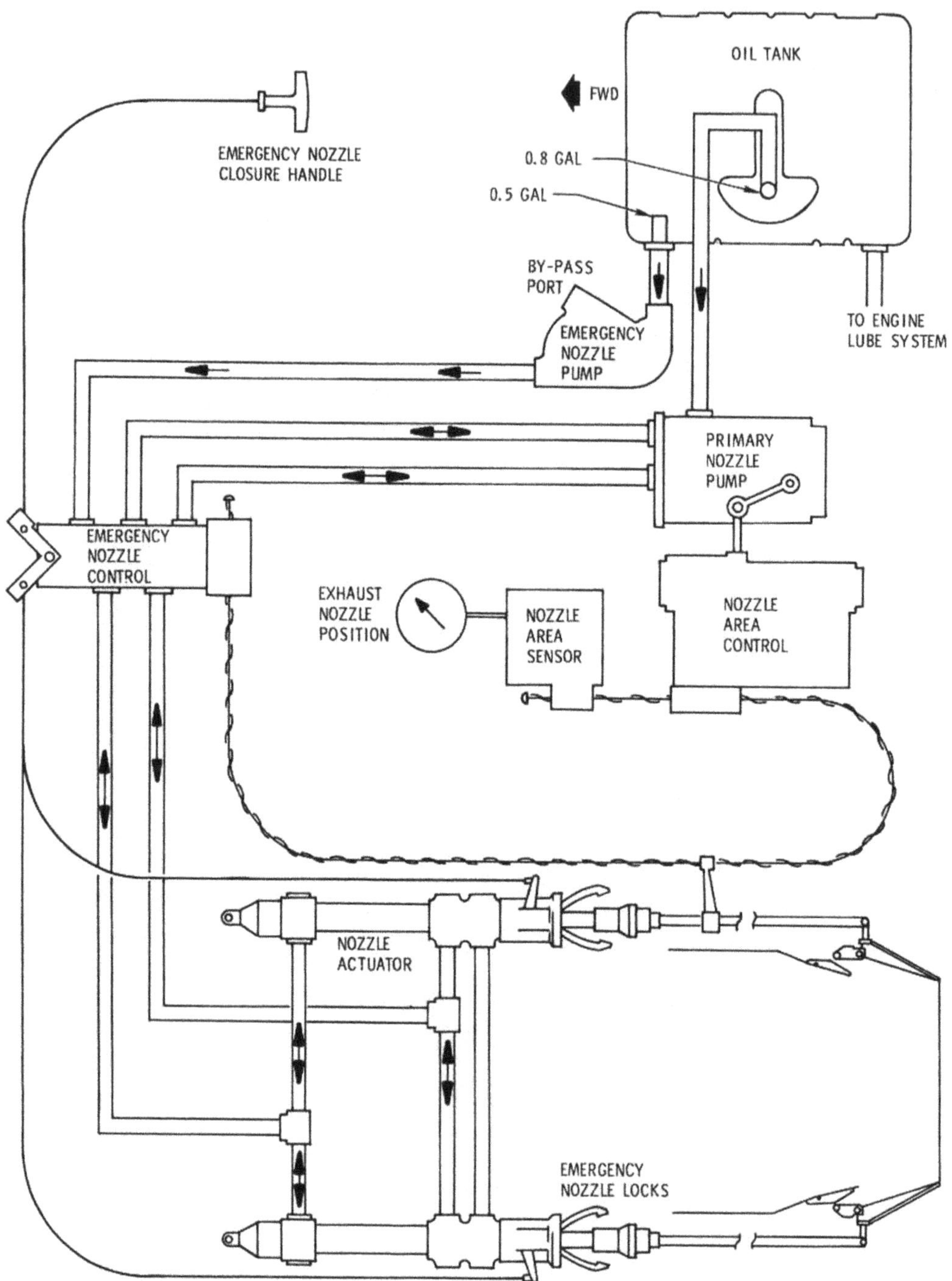

Figure 1-11

regions. There is a mechanical schedule according to which the nozzle area control starts closing the exhaust nozzle immediately following the idle range of throttle position and continuing to the Military thrust position. (See figure 1-10.) When the nozzle is at its smallest scheduled opening, the temperature control system begins to control the EGT by opening the nozzle above the position called for by the mechanical schedule and continues to determine nozzle position throughout the Military and afterburner ranges. The nozzle mechanical schedule causes an increase in the minimum nozzle area, above that called for in the Military setting, as throttle is advanced into the afterburner range to prevent severe overtemperature or stall if the nozzle fails in the closed direction. This mechanical schedule causes the nozzle to remain open whenever afterburner is selected even if afterburner fails to light, or blows out.

Temperature Amplifier.

The temperature amplifier provides an electrical signal to the nozzle area control. This signal overrides the "mechanical schedule" signal to the primary nozzle and prevents overtemperature operation of the engine. It also senses rate of change of engine speed, exhaust gas temperature, transients to open or close the nozzle to improve engine acceleration, and reduce speed roll back during afterburner light-off. The amplifier receives power from the control alternator (separate from the airplane electrical system) and an electrical signal representing actual exhaust gas temperature from the thermocouples. The thermocouples' generated signal is compared with a signal representing desired exhaust gas temperature. The difference in voltage is amplified and delivered to the torque motor of the nozzle area control.

Nozzle Pump. The nozzle hydraulic pump is a variable pressure, variable displacement pump driven by a single engine shaft. The amount and direction of flow are determined by a mechanical push-pull signal from the nozzle area control.

Exhaust Nozzle Flap Actuators. There are four nozzle hydraulic actuators. The actuators are supplied with high pressure oil from the nozzle hydraulic pump. The four equally spaced actuators are located on the tailpipe and mechanically open and close the nozzles automatically through a series of rods and levers.

Exhaust Nozzle Control Switch. 3B An exhaust nozzle control switch (9, figures 1-14, 1-15, 1-18) is located on the left side of the cockpit just forward of the throttle quadrant. The switch is labeled NOZZLE CONTROL and has two positions, AUTO and MANUAL. In the AUTO position (normal) the electronic temperature control of the nozzle area control system is energized. With the switch in MANUAL, the area of the exhaust nozzle depends on the throttle position directly. If the electronic temperature control system should malfunction, the pilot may override the automatic feature and close the exhaust nozzle to the mechanical schedule by placing the switch in MANUAL. The switch is powered from the dc emergency bus.

Note

> A failure of the hydraulic-mechanical portion of the nozzle area control system is also a possibility. Under this condition, control of the exhaust nozzle may not be possible.

Exhaust Nozzle Position Indicator. An indicator (18, 16, figures 1-12, 1-13 and 20, 16 figures 1-22, 1-23), located on the right side of the instrument panel, shows the relative size of the exit area of the exhaust nozzle. The instrument, placarded JET NOZZLE POSITION, is calibrated from MIN. AREA in ¼th increments (or 0 through 10 on later aircraft) to MAX AREA. Power for the instrument is supplied by the instrument ac bus.

EXHAUST NOZZLE EMERGENCY CLOSURE SYSTEM.  *(See figure 1-11)*

An emergency exhaust nozzle lock system and a priority oil supply system is installed. The emergency exhaust lock system incorporates lock assemblies that are mounted on the No. 2 and 4 nozzle actuators. This system locks the nozzle to prevent it from exceeding the cruise position of approximately an indicated nozzle position of 3, thus preventing a full-open nozzle should the emergency nozzle closure system become inoperative as a result of an excessive oil loss.

The priority oil-supply system consists of a lube tank, modified to incorporate an emergency hydraulic port, and a standpipe which extends within the tank to the 4-pint level. This system separates the engine lubrication system from the emergency nozzle closure system supply ports and provides a reserve supply of 4 pints of oil for engine lubrication. During normal engine operation, the primary nozzle hydraulic system regulates the exhaust.

Engine Exhaust Nozzle Locks. 

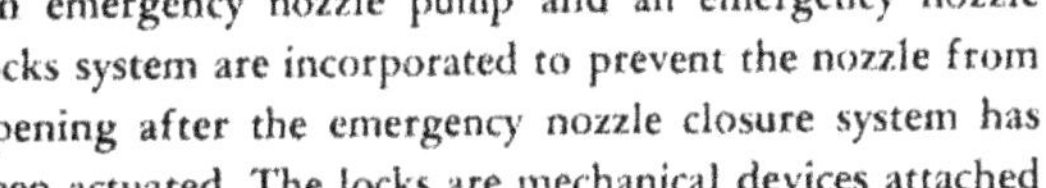

An emergency nozzle pump and an emergency nozzle locks system are incorporated to prevent the nozzle from opening after the emergency nozzle closure system has been actuated. The locks are mechanical devices attached to two of the nozzle actuators and connected directly to an emergency nozzle closure handle. The combination of the emergency nozzle pump and the emergency nozzle locks provide for hydraulic failures such as nozzle area control or nozzle pump, upstream of the transfer valve in the normal system, or an electric failure in the temperature amplifier. Neither system will close a nozzle which has failed because of an actuator failure, or a break in the actuator lines downstream of the transfer valve. If a break occurs anywhere in the lubrication or nozzle system, the oil supply will be quickly depleted. The extent of the loss will depend upon the location of the leak. If the leak is in the lubrication lines, complete oil loss will occur, since the oil outlet is in the bottom of the tank. If the leak is in the nozzle system, the oil level will deplete to the 0.8 gallon level at the pendulum outlet. Pressure loss in the nozzle lines will then cause the ENGINE OIL LEVEL LOW warning light to illuminate, and the nozzles to open. Pulling the emergency nozzle handle will cock the nozzle locks and unless the failure is aft of the transfer valve, will actuate the emergency nozzle pump and close the nozzles. The oil supply for the emergency nozzle pump is the 0.3 gallons contained between the 0.8 gallon pendulum outlet, and the 0.5 gallon standpipe extending from the bottom of the tank. If the oil leak is downstream of the transfer valve, pulling the T-handle will not close the nozzles, and the 0.3 gallons will be quickly depleted. If the leak is upstream of the transfer valve, the nozzle will close and stay closed for approximately two minutes before the 0.3 gallons of oil is lost. This is due to a calibrated cooling leak in the nozzle actuators. When oil pressure from the emergency nozzle pump drops, the nozzles will again open, but will be stopped when the collars on the nozzle actuating rods engage the nozzle locks. The collars which engage the nozzle locks are so designed that they will ride through the cocked nozzle locks when the T-handle is pulled, but will engage the locks when pressure to the nozzle actuators is lost.

Note

- The 0.5 gallon reserve below the standpipe is reserved for engine lubrication and cannot be lost to the nozzle closure system.
- A common engine drive shaft drives the engine oil supply system pump and the emergency nozzle system pump.

Emergency Nozzle Closure Handle.

7A

A T-handle (23, 19, figures 1-12, 1-13 and 26, 22, figures 1-22, 1-23), is installed on the lower instrument panel labeled EMERGENCY NOZZLE CLOSURE. This handle is connected by flexible cable to a transfer valve in the nozzle area control system, and to the emergency nozzle locks. The transfer valve permits selecting either the normal or the emergency system for controlling the nozzle. When the emergency nozzle closure handle is in the NORMAL (forward detent) position the nozzle locks are uncocked, and the transfer valve allows free flow of oil between the normal nozzle pump and the nozzle actuators; nozzle area is therefore controlled by the normal control system. Pulling the T-handle to the EMERGENCY (aft detent) position mechanically cocks the nozzle locks, and positions the transfer valve to direct oil from the emergency nozzle pump to the nozzle actuators, closing the nozzles to a preset position of approximately 2.5 on the nozzle position indicator. Some modulation of the nozzle opening will still occur as a result of changes in thrust setting (exhaust gas pressure variation). If oil pressure in the emergency system is lost, the nozzles will attempt to open, but will be stopped by the emergency nozzle locks at a reading of approximately 3.5 on the exhaust nozzle position indicator. Under this condition, the handle cannot be pushed in until the aerodynamic loads in the nozzle are relieved.

ENGINE STARTER AND IGNITION SYSTEMS.

Engine Starter System.

The engine is equipped with an air-driven starter which requires air from a ground turbine compressor. The receptacle for connecting the air supply line is located in the right main wheel well. A special electrical receptacle located adjacent to this air connector is provided to permit electrical connection of the start switches to the electrically controlled air valve on the ground starting unit. If this electrical connection is made, the pilot has control of the start; starting air to the engine starter is provided through electrical operation of the valve by the pilot. A centrifugal switch closes the air valve to disengage the starter automatically when engine rpm increases to between 42 and 47 percent. If this electrical connection is not made, the ground crew must manually position the valve to open and close on signal from the pilot.

Engine Ignition System.

Dual ignition systems are provided for air start reliability. Each system has an individual battery, battery bus, switch, and spark plug. When energized, the ignition circuit selected will supply power to its respective spark plug for 45 seconds or until the start switch is moved to the STOP—START position. The spark plug will ignite the fuel—air mixture in its vicinity. Ignition is propagated through combustion chamber crossfire tubes. During armament firing, the ignition circuit is energized when the trigger is depressed and remains energized for 10 to 15 seconds after release. This provides stand-by ignition for immediate engine relight if flameout occurs.

Start Switches. Two start switches (figures 1-20, 1-21) are located on the left forward panel and are labeled No. 1 and No. 2. The switches have a START, STOP–START and a center NEUTRAL position. The switches are spring loaded from the START and STOP–START positions to NEUTRAL. By momentarily moving either start switch to START, battery bus power is supplied to energize the ignition circuit and begin the 45-second ignition cycle. During an ignition cycle the start switches may be used to begin a completely new 45-second cycle. Placing the start switch to the STOP–START position discontinues ignition. Both switches are used simultaneously to energize the ignition systems during air starts. This provides dual air start reliability. When the special electrical connection is made between the aircraft and the control valve, the start switch also controls starting air.

Engine Motoring Switch. The engine motoring switch (9, figures 1-16, 1-17 and 6, figures 1-26, 1-27), located on the right console, is spring loaded from ON to OFF. It is provided to energize the ground turbine compressor air valve which diverts compressor air to the engine starter for motoring the engine without ignition. The engine motoring switch is electrically powered by the No. 1 battery bus. (Refer to Engine Starter System in this section for information on the ground turbine compressor and engine starter.)

Fuel Flow Indicator. The fuel flow indicator (25, 21, figures 1-12, 1-13, and 22, 17, figures 1-27, 1-23), located on the lower right instrument panel is operated by a flowmeter installed in the engine fuel line. This instrument indicates fuel consumption rate in pounds per hour and is calibrated to 12,000 pounds. The system receives 26-volt ac power from the instrument ac bus through the instrument autotransformer and fuses on the electronic compartment circuit breaker panel. The instrument does not indicate afterburner fuel flow.

Engine Air Inlet Temperature Gage (CIT). A temperature gage (2, 4, figures 1-12, 1-13, and 2, figures 1-22, 1-23), located on the upper left side of the instrument panel, measures compressor inlet temperature (CIT). The temperature detector is located in the right 20 kva ac generator blast tube which carries engine inlet air from the right intake duct. The instrument is calibrated from -70°C to +150°C and receives power from the 28 volt dc monitored bus.

CIT Warning Light. A placard-type compressor inlet temperature warning light (7, 5, figures 1-12, 1-13, and 6, 5, figures 1-22, 1-23), located on the upper left side of the main instrument panel, is powered by the dc emergency bus. This light is energized when CIT exceeds the allowable limit. This may or may not coincide with the CIT limit indication on the gage. When the light is energized the word SLOW will flash on and off and alert the pilot to slow the airplane and avoid engine damage. This may or may not coincide with the CIT gage limit indication.

Exhaust Gas Temperature Gage. An exhaust gas temperature gage (17, 15, figures 1-12, 1-13 and 19, 15, figures 1-22, 1-23), located on the right side of the main instrument panel is calibrated from 0° to 1000°C A B and 0° to 1200°C. C D. The unit is operated electrically by self-generating thermocouples and provides visual indications of exhaust gas temperature.

Tachometer. The tachometer (16, 13, figures 1-12, 1-13 and 18, 14, figures 1-22, 1-23) mounted on the right side of the main instrument panel, registers engine speed in percentage of maximum rated rpm. The instrument is powered by a tachometer generator which generates a frequency proportional to the engine speed and therefore does not require power from the airplane electrical system.

AFTERBURNER SYSTEM. 

The afterburner section is located just aft of the turbine section and comprises the tailpipe, guided expansion exhaust nozzle, torch igniter, spray bars, and manifold. The purpose of the afterburner is to provide thrust augmentation by injecting additional fuel into the exhaust gases and igniting the mixture. The turbine exhaust gases are heated and discharged into the jet nozzle. The system provides quick light-off at low afterburner fuel flow with no discernible thrust jump and fully modulated thrust capability to maximum afterburner.

AFTERBURNER SYSTEM. 

The afterburner section of the engine is located just aft of the turbine section and consists of the tail pipe, aerodynamic variable area exhaust nozzle, torch igniter, spray bars, and manifold. The purpose of the afterburner is to provide thrust augmentation by injecting additional fuel into the exhaust gases and igniting the mixture.

AFTERBURNER FUEL SYSTEM.  

Fuel flows from the aircraft tanks through the on-off valve, the afterburner fuel pump, the check-and-vent valve, and the afterburner fuel filter to the afterburner fuel control. The control splits the fuel into "core" and "annulus" flow. Core fuel passes through the oil-cooler to a pressurizing valve. Annulus fuel flows directly to the pressurizing valve. The pressurizing valve then splits both core and annulus flows into primary and secondary paths to the full-ring manifolds and their respective spraybars.

TYPICAL INSTRUMENT PANEL A FORWARD COCKPIT B

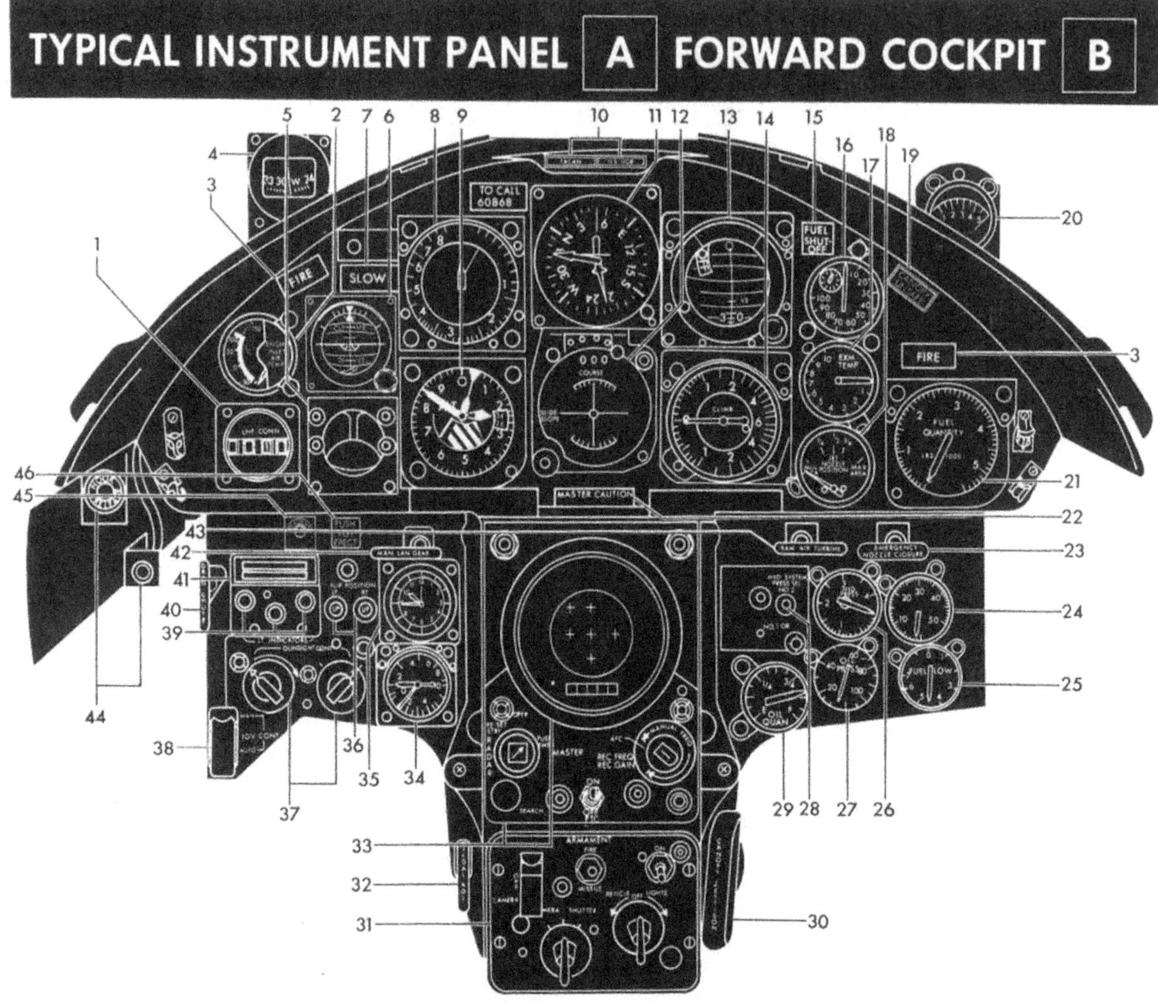

1 REMOTE CHANNEL FREQUENCY INDICATOR
2 COMPRESSOR INLET TEMPERATURE GAGE
3 FIRE WARNING LIGHT (2)
4 STANDBY COMPASS
5 TURN-AND-SLIP INDICATOR
6 STANDBY ATTITUDE INDICATOR
7 COMPRESSOR INLET TEMPERATURE WARNING LIGHT
8 AIRSPEED AND MACH NUMBER INDICATOR
9 ALTIMETER
10 TACAN-ILS/VOR INDICATOR LIGHTS
11 BEARING DISTANCE HEADING INDICATOR (ID-526)
12 COURSE INDICATOR
13 ATTITUDE INDICATOR
14 VERTICAL VELOCITY INDICATOR
15 MAIN FUEL SHUTOFF VALVE WARNING LIGHT
16 TACHOMETER
17 EXHAUST GAS TEMPERATURE GAGE
18 EXHAUST NOZZLE POSITION INDICATOR
19 CANOPY UNSAFE (FLASHING) WARNING LIGHT
20 AUTOMATIC PITCH CONTROL INDICATOR
21 FUEL QUANTITY INDICATOR
22 MASTER CAUTION LIGHT AND RESET BAR
23 EMERGENCY NOZZLE CLOSURE HANDLE **19**
24 CABIN ALTIMETER
25 FUEL FLOW INDICATOR
26 HYDRAULIC SYSTEMS PRESSURE GAGE
27 OIL PRESSURE GAGE
28 HYDRAULIC SYSTEM PRESSURE GAGE SELECTOR SWITCH
29 NUCLEONIC OIL QUANTITY INDICATOR
30 CANOPY JETTISON HANDLE
31 ARMAMENT CONTROL PANEL **A**
32 RUDDER PEDAL ADJUSTMENT HANDLE
33 RADAR INDICATOR AND CONTROL PANEL
34 ACCELEROMETER
35 CLOCK
36 WING FLAP POSITION INDICATORS
37 GUNSIGHT CONTROL SWITCHES
38 INLET GUIDE VANES SWITCH **3B**
39 LANDING GEAR POSITION INDICATOR LIGHTS
40 DRAG CHUTE HANDLE
41 STABILIZER AND AILERON TAKE OFF TRIM INDICATOR LIGHTS
42 MANUAL LANDING GEAR RELEASE HANDLE
43 RAM AIR TURBINE EXTENSION HANDLE
44 ARRESTING HOOK RELEASE BUTTON AND ARRESTING HOOK DOWN WARNING LIGHT
45 RADAR LOCK-ON SENSITIVITY CONTROL
46 VGI PUSH-TO-ERECT

F52-0-1-10

Figure 1-12

TYPICAL AFT COCKPIT - INSTRUMENT PANEL B

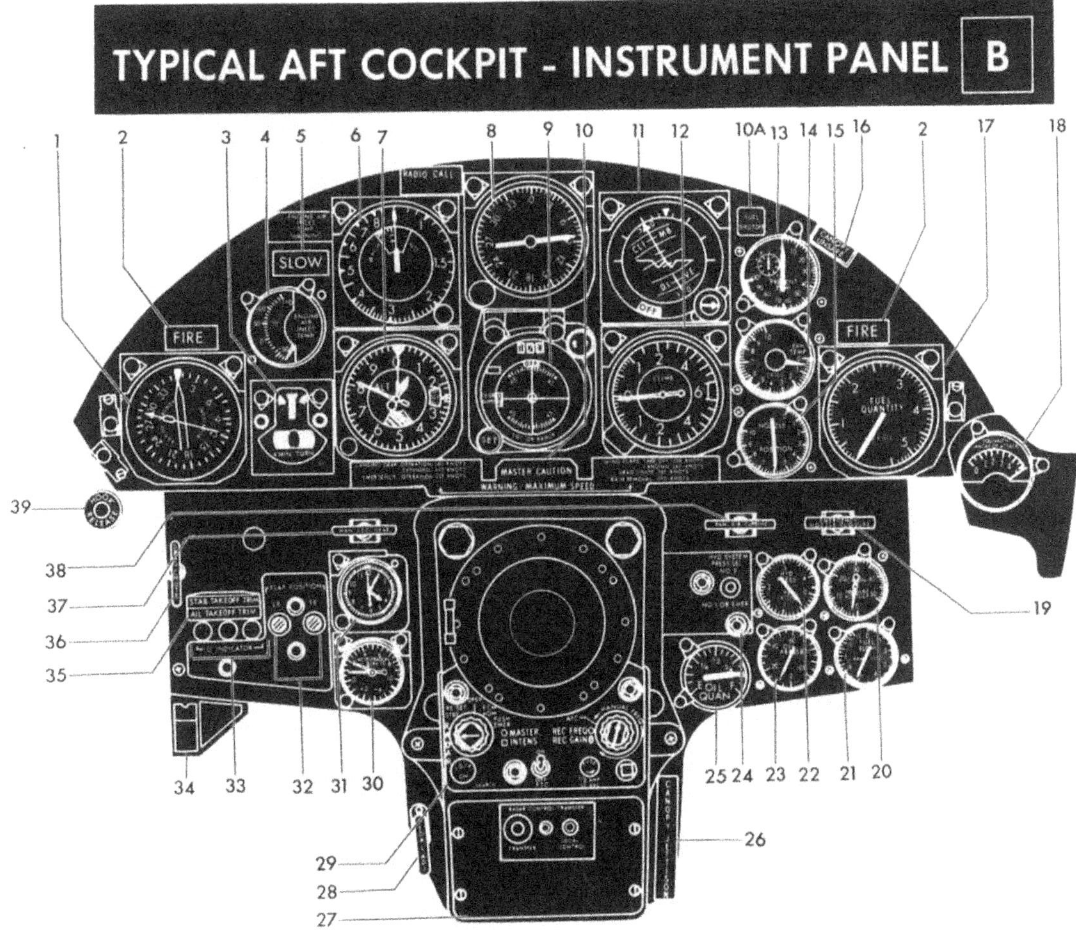

1	RADIO MAGNETIC INDICATOR *
2	FIRE WARNING LIGHT (2)
3	TURN-AND-SLIP INDICATOR
4	COMPRESSOR INLET TEMPERATURE GAGE
5	COMPRESSOR INLET TEMPERATURE WARNING LIGHT
6	AIRSPEED AND MACH NUMBER INDICATOR
7	ALTIMETER
8	HEADING INDICATOR
9	COURSE INDICATOR
10	MASTER CAUTION LIGHT AND RESET BAR
10A	MAIN FUEL SHUTOFF VALVE WARNING LIGHT
11	ATTITUDE INDICATOR
12	VERTICAL VELOCITY INDICATOR
13	TACHOMETER
14	EXHAUST GAS TEMPERATURE GAGE
15	EXHAUST NOZZLE POSITION INDICATOR
16	CANOPY UNSAFE (FLASHING) WARNING LIGHT
17	FUEL QUANTITY INDICATOR
18	AUTOMATIC PITCH CONTROL INDICATOR
19	EMERGENCY NOZZLE CLOSURE HANDLE 19
20	CABIN ALTIMETER
21	FUEL FLOW INDICATOR
22	HYDRAULIC SYSTEMS PRESSURE INDICATOR
23	OIL PRESSURE GAGE
24	HYDRAULIC SYSTEMS PRESSURE SELECTOR SWITCH
25	NUCLEONIC OIL QUANTITY INDICATOR
26	CANOPY JETTISON HANDLE
27	RADAR CONTROL TRANSFER PANEL
28	RUDDER PEDAL ADJUSTMENT HANDLE
29	RADAR INDICATOR AND CONTROL PANEL
30	ACCELEROMETER
31	CLOCK
32	WING FLAP POSITION INDICATORS
33	LANDING GEAR POSITION INDICATOR LIGHTS
34	INLET GUIDE VANES SWITCH 3B
35	STABILIZER AND AILERON TAKEOFF TRIM INDICATOR LIGHTS
36	DRAG CHUTE HANDLE
37	MANUAL LANDING GEAR RELEASE HANDLE
38	RAM AIR TURBINE EXTENSION HANDLE
39	ARRESTING HOOK RELEASE BUTTON

F52-0-1-11A

Figure 1-13

TYPICAL COCKPIT - LEFT SIDE A

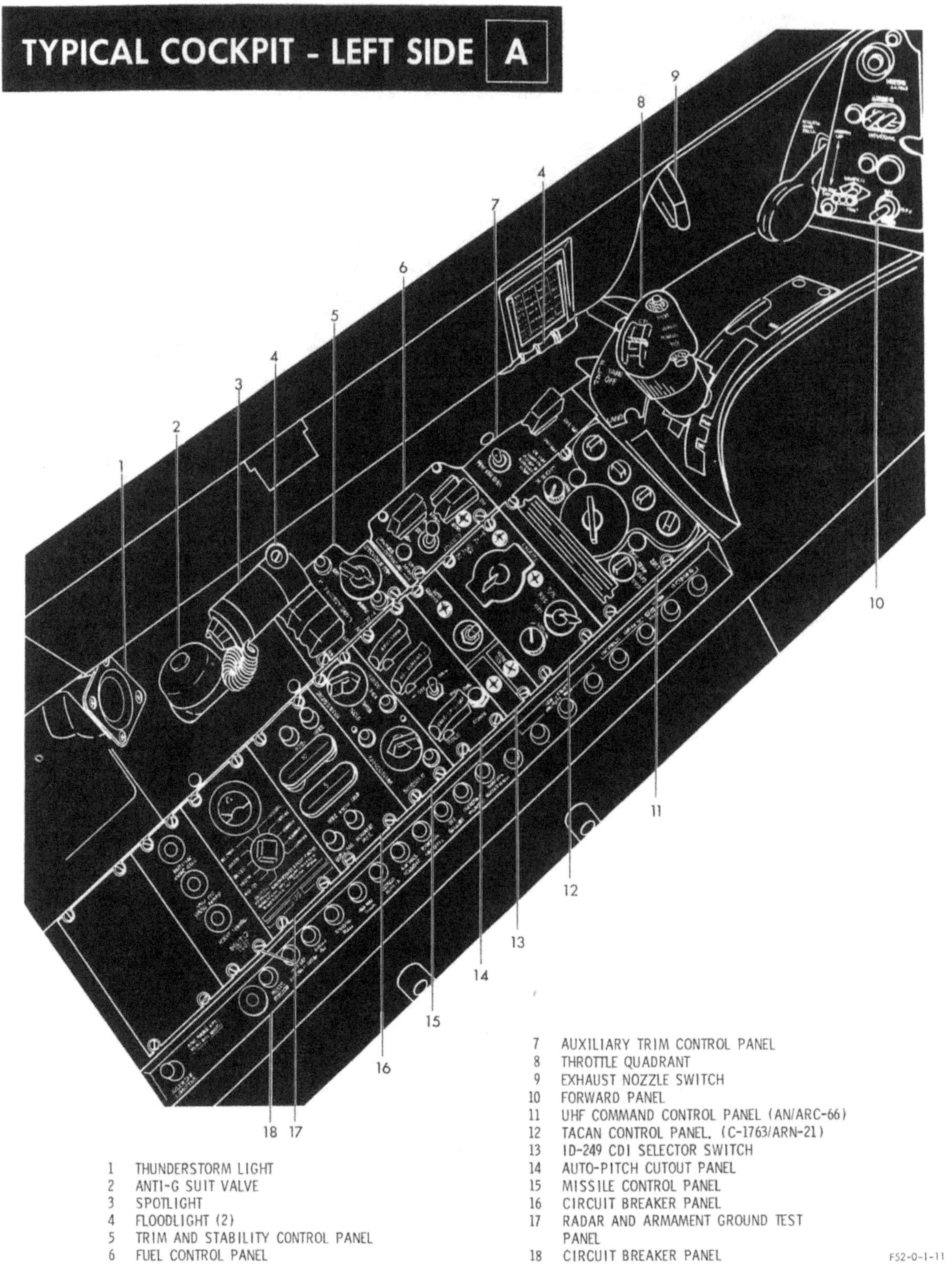

1 THUNDERSTORM LIGHT
2 ANTI-G SUIT VALVE
3 SPOTLIGHT
4 FLOODLIGHT (2)
5 TRIM AND STABILITY CONTROL PANEL
6 FUEL CONTROL PANEL
7 AUXILIARY TRIM CONTROL PANEL
8 THROTTLE QUADRANT
9 EXHAUST NOZZLE SWITCH
10 FORWARD PANEL
11 UHF COMMAND CONTROL PANEL (AN/ARC-66)
12 TACAN CONTROL PANEL (C-1763/ARN-21)
13 ID-249 CDI SELECTOR SWITCH
14 AUTO-PITCH CUTOUT PANEL
15 MISSILE CONTROL PANEL
16 CIRCUIT BREAKER PANEL
17 RADAR AND ARMAMENT GROUND TEST PANEL
18 CIRCUIT BREAKER PANEL

F52-0-1-11

Figure 1-14

TYPICAL FORWARD COCKPIT - LEFT SIDE B

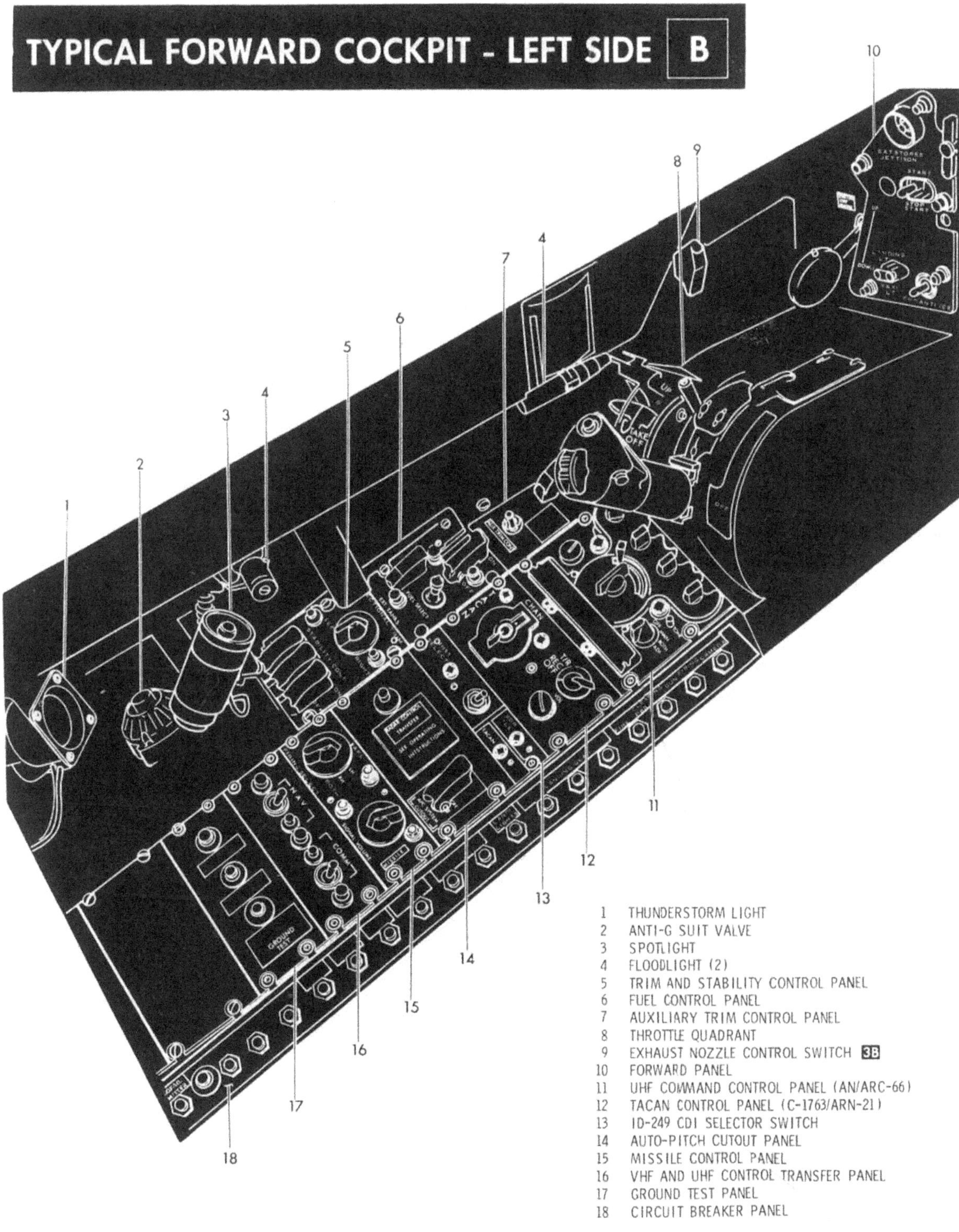
1 THUNDERSTORM LIGHT
2 ANTI-G SUIT VALVE
3 SPOTLIGHT
4 FLOODLIGHT (2)
5 TRIM AND STABILITY CONTROL PANEL
6 FUEL CONTROL PANEL
7 AUXILIARY TRIM CONTROL PANEL
8 THROTTLE QUADRANT
9 EXHAUST NOZZLE CONTROL SWITCH 3B
10 FORWARD PANEL
11 UHF COMMAND CONTROL PANEL (AN/ARC-66)
12 TACAN CONTROL PANEL (C-1763/ARN-21)
13 ID-249 CDI SELECTOR SWITCH
14 AUTO-PITCH CUTOUT PANEL
15 MISSILE CONTROL PANEL
16 VHF AND UHF CONTROL TRANSFER PANEL
17 GROUND TEST PANEL
18 CIRCUIT BREAKER PANEL
F52-0-1-13

Figure 1-15

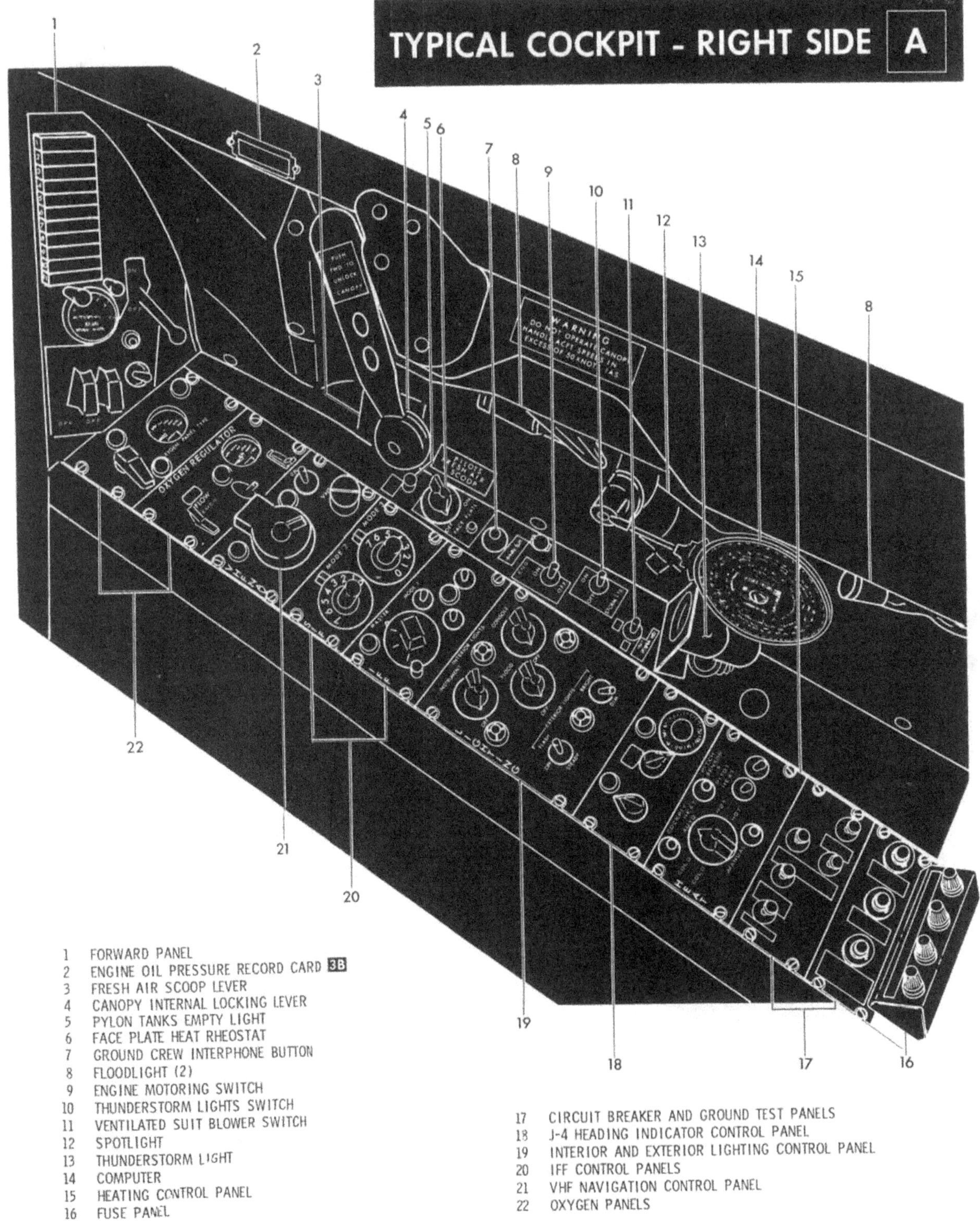

1 FORWARD PANEL
2 ENGINE OIL PRESSURE RECORD CARD 3B
3 FRESH AIR SCOOP LEVER
4 CANOPY INTERNAL LOCKING LEVER
5 PYLON TANKS EMPTY LIGHT
6 FACE PLATE HEAT RHEOSTAT
7 GROUND CREW INTERPHONE BUTTON
8 FLOODLIGHT (2)
9 ENGINE MOTORING SWITCH
10 THUNDERSTORM LIGHTS SWITCH
11 VENTILATED SUIT BLOWER SWITCH
12 SPOTLIGHT
13 THUNDERSTORM LIGHT
14 COMPUTER
15 HEATING CONTROL PANEL
16 FUSE PANEL
17 CIRCUIT BREAKER AND GROUND TEST PANELS
18 J-4 HEADING INDICATOR CONTROL PANEL
19 INTERIOR AND EXTERIOR LIGHTING CONTROL PANEL
20 IFF CONTROL PANELS
21 VHF NAVIGATION CONTROL PANEL
22 OXYGEN PANELS

F52-0-1-12(1)

Figure 1-16

TYPICAL FORWARD COCKPIT - RIGHT SIDE B

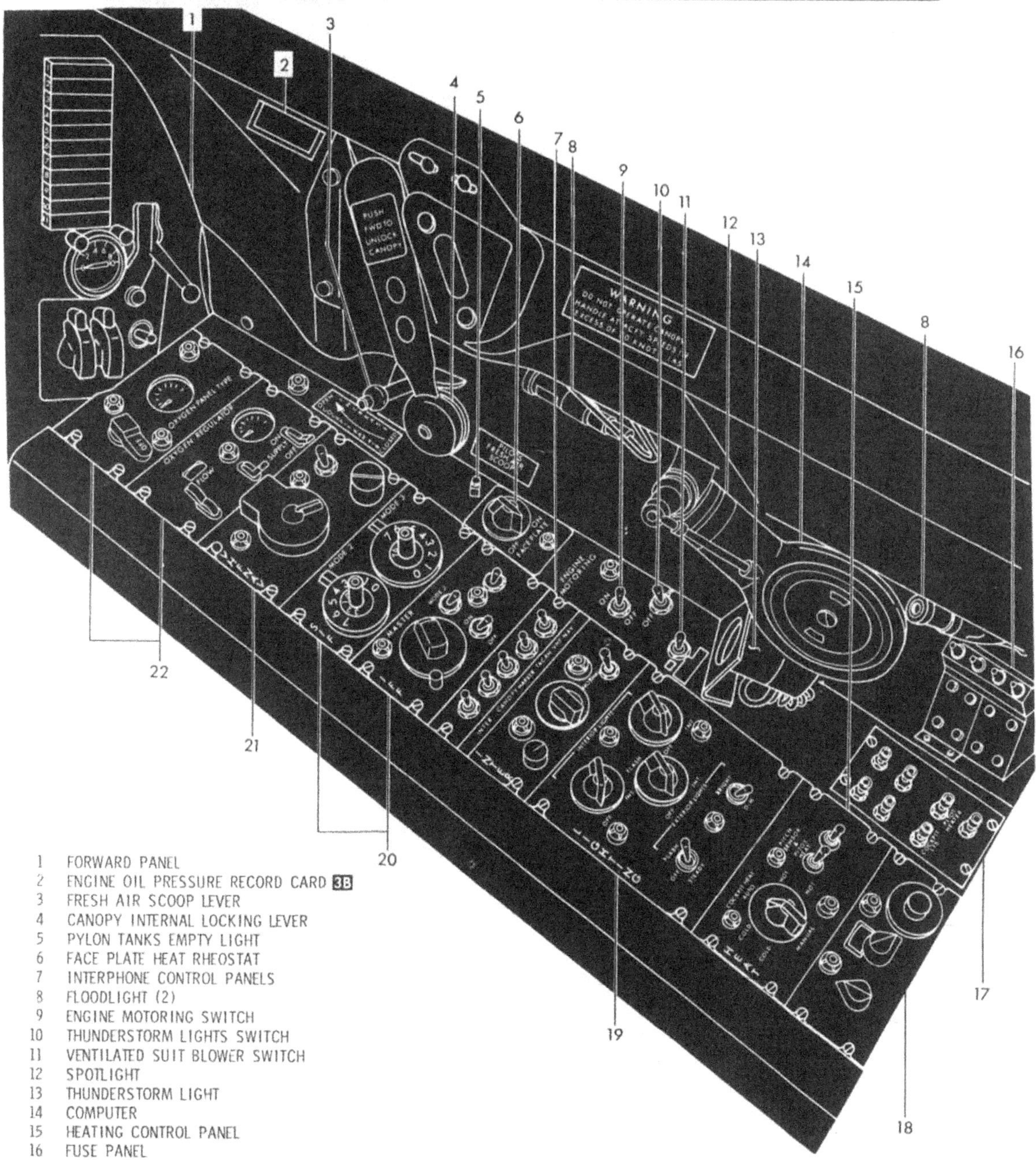

1. FORWARD PANEL
2. ENGINE OIL PRESSURE RECORD CARD 3B
3. FRESH AIR SCOOP LEVER
4. CANOPY INTERNAL LOCKING LEVER
5. PYLON TANKS EMPTY LIGHT
6. FACE PLATE HEAT RHEOSTAT
7. INTERPHONE CONTROL PANELS
8. FLOODLIGHT (2)
9. ENGINE MOTORING SWITCH
10. THUNDERSTORM LIGHTS SWITCH
11. VENTILATED SUIT BLOWER SWITCH
12. SPOTLIGHT
13. THUNDERSTORM LIGHT
14. COMPUTER
15. HEATING CONTROL PANEL
16. FUSE PANEL
17. CIRCUIT BREAKER PANEL
18. J-4 HEADING INDICATOR CONTROL PANEL
19. INTERIOR AND EXTERIOR LIGHTING CONTROL PANEL
20. IFF CONTROL PANELS
21. VHF NAVIGATION CONTROL PANEL
22. OXYGEN PANELS

F52-0-1-14(1)

Figure 1-17

TYPICAL AFT COCKPIT - LEFT SIDE B

NOTE

ITEMS 12, 13, 14, AND 15 APPEAR IN A AND FORWARD COCKPIT B ONLY

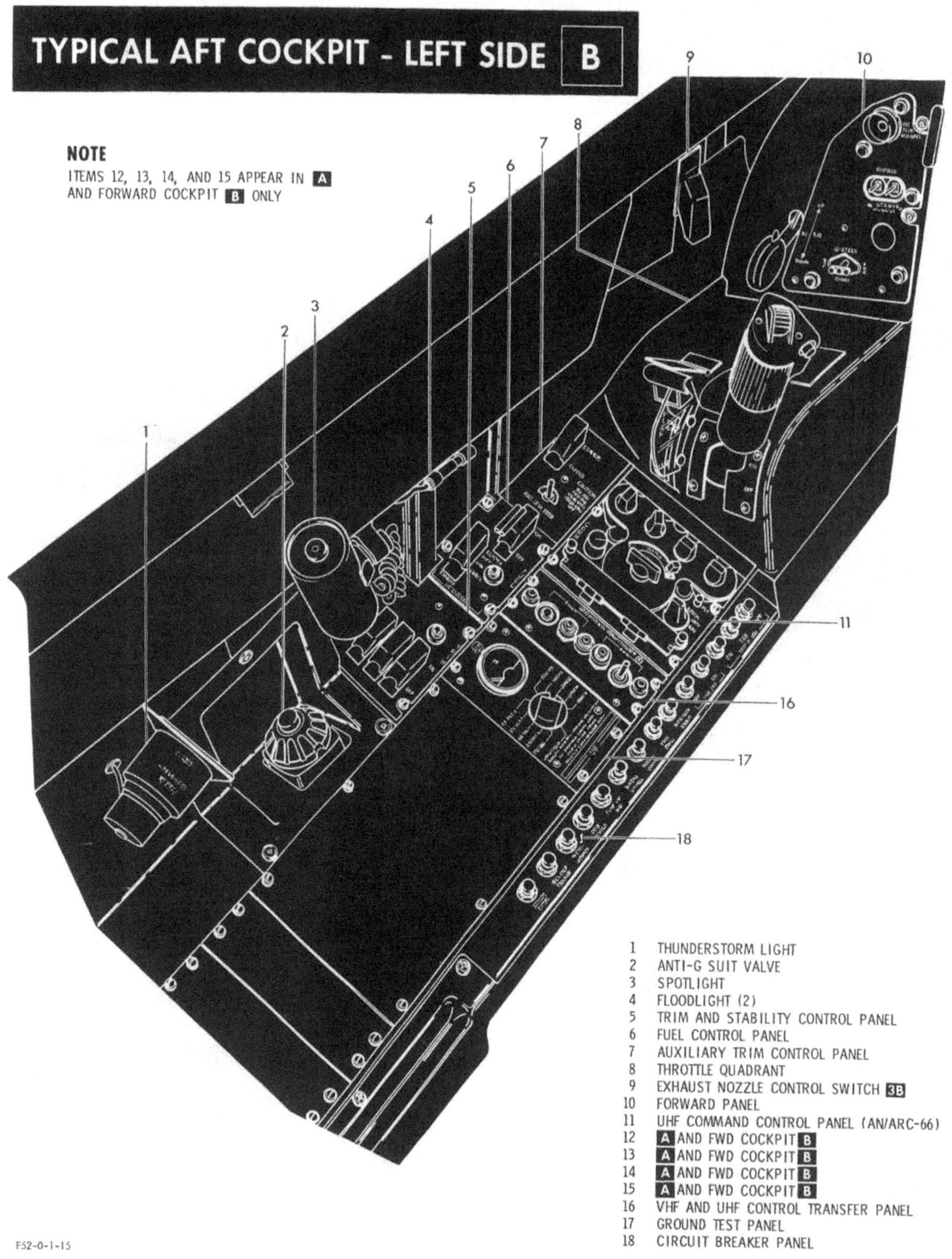

1 THUNDERSTORM LIGHT
2 ANTI-G SUIT VALVE
3 SPOTLIGHT
4 FLOODLIGHT (2)
5 TRIM AND STABILITY CONTROL PANEL
6 FUEL CONTROL PANEL
7 AUXILIARY TRIM CONTROL PANEL
8 THROTTLE QUADRANT
9 EXHAUST NOZZLE CONTROL SWITCH 3B
10 FORWARD PANEL
11 UHF COMMAND CONTROL PANEL (AN/ARC-66)
12 A AND FWD COCKPIT B
13 A AND FWD COCKPIT B
14 A AND FWD COCKPIT B
15 A AND FWD COCKPIT B
16 VHF AND UHF CONTROL TRANSFER PANEL
17 GROUND TEST PANEL
18 CIRCUIT BREAKER PANEL

F52-0-1-15

Figure 1-18

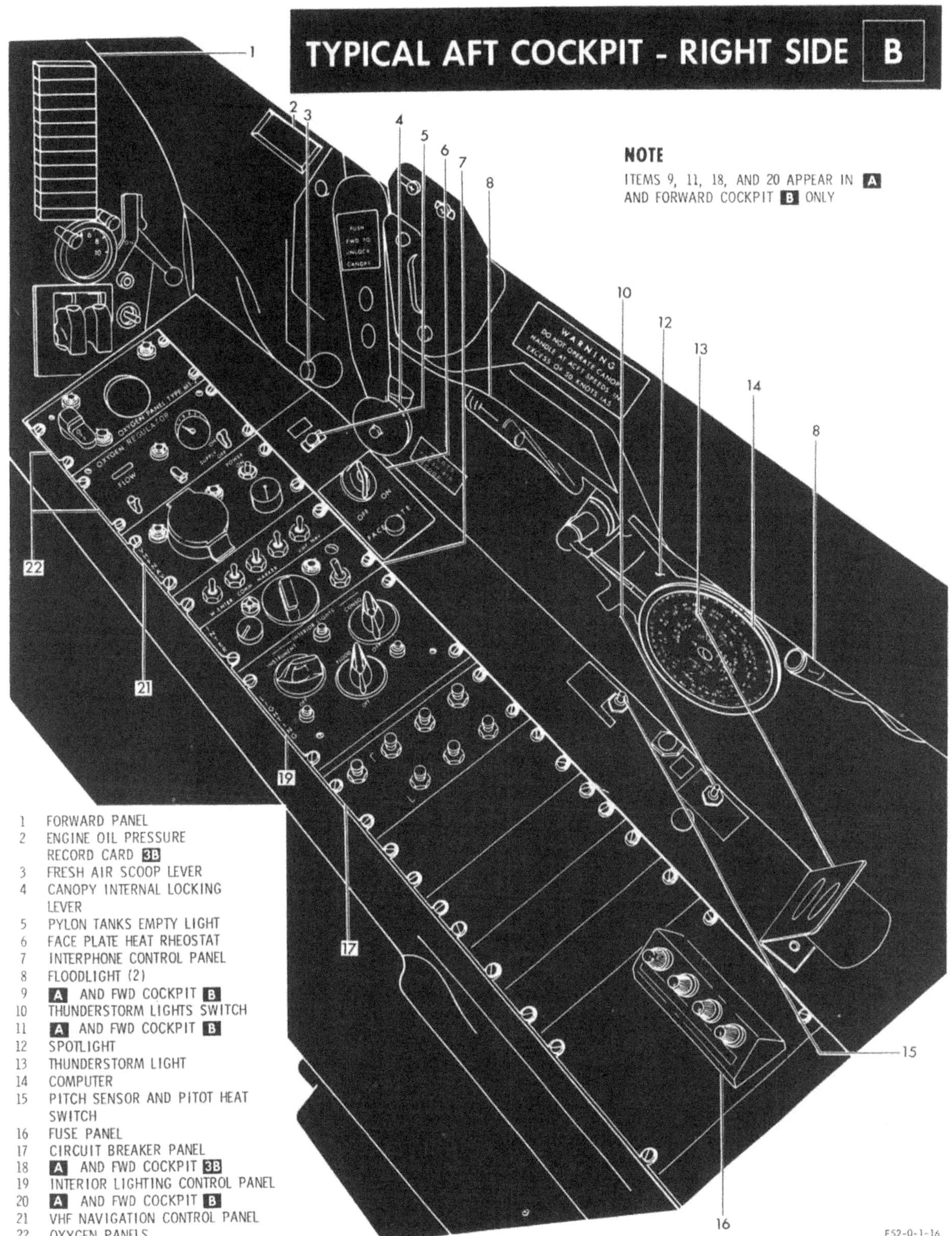
TYPICAL AFT COCKPIT - RIGHT SIDE B
NOTE
ITEMS 9, 11, 18, AND 20 APPEAR IN A AND FORWARD COCKPIT B ONLY
PUSH FWD TO UNLOCK CANOPY
WARNING DO NOT OPERATE CANOPY HANDLE AT ACFT SPEEDS IN EXCESS OF 50 KNOTS IAS
OXYGEN PANEL TYPE MD-1
OXYGEN REGULATOR
1 FORWARD PANEL
2 ENGINE OIL PRESSURE RECORD CARD 3B
3 FRESH AIR SCOOP LEVER
4 CANOPY INTERNAL LOCKING LEVER
5 PYLON TANKS EMPTY LIGHT
6 FACE PLATE HEAT RHEOSTAT
7 INTERPHONE CONTROL PANEL
8 FLOODLIGHT (2)
9 A AND FWD COCKPIT B
10 THUNDERSTORM LIGHTS SWITCH
11 A AND FWD COCKPIT B
12 SPOTLIGHT
13 THUNDERSTORM LIGHT
14 COMPUTER
15 PITCH SENSOR AND PITOT HEAT SWITCH
16 FUSE PANEL
17 CIRCUIT BREAKER PANEL
18 A AND FWD COCKPIT 3B
19 INTERIOR LIGHTING CONTROL PANEL
20 A AND FWD COCKPIT B
21 VHF NAVIGATION CONTROL PANEL
22 OXYGEN PANELS
F52-0-1-16

Figure 1-19

TYPICAL LEFT AND RIGHT FORWARD PANELS  

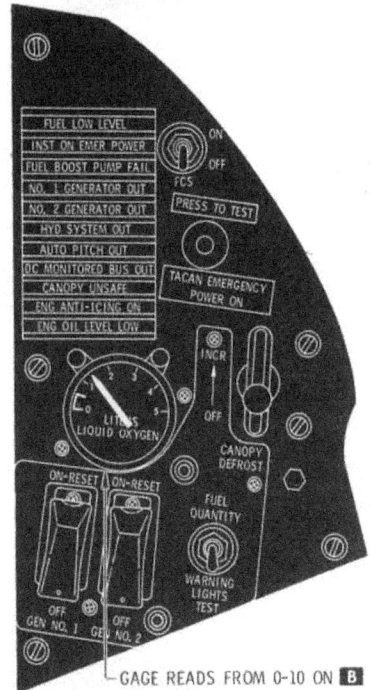

A AND FWD COCKPIT B

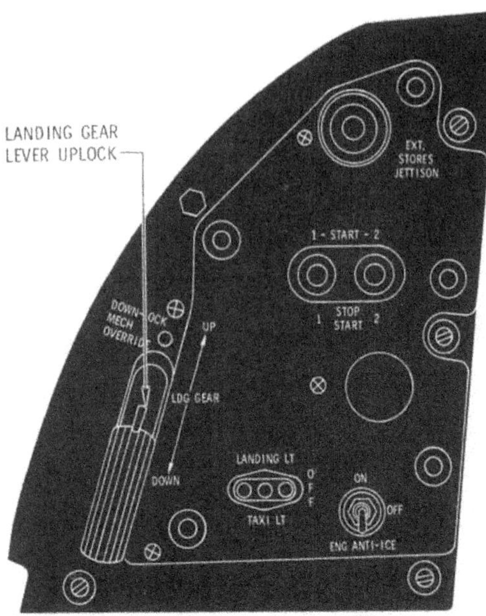

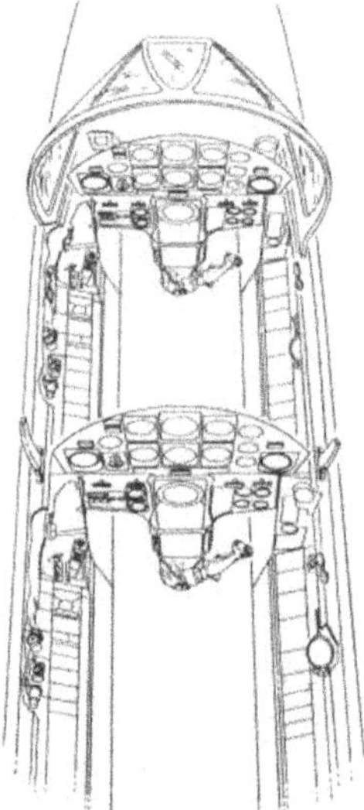

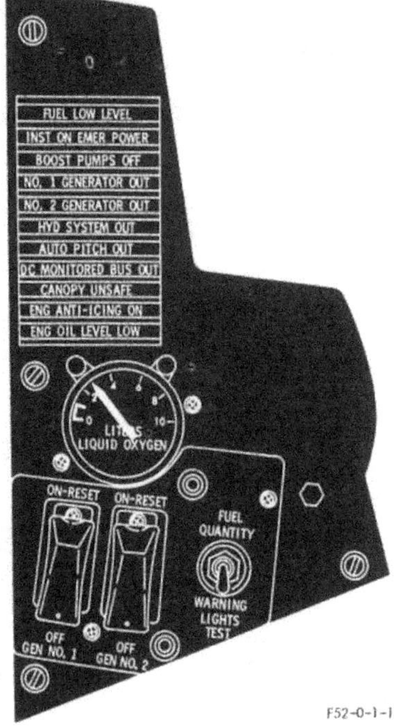

AFT COCKPIT B

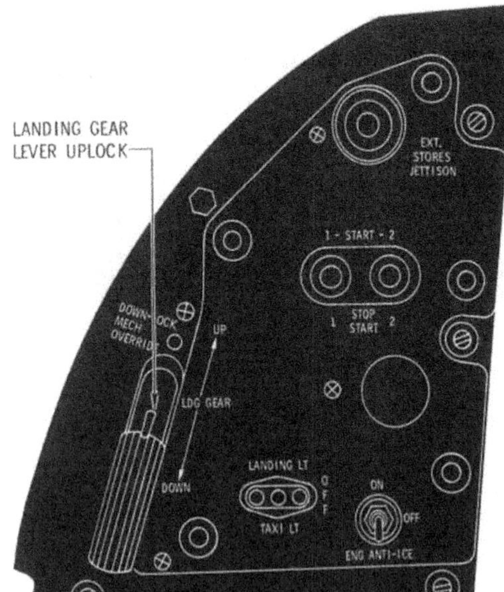

F52-0-1-18

Figure 1-20

TYPICAL LEFT AND RIGHT FORWARD PANELS (C) (D)

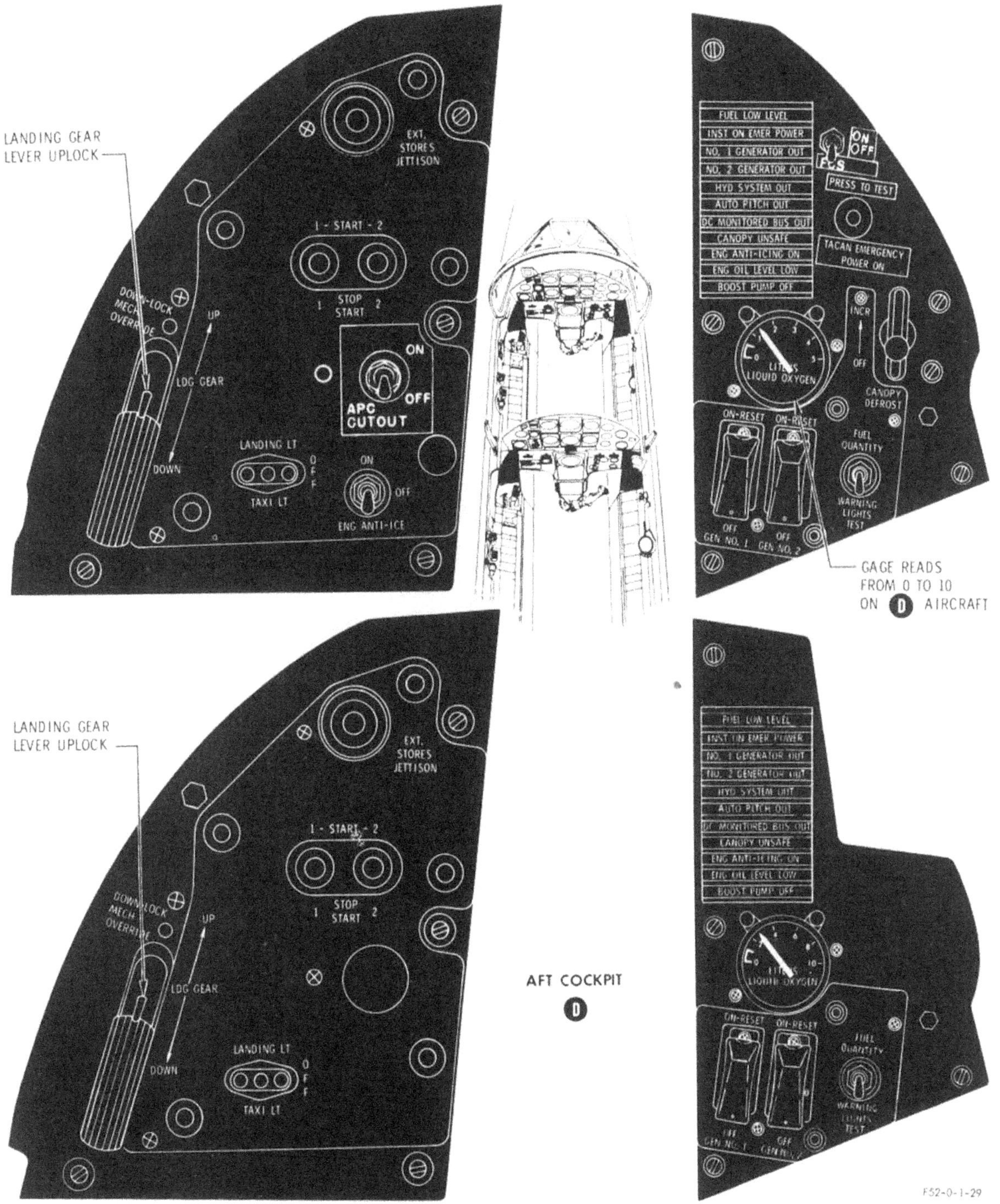
LANDING GEAR LEVER UPLOCK
EXT. STORES JETTISON
1 - START - 2
1 STOP START 2
DOWN-LOCK MECH OVERRIDE
UP
LDG GEAR
DOWN
ON
OFF
APC CUTOUT
LANDING LT
OFF
TAXI LT
ENG ANTI-ICE
FUEL LOW LEVEL
INST ON EMER POWER
NO. 1 GENERATOR OUT
NO. 2 GENERATOR OUT
HYD SYSTEM OUT
AUTO PITCH OUT
DC MONITORED BUS OUT
CANOPY UNSAFE
ENG ANTI-ICING ON
ENG OIL LEVEL LOW
BOOST PUMP OFF
FCS
PRESS TO TEST
TACAN EMERGENCY POWER ON
INCR
CANOPY DEFROST
LITERS LIQUID OXYGEN
ON-RESET
FUEL QUANTITY
WARNING LIGHTS TEST
GEN NO. 1
GEN NO. 2
GAGE READS FROM 0 TO 10 ON (D) AIRCRAFT
AFT COCKPIT (D)
F52-0-1-29

Figure 1-21

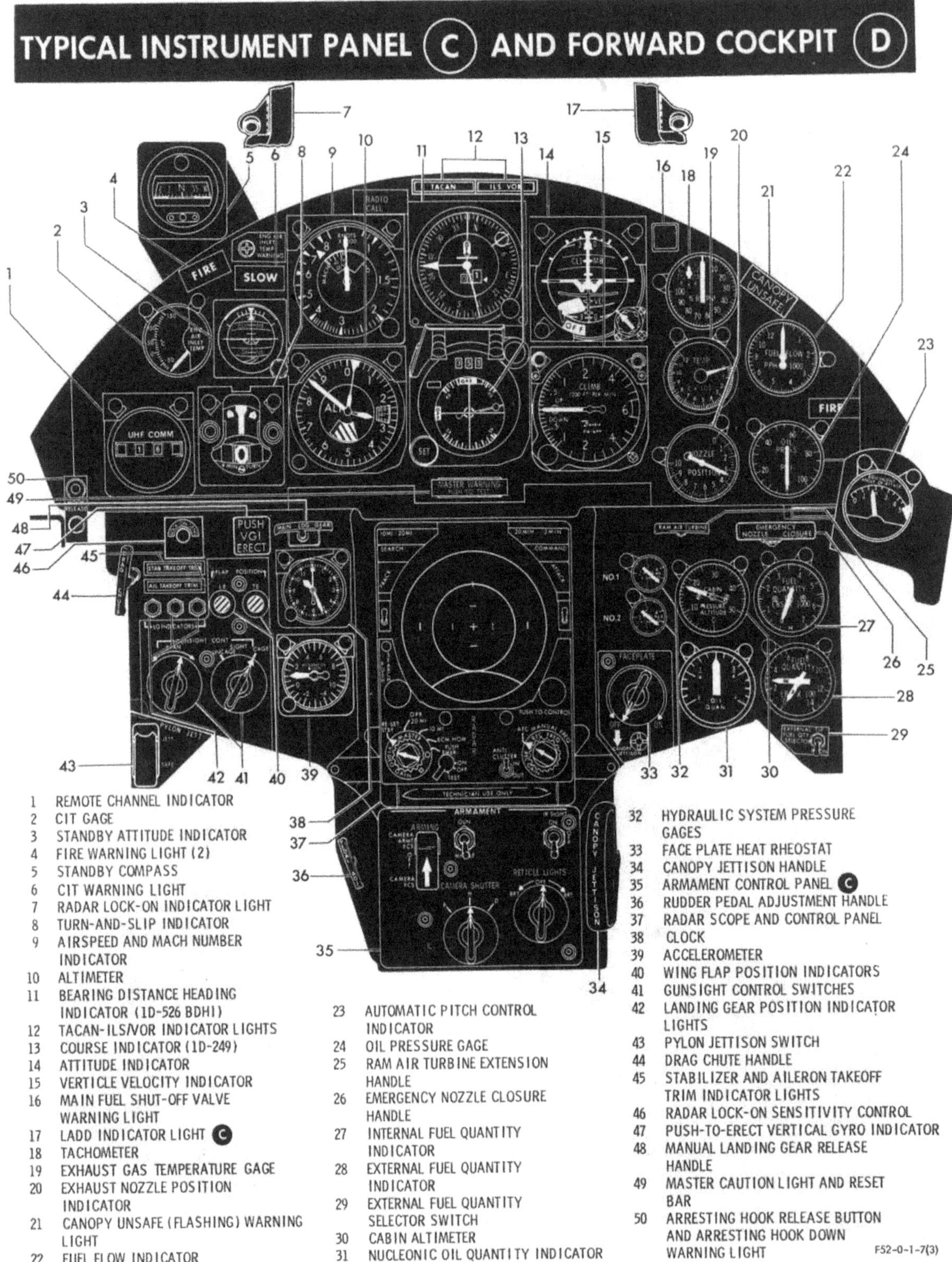
TYPICAL INSTRUMENT PANEL (C) AND FORWARD COCKPIT (D)
1 REMOTE CHANNEL INDICATOR
2 CIT GAGE
3 STANDBY ATTITUDE INDICATOR
4 FIRE WARNING LIGHT (2)
5 STANDBY COMPASS
6 CIT WARNING LIGHT
7 RADAR LOCK-ON INDICATOR LIGHT
8 TURN-AND-SLIP INDICATOR
9 AIRSPEED AND MACH NUMBER INDICATOR
10 ALTIMETER
11 BEARING DISTANCE HEADING INDICATOR (1D-526 BDHI)
12 TACAN-ILS/VOR INDICATOR LIGHTS
13 COURSE INDICATOR (1D-249)
14 ATTITUDE INDICATOR
15 VERTICLE VELOCITY INDICATOR
16 MAIN FUEL SHUT-OFF VALVE WARNING LIGHT
17 LADD INDICATOR LIGHT (C)
18 TACHOMETER
19 EXHAUST GAS TEMPERATURE GAGE
20 EXHAUST NOZZLE POSITION INDICATOR
21 CANOPY UNSAFE (FLASHING) WARNING LIGHT
22 FUEL FLOW INDICATOR
23 AUTOMATIC PITCH CONTROL INDICATOR
24 OIL PRESSURE GAGE
25 RAM AIR TURBINE EXTENSION HANDLE
26 EMERGENCY NOZZLE CLOSURE HANDLE
27 INTERNAL FUEL QUANTITY INDICATOR
28 EXTERNAL FUEL QUANTITY INDICATOR
29 EXTERNAL FUEL QUANTITY SELECTOR SWITCH
30 CABIN ALTIMETER
31 NUCLEONIC OIL QUANTITY INDICATOR
32 HYDRAULIC SYSTEM PRESSURE GAGES
33 FACE PLATE HEAT RHEOSTAT
34 CANOPY JETTISON HANDLE
35 ARMAMENT CONTROL PANEL (C)
36 RUDDER PEDAL ADJUSTMENT HANDLE
37 RADAR SCOPE AND CONTROL PANEL
38 CLOCK
39 ACCELEROMETER
40 WING FLAP POSITION INDICATORS
41 GUNSIGHT CONTROL SWITCHES
42 LANDING GEAR POSITION INDICATOR LIGHTS
43 PYLON JETTISON SWITCH
44 DRAG CHUTE HANDLE
45 STABILIZER AND AILERON TAKEOFF TRIM INDICATOR LIGHTS
46 RADAR LOCK-ON SENSITIVITY CONTROL
47 PUSH-TO-ERECT VERTICAL GYRO INDICATOR
48 MANUAL LANDING GEAR RELEASE HANDLE
49 MASTER CAUTION LIGHT AND RESET BAR
50 ARRESTING HOOK RELEASE BUTTON AND ARRESTING HOOK DOWN WARNING LIGHT
F52-0-1-7(3)

Figure 1-22

TYPICAL AFT COCKPIT INSTRUMENT PANEL (D)

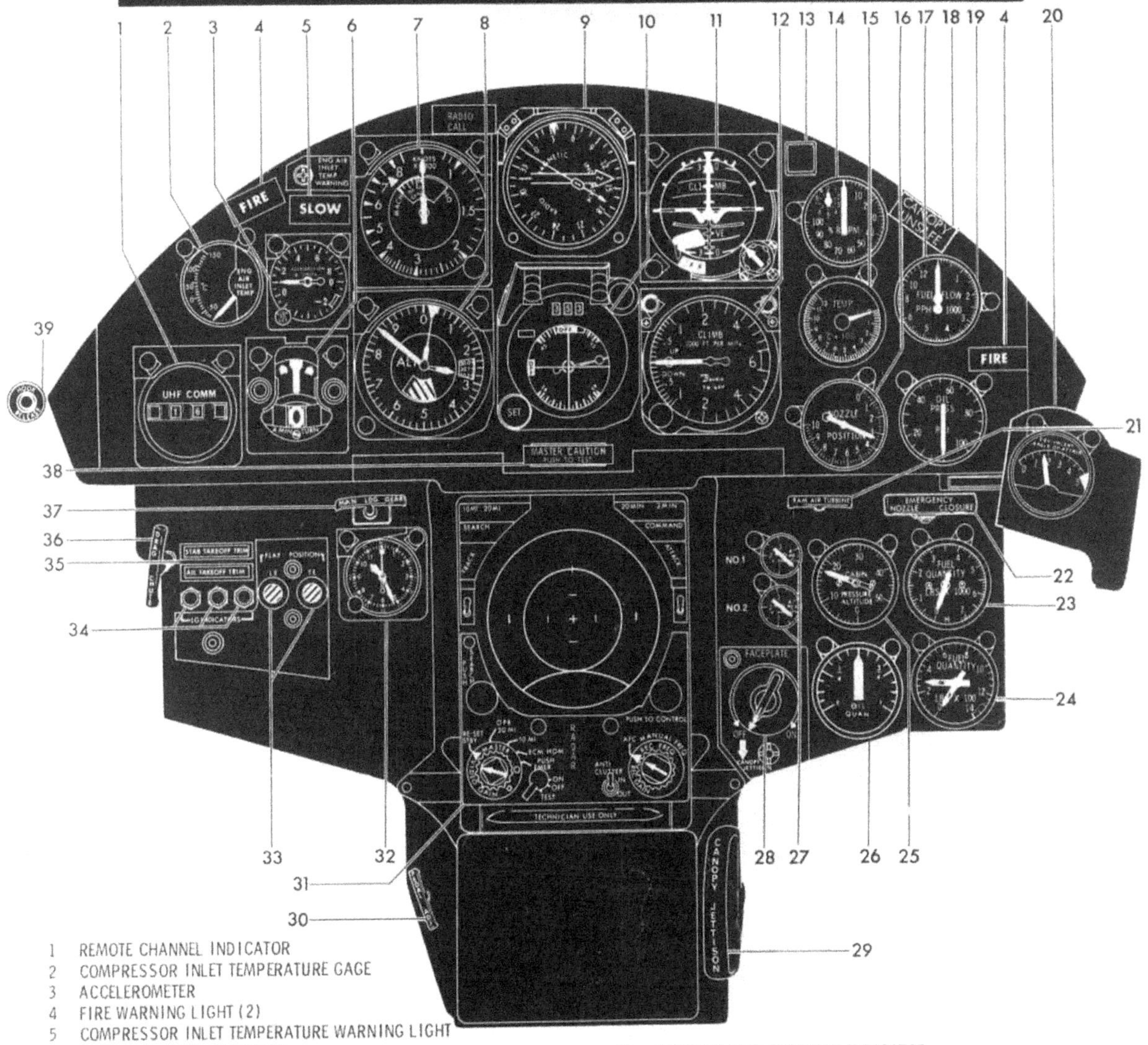

1 REMOTE CHANNEL INDICATOR
2 COMPRESSOR INLET TEMPERATURE GAGE
3 ACCELEROMETER
4 FIRE WARNING LIGHT (2)
5 COMPRESSOR INLET TEMPERATURE WARNING LIGHT
6 TURN-AND-SLIP INDICATOR
7 AIRSPEED AND MACH NUMBER INDICATOR
8 ALTIMETER
9 RADIO MAGNETIC INDICATOR (ID-250)
10 COURSE INDICATOR (ID-249)
11 ATTITUDE INDICATOR
12 VERTICAL VELOCITY INDICATOR
13 MAIN FUEL SHUT-OFF VALVE WARNING LIGHT
14 TACHOMETER
15 EXHAUST GAS TEMPERATURE GAGE
16 EXHAUST NOZZLE POSITION INDICATOR
17 FUEL FLOW INDICATOR
18 CANOPY UNSAFE (FLASHING) WARNING LIGHT
19 OIL PRESSURE GAGE
20 AUTOMATIC PITCH CONTROL INDICATOR
21 RAM AIR TURBINE EXTENSION HANDLE
22 EMERGENCY NOZZLE CLOSURE HANDLE
23 INTERNAL FUEL QUANTITY INDICATOR
24 EXTERNAL FUEL QUANTITY INDICATOR
25 CABIN ALTIMETER
26 NUCLEONIC OIL QUANTITY INDICATOR
27 HYDRAULIC SYSTEM PRESSURE GAGES
28 FACE PLATE HEAT RHEOSTAT
29 CANOPY JETTISON HANDLE
30 RUDDER PEDAL ADJUSTMENT HANDLE
31 RADAR SCOPE AND CONTROL PANEL
32 CLOCK
33 WING FLAP POSITION INDICATORS
34 LANDING GEAR POSITION INDICATOR LIGHTS
35 STABILIZER AND AILERON TAKEOFF TRIM INDICATOR
36 DRAG CHUTE HANDLE
37 MANUAL LANDING GEAR RELEASE HANDLE
38 MASTER CAUTION LIGHT AND RESET BAR
39 ARRESTING HOOK RELEASE BUTTON

F52-0-1-8

Figure 1-23

TYPICAL COCKPIT - LEFT SIDE (C)

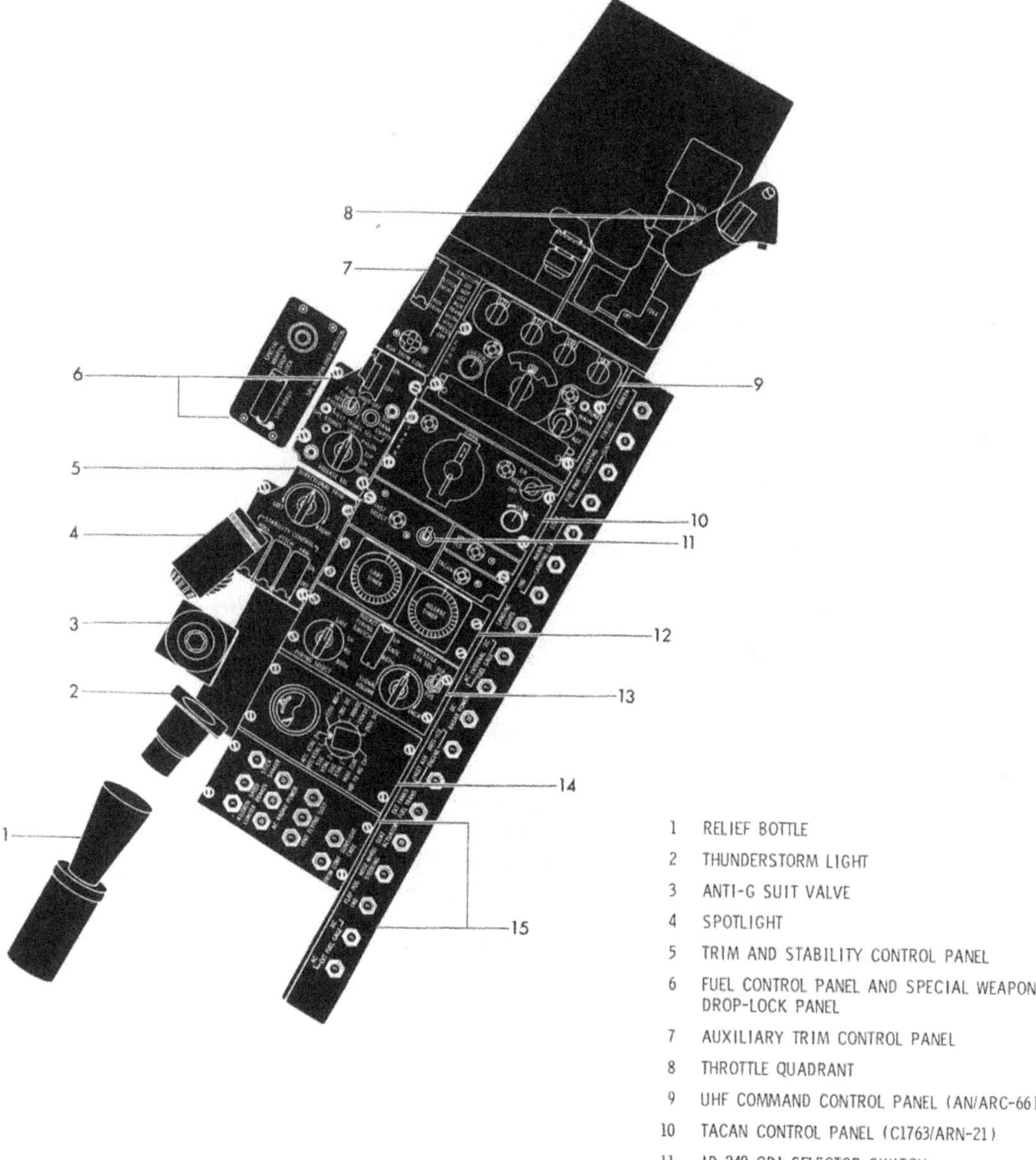

1 RELIEF BOTTLE
2 THUNDERSTORM LIGHT
3 ANTI-G SUIT VALVE
4 SPOTLIGHT
5 TRIM AND STABILITY CONTROL PANEL
6 FUEL CONTROL PANEL AND SPECIAL WEAPON DROP-LOCK PANEL
7 AUXILIARY TRIM CONTROL PANEL
8 THROTTLE QUADRANT
9 UHF COMMAND CONTROL PANEL (AN/ARC-66)
10 TACAN CONTROL PANEL (C1763/ARN-21)
11 ID-249 CDI SELECTOR SWITCH
12 DUAL TIMERS
13 MISSILE CONTROL PANEL
14 RADAR TEST PANEL
15 CIRCUIT BREAKER PANELS

F52-0-1-22A

Figure 1-24

TYPICAL FORWARD COCKPIT - LEFT SIDE (D)

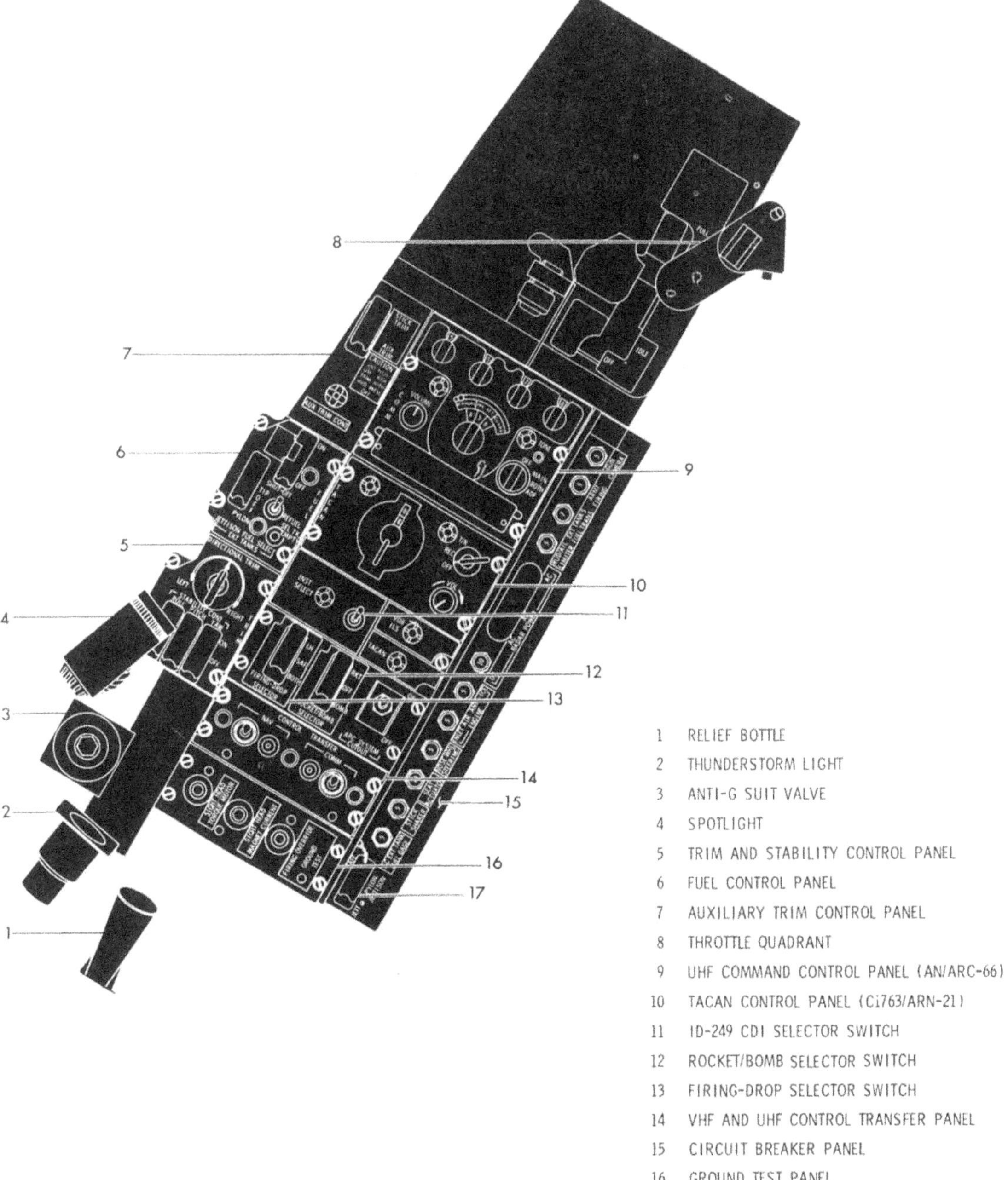

1 RELIEF BOTTLE
2 THUNDERSTORM LIGHT
3 ANTI-G SUIT VALVE
4 SPOTLIGHT
5 TRIM AND STABILITY CONTROL PANEL
6 FUEL CONTROL PANEL
7 AUXILIARY TRIM CONTROL PANEL
8 THROTTLE QUADRANT
9 UHF COMMAND CONTROL PANEL (AN/ARC-66)
10 TACAN CONTROL PANEL (C1763/ARN-21)
11 ID-249 CDI SELECTOR SWITCH
12 ROCKET/BOMB SELECTOR SWITCH
13 FIRING-DROP SELECTOR SWITCH
14 VHF AND UHF CONTROL TRANSFER PANEL
15 CIRCUIT BREAKER PANEL
16 GROUND TEST PANEL
17 PYLON JETTISON SWITCH

F52-0-1-30A

Figure 1-25

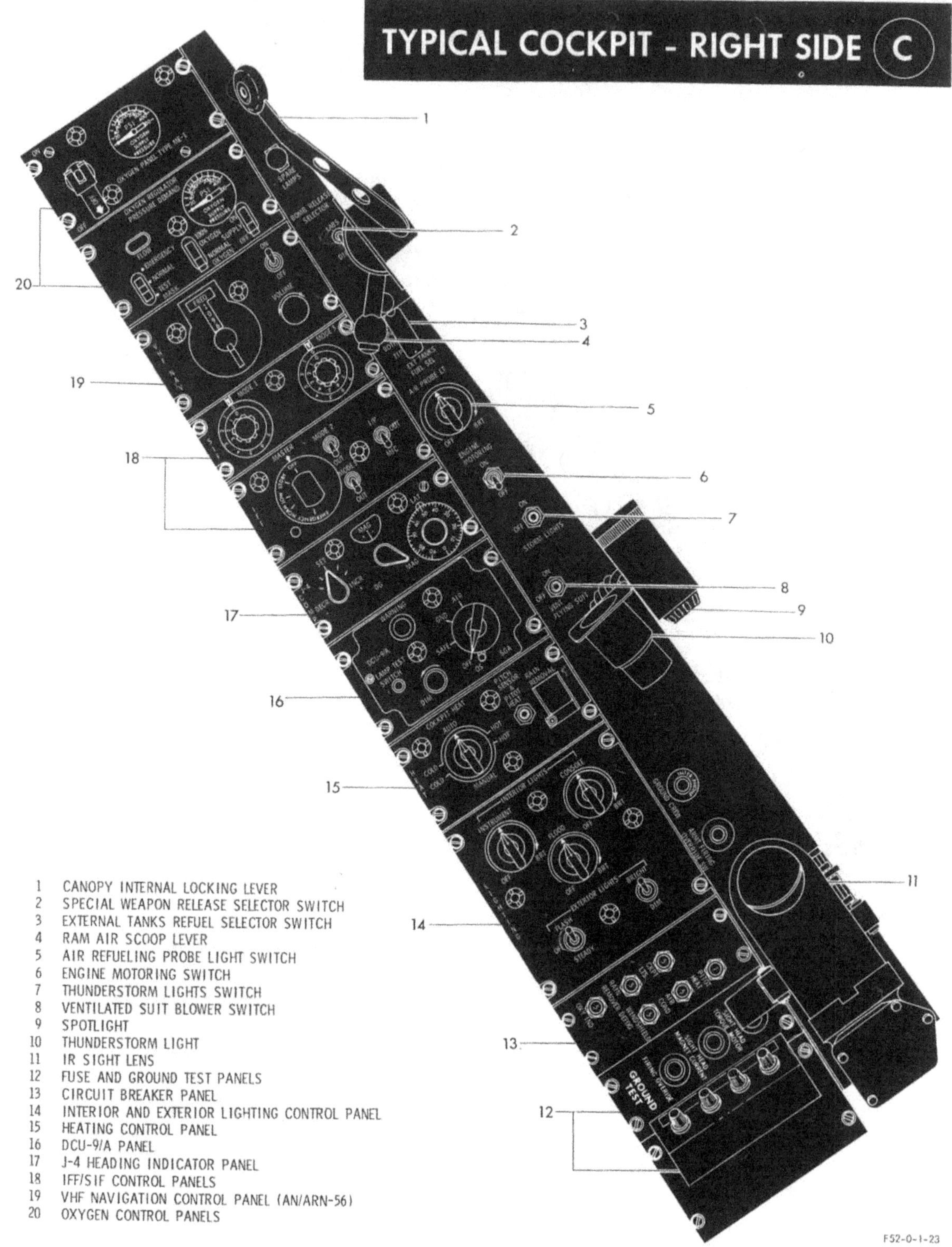
TYPICAL COCKPIT - RIGHT SIDE C
1 CANOPY INTERNAL LOCKING LEVER
2 SPECIAL WEAPON RELEASE SELECTOR SWITCH
3 EXTERNAL TANKS REFUEL SELECTOR SWITCH
4 RAM AIR SCOOP LEVER
5 AIR REFUELING PROBE LIGHT SWITCH
6 ENGINE MOTORING SWITCH
7 THUNDERSTORM LIGHTS SWITCH
8 VENTILATED SUIT BLOWER SWITCH
9 SPOTLIGHT
10 THUNDERSTORM LIGHT
11 IR SIGHT LENS
12 FUSE AND GROUND TEST PANELS
13 CIRCUIT BREAKER PANEL
14 INTERIOR AND EXTERIOR LIGHTING CONTROL PANEL
15 HEATING CONTROL PANEL
16 DCU-9/A PANEL
17 J-4 HEADING INDICATOR PANEL
18 IFF/SIF CONTROL PANELS
19 VHF NAVIGATION CONTROL PANEL (AN/ARN-56)
20 OXYGEN CONTROL PANELS
F52-0-1-23

Figure 1-26

TYPICAL FORWARD COCKPIT - RIGHT SIDE (D)

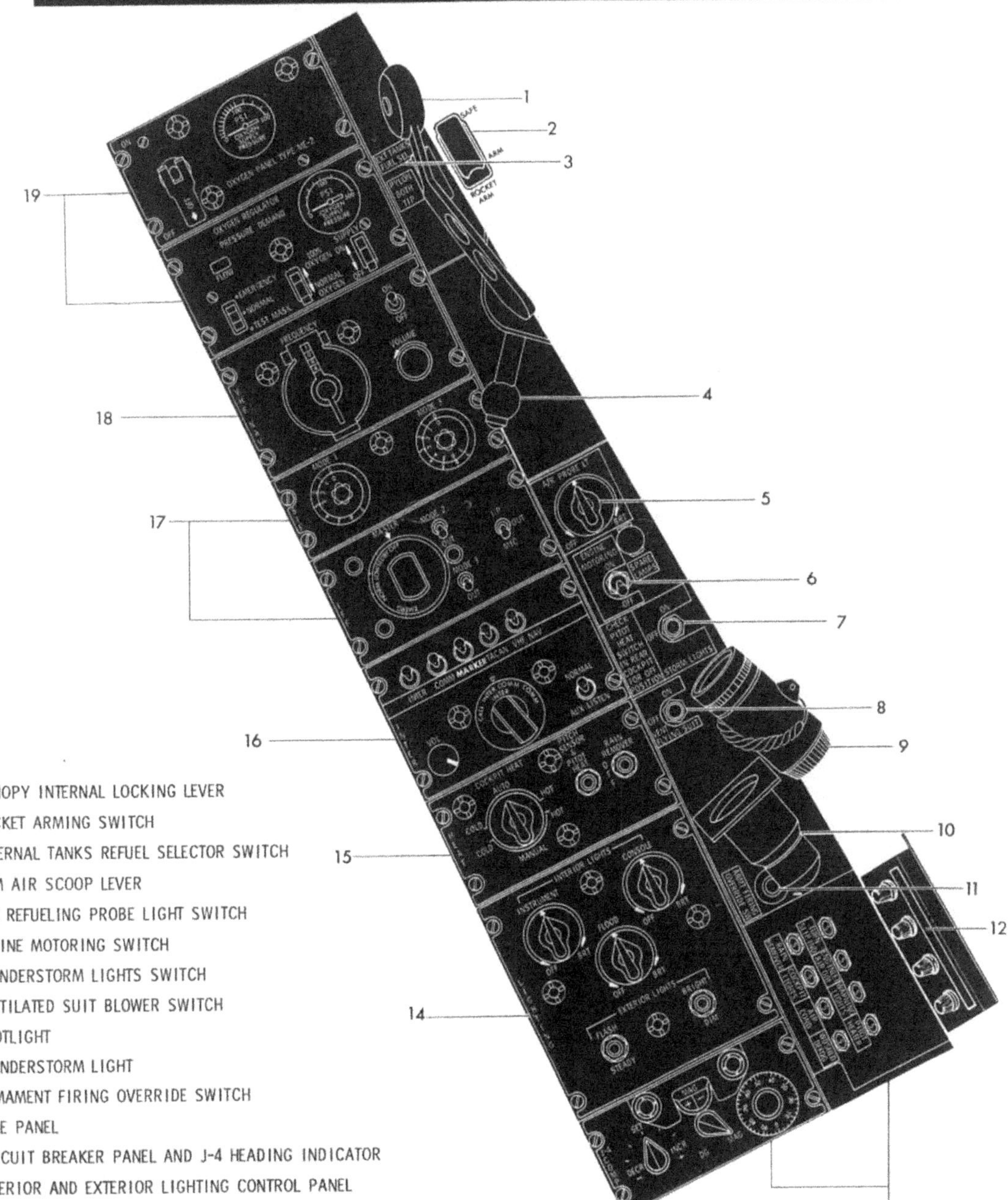

1 CANOPY INTERNAL LOCKING LEVER
2 ROCKET ARMING SWITCH
3 EXTERNAL TANKS REFUEL SELECTOR SWITCH
4 RAM AIR SCOOP LEVER
5 AIR REFUELING PROBE LIGHT SWITCH
6 ENGINE MOTORING SWITCH
7 THUNDERSTORM LIGHTS SWITCH
8 VENTILATED SUIT BLOWER SWITCH
9 SPOTLIGHT
10 THUNDERSTORM LIGHT
11 ARMAMENT FIRING OVERRIDE SWITCH
12 FUSE PANEL
13 CIRCUIT BREAKER PANEL AND J-4 HEADING INDICATOR
14 INTERIOR AND EXTERIOR LIGHTING CONTROL PANEL
15 HEATING CONTROL PANEL
16 INTERPHONE CONTROL PANEL
17 IFF/SIF CONTROL PANELS
18 VHF NAVIGATION CONTROL PANEL
19 OXYGEN PANELS

F52-0-1-30

Figure 1-27

TYPICAL AFT COCKPIT - LEFT SIDE (D)

NOTE

ITEMS 1, 10, 11, 12, AND 13 APPEAR IN (C) AND FORWARD COCKPIT (D) ONLY

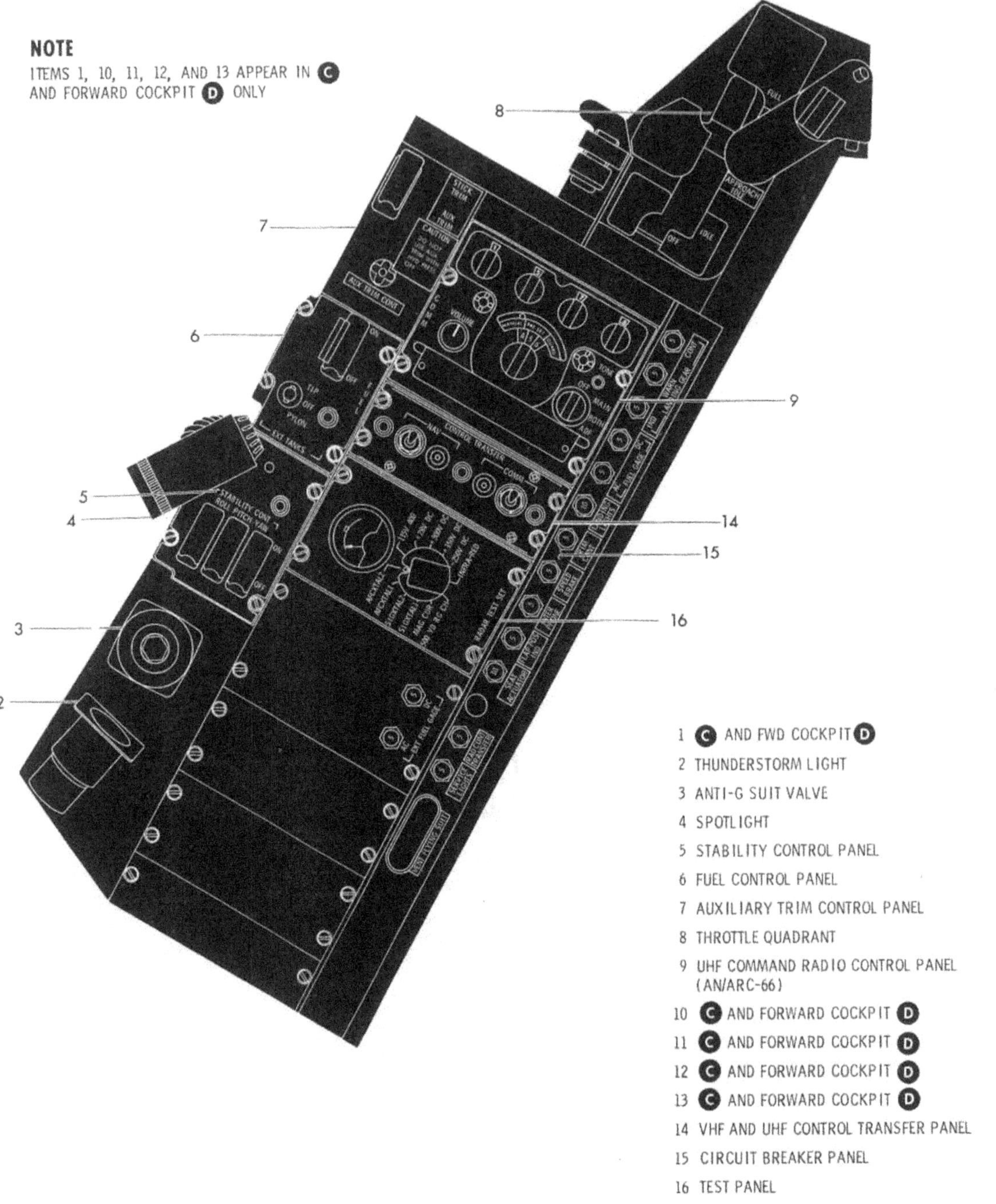

1 (C) AND FWD COCKPIT (D)
2 THUNDERSTORM LIGHT
3 ANTI-G SUIT VALVE
4 SPOTLIGHT
5 STABILITY CONTROL PANEL
6 FUEL CONTROL PANEL
7 AUXILIARY TRIM CONTROL PANEL
8 THROTTLE QUADRANT
9 UHF COMMAND RADIO CONTROL PANEL (AN/ARC-66)
10 (C) AND FORWARD COCKPIT (D)
11 (C) AND FORWARD COCKPIT (D)
12 (C) AND FORWARD COCKPIT (D)
13 (C) AND FORWARD COCKPIT (D)
14 VHF AND UHF CONTROL TRANSFER PANEL
15 CIRCUIT BREAKER PANEL
16 TEST PANEL

F52-0-1-31

Figure 1-28

AFT COCKPIT-RIGHT SIDE (D)

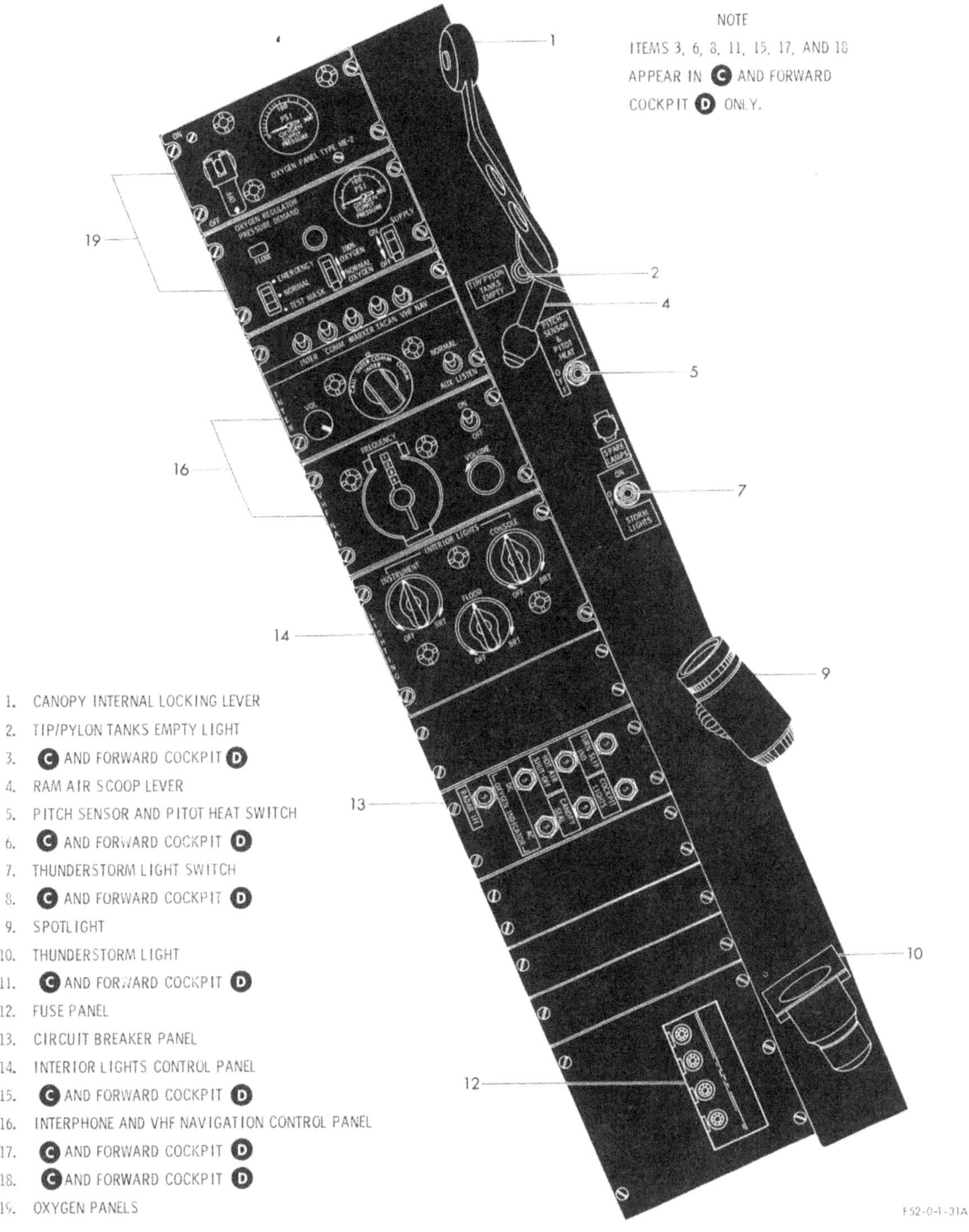

1. CANOPY INTERNAL LOCKING LEVER
2. TIP/PYLON TANKS EMPTY LIGHT
3. (C) AND FORWARD COCKPIT (D)
4. RAM AIR SCOOP LEVER
5. PITCH SENSOR AND PITOT HEAT SWITCH
6. (C) AND FORWARD COCKPIT (D)
7. THUNDERSTORM LIGHT SWITCH
8. (C) AND FORWARD COCKPIT (D)
9. SPOTLIGHT
10. THUNDERSTORM LIGHT
11. (C) AND FORWARD COCKPIT (D)
12. FUSE PANEL
13. CIRCUIT BREAKER PANEL
14. INTERIOR LIGHTS CONTROL PANEL
15. (C) AND FORWARD COCKPIT (D)
16. INTERPHONE AND VHF NAVIGATION CONTROL PANEL
17. (C) AND FORWARD COCKPIT (D)
18. (C) AND FORWARD COCKPIT (D)
19. OXYGEN PANELS

F52-0-1-31A

Figure 1-29

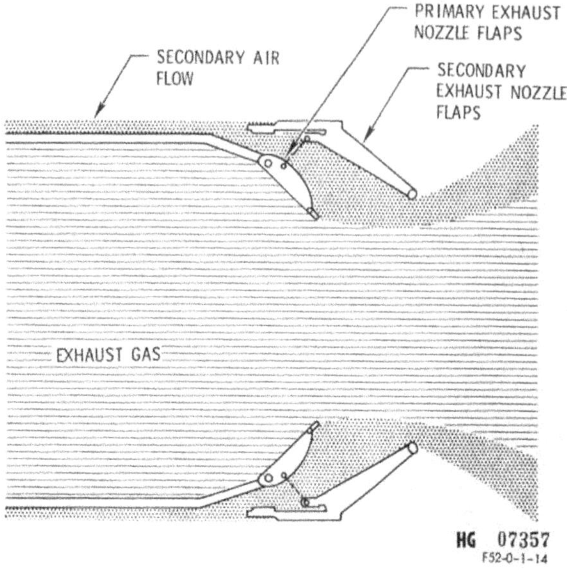

Figure 1-30

GUIDED EXPANSION EXHAUST NOZZLE 19

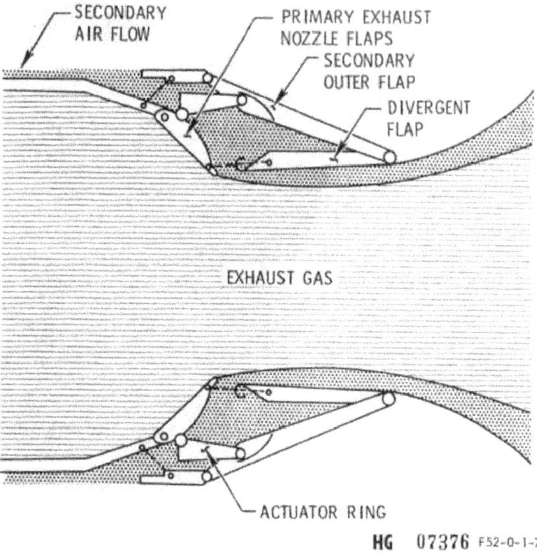

Figure 1-31

AFTERBURNER FUEL SYSTEM. 

Fuel from the aircraft fuel tanks is admitted to the afterburner on-off valve, and when the afterburner system is operating the fuel passes through this valve and into the afterburner fuel pump. (See figure 1-8.) From the afterburner fuel pump the fuel passes to the afterburner fuel control and then to the afterburner fuel oil-cooler. From the cooler the fuel passes through a filter to the flow divider and selector valve and on to the spray bars. Fuel flow is taken immediately downstream of the pressurizing and drain valve in the engine fuel system and is used for ignition purposes. The ignition system receives power from the No. 2 ac bus.

Afterburner On-Off Valve.

The afterburner on-off valve is located at the inlet of the afterburner fuel pump and allows fuel to pass into the fuel pump on a high-pressure fuel signal from the engine fuel control unit. This signal is affected first by throttle position, and second by engine speed. If the throttle is advanced into the afterburner region, the high pressure fuel signal will be applied to the engine speed control valve in the engine fuel control unit. If engine speed is high enough the signal will pass through this valve and into the afterburner on-off valve, thereby actuating it. If there is no signal the valve will remain closed and no fuel will enter the afterburner pump.

Afterburner Fuel Pump.

The afterburner fuel pump is an engine-driven centrifugal pump. It rotates continuously, discharging fuel to the afterburner fuel system only when the afterburner on-off valve is open.

Afterburner Fuel Control. 

The afterburner fuel control is a hydromechanical device which meters total fuel flow as a function of throttle lever position and compressor discharge pressure. The control meters the proper quantity of fuel and directs the flow to the core and annulus manifolds. No flow interruption occurs during the transition from core to core-and-annulus operations. The change from single (core) manifold operation to dual (core plus annulus) manifold operation is accomplished by increasing the throttle lever beyond a predetermined setting. During this throttle advance, the core flow is maintained constant while the annulus flow is increased.

Afterburner Pressurizing Valve. 3B 19 The flow out of the core and annulus discharge ports of the control enter the core and annulus inlet ports of the afterburner pressurizing valve. Four spring-loaded valves in the pressurizing valve split the core and annulus flows into primary and secondary fuel flows as a function of fuel pressure.

Afterburner Core Burning Sequence. (*See figures 1-32 and 1-7*) 3B

Four full-circle manifolds supply fuel to 20 four-tube spraybars. Each manifold supplies fuel to one spraybar at each of the 20 locations. At low augmentation power settings, fuel is delivered through the primary and secondary core spraybars in a circular area consisting of about 40 percent of the tailpipe cross-sectional area. As throttle angle is increased past 90 degrees, annulus flow begins, supplying fuel to the remainder of the area. The burning in the annulus increases as the fuel flow increases until, at 113 degrees throttle angle, the fuel—air ratio is equal to that in the core and burning is uniform.

Core Burner System (*See figures 1-32 and 1-7*) 19

At initiation of afterburning, fuel is introduced at the core of the gas stream. As more thrust is demanded, the fuel/air ratio in the core is held constant, and additional fuel is introduced into the annulus surrounding the core until Maximum thrust is achieved. This provides afterburner light-off at low fuel flows with minimal thrust jump, and fully modulated thrust to maximum power.

The system is composed of twenty-one quadruple spraybars which are mounted on the forward exhaust duct and supported by bushings on the inner exhaust cone. The spraybars have four tubes each, for primary and secondary flow for the core and the annulus respectively. Fuel flow can be modulated from 2700 pounds per hour to 34,000 pounds per hour. Full circle manifolds, with hinge mounts designed to minimize thermal stresses and damp vibratory loads, supply fuel to the spraybars.

Fuel Manifolds and Spraybars. During light-off and low afterburner power settings, fuel is distributed only to the core manifolds and core tubes of the spraybars. This fuel is distributed in the afterburner in a circular area which is approximately 40% of the total afterburner area inside the liners of the duct. Fuel burns in this circular area in the core of the exhaust duct. As the throttle is advanced, fuel flow to the core increases until the core fuel/air ratio reaches a predetermined value. Core fuel flow and fuel/air ratio are then held constant, and increased fuel flow is directed to the annulus manifolds and spraybar tubes. These spraybar tubes distribute fuel to the annular area formed by the outer periphery of the core and exhaust duct liners. This area is approximately 60% of the total area of the afterburner. As fuel flow is increased, the burning in the annulus increases until at maximum power, fuel/air ratio in the annulus is the same as that in the core, and afterburning is uniform.

The use of primary and secondary tubes in the core and annulus provides improved burning at altitude. As altitude increases, air flow decreases and therefore fuel flow decreases. With lower fuel flow in the secondary tubes, secondary pressures decrease and the possibility of fuel vaporization increases. To prevent such vaporization, fuel flow in the secondary manifolds is restricted at compressor discharge pressure of less than 76 psia. In such cases all fuel is distributed by the primary manifolds, and the primary fuel pressures are sufficient to prevent fuel vaporization at high altitude.

AFTERBURNER IGNITION SYSTEM.

Afterburner ignition is controlled by a throttle-actuated ignition switch. The afterburner ignition unit receives power from the No. 2 ac bus when the throttle is moved to any position in the afterburner range. A spark plug located within the torch igniter operates continuously during afterburning, assuring positive ignition of the torch igniter.

Afterburner Ignition Switch (If installed) 3B

The afterburner ignition control switch (figures 1-14, 1-15) is a two-position (ON-OFF) switch located on the left console. It is used to disconnect electrical power from the afterburner spark plug. This switch is used primarily by maintenance personnel to disconnect the continuous ignition feature when external power is supplied to the aircraft. This switch should be ON during flight.

Afterburner Fuel Control. 

The afterburner fuel control is linked mechanically to the engine fuel control unit. Fuel entering the afterburner fuel control is metered by the fuel control in response to throttle movement and changes in compressor discharge pressure (optimum fuel—air ratio). The afterburner fuel control is made to hold a constant pressure drop across an orifice while the area of that orifice is varied in accordance with throttle position and compressor discharge pressure.

AFTERBURNER FUEL MANIFOLD 3B 19

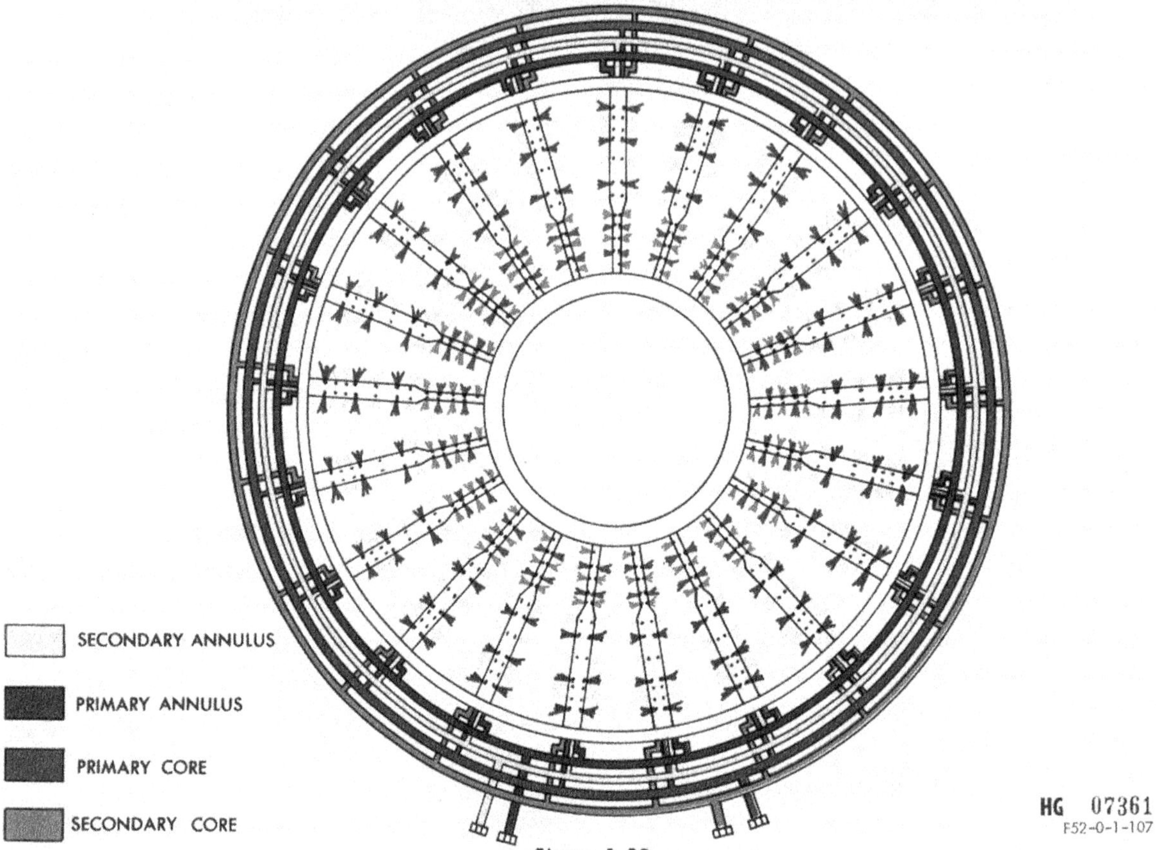

SECONDARY ANNULUS

PRIMARY ANNULUS

PRIMARY CORE

SECONDARY CORE

HG 07361
F52-0-1-107

Figure 1-32

Afterburner Fuel Oil-Cooler. Fuel from the afterburner fuel control passes through the fuel oil-cooler which removes heat from the engine oil in much the same manner as the fuel oil-cooler in the engine fuel system.

Flow Divider and Selecter Valve. 7A Metered fuel from the afterburner fuel control passes through the fuel oil-cooler and fuel filter to the inlet of the flow divider and selector valve. Here, fuel is distributed to the various sectors of the afterburner to obtain the best spray pattern for the condition of afterburning required.

Afterburner Sector Light-Up. 7A

The flow divider and selector valve assembly distributes the fuel to the spray bars in sequence. (See figure 1-33.)

There are four stages of fuel flow:

1. Primary sector.
2. Secondary sector.
3. Primary uniform.
4. Secondary uniform.

When the throttle is first advanced to the afterburner position, the primary sector lights up. Further advancement causes the secondary sector to light up. When the throttle is advanced still more a distinct increase in thrust occurs. As the throttle is advanced to the maximum afterburner position, the final (secondary uniform) manifold receives fuel. This is full uniform burning.

COMPRESSOR AND VARIABLE STATOR OPERATION. 3B 7A

To understand the J79 engine it is important that the pilot understand the need for the variable inlet guide vane and stator system. In order to optimize subsonic cruise performance in supersonic engines a high-pressure-ratio compressor is desirable. High-pressure-ratio compressors, however, can be designed to operate efficiently in only one speed range without incorporating some type

AFTERBURNER FUEL MANIFOLD (7A)

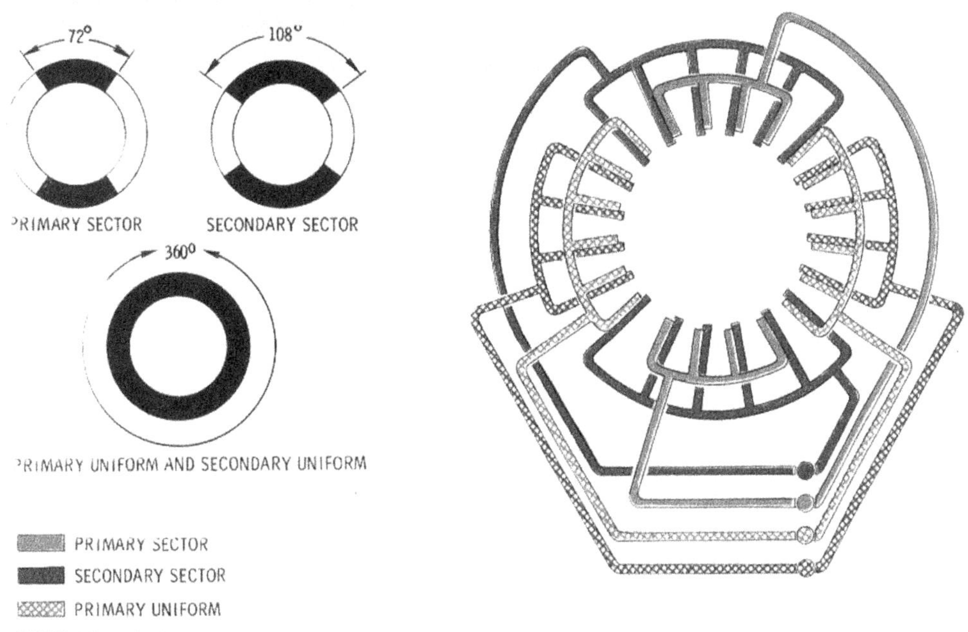

Figure 1-33

of compensating device. This compensation can be accomplished by several methods, most common of which are the dual-compressor system and the variable stator system (as used in the J79 engine). The J79 was designed for maximum operating efficiency at the higher rpm settings. With a fixed guide vane position, the higher the engine rpm the lower the effective angle of attack of the compressor blades, and conversely, as the rpm is reduced the effective angle of attack is increased to the point that blade stall will occur in a manner comparable to an airplane wing stall. The variable inlet guide vane and stator system (referred to only as IGV) was incorporated in the J79 engine to allow stall-free operation throughout the entire speed range. As rpm is reduced from Military, the IGV will start to close and track closed as a function of rpm at any given air inlet temperature. At sea level standard-day conditions the IGV will be fully open above 94.5 percent rpm; below 94.5 percent rpm they will track as a function of rpm to the closed position, reaching the closed position at 67 percent rpm. The IGV track through a total of 35 degrees of travel from open to closed. The closing of the IGV avoids the stall area by directing airflow against the compressor blades at an angle less than the critical angle as rpm is varied. In addition, total airflow through the compressor is reduced as rpm decreases and the IGV shift toward closed, relieving the load on the rear stages of the compressor and thereby avoiding compressor stalls. The IGV control senses compressor inlet temperature (CIT) as well as physical rpm of the engine. The IGV schedule follows a constant slope as a function of engine rpm; however, the slope is shifted as a result of CIT. At higher CIT values the IGV will start to close at a higher indicated rpm, and conversely, will start to close at a lower rpm when the CIT is below standard.

CORRECTED RPM.  

The term "corrected rpm" is often encountered and needs clarification to further understand the operation of the J79. The pumping characteristics of the compressor are affected by the temperature of the air entering the compressor, since temperature affects the density. An increase in CIT is effectively the same as a reduction in rpm as far as the compressor is concerned, and conversely, a decrease in CIT is effectively the same as an increase in rpm. To maintain a constant mass flow of air through the engine the physical rpm must be varied directly as a function of compressor inlet temperature. As an example, 100 percent indicated rpm with a 15°C inlet temperature is 100 percent "corrected rpm." A 100 percent indicated rpm with an inlet temperature at 95°C corrects to an effective, or corrected, rpm of 88.5 percent while 100 percent indicated rpm at −28°C is a corrected rpm of 108.6 percent.

ENGINE SPEED CONTROL FEATURES. 

In addition to its normal governing functions, the engine fuel control unit senses CIT, the value of which is integrated with the rpm signal and a corrected rpm is computed mechanically within the unit. This information is used to vary the IGV angle and limits corrected engine rpm to a preset maximum.

HIGH CORRECTED RPM AND RPM CUTBACK. 

With a set rpm of 100 percent engine speed the corrected rpm increases as CIT decreases. At approximately −12°C, 100 percent indicated rpm is equal to 105 percent corrected rpm. At this point the engine fuel control unit begins to reduce fuel flow to the engine, thereby reducing engine speed, limiting corrected rpm to a maximum of 108.6 percent. The reduction in rpm as the aircraft climbs into colder ambient air conditions is not an rpm droop, as was prevalent with earlier jet engines but rather is a scheduled reduction in engine speed to maintain corrected rpm within limits (See figure 1-34).

LOW CORRECTED RPM AND T_2 RESET. 3B 

As CIT is increased, the corrected rpm decreases and would decrease to the point where a low corrected rpm stall would be encountered if no compensating action were taken. The IGV schedule is designed to follow corrected engine rpm and will close to provide a stall margin. Increasing engine rpm also increases corrected rpm for an increased stall margin and at the same time increases the maximum available thrust. This increase in rpm to a maximum of 103.5 (±1.0) percent indicated is referred to as T_2 reset.

3B T_2 reset is initiated at approximately 79°C CIT. Indicated rpm will increase from 100% at 79°C to 103.5% (±1.0%) at CIT of 82°C, or above. The flight idle fuel flow schedule is also raised as a function of CIT. This results in flight idle rpm being the same as maximum rpm at 79°C and above. A throttle "chop" below Military thrust will not produce a reduction in rpm. This feature was incorporated to prevent a sudden reduction in rpm at high Mach numbers which would decrease engine air flow, thereby causing duct buzz.

Note 3B

There are currently two types of main fuel controls in use and their T_2 reset functions differ. The earlier main fuel control starts reset at a higher CIT and resets slowly. Newer main fuel controls start reset at a lower CIT and engine speed will increase rapidly, as shown in figure 1-34.

7A T_2 reset is initiated at approximately 92°C CIT. Indicated rpm will increase from 100 percent at 92°C to 103.5 (±1.0) percent at CIT of 105°C or above. This flight idle fuel flow schedule is also raised as a function of CIT and flight idle rpm is the same as maximum rpm at 92°C and above. Therefore a throttle "chop" below Military thrust will not produce an immediate rpm reduction. This feature was incorporated to prevent a sudden reduction in rpm at high Mach numbers which would decrease engine airflow, thereby causing duct buzz. (See figure 1-34.)

Note 

T_2 reset can start as low as 70°C due to temperature lag or cockpit gage error.

CAUTION

EGT must be monitored closely during T_2 reset operation to avoid exceeding limits.

CDP LIMITER. 

When the maximum airspeed region of the airplane is approached at low altitude, compressor inlet pressure is drastically increased. Compressor discharge pressure (CDP) approaches the maximum value permitted by the physical strength of the engine components. A CDP limiter incorporated in the engine fuel control unit, senses CDP and reduces fuel flow to the engine thus allowing rpm to decrease when the maximum CDP limit is reached.

CIT SENSOR.  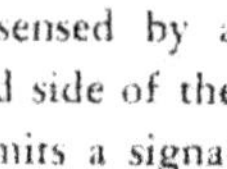

Compressor inlet temperature (CIT) is sensed by a capillary tube located in the lower left-hand side of the compressor inlet. This capillary unit transmits a signal to the engine fuel control unit, reacts on internal portions of the fuel controller, and modifies IGV and fuel flow schedules as a function of CIT.

T_2 RESET AND CUTBACK VS ENGINE RPM

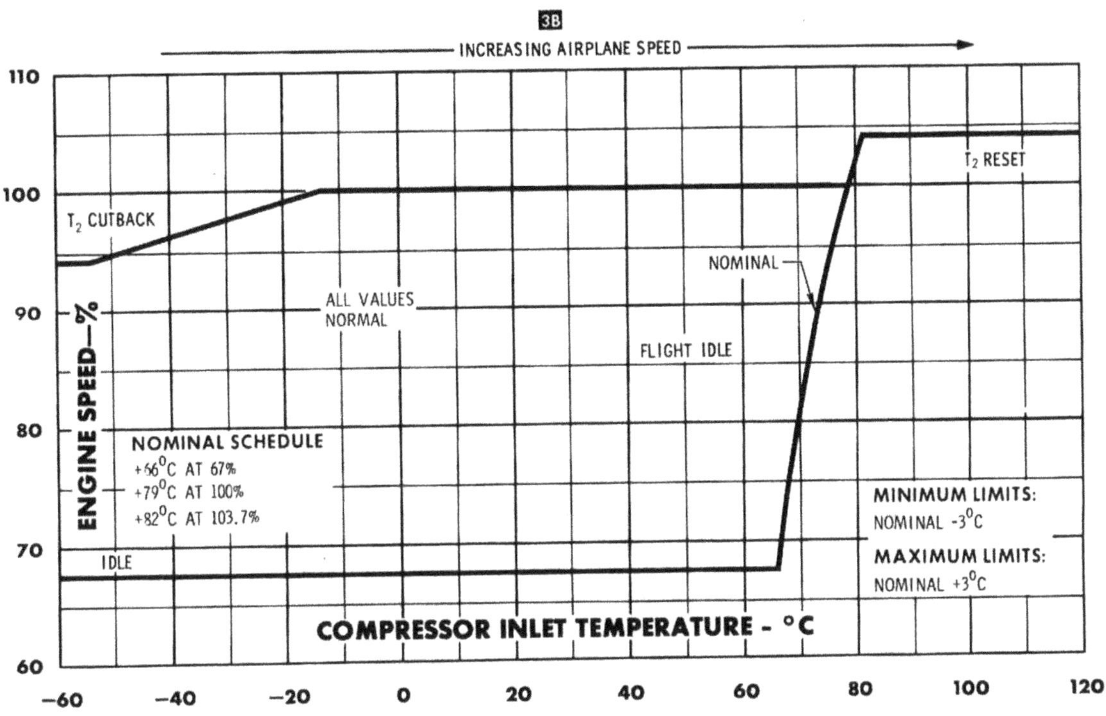

3B
INCREASING AIRPLANE SPEED
T2 CUTBACK
T2 RESET
NOMINAL
ALL VALUES NORMAL
FLIGHT IDLE
ENGINE SPEED—%
NOMINAL SCHEDULE
+66°C AT 67%
+79°C AT 100%
+82°C AT 103.7%
IDLE
MINIMUM LIMITS:
NOMINAL -3°C
MAXIMUM LIMITS:
NOMINAL +3°C
COMPRESSOR INLET TEMPERATURE - °C

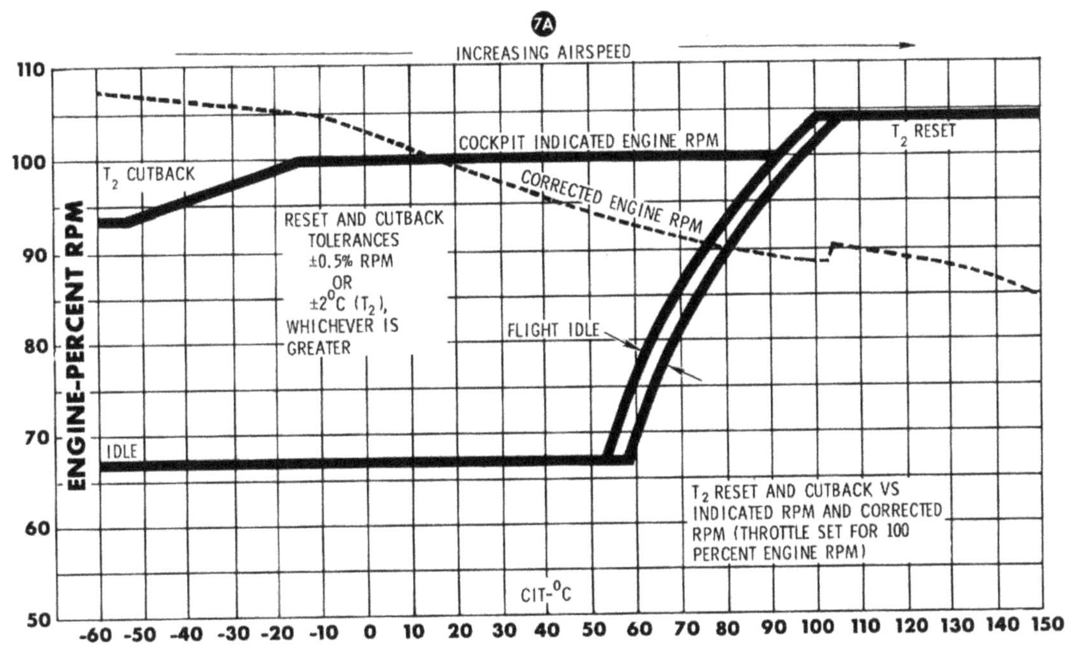

7A
INCREASING AIRSPEED
COCKPIT INDICATED ENGINE RPM
T2 RESET
T2 CUTBACK
CORRECTED ENGINE RPM
RESET AND CUTBACK TOLERANCES ±0.5% RPM OR ±2°C (T2), WHICHEVER IS GREATER
FLIGHT IDLE
ENGINE-PERCENT RPM
IDLE
T2 RESET AND CUTBACK VS INDICATED RPM AND CORRECTED RPM (THROTTLE SET FOR 100 PERCENT ENGINE RPM)
CIT-°C

F52-0-1-102

Figure 1-34

IGV RESET SWITCH. 3B

Since failures of the CIT sensing system could occur because of breakage of the capillary tube, resulting in a loss of fluid, an IGV reset switch has been incorporated as an emergency device. Loss of the capillary fluid would result in the CIT sensor giving a −65°F signal to the fuel control unit. This would schedule the IGV to open more than required in the intermediate speed range and would produce engine stalls when the throttle was retarded. Should the CIT sensor fail, and schedule the IGV to the −65°F point, the IGV reset switch may be activated to introduce to the engine fuel control unit a false signal corresponding to an inlet temperature of +145°F. When the CIT is below this value the IGV will be operating more closed than required; this will result in increased stall margin. It must be stressed that the IGV do not go to a fixed position when this switch is activated, but rather follow the same schedule rpm as they would with normal operation with an inlet temperature of +145°F.

ENGINE COMPRESSOR STALLS. 

Engine compressor stalls can be caused by various factors, such as engine fuel control malfunction, IGV misrigging, CIT sensor cold shift, or afterburner surging. Regardless of the cause, the result is that the compressor blades stall in much the same manner as the wings of an aircraft. During normal operation, the compressor blades generate axial airflow from the front of the compressor to the rear, at ever-increasing pressure. This pressurized air is delivered to the combustion chamber, where it is heated, and exhausted through the nozzle at a greater velocity than it had at the compressor inlet, thus producing thrust. A compressor stall occurs whenever this axial airflow is interrupted in its normal rearward travel and slows or stops at some stage of compression, thus stalling the airfoil-shaped compressor blades. Some of the reasons for this airflow interruption are the following:

1. Foreign object damage which destroys the airfoil shape of the compressor blades, eliminating their ability to pump air.
2. Corrosion on the compressor blades and stators which reduces their capability to pump air at ever-increasing pressure, the same way frost destroys the ability of an aircraft wing to produce lift.
3. If the fuel "schedule" during a throttle burst is too high, pressures in the combustion chamber may increase to the point beyond which the compressor cannot pump air and the axial velocity of the air slows to the point where the blades stall.
4. If the inlet guide vanes are too wide open for a given engine condition, the front of the compressor will pump too much air and overflow the rear of the compressor, resulting in a pile-up of air which decreases the axial airflow velocity, and the compressor will stall.

Other factors such as aircraft high G load, high angle-of-attack with its resulting compressor inlet pressure distortion, or operation at high Mach numbers and CIT outside the prescribed limits can also lead to compressor stall.

Primarily, there are two types of engine compressor stalls, both of which are relatively easy to recognize. The first type, most commonly associated with high Mach number flight, is characterized by loud banging and chugging sounds which are definitely noticeable in the cockpit. This type of stall can be eliminated by retarding the throttle below Military thrust. The second type of stall is normally associated with subsonic flight. It is not violent, and the only evidence of this stall is a mild rumble which can be felt by the pilot and a noticeable loss of thrust. While these sounds and symptoms are usually good indicators, they are not always present; however, when they do exist, these clues and indications should always be confirmed by the gages. The EGT gage should be the first instrument checked when a stall is suspected. If the gage reading is abnormally high, a stall probably exists. In a low-altitude stall, the rpm will also be unwinding or hungup. Combined with the high EGT and unwinding or hungup rpm, will be a wide-open nozzle. The nozzle is not open due to a nozzle malfunction, but because it is attempting to reduce the overtemperature accompanying the stall; therefore, EGT, rpm, and nozzle position must always be considered to properly diagnose a stall. (Refer to Section III for Stall Clearing Procedures.)

Low Altitude Stall—Subsonic.  

Low-altitude stall (below 15,000 feet) normally begins with a chug or pop, followed by mild vibration, as distinguished from the loud banging characteristics of a high-Mach-number stall. Thrust loss is immediate as evidenced by rapid aircraft deceleration. The engine gages will give the following positive indications of the stall:

1. EGT will be 700° to 800°C or higher.
2. RPM will decrease and hangup in the 70 to 75 percent range.
3. Nozzle will indicate 9 to 10 units as the nozzle goes to wide open in an attempt to lower EGT.

Engine response to throttle manipulation will not be normal, and a throttle advance may only increase the overtemperature and the intensity of the vibration. This simultaneous existence of high EGT, low rpm, and wide-open nozzle is conclusive proof that a stall exists. Compressor stall is easily distinguished from open nozzle failure, in which case the open nozzle is accompanied by low EGT and normal rpm response.

High Altitude Stall—Supersonic. 3B 7A

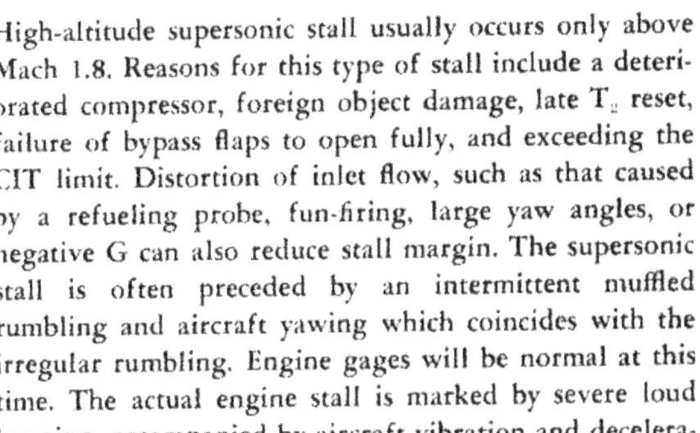

High-altitude supersonic stall usually occurs only above Mach 1.8. Reasons for this type of stall include a deteriorated compressor, foreign object damage, late T_2 reset, failure of bypass flaps to open fully, and exceeding the CIT limit. Distortion of inlet flow, such as that caused by a refueling probe, fun-firing, large yaw angles, or negative G can also reduce stall margin. The supersonic stall is often preceded by an intermittent muffled rumbling and aircraft yawing which coincides with the irregular rumbling. Engine gages will be normal at this time. The actual engine stall is marked by severe loud banging, accompanied by aircraft vibration and deceleration. EGT fluctuation between approximately 550° to 700°C will occur concurrently with the banging.

High Altitude Stall—Subsonic. 3B 7A

High-altitude subsonic stall may not be recognized since an immediate flameout usually occurs. This stall will usually occur only if aircraft flight speed is decreased below minimum level-flight speeds at altitudes above 40,000 feet, and engine transients, such as a throttle burst, afterburner light, or switchover, are made. If the angle-of-attack is high, and a large pitch rate or yaw angle is induced, compressor inlet pressure distortion may cause the engine to stall. These conditions could be created when trying to top a thunderhead or when simulating combat maneuvers at low subsonic speeds. If the aircraft is operated within the speed limits shown in figure 6-7, this condition will not occur. When operating near the minimum-speed line, use full afterburner rather than partial afterburner, since full uniform afterburning will not blow out anywhere in the steady-state maximum thrust envelope (figure 6-7). If partial afterburner is used at extreme high altitudes and low speeds, the afterburner could blow out and the resulting engine transient could cause a stall. Since this stall is usually followed immediately by an engine flameout, it is easily recognized by a slight bump or pop followed by silence and a sinking sensation. Engine speed will be unwinding rapidly and EGT will be low. If an engine air start procedure (Section III) is initiated immediately, the engine may be started before the rpm drops below 90 percent, thus avoiding the discomfort of loss of pressurization. If the stall occurs during an afterburner light or throttle burst to Military thrust, retard the throttle out of that position so the condition will not be repeated after air start.

RPM Hangup.

If the rpm decreases below flight idle, before an air start is accomplished, an rpm hangup may occur at approximately 70 to 75 percent following light-off. EGT will be moderate but rising abnormally, and a slight buzzing or high frequency vibration will be felt. Hangup occurs because the engine minimum flow is slightly high for the high altitude and low airspeed existing at light-off. This usually occurs only above 35,000 feet and as the aircraft descends at best glide speed, start conditions improve rapidly. Refer to Air Start procedure in Section III.

Note

> When flying with the RAT extended the throttle should not be handled as casually as under normal conditions. Since a throttle retard below 90 percent brings a normal engine closest to the stall line, it is a good idea to avoid this condition during critical phases of flight such as landing. If possible, fly a precautionary pattern. Refer to Flight With RAT Extended in Section III.

In the final analysis of compressor stalls the best protection is summarized as follows:

1. Knowledge of aircraft maneuvers and engine transients which can contribute to compressor stall, and knowledge of the areas of least stall margin in the F-104 envelope.

2. Knowledge of the engine symptoms which identify compressor stall.

3. Knowledge of correct stall-clearing procedures.

COMPRESSOR AND VARIABLE STATOR OPERATION. 19

In order to optimize subsonic cruise performance, a high-pressure-ratio compressor is provided. This is accomplished by the variable stator system. The engine was designed for maximum operating efficiency at high rpm settings. The variable IGV and stator system allows stall-free operation throughout the entire speed range. As rpm is reduced from Military, the IGV and variable stators (hereafter referred to only as IGV) will start to close and track closed as a function of rpm at any given air inlet temperature. At sea level standard day conditions, the IGV will be fully open above 95.3% rpm; below 93.5% they will track as a function of rpm to the closed position, reaching the closed position at 61.3% rpm. The IGV track through a total of 38.1% degrees of travel from open to closed. Closing the IGV, avoids the stall area by directing airflow against the compressor blades at an angle below that which is critical as rpm is varied. In addition, total airflow through the compressor is reduced as rpm decreases and the IGV shift toward closed, relieving the load on the rear stages of the compressor, thereby avoiding compressor stalls. The IGV control senses compressor inlet temperature (CIT) and engine rpm. The IGV schedule follows a constant slope as a function of engine rpm; however, the slope is shifted as a result of CIT. At higher CIT values, the IGV will start to close at a higher indicated rpm, and conversely, will start to close at a lower rpm when the CIT is below standard.

CORRECTED RPM. 19

The pumping characteristics of the compressor are affected by the temperature of the air entering the compressor, since temperature affects the density. An increase in CIT is effectively the same as a decrease in rpm as far as the compressor is concerned; conversely, a decrease in CIT is effectively the same as an increase in rpm. To maintain a constant mass flow of air through the engine, the rpm must be varied directly as a function of CIT. As an example, 100% indicated rpm with a 15°C CIT, is a 100 percent, corrected rpm. Indicated rpm of 103%, with a CIT of 95°C corrects to an effective or corrected rpm of 91.2% while 96.2% indicated rpm at −28°C corrects to an rpm of 104.3%.

ENGINE SPEED CONTROL FEATURES. 19

In addition to its normal governing functions, the engine fuel control unit senses and integrates CIT with rpm signals and a corrected rpm is computed mechanically within the unit. This intelligence is used to vary the IGV angle and limit corrected engine rpm to a preset maximum.

HIGH CORRECTED RPM AND RPM CUTBACK. 19

With a set engine speed of 103% rpm, corrected speed increases as CIT decreases and at approximately 45°C, 103% indicated rpm is a corrected rpm of 98.1%. At this point the main fuel control schedules reduced engine speed, limiting corrected rpm to a maximum of 105% to insure adequate high corrected speed stall margin.

LOW CORRECTED RPM. 19

As CIT is increased, corrected rpm decreases to a point where a low corrected-speed stall would be encountered if no compensating action were provided. The IGV schedule is designed to follow corrected engine speed and close to provide a stall margin. Normal operating engine rpm is 103% above a CIT of approximately 45°C. This speed schedule also provides for engine stall margin.

Flight idle fuel flow is scheduled to maintain 103% rpm at approximately 105°C CIT. A throttle chop below Military thrust during flight which results in a CIT higher than approximately 105°C will not produce an immediate reduction in rpm. This feature is incorporated to reduce the possibility of inlet duct buzz caused by decreased engine air flow requirements at lower rpm for high Mach number conditions.

EGT (T_5) RESET. 19

The engine control system includes an EGT (T_5) reset function to preclude burning the flame holder during afterburning operation while at low altitude and high Mach numbers. During T_5 reset operation, EGT is automatically decreased to approximately 610°C. The portion of the flight regime where T_5 reset is effective is limited, and corresponds to speeds above Mach .95 at sea level and above Mach 1.13 at 10,000 feet.

CDP LIMITER. 19

When maximum airspeed is approached at low altitude, compressor inlet pressure is drastically increased and compressor discharge pressure (CDP) approaches the maximum value permitted by the physical strength of the engine components. A CDP limiter, in the engine fuel control unit, senses CDP and reduces fuel flow to the engine, thus allowing rpm to decrease when the maximum CDP limit is reached.

CIT SENSOR. 19

Compressor inlet temperature is sensed by a capillary tube located in the lower left side of the compressor inlet. This capillary unit transmits a signal to the engine fuel control unit, reacts on internal portions of the fuel control, and modifies IGV and fuel flow schedules as a function of CIT.

ENGINE COMPRESSOR STALLS. 19

Engine compressor stalls can be caused by various factors, such as engine fuel control malfunction, IGV misrigging, CIT sensor cold shift, or afterburner surging. Regardless of the cause, the result is that the compressor blades stall in much the same manner as the wings of an aircraft.

During normal operation, the compressor blades generate axial airflow from the front of the compressor to the rear, at ever-increasing pressure. This pressurized air is delivered to the combustion chamber, where it is heated, and exhausted through the nozzle at a great velocity than it had at the compressor inlet, thus producing thrust. A compressor stall occurs whenever this axial airflow is interrupted in its normal rearward travel and slows or stops at some stage of compression, thus stalling the airfoil-shaped compressor blades. Some of the reasons for this airflow interruption are the following:

1. Foreign object damage which destroys the airfoil shape of the compressor blades, eliminating their ability to pump air.

2. Corrosion on the compressor blades and stators which reduces their capability to pump air at ever-increasing pressure, the same way frost destroys the ability of an aircraft wing to produce lift.

3. If the fuel schedule during a throttle burst is too high, pressures in the combustion chamber may increase to the point beyond which the compressor cannot pump air and the axial velocity of the air slows to the point where the blades stall.

4. If the inlet guide vanes are too far open for a given engine condition, the front of the compressor will pump too much air and overflow the rear of the compressor, resulting in a pile-up of air which decreases the axial airflow velocity, and the compressor will stall.

Other factors such as aircraft high G load, high angle-of-attack with its resulting compressor inlet pressure distortion, or operation at high Mach numbers and CIT outside the prescribed limits can also lead to compressor stall.

Primarily, there are two types of engine compressor stalls, both of which are relatively easy to recognize. The first type, most commonly associated with high Mach number flight, is characterized by loud banging and chugging sounds which are definitely noticeable in the cockpit. This type of stall can be eliminated by retarding the throttle below Military thrust. The second type of stall is normally associated with subsonic flight. It is not violent, and the only evidence of this stall is a mild rumble which can be felt by the pilot and a noticeable loss of thrust. While these sounds and symptoms are usually good indicators, they are not always present; however, when they do exist, these clues and indications should always be confirmed by the gages. The EGT gage should be the first instrument checked when a stall is suspected. If the gage reading is abnormally high, a stall probably exists. In a low-altitude stall, the rpm will also be unwinding or hungup. Combined with the high EGT and unwinding or hungup rpm, will be a wide-open nozzle. The nozzle is not open due to a nozzle malfunction, but because it is attempting to reduce the overtemperature accompanying the stall; therefore, EGT, rpm, and nozzle position must always be considered to properly diagnose a stall. Refer to Section III for Stall Clearing Procedures.

Low Altitude Stall—Subsonic. 

Low-altitude stall (below 15,000 feet) normally begins with a chug or pop, followed by a mild vibration, as distinguished from the loud banging characteristics of a high-Mach-number stall. Thrust loss is immediate as evidenced by a rapid aircraft deceleration. The engine gages will give the following positive indications of the stall:

1. EGT will be 750° to 800°C or higher.

2. RPM will decrease and hangup in the 70 to 75 percent range.

3. Nozzle will indicate 9 to 10 as the nozzle opens in an attempt to lower EGT.

Engine response to throttle manipulation will not be normal, and a throttle advance may only increase the overtemperature and the intensity of the vibration. This simultaneous existence of high EGT, low rpm, and open nozzle is conclusive proof that a stall exists. Compressor stall is easily distinguished from open nozzle failure, in which case the open nozzle is accompanied by low EGT and normal rpm response.

High Altitude Stall—Supersonic. 

High-altitude supersonic stall usually occurs only above Mach 1.8. Reasons for this type of stall include a deteriorated compressor, foreign object damage, failure of bypass flaps to open fully, and exceeding the CIT limit. Distortion of inlet flow, such as that caused by a refueling probe, gun-firing, large yaw angles, or negative G can also reduce stall margin. The supersonic stall is often preceded by an intermittent muffled rumbling and aircraft yawing which coincides with the irregular rumbling. Engine gages will be normal at this time. The actual engine stall is marked by severe loud banging, accompanied by aircraft vibration and deceleration. EGT fluctuation between approximately 650° to 750°C will occur concurrently with the banging.

High Altitude Stall—Subsonic. 

High-altitude subsonic stall may not be recognized since an immediate flameout usually occurs. This stall will usually occur only if aircraft flight speed is decreased below minimum level-flight speeds at altitudes above 40,000 feet, and engine transients, such as a throttle burst, or afterburner light are made. If the angle-of-attack is high, and a large pitch rate or yaw angle is induced, compressor inlet pressure distortion may cause the engine to stall. These conditions could be created when trying to top a thunderhead or when simulating combat maneuvers at low subsonic speeds. If the aircraft is operated within the speed limits shown in figure 6-8, this condition will not occur. When operating near the minimum-speed line, use full afterburner rather than partial afterburner, since full afterburning will not blow out anywhere in the steady-state Maximum thrust envelope (figure 6-8). If partial afterburner is used at extremely high altitudes and low speeds, the afterburner could blow out and the resulting engine transient could cause a stall. Since this stall is usually followed immediately by an engine flameout, it is easily recognized by a slight bump or pop followed by silence and sinking sensation. Engine speed will be unwinding rapidly and EGT will be low. If an engine air start procedure (Section III of basic manual) is initiated immediately, the engine may be started before the rpm drops below 90 percent, thus avoiding the discomfort of loss of pressurization. If the stall occurs during an afterburner light or throttle burst to Military thrust, retard the throttle out of that position so the condition will not be repeated after air start.

RPM Hangup. 19

If the rpm decreases below flight idle, before an air start is accomplished, an rpm hangup may occur at approximately 70 to 75 percent following light-off. EGT will be moderate but rising abnormally, and a slight buzzing or high frequency vibration will be felt. Hangup occurs because the engine minimum flow is slightly high for the high altitude and low airspeed existing at light-off. This usually occurs only above 35,000 feet. As the aircraft descends at best glide speed, start conditions improve rapidly. Refer to Air Start procedure in Section III of basic manual.

Note

> When flying with the RAT extended the throttle should not be handled as casually as under normal conditions. Since a throttle retard below 90 percent brings a normal engine closest to the stall line, it is a good idea to avoid this condition during critical phases of flight such as landing. If possible, fly a precautionary pattern. Refer to Flight With RAT Extended in Section III of basic manual.

In the final analysis of compressor stalls the best protection is summarized as follows:

1. Knowledge of aircraft maneuvers and engine transients which can contribute to compressor stall, and knowledge of the areas of least stall margin in the operating envelope.
2. Knowledge of the symptoms to identify engine compressor stall.
3. Knowledge of correct stall-clearing procedures. Refer to Engine Stall Clearing in Section III.

OIL SUPPLY SYSTEM.

The engine oil system is a closed and automatically operated system. The system is normally serviced with 28 pints stored in the oil tank. In addition to engine lubrication, engine oil is used to operate the exhaust nozzle actuators. The flow of oil for the exhaust nozzle actuators is automatically controlled by the nozzle area control system. The oil tank has two outlets 3B and three outlets 19 and 7A . One outlet (0.8 gallons) is for the normal exhaust nozzle pump and one is for engine lubrication (bottom of tank). The third outlet (0.5 gallons) is for the emergency nozzle pump. The normal nozzle pump outlet is located on a pendulum, 0.8 gallons from the bottom of the tank. Oil for engine lubrication is drawn from the outlet at the bottom of the tank 19 7A . The addition of an emergency nozzle pump and an emergency nozzle lock system provides for nozzle area control system hydraulic failure. Oil for the emergency pump is acquired from a standpipe outlet located 0.5 gallons from the bottom of the tank. This oil supply is the 0.3 gallons contained between the 0.8 gallons pendulum outlet and the 0.5 gallon standpipe extending from the bottom of the pump.

Access to the oil quantity dipstick is provided on the top surface of the fuselage directly over the wing. See figure 2-8. Refer to Strange Field Procedures, Section II, for oil grades and specifications.

ENGINE OIL PRESSURE. 19

Abnormal engine oil pressure is frequently an early indication of engine malfunction. It is important to detect a difference in oil pressure indication for a given rpm from the value that has been considered normal. The oil pressure gage is marked for each engine/airframe combination. The oil pressure gage markings are based on the placard oil pressure at 100 percent engine rpm. Indicated oil pressure at 100 percent rpm must be equal to placard oil pressure ±5 psi. With engine speed in excess of 100 percent rpm, indicated oil pressure may be placard psi ±5 psi +3 psi. During engine check, if rpm is not 100 percent, oil pressure may be corrected to placard oil pressure as follows:

With engine speed above 100 percent rpm, subtract one psi from the indicated oil pressure for each one percent above 100 percent rpm.

Note

Insufficient tire traction to hold the aircraft may be a factor with the engine operating in the higher rpm regions. On days when the temperature is above 59°F (15°C), 100 percent rpm can be obtained by retarding the throttle for a quick check of indicated oil pressure versus placard pressure.

With engine below 100 percent rpm, add one psi to the indicated oil pressure for each one percent below 100 percent rpm.

CAUTION

If indicated oil pressure corrected to 100 percent rpm or indicated oil pressure at 100 percent rpm is not placard psi ±5 psi, abort the flight and have the engine inspected.

ENGINE OIL PRESSURE. 

When a new engine is run up for the first time the pilot should take note of the characteristic readings of the various engine operating instruments. This will assist in recognizing a malfunction so that quick remedial action can be taken. Abnormal engine oil pressure is frequently an early indication that something is wrong with the engine. The important thing is to notice a difference in the oil pressure reading for a given rpm from the value that was considered normal. If during preflight engine check at 100 percent rpm the indicated oil pressure varies within limits (± 5 psi) from the normal pressure stated on the record card, use the indicated pressure observed during the 100 percent rpm check as the normal oil pressure in lieu of the pressure stated on the record card.

CAUTION

If the indicated oil pressure varies more than ±5 psi from that listed on the record card, abort the flight and perform an engine inspection.

An oil pressure increase of approximately 11 psi above placard psi can be expected with full T_2 reset.

ENGINE OIL PRESSURE RECORD CARD.  

An engine oil pressure record card is located on the forward right side of the cockpit. This card lists the normal engine oil pressure at 100 percent rpm for each engine-airplane combination.

OIL PRESSURE GAGE.

An oil pressure gage (27, 23, figures 1-12, 1-13 and 24, 19, figures 1-22, 1-23) is located on the right side of the instrument panel. The gage registers oil pressure in pounds per square inch. The gage receives fixed-frequency ac power from the instrument ac bus through a 115-26 volt ac autotransformer.

NUCLEONIC OIL QUANTITY INDICATING SYSTEM.

An engine oil quantity indicating system is installed in modified aircraft. The system employs a low energy level radiation source and a detector tube mounted externally on the engine oil tank. The radiation source is positioned to provide an even distribution of emitted radiation through the tank wall and oil, to the detector. The oil contained in the tank absorbs a portion of the emitted radiation proportional to oil quantity, and the remainder is received by the detector. From the amount of this absorption and detection, the system can determine the quantity of oil in the tank. Quantity indication may be affected by aircraft attitude and speed changes.

NUCLEONIC OIL QUANTITY INDICATOR.

The indicator is located on the right side of the lower instrument panel (29, 25 figures 1-12, 1-13 and 31, 26 figures 1-22, 1-23) and is marked in one quarter increments from empty to full. Each graduation on the indicator represents two pints and full represents tank capacity of 32 pints. In addition to providing continuous oil quantity indication to the pilot, the indicator provides a signal to operate the oil level low warning light when oil quantity drops to 14 pints (one mark below 1/2 indication) or less. It also provides a signal to operate a repeater indicator in the aft cockpit. Three adjustment screws are provided on the back of the instrument to calibrate the full and empty level and to adjust action of the warning light switch to the 14 pint level. The indicator is powered from the instrument ac bus.

Note

During normal operation, a slow fluctuation of the pointer may be expected. Also, indicator response to oil level changes within the tank are somewhat retarded due to the inherent lag in the system.

NUCLEONIC ENGINE OIL LEVEL LOW WARNING LIGHT.

Engine oil level low warning indication is provided in each cockpit by the existing warning and master caution lights. The signal to operate the warning lights is provided by the forward cockpit oil quantity indicator only. The lights are activated on decreasing oil level at 14 pints or less and go out at 18 pints on increasing oil level.

ENGINE OIL LOW LEVEL WARNING LIGHT 2.4 GALLON SYSTEM.

Oil tanks on engines with 2J-J79-729C/W, provide an indication during level flight, when the oil tank level has dropped to 2.4 gallons or less. On aircraft with 805C/W the warning system by providing a 4.5 second time delay relay to prevent flickering of the oil level low light on the warning panel. Due to the location of the oil level sensing switch, a deceleration force lasting approximately 4.5 seconds or more, and of sufficient magnitude to cause oil level variance in the oil tank, can result in illumination of the warning light. This will normally be encountered during deceleration from high indicated airspeed when coming out of afterburner, making large throttle reductions or deceleration from extending the speed brakes. As the deceleration force diminishes or is removed, the warning light will go out. Application of negative "G" force or nose low attitude has a tendency to prolong the time the warning light remains on, even though the deceleration force has ceased. Illumination of the warning light during deceleration is not considered an emergency as it is quickly discernible from an actual oil loss by application of a momentary positive G load. The light will go out, if illumination was due to deceleration forces.

FUEL SUPPLY SYSTEM.

The aircraft fuel system (figures 1-35, 1-36) consists of one main fuel tank containing four separate interconnected bladder-type non-self-sealing cells, four tank-mounted submerged booster pumps, a shutoff valve, a strainer, and the necessary plumbing and electrical circuits. Flapper valves are installed between the forward main and aft center cells and permit fuel flow by gravity from the aft cells to the forward main cell. All necessary plumbing and electrical circuits are provided for the installation of tip and pylon tanks. On A C aircraft an auxiliary fuel cell located forward of the main fuel cell transfers fuel by means of a gravity flow connection, a transfer pump, and transfer float valve to the forward main cell. On D aircraft, AF Serials 57-1320 and subsequent, three interconnected auxiliary fuel cells transfer fuel by gravity flow to the forward main cell. On all C aircraft and D aircraft, AF Serial 57-1320 and subsequent, all internal and external fuel tanks may be serviced by single-point pressure refueling and can be refueled in flight through a probe mounted on the left side of the fuselage. Refer to Ground Refueling and Air Refueling in Section IV. If pressure refueling ground equipment is not available, the internal fuel tanks can be refueled through two filler wells (figure 2-8). The pylon tanks can be refueled through individual filler wells. Each tip tank is refueled through two filler wells. Refer to Strange Field Procedures in Section II for fuel specifications and grades. See figure 1-38 for fuel tank capacities.

Note

No single point pressure refueling capabilities are provided for A and B aircraft.

FORWARD MAIN FUEL CELL.

All of the fuel that goes to the engine is fed from the forward main fuel cell. Fuel from the aft center fuel cell enters the forward main fuel cell through two flapper-type check valves. Fuel from the external tanks enters the forward main fuel cell through a transfer float valve. Fuel from the auxiliary fuel cell also enters the forward main fuel cell through a flapper-type check valve and a transfer float valve. A now-level warning switch, quantity transmitter, four boost pumps, two vent valves, and a fuel manifold are located inside the cell. Drain valves are located in the pump wells of the cell and are accessible from outside the aircraft.

AFT CENTER FUEL CELL.

The aft center fuel cell is located between the engine inlet ducts. Two vent valves, a dual fuel-level control valve, a quantity transmitter, and two drain valves are in the cell. The drain valves are at the forward bottom end of the cell and are accessible from the forward end of the wheel well.

RIGHT AND LEFT AFT FUEL CELLS.

The right and left aft fuel cells fit around the engine air inlet ducts, outboard of the aft center fuel cell. Each cell is connected by tubes, at the bottom and top, to the aft center fuel cell. Fuel flows to the aft center fuel cell through the bottom tube. The top tube serves as a vent connection. These cells and the aft center fuel cell will hereafter be considered and referred to as the aft main fuel cell.

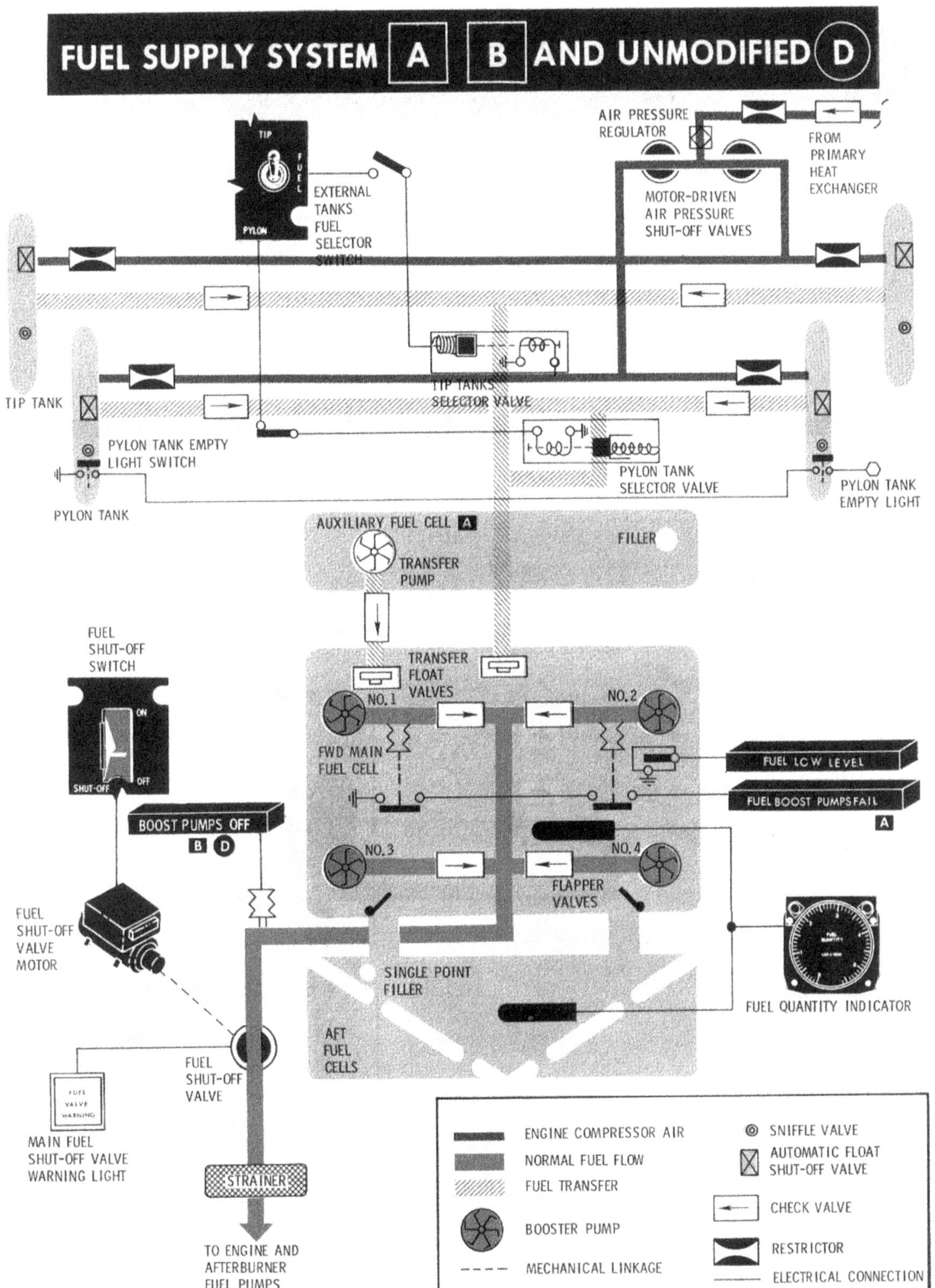
FUEL SUPPLY SYSTEM A B AND UNMODIFIED D
AIR PRESSURE REGULATOR
FROM PRIMARY HEAT EXCHANGER
MOTOR-DRIVEN AIR PRESSURE SHUT-OFF VALVES
TIP
FUEL
PYLON
EXTERNAL TANKS FUEL SELECTOR SWITCH
TIP TANKS SELECTOR VALVE
TIP TANK
PYLON TANK EMPTY LIGHT SWITCH
PYLON TANK
PYLON TANK SELECTOR VALVE
PYLON TANK EMPTY LIGHT
AUXILIARY FUEL CELL A
FILLER
TRANSFER PUMP
FUEL SHUT-OFF SWITCH
ON
OFF
SHUT-OFF
TRANSFER FLOAT VALVES
NO. 1
NO. 2
FWD MAIN FUEL CELL
FUEL LOW LEVEL
FUEL BOOST PUMPS FAIL
A
BOOST PUMPS OFF
B D
NO. 3
NO. 4
FLAPPER VALVES
FUEL SHUT-OFF VALVE MOTOR
SINGLE POINT FILLER
FUEL QUANTITY INDICATOR
AFT FUEL CELLS
FUEL SHUT-OFF VALVE
MAIN FUEL SHUT-OFF VALVE WARNING LIGHT
STRAINER
TO ENGINE AND AFTERBURNER FUEL PUMPS
ENGINE COMPRESSOR AIR
NORMAL FUEL FLOW
FUEL TRANSFER
BOOSTER PUMP
MECHANICAL LINKAGE
SNIFFLE VALVE
AUTOMATIC FLOAT SHUT-OFF VALVE
CHECK VALVE
RESTRICTOR
ELECTRICAL CONNECTION
F52-0-1-22

Figure 1-35

FUEL SUPPLY SYSTEM (C) AND AIR REFUELABLE (D)

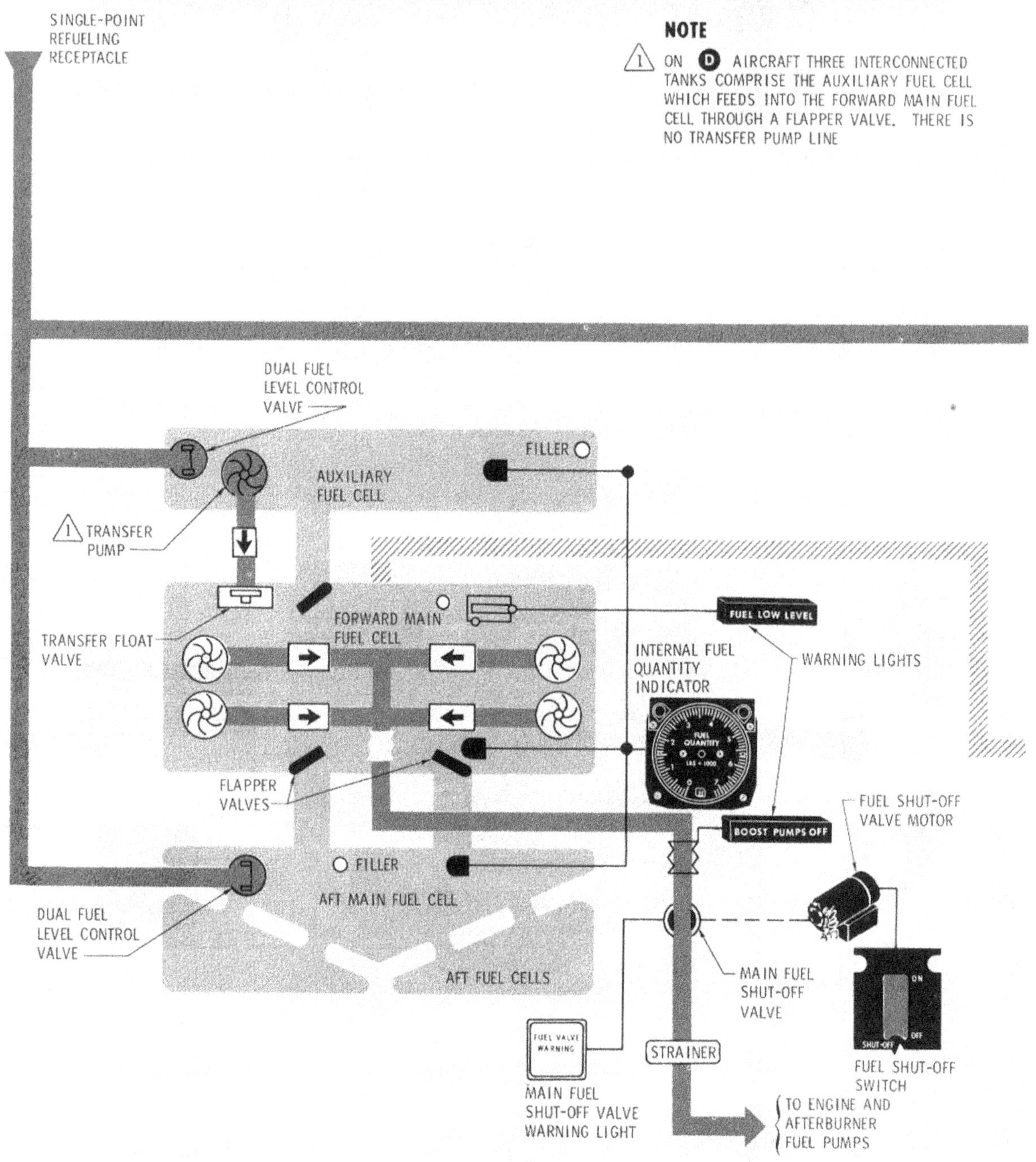
SINGLE-POINT REFUELING RECEPTACLE
NOTE
1 ON D AIRCRAFT THREE INTERCONNECTED TANKS COMPRISE THE AUXILIARY FUEL CELL WHICH FEEDS INTO THE FORWARD MAIN FUEL CELL THROUGH A FLAPPER VALVE. THERE IS NO TRANSFER PUMP LINE
DUAL FUEL LEVEL CONTROL VALVE
FILLER
AUXILIARY FUEL CELL
1 TRANSFER PUMP
FORWARD MAIN FUEL CELL
FUEL LOW LEVEL
TRANSFER FLOAT VALVE
INTERNAL FUEL QUANTITY INDICATOR
WARNING LIGHTS
FLAPPER VALVES
FUEL SHUT-OFF VALVE MOTOR
BOOST PUMPS OFF
FILLER
AFT MAIN FUEL CELL
DUAL FUEL LEVEL CONTROL VALVE
AFT FUEL CELLS
MAIN FUEL SHUT-OFF VALVE
ON
OFF
SHUT-OFF
FUEL VALVE WARNING
STRAINER
FUEL SHUT-OFF SWITCH
MAIN FUEL SHUT-OFF VALVE WARNING LIGHT
TO ENGINE AND AFTERBURNER FUEL PUMPS
F52-0-1-18(1)

Figure 1-36 (Sheet 1 of 2)

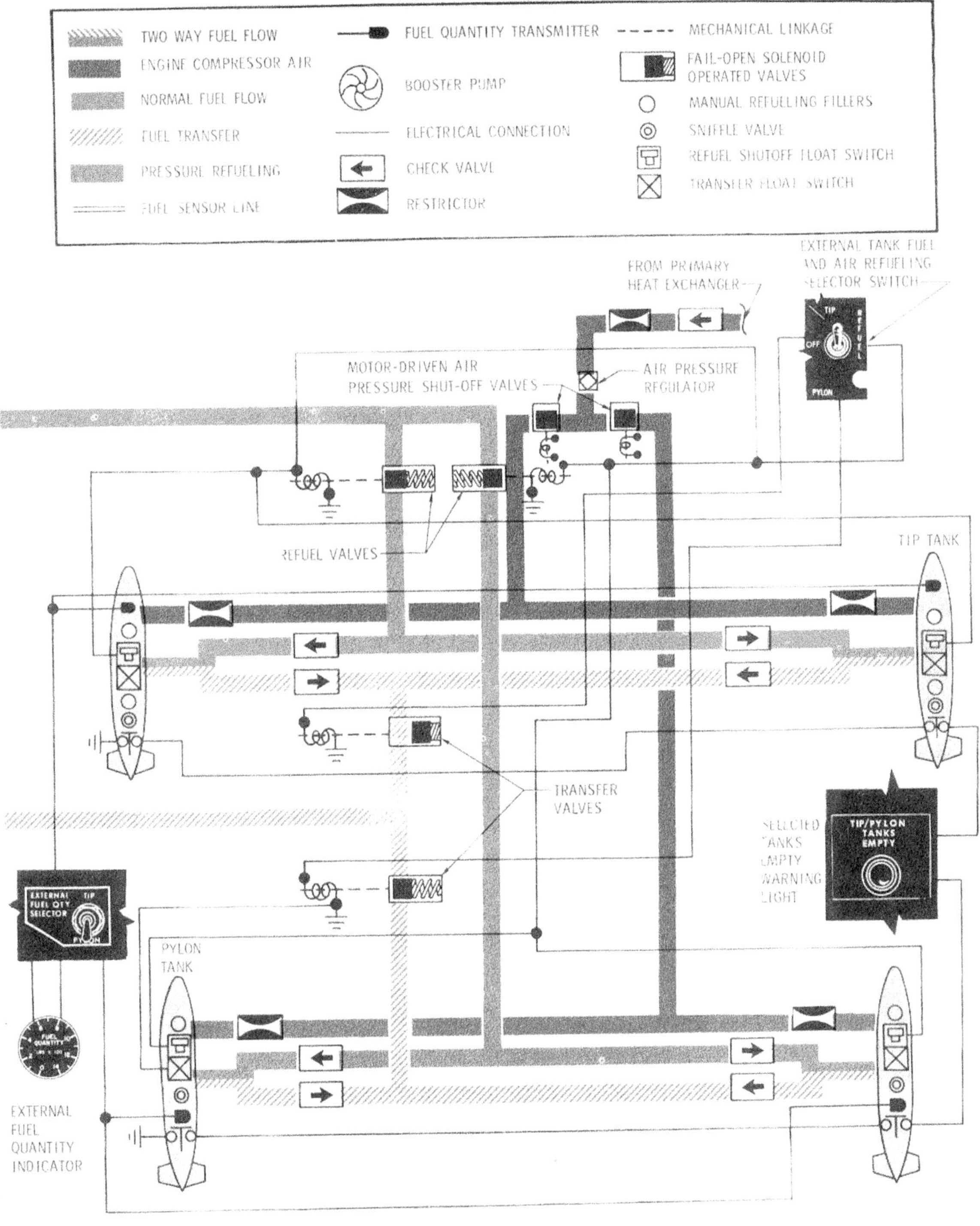

TWO WAY FUEL FLOW
ENGINE COMPRESSOR AIR
NORMAL FUEL FLOW
FUEL TRANSFER
PRESSURE REFUELING
FUEL SENSOR LINE
FUEL QUANTITY TRANSMITTER
BOOSTER PUMP
ELECTRICAL CONNECTION
CHECK VALVE
RESTRICTOR
MECHANICAL LINKAGE
FAIL-OPEN SOLENOID OPERATED VALVES
MANUAL REFUELING FILLERS
SNIFFLE VALVE
REFUEL SHUTOFF FLOAT SWITCH
TRANSFER FLOAT SWITCH
FROM PRIMARY HEAT EXCHANGER
EXTERNAL TANK FUEL AND AIR REFUELING SELECTOR SWITCH
TIP
OFF
REFUEL
PYLON
MOTOR-DRIVEN AIR PRESSURE SHUT-OFF VALVES
AIR PRESSURE REGULATOR
REFUEL VALVES
TIP TANK
TRANSFER VALVES
SELECTED TANKS EMPTY WARNING LIGHT
TIP/PYLON TANKS EMPTY
EXTERNAL FUEL QTY SELECTOR
PYLON TANK
FUEL QUANTITY
EXTERNAL FUEL QUANTITY INDICATOR
52-0-1-18(2)

Figure 1-36 (Sheet 2 of 2)

AUXILIARY FUEL CELLS. A C

A 145-gallon auxiliary fuel cell is located ahead of the forward main fuel cell. Fuel is transferred automatically by means of a transfer pump through a transfer float valve and a gravity flow connection to the forward main fuel cell. The auxiliary fuel cell also contains a dual fuel-level control valve, a vent float valve, two drain valves, and a low level pump cutoff float switch. The drain valves are accessible from beneath the aircraft. The transfer pump is powered by the No. 2 ac bus when the airplane electrical system is energized and there is fuel in the tank. It shuts off automatically when the cell is empty. The transfer pump is energized automatically when the external tanks are empty or when the external tank fuel and air refueling selector switch is in the OFF or REFUEL position.

D On AF Serials 57-1320 and subsequent, three auxiliary fuel cells are installed. These interconnected cells have a combined capacity of 98 gallons and feed by gravity to the forward main fuel cell. A flapper valve is installed in the lowest auxiliary cell to prevent reverse flow from the forward main fuel cell.

FUEL BOOST PUMPS.

Four boost pumps, operated by 3-phase ac motors, are installed, one in each corner, in the forward main fuel cell. Power for operation of the No. 1 boost pump is supplied from the emergency ac bus. The No. 2 boost pump is on the No. 2 ac bus. No. 3 and No. 4 boost pump power is supplied from the No. 1 ac bus. The pumps are manifolded together through check valves into the main fuel supply line to the engine. The main fuel supply line is routed from the forward cell aft to the shutoff valve at the firewall. A line connects the shutoff valve to the fuel strainer aft of the firewall. A drain valve and an overboard drain line is plumbed from the strainer sump. The fuel from the strainer is routed through a flexible hose to the engine and afterburner fuel pumps. The boost pump circuits are energized whenever the airplane electrical system is energized and the circuit breakers are in. The pumps supply fuel at 35 psi. No fuel pressure indicating system is provided in the cockpit.

Fuel Boost Pumps Failure Warning Light. A

Two pressure switches are installed in the forward fuel cell. One switch is connected to the pressure feed line from the left forward pump (No. 1) and one into the line from the right forward pump (No. 2). The pressure switches are connected in series to the 28-volt dc emergency bus through the warning light circuit breaker on the electronics compartment panel. The switches are normally closed; they open when the forward pumps are in normal operation. The switches close if the pumps fail, lighting the BOOST PUMP FAIL warning indicator light on the warning light panel (figure 1-20). The MASTER CAUTION indicator light will go on also. Pressure from both forward pumps must decrease to a preset value to energize the warning circuits. The warning system is connected to the two front pumps because these are the critical pumps in the approach or nose-down attitude of the airplane.

Fuel Boost Pumps OFF Warning Light. B C D

A pressure switch, installed downstream of the aircraft boost pumps, monitors the fuel pressure in the lines to the engine. The switch is normally closed but opens when the fuel boost pumps are in operation. If fuel pressure at the switch falls below a preset value, the switch will close and the BOOST PUMPS OFF warning light will illuminate on the warning light panel (figures 1-20, 1-21). The MASTER CAUTION warning light will illuminate simultaneously. The system receives power from the dc emergency bus.

Note

With the fuel boost pumps inoperative, the engine will operate at Military thrust up to 25,000 feet and at maximum thrust up to 12,000 feet using gravity fuel flow. Above these altitudes, there may not be sufficient fuel flow to maintain normal engine operation.

FUEL TANK PRESSURIZATION AND VENT SYSTEM.

The vent system vents the internal fuel cells, provides self-pressurization of the cells in a climb to prevent loss of fuel, and provides controlled pressurization of the cells in a dive.

Vent Float Valves.

Five vent float valves are installed in the system, two are in the forward main fuel cell, two in the aft center fuel cell, and one in the auxiliary fuel cell. The valves are float-actuated and close the respective fuel cell vent in all attitudes of flight when the fuel reaches a predetermined level at the valve. This prevents fuel from flowing out the vent.

Pressure Regulator.

A dual air pressure regulator is installed to maintain an air pressure differential between the fuel cell cavity and the inside of the fuel cell. Either side of the dual regulator is capable, by itself, of fulfilling the entire requirement. The regulator senses pressure both within the cells and in the cell cavity and closes when the pressure within the cells exceeds the cell cavity pressure by a preset valve.

EXTERNAL FUEL TANKS.

Provisions are included for carrying tip tanks and pylon tanks on each wing. A means of jettisoning tip tanks, pylons, pylon racks, and pylon tanks is provided. All stores are jettisoned by electrically actuated cartridges. An automatic drop system is provided for tip stores only.

Automatic Fuel Transfer Shut-Off. Fuel in the tip tanks moves from an aft compartment to a forward compartment through a tube. Fuel in the pylon tanks moves forward and aft through flapper valves to the center section. The fuel outlet to the transfer line and to the fuselage tank is in the forward compartment. Each tank contains a low-level float switch which shuts off the transfer valve and pressurizing air when the tanks become empty. The shutoff prevents engine bleed air from entering the fuel transfer lines and internal cells when the tip tanks are empty.

EXTERNAL FUEL TRANSFER SYSTEM.

The fuel transfer system provides a means of transferring fuel from the tip and pylon tanks to the forward main fuel cell. The fuel is transferred by using air pressure supplied by the engine compressor. Air is cooled by the primary heat exchanger and is controlled by a pressure regulator set to maintain a constant psi. The air passes through motor-driven air shutoff valves. The shutoff valves are controlled by low-level float switches and are open when the tanks are installed and have fuel in them. Plumbing is arranged so that is is symmetrical about the airplane centerline to provide equal flow from both tanks. Sniffle valves are located in the tip and pylon tanks. They act as relief valves in case of a malfunctioning regulator. A failure in the regulator will cause it to fail to the open position. The unit is vented to the atmosphere by a line on the left side of the fuselage.

Note

- A nominal amount of fuel may be vented overboard through the fuselage overboard vent at the time the tip tanks become empty.
- A thumping noise may be heard during fuel transfer when the fuel lines run dry. This phenomenon is harmless and no corrective action is necessary.

Air Shutoff Valves.

Two air shutoff valves are installed in the engine compartment on the left side. One valve shuts off the supply of engine compressor air to the tip tanks and the other shuts off the air to the pylon tanks. The valves are motor-operated and controlled by low-level float switches in the external tanks.

Fuel Transfer Float Valves.

A fuel transfer float valve is installed in the forward main fuel cell. The valve controls fuel transfer from the external fuel tanks. The level of fuel in the forward main fuel cell is maintained by movement of a float inside the valve that opens and closes the valve by its movement until external fuel is exhausted.

External Stores Automatic Drop System.

A tip store automatic drop system is provided. If a tip tank should be disengaged accidentally, the system will automatically jettison both the disengaged tank and the corresponding tank on the opposite wing, provided the airplane electrical system is in operation. The system is powered from the dc emergency bus. To prevent the automatic drop system from operating on the ground when one tank is intentionally removed, safety pins are provided for the tip tanks to disarm the system. The pins are inserted under each wing for the tip tanks.

Note

The automatic drop system is in operation when missiles are on the wing tips. Only in the event of a missile launcher becoming disengaged will the automatic drop system function as described. Missile firing will not activate the system.

Fuel Shutoff Switch.

The fuel shutoff switch (figure 1-37) is located on the left console; it is guarded to the ON position. The switch (battery bus powered) may be used to electrically actuate the fuel shutoff valve, located just aft of the main fuel cell. The valve is motor-driven. The motor is connected through the fuel shutoff switch and through a circuit breaker in the electronic compartment of the battery bus. The valve provides a means of shutting off fuel to the engine in case of fire, for crash landing, or for ground maintenance.

FUEL CONTROL PANELS

C

D AF SERIALS 57-1320 AND SUBSEQUENT

NOTE

EXTERNAL TANK FUEL AND AIR REFUELING SELECTOR SWITCH IN FORWARD COCKPIT ONLY

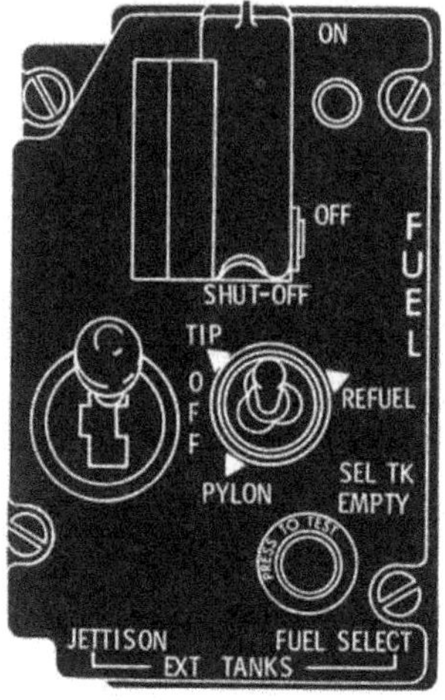

A B AND AF SERIALS D PRIOR TO 57-1320

NOTE

EXTERNAL FUEL SELECTOR SWITCH IN FORWARD COCKPIT ONLY

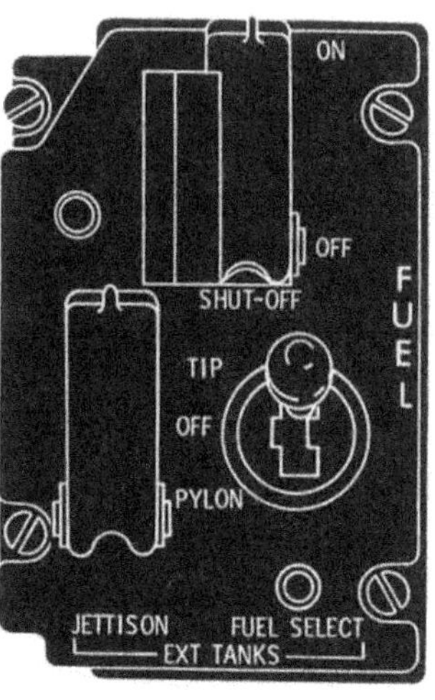

Figure 1-37

Fuel Shutoff Valve Warning Light.

On aircraft with 865 C/W, a fuel shutoff valve warning light is installed on the upper right instrument panels (15, 14 figures 1-12, 1-13 and 16, 13, figures 1-22, 1-23). The light will illuminate the words FUEL VALVE WARNING any time the position of the main fuel shutoff valve does not agree with the position of the main fuel shutoff switch. The light may be tested by operating the press-to-test feature.

External Tank Fuel Selector Switch.

A B and AF Serials prior to 57-1320 D.

An over-center, two-position, external tank fuel selector switch (figure 1-37) labeled TIP and PYLON is provided on the fuel control panel. The switch is used to control motor- or solenoid-operated external fuel selector valves which permit fuel to be transferred from both tip tanks or from both pylon tanks. The selector valves are connected to the dc monitored bus through air shutoff valve relays, the fuel selector switch, and a circuit breaker on the electronic compartment panel.

Note

- The fuel selector valves on unmodified AF Serials 55-2955 through 56-747 A, have solenoid-operated selector valves which will fail to the closed position. Unmodified AF Serials 56-748 through 56-877 A, and unmodified AF Serials 56-3719 through 57-1302 B, have motor-operated selector valves which will fail to the position they are in at the time of failure.
- AF Serials 56-878 and subsequent A, modified A, AF Serials 57-1303 and subsequent B, modified B and all D, incorporate solenoid-operated external fuel selector valves which fail to the open position, so that if electrical power fails, remaining external fuel will be available.

The PYLON or TIP position controls selector valve operation as long as external tanks are installed. A transfer float valve in the forward main cell allows fuel transfer from the selected external tanks when fuel level in the forward main cell is lowered.

Note A B

If both tip and pylon tanks are installed, fuel will automatically transfer from the remaining tanks after the selected tanks become empty. If only one set of tanks is installed or if one set of tanks is jettisoned, fuel will automatically transfer from the installed tanks, regardless of selector switch position.

External Tank Fuel and Air Refueling Selector Switch.

C and AF Serials 57-1320 and subsequent D.

A four-position switch (figure 1-37) on the fuel control panel, is used to control solenoid-operated external fuel selector valves and permit fuel to be transferred from both tip tanks or from both pylon tanks. The selector valves are connected to the dc monitored bus through air shutoff valve relays, the fuel selector switch and a circuit breaker on the electronic compartment panel. The four-position external tank fuel and air refueling selector switch is labeled PYLON, OFF, TIP, and REFUEL. The TIP, PYLON, and OFF positions control valve operation as long as external tanks are installed.

A transfer float valve in the forward main fuel cell allows fuel transfer from the selected external tanks when the fuel level in the forward main fuel cell is lowered. The REFUEL position is used for ground and air refueling. (Refer to External Tank Fuel And Air Refueling Selector Switch paragraph in Section IV.)

External Tanks Fuel (Refuel) Selector Switch.

C and AF Serials 57-1320 and subsequent D.

An external tanks refuel selector switch (3, figures 1-26, 1-27) labeled TIP, PYLON and BOTH is located on the right console (forward cockpit D) and is guarded to the BOTH position. On early aircraft the switch was located externally in the refueling precheck switch panel. The switch provides a method of selective refueling of the external tanks. Electrical power is provided by the dc monitored bus.

External Stores Release Rotary Selector Switch. C

A six-position, external stores, rotary selector switch located on the fuel control panel (figure 1-37) is provided for selection of regular droppable stores and special droppable stores that are released by using the bomb/rocket button. The switch positions (clockwise) are as follows:

SPL STORES	Selects droppable stores carried on the fuselage underside.
OFF	Disarms the circuitry (except for emergency jettisoning) for release of both regular and special droppable stores using the bomb/rocket button.
PYLON	Selects pylon stores, including tanks, rocket launchers, and bombs; bombs are dropped unarmed from this position.
TIP	Selects simultaneous release of all wing tip stores.
LH	Selects the left-hand pylon store. If the pylon stores are bombs, the left-hand bomb will be armed and released when the bomb/rocket button is pressed. After releasing the LH bomb the rotary selector switch must be moved to the BOTH position in order to release the right-hand store.
BOTH	Selects both pylon stores, or right hand store if LH store has been released. Differs from the pylon position in that the bombs will be armed for release. When the button is pressed, both bombs will be released.

Note

- In the PYLON and BOTH positions a separate, 50-millisecond time delay relay is installed in the right-hand pylon release circuitry to separate conventional bombs and eliminate the possibility of their colliding.
- The catamaran is not jettisonable.

Lock Release Button. (2083 N/C/W) C

A lock release button located to the left of the external stores release rotary selector switch is provided to prevent inadvertent selection of special stores. The button must be depressed before the rotary selector switch can be moved counterclockwise from the OFF to the SPL STORES position. If 2083 has been C/W, the lock release button has been removed allowing the rotary selector switch to be moved to the SPL STORES by turning the selector switch counterclockwise.

External Stores Release Selector Switch. A B D

A guarded selector switch, located on the fuel control panel (figure 1-37), is provided for selection of the droppable stores that may be released using the bomb/rocket button. The switch has three positions PYLON, OFF, and TIP.

CAUTION

The external fuel tank selector switch and the external stores release selector switch are adjacent to each other and use the common placard positions of TIP, and PYLON.

External Stores Release Button (Bomb/Rocket Button).

The external stores release button located on the control stick grip (2, figure 1-44) is provided to release the selected droppable stores. The system is powered from the battery bus. Pressing the release button closes the selected circuit by the selector switch, causing the selectors to jettison the stores. In order to release the pylons after the pylon stores are released, the external stores release button must be released and pressed again.

Note 

- The external stores release button will operate only in the cockpit in which the system has been armed by the external stores release selector switch.
- On the ground, the ground air safety switch must be overridden by the armament firing override switch to utilize the bomb/rocket button after the external stores release rotary selector switch has been positioned.

External Stores Jettison Button. 

An external stores jettison button (figure 1-20) is provided on the left forward panel to jettison all external stores (except pylon racks) in an emergency. The jettison circuit is connected directly to the battery bus through a circuit breaker in the electronic compartment and is energized any time the circuit breaker is pushed in and a battery installed. By pushing the button both tip and pylon stores may be jettisoned. The external stores release button is the only means of jettisoning the pylon racks.

External Stores Jettison Button. 

The external stores jettison button located on the left forward panel (figure 1-21) is provided to jettison all external stores except pylon racks, fuselage mounted AIM-9B missile adapter, special stores and bomb dispenser. The pylon racks are jettisoned by means of the pylon jettison switch on the left console. The external stores jettison button is the only means of jettisoning fuselage-mounted missiles; however, fuselage-mounted launchers cannot be jettisoned if missiles are not attached.

WARNING

The circuit is connected directly to the battery bus through a circuit breaker in the electronic compartment and is energized any time the circuit breaker is pushed in and a battery is installed. Two pounds of pressure are sufficient to actuate the switch. Therefore, care should be exercised to prevent inadvertent jettison of external stores.

Pylon Jettison Switch 

The pylon jettison switch (43, figure 1-22 and 17, figure 1-25) is a guarded two-position switch. It is placarded JETT and SAFE and is normally safety-wired in the forward, guarded, SAFE position. To jettison the pylons, the guard is raised, breaking the safety wire and the switch is placed in the JETT position. The pylon will not jettison if a store or tank is attached to the pylon. The store or tank must be jettisoned separately before the pylon can be jettisoned.

Tip/Pylon Tanks Empty Light. 

AF Serials 57-1320 and subsequent Ⓓ.

A red push-to-test light (figure 1-37) is located on the fuel control panel. The light illuminates when the selected external tanks are empty. The light is powered from the dc emergency bus. It is labeled SEL. TANK EMPTY.

Pylon Tanks Empty Light.

(AF Serials 56-772 and subsequent and earlier modified aircraft, [A] all [B], and unmodified AF Serials prior to 57-1320 Ⓓ.)

A red light (5, figures 1-16, 1-17, 1-19 and 2, figure 1-29) located on the right console in each cockpit. illuminates when the pylon tanks are empty. The light is powered from the dc emergency bus.

Internal Fuel Quantity Indicator.

The internal fuel quantity indicating system indicates in pounds the internal fuel quantity remaining in the internal fuel cells. The system consists of an indicator (21, 17, figures 1-12, 1-13 and 27, 23, figures 1-22, 1-23), on the right side of the main instrument panel, and fuel quantity transmitters, one in the forward cell, one in the aft cell, and on Ⓒ aircraft one in the auxiliary cell. The transmitter in the forward cell is combined with a fuel density compensating unit. The system receives power from the No. 2 ac bus and the dc emergency bus through circuit breakers on the left circuit breaker panel. On Ⓓ aircraft, AF Serials 57-1320 and subsequent, three fuel quantity transmitters are located in the auxiliary fuel cells. On Ⓓ aircraft prior to AF Serial 57-1320 auxiliary fuel cells are not installed.

External Fuel Quantity Indicator. 

The external fuel quantity indicating system indicates in pounds the external fuel remaining in the individual tip and pylon tanks. The system consists of a two-pointer

FUEL QUANTITY DATA

DATA BASIS:
GROUND TEST,
STANDARD DAY
CONDITIONS WITH
CONVERSION FACTOR
6.5 LBS/GAL

REMARKS:
LEVEL FLIGHT
ATTITUDE — TOP OF
FUSELAGE 3° NOSE
UP, STATIC
ATTITUDE — TOP OF
FUSELAGE 0°

	USABLE FUEL IN LEVEL FLIGHT ATTITUDE				FULLY SERVICED IN STATIC ATTITUDE			
	LBS		U. S. GALS		LBS		U. S. GALS	
	A C	B D	A C	B D	A C	B D	A C	B D
INTERNAL FUEL MAIN FUEL CELLS	4901	4257	754	655	4959	4303	763	662
AUXILIARY FUEL CELL	923	630	143	97	929	637	144	98
TIP TANKS (EACH)	1105	1105	170	170	1137	1137	175	175
PYLON TANKS (EACH)	1267	1267	195	195	1293	1293	199	199

TOTAL USABLE FUEL IN LEVEL FLIGHT ATTITUDE	LBS		GALS	
	A C	B D	A C	B D
INTERNAL FUEL	5824	4257	896	655
WITH TIP TANKS	8034	6467	1236	995
WITH PYLON TANKS	8359	6792	1286	1045
WITH PYLON AND TIP TANKS	10569	9002	1626	1385

NOTE

D AIRCRAFT, AF SERIALS 57-1320 AND SUBSEQUENT HAVE AUXILIARY TANKS INSTALLED. SUBTRACT 97 GALLONS OR 630 LBS FROM ABOVE FIGURES TO DETERMINE FUEL CAPACITIES OF UNMODIFIED AIRCRAFT

F52-0-1-23

Figure 1-38

indicator (28, 24, figures 1-22, 1-23) located on the right side of the main instrument panel and ten fuel cell transmitters; two in each tip tank and three in each pylon tank. The system receives power from the No. 2 ac bus and the dc emergency bus.

External Fuel Quantity Selector Switch. C D

The external fuel quantity selector switch (29, figure 1-22) located on the lower right instrument panel is labeled EXTERNAL FUEL QTY. SELECTOR (forward cockpit D). The two positions are TIP and PYLON. The switch is used to connect the external fuel quantity indicator to either the tip tanks or pylon tanks. The external fuel quantity indicator indicates the amount of fuel (in pounds) remaining in the respective tanks, depending on the position of the switch.

Fuel Quantity System Test Switch.

A test switch (figures 1-20, 1-21) is located on the right forward panel. When the airplane electrical system is energized, placing the switch in the FUEL QUANTITY (up) position grounds the system power supply, which will cause the internal and external fuel quantity gage pointer to go toward zero if the system is functioning properly. This will not activate the low-level warning indication as the systems are independent. The switch is also used to check the warning light circuits in the WARNING LIGHTS TEST (down) position.

Fuel Low-Level Warning Light.

A low-level warning system is installed to indicate to the pilot that the fuel level in the forward main fuel cell has decreased to a critical level. The system includes a float-actuated switch installed in the forward main fuel cell, and a light on the warning panel. When the fuel level falls to approximately 1275 (±250) pounds in level flight, the switch closes the circuit and energizes the FUEL LOW LEVEL warning light (figures 1-20, 1-21) and the MASTER CAUTION light. The system receives electrical power from the dc emergency bus.

Note

> Changes in aircraft attitude or acceleration will cause the fuel low-level warning light to illuminate when the fuel level is close to the warning actuation level. Illumination of the light should be considered as a caution indication only. As soon as possible, check the fuel quantity gage indication during steady-state straight-and-level flight.

ELECTRICAL POWER SUPPLY SYSTEMS.

The aircraft electrical systems obtain power primarily from two engine-driven alternating current generators. This power is utilized by the main ac electrical system, a dc electrical system, and inverters. Emergency power is supplied by a ram-air turbine-driven ac generator and (one A B and two C D) small 3.6-ampere-hour batteries. For ground operation, the external power receptacle on the lower right side of the fuselage provides a means for connecting an external ac power source to the aircraft. Electrical power is distributed to the individual systems through an ac bus for each of the generators, an emergency ac bus, and a dc monitored bus. Power to the dc monitored bus is provided by a (100-ampere A B, 120-ampere C D) transformer—rectifier. The inverters receive power from the dc monitored bus during normal operation and supply fixed frequency ac power to the instrument ac bus, the three-axes control damper and TACAN equipment. The dc monitored bus also supplies power to a dc essential bus and a dc emergency bus during normal operation. The battery bus A B and battery buses C D receive power from the 20-ampere transformer—rectifier through blocking rectifiers. During emergency operation both the instrument ac bus and TACAN equipment receive power from the emergency ac bus through an emergency instrument transformer, while the dc essential bus, dc emergency bus and battery bus A B or buses C D, receive their power from the emergency ac bus through a 20-ampere transformer—rectifier. In the event that even the emergency power supply is lost, the 3.6-ampere-hour batteries will furnish sufficient power to operate those items on the battery buses for a limited period of time.

AC ELECTRICAL POWER SUPPLY.

Two 20 kva engine-driven generators serve as the primary source of ac electrical power for the aircraft. They are located on the accessory section of the engine. The generators supply 200 and 115 volt 3-phase variable frequency power to the aircraft electrical system when the engine is running and the ground power supply is disconnected. This generator output is controlled by means of a voltage regulator, protection panel, relays for automatic transfer of the two ac buses from one generator to the other, and a control switch for each generator. Normally, the No. 1 generator output goes to the No. 1 ac bus and the No. 2 generator output to the No. 2 ac bus. In addition to this, the No. 2 generator normally provides power for the emergency ac bus. In cases where an undervoltage or an overvoltage condition exists for either generator, that generator is automatically removed from its bus; the bus is automatically transferred to the other generator, and the warning light panel in the cockpit is illuminated, indicating which generator is not operating. The automatic bus transfer system provides for five possible modes of operation as indicated in figure 1-39. Various electrically operated units take their power directly from the No. 1 and No. 2 ac buses. (See figure 1-39.) The No. 1 ac bus also directs generator output to the 100 A B or 120 C D ampere transformer—rectifier where ac is converted to 28-volt dc before being sent to the dc monitored bus. If either the instrument or TACAN inverter fails, variable frequency ac power will be supplied automatically from the emergency ac bus through the instrument emergency power transformer.

Note

> The electrical supply system is equipped with under-frequency relays which cut the two 20-kva generators off the buses when the engine rpm drops below approximately 65 percent. Under this condition, all electrically operated equipment except the No. 2 boost pump and the battery buses will be inoperative. The No. 2 boost pump will continue to operate at lower engine rpm (down to approximately 40 percent). This feature ensures sufficient boost pump pressure for high altitude air starts.

Emergency AC Power Supply.

The airplane is equipped with a normally concealed ram-air turbine which, when extended, supplies emergency electrical and hydraulic power as required. Once extended, the ram-air turbine cannot be retracted in flight. If both the No. 1 and No. 2 generators fail, the ram-air turbine-driven ac generator (5.5 kva) will supply variable frequency ac power for the emergency bus. It will also furnish power for the instrument ac bus and TACAN equipment through the instrument emergency power transformer. In addition to this, the emergency ac bus will direct power to the dc essential bus, dc emergency bus, bus A B and buses C D through a 20-ampere transformer—rectifier.

During emergency operation, a cut-out relay to the dc emergency bus insures adequate power to the wing flap motors for flap extension by cutting out automatically all power to those systems operated by the dc emergency bus during flap sequencing.

External Power Supply.

The aircraft is equipped with a receptacle for connecting an external ac power source to the electrical system. This receptacle (figure 2-8) is located on the lower right side of the fuselage and is accessible through a door above the hydraulic panel. When the external power supply is connected to the aircraft, the generators are automatically disconnected from their respective buses, and all three ac buses receive power from the external ac power source. In order to prevent unnecessary operation of the inverters, a system of protective relays operates automatically whenever external power is applied. One of the functions of these relays is to disconnect the inverters from the dc monitored bus. Power for the TACAN equipment and bus is then supplied automatically through the emergency ac bus and the emergency instrument power transformer. It is possible for ground personnel to test operation of the inverters by means of the inverter ground test switch located on the electronics compartment junction box. When the switch is held ON, the instrument bus and TACAN equipment are connected to their respective inverters through the instrument power relay.

DC ELECTRICAL POWER SUPPLY.

The direct current requirements of the aircraft normally are supplied from the No. 1 ac bus through a 100 A B , 120 C D ampere transformer—rectifier. This changes the 200/115 volt ac to 28-volts dc which is directed to the dc monitored bus. Power is drawn directly from this bus to operate various units (figure 1-39) including the inverters. The dc essential bus and the dc emergency bus are also connected to the dc monitored bus during normal operation. The dc essential and dc emergency buses furnish power to units which are considered necessary for safe operation of the aircraft. Therefore, an alternate source of power to these buses is provided in the event that power from the dc monitored bus is disrupted. Under this condition the dc emergency and dc essential buses will be connected automatically to the 20-ampere transformer—rectifier unit which receives power from the ac emergency bus. When the ram-air turbine-driven ac generator is operative (emergency mode), it is important that the load on the emergency ac bus be minimized when using the aircraft leading and trailing edge flaps since they are powered directly from the emergency ac bus. To reduce loads and ensure maximum flap effectiveness, the dc emergency bus is automatically disconnected from the 20-ampere transformer—rectifier while the flaps are in operation. Those units which are powered from the dc emergency bus, including UHF command radio, will be inoperative during flap operation.

Emergency DC Power Supply.

Note

> A B aircraft are equipped with one 3.6-ampere-hour battery and a battery bus. C D aircraft are equipped with two 3.6-ampere-hour batteries and two battery buses.

ELECTRICAL POWER DISTRIBUTION

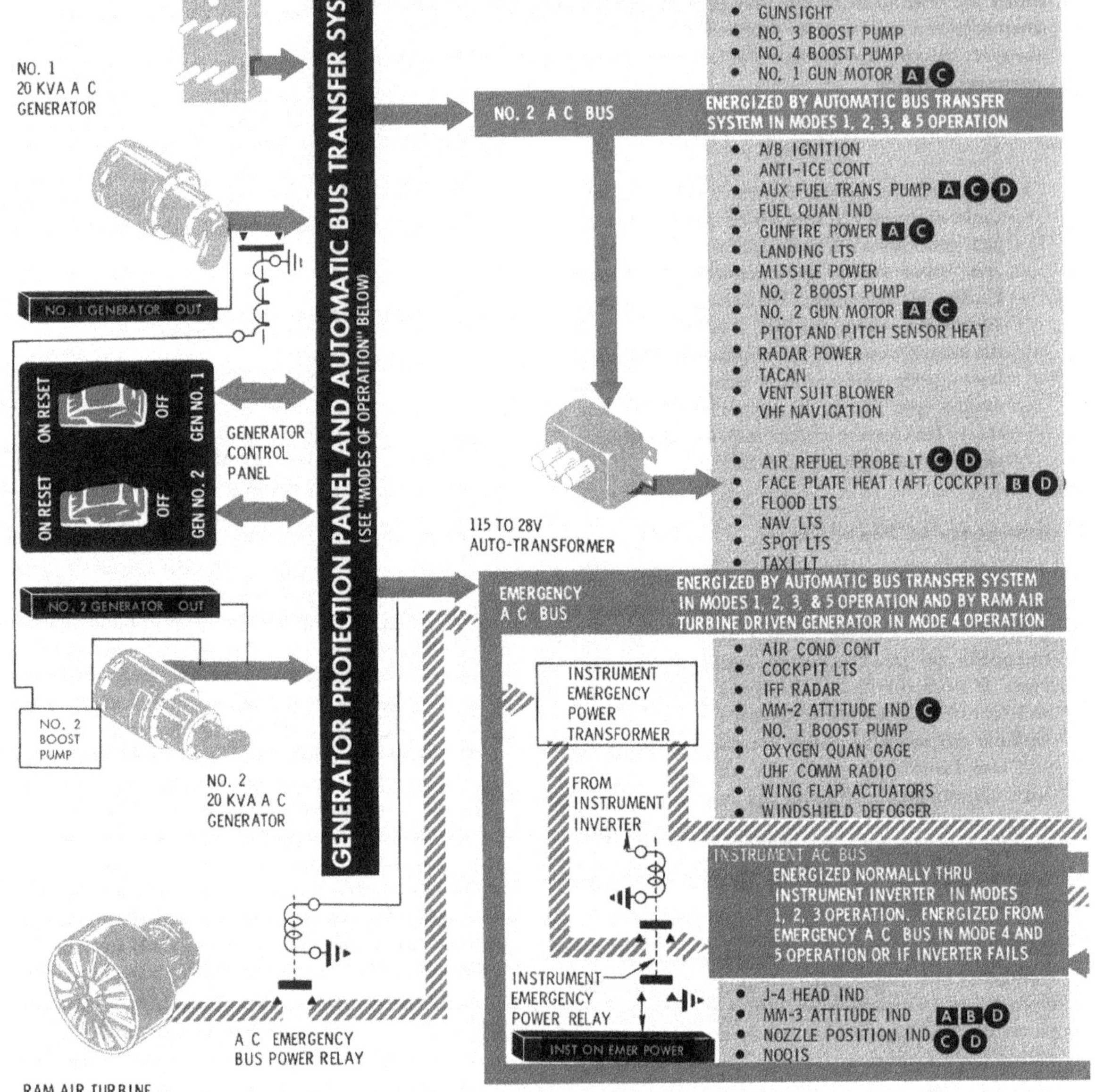

MODES OF OPERATION

MODE 1 - NORMAL OPERATION	MODE 2 - NO. 1 GENERATOR OUT	MODE 3 - NO. 2 GENERATOR OUT	MODE 4 - EMERGENCY OPERATION	MODE 5 - GROUND POWER OPERATION
• NO. 1 GENERATOR ON NO. 1 A C BUS • NO. 2 GENERATOR ON NO. 2 A C BUS AND EMERGENCY BUS	• NO. 2 GENERATOR ON ALL BUSSES	• NO. 1 GENERATOR ON ALL BUSSES	• NO. 1 & 2 BUSSES OUT • NO. 1 & 2 GENERATORS OUT • EMERGENCY GENERATOR ON EMERGENCY A C BUS	• ALL BUSSES ENERGIZED BY EXTERNAL POWER SOURCE

Figure 1-39 (Sheet 1 of 2)

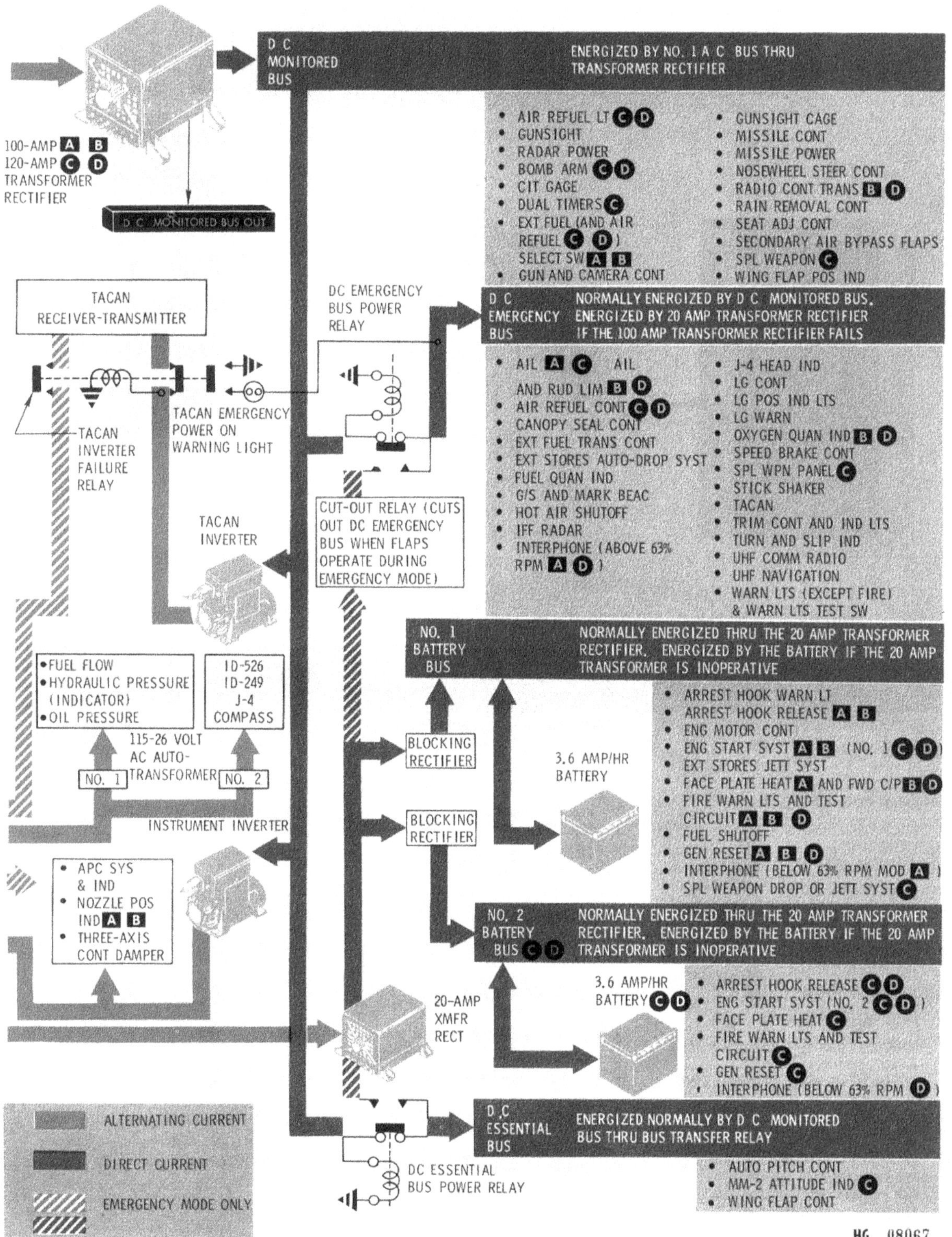
D C MONITORED BUS
ENERGIZED BY NO. 1 A C BUS THRU TRANSFORMER RECTIFIER
100-AMP A B
120-AMP C D
TRANSFORMER RECTIFIER
D C MONITORED BUS OUT
• AIR REFUEL LT C D
• GUNSIGHT
• RADAR POWER
• BOMB ARM C D
• CIT GAGE
• DUAL TIMERS C
• EXT FUEL (AND AIR REFUEL C D) SELECT SW A B
• GUN AND CAMERA CONT
• GUNSIGHT CAGE
• MISSILE CONT
• MISSILE POWER
• NOSEWHEEL STEER CONT
• RADIO CONT TRANS B D
• RAIN REMOVAL CONT
• SEAT ADJ CONT
• SECONDARY AIR BYPASS FLAPS
• SPL WEAPON C
• WING FLAP POS IND
TACAN RECEIVER-TRANSMITTER
DC EMERGENCY BUS POWER RELAY
D C EMERGENCY BUS
NORMALLY ENERGIZED BY D C MONITORED BUS. ENERGIZED BY 20 AMP TRANSFORMER RECTIFIER IF THE 100 AMP TRANSFORMER RECTIFIER FAILS
• AIL A C AIL AND RUD LIM B D
• AIR REFUEL CONT C D
• CANOPY SEAL CONT
• EXT FUEL TRANS CONT
• EXT STORES AUTO-DROP SYST
• FUEL QUAN IND
• G/S AND MARK BEAC
• HOT AIR SHUTOFF
• IFF RADAR
• INTERPHONE (ABOVE 63% RPM A D)
• J-4 HEAD IND
• LG CONT
• LG POS IND LTS
• LG WARN
• OXYGEN QUAN IND B D
• SPEED BRAKE CONT
• SPL WPN PANEL C
• STICK SHAKER
• TACAN
• TRIM CONT AND IND LTS
• TURN AND SLIP IND
• UHF COMM RADIO
• UHF NAVIGATION
• WARN LTS (EXCEPT FIRE) & WARN LTS TEST SW
TACAN EMERGENCY POWER ON WARNING LIGHT
TACAN INVERTER FAILURE RELAY
TACAN INVERTER
CUT-OUT RELAY (CUTS OUT DC EMERGENCY BUS WHEN FLAPS OPERATE DURING EMERGENCY MODE)
NO. 1 BATTERY BUS
NORMALLY ENERGIZED THRU THE 20 AMP TRANSFORMER RECTIFIER. ENERGIZED BY THE BATTERY IF THE 20 AMP TRANSFORMER IS INOPERATIVE
•FUEL FLOW
•HYDRAULIC PRESSURE (INDICATOR)
•OIL PRESSURE
ID-526
ID-249
J-4
COMPASS
115-26 VOLT AC AUTO-TRANSFORMER
NO. 1
NO. 2
INSTRUMENT INVERTER
BLOCKING RECTIFIER
BLOCKING RECTIFIER
3.6 AMP/HR BATTERY
• ARREST HOOK WARN LT
• ARREST HOOK RELEASE A B
• ENG MOTOR CONT
• ENG START SYST A B (NO. 1 C D)
• EXT STORES JETT SYST
• FACE PLATE HEAT A AND FWD C/P B D
• FIRE WARN LTS AND TEST CIRCUIT A B D
• FUEL SHUTOFF
• GEN RESET A B D
• INTERPHONE (BELOW 63% RPM MOD A)
• SPL WEAPON DROP OR JETT SYST C
• APC SYS & IND
• NOZZLE POS IND A B
• THREE-AXIS CONT DAMPER
NO. 2 BATTERY BUS C D
NORMALLY ENERGIZED THRU THE 20 AMP TRANSFORMER RECTIFIER. ENERGIZED BY THE BATTERY IF THE 20 AMP TRANSFORMER IS INOPERATIVE
20-AMP XMFR RECT
3.6 AMP/HR BATTERY C D
• ARREST HOOK RELEASE C D
• ENG START SYST (NO. 2 C D)
• FACE PLATE HEAT C
• FIRE WARN LTS AND TEST CIRCUIT C
• GEN RESET C
• INTERPHONE (BELOW 63% RPM D)
ALTERNATING CURRENT
DIRECT CURRENT
EMERGENCY MODE ONLY
D C ESSENTIAL BUS
ENERGIZED NORMALLY BY D C MONITORED BUS THRU BUS TRANSFER RELAY
DC ESSENTIAL BUS POWER RELAY
• AUTO PITCH CONT
• MM-2 ATTITUDE IND C
• WING FLAP CONT
HG 08067
F52-0-1-24(2)

Figure 1-39 (Sheet 2 of 2)

CIRCUIT BREAKER PANELS A B

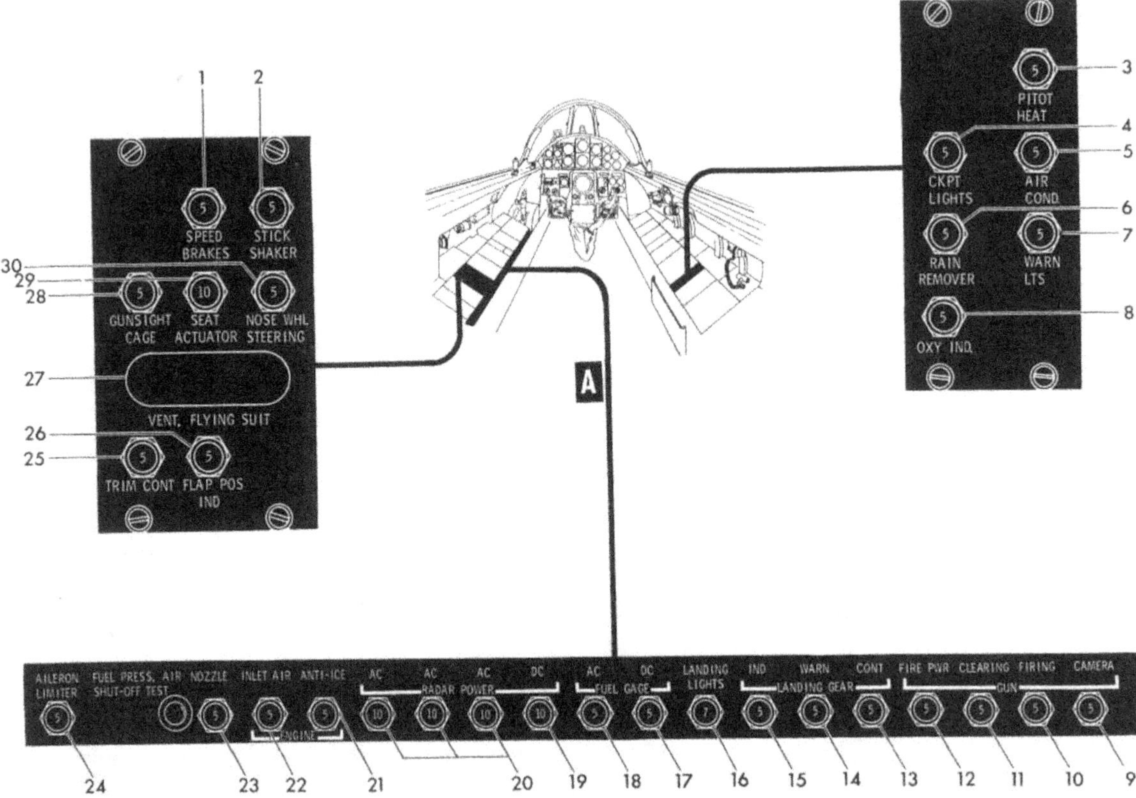

1 SPEED BRAKE VALVE
SPEED BRAKE CONTROL RELAY

2 STICK SHAKER MOTOR
STICK SHAKER RELAY
STICK SHAKER POWER FAIL RELAY

3 PITOT HEATER
ANGLE OF ATTACK TRANSDUCER HEATER
STICK SHAKER TRANSDUCER HEATER

4 CONSOLE LIGHTS
INSTRUMENT LIGHTS

5 AIR CONDITIONING SYSTEM

6 RAIN REMOVER SOLENOID

7 WARNING LIGHT TEST AND DIM RELAYS
MASTER CAUTION LIGHT
ANNUNCIATOR PANEL WARNING LIGHTS

8 LIQUID OXYGEN INDICATOR

9 N-9 GUN CAMERA

10 GUN FIRING INITIATOR
MISSILE FIRING
IGV CONTROL (DURING GUN FIRING)
GUN PURGE VALVE AND TIMER INITIATION

11 DELETED

12 GUN FIRE POWER SUPPLY (GUN IGNITION)

13 LANDING GEAR DOOR AND GEAR SELECT VALVES

14 LANDING GEAR WARNING SIMULATOR
LANDING GEAR WARNING LIGHTS

15 LANDING GEAR DOWN POSITION LIGHTS
LANDING GEAR UPLOCK, DOWNLOCK AND GROUND-AIR SAFETY RELAYS
LANDING LIGHT CUTOUT RELAY

16 LH AND RH LANDING LIGHTS
LANDING LIGHTS AUTO TRANSFORMER

17 FUEL QUANTITY SYSTEM (DC)

18 FUEL QUANTITY SYSTEM (AC)

19 MA-10 RADAR (DC)
RADAR COOLING BLOWER RELAY
(INDIRECTLY) COCKPIT PRESSURE DUMP VALVE

20 MA-10 RADAR (AC)
RADAR COOLING BLOWER

21 ENGINE ANTI-ICE VALVE

22 ENGINE INLET AIR INDICATOR

23 NOZZLE POSITION INDICATOR (EXCEPT AS MODIFIED BY T.O. 1F-104-580)

24 AILERON LIMITER (AFTER INCORP SB 747, TE FLAP CONTROL C/B ALSO CONTROLS AILERON LIMITER)

25 AILERON TRIM MOTOR.
STABILIZER TRIM MOTOR

26 TE AND LE FLAP POSITION INDICATORS AFTER INCORP SB 747, SYSTEM ALSO AFFECTED BY TE FLAP CONTROL C/B

27 VENT. FLYING SUIT BLOWER
VENT. FLYING SUIT RELAY

28 CAGE OPTICAL SIGHT

29 SEAT ACTUATOR

30 NOSE WHEEL STEERING S/O VALVE (SOLENOID)

F52-0-1-21(1)

Figure 1-40 (Sheet 1 of 2)

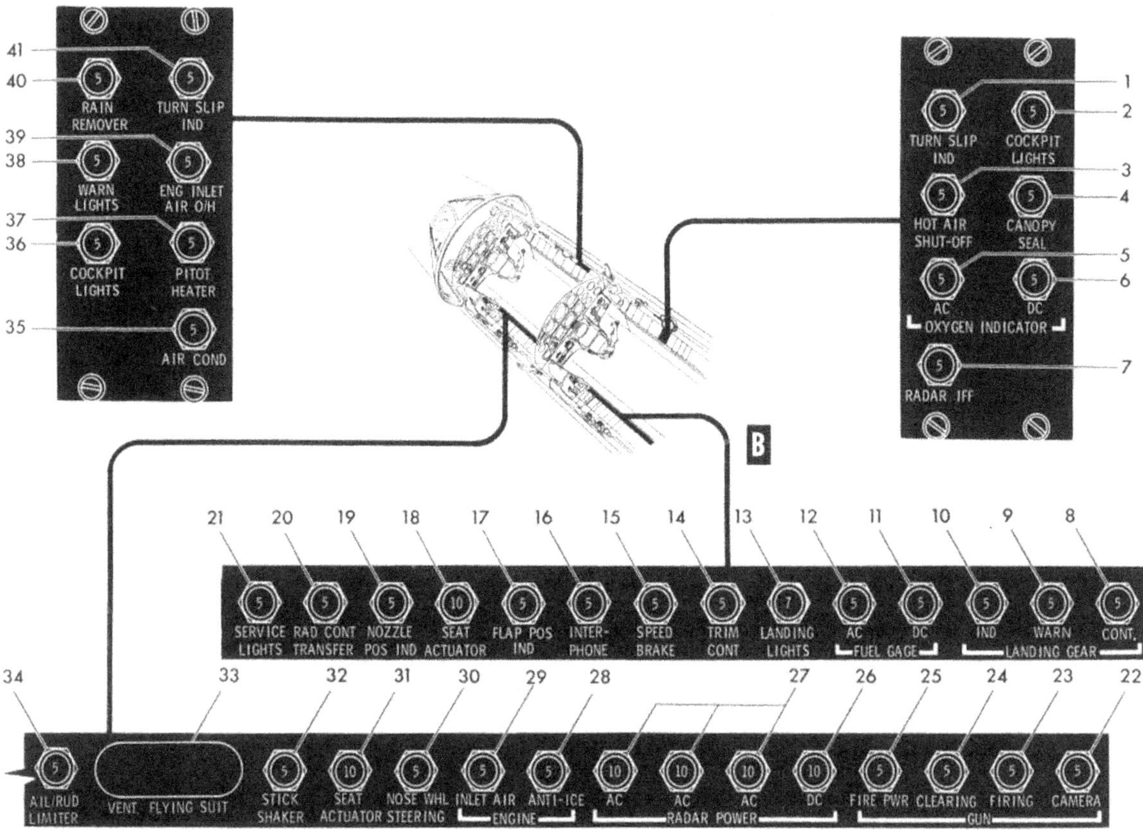

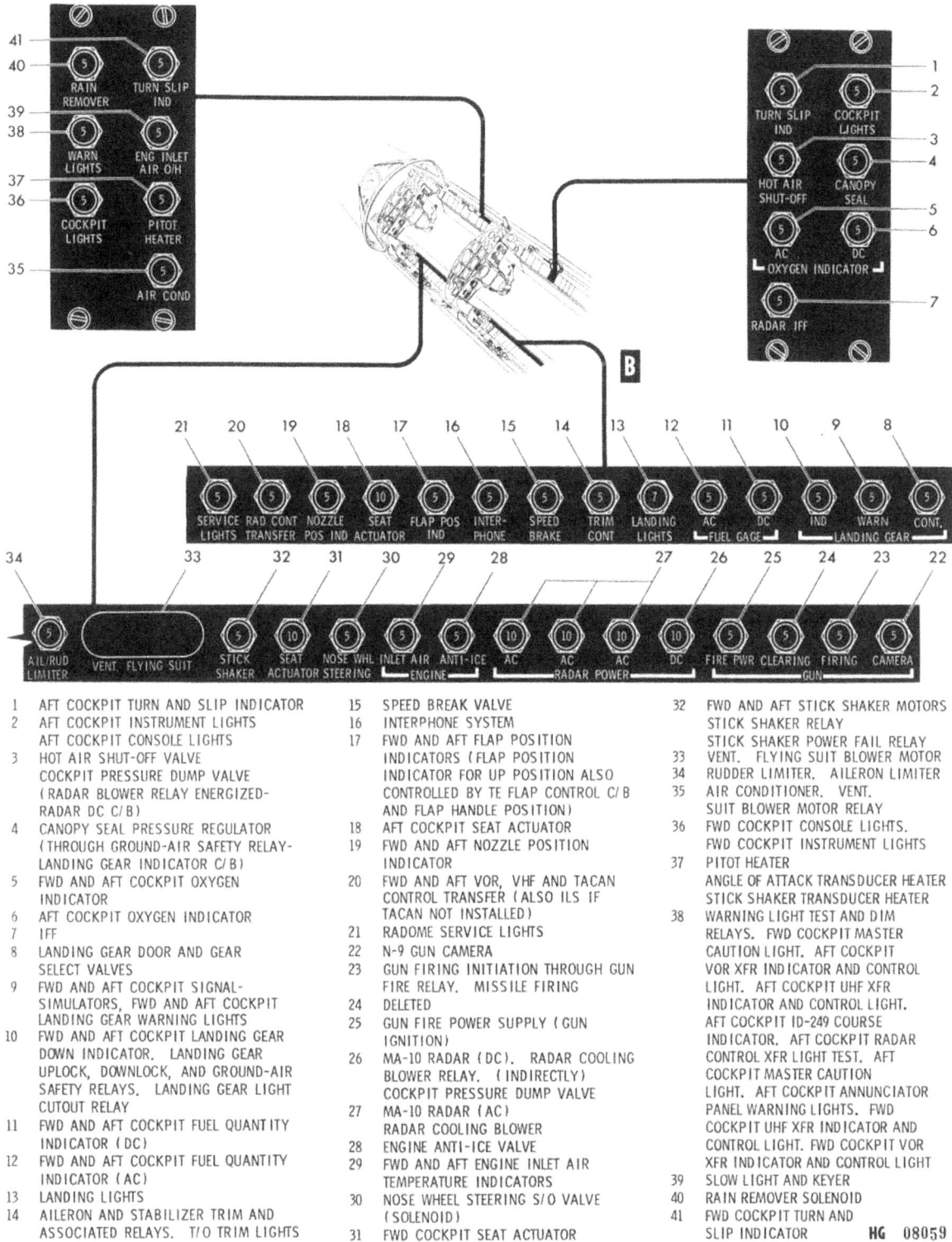

1 AFT COCKPIT TURN AND SLIP INDICATOR
2 AFT COCKPIT INSTRUMENT LIGHTS
AFT COCKPIT CONSOLE LIGHTS
3 HOT AIR SHUT-OFF VALVE
COCKPIT PRESSURE DUMP VALVE
(RADAR BLOWER RELAY ENERGIZED-RADAR DC C/B)
4 CANOPY SEAL PRESSURE REGULATOR
(THROUGH GROUND-AIR SAFETY RELAY-LANDING GEAR INDICATOR C/B)
5 FWD AND AFT COCKPIT OXYGEN INDICATOR
6 AFT COCKPIT OXYGEN INDICATOR
7 IFF
8 LANDING GEAR DOOR AND GEAR SELECT VALVES
9 FWD AND AFT COCKPIT SIGNAL-SIMULATORS, FWD AND AFT COCKPIT LANDING GEAR WARNING LIGHTS
10 FWD AND AFT COCKPIT LANDING GEAR DOWN INDICATOR. LANDING GEAR UPLOCK, DOWNLOCK, AND GROUND-AIR SAFETY RELAYS. LANDING GEAR LIGHT CUTOUT RELAY
11 FWD AND AFT COCKPIT FUEL QUANTITY INDICATOR (DC)
12 FWD AND AFT COCKPIT FUEL QUANTITY INDICATOR (AC)
13 LANDING LIGHTS
14 AILERON AND STABILIZER TRIM AND ASSOCIATED RELAYS. T/O TRIM LIGHTS
15 SPEED BREAK VALVE
16 INTERPHONE SYSTEM
17 FWD AND AFT FLAP POSITION INDICATORS (FLAP POSITION INDICATOR FOR UP POSITION ALSO CONTROLLED BY TE FLAP CONTROL C/B AND FLAP HANDLE POSITION)
18 AFT COCKPIT SEAT ACTUATOR
19 FWD AND AFT NOZZLE POSITION INDICATOR
20 FWD AND AFT VOR, VHF AND TACAN CONTROL TRANSFER (ALSO ILS IF TACAN NOT INSTALLED)
21 RADOME SERVICE LIGHTS
22 N-9 GUN CAMERA
23 GUN FIRING INITIATION THROUGH GUN FIRE RELAY. MISSILE FIRING
24 DELETED
25 GUN FIRE POWER SUPPLY (GUN IGNITION)
26 MA-10 RADAR (DC). RADAR COOLING BLOWER RELAY. (INDIRECTLY) COCKPIT PRESSURE DUMP VALVE
27 MA-10 RADAR (AC)
RADAR COOLING BLOWER
28 ENGINE ANTI-ICE VALVE
29 FWD AND AFT ENGINE INLET AIR TEMPERATURE INDICATORS
30 NOSE WHEEL STEERING S/O VALVE (SOLENOID)
31 FWD COCKPIT SEAT ACTUATOR
32 FWD AND AFT STICK SHAKER MOTORS
STICK SHAKER RELAY
STICK SHAKER POWER FAIL RELAY
33 VENT. FLYING SUIT BLOWER MOTOR
34 RUDDER LIMITER. AILERON LIMITER
35 AIR CONDITIONER. VENT. SUIT BLOWER MOTOR RELAY
36 FWD COCKPIT CONSOLE LIGHTS. FWD COCKPIT INSTRUMENT LIGHTS
37 PITOT HEATER
ANGLE OF ATTACK TRANSDUCER HEATER
STICK SHAKER TRANSDUCER HEATER
38 WARNING LIGHT TEST AND DIM RELAYS. FWD COCKPIT MASTER CAUTION LIGHT. AFT COCKPIT VOR XFR INDICATOR AND CONTROL LIGHT. AFT COCKPIT UHF XFR INDICATOR AND CONTROL LIGHT. AFT COCKPIT ID-249 COURSE INDICATOR. AFT COCKPIT RADAR CONTROL XFR LIGHT TEST. AFT COCKPIT MASTER CAUTION LIGHT. AFT COCKPIT ANNUNCIATOR PANEL WARNING LIGHTS. FWD COCKPIT UHF XFR INDICATOR AND CONTROL LIGHT. FWD COCKPIT VOR XFR INDICATOR AND CONTROL LIGHT
39 SLOW LIGHT AND KEYER
40 RAIN REMOVER SOLENOID
41 FWD COCKPIT TURN AND SLIP INDICATOR

HG 08059
F52-0-1-21(2)

Figure 1-40 (Sheet 2 of 2)

CIRCUIT BREAKER PANELS TYPICAL (C)

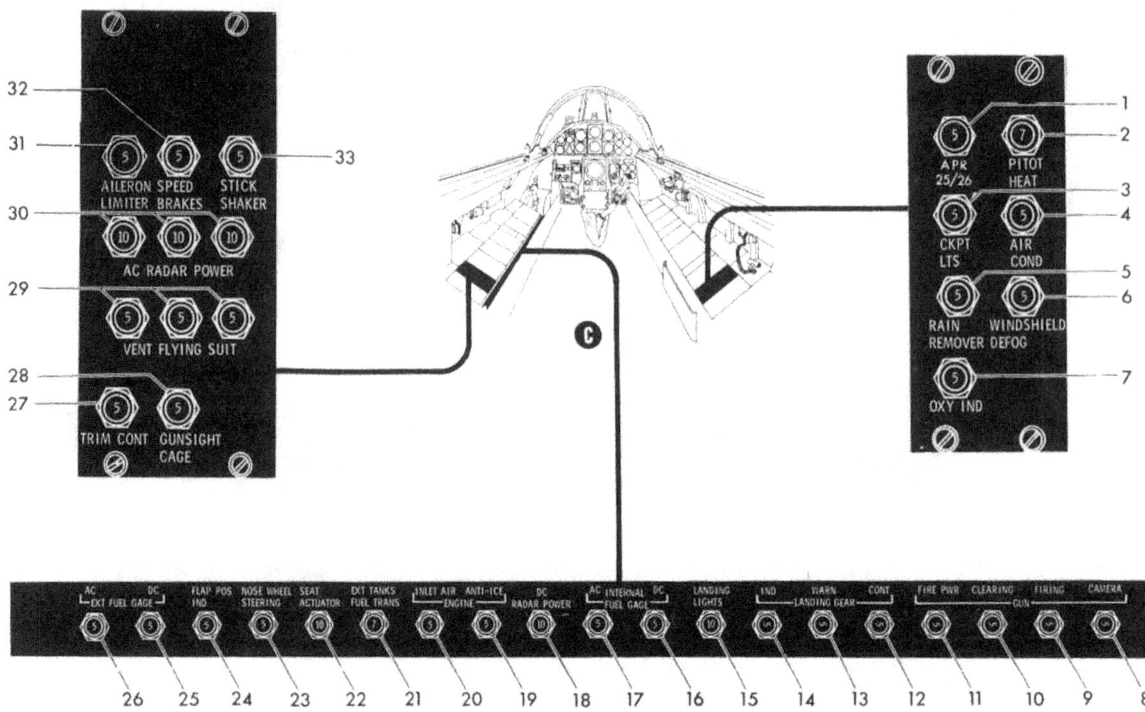

1 APR - 25/26

2 PITOT HEATER
ANGLE OF ATTACK TRANSDUCER HEATER
STICK SHAKER TRANSDUCER HEATER

3 CONSOLE LIGHTS. INSTRUMENT LIGHTS

4 AIR CONDITIONING SYSTEM

5 RAIN REMOVER VALVE SOLENOID

6 HEATED WINDSHIELD POWER

7 LIQUID OXYGEN INDICATOR

8 N-9 GUN CAMERA

9 GUN FIRING INITIATION
MISSILE FIRING
IGV CONTROL (DURING GUN) FIRING, GUN PURGE VALVE AND TIMER INITIATION, ENGINE IGNITION PLUS ASSOCIATED RELAYS

10 DELETED

11 GUN FIRE POWER SUPPLY (GUN IGNITION)

12 LANDING GEAR DOOR AND GEAR SELECT VALVES
ARMAMENT CUTOUT RELAY

13 LANDING GEAR WARNING SIMULATOR(S)
LANDING GEAR WARNING LIGHT(S)

14 LANDING GEAR DOWN POSITION LIGHT(S)
LANDING GEAR UPLOCK, DOWNLOCK AND GROUND-AIR SAFETY RELAYS
LANDING LIGHTS CUTOUT RELAY

15 LH AND RH LANDING LIGHTS
LANDING LIGHTS AUTO TRANSFORMER

16 INTERNAL FUEL QUANTITY SYSTEM DC

17 INTERNAL FUEL QUANTITY SYSTEM AC

18 MA-10 RADAR
RADAR COOLING BLOWER RELAY (INDIRECTLY). COCKPIT PRESSURE DUMP VALVE

19 ENGINE ANTI-ICE VALVE

20 ENGINE INLET AIR TEMPERATURE INDICATOR

21 EXTERNAL FUEL TANK AIR S/O AND FUEL VALVES, FUEL AND AIR REFUEL CONTROL

22 SEAT ACTUATOR

23 NOSE WHEEL STEERING S/O VALVE (SOLENOID)

24 TE AND LE FLAP POSITION INDICATORS AFTER INCORPORATING SB 747
TE SYSTEM ALSO AFFECTED BY TE FLAP CONTROL C/B

25 EXTERNAL FUEL QUANTITY INDICATOR DC

26 EXTERNAL FUEL QUANTITY INDICATOR AC

27 STABILIZER AND AILERON TRIM MOTOR

28 OPTICAL SIGHT GAGE

29 VENT. FLYING SUIT BLOWER
VENT. FLYING SUIT RELAY

30 MA-10 RADAR
RADAR COOLING BLOWER

31 AILERON LIMITER AFTER INCORPORATING SB 747, TE FLAP CONTROL C/B ALSO CONTROLS AILERON LIMITER

32 SPEED BRAKE SELECTOR VALVE
SPEED BRAKE CONTROL RELAY

33 STICK SHAKER MOTOR(S)
STICK SHAKER RELAY
STICK SHAKER POWER FAIL RELAY

F52-0-1-21(3)

Figure 1-41 (Sheet 1 of 2)

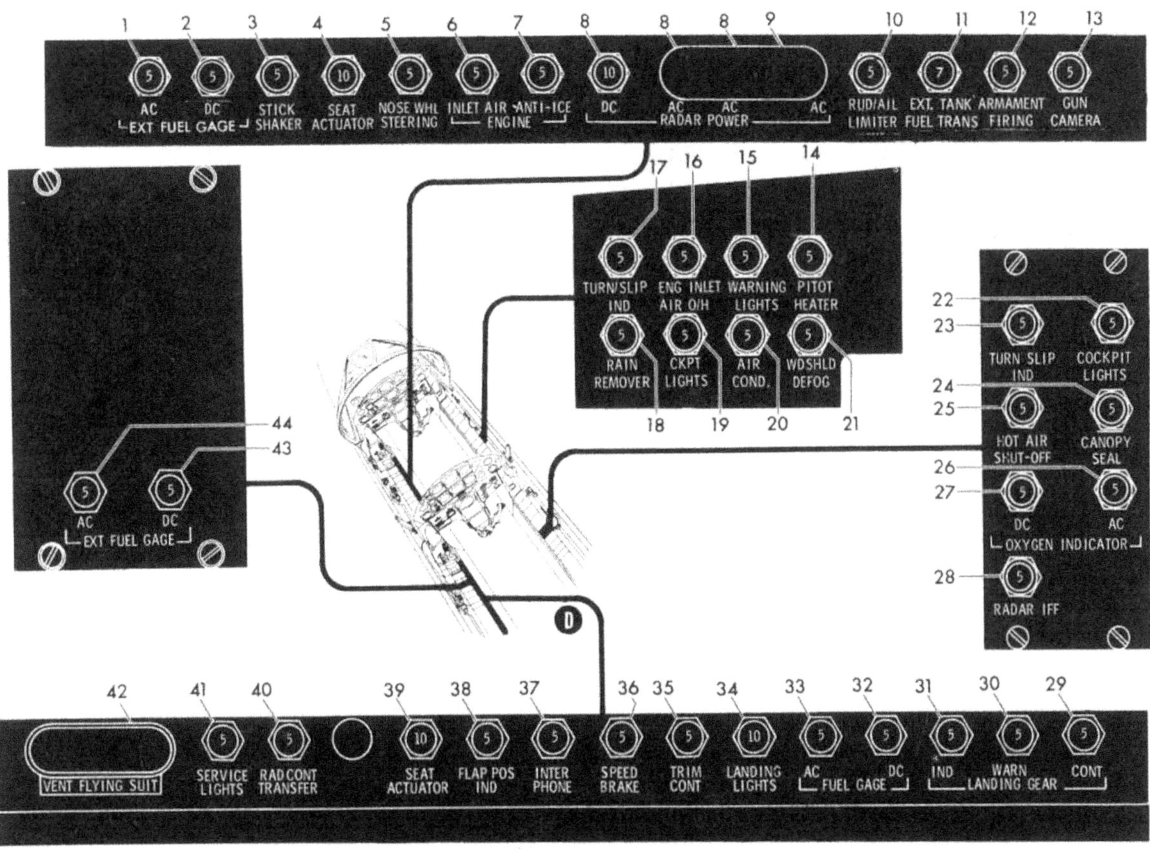

1 EXTERNAL FUEL QUANTITY INDICATOR AC
2 EXTERNAL FUEL QUANTITY INDICATOR DC
3 STICK SHAKER MOTOR(S)
STICK SHAKER RELAY
STICK SHAKER POWER FAIL RELAY
4 FORWARD COCKPIT SEAT ACTUATOR
5 NOSE WHEEL STEERING S/O VALVE (SOLENOID)
6 FWD AND AFT ENGINE INLET AIR TEMPERATURE INDICATORS
7 ENGINE ANTI-ICE VALVE
8 MA-10 RADAR.
RADAR COOLING BLOWER
9 MA-10 RADAR. RADAR COOLING BLOWER RELAY (INDIRECTLY). COCKPIT PRESSURE DUMP VALVE
10 RUDDER LIMITER. AILERON LIMITER
11 EXTERNAL FUEL TANK AIR S/O AND FUEL VALVES, FUEL AND AIR REFUEL CONTROL
12 GUN FIRING INITIATION THROUGH GUN FIRE RELAY. MISSILE FIRING
13 N-9 GUN CAMERA
14 PITOT HEATER
ANGLE OF ATTACK TRANSDUCER HEATER
STICK SHAKER TRANSDUCER HEATER
15 WARNING LIGHT TEST AND DIM RELAYS
FWD COCKPIT ANNUNCIATOR PANEL WARNING LIGHTS. FWD COCKPIT MASTER CAUTION LIGHT. AFT COCKPIT COMM AND NAV CONTROL INDICATOR LIGHT. (FWD AND AFT COCKPIT) ID-249 COURSE INDICATOR. AFT COCKPIT RADAR TRANSFER AND INDICATOR LIGHT. AFT COCKPIT MASTER CAUTION LIGHT. AFT COCKPIT ANNUNCIATOR PANEL WARNING LIGHTS. FWD COCKPIT COMM AND NAV CONTROL INDICATOR LIGHT.
PYLON TANK EMPTY INDICATOR
16 SLOW LIGHT AND KEYER
17 FWD COCKPIT TURN AND SLIP INDICATOR
18 RAIN REMOVER VALVE SOLENOID
19 FWD COCKPIT CONSOLE AND INSTRUMENT LIGHTS
20 AIR CONDITIONER.
VENT. SUIT BLOWER MOTOR RELAY
21 HEATED WINDSHIELD POWER
22 AFT COCKPIT CONSOLE AND INSTRUMENT LIGHTS
23 AFT COCKPIT TURN AND SLIP INDICATOR
24 CANOPY SEAL PRESSURE REGULATOR (THROUGH GROUND AIR SAFETY RELAY- LANDING GEAR INDICATOR C/B)
25 HOT AIR SHUT-OFF VALVE.
COCKPIT PRESSURE DUMP VALVE (RADAR BLOWER RELAY ENERGIZED- RADAR DC C/B)
26 FWD AND AFT COCKPIT OXYGEN INDICATOR
27 AFT COCKPIT OXYGEN INDICATOR
28 IFF/SIF
29 LANDING GEAR AND DOOR SELECTOR VALVES. ARMAMENT CUTOUT RELAY. (SERIALS 5033 THRU 5046) GROUND-AIR SAFETY RELAY
30 LANDING GEAR WARNING SIMULATOR(S)
LANDING GEAR WARNING LIGHT(S)
31 LANDING GEAR DOWN POSITION LIGHT(S)
LANDING GEAR UPLOCK, DOWNLOCK AND GROUND-AIR SAFETY RELAYS.
LANDING LIGHTS CUTOUT RELAY
32 FWD AND AFT COCKPIT INTERNAL FUEL QUANTITY INDICATORS DC
33 FWD AND AFT COCKPIT INTERNAL FUEL QUANTITY INDICATORS AC
34 LANDING LIGHTS
35 AILERON AND STABILIZER TRIM AND ASSOCIATED RELAYS. T/O TRIM LIGHTS
36 SPEED BRAKE SELECTOR
SPEED BRAKE CONTROL RELAY
37 INTERPHONE SYSTEM
38 FWD AND AFT COCKPIT FLAP POSITION INDICATORS. (FLAP POSITION INDICATORS FOR UP POSITION ALSO CONTROLLED BY TE FLAP CONTROL C/B AND FLAP HANDLE POSITION)
39 AFT COCKPIT SEAT ACTUATOR
40 FWD AND AFT COCKPIT VOR AND UHF CONTROL TRANSFER (ALSO ILS IF TACAN NOT INSTALLED)
41 RADOME SERVICE LIGHTS
42 VENTILATED FLYING SUIT BLOWER (CONTROLLED BY VENTILATED SUIT BLOWER SWITCH AND AIR CONDITIONER C/B IN FWD COCKPIT)
43 EXTERNAL FUEL QUANTITY INDICATOR DC
44 EXTERNAL FUEL QUANTITY INDICATOR AC

HG 08068 F52-0-1-21(4)

Figure 1-41 (Sheet 2 of 2)

If all three generators (No. 1, No. 2, and RAT) fail, the batteries will furnish a supply of direct current to the battery buses. The batteries are the only independent source of direct current in the aircraft electrical system. Normally, the batteries and battery buses are paralleled with the 20-ampere transformer—rectifier, and the batteries are thereby maintained in a fully charged condition. In emergency operation, battery output is prevented from discharging to the 20-ampere transformer—rectifier by blocking rectifiers in order to conserve the limited power supply for those units connected directly to the battery buses. There is no battery control switch in the cockpit, and operation of the battery system is entirely automatic. A fully charged battery may last as long as 30 minutes.

INSTRUMENT POWER SUPPLY.

Alternating current necessary for operation of the various aircraft flight instruments is furnished normally by an instrument inverter located in the electronics compartment. The inverter functions to convert 28-volt dc from the dc monitored bus to 115-volt, 400-cycle, fixed frequency ac power for the instrument ac bus. Failure of the instrument inverter actuates a transfer system and automatically connects the instrument ac bus to the emergency ac bus through the instrument emergency power transformer so that there will be no interruption of instrument operation. The inverter is disconnected from the dc monitored bus whenever an external power source is connected to the aircraft electrical system. Ground personnel may test the inverter for proper operation by operating the inverter ground test switch in the electronics compartment. During external power operation, alternating current for the instruments is supplied by the ground power unit through the emergency ac bus and instrument emergency power transformer.

TACAN POWER SUPPLY.

Variable-frequency, 115-volt ac power is supplied to the TACAN system from the No. 2 ac bus. Fixed-frequency, 115-volt ac power from the TACAN inverter is supplied to the TACAN system through closed contacts of the TACAN inverter failure relay. The TACAN inverter is energized by 28-volt dc power from the dc monitored bus. The TACAN controls are operated by dc power from the emergency dc bus. When the TACAN inverter or its dc monitored bus power source fails, the TACAN inverter failure relay is deenergized and operates to connect variable-frequency ac power from the instrument emergency power transformer to the TACAN system. When the TACAN is operating on emergency power the TACAN EMERGENCY POWER ON warning light is illuminated.

Note

On emergency ac variable frequency power, TACAN information becomes degraded and may be unreliable.

Circuit Breakers.

The circuit breaker panels (figures 1-40, 1-41) on the left and right consoles contain push-to-reset, pullout type breakers for certain ac and dc circuits. All of the distribution circuits in the electrical system are protected by circuit breakers of various types. Circuit breaker panels which are not accessible during flight, but which should be inspected before flight, are located in the electronics compartment behind the cockpit and in the electrical load center on the right side of the fuselage.

CAUTION

Circuit breakers should not be pulled or reset without a complete understanding of all the effects and results of so doing. Pulling circuit breakers indiscriminately can eliminate from the system some related warning system, interlocking circuit, or canceling signal, which could result in an undesirable reaction.

Generator Switches.

A generator switch is provided for each of the 20-kva generator systems. These switches (figures 1-20, 1-21) are identical and are located on the right forward panel. They are powered from the battery bus. Each switch has three positions, ON—RESET, OFF, and a center NEUTRAL position which is the normal position of the switch when covered by the guard. The switches are spring loaded to return to the NEUTRAL position. Moving the switch up to the ON—RESET position returns the generator to normal operation if it has been removed from the line for any reason other than complete generator failure. When moved down to the OFF position, the switch energizes the generator control relay which then removes the generator from its associated bus.

Ram Air Turbine Extension Handle.

Emergency ac power is made available by extending the ram air turbine (RAT) into the aircraft slipstream. The turbine is extended by pulling the yellow ram air turbine extension handle (43, 38, figures 1-12, 1-13, and 25, 21, figures 1-22, 1-23) located at the lower right side of the instrument panel. The handle requires a firm pull of about 4 inches to the stop for extension.

Note

The ram air turbine cannot be retracted in flight.

Generator-Out Warning Lights.

Two generator-out warning lights (figures 1-20, 1-21), one for each of the 20-kva generators, are located on the warning light panel. The lights are placarded No. 1 GENERATOR OUT and No. 2 GENERATOR OUT. Each light is powered by the 28-volt dc emergency bus and will illuminate whenever its respective generator is not generating. The MASTER CAUTION light also illuminates when either generator-out warning light illuminates.

Note

- With both generators off and the RAT retracted, all warning lights (including generator out warning lights) except the tail arresting hook, main fuel shutoff valve, and fire warning lights are inoperative.
- If the No. 1 main generator fails the power source for the No. 1 ac bus is automatically transferred to the No. 2 generator by the automatic bus transfer system. When this occurs, both the INST ON EMER POWER and TACAN EMERGENCY POWER ON warning lights may flicker momentarily then go out. This is because of the momentary interruption of power during bus transfer operation.

DC Monitored Bus-Out Warning Light.

The dc monitored bus-out warning light (figures 1-20, 1-21), located on the warning light panel, is energized by the 28-volt dc emergency bus. The light is placarded DC MONITORED BUS OUT and illuminates any time power to the dc monitored bus is interrupted during normal operation. The MASTER CAUTION light, INST ON EMER POWER and TACAN EMERGENCY POWER ON warning lights also illuminate when the dc monitored warning light illuminates. (See figure 1-xx for units which will be operative when the dc monitored bus-out warning light is on.)

Instruments On Emergency Power Warning Light.

The instruments on emergency power warning light (figures 1-20, 1-21), located on the warning light panel, is energized by the 28-volt dc emergency bus. The light is placarded INST ON EMER POWER and illuminates any time power from the instrument inverter is interrupted and the instrument emergency power transformer is supplying power to the instrument ac bus. The MASTER CAUTION light also illuminates when the warning light illuminates.

TACAN Emergency Power On Warning Light.

The TACAN EMERGENCY POWER ON warning light (figures 1-20, 1-21) is energized by the 28-volt dc emergency bus. It will illuminate any time fixed-frequency ac power from the TACAN inverter is interrupted and the instrument emergency power transformer is supplying power to the TACAN system. The MASTER CAUTION light will also illuminate when the TACAN EMERGENCY POWER ON warning light is illuminated.

HYDRAULIC POWER SUPPLY SYSTEMS.

Two completely independent main hydraulic systems and a utility system provide power to the various hydraulically actuated units in the aircraft. (See figures 1-42, 1-43.) The No. 1 and No. 2 systems are in simultaneous operation during all normal operating conditions and supply fluid at 3000 psi pressure to their respective hydraulically actuated units. Both No. 1 and No. 2 systems are provided with separate reservoirs which differ only in size and location with the No. 2 reservoir the larger. Both reservoirs are pressurized to prevent pump cavitation. In addition, each system includes an engine-driven pump, a cylindrical accumulator, a pressure transmitter, a pressure switch, and filters. In case of failure of either system 1 or system 2, the system that remains will maintain fluid pressure for flight control at a reduced rate. If systems 1 and 2 both fail, the emergency ram air turbine-driven pump will furnish enough fluid pressure through system 1 for flight control at a reduced rate.

Accumulators.

The cylindrical accumulators are charged at approximately 1000 psi and are provided with an air valve and an air pressure gage. The accumulator function is to store a supply of high pressure fluid and also to act as surge chambers. The accumulators and pressure gages for systems 1 and 2 are accessible upon opening a large engine access door (figure 2-8) on the underside of the fuselage below the engine. Graduations on the gage dial are in increments of 100 from 0 to 4000 psi. The pressure gage shows the intitial charge (1000 psi) in the accumulator only when system hydraulic pressure is zero.

Air Oil Separators.

An air oil separator is installed in the return line of both the No. 1 and No. 2 hydraulic systems (figure 1-42). The separators remove excess air from the hydraulic fluid which helps to prevent nosewheel shimmy and speed brake shudder.

HYDRAULIC SYSTEM

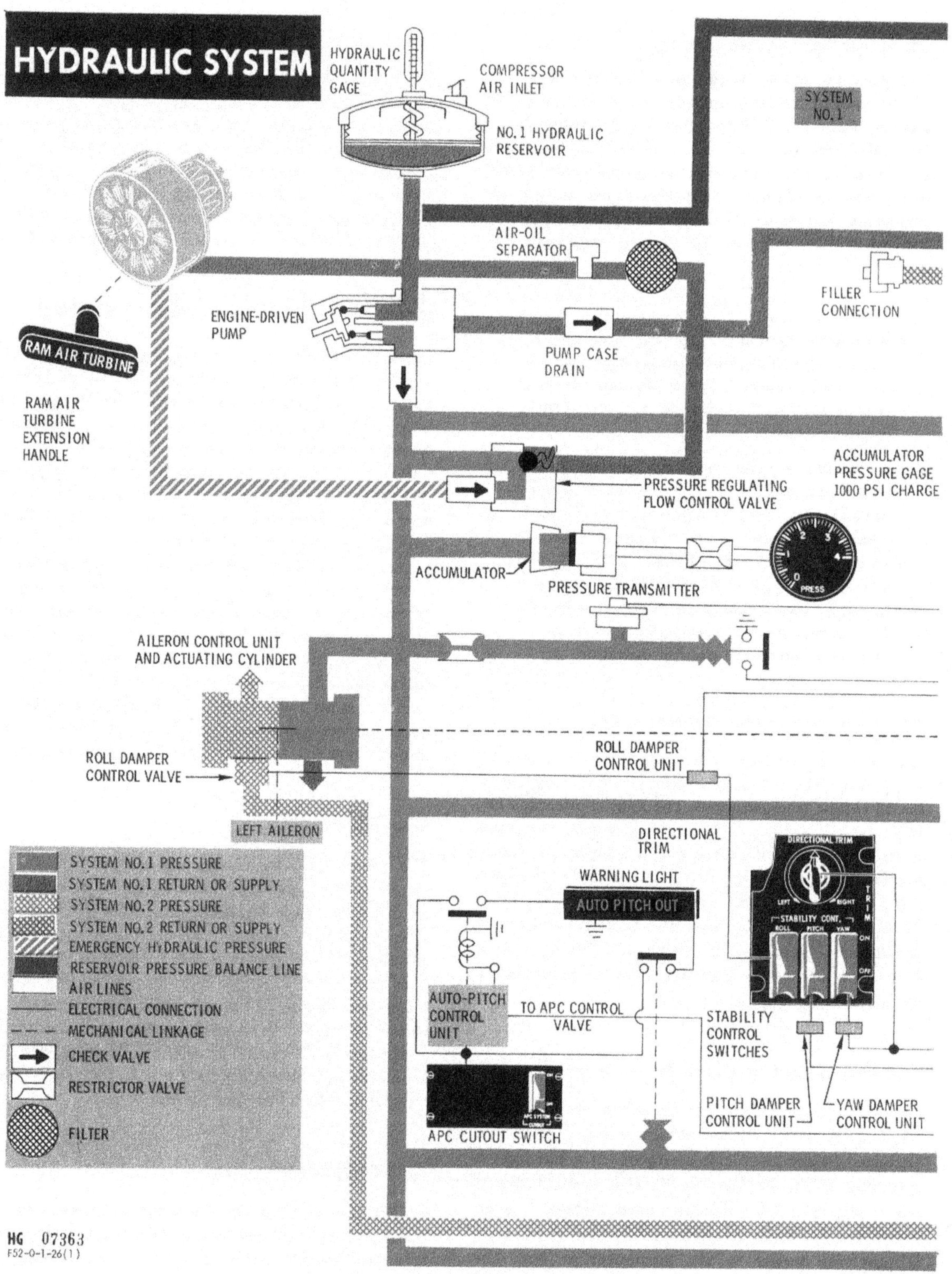
HYDRAULIC QUANTITY GAGE
COMPRESSOR AIR INLET
SYSTEM NO.1
NO.1 HYDRAULIC RESERVOIR
AIR-OIL SEPARATOR
FILLER CONNECTION
ENGINE-DRIVEN PUMP
RAM AIR TURBINE
PUMP CASE DRAIN
RAM AIR TURBINE EXTENSION HANDLE
ACCUMULATOR PRESSURE GAGE 1000 PSI CHARGE
PRESSURE REGULATING FLOW CONTROL VALVE
ACCUMULATOR
PRESSURE TRANSMITTER
AILERON CONTROL UNIT AND ACTUATING CYLINDER
ROLL DAMPER CONTROL VALVE
ROLL DAMPER CONTROL UNIT
LEFT AILERON
DIRECTIONAL TRIM
WARNING LIGHT
AUTO PITCH OUT
SYSTEM NO.1 PRESSURE
SYSTEM NO.1 RETURN OR SUPPLY
SYSTEM NO.2 PRESSURE
SYSTEM NO.2 RETURN OR SUPPLY
EMERGENCY HYDRAULIC PRESSURE
RESERVOIR PRESSURE BALANCE LINE
AIR LINES
ELECTRICAL CONNECTION
MECHANICAL LINKAGE
CHECK VALVE
RESTRICTOR VALVE
FILTER
AUTO-PITCH CONTROL UNIT
TO APC CONTROL VALVE
STABILITY CONTROL SWITCHES
APC CUTOUT SWITCH
PITCH DAMPER CONTROL UNIT
YAW DAMPER CONTROL UNIT
HG 07363
F52-0-1-26(1)

Figure 1-42 (Sheet 1 of 2)

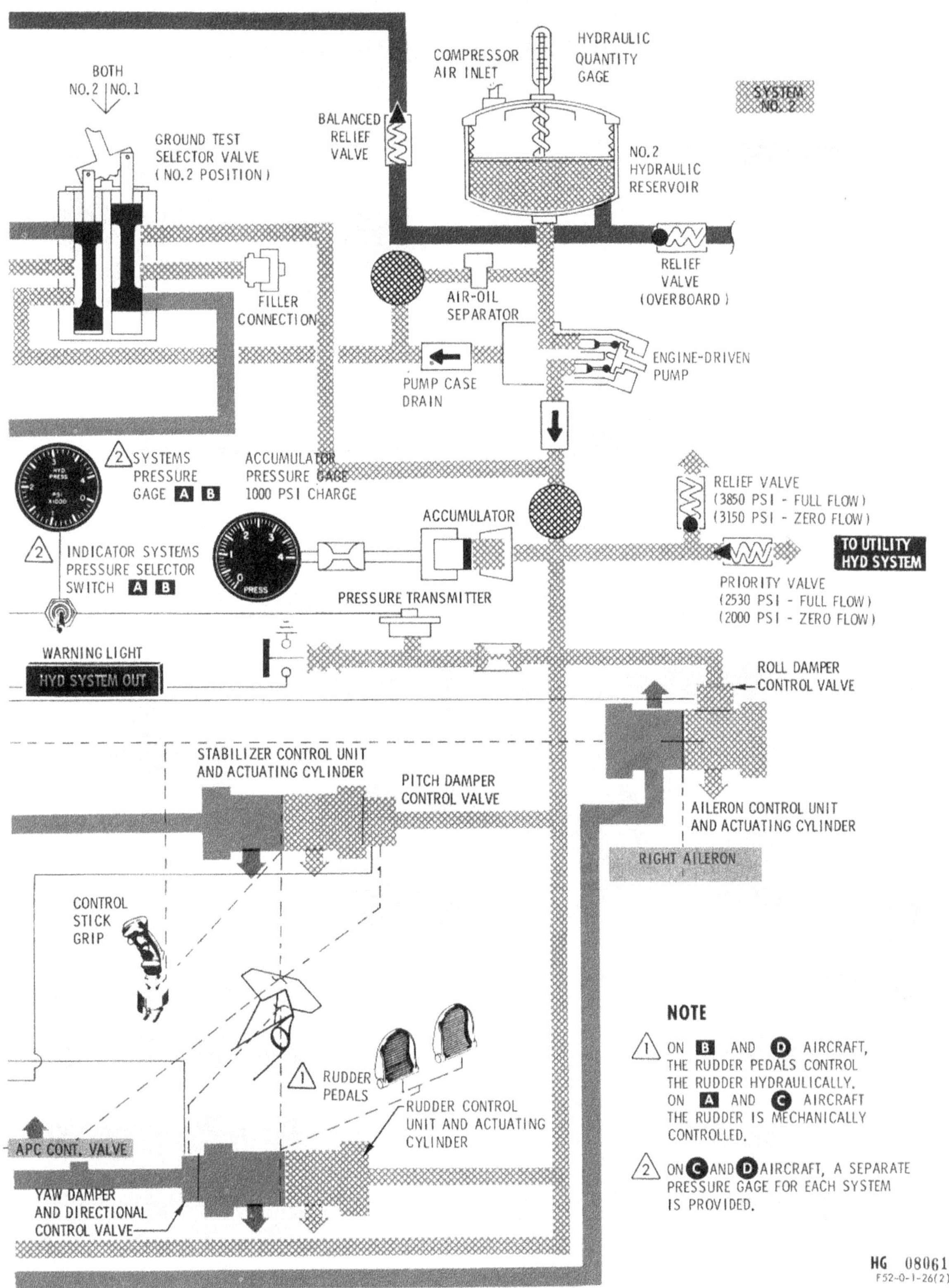

SYSTEM NO. 2
BOTH
NO.2 | NO.1
GROUND TEST SELECTOR VALVE (NO.2 POSITION)
BALANCED RELIEF VALVE
COMPRESSOR AIR INLET
HYDRAULIC QUANTITY GAGE
NO.2 HYDRAULIC RESERVOIR
RELIEF VALVE (OVERBOARD)
FILLER CONNECTION
AIR-OIL SEPARATOR
PUMP CASE DRAIN
ENGINE-DRIVEN PUMP
2 SYSTEMS PRESSURE GAGE A B
ACCUMULATOR PRESSURE GAGE 1000 PSI CHARGE
ACCUMULATOR
RELIEF VALVE (3850 PSI - FULL FLOW) (3150 PSI - ZERO FLOW)
TO UTILITY HYD SYSTEM
PRIORITY VALVE (2530 PSI - FULL FLOW) (2000 PSI - ZERO FLOW)
2 INDICATOR SYSTEMS PRESSURE SELECTOR SWITCH A B
PRESSURE TRANSMITTER
WARNING LIGHT
HYD SYSTEM OUT
ROLL DAMPER CONTROL VALVE
STABILIZER CONTROL UNIT AND ACTUATING CYLINDER
PITCH DAMPER CONTROL VALVE
AILERON CONTROL UNIT AND ACTUATING CYLINDER
RIGHT AILERON
CONTROL STICK GRIP
1 RUDDER PEDALS
RUDDER CONTROL UNIT AND ACTUATING CYLINDER
APC CONT. VALVE
YAW DAMPER AND DIRECTIONAL CONTROL VALVE
NOTE
1 ON B AND D AIRCRAFT, THE RUDDER PEDALS CONTROL THE RUDDER HYDRAULICALLY. ON A AND C AIRCRAFT THE RUDDER IS MECHANICALLY CONTROLLED.
2 ON C AND D AIRCRAFT, A SEPARATE PRESSURE GAGE FOR EACH SYSTEM IS PROVIDED.
HG 08061
F52-0-1-26(2)

Figure 1-42 (Sheet 2 of 2)

UTILITY HYDRAULIC SYSTEM

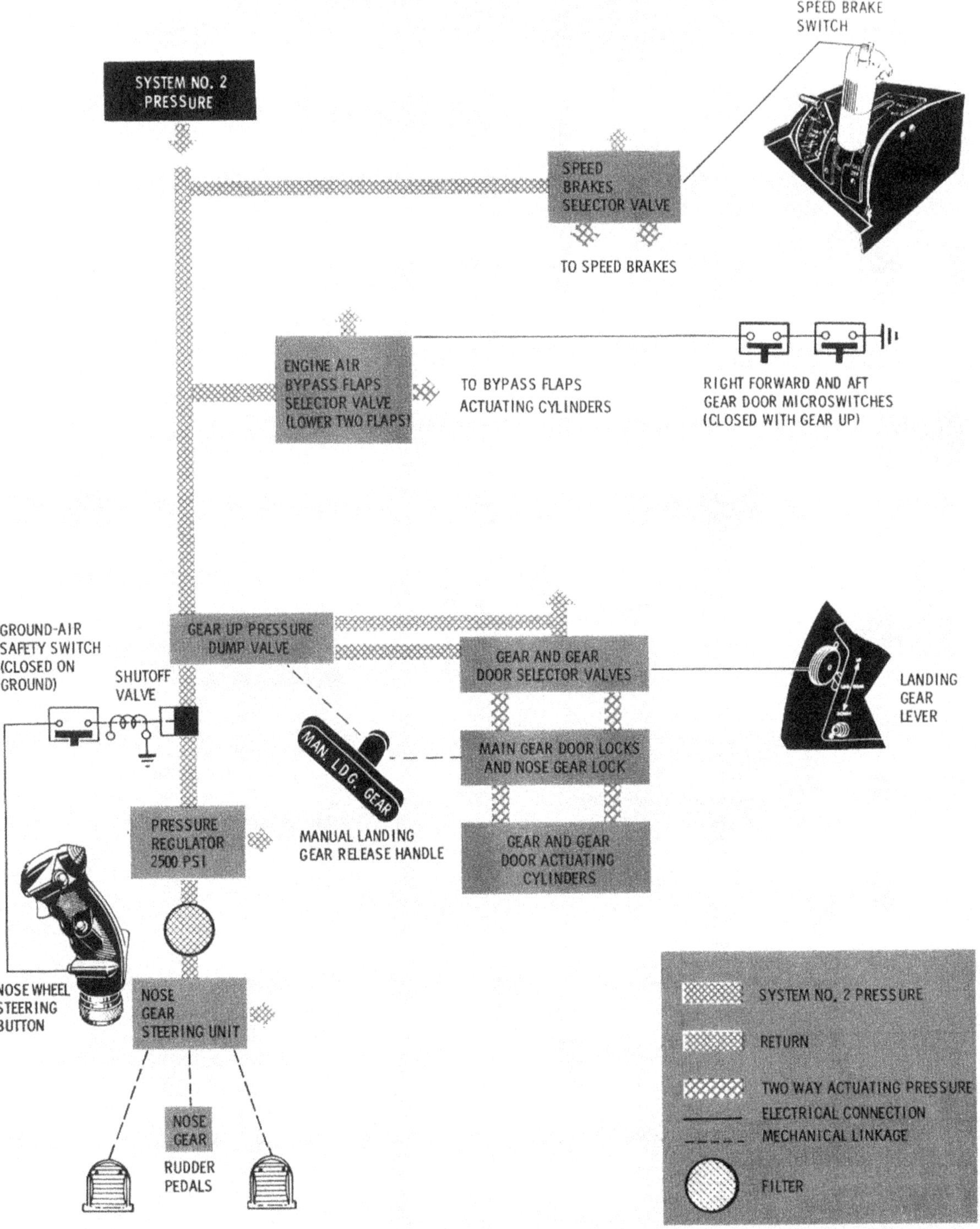
SPEED BRAKE SWITCH
SYSTEM NO. 2 PRESSURE
SPEED BRAKES SELECTOR VALVE
TO SPEED BRAKES
ENGINE AIR BYPASS FLAPS SELECTOR VALVE (LOWER TWO FLAPS)
TO BYPASS FLAPS ACTUATING CYLINDERS
RIGHT FORWARD AND AFT GEAR DOOR MICROSWITCHES (CLOSED WITH GEAR UP)
GROUND-AIR SAFETY SWITCH (CLOSED ON GROUND)
SHUTOFF VALVE
GEAR UP PRESSURE DUMP VALVE
GEAR AND GEAR DOOR SELECTOR VALVES
LANDING GEAR LEVER
MAN. LDG. GEAR
MAIN GEAR DOOR LOCKS AND NOSE GEAR LOCK
PRESSURE REGULATOR 2500 PSI
MANUAL LANDING GEAR RELEASE HANDLE
GEAR AND GEAR DOOR ACTUATING CYLINDERS
NOSE WHEEL STEERING BUTTON
NOSE GEAR STEERING UNIT
NOSE GEAR
RUDDER PEDALS
SYSTEM NO. 2 PRESSURE
RETURN
TWO WAY ACTUATING PRESSURE
ELECTRICAL CONNECTION
MECHANICAL LINKAGE
FILTER
F53-0-1-26

Figure 1-43

HYDRAULIC PANEL.

Most of the hydraulic units are mounted directly on a hydraulic panel on the inside face of the engine access door. Upon opening the door the various units are exposed for servicing, testing, and checking quantity indicators.

Ground Test Selector Valve.

The manually controlled ground test selector valve (on the hydraulic panel) is the only link between systems 1 and 2. A three-position lever extends from the top of the valve. Mechanical linkage from this lever to a fixed bracket inside the fuselage ensures that the lever is placed and locked in the No. 2 position whenever the engine access door is closed.

HYDRAULIC SYSTEM INTERFLOW.

Flow of hydraulic fluid between systems after engine shutdown on the ground is caused by unequal pressure decay in the hydraulic reservoir air system. More rapid loss of air pressure in one reservoir air system than the other can create a pressure differential in the return systems as great as 35 psi. This will generate flow of fluid in either direction. At the time of engine shutdown if the No. 1 system reservoir has reached the point of complete collapse of the bellows as a result of in-flight interflow, the discharging of the No. 1 system accumulator can cause the No. 1 reservoir relief valve to open, resulting in loss of fluid overboard. On modified aircraft, in-flight hydraulic system interflow is accommodated by installing a balanced relief valve between the two reservoirs to return the fluid to the No. 2 reservoir during flight.

NO. 1 HYDRAULIC POWER SUPPLY SYSTEM.

The No. 1 hydraulic system (figure 1-42) supplies fluid under regulated pressure exclusively to the flight controls. Power is supplied to the stabilizer aft cylinder, the five inboard cylinders for each aileron, the APC actuator, the yaw damper (including direction trim), and on B D aircraft, the rudder bottom cylinder. The system includes a reservoir, an engine-driven pump, a cylindrical accumulator, pressure transmitter, a pressure switch, a pressure-regulating flow control valve, and a filter. Fluid is supplied to the pump by the reservoir, pressurized to prevent pump cavitation. Fluid from the pump is supplied, under 3000 psi pressure, directly to the flight control components. The pressure-regulating flow-control valve is connected to the pressure line. This valve contains a relief valve which relieves system pressure to the return line in case of a pressure surge. When the emergency pump is in use, the pressure-regulating flow control valve also regulates the pressure, maintaining near-constant flow of fluid from the emergency pump to the No. 1 system if sufficient hydraulic fluid is available in the No. 1 system.

EMERGENCY HYDRAULIC POWER SUPPLY SYSTEM.

The emergency hydraulic system (figure 1-42) consists of a pump supplied fluid by the No. 1 system reservoir. The pump delivers fluid under pressure to the No. 1 system through the pressure-regulating flow control valve. The pump is a constant-volume, piston type powered by the ram air turbine. The pressure-regulating flow control valve diverts emergency pump fluid to a return line until the ram air turbine emergency pump has reached operating speed. Thus, a hydraulic load cannot be imposed on the turbine before it has reached a speed sufficient to handle the load. With the turbine and pump operating at the proper speed, fluid is then fed upon demand to system 1.

Note

In addition to furnishing emergency hydraulic power, the ram air turbine will furnish emergency electrical power, if necessary. Once extended, the ram air turbine cannot be retracted in flight.

NO. 2 HYDRAULIC POWER SUPPLY SYSTEM.

The No. 2 hydraulic system (figure 1-42) supplies fluid under regulated pressure to the flight controls, pitch and roll damper control valves, landing gear, nosewheel steering, engine air bypass flaps, and speed brakes. The system includes a reservoir, an engine-driven pump, a cylindrical accumulator, a pressure transmitter, a pressure switch, a relief valve, a priority valve, and two filters. Fluid is supplied to the pump from the reservoir, pressurized to prevent pump cavitation. Fluid from the pump is supplied, under 3000 psi pressure, through a filter directly to the accumulator and flight control components (five outboard cylinders for each aileron, the stabilizers forward cylinder, and on B D aircraft, the rudder top cylinder). A line connected to the pressure line immediately downstream of the filter feeds through a restrictor valve to the pressure switch and pressure transmitter. Another pressure line connected to the outlet port of the filter is routed to the pressure relief valve and the priority valve. The pressure relief valve relieves system pressure to the return line if a pressure surge occurs. The priority valve is installed in order to reserve a minimum of 2000 psi for the flight controls. The pressure line from the priority valve outlet carries fluid to the utility hydraulic system (figure 1-43) which includes the engine-air bypass flaps, landing gear system, nosewheel steering system, and speed brake selector valve. The priority valve starts to close at 2350 psi. At 2000 psi the priority valve is fully closed thus retaining all system pressure below this range for the flight controls.

Hydraulic Systems Pressure Gage. A B

The hydraulic systems pressure gage (26, 22, figures 1-12, 1-13), located adjacent to the hydraulic systems pressure gage selector switch, provides a visual indication of the pressure available from the hydraulic systems. The system receives 26-volt ac power from the instrument ac bus autotransformer through fuses on the electronics compartment circuit breaker panel. The gage dial is calibrated from 0 to 4000 psi in increments of 100.

Hydraulic Systems Pressure Gage Selector Switch. 

The hydraulic systems pressure gage selector switch (28, 24, figures 1-12, 1-13) located on the lower right instrument panel is labeled HYD SYSTEM PRESS. SEL. The up position is NO. 2 and the down position is NO. 1. The switch may be used to connect the pressure gage to either the No. 1 or the No. 2 pressure transmitter. The No. 1 transmitter measures No. 1 hydraulic system pressure when the system is on normal or emergency operation. The No. 2 transmitter measures No. 2 hydraulic system pressure. A signal voltage is induced in the transmitter which varies in proportion to the amount of hydraulic pressure available in the system. This signal voltage is transmitted to the gage where it is converted to a scale reading of pressure in psi.

Hydraulic Systems Pressure Gages. 

The hydraulic systems pressure gages (32, 27, figures 1-22, 1-23), located on the lower right subpanel, provide a visual indication of the pressure available from the hydraulic systems. The system receives 26-volt ac power from the instrument ac bus autotransformer through fuses on the electronic compartment circuit breaker panel. The gage dials are calibrated in increments of 500 from 0 to 4000 psi.

Ram Air Turbine Extension Handle.

A yellow handle (43, 38, figures 1-12, 1-13 and 25, 21, figures 1-22, 1-23), located below the main instrument panel on the right side, is used to extend the ram air turbine (RAT) which powers the emergency hydraulic pump. The handle is labeled RAM AIR TURBINE and requires a firm pull of about 4 inches to the stop for extension. With the ram air turbine extended into the airstream, the emergency hydraulic pump will supply pressure through system 1 for operation at about one-sixth the normal rate of the various hydraulic units normally operated by system 1.

HYD SYSTEM OUT Warning Light.

The HYD SYSTEM OUT warning light, located on the warning light panel (figures 1-20, 1-21) illuminates when either hydraulic system 1 or 2 decreases to approximately 1250 psi. The hydraulic pressure indicating system can be used to determine which system is out. The warning light is powered from the emergency dc bus through a circuit breaker in the electronics compartment. The MASTER CAUTION light also illuminates when the HYD SYSTEM OUT warning light illuminates.

FLIGHT CONTROL SYSTEM.

The flight control system is composed of conventional cables and pushrods, mechanical and electro-hydraulic servos, electrical trim devices, electrical control circuits, and hydraulic control circuits. The primary flight control surfaces include the ailerons, a rudder, a yaw damper, and a pivoted one-piece controllable horizontal stabilizer. On A C aircraft the rudder is the only primary control surface directly controlled by pilot effort, through a cable system. Rudder travel is limited to 25 degrees on either side of neutral.

FULL POWER IRREVERSIBLE CONTROL SYSTEM.

The ailerons and horizontal stabilizer, and on B D aircraft the rudder, are dependent upon a complete hydraulic power control system for operation. Movement of the controls in any direction, even to the slightest degree, immediately affects a servomechanism. This servomechanism immediately responds and directs hydraulic pressure to the control surface cylinders which move in the required direction. As soon as the control surface begins to move a followup linkage begins to cancel the original control signal, called for by control motion, to stop the control surfaces at the required deflection. When the required deflection of the control surface is reached it stops and is hydraulically locked in position by the actuating cylinders. The surface then cannot be moved by external forces acting upon it. Built into the rudder on A C aircraft is an irreversible feature in the form of a centering spring which aids in returning the rudder to neutral and a lock that maintains the rudder in that position. The lock is provided to cancel aerodynamic forces on the rudder induced by the action of the yaw damper surface. The rudder cannot be moved by external forces acting upon it, but can be moved out of the neutral position by moving the rudder pedals.

ARTIFICIAL FEEL SYSTEM.

The use of a full-power, irreversible control system for actuating the flight controls prevents air loads and resulting feel from reaching the cockpit control. Therefore, an artificial feel system is installed to provide a sense of control feel under all flight conditions. Normal forces are simulated by a system of cams and centering springs. This system applies loads to the controls in proportion to the degree of control deflection or proportionally to the number of G's.

CONTROL STICK.

The control stick is mechanically connected (by means of control cables and pushrods) to hydraulic control valves at the aileron and horizontal stabilizer hydraulic actuators. Movement of the stick positions these control valves so that power from the flight control hydraulic systems is directed to the control surface actuators to move the control surfaces. A followup system automatically closes off the flow of hydraulic fluid to the actuators when the desired control surface deflection is obtained. The control-stick grip (figure 1-44) incorporates the primary aileron and horizontal stabilizer trim switch, nosewheel steering button, camera-armament trigger switch, external stores release button, and radar track action button.

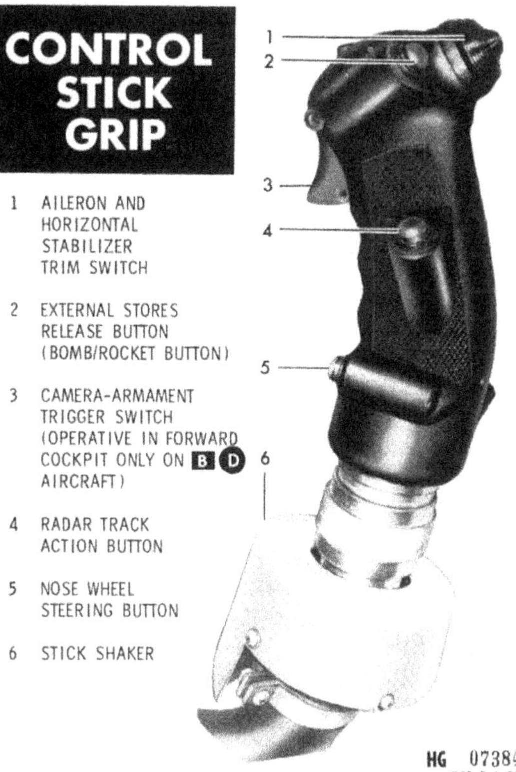

Figure 1-44

AILERON LIMITING SYSTEM.

A device is installed in the control stick mechanism that limits aileron travel when the flap handle is in the UP position. This means that the aileron travel is reduced from ±15 to ±9.75 degrees when flaps UP is selected with the flap handle. An additional 5 degrees of travel may be obtained with the limiters engaged by applying aileron trim. The limiter mechanism is actuated by an electrically energized solenoid. When the trailing edge flaps leave the UP position, the solenoid is deenergized and full aileron travel is available. The solenoid operated system receives power from the No. 1 emergency dc bus through a circuit breaker labeled AILERON LIMITER A C and RUD/AIL LIMITER B D. It is located on the left console A C and front cockpit left console B D and when pulled provides full aileron travel of ±15 degrees.

CAUTION B D

Pulling the RUD/AIL LIMITER circuit breaker also provides full rudder travel of ± 20 degrees.

If loss of electrical power occurs, aileron travel will be unlimited. Refer to Section VI for additional information. Also, operation of the trailing edge flap asymmetry detection system will automatically disengage the aileron limiters.

WARNING

The use of full unlimited aileron or rudder travel in maneuvers at speeds above 300 KIAS can result in structural damage and possible loss of the aircraft.

If full surface control has been applied with limiter engaged, it may not be possible to attain additional travel when the limiter is disengaged. This is caused by the control input interfering with the limiter stop which will hold it in the limited position. Therefore, it may be necessary to relax the control input toward neutral slightly so that the limiter will retract.

RUDDER PEDALS. A C

Primary control for the rudder consists of conventional hanging-type rudder pedals, which are connected to cables running aft through the fuselage to a rudder lock assembly. Movement of the pedals causes the cables to operate the rudder lock and rudder. The rudder lock maintains the rudder in neutral and a centering spring aids in restoring the rudder to a neutral position. The rudder pedals can be adjusted fore and aft by use of a gray handle (36, 32, figures 1-12, 1-22 labeled PEDAL ADJ. located to the left of the center control panel. The wheel brakes are applied conventionally by toe action on the rudder pedals. Rudder pedal movement also controls nosewheel steering. (Refer to Nosewheel Steering System paragraph.)

RUDDER PEDALS. B D

Primary control for the rudder consists of conventional rudder pedals, mechanically connected to a hydraulic control valve at the rudder hydraulic actuator. Movement of the rudder pedals positions the valve so that power from the flight control hydraulic systems is directed to the control surface actuators to move the rudder. A followup system automatically closes off the flow of hydraulic fluid to the actuators when the desired rudder deflection is obtained. The rudder pedals can be adjusted by use of rudder pedal adjustment handles (32, 28, figures 1-12, 1-13, and 36, 30, figures 1-22, 1-23), labeled PEDAL ADJ., located to the left of the center control panels. The wheel brakes are applied conventionally by toe action on the rudder pedals. Rudder pedal movement also controls nosewheel steering. Refer to Nosewheel Steering System paragraph.

Rudder Traveling Limiting System. B D

A device is installed on the rudder pedals in the aft cockpit that limits rudder travel when the gear is UP. This means that rudder travel is reduced from ±20 to ±6 degrees when the gear is retracted. An additional 4 degrees of rudder travel may be obtained with limiters engaged by using rudder trim. The limiter mechanism is actuated electrically by micro-switches located on the left main gear door and left forward gear door. When the gear doors are open, rudder travel is 20 degrees either side of neutral. When the landing gear is up, and the doors are closed, rudder travel is limited to 6 degrees either side of neutral. The system receives power from the No. 1 emergency dc bus through the RUD/AIL LIMITER circuit breaker located on the front cockpit left console. Pulling this circuit breaker provides full rudder travel of ±20 degrees.

CAUTION

Pulling the RUD/AIL LIMITER circuit breaker also provides full aileron travel of ±15 degrees.

If loss of electrical power occurs, rudder travel will be unlimited. Refer to Section VI for additional information. Also, operation of the trailing edge flap asymmetry detector will automatically disengage the aileron and rudder limiters.

WARNING

The use of full unlimited aileron or rudder travel in maneuvers at speeds above 300 KIAS can result in structural damage and possible loss of the aircraft.

If full surface control has been applied with limiter engaged, it may not be possible to attain additional travel when the limiter is disengaged. This is caused by the control input interfering with the limiter stop which will hold it in the limited position. Therefore, it may be necessary to relax the control input toward neutral slightly so that the limiter will retract.

STABILITY AUGMENTATION CONTROL SYSTEM. Roll, Pitch, and Yaw.

A three-axes stability augmentation control system is provided to compensate for and correct small and rapid changes of rate in fundamental airplane stability due to speed or attitude change. Normal electrical power is supplied from the dc monitored bus through the instrument inverter. Emergency electrical power is supplied from the ac emergency bus through the instrument emergency power transformer and instrument ac bus. The system measures the rate of change of airplane stability and generates an electrically amplified signal.

This signal moves a system of valves which in turn direct hydraulic flow and pressure to the actuating cylinders to move the yaw damper (or rudder B D) stabilizer, or ailerons to a position relative to the amount of correction necessary. This operation does not move the normal surface control linkage or have any effect upon the cockpit control. The ailerons move for corrections about the roll axis and the stabilizer moves for corrections about the pitch axis. Corrections about the yaw axis are made by either the yaw damper **A** **C** or the rudder **B** **D**. On **A** **C** aircraft the yaw damper surface (14, figure 1-2) is installed directly below the rudder and is powered normally by the instrument inverter.

The total area of the yaw damper is approximately one square foot and is operated through ±20 degrees by a hydraulic actuator controlled in the same manner as the actuators used in the pitch and roll system. The stability augmentation system also contains a "washout" circuit. The washout circuit is provided to allow the pilot to execute maneuvers without interference by the stability augmentation devices. The stability augmentation system causes the control surfaces to be deflected to correct for small, rapid disturbances. The washout circuit cancels these signals in favor of pilot-initiated signals. In order to decrease the possibility of excessive pitch roll changes with resultant high negative-G forces, there is no washout circuit incorporated in the pitch axis.

AUTOMATIC PITCH CONTROL (APC) SYSTEM.

An automatic pitch control actuator (kicker) is installed to provide an artificial stall warning and to prevent inadvertent stalls by moving the control stick forward to neutral when either the pitch velocity, angle of attack, or a combination of both reaches a critical value. Signals to effect stick movement come from a rate gyro and a vane-actuated, angle-of-attack detecting system. These signals are amplified and when a critical value is reached they trigger a solenoid valve and operate a small hydraulic cylinder, which in turn causes the stabilizer to assume an airplane nose-down deflection and the control stick to move forward. (This is the only control surface deflection that is ever transmitted back through the control system to the control stick.) Thus, the pilot is immediately made aware of an approaching aircraft stall attitude. A force of approximately 32 pounds applied to the stick can override the automatic pitch system. The automatic pitch control vane is located on the right side of the fuselage just forward of the canopy. Electrical power for the automatic pitch control system is supplied by the instrument inverter through the three-axis control damper. Hydraulic power is supplied from the No. 1 hydraulic system. The APC system can operate with the flaps in the TAKE OFF position when the landing gear is up and locked. This allows the use of TAKE OFF flaps for increased maneuverability while retaining the stick kicker warning feature. (Refer to Sections V and VI for additional information.) APC operation is dependent upon gear and flap configuration, as follows:

Gear	*Flaps*	*Kicker*	*Shaker*
UP	UP	Yes	Yes
DOWN	UP	Yes	Yes
*UP	TAKE OFF	Yes	Yes
DOWN	TAKE OFF	No	Yes
UP	LAND	No	Yes
DOWN	LAND	No	Yes

*When the flap lever is in the TAKE OFF position and the right forward gear door is up and locked, the uplock switch is closed, thus completing the kicker operation circuit. If the door is not up and positively locked, the kicker will be inoperative.

WARNING

With TAKE OFF flaps extended and a gear unsafe indication, the pilot must assume that the kicker is inoperative.

APC System Cutout Switch.

The OFF position of the APC cut-out switch (14, figures 1-14, 1-15 and figure 1-21) may be used to deenergize the APC system if necessary. Power for the switch is received from the instrument inverter through the three-axes control damper. When the switch is placed in the OFF position the AUTO PITCH OUT warning light and MASTER CAUTION light are energized.

Note

- The APC cutout switch is provided to deenergize the system because of malfunction or for ground maintenance.
- The APC cutout switch does not deactivate the stick shaker.
- The APC switch should be turned OFF for low level weapons delivery and low level navigation missions to prevent any inadvertent kicker operation at low altitudes.

Automatic Pitch Control Indicator.

An APC indicator (20, 18, figures 1-12, 1-13 and 23, 20, figures 1-22, 1-23), located on the right side of the glare shield and powered by the instrument inverter, will give an indication of equivalent angle of attack. The indicator, which is activated by the right vane only, may also be used throughout the flight to ascertain operation of the APC system as well as to inform the pilot of the relation of the airplane to the stall condition. The indicator dial is graduated from 0 to 5 with a red area at 5, the point at which the kicker becomes effective. Since the stick shaker (paragraph below) will be activated prior to kicker operation, experience with the indicator will aid the pilot in obtaining maximum performance from the aircraft.

AUTO PITCH OUT Warning Light.

A dc emergency bus powered, AUTO PITCH OUT warning light on the warning panel (figure 1-20, 1-21) and the MASTER CAUTION light illuminate if the APC system malfunctions, or the No. 1 hydraulic system becomes inoperative. This will warn the pilot to exercise caution to avoid pitchup during maneuvering flight or at low airspeed. If the APC cutout switch is moved to the OFF position, or the stick shaker circuit breaker is pulled out, the AUTO PITCH OUT warning light and MASTER CAUTION light will illuminate.

Note

The light may blink during normal operation when approaching the range of kicker operation.

STICK SHAKER SYSTEM.

A control stick shaker stall warning system has been incorporated into the flight control system. The system is energized when pitch velocity, angle of attack, or a combination of both reaches a value which is less than the automatic-pitch control activating system requires. When energized, electrical power from the dc emergency bus activates an eccentric motor on the control stick which agitates it in a forward and aft motion. This shaking is a pre-warning to a stall and will commence before the APC is actuated. Refer to Section VI for additional information on this system.

Note

No switch is provided to deenergize the stick shaker; however, a circuit breaker (figures 1-40, 1-41) on the left console (forward cockpit B D) can be used to deenergize the system if necessary. Pulling the circuit breaker causes the AUTO PITCH OUT light to illuminate. The APC system, however, remains operational.

TRIM CONTROL SYSTEM.

Aileron and Stabilizer.

The trim actuators are mechanically connected to the trim motors by flexible driveshafts and provide electrical trim of the control surfaces by movement of the servo valve assembly input linkage arms. This operation causes deflection of the control surfaces to a trimmed position but does not move the control stick. The trim motors are dc emergency bus powered and contain cam-actuated, up-and-down limit switches and a takeoff trim indicator light switch.

Yaw Damper. A 

The trim system for the yaw damper is provided to allow electrical directional trim control of the airplane in the yaw axis. Trim control on the yaw damper has a range of ±10 degrees. The system for trim of the yaw damper reacts in the same manner as for augmentation control except that the electrical signals originate in a trim potentiometer located on the trim and stability control panel (figure 1-45) and are controlled by the pilot instead of from the yaw damper rate gyro.

Rudder.  

An electrical trim system for the rudder provides directional trim control of the airplane. The trim system for the rudder reacts in the same manner as the stability augmentation control system except that the electrical signals originate in a trim potentiometer located on the trim and stability control panel (figure 1-45) and are controlled by the pilot instead of by the yaw damper rate gyro. There is ±2.8 degrees of rudder deflection for trim purposes.

Aileron and Horizontal Stabilizer Trim Switch.

Lateral and longitudinal trim control is provided by a four-position, spring-loaded, thumb-actuated switch with a center OFF position, located on top of the control stick grip (1, figure 1-44). The switch is used to control dc emergency bus powered trim motors. Lateral movement of the switch to the left causes a left aileron up, right aileron down operation of the trim motor and trim actuators. Lateral movement to the right causes the reverse. Forward movement of the switch causes a stabilizer leading edge up (aircraft nose down) operation of the trim motor and actuator. Aft movement causes the reverse action.

TRIM AND STABILITY CONTROL PANELS

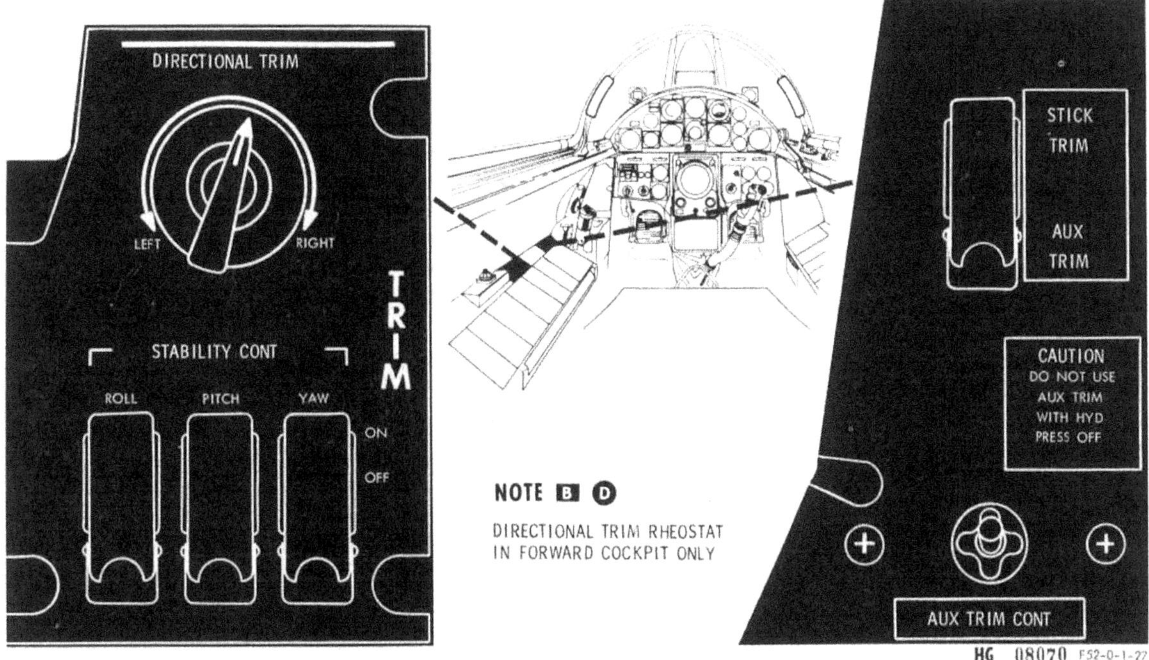

Figure 1-45

Note

A pressure switch in the No. 1 hydraulic system prevents operation of the aileron and horizontal stabilizer trim switch without hydraulic pressure. Failure of the No. 1 hydraulic system in flight will necessitate the use of the auxiliary trim system to trim ailerons and stabilizer.

Auxiliary Trim Selector Switch.

A two-positioned, guarded trim selector switch (figure 1-45) is located on the left console and labeled STICK TRIM and AUX. TRIM. The switch is powered by the dc emergency bus and may be used to override the control stick trim switch. In the event of failure of the control stick trim switch, the selector switch allows selection of the auxiliary trim switch for control of the stabilizer and aileron trim circuits.

Auxiliary Trim Control Switch.

A four-position, spring-loaded switch (figure 1-45) with a center OFF position is located aft of the auxiliary trim selector switch. This switch (dc emergency bus powered) produces the same effects as the control stick trim switch, provided the auxiliary trim selector switch is in AUX. TRIM position. The switch is labeled AUX. TRIM CONT. and is provided as an auxiliary, or standby switch, should the control stick trim switch fail.

Note

The forward and aft cockpit trim switches may be used independently; however, primary trim control is in the aft cockpit and will override any trim control operation in the forward cockpit.

CAUTION

The auxiliary trim control switch should not be operated without hydraulic pressure available as this may change the trim motor.

Directional Trim Rheostat.

A rheostat (figure 1-45) placarded DIRECTIONAL TRIM, located on the trim and stability control panel on the left console (forward cockpit B D), is provided to allow electrical directional trim control of the airplane around the yaw axis. Electrical signals from the rheostat are amplified and transmitted to the yaw damper servo valve assembly. The yaw damper (rudder B D) mechanism reacts in the same manner as it does for stability augmentation control except that the rheostat adjusts yaw signal output from the three-axes control damper amplifier. Power for the three-axes control damper amplifier originates in the ac instrument bus.

Roll, Pitch, and Yaw Damper Switches.

Three guarded switches (figure 1-45) placarded (STABILITY CONT.) ROLL, PITCH, and YAW, are located on the left console. These switches are guarded to the ON position but may be used to disconnect the stability augmentation control system in any or all three axes at any time it may be required, by placing them in OFF position. Any one or two of the systems may be disconnected without adversely affecting stability augmentation control of the remaining system. All three systems can be disconnected without seriously disturbing flight control; however, the systems are especially desirable for aircraft stability during use of the fire control system. A slight change in trim will occur when the dampers are disconnected. (Refer to Section VI for flight characteristics with and without stability augmentation control.)

Note B D

The forward and aft cockpit switches must both be ON to obtain system operation.

Stabilizer and Aileron Takeoff Trim Indicator Lights.

Two dc emergency bus powered takeoff trim indicator lights (41, 36, figures 1-12, 1-13 and 45, 35, figures 1-22, 1-23) are located on the left side of the lower instrument panel. With the airplane on the ground, the electrical system energized, and hydraulic systems under pressure, the trim indicator lights can be energized either by use of the control stick trim switch, the auxiliary trim control switch, or by the warning light system test switch. The lights are provided to indicate aileron and stabilizer takeoff trim position. When the lights are energized the words STAB. TAKEOFF TRIM are illuminated on the upper light and AIL. TAKEOFF TRIM are illuminated on the lower light. The lights illuminate whenever the trim motors are run through the takeoff trim position of the aileron or stabilizer by action of the trim switches. The light will go out when the trim switch is released.

Note

On aircraft with 1006 C/W, the stabilizer trim light circuitry has been changed so that the light will remain on when takeoff trim is set and the stabilizer trim switch is released.

The stabilizer takeoff trim light cannot operate once the airplane is airborne due to a landing gear actuated ground-air safety switch. The aileron takeoff trim indicator light may be energized in the air. This provides an additional means of checking a suspected asymmetric tip tank fuel loading.

Horizontal Stabilizer Trim Marker.

A black T painted on the right side of the vertical stabilizer is used as a takeoff trim index. When trim is set for takeoff, the leading edge of the horizontal stabilizer should be aligned with the index. This enables ground personnel to assure the pilot that the stabilizer is in the correct position for takeoff. The black circle painted on the right side of the vertical stabilizer above the black T is used by maintenance personnel for rigging purposes only.

WING FLAP SYSTEM.

The wing flap system comprises a set of trailing edge flaps and a set of leading edge flaps. The trailing edge flaps are attached to the aft beam of each wing panel, between the wing fillets and the inboard end of the ailerons and are hinged at the forward lower edge. The leading edge flaps form the leading edge of each wing, between the fuselage and the wing-tip fairings; they are hinged at the aft lower edge. Both sets of flaps are actuated when the flap lever is operated. Each set is electrically connected by a control circuit, and mechanically connected by flexible driveshafts; the trailing edge and leading edge flaps are only electrically interconnected by the control circuit. Each set of flaps is operated by two ac motor powered actuators. One motor is capable of operating a set of flaps, at a reduced rate, if the other is inoperative. However, when only one actuator is functional and the flaps are extended at high airspeeds the actuator motor will disengage from the flap gear train, the flaps will stop in an intermediate extended position, and a continuous barber pole indication will appear on the flap position indicator. The trailing edge actuator disconnect disengages only when the flaps are extended at high airspeeds; however, the leading edge flap actuator disconnect disengages on retraction or extension of flaps, depending on airspeed and load factor.

CAUTION

Because the actuator motor will continue to run under this condition, the flaps should not be left in an intermediate position for a prolonged period. Corrective action is to return the flap lever to the prior position, (thus reversing the motor), then after the aircraft is slowed, move to the desired position. If barber pole position persists, return flap selector to the original position. Do not exceed flap limit speed.

A leading edge flap lock is incorporated in the flap system to lock the flaps up. Each leading edge flap is provided with a locking assembly and lock actuator, the left flap lock and actuator being driven by a No. 2 emergency dc bus-powered motor, and the right flap lock actuator by the left lock actuator through an interconnecting flexible driveshaft. A boundary layer control system is automatically operated when the wing flaps are in the landing configuration. Whenever the ram air turbine is extended for electrical power, and the wing flap lever is moved to the TAKEOFF position, a wing flap sequencing system operates automatically to prevent electrical power from going to the leading edge flaps until the trailing edge flaps have moved to TAKEOFF position. This sequence reduces the electrical demands on the ram air turbine-driven generator under emergency conditions. The control circuit for the flaps receives power from the No. 2 emergency dc bus and the actuating power is from the emergency ac bus.

Trailing Edge Flap Asymmetry Detection System.

The trailing edge wing flap asymmetry detection system consists of a cam-actuated switch assembly mounted on a plate which is driven by the right-hand flap. The left-hand flap drives a disc cam. During symmetrical flap travel, the switch roller rides in the cam detent. In the event of asymmetrical flap travel in excess of 5 degrees, the switch roller rides out of the detent causing the switch to open the trailing edge flap control circuit stopping further flap travel. Once the detection system has been activated power is no longer available to the trailing edge flaps; consequently the landing must be accomplished in whatever flap configuration existed at the time the asymmetry occurred.

Note

The trailing edge flap asymmetry detection system will not detect asymmetry nor affect operation of the leading edge flaps.

Wing Flap Lever.

The wing flap lever (1, figure 1-9) is located immediately to the left of the throttle. The positions are UP, TAKEOFF, and LAND. The lever is powered by the dc essential bus. A spring-loaded guard prevents G loads from pulling the wing flap lever out of the UP position. Both leading and trailing edge flaps are controlled by the flap lever. Selection of the TAKEOFF position causes the leading edge flaps and trailing edge flaps to extend 15 degrees from the faired position. When in the LAND position, the leading edge flaps extend 30 degrees from the faired position and the trailing edge flaps extend 45 degrees. When the flap lever is in the UP position both sets of flaps retract to the UP (faired) position. When moving the flap lever from the LAND to the UP position, the lever will latch at the TAKEOFF position. In order to release the latch, the lever must be pulled back (toward LAND) approximately 1/4 inch after which the lever can be moved forward to the UP position. On **B** **D** aircraft the forward and aft cockpit wing flap levers are mechanically interconnected.

Note

When the wing flap lever is moved from the UP to the TAKEOFF position, the flaps are extended 15 degrees from the faired position. However, if the wing flap lever is moved from the LAND position to the TAKEOFF position, the flaps will be extended slightly more than 15 degrees from the faired position. This results from hysteresis in the electrical switching of the wing flap system.

Wing Flap Position Indicators.

Position indicators (36, 32, figures 1-12, 1-13 and 40, 33, figures 1-22, 1-23) for the trailing and leading edge flaps are located on the left side of the lower instrument panel. The left indicator is for the leading edge flaps and the right indicator is for the trailing edge flaps. Two windows are provided, labeled FLAP POSITION, LE and TE. Flap position indications for leading and trailing edge flaps are given in their respective windows. The legend, UP, T.O., or LAND rotates into view in each window to correspond with the flap deflection. A crosshatched indication is visible when the flaps are in any position other than that selected or when the electrical system is not energized. The indicators are powered by the 28-volt dc monitored bus.

Note

The LE flap position indicator will not indicate UP until the left leading edge flap is fully retracted and locked.

Emergency Wing Flap Operation.

Partial flap extension is obtainable for landing when alternating current is being furnished under emergency conditions by the ram air turbine. With the RAT extended, wing flap extension is obtained by placing the wing flap lever in the TAKEOFF position. The flaps are then extended in sequence (trailing edge first) to the takeoff position, thereby reducing the RAT momentary electrical load.

BOUNDARY LAYER CONTROL DUCT SECTION

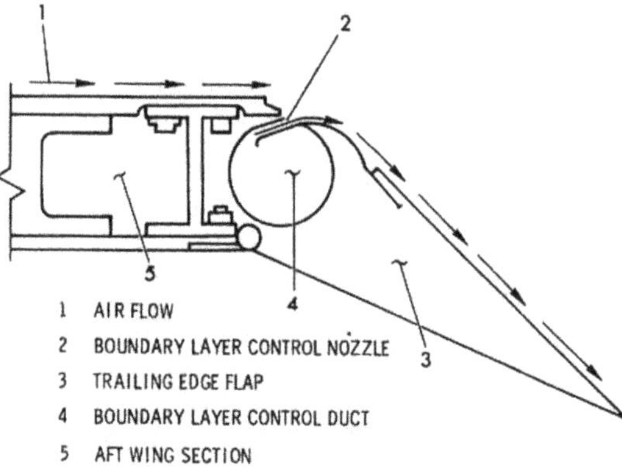

Figure 1-46

CAUTION

Power from the ram air turbine is only capable of sequencing flaps from UP to TAKEOFF. An attempt to sequence the flaps in any other direction will likely overload the ram air turbine resulting in a loss of emergency electrical and hydraulic power.

BOUNDARY LAYER CONTROL SYSTEM.

Air is bled from the last compressor stage of the engine and ducted to the boundary layer control manifold, located above the trailing edge flap hinge line. (See figure 1-46.) The boundary layer control manifold has a series of nozzles that direct this high-pressure, high temperature air over the upper surface of the flap when the LAND position is used. The high velocity created by this jet of air causes it to adhere to the curved fairing and bend around and pass over the upper surface of the flap. This curving jet attracts the adjacent layer of air and causes it to bend through the flap-deflection angle, thus preventing airflow separation and resulting in a reduced landing speed. The system operation is completely automatic.

Boundary Layer Control Valve.

Since boundary layer control is used only with a 45 degree flap setting there is no airflow for flap angles of 15 degrees or less. The airflow is controlled by a valve which is mechanically driven by the flap actuator; thus, the position of the valve depends on the flap position. The valve butterfly remains closed from 0 to 15 degrees flap angle. For flap angles greater than 15 degrees the valve moves proportionally to full open at 45 degrees.

SPEED BRAKE SYSTEM.

The speed brakes consist of two flaps, one on the left and one on the right side of the fuselage, just aft of the trailing edge of each wing. Total projected area of the speed brakes is approximately 8.25 square feet. The flaps move both outward and aft as they are extended by hydraulic cylinders. Maximum outward deflection is approximately 60 degrees from the retracted (faired) position. The speed brakes are electrically controlled from the dc emergency bus and hydraulically actuated by the No. 2 hydraulic system through the priority valve. The priority valve will close and prevent speed brake operation if the No. 2 hydraulic system pressure drops to less than 2000 psi. No position indication is provided for the speed brakes. In the event of electrical power loss, the solenoid-operated valve in the system fails to the closed position, allowing normal hydraulic pressure or windmilling engine hydraulic pressure to close the speed brakes. The No. 2 hydraulic system pressure must be above approximately 2000 psi.

Speed Brake Switch.

The speed brake switch (4, figure 1-9) is a thumb-actuated, slide type switch located in the top of the throttle lever and powered by the dc emergency bus. The three positions are IN, NEUTRAL, and OUT. Incremental positioning of the speed brakes is possible by moving the switch back to the NEUTRAL position, which hydraulically locks the speed brakes in any position between out and in. On B D aircraft the aft cockpit switch is a momentary, spring-loaded, neutral type switch and is the primary control for the speed brakes; however, the speed brakes will return to the position selected in the forward cockpit when the aft cockpit switch is released.

LANDING GEAR SYSTEM.

The aircraft is equipped with two main landing gears and a nose landing gear. Normally, the landing gear

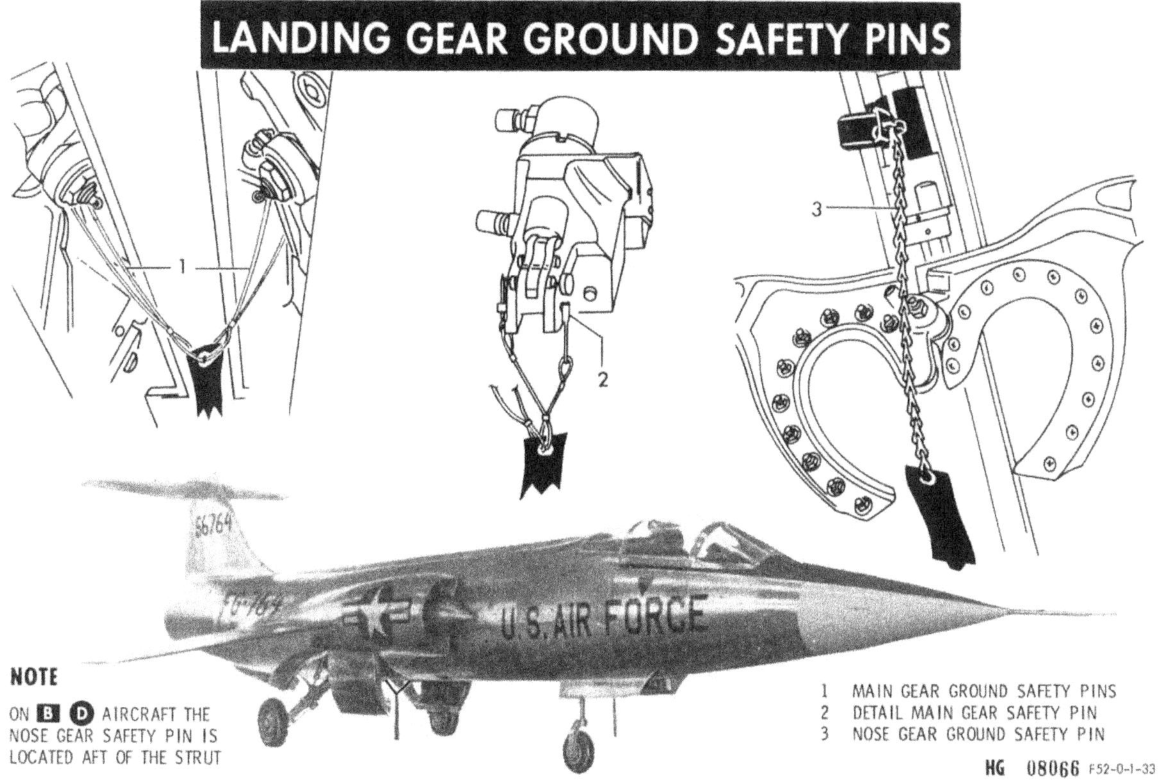

Figure 1-47

system is hydraulically operated and electrically controlled by the dc emergency bus. Normal extension or retraction time of the landing gear is 4 to 5 seconds. A manual release system is provided for emergency extension of the gear which also requires 4 to 5 seconds. There is no means of retracting the landing gear in flight after an emergency extension. The gear may be recycled, if necessary, before reaching either the full UP or full DOWN position.

MAIN LANDING GEAR.

The main landing gear retracts forward and inward into the fuselage wheel wells. A linkage causes the wheels to rotate 90 degrees during retraction so that they fit into the wheel wells. Each main gear, when retracted, is enclosed by a forward and aft door. The forward door is hydraulically operated. The aft door is mechanically linked to the gear and travels up and down with the gear. The doors are locked in the closed position by four latches on the fuselage structure. The latches also serve as main gear uplocks because, in the event of loss of hydraulic pressure, the doors support the gear in the closed position. The forward door is held open by hydraulic pressure and air loads while the gear is being extended. During normal operation, after the gear is extended, the forward door is returned to within 4 inches of the fully closed position and held there by a mechanical detent. The main gear is locked in the down position by the drag strut cylinder assembly. Barrier engagement fingers are located on the forward doors to retain the barrier cable during low-speed engagements. When the gear is extended by the manual release, the forward doors remain in the open position. Ground safety lockpins are provided for manual installation in the downlock linkage at the forward end of the drag strut cylinder (1, figure 1-47) of each gear.

NOSE LANDING GEAR.

The nose gear retracts (forward on A C aircraft and aft on B D aircraft) into a wheel well aft of the cockpit. The nose gear incorporates a conventional air–oil shock strut. When the nose gear is retracted, it is enclosed by two doors that are mechanically operated through contact with the nose gear strut. When the gear is extended, a downlock mechanism serves to lock the knee joint in the extended position. On B D aircraft, emergency extension of the nose gear is accomplished mechanically by a bungee spring. An uplock cylinder is mounted on the drag strut support beam and is linked to an uplock hook mounted on the upper drag strut pin. The uplock hook engages a lug on the nosewheel fork to lock the gear up. A ground safety pin is provided for manual installation on the downlock stop cartridge (3, figure 1-47). The nose gear is steerable through the use of the rudder pedals. Refer to Nosewheel Steering System paragraph.

Landing Gear Lever.

The landing gear lever (figures 1-20, 1-21) is located on the left forward panel. The lever has two positions, UP, and DOWN. The lever electrically controls the landing gear and landing gear door hydraulic selector valves.

When the lever is moved to the UP position, 28-volt dc emergency bus power is directed to selector valves, electrically sequenced to direct hydraulic pressure to open the main gear forward doors, retract the nose gear and main gear (and aft doors), and reclose the main gear forward doors. The nose gear doors are mechanically connected to the nose gear strut and open and close with nose gear extension and retraction. When the landing gear lever is placed in the DOWN position the selector valves direct hydraulic pressure to lower the nose gear, open the main gear forward doors, and lower the main landing gear (which opens the aft main gear doors). When the gear reaches the down-and-locked position, hydraulic pressure is automatically selected to close the main forward doors to the mechanical detent position. On B D aircraft the forward and aft cockpit landing gear levers are mechanically interconnected.

Landing Gear Lever Uplock. A landing gear lever uplock mechanism is provided. A trigger (figures 1-20, 1-21) which extends upward from the top of the lever is used to release the lever uplock mechanism. The lock is provided to prevent the gear lever from being lowered inadvertently.

Landing Gear Lever Override Button. A landing gear lever override button (figures 1-20, 1-21) is provided just above the landing gear lever. The button may be used in an emergency to override the lever downlock if it becomes necessary to raise the gear when the weight of the aircraft is on the landing gear. When the airplane is on the ground with the gear down and locked, a solenoid-operated locking mechanism locks the landing gear lever in the DOWN position. This locking mechanism is provided with a mechanical downlock bypass, operated by the button. When the weight of the aircraft is off the landing gear, 28-volt dc emergency bus power is directed to the control lock solenoid which permits the lever to be moved to the UP position.

Note

Under extreme cold weather conditions, the landing gear strut may not fully extend after takeoff. Use of the override button may be necessary in order to retract the landing gear.

Manual Landing Gear Release Handle.

A yellow manual landing gear release handle (42, 37, figures 1-12, 1-13 and 48, 37, figures 1-22, 1-23), located below the main instrument panel on the left side, is labeled MAN. LDG. GEAR. The handle is provided to release the main landing gear door uplocks and the nose gear uplocks which allows the gear to lower by gravity and air load forces. The gear is then locked down by spring-loaded downlocks. Approximately a 10-inch pull to the stop is required to release the gear. On B D aircraft the nose gear is forced down by a bungee spring. The landing gear cannot be retracted in flight after being lowered by means of the manual landing gear release handle. If the manual landing gear release handle is used, a notation must be made in Form 781 so that the system valves will be repositioned prior to the next flight.

Landing Gear Position Indicator Lights.

Three green landing gear position indicator lights (39, 33, figures 1-12, 1-13 and 42, 34, figures 1-22, 1-23) are installed on the left side of the lower instrument panel. When the lights are illuminated they indicate that the landing gear is down and locked. The lights are labeled LH GEAR DOWN, NOSE GEAR DOWN, and RH GEAR DOWN. As each gear reaches the down-and-locked position, 28-volt dc power from the emergency bus is directed through the warning light dimming circuit to illuminate the indicator lights. The lights go off any time the gear is not down and locked except when energized by the warning light test switch.

Landing Gear System Malfunction Light.

A red warning light is installed in the transparent knob on the landing gear lever (figures 1-20, 1-21). This light provides the pilot with a visual signal whenever the landing gear is not up and locked or down and locked. The light receives power from the 28-volt dc emergency bus.

On aircraft with 947 C/W, the main landing gear electrical control system has been modified so that inadvertent opening of the doors due to improper tolerances in the microswitches will be prevented. Once the landing gear is retracted and the unsafe warning light is out, the landing gear circuit becomes insensitive to sequencing switch malfunctions. The landing gear and doors will remain in the up and locked position until the landing gear handle is placed in the DOWN position.

Once the gear is up and locked a flickering gear unsafe warning light indicates improper tolerances in the door microswitches; however, the gear and doors will remain up and locked. If this happens, the mission can be continued but the incident must be noted in Form 781-1.

A steady gear unsafe warning light could mean a malfunction of the uplock relays and the sequencing switches could be controlling the gear and gear doors. High positive or negative g maneuvers should be avoided and the mission aborted.

Landing Gear Warning Signal.

An engine-speed and pitot-static-operated landing gear warning signal is produced in the pilot's earphones through the interphone system when the landing gear is not in the down-and-locked position. When the throttle is retarded below 95 to 97 percent, the altitude is below 10,000 (±1000) feet, and the airspeed is below 220 (±10) knots, the warning signal will sound. Power for the signal system is delivered from the dc emergency bus.

NOSEWHEEL STEERING SYSTEM.

The nosewheel steering system provides power steering for the nosewheel when the airplane is on the ground. The nosewheel is steerable 25 degrees either side of center. Steering is accomplished by a hydraulically powered steer–damper unit that is controlled by the rudder pedals through a cable system. No. 2 hydraulic system pressure from the landing-gear-down line is routed to the steering system through a solenoid shutoff valve and a pressure-reducing valve that reduces system pressure from 3000 psi to 2500 psi. The solenoid shutoff valve is controlled by a switch on the control-stick grip. The system is irreversible, in that forces on the nosewheel cannot be transmitted back to the rudder pedals. Upon retraction, the nosewheel automatically centers itself.

WARNING

Under no circumstances will an attempt be made to restore nosewheel steering by rotating the hydraulic dump valve to the normal position after an emergency landing gear extension since the forward landing gear doors will immediately travel to the part closed position. In addition, there exists the possibility that this action will cause the landing gear to retract.

Note

- The ground–air safety switch and relay are connected to the shutoff valve circuit in a way which ensures that the steering system is inoperative unless the weight of the aircraft is on the main landing gear.
- If the manual landing gear release handle is used to lower the gear, hydraulic pressure to the nosewheel steering system is lost and nosewheel steering is inoperative.

STEER—DAMPER UNIT.

A steer–damper unit transforms hydraulic pressure into steering force when the unit is pressurized and when nosewheel steering is engaged. When unpressurized, the unit absorbs shock loads and dampens nosewheel shimmy. The air oil separator installed in the No. 2 hydraulic system removes air from the hydraulic fluid oil which also helps prevent nosewheel shimmy. When pressure is applied an internal clutch engages the unit with the rudder cables through a control pulley.

Note

The clutch will engage only when the nosewheel and rudder pedals are aligned.

Nosewheel Steering Button.

A pushbutton (5, figure 1-44) mounted on the control stick grip, engages the nosewheel steering system. When the button is depressed and held, dc-monitored bus power is directed to a shutoff valve which directs No. 2 hydraulic system pressure to the nosewheel steering unit. A clutch is then engaged hydraulically to link the rudder cable with the steering unit when rudder pedals and nosewheel are aligned.

Note

- The nosewheel steering button is operable only if dc-monitored-bus power is available and the weight of the aircraft is on the main landing gear.
- If the manual landing gear release handle is used to lower the gear, hydraulic pressure to the steer-damper unit is lost if nose wheel steering button is depressed.

DECELERATION SYSTEMS.

WHEEL BRAKE SYSTEM.

Each main gear incorporates a hydraulic brake assembly. The brakes are the self-adjusting, segmented rotor type.

The self-contained brake hydraulic system is independent of the aircraft hydraulic system. Each brake is operated conventionally by toe action on the rudder pedals linked to master brake cylinders. Fluid reservoirs are incorporated as part of each brake valve. A fluid quantity sight gage (figure 2-8) is mounted on the front of the pressure bulkhead and is accessible by sliding the nose section forward. The gage is connected by tubing to both master brake cylinders and is used to fill the system. No parking brakes are provided. On **B** **D** aircraft a fluid sight gage is also located on the bulkhead between the cockpits.

DRAG CHUTE SYSTEM.

A drag chute is provided to reduce the landing roll. The chute, packed in a deployment bag, is stowed in a compartment located in the lower surface of the aft fuselage and is mechanically controlled from the cockpit. A shear link is provided which will shear and release the drag chute if deployed at airspeeds in excess of the aircraft structural limit.

CAUTION

Due to the location of the drag chute, it causes an aircraft nose-down pitching moment when deployed; therefore, it should not be deployed until the nosewheel is on the ground and speed is below the link shear limit.

Drag Chute Handle.

The drag chute handle (40, 35, figures 1-12, 1-13 and 44, 36, figures 1-22, 1-23) is located at the left of the lower instrument panel. When pulled straight aft (about 2 inches) to the stop (without turning the handle) the spring-loaded drag chute door opens and a pilot chute is deployed; the pilot chute in turn, depolys the drag chute. The drag chute can then be jettisoned at any time by turning the handle 90 degrees clockwise and pulling to the next stop (about 4 inches). The handle is under spring tension during the final pull. When the handle is released it will retract to the first stop.

ARRESTING HOOK SYSTEM.

WARNING

Stay clear of arresting hook when it is in stowed or intermediate position as inadvertent release could cause serious injury.

The arresting hook system is an emergency system designed to engage a barrier cable and bring the aircraft to an emergency stop. The system consists of the arresting hook assembly, piston assembly, snubber assembly, latching mechanism, and an electrically operated solenoid. Part of the arresting hook is submerged in the fuselage to reduce aerodynamic drag. In the stowed position the hook lays immediately beneath the drag chute door. This location requires the hook to drop to an intermediate position when the drag chute is deployed. The intermediate position is achieved by a cable linkage when the drag chute handle is pulled. The hook will extend to the emergency position from either the intermediate or the stowed position.

Arresting Hook Release Button.

The arresting hook is extended by use of the HOOK RELEASE button (46, 39, figures 1-12, 1-13 and 50, 39, figures 1-22, 1-23), located on the left windshield sill (**B** **D** both cockpits). To release the arresting hook, the HOOK RELEASE button must be pressed.

Tail Arrestor Hook Warning Light.

A push-to-test HOOK DOWN warning light (46, 50, figures 1-12, 1-22), located below the hook release button (**B** **D** forward cockpit only) illuminates anytime the hook extends below the drag-chute deployment (intermediate) position. The light is powered from the No. 1 battery bus.

Note

The arresting hook is not retractable from the cockpit either in flight or on the ground. The hook must be retracted and latched manually by the ground crew.

INSTRUMENTS.

Most of the instruments are electrically powered by the ac and dc electrical systems, or both. For information regarding instruments that are an integral part of a particular system, refer to applicable paragraphs in this section and Section IV.

PITOT PRESSURE AND STATIC SYSTEMS.

The pitot pressure and static systems operate the airspeed indicator, altimeter, and vertical velocity indicator. The system is also connected to the gunsight pressure transmitters. The pitot-static head is mounted on a boom extending forward from the nose radome. The head is electrically heated. The heating element in the head is controlled by a switch (figure 4-3) on the right console. Refer to Defrosting and Anti-Icing Systems paragraphs in Section IV.

AIRSPEED/MACH NUMBER INDICATORS.

The airspeed and mach indicator (figure 1-48) presents indicated mach and maximum allowable airspeed. The instrument contains a pressure diaphragm which drives the airspeed and mach pointer and two altitude aneroids. One aneroid rotates the mach scale to allow indicated airspeed and mach number to be read simultaneously. The second aneroid drives the maximum allowable airspeed pointer. This pointer is preset to the aircraft's maximum equivalent airspeed and increases with altitude. A set knob is available to set the movable airspeed marker to a desired airspeed.

ALTIMETER.

The altimeter (9, 7, figures 1-12, 1-13 and 10, 8, figures 1-22, 1-23) has three pointers. To determine your indicated altitude, read the long thin pointer first (with the inverted triangle on the end), then the small pointer and the large pointer last. The thin pointer indicates tens of thousands of feet, the small pointer thousands of feet and the large pointer hundreds of feet. The striped area, called the low altitude warning symbol, becomes visible only at altitudes below 16,000 feet.

ACCELEROMETER:

A three-pointer accelerometer (34, 30, figures 1-12, 1-13 and 39, 3, figures 1-22, 1-23) indicates positive-G and negative-G loads. In addition to the conventional indicating pointer there are two recording pointers (one for positive-G loads and one for negative-G loads) which follow the indicating pointer to its maximum attained travel. The recording pointers remain at the maximum travel positions reached by the indicating pointer, thus providing a record of maximum G-loads encountered. To return the recording pointers to the normal 1G position, press the knob on the lower left corner of the instrument.

STANDBY COMPASS.

A standby magnetic compass (4, 5, figures 1-12, 1-22) is provided for navigation if the electrical system fails, or to check the heading indicator. The compass is located on the left side above the instrument panel glare shield (forward cockpit B D), and is hinged to fold forward when not in use. The light within the compass case is controlled by a rheostat on the right console interior lights panel (figure 4-15). The standby compass is unreliable when the air refueling probe is installed.

MM-3 ATTITUDE INDICATOR. A B D

MM-3 attitude indicators (13, 11, figures 1-12, 1-13 and 11, figure 1-23) provide the pilots with a pictorial representation of aircraft attitude. The installation consists of

AIRSPEED/MACH INDICATOR

Figure 1-48

indicators mounted on the instrument panels, remotely located indicator amplifiers, an MD-1 gyro control and an MC-1 rate gyro. The indicators are operated independently by a common MC-1 gyro control and MD-1 rate gyro through individual indicator amplifiers. The MD-1 gyro control senses pitch and bank angles and incorporates a pitch-and-bank erection system. The MC-1 rate gyro senses rate of turn. Any angular motion of the aircraft with respect to the vertical reference established by the gyro is detected by the MD-1 gyro control and electrically transmitted through the indicator amplifiers to the universally mounted sphere on the indicator assembly.

The gyro is so mounted that aircraft attitude is shown accurately through 360 degrees of roll and plus or minus 82 degrees of pitch. The pitch-and-bank erection system, together with the rate gyro, reduces turning errors to a minimum. Acceleration and deceleration will cause slight errors in pitch indications which will be most noticeable on takeoff.

Indications of aircraft attitude are presented by movement of the universally mounted sphere which serves as a background for a miniature reference airplane. The horizon, represented by a white line on the sphere, separates sky and earth representations which are light grey and black, respectively. Both the sky and earth areas are marked with horizontal lines in 5-degree increments, enabling the pilot to determine accurately his pitch attitude up to 82 degrees of climb or dive. The scale is expanded to amplify pitch displacement, providing quick readability within 1 degree of pitch attitude. Bank angles are indicated by the position of the pointer at the top of the sphere in relation to the semicircular bank scale around the upper half of the instrument. An adjustment knob, located on the lower right side of the instrument, permits the horizontal lines on the sphere to be alined with the miniature reference airplane. Turning the knob causes the sphere to be electrically rotated so that a relationship between reference lines and the miniature airplane may be established to provide greater ease in maintaining a desired pitch attitude. The OFF flag at the lower left of the instrument will be visible whenever ac power to the instrument is disrupted. The system starts operating as soon as 115 volts ac from the instrument bus is available, but the OFF flag will not retract until a warm-up period of approximately 60 seconds has elapsed. The OFF flag will appear in case of a complete ac power failure. However, a slight reduction in ac power, or failure of certain electrical or mechanical components within the system, *will not* cause the OFF flag to appear, even though the system is not functioning properly.

WARNING

It is possible that a malfunction of the attitude indicator can be detected only by checking it with the heading indicator and the turn-and-slip indicator.

Gyro erection is done automatically by the pitch-and-bank erection system, thereby elminating the necessity for manual caging provisions. If the pitch limit of 82 degrees is exceeded, the sphere will roll 180 degrees, reversing the normal position of the sky and earth reference area, but still providing an accurate indication of aircraft attitude. As soon as the aircraft returns below the 82-degree limit, the sphere will roll back to its normal position without introducing any errors into the system.

MM-2 ATTITUDE INDICATOR. G

An MM-2 attitude indicator (14, figure 1-22), provides the pilot with a remote reference pictorial presentation of aircraft attitudes. The installation consists of an indicator assembly, mounted on the instrument panel, and a remotely located K-4B control assembly which incorporates a vertical gyro, rate-of-turn gyro, pitch-and-bank erection system, and associated components. Any angular motion of the aircraft with respect to the vertical reference established by the gyro is detected by the control assembly and electrically transmitted to the universally mounted attitude sphere on the indicator assembly. The gyro is mounted so that aircraft attitude is shown accurately through 360 degrees of roll and plus or minus 85 degrees of pitch. The pitch-and-bank erection system together with the rate of turn gyro reduces turning errors to a minimum. Acceleration and deceleration will cause slight errors in pitch indications which will be most noticeable on takeoff.

Indications of aircraft attitude are presented by movement of the universally mounted attitude sphere which serves as a background for a miniature aircraft. The horizon is represented by a white line on the attitude sphere and separates sky and earth presentations which are light-gray and black, respectively. Both the sky and earth areas are marked with horizontal lines in 5-degree increments, enabling the pilot to determine accurately his pitch attitude up to 85 degrees of climb or dive. The scale is expanded to amplify pitch displacement, providing quick readability within 1 degree of pitch attitude. Bank angles are indicated by the position of the bank pointer at the top of the attitude sphere in relation to the semicircular bank index scale around the upper half of the instrument. An adjustment knob, located on the lower right side of the instrument, permits alinement of the horizon on the attitude sphere with the miniature aircraft. Turning the knob causes the attitude sphere to be electrically rotated so that a relationship between the horizon and the miniature aircraft may be established to provide greater ease in maintaining a desired pitch attitude. The OFF flag in the upper left corner of the instrument will be visible whenever dc or ac power to the instrument is interrupted.

The system starts operating as soon as 28-volt dc essential bus power and 115-volt ac from the emergency bus are available, but the OFF flag will not retract until a warm-up period of approximately 2½ minutes has elapsed. The OFF flag will appear in case of a complete ac or dc power failure; however, a slight reduction in ac or dc power, or failure of certain electrical or mechanical components within the system *will not* cause the OFF flag to appear, even though the system is not functioning properly.

Gyro erection is accomplished automatically by the pitch-and-bank erection system, thereby eliminating the necessity for manual caging provisions. If the pitch limit of 85 degrees is exceeded, the sphere will roll 180 degrees, reversing the normal position of the sky and earth reference area, but still providing an accurate indication of aircraft attitude. As soon as the aircraft returns below the 85-degree limit, the sphere will roll back to its normal position without introducing any errors into the system.

WARNING

- It is possible that a malfunction of the attitude indicator can be detected only by checking it with the directional indicator and the turn-and-slip indicator.
- A slight amount of pitch error in the indication of the Type MM-2 attitude indicator will result from accelerations or decelerations. It will appear as a slight climb indication after a forward acceleration and as a slight dive indication after a deceleration when the airplane is flying straight and level. This error is most noticeable at the time the airplane breaks ground during the takeoff run. At this time, a climb indication error of about 1½ bar widths will normally be noticed; however, the exact amount of error will depend upon the acceleration and elapsed time of each individual takeoff. The erection system will automatically remove the error after the acceleration ceases.

TURN-AND-SLIP INDICATOR.

A conventional turn-and-slip indicator (5, 3, figures 1-12, 1-13 and 8, 6, figures 1-22, 1-23) is mounted on the main instrument panel. The instrument is electrically driven by 28-volt dc power from the dc emergency bus.

Note

Expect a momentary indication of a turn opposite to the direction of bank when originating a turn.

VERTICAL VELOCITY INDICATOR.

The vertical velocity indicator (14, 12, figures 1-12, 1-13 and 15, 12, figures 1-22, 1-23) is mounted on the main instrument panel. The indicator registers the rate of climb or descent in feet per minute and is operated by the static air system.

WARNING LIGHT SYSTEM.

WARNING PANEL LIGHTS SYSTEM.

The warning panel lights system functions to give the pilot visual indication of failure of certain critical power equipment and in case of failure or unsafe conditions in critical areas of the aircraft. The system consists of a warning light panel (figures 1-20, 1-21), a MASTER CAUTION light and reset bar, and the associated equipment to automatically operate amber placard-type lights on the warning panel and caution bar. The warning panel contains placard-type warning lights, each having its own operating circuit to indicate a particular condition in the aircraft. If a failure occurs in one of the systems, the warning light for that particular system remains on until the failure is corrected. The warning panel lights system is powered by the emergency dc bus. Refer to the particular system associated with each warning light in this section.

Note

With both generators off and the RAT retracted, all of the warning lights are inoperative except the tail arrestor hook, main fuel shutoff valve and fire warning lights.

MASTER CAUTION LIGHT.

The MASTER CAUTION light (22, 10, figures 1-12, 1-13 and 49, 38, figures 1-22, 1-23) illuminates when any of the warning panel lights are energized. A reset bar on which the MASTER CAUTION light is mounted, permits the pilot to push and deenergize the MASTER CAUTION light even though a malfunction continues and the individual warning panel light stays on. This permits the MASTER CAUTION light to indicate a second malfunction if one should occur while the first malfunction is still present. The MASTER CAUTION light, however, cannot be cancelled when the FUEL LOW LEVEL warning light illuminates.

Warning Panel Indicator Lights.

The following indicator lights are located on the warning panel:

FUEL LOW LEVEL

INST ON EMER POWER

FUEL BOOST PUMP FAIL A (BOOST PUMPS OFF B)

NO. 1 GENERATOR OUT

NO. 2 GENERATOR OUT

HYD SYSTEM OUT

AUTO PITCH OUT

DC MONITORED BUS OUT

CANOPY UNSAFE

ENG ANTI-ICING ON

ENG OIL LEVEL LOW

BOOST PUMPS OFF C D

WARNING LIGHTS DIMMING SYSTEM.

The warning lights dimming circuit provides a means for reducing the brilliance of all warning lights with a single rheostat. The warning light dimming relay coil is connected to the emergency dc bus through the WARN LTS. circuit breaker and the instrument lights rheostat. When the rheostat is in the OFF position, as it is for daylight flying, full bus voltage is directed to the warning lights and they burn at maximum brilliance when energized. When the switch is moved from OFF, the warning light dimming relay is energized and bus voltage is directed to the warning lights through a dimming resistor and the lights operate at reduced brilliance. Once the aircraft electrical system has been deenergized the warning light dimming relay automatically returns the warning lights to full brilliance, regardless of the position of the rheostat.

Warning Lights Dimming Rheostat (Instrument Light Dimming Rheostat).

A rheostat on the right console lighting panel (figure 4-15) labeled INSTRUMENT, OFF, and BRT, may be used to dim the warning lights. When the rheostat is in the OFF position, as it is for daylight flying, full bus voltage is applied to the warning lights and they burn at maximum brilliance when energized. When the switch is moved from OFF, the warning light dimming relay is energized and bus voltage is directed to the warning lights through a dimming resistor and the lights operate at a reduced brilliance. Once the airplane's electrical system has been deenergized the warning lights dimming relay automatically returns the warning lights to full brilliance, regardless of the position of the rheostat.

Note

To re-dim the warning lights the rheostat must be returned to the OFF position and again moved out of the OFF position.

The following lights are dimmed by use of this rheostat:

FIRE WARNING LIGHT, SLOW LIGHT, LANDING GEAR WARNING LIGHTS, LANDING GEAR INDICATOR LIGHTS, ALL WARNING PANEL LIGHTS, TRIM LIGHTS, RADAR INDICATOR LIGHTS, and MASTER CAUTION LIGHT.

CAUTION

If the instrument lights rheostat is inadvertently moved out of the OFF position the warning lights may not be visible during daylight operation.

WARNING LIGHT TEST SYSTEM.

The warning light test circuit provides a means for checking warning light filaments simultaneously by operating a single switch. The warning light test relay coils are tied to the dc emergency bus through a circuit breaker and test switch.

Warning Light Systems Test Switch.

A warning light system test switch (figures 1-20, 1-21) is located on the right forward panel. (The switch is also used to check the fuel quantity indicating system.) When the test switch is moved to WARNING LIGHTS TEST position the fire warning, engine air inlet temperature warning, landing gear warning, landing gear indicator, aileron and stabilizer takeoff trim indicator, AN/ASG-14 system target lockon, MASTER CAUTION light, and the warning panel lights are energized. The warning lights test switch is powered by the dc emergency bus. The fire warning lights are energized through the battery bus.

TACAN Emergency Power On Warning Light.

Refer to Electrical Power supply System, this Section.

ENGINE FIRE DETECTOR WARNING SYSTEM.

The aircraft is equipped with a system to give a visual warning in the cockpit of an overtemperature condition in the engine compartment or the tail section. The system consists of 11 temperature-sensing detectors in the engine compartment, 4 detectors in the tail section, and 2 fire warning lights (each cockpit B D). The system is powered by the dc battery bus through a circuit breaker in the electronics compartment.

Fire Warning Lights.

Two fire warning lights (3, 2, figures 1-12, 1-13 and 4, figures 1-22, 1-23) are located on the main instrument panel. The word FIRE will be illuminated by these lights if any of the overtemperature detectors close. The detectors in the engine compartment close at 450°F and those in the tail section at 650°F. Because of the secondary airflow used with this engine installation it is impossible to install a secondary firewall between the hot and cold ends of the engine. Due to the high compression ratio of the engine, the aft end of the compressor section is as hot as the combustion chamber on many conventional engines. A secondary firewall would not effectively separate that portion of the engine containing fuel and oil system components from a high temperature region; therefore, no overheat warning lights have been provided.

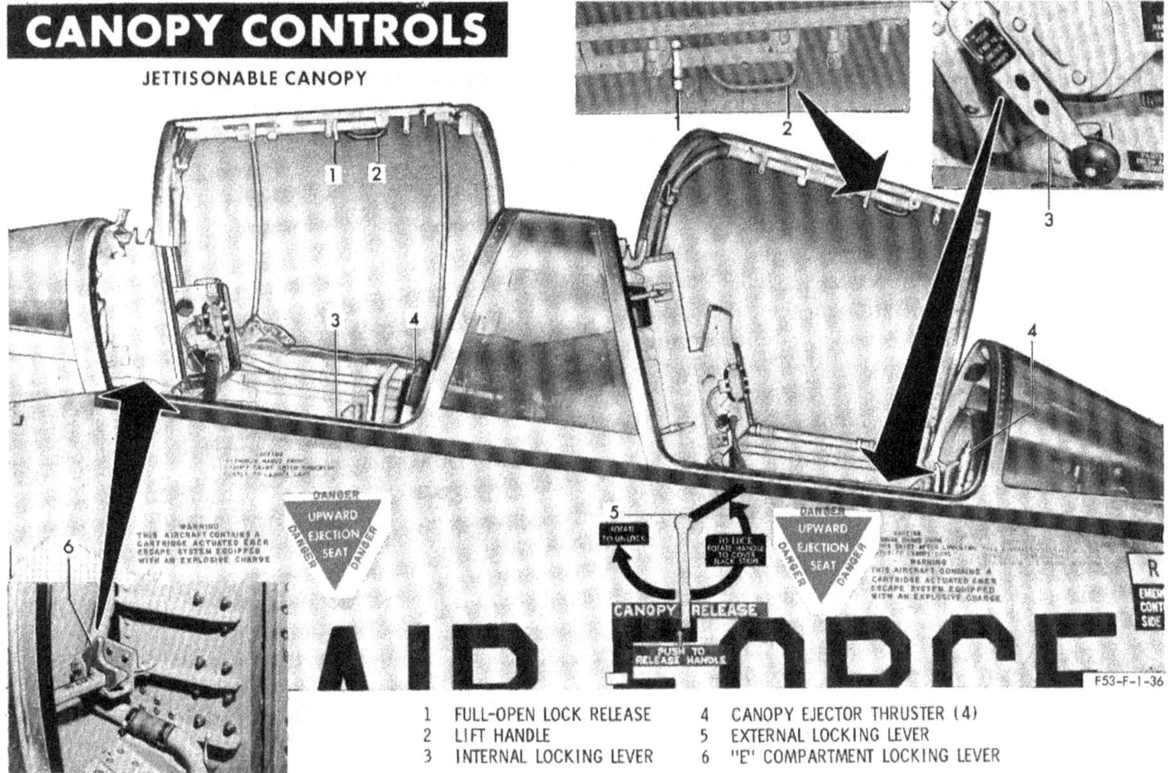

Figure 1-49

CIT WARNING SYSTEM.

The aircraft is equipped with a system to give visual warning in the cockpit when engine air inlet temperature increases to a critical value. The system consists of a temperature-sensing detector, a warning light, and a warning flasher. The detector is located in the left 20-kva ac generator blast tube which carries engine inlet air from the left duct.

CIT Warning Light.

A warning light (7, 5, figures 1-12, 1-13 and 6, 5, figures 1-22, 1-23) is located on the upper left on the main instrument panel. The light is decaled ENGINE AIR INLET TEMP WARNING. A flasher is connected in series with the detector and the warning light. The flasher alternately opens and closes to flash the light on and off whenever the detector is closed. When the light is on, the word SLOW is illuminated. The detector closes when compressor inlet temperature reaches the allowable limit which may or may not coincide with the compressor inlet temperature gage limit indication. The light is powered by the emergency bus through a circuit breaker in the electronics compartment.

CANOPY.

The canopy consists of a single piece of transparent plastic secured within a frame hinged to the left cockpit sill. Normal operation of the canopy is entirely manual. Cartridge-type charges are provided for jettisoning the canopy during an emergency. When jettisoned, the canopy is released from both sides and is raised about 2 inches above the canopy sills by the canopy unlatching thruster. The canopy unlatching thruster in turn fires the canopy ejector thrusters on the forward canopy sills to ensure upward rotation of the canopy. From this point the canopy is automatically hinged at the upper rear, allowing it to rotate upward and backward. The canopy is jettisoned automatically during the pilot escape ejection sequence by actuating the ejection ring on the seat.

WARNING

Canopy loss experience has shown that even if the canopy is in the open position and the canopy thrusters are not in a position to make the thruster pad contact, immediately jettisoning the canopy will release the canopy hinge on the left canopy rail and greatly lessen engine foreign object damage and pilot disorientation.

CANOPY SEAL.

An inflatable rubber seal is installed in the edge of the canopy frame and seats against the mating surfaces of the canopy sill and windshield to provide sealing for cockpit pressurization. The seal pressurization switch is actuated by the center canopy latch when the canopy is down and locked and by a landing gear actuated switch when the aircraft weight is off the gear. The switches operate a valve which allows engine compressor air to inflate the seal. Seal pressure will be dumped when the weight of the aircraft is on the landing gear or when the canopy is in the unlocked position or when seat ejection is initiated. Electrical power is supplied to the switches from the dc emergency bus.

CANOPY FULL OPEN LOCK RELEASE.

The canopy is released from the full OPEN position by depressing a small canopy lock release lever (1, figure 1-49) attached to a handle mounted on the right canopy frame. This allows the canopy to be lowered until it comes to rest on two lifter cams which protrude through the right canopy sill and hold the canopy approximately 2 inches from the sill. This places the canopy in position to be locked closed by use of the internal locking lever.

CANOPY INTERNAL LOCKING LEVER.

A lever (3, figure 1-49) located below the canopy sill on the right forward side of the cockpit is used to lock or unlock the canopy. After the canopy has been lowered so that it rests on the lifter cams it may be fully locked by moving the locking lever to the full-locked position. A very positive overcenter feel will be noticed as lever is moved aft, and as the lever is moved aft, the lifter cams retract and the canopy lowers by gravity to the sill where three hooks will engage three canopy brackets. The engagement of these hooks has been designed so that it can be observed by the pilot to ensure proper operation.

CAUTION

- The canopy opening and closing operation is designed to work smoothly and effortlessly. If the canopy is slammed shut or open, the system may be damaged. If any forcing is necessary to promote hook engagement, the canopy is either out of rig or improperly fitted, and corrective action must be taken before flight.
- The canopy should not be opened in flight because there is no latching mechanism allowing the canopy to be positioned in the part-open position.

CANOPY EXTERNAL LOCKING LEVER.

An external flush-mounted yellow lever (5, figure 1-49) provides external control of the canopy identical with the internal locking lever in the cockpit. The external locking lever is placarded CANOPY RELEASE and is located on the right side of the fuselage below the windshield. The handle may be extended for use by pushing on the release at the lower end of the handle.

Note  

For solo flight, make sure that the yellow canopy external locking lever is rotated counterclockwise through its full travel and latched. Visually check locking hooks and canopy locking handle postion inside rear cockpit.

CANOPY INTERNAL JETTISON HANDLE.

A yellow canopy jettison handle (30, 26, figures 1-12, 1-13 and 34, 29, figures 1-22, 1-23) located on the lower right instrument panel may be used by the pilot to jettison the canopy independently of the automatic canopy—seat ejection system. The canopy may be jettisoned with the canopy emergency jettison handle even if the ejection seat safety pin is installed.

Note  

The internal canopy jettison handle in the front cockpit, when pulled will blow instantaneously only in the front canopy. It will not blow the rear canopy. The internal canopy jettison handle in the rear cockpit, when pulled, will blow the rear canopy only, 3 seconds after actuation. It will not blow the front canopy.

CANOPY EXTERNAL JETTISON LANYARD.

The canopy external jettison lanyard (figure 3-1), located on the left side of the fuselage, permits ground rescue personnel to jettison the canopy from the airplane for emergency entrance. The handle cover is labeled EMERGENCY CANOPY JETTISON ACCESS DOOR. Actuating the T-handle jettisons the canopy, using the same linkage as used to fire the canopy by means of the canopy jettison handle.

Note 

The external canopy jettison lanyard, when pulled, will blow the front canopy instantaneously and fire another initiator that will blow the aft cockpit canopy 3 seconds later.

CANOPY UNSAFE WARNING LIGHT.

If the canopy is not properly locked, microswitches in the canopy locking mechanism and right canopy rail illuminate the CANOPY UNSAFE warning light on the warning panel (figures 1-20, 1-21) together with the MASTER CAUTION light. Power for the warning light is derived from the emergency dc bus.

Modified aircraft have an additional canopy unsafe warning light (19, 21, figures 1-12, 1-22) (push-to-test) installed on the instrument panel glare shield. A microswitch in the forward cockpit throttle quadrant completes the circuit to illuminate flashing canopy unsafe warning light. The light will flash when the throttle is advanced to approximately 95% rpm if the canopy is not properly locked. Power for the warning light is derived from the emergency dc bus through the existing warning circuit.

EJECTION SEAT.

The ejection seat system has a zero elevation escape capability in level flight provided 120 knots or more is achieved prior to ejection. (See figure 3-3) for minimum ejection altitude for various dive angles and airspeeds. The seats incorporate a pilot—seat separation device which eliminates the problem of kicking free of the seat after ejection. The seat (figure 1-50) also incorporates an ejection ring, headrest, knee guards, vertical seat adjustment, arm nets, automatic foot retractors, automatic foot retention separation, shoulder harness, inertia reel lock assembly, and an initiator-operated automatic opening lap belt. An initiator-operated thruster and an initiator-operated catapult provide initial power for ejection. The seat rails support the seat and provide tracks up which the seat slides during ejection. At a predetermined point in the upward travel of the seat, a rocket charge is ignited by the initial charge and provides additional upward thrust to the seat. Quick-disconnect fittings installed on the bottom of the survival kit permit single-point disconnection for the microphone, headset, faceplate lead, and oxygen line. Another similar fitting on the left side of the seat contains the G-suit and ventilated suit hose quick-disconnect. A secondary backup system, operated by the single pull of the ejection ring, fires a 1-second delay initiator directly into the catapult and a 2-second delay initiator into the foot cable cutters. A yellow ring, located on the right side of the headrest, provides a means for manually activating the cable cutter initiator.

Note

Use of incorrect seat cushions or kits increases the chance of back injury upon ejection or crash landing. The rigid seat-style survival and oxygen kit container is contractor furnished equipment. No parachute support block is required because the aft section of the kit has a parachute support. If aircraft are furnished without kit containers, either the MC-2 seat cushion or the MD-1 contoured seat style survival kit container should be used. When the MD-1 container is used, the parachute support block is required.

PRE-EJECTION SEQUENCE.

When the ejection ring is pulled, firing the initiators, the emitted gas pressure operates the thrusters which cause the following sequence of events: The knee guards are raised and the arm nets are deployed, the pilot's feet are pulled back into the foot rests, the inertia reel is locked, and the canopy is jettisoned. If a pressure suit is worn, the emergency oxygen supply is automatically actuated by movement of the ejection seat during the ejection sequence. The ejection ring is connected to the initiators by cables having 3 inches of slack.

Note

- The linkage slack ensures that the initiators will not fire if the ejection ring is inadvertently knocked or pulled. Also, the slack in the system places the hands and arms in the most advantageous position for a safe ejection.
- The ejection ring cables are restrained by a spring cartridge designed to absorb the sudden shock of the airloads which could cause the pilot to lose his grip on the ring.

PILOT—SEAT SEPARATION.

The ejection seat is provided with a pilot—seat separation system which operates in conjunction with the automatic seat belt release system. The system consists of a windup reel mounted aft of the headrest, a nylon webbing arrangement, and an initiator. A single nylon web (4, figure 1-50) is routed from the reel half-way down the forward face of the seat back. From this point two separate nylon straps continue down, pass under the survival kit, and then are secured to the forward seat bucket lip. After ejection, as the seat belt is released, gas pressure is supplied to the rotary actuator. A cartridge is then fired and the resulting gas pressure exerts the necessary force to cause the webbing to be wound in. As the webbing becomes taut the seat occupant is forcibly separated from the seat.

EJECTION SEAT

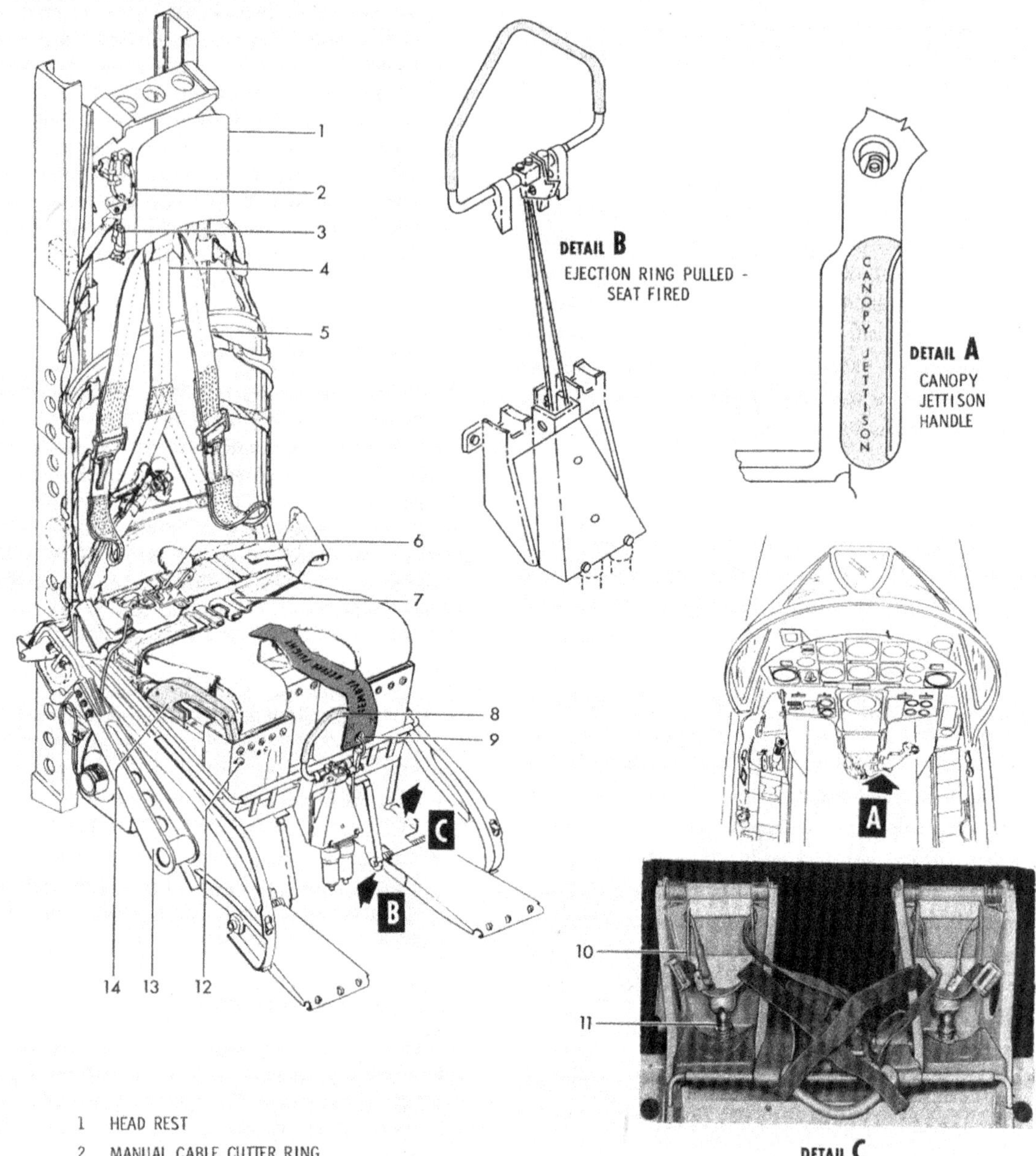

1 HEAD REST
2 MANUAL CABLE CUTTER RING
3 BALLISTIC PARACHUTE ARM/RELEASE ACTUATOR. (CONNECTION FOR DROGUE-GUN ARMING CABLE 980 C/W).
4 PILOT-SEAT SEPARATOR
5 SHOULDER HARNESS
6 AUTOMATIC LAP BELT
7 SURVIVAL KIT ATTATCHMENT STRAP
8 EJECTION RING
9 SEAT GROUND SAFETY PIN
10 FOOT SPURS
11 FOOT RETRACTOR FITTING (2)
12 OXYGEN SYSTEM PRESSURE TEST BUTTON
13 KNEE GUARD (STOWED POSITION)
14 SURVIVAL KIT RELEASE HANDLE

F52-0-1-17

Figure 1-50

AUTOMATIC SEAT BELT.

The ejection seat is equipped with a modified MA-6 automatic-opening seat belt (figure 1-51) which facilitates pilot separation from the seat following ejection. Belt opening is automatically accomplished as part of the normal ejection sequence and requires no additional effort on the part of the pilot. As the seat travels up the rails during ejection, a mechanical trip bar fires a 1-second delay initiator which actuates the foot cable cutters. This initiator fires a second initiator which passes gas pressure to the lap belt buckle and releases the lap belt and shoulder harness. The second initiator also fires a rotary actuator in the pilot–seat separation system. Refer to Pilot–Seat Separation paragraph in this section.

WARNING

If the primary 1-second delay initiator fails to fire, a secondary 2-second delay initiator fires. The secondary initiator which fires when the ejection ring is pulled will only actuate the foot cable cutters. In this case there will be no automatic lap-belt release or pilot-seat separation. The pilot will be required to release the lapbelt, push free of the seat, and deploy the parachute after ejection.

SEAT BELT, PARACHUTE ATTACHMENTS.

If the pilot is wearing an automatic-opening aneroid type parachute, the parachute lanyard anchor from the parachute-opening device must be attached to the swivel link. As the pilot separates from the seat, the lanyard which is attached to the belt, serves as a static line to arm the parachute-opening device. The parachute will then open at the preset time lapse or altitude.

SEAT VERTICAL ADJUSTMENT SWITCH.

The seat is adjusted vertically by means of an electric actuator mounted on the lower end of the catapult. The switch is located on the right side of the seat bucket. Power for seat adjustment is derived from the 28-volt dc monitored bus.

SHOULDER HARNESS INERTIA REEL LOCK LEVER.

The shoulder harness inertia reel lock lever, on the left side of the seat bucket, is a conventionally operated manual device for locking and unlocking the shoulder harness. The lever has two positions, LOCKED and UNLOCKED. Each position is spring-loaded to hold the lever in the selected position. An inertia reel, located on the back of the seat, will maintain a constant

AUTOMATIC SEAT BELT

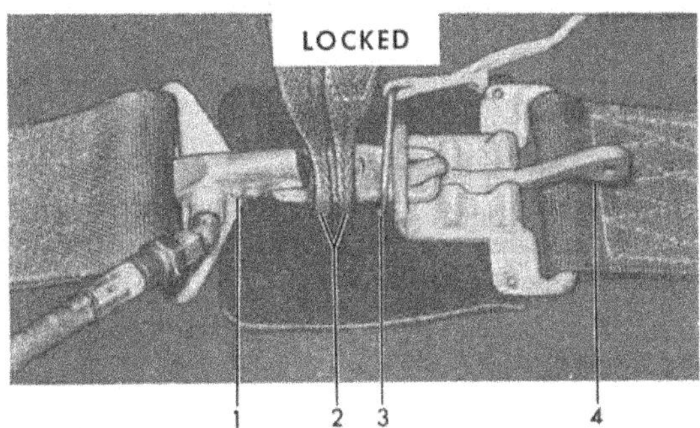

1 AUTOMATIC RELEASE
2 SHOULDER HARNESS
3 PARACHUTE LANYARD ANCHOR
4 MANUAL RELEASE

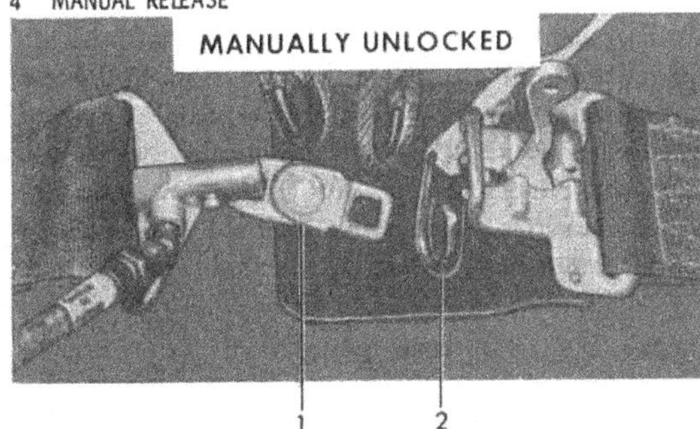

1 SWIVEL LINK
2 PARACHUTE LANYARD ANCHOR FREE

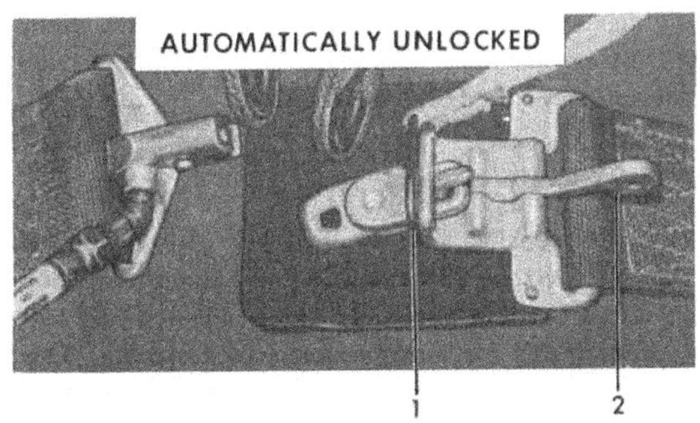

1 PARACHUTE LANYARD ANCHOR RETAINED BY SHOULDER ON SWIVEL LINK
2 MANUAL RELEASE LEVER LOCKED

HG 07380
F52-0-1-36

Figure 1-51

tension on the shoulder straps to keep them from becoming slack upon backward movement. This inertia reel also incorporates a locking mechanism which locks the shoulder harness when a 2G or 3G body force has been exerted in a forward direction. When the reel is locked in this manner, it will remain locked until the lock lever is moved to the LOCKED position and then returned to the UNLOCKED position.

EJECTION RING.

An ejection ring (8, figure 1-50) located on the front of the seat bucket is the primary ejection control. The ejection system safety pin (11, figure 1-50) is installed in the ejection ring housing bracket.

FOOT SPURS.

Foot spurs (9, figure 1-50) attached to the pilot's shoes are connected to the ejection seat by cables. Normal foot movement is in no way restricted as the cables are under a slight spring tension and reel in and out freely. When the ejection ring is pulled and the knee guards rotate out of their stowed position, the cables to the foot spurs are reeled in, pulling the feet into the foot rests. As the seat moves up the rails, a mechanical trip bar fires a 1-second delay initiator which activates the foot cable cutters and actuates the pilot—seat separation system. A secondary backup cable cutter system with a 2-second delay initiator also fires automatically when the ejection ring is pulled.

MANUAL CABLE CUTTER RING.

All ejection seats incorporate an emergency means for cutting the foot retractor cables. A yellow ring (2, figure 1-50) located to the right of the seat headrest has been connected to an initiator which operates the cable cutters. This provides a manual means for activating the cable cutters initiator should the automatic cable cutter systems fail or if a rapid abandonment from the aircraft is required on the ground.

ONE-AND-ZERO SYSTEM.

In order to provide an improved low altitude escape capability, a system incorporating a 1-second lap belt delay and a 0-second parachute delay (one-and-zero system) is provided for ejection seat escape systems. This system makes use of a detachable lanyard that connects the parachute timer knob to the parachute ripcord handle. At very low altitudes and airspeeds this zero-delay lanyard must be connected to provide parachute deployment immediately after separation of the pilot from the ejection seat. At other altitudes the lanyard MUST BE DISCONNECTED from the parachute ripcord handle to allow the parachute timer-aneroid to actuate the parachute at the altitude set into the aneroid mechanism. A ring attached to the parachute harness is provided for stowage of the lanyard hook when it is not connected to the parachute ripcord handle. THIS HOOK UP and UNHOOK OF THE LANYARD MUST BE DONE MANUALLY BY THE PILOT. The following requirements are mandatory for use with the one-and-zero escape system. Before takeoff, the lanyard must be hooked up to the parachute ripcord handle. A check should be made as part of the pilot's cockpit check sequence prior to takeoff, to ensure that the lanyard is connected. After takeoff the lanyard must be unhooked and stowed by the pilot, in accordance with zero-delay lanyard connection requirements in Section III.

WARNING

The lanyard must be disconnected whenever operating at high altitudes in order that the safety delay provided by the parachute aneroid mechanism will not be overridden.

EJECTION SYSTEM IMPROVED CAPABILITY

Aircraft with 980 C/W have improved ejection capabilities consisting of the following:

a. More powerful rocket-catapult.
b. More powerful seat-man separation actuator.
c. Automatic ballistically-deployed parachute.
d. An ejection ring cable-cutter.
e. Positive personal leads separation system.

The increase in energy derived from the new rocket-catapult amounts to approximately 60 percent.

The improved seat-man separator provides approximately 25 percent more energy resulting in more positive seat-man separation.

Automatic Ballistically-Deployed Parachute.

The improved version includes provisions for an automatic ballistically-deployed parachute. This parachute incorporates a drogue-gun device which is actuated by gas pressure from a seat-mounted initiator. The drogue-gun has an arming cable, which is also a part of the parachute-pack assembly. The drogue-gun arming cable housing must be attached to the drogue-gun arming actuator (3, figure 1-50) before takeoff. The location of this actuator is on the right side of the seat below the manual foot cable cutter D-ring. During the seat-man separation process, the initiator fires providing gas pressure to arm the drogue-gun through the drogue-gun arming cable. The cable then automatically disconnects from the seat.

When ejection altitude is less than 15,000 feet, a one-second delay cartridge in the drogue gun is energized. If the ejection altitude is above 15,000 feet an aneroid barometer within the drogue gun prevents the one-second delay cartridge from energizing until the pilot free-falls to an elevation of 15,000 feet. After the one-second delay, the cartridge propels a slug diagonally outward from the upper left side of the parachute. The slug is attached by a line to the pilot-chute which it pulls along with the main parachute allowing rapid deployment of the parachute canopy.

Ejection Ring Cable-Cutter.

The ejection ring cable-cutter unit which fires during the seat-man separation process, contains a cartridge which drives a knife against an anvil, severing the ejection ring cable. This precludes the possibility of the pilot holding onto the ring and delaying seat-man separation.

Personal Leads Separation System.

An improved personal leads separation system is included. The design uses energy from the seat catapult to pull the fittings from their detents and provides positive separation of the leads by spring impulse while the seat is still in the rails.

Escape Capabilities.

When the canopy is jettisoned as part of the ejection sequence, ground level escape capability requires a minimum speed of 60 knots. When the canopy is jettisoned manually prior to seat ejection, zero-speed, zero-altitude capability is provided.

Ground level escape capability at high speed is limited to approximately 400 KIAS. At speeds greater than 400 KIAS, an altitude of 50 feet or more must be attained to provide the necessary time/altitude required for proper parachute deployment.

SURVIVAL KIT.

A reinforced fiberglas survival kit (figure 1-52) container fits into the seat bucket. The container is divided into two main sections. The aft section contains two emergency oxygen bottles, an oxygen regulator, and associated oxygen equipment. Refer to Section IV for information on the oxygen system. A door on the top--back of this section provides access to the components within. The aft section of the survival kit container also serves as a support for the backpack-type parachute. The forward section of the container holds survival gear such as gun, food, and fishing kit, packed in a waterproof plastic bag attached to a 20 foot retention lanyard. If an over-water flight is anticipated, a life raft may be stowed on top of the plastic bag and attached to the 20 foot retention lanyard. During ejection, a ship-to-kit disconnect automatically actuates the emergency oxygen supply and arms the lift raft inflating device. Following ejection, the survival kit release handle should be pulled before reaching the ground; this action separates the survival gear from the pilot and inflates the life raft. The survival gear and life raft remain attached to the parachute harness by the retention lanyard. During a rapid abandonment of the aircraft on the ground, the survival kit release handle may be used to free the pilot of the survival kit (including the lanyard) without inflating the life raft.

A modification exists which installs a new survival kit. Operation of the kit remains the same except that during ejection, the life raft inflating device is armed by an arming foot located on the left outside center of the kit. The arming foot should be inspected to insure that the arming foot ground handling pin has been removed.

During the initial ejection sequence, quick-disconnect fittings installed on the bottom of the survival kit container permit single-point disconnection for the microphone, headset, faceplate lead (if worn), and oxygen line. If a pressure suit is worn, the oxygen unit in the kit is automatically activated, furnishing breathing oxygen and pressure.

If the pressure suit is not worn, the only source of oxygen is the manually activated bail-out bottle.

AUXILIARY EQUIPMENT.

Information concerning the following auxiliary equipment is supplied in Section IV: Air-Conditioning and Pressurization System, Defrosting and Rain Removal System, Anti-icing System, Communications and Associated Electronic Equipment, Lighting Equipment, Oxygen System, Navigation Equipment, Armament Equipment, Pressure Refueling System, and Miscellaneous Equipment.

SURVIVAL KIT

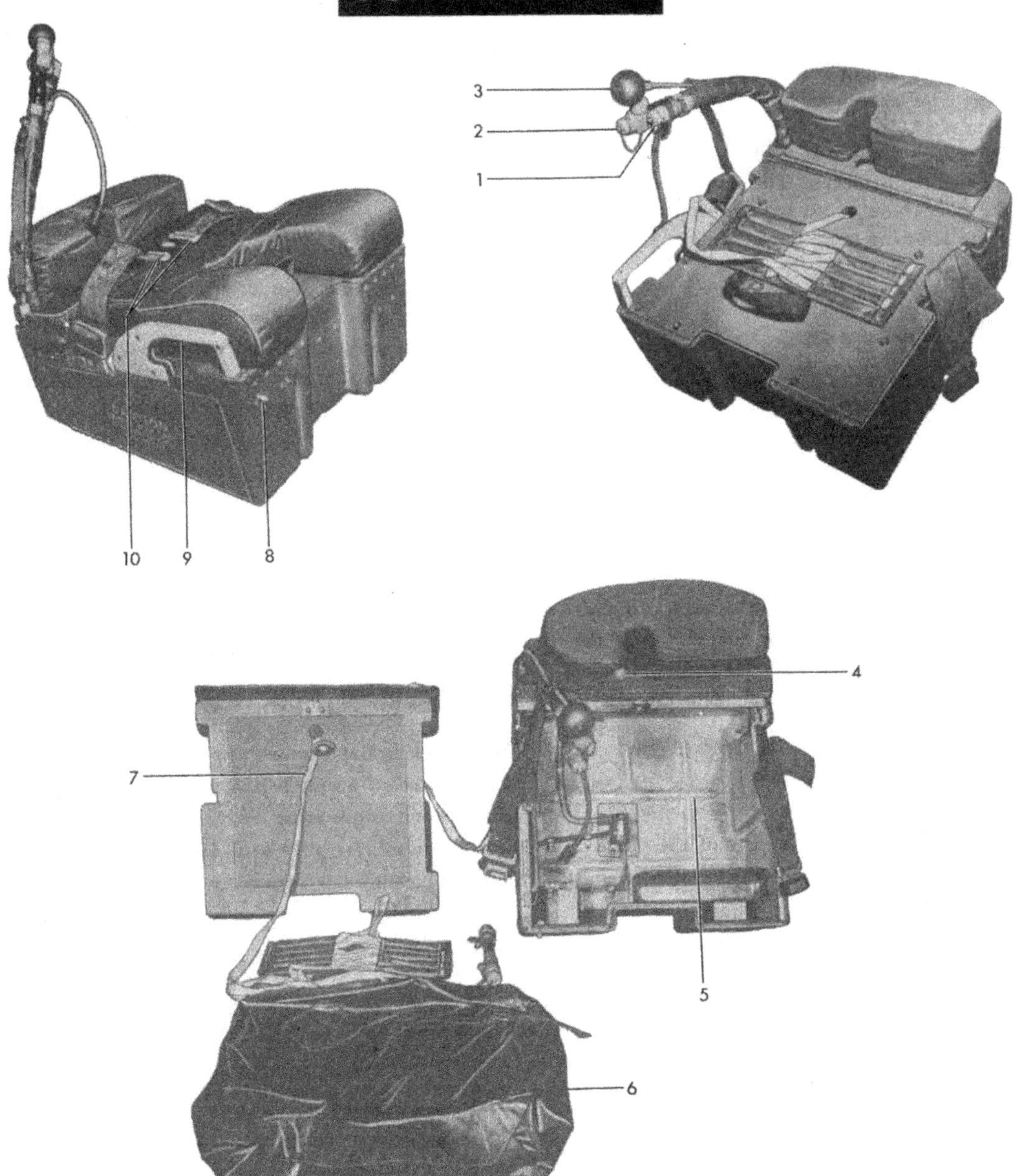

1 OXYGEN AND RADIO CONNECTIONS
2 PRESSURE SUIT CONNECTION
3 MANUAL EMERGENCY OXYGEN SUPPLY ACTUATOR
4 EMERGENCY OXYGEN PRESSURE INDICATOR
5 SURVIVAL KIT CONTAINER
6 SURVIVAL GEAR (CONTENTS TO BE DETERMINED BY MISSION OR COMMAND)
7 LANYARD TO PILOTS PERSONAL GEAR
8 OXYGEN SYSTEM PRESSURE TEST BUTTON
9 SURVIVAL KIT RELEASE AND LIFE RAFT ACTUATION HANDLE
10 PARACHUTE ATTACHMENTS

F53-8-1-35

Figure 1-52

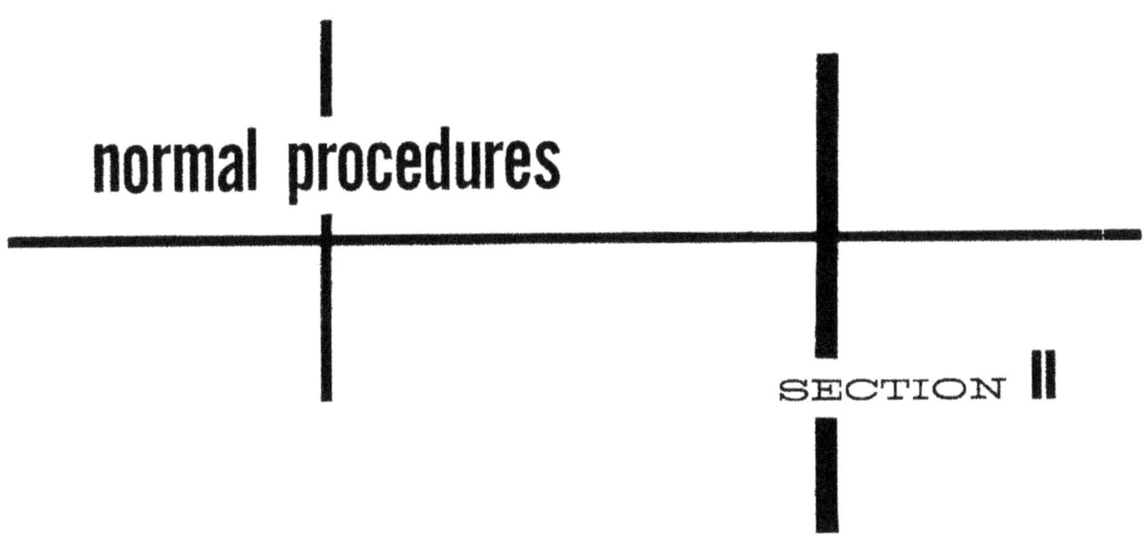

TABLE OF CONTENTS

PREPARATION FOR FLIGHT.

FLIGHT RESTRICTIONS.

Refer to Section V for detailed airplane and engine limitations.

FLIGHT PLANNING.

Refer to Appendix I, II or III as applicable to determine the fuel quantity, engine settings, and airspeeds that are required to complete the mission.

TAKEOFF AND LANDING DATA CARDS.

Refer to Appendix I, II or III as applicable for information necessary to fill out Takeoff and Landing Data Cards before each flight.

WEIGHT AND BALANCE.

Refer to Section V for weight limitations. For loading information, refer to Handbook of Weight and Balance Data, T.O. 1-1B-40.

PREFLIGHT CHECK.

BEFORE EXTERIOR INSPECTION.

The following checks apply to **A** **C** aircraft and both cockpits of **B** **D** aircraft.

1. Form 781 — Check for engineering status and servicing.

EXTERIOR INSPECTION.

Perform exterior inspection as outlined in figure 2-1. If partial filling of the tip tanks is necessary, the pilot should insure by visual inspection that the forward compartment has been serviced to full capacity prior to adding any fuel to the rear compartment.

WARNING

As little as six gallons of fuel in the rear compartment, when the forward compartment is less than one half full, will shift the center of gravity far enough aft to excite a divergent flutter of the tip tank, which could lead to wing failure. This condition becomes worse with a greater aft fuel quantity differential, and the rate of divergence increases with velocity. Flutter is considered to be impossible with empty tanks or with all fuel aboard in the forward compartment of the tip tanks.

AFT COCKPIT CHECK (SOLO FLIGHTS). B D

The following aft cockpit inspection must be made before solo flights.

1. Seat belt, tiedown strap, shoulder harness, and all personal leads—Secured.
2. Circuit breakers—In.
3. Stability control switches—ON.
4. External stores release selector switch—OFF.
5. Fuel shutoff switch—ON (Guard down, secure).
6. Auxiliary trim selector switch—STICK TRIM.
7. UHF command radio—ON and select Guard.
8. Exhaust nozzle control switch—AUTO, guard down. 3B
9. Speed brake switch—NEUTRAL.
10. IGV switch—Guard down and safetied. 3B
11. Landing and taxi lights switch—OFF.
12. Drag chute handle—Stowed.
13. Manual landing gear release handle—Stowed.
14. RAT extension handle—Stowed.
15. Canopy jettison handle—Stowed.
16. Radar master selector switch—RESET STBY.
17. Faceplate heat rheostat—OFF.
18. Generator switches—NEUTRAL (guards down).
19. Oxygen supply lever—OFF.
20. VHF navigation radio—On (set frequency and increase volume).
21. Ram air scoop lever—CLOSED.

Press the button on the lever and make sure lever is in last detent.

22. Pitch sensor and pitot heat switch—OFF.
23. Thunderstorm lights switch—OFF.
24. Circuit breakers—IN.
25. Electronics bay locking lever—LOCKED (check locking pin retracted).
26. Aft canopy—LOCKED.

Insure canopy external locking handle is rotated to locking index radius stripe and visually check locking hooks position and canopy locking handle position inside rear cockpit.

BEFORE ENTERING COCKPIT.

1. Armament switches—OFF.
2. Start switches—Check.

Check individually for audible ignition.

WARNING

If either ignition system is found to be defective, abort the flight.

3. Fire and tail arrestor hook warning lights—Check.
4. Canopy—Check.

Check for cracks, cleanliness and distortion.

5. Manual cable cutter ring—Secure.
6. Ejection ring in position and seat safety pin installed—Check.

Safety pin installed from left side.

Note

Care should be taken to insure that the ejection ring is in proper position and the pin is properly installed in the ejection ring housing bracket.

7. Ejection seat and seat belt initiator hoses—Inspect.
8. Canopy jettison initiator hose — Condition; quick disconnect properly seated and safety wired.

WARNING

If the canopy jettison initiator hose quick disconnect is not properly connected, and the pilot pulls the ejection ring without first jettisoning the canopy with the canopy jettison handle, the pilot will be ejected through the canopy.

EXTERIOR INSPECTION

NOTE

WHILE MAKING EXTERIOR INSPECTION, CHECK ALL SURFACES FOR CRACKS, DISTORTION, LOOSE FASTENERS, AND DAMAGE; CHECK FOR FUEL, OIL, AND HYDRAULIC LEAKS. REMOVE ALL GROUND SAFETY GUARDS AND COVERS

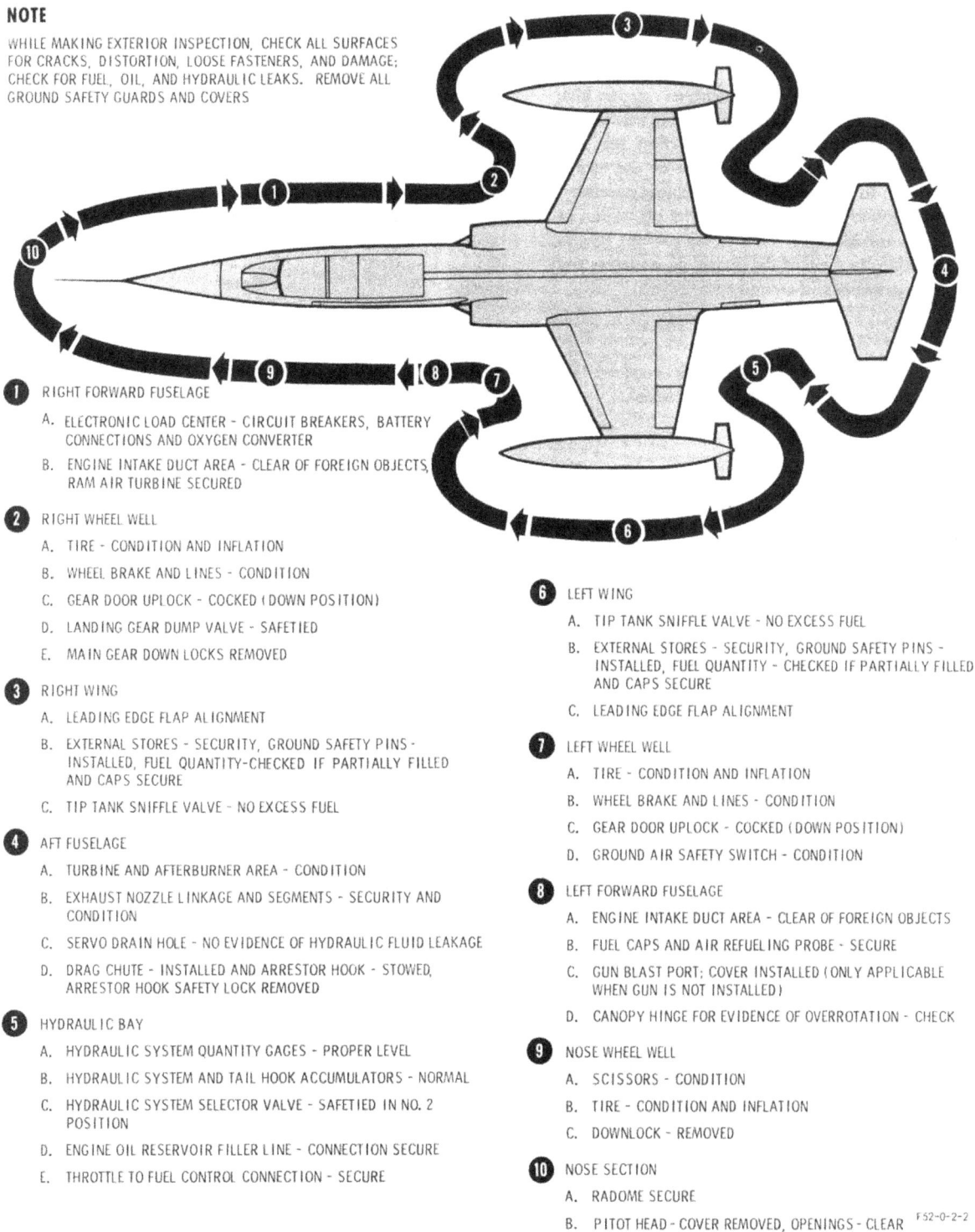

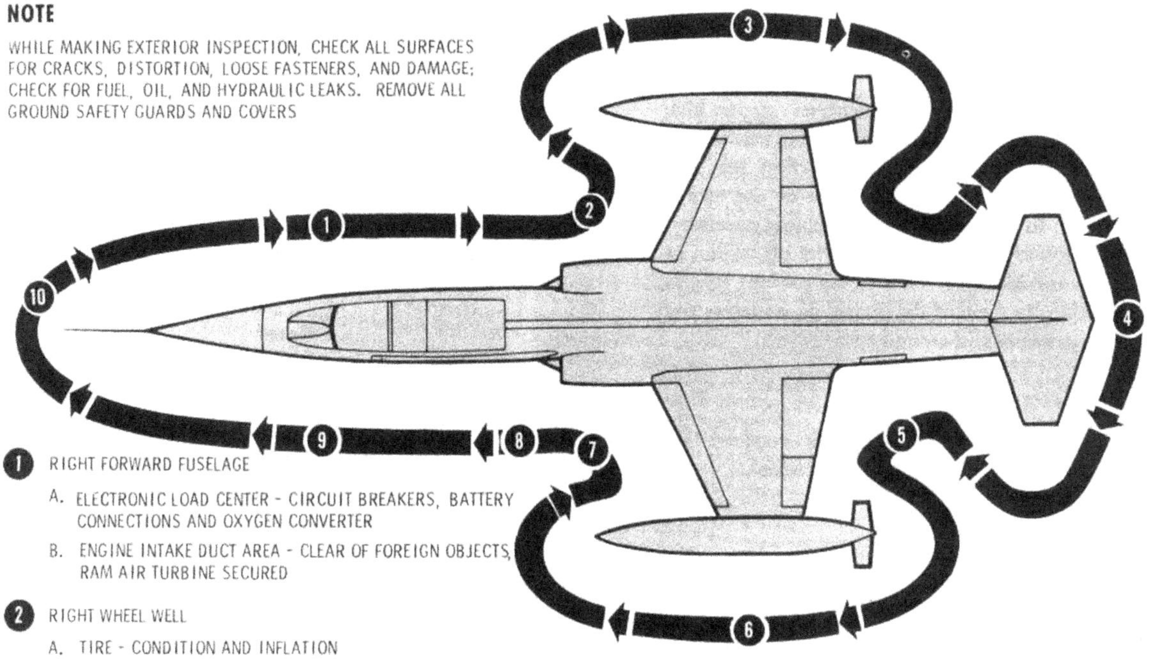

1 RIGHT FORWARD FUSELAGE

A. ELECTRONIC LOAD CENTER - CIRCUIT BREAKERS, BATTERY CONNECTIONS AND OXYGEN CONVERTER

B. ENGINE INTAKE DUCT AREA - CLEAR OF FOREIGN OBJECTS, RAM AIR TURBINE SECURED

2 RIGHT WHEEL WELL

A. TIRE - CONDITION AND INFLATION

B. WHEEL BRAKE AND LINES - CONDITION

C. GEAR DOOR UPLOCK - COCKED (DOWN POSITION)

D. LANDING GEAR DUMP VALVE - SAFETIED

E. MAIN GEAR DOWN LOCKS REMOVED

3 RIGHT WING

A. LEADING EDGE FLAP ALIGNMENT

B. EXTERNAL STORES - SECURITY, GROUND SAFETY PINS - INSTALLED, FUEL QUANTITY-CHECKED IF PARTIALLY FILLED AND CAPS SECURE

C. TIP TANK SNIFFLE VALVE - NO EXCESS FUEL

4 AFT FUSELAGE

A. TURBINE AND AFTERBURNER AREA - CONDITION

B. EXHAUST NOZZLE LINKAGE AND SEGMENTS - SECURITY AND CONDITION

C. SERVO DRAIN HOLE - NO EVIDENCE OF HYDRAULIC FLUID LEAKAGE

D. DRAG CHUTE - INSTALLED AND ARRESTOR HOOK - STOWED, ARRESTOR HOOK SAFETY LOCK REMOVED

5 HYDRAULIC BAY

A. HYDRAULIC SYSTEM QUANTITY GAGES - PROPER LEVEL

B. HYDRAULIC SYSTEM AND TAIL HOOK ACCUMULATORS - NORMAL

C. HYDRAULIC SYSTEM SELECTOR VALVE - SAFETIED IN NO. 2 POSITION

D. ENGINE OIL RESERVOIR FILLER LINE - CONNECTION SECURE

E. THROTTLE TO FUEL CONTROL CONNECTION - SECURE

6 LEFT WING

A. TIP TANK SNIFFLE VALVE - NO EXCESS FUEL

B. EXTERNAL STORES - SECURITY, GROUND SAFETY PINS - INSTALLED, FUEL QUANTITY - CHECKED IF PARTIALLY FILLED AND CAPS SECURE

C. LEADING EDGE FLAP ALIGNMENT

7 LEFT WHEEL WELL

A. TIRE - CONDITION AND INFLATION

B. WHEEL BRAKE AND LINES - CONDITION

C. GEAR DOOR UPLOCK - COCKED (DOWN POSITION)

D. GROUND AIR SAFETY SWITCH - CONDITION

8 LEFT FORWARD FUSELAGE

A. ENGINE INTAKE DUCT AREA - CLEAR OF FOREIGN OBJECTS

B. FUEL CAPS AND AIR REFUELING PROBE - SECURE

C. GUN BLAST PORT; COVER INSTALLED (ONLY APPLICABLE WHEN GUN IS NOT INSTALLED)

D. CANOPY HINGE FOR EVIDENCE OF OVERROTATION - CHECK

9 NOSE WHEEL WELL

A. SCISSORS - CONDITION

B. TIRE - CONDITION AND INFLATION

C. DOWNLOCK - REMOVED

10 NOSE SECTION

A. RADOME SECURE

B. PITOT HEAD - COVER REMOVED, OPENINGS - CLEAR

F52-0-2-2

Figure 2-1

9. Survival kit emergency oxygen – Check (if required).

WARNING

Stowage of items such as maps, navigation kits, flying clothes, etc. under the survival kit cushion and under and around the ejection seat can interfere with normal operation of the escape system. In the event ejection becomes necessary, this stowed material could restrict separation of pilot and kit from the seat, or prevent proper ejection. In view of the above, do not stow any equipment in and around ejection seat.

10. Landing gear lever–DOWN.

11. Electronics bay–Check circuit breakers, absence of fuel fumes, and hatch closed and locked.

INTERIOR CHECK.

The following checks apply to **A** **C** aircraft and the forward cockpit of **B** **D** aircraft. For dual flights in **B** **D** aircraft, all items marked with an asterisk must be checked in the aft cockpit also.

*1. Foot retractors–Attach.

*2. Strap in.

Survival kit arming foot ground handling pin–Check removed (later kits).

Attach straps as follows:

a. Route the pilot's anti-G suit hose under the lap belt.

b. Route the aircraft's anti-G suit hose over the lap belt and connect to the pilot's hose.

WARNING

If the anti-G suit hose is not routed as indicated in a. and b. above, the hose may open the manual side of the lap belt during ejection, thereby preventing automatic operation of the parachute. A satisfactory connection may not be maintained if both anti-G suit hoses are routed under the lap belt.

c. If the aircraft anti-G suit hose is not used, it must be routed to lie under the lap belt and along the pilot's thigh.

d. Other aircraft personal leads (radio, oxygen, and vent suit) must be routed under the lap belt when there is a possibility they may fall over the seat belt and to the left of the seat belt release handle. Survival kit leads when not used should be removed and stored in the kit.

WARNING

Care must be taken to ensure that flight clothing, such as sleeves, will not catch and release the seat belt during separation.

Note

- The oxygen hose from the mask to the quick disconnect should be routed under the right shoulder harness strap before connecting to the quick disconnect. This helps to prevent the shoulder harness from snagging the oxygen hose during seat separation.
- The zero-second lanyard may be of such length as to hang down and to the left of the seat belt release. Care must be taken to insure this does not happen.
- Aircraft with 980 C/W have provisions installed on the seat for connecting the drogue gun arming cable for the ballistically deployed parachute. The zero-delay lanyard is not used with this parachute.

e. Place the right and left shoulder harness loops over the manual release end of the swivel link.

f. Place the automatic parachute lanyard anchor over the manual release end of the swivel link.

g. Fasten the lap belt by locking the manual release lever.

WARNING

- Failure to attach the straps in the correct sequence may prevent separation from the ejection seat after ejection.
- After the shoulder harness is properly adjusted, assure that the loose ends are secured to the shoulder harness webbing and that all other loose strap ends are also secured in order to lessen the possibility of seat/man entanglement during ejection.

*3. Zero-delay lanyard—Connect (980 N/C/W). Drogue-gun arming cable—Connect (980 C/W, Ballistic Parachute).

*4. Interphone—Check operation on battery power. B D

Note B D

Interphone power can be transferred from the emergency dc bus to the battery bus by pulling the landing gear control circuit breaker.

5. MA-2 or MD-3 external power unit—Connected and operating, external electrical power—ON.

Note

- The following warning lights will illuminate until engine is started:

  MASTER CAUTION LIGHT
  INST ON EMERGENCY POWER
  TACAN EMERGENCY POWER ON
  HYD SYSTEM OUT
  AUTO PITCH OUT
  NO. 1 GENERATOR OUT
  NO. 2 GENERATOR OUT
  CANOPY UNSAFE
  ENGINE OIL LEVEL LOW

- Engine oil level low warning light will not be illuminated on aircraft with the nucleonic quantity indicator.

*6. Left console circuit breaker—IN.

Note

Gun firing circuit breaker may be positioned as required.

7. Pylon jettison switch—Guard down and safetied. C

*8. Radio control transfer switches—As desired. B D

*9. Stability control switches (roll, pitch, and yaw)—ON.

10. Rocket firing selector switch—SAFE. C

11. Missile station selector switch—TIP or FUS, as desired. C

12. Missile firing selector switch—SAFE. A C

13. Rocket-Bomb selector switch—As desired. D

14. Firing drop selector switch—SAFE. D

15. Dual timers—Adjust as required. C

16. Selected tanks empty indicator light—Push to test. C. If installed D.

*17. External stores release selector switch—OFF.

18. External tank fuel selector switch—As required. A B and unmodified D

19. External tank fuel and air refueling selector switch—As required C and air refuelable D.

*20. Fuel shutoff switch—Guard down and secured, warning light Off.

21. Special weapon droplock switch—SAFE. C

*22. Auxiliary trim selector switch—STICK TRIM.

CAUTION

Do not use the auxiliary trim control without hydraulic pressure because the trim motor may be damaged.

23. CDI selector switch—As required. (Verify indicator light agrees with selected switch position, 923 C/W).

Note

If the TACAN and VOR/ILS equipment are energized, the aural signal and ID-249 course deviation indications will be received by either the TACAN or VOR/ILS station as selected by the CDI selector switch. However, CDI selector switch panel lights will illuminate only when the switch is in the VOR/ILS position.

24. Radar dc power switch—OFF (if installed). A

25. Emergency cockpit light—NORMAL (if installed). A

26. TACAN—OFF.

*27. UHF command radio—OFF.

*28. Wing flap lever—UP (check indicator).

*29. Throttle—OFF.

30. Speed brake switch—IN.

*31. Exhaust nozzle control switch—AUTO, guard down. 3B

*32. Red landing gear warning light—Off.

*33. Green landing gear indicator lights—Illuminated.

*34. Landing and taxi lights switch—OFF.

35. Engine anti-ice switch—OFF.

*36. IGV switch—AUTO (safetied). 3B

37. APC cutout switch—ON.

*38. Drag chute handle—Stowed.

*39. Manual landing gear release handle—Stowed.

40. Gunsight mechanical cage switch—CAGE.

*41. Accelerometer—RESET.

*42. Clock—Check.

*43. Airspeed marker—Set as desired.

*44. Altimeter—Set.

WARNING

It is possible to rotate the barometric set knob through full travel so that the 10,000-foot pointer is 10,000 feet in error. Special attention should be given the altimeter to ensure that the 10,000 foot pointer is reading correctly.

*45. Attitude indicators—Check.

a. Warning OFF flag for MM-2 retracted within 2½ minutes. For MM-3 retracted within 1½ minutes.

b. Attitude sphere for proper attitude and freedom from oscillation (energized).

c. Attitude sphere for proper response to trim knob.

WARNING

If the warning OFF flag for MM-2 requires longer than 2½ minutes to retract or longer than 1½ minutes for the MM-3, or if any oscillations are noted on the indicator after the OFF flag has retracted, a possible malfunction exists. Either of the above is cause to not use the indicator and notice should be entered in Form 781.

*46. Radar—STANDBY.

*47. Canopy unsafe warning light—Check (push-to-test, 974 C/W).

*48. Armament panel security—Check.

49. Arming switch—OFF.

50. Weapon selector switch—As required.

51. IR sight switch—OFF.

52. Camera shutter selector switch—As desired.

*53. Canopy jettison handle—Stowed.

*54. Faceplate heat rheostat—As required.

*55. Hydraulic systems pressure gage selector switch—No. 1 A B

*56. RAT extension handle—Stowed.

*57. Emergency nozzle closure handle—Stowed. 19

*58. Generator switches—ON.

59. Canopy defroster lever—As required.

*60. Oil, fuel quantity and fuel indicating and warning light system—Check.

61. External fuel quantity selector switch—As desired. C D

Note

All C D (953 N/C/W) require special external fuel transfer management to prevent the internal aft fuel cell from being subjected to excessive pressure. The external tank fuel and air refueling selector switch must be OFF prior to engine start and remain OFF until approximately 200 pounds of internal fuel has been used. The external tank fuel and air refueling selector switch must then be turned to the desired external tanks. After verifying that external fuel is transferring normally, return selector switch to OFF. Leave the selector switch in OFF until 3500 pounds internal fuel C and 2500 pounds internal fuel D has been used.

*62. Oxygen pressure gage—Approximately 70 psi A C, and 295-315 psi B D.

*63. Liquid oxygen quantity gage—2 liters minimum A C, 4 liters minimum B D.

*64. Oxygen System—Normal oxygen.

WARNING

If the airplane is to be operated on the ground under possible conditions of carbon monoxide contamination, use 100% oxygen.

Refer to Oxygen System Preflight Check in Section IV.

Note

If the diluter demand oxygen system is not to be used, the supply lever on the oxygen regulator panel must be placed in the OFF position. If left in the ON position, the regulator will automatically allow positive pressure oxygen flow above 25,000 feet cockpit altitude, which will rapidly deplete the oxygen supply.

*65. VOR/ILS equipment—OFF.

66. SIF panel—As required.

67. IFF master switch—OFF.

*68. Interphone control panel—As desired B D.

*69. Ram air scoop lever—CLOSED (lever in last aft detent).

CAUTION

It is recommended that the ram air scoop lever be in the CLOSED position during the preflight check and during all ground operation. This will provide sufficient cooling air for the electronic equipment. If the ram air scoop is opened on the ground, the supply of cooling air to the electronics compartment is shut off and the electronics equipment may reach overtemperature limits.

70. External tanks refuel selector switch—BOTH. C and air refuelable D

71. Air refueling probe light switch—OFF. C and air refuelable D

*72. Thunderstorm light switch—OFF.

73. Ventilated suit blower switch—As desired.

*74. Interior lights rheostats—As desired.

75. Exterior lights switches—As desired.

76. Cockpit heat rheostat — AUTO (position as desired.)

*77. Pitch sensor and pitot heat switch—OFF.

78. Rain removal switch—OFF.

79. Heading indicator function selector switch—MAG.

*80. Right console circuit breakers—IN.

BEFORE STARTING ENGINE.

Before starting engine, make sure danger areas (figure 2-2) fore and aft of aircraft are clear of personnel, aircraft, and vehicles. The boundary layer control outlet for the intake ducts on each side of the lower fuselage will have a strong suction when the engine is started, strong enough to draw articles of clothing or loose equipment into the engine. Start engine with airplane heading into the wind when practicable. An external electric power source should be used when starting the engine under all normal circumstances.

CAUTION

The automatic start control cable, between the aircraft and the automatic start control valve, should be connected so that the start switches control starting air. If the automatic start control cable is not connected, the pilot has no cockpit control over starting air with which to prevent starter overspeed. Repeated exposure to overspeed conditions (above 40 percent rpm) will cause starter fatigue and subsequent disintegration of the starter. This can result in serious damage to the airplane.

STARTING ENGINE.

Occasionally it may be necessary to start the engine without the recommended ground starting equipment. Basically there are three types of starts that may be made, automatic, manual, and battery. The following chart shows the difference between the automatic, manual, and battery starts, and how existing equipment may be utilized to effect a start.

Type of Start	*Automatic Start Control Cable Connected*	*Air Compressor Connected*	*External Electrical Power Connected*
Automatic	Yes	Yes	Yes
Manual	No	Yes	Yes
Battery	Yes or No	Yes	No

CAUTION

During any start it is imperative that pilot and ground crewman coordinate their actions to prevent starter overspeed. The pilot must signal the ground crewman at 40 percent engine rpm to disconnect external air immediately.

AUTOMATIC OR MANUAL START.

Note

- The automatic starting feature shall be used whenever possible. If the automatic start system malfunctions, the mission need not be aborted. However, the malfunction must be corrected prior to the next flight.
- Without the automatic start control cable connected, no automatic cockpit control is available to control starting air. The procedures for a manual start are the same as an automatic start except that starting air should be supplied prior to actuating the start switch.

DANGER AREAS

WARNING

- THE AREA NEAR THE INTAKE DUCTS AND THE EXHAUST IS VERY DANGEROUS - KEEP CLEAR.
- DURING START AND RUNUP AVOID PLANE OF STARTER TURBINE AND ENGINE TURBINE WHEELS.
- DURING RUNUP, ENGINE NOISE CAN CAUSE PERMANENT DAMAGE TO EARS. WITHIN 100 FEET USE EAR PLUGS. WITHIN 50 FEET USE EAR PLUGS AND PROTECTIVE COVERS.
- IF BLAST DEFLECTOR IS NOT AVAILABLE, CLEAR AREA FOR 250 FEET.

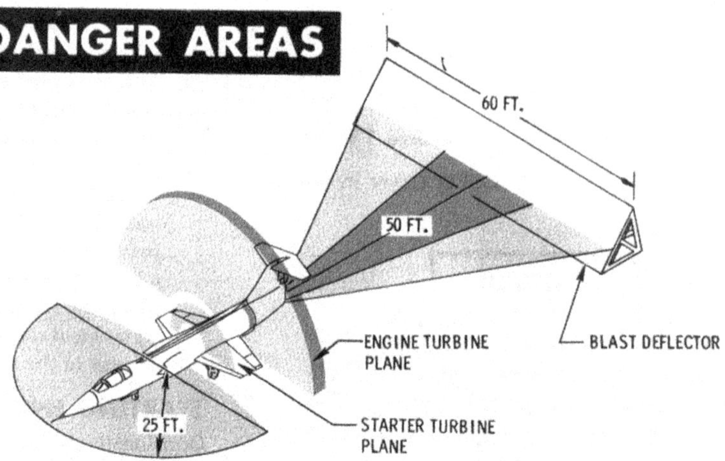

IDLE THRUST

TEMPERATURE DISTRIBUTION - °F

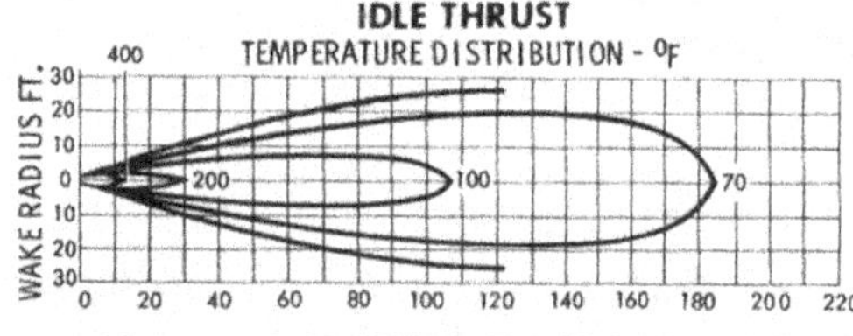

VELOCITY DISTRIBUTION - FT/SEC

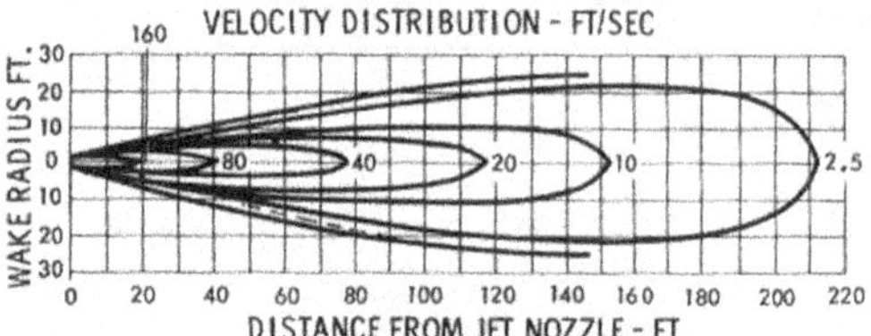

TAXI THRUST

TEMPERATURE DISTRIBUTION - °F

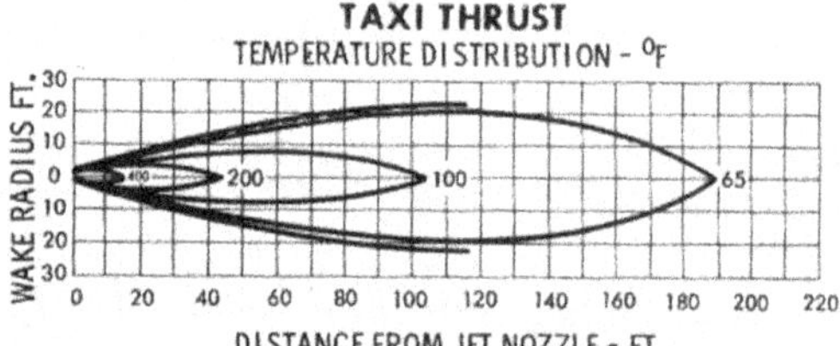

VELOCITY DISTRIBUTION - FT/SEC

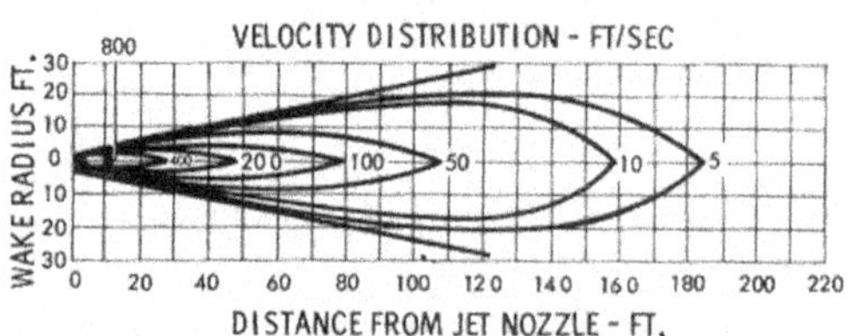

MILITARY THRUST

TEMPERATURE DISTRIBUTION - °F

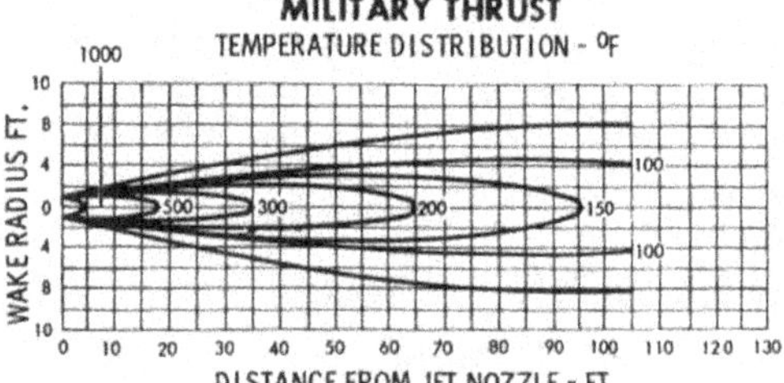

VELOCITY DISTRIBUTION - FT/SEC

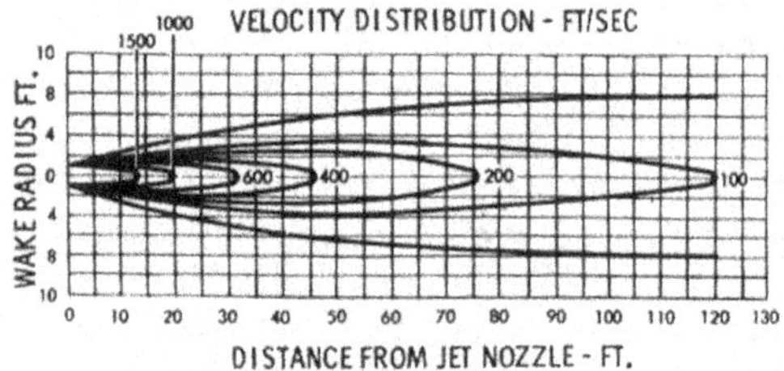

MAXIMUM THRUST

TEMPERATURE DISTRIBUTION - °F

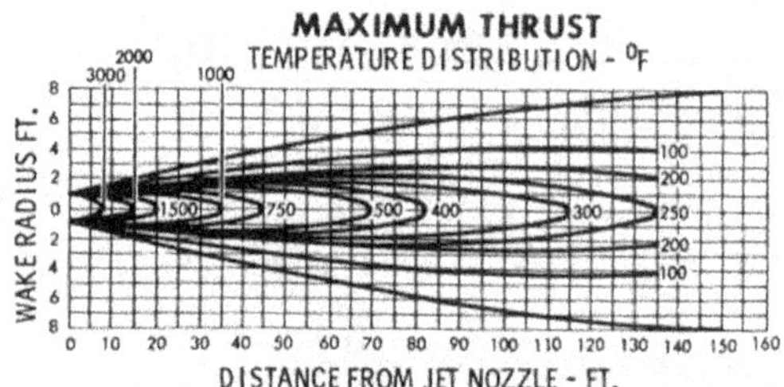

VELOCITY DISTRIBUTION - FT/SEC

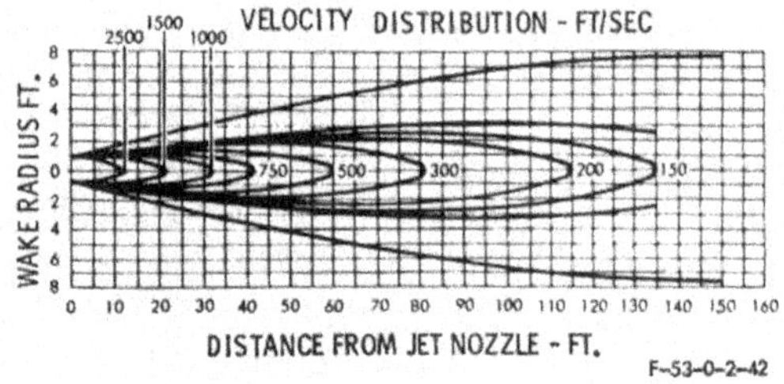

Figure 2-2

Start engine as follows:

1. Ground turbine compressor—ON (auto-start cable—Connected as necessary).

2. Start switch—START and release.

Note

- Alternate engine starts between ignition systems. This procedure will serve as a check on system operation.
- The maximum starting time should not exceed 60 seconds from the time the start switch is actuated until reaching idle rpm.

3. Throttle—IDLE.

At first indication of engine rotation 3B 7A and at 10 percent rpm 19 , advance throttle beyond IDLE detent and then retard to IDLE detent.

4. Fuel flow—400-800 pounds per hour 3B 7A and 250-800 pounds per hour 19 .

CAUTION

- If fuel flow exceeds 800 pounds per hour, a hot start may result. If fuel flow is less than 400 pounds per hour 3B 7A and 250 pounds per hour 19 for ground starts, a hung start may result. If these conditions occur, the aircraft should be cleared by maintenance personnel before flight.
- Combustion normally occurs at about 12 percent rpm, 3B 7A and between 16 and 18% rpm 19 , but may occur anywhere between 10 and 16 percent rpm. If combustion does not occur by 20 percent rpm or 20 seconds after fuel flow indication, or the engine fails to accelerate to normal idle rpm, or exhaust gas temperature exceeds starting limits, proceed as indicated in False, Hanging Or Hot Start Procedures in this section.

5. Start switches—STOP-START at 40 percent rpm. At 40 percent rpm, simultaneously move both start switches to the STOP-START position and signal ground crew to stop air flow.

CAUTION

- The only positive indication of air flow shutoff is to visually observe starting air hose deflation.
- If the throttle is unintentionally retarded to OFF, a flameout will occur immediately. Do not reopen throttle, as relight is impossible and the resultant flow of unburned fuel into the engine creates a fire hazard.

6. External electrical power and ground turbine compressor—Disconnect at idle rpm.

Note

If the INST ON EMER POWER, TACAN EMERGENCY POWER ON, NO. 1 GENERATOR OUT, and NO. 2 GENERATOR OUT warning lights remain on, ground power unit is still connected.

7. Engine instruments for proper indications—Check.

   a. Nozzle position—Approximately 8.5.

   b. Tachometer—67 ± 1.0 percent rpm.

   c. Exhaust gas temperature—320°-420°C.

Note

In extremely hot weather with ramp temperatures in excess of 38°C, EGT may increase as high as 500°C. In extremely cold weather with ramp temperatures as low as minus 40°C, EGT may be as low as 120°C.

   d. Oil pressure—12 psi minimum.

   e. Fuel flow—1000-1300 lb/hr.

   f. Oil quantity indicator—28 pints (7/8).

BATTERY START.

A battery start is accomplished with only the air compressor unit connected and with or without the automatic start control cable connected. With the automatic start control cable connected, the starting procedure is the same as during an automatic start. Without the automatic start control cable connected, the starting procedure is the same as during a manual start.

CAUTION

During a battery start, the only instruments available will be the exhaust gas temperature gage and the tachometer until the generators reach operating speed. Therefore, exhaust gas temperature must be monitored closely to prevent engine overtemperature.

FALSE, HANGING OR HOT START PROCEDURES.

1. Throttle—OFF.

2. Both start switches—STOP-START.

Simultaneously move both start switches to the STOP-START position and signal ground crew to stop air flow.

3. Check for absence of fuel in tailpipe.

CAUTION

- Wait until the engine stops rotating before checking for fuel in the tailpipe. If fuel is present, motor engine.
- The starter is limited to 1 minute of continuous operation after which 2 minutes must be allowed for cooling before using the starter again.

4. Attempt restart.

GROUND OPERATION.

With the assistance of ground personnel, proceed as follows:

1. Generators—Check to ensure operation of the generator bus transfer circuits. Check as follows:

a. No. 1 generator—OFF; check warning light and reset.

b. No. 2 generator—OFF; check warning light.

c. Fuel quantity—Test. If fuel quantity indicator does not test properly, automatic bus transfer relay may be inoperative.

d. No. 2 generator—Reset.

2. UHF, VOR, TACAN, and IFF/SIF—As required.

3. Hydraulic system—Check.

To ensure that the hydraulic systems are operating properly, perform the following checks:

a. At IDLE rpm, move stabilizer only through a complete cycle. Pressure indications should drop to approximately 2700 psi, then rise to 3300 psi maximum and return to normal.

Note

If there are no hydraulic pressure fluctuations during fore and aft movement of the control stick, shut down the engine and investigate.

b. Move ailerons only through complete cycle. Pressure indications should drop to approximately 2600 psi, then rise to 3300 psi maximum and return to normal. Also note that aileron limiters are engaged.

c. Move rudder through maximum travel and check that hydraulic pressure drops, rises, and returns to normal. B D

d. Hydraulic systems pressure gage selector switch —No. 2 and repeat steps a, b and c. A B .

e. Speed brakes — At 75 percent rpm, operate through one complete cycle. Pressure indication on No. 2 system should drop quickly to approxixmately 2150 psi, then rise momentarily to approximately 3300 psi and return to normal.

4. Minimum fuel flow—Check.

(On B D accomplish from aft cockpit if occupied by qualified person.) Rapidly retard throttle to IDLE while checking fuel flow. Fuel flow should drop momentarily to 400-800 lb/hr. 3B 7A and 250-800 lb/hr. 19 . If fuel flow is not within these limits abort the flight.

5. APC—Check.

a. Rotate right vane clockwise until the stick shaker operates at 4¼ to 4¾.

b. Continue rotation until the kicker operates at 5.

c. Overpower APC with a strong steady force — Stick will move to full aft position.

d. Set right vane 1 degree below position where the kicker operates and sharply lift nose of aircraft until kicker operates.

e. Check left vane for shaker only.

6. Wing flap lever—LAND. Have ground crew check BLC airflow (check that flap extension time does not exceed 20 seconds maximum).

7. Wing flap lever—TAKEOFF. Have ground crew verify flap position, check absence of BLC airflow and rotate right vane to assure that kicker is inoperative with gear and flaps down. Note aileron limiters are disengaged.

8. Trim—Check operation and set for takeoff.

Note

- The pilot and ground crew should visually check that all surfaces move in the proper direction during the trim system check.
- To assure full stabilizer travel for nosewheel liftoff, takeoff trim is required.

CAUTION

It is possible to damage the trim mechanism by operating the trim controls with the control stick in the full-throw position. To preclude this possibility, make all trim system checks with control stick neutral.

Note

- Takeoff trim indicator lights should illuminate momentarily as trim motors pass through takeoff setting. On modified aircraft the stabilizer takeoff trim indicator light will remain on when takeoff trim is set and the trim switch is released, but will go out when airborne. Have ground crew verify all trim surfaces for proper trim position.
- Leading edge of horizontal stabilizer should be aligned with black T index painted on the vertical stabilizer.

WARNING

An improperly installed or defective trim switch is subject to sticking in any or all of the actuated positions, resulting in application of extreme trim. If this condition occurs during preflight check and the switch does not return to the center OFF position, abort mission and make entry in Form 781.

a. Directional trim rheostat—Operate through full travel and return to neutral.

9. Stability augmenters—Check.

a. Stability augmenters—OFF, then ON, one at a time. Note stick kick in pitch and roll. (Rudder kick in yaw B D) as respective switches are turned ON. Crew chief verifies operation.

10. Hydraulic bay door—Security, verified by ground crew.

11. Emergency nozzle closure system—Check. 19

a. Throttle—IDLE.

b. Emergency nozzle closure handle—Pull.

Note

Movements of the T-handle in or out should be made as rapidly as possible.

c. Nozzle position indicator—1 to 3. Check that nozzle closes and stabilizes at an indicated 1 to 3.

d. Emergency nozzle closure handle—Push in.

CAUTION

If the nozzle closure handle is pushed in too slowly, the nozzle may lock up before the locks have retracted. This is due to the mechanical sequencing of the nozzle locks and the nozzle pump. If the nozzle handle does not return to the fully stowed position, immediately pull the nozzle handle out. If the nozzle cannot be returned to the stowed position, immediately shut down the engine and abort the mission.

e. Nozzle position indicator—Check for return to normal.

12. Engine anti-ice, canopy defrost, pitch sensor, pitot heat, and rain remover—Check if flight through IFR conditions is anticipated.

BEFORE TAXIING.

1. Canopy—Locked or full-open.

During all pre-takeoff operations the canopy should be full-open or closed and locked. When locking the canopy, visually check that the three locking hooks are over the three canopy brackets and that canopy unsafe lights are out.

CAUTION

The canopy can be damaged during lowering operations if a firm grip is not maintained on the canopy lift handle. As the canopy passes over top dead center, the weight of the canopy and high or gusty winds can cause the canopy to slam shut.

2. Seat safety pin—Removed and stowed.

3. Wheel chocks—Removed.

4. External stores automatic drop system safety pins—Removed.

It may be advisable to taxi clear of congested areas prior to removing pins.

TAXIING.

1. Nosewheel steering— Engage.

The nosewheel and rudder pedals must be in the same relative position before the steering mechanism can be engaged.

MILITARY THRUST FUEL FLOW 3B (7A)

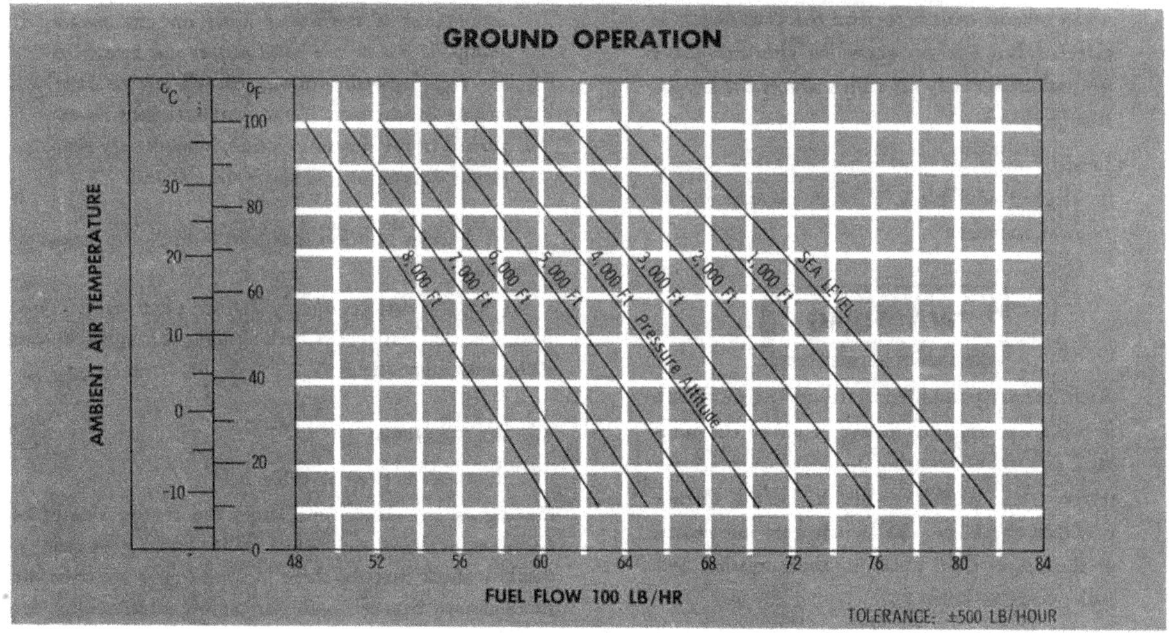

HG 07377 F52-0-2-41

Figure 2-3

CAUTION

If speed brakes are operated at the same time the nosewheel steering system receives an input, such as initiating a turn, nosewheel steering may become inoperative momentarily because of the drop in hydraulic pressure. Reengagement of the steering may be necessary.

2. Brakes—Check.

CAUTION

Taxi far enough away from the edge of the ramp and taxiways to minimize the possibility of foreign object damage.

3. Flight instruments and navigation equipment—Check.

4. External tank fuel and air refueling selector switch—OFF after verifying that fuel from the selected external tanks is transferring normally (953 N/C/W (C) (D)).

5. External fuel quantity indicator—Note quantity. (C) (D)

BEFORE TAKEOFF.

AIRPLANE CHECK.

After taxiing to takeoff area, complete the following checks:

1. Canopy—Locked, warning light out. Check locks visually.

WARNING

Even though the canopy unsafe warning light is out, observe that hooks are properly engaged for positive indication that canopy is locked.

2. Speed brake switch—IN.

To prevent inadvertent extension, switch should be positioned to IN when speed brakes are not being used.

3. Stabilizer takeoff trim indicator light—Check (1006 C/W).

90 PERCENT RPM FUEL FLOW 19

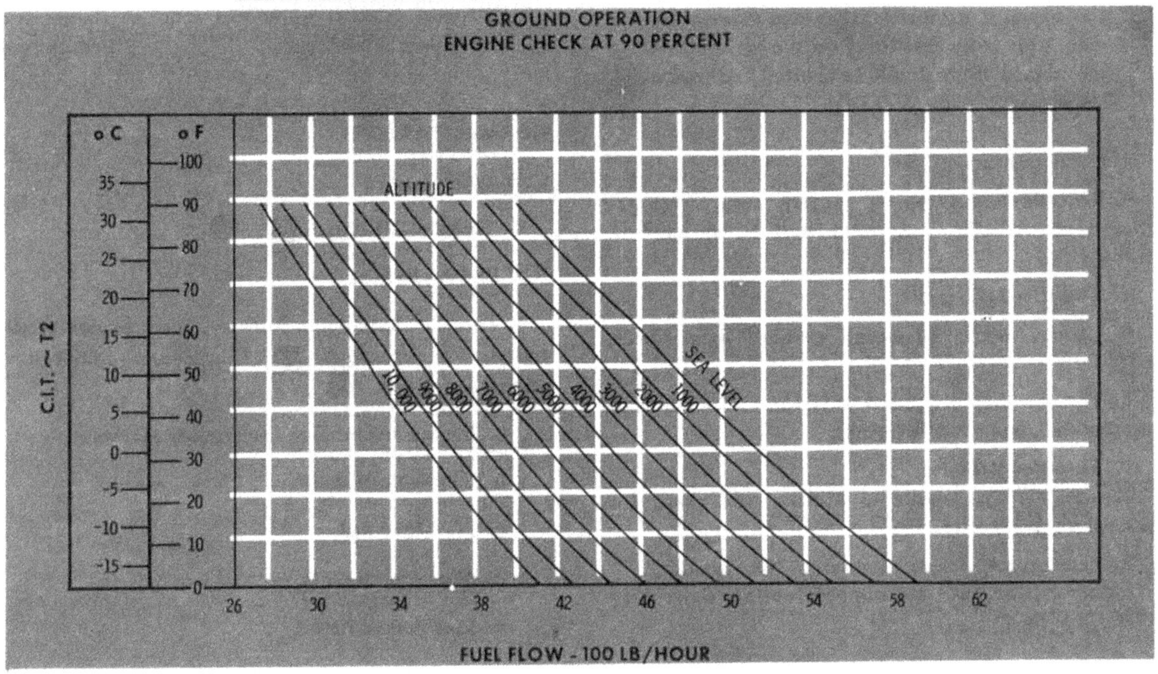

F52-0-2-1

Figure 2-4

4. Wing flap lever—TAKEOFF (check indicators).
5. Pitot heat, rain removal, and canopy defrost—As required.

Note

Moisture can collect in the pitot static tube after exposure to precipitation or high humidity. Heating the tube will help to eliminate the entrapped moisture.

CAUTION

Rain remover must be off during takeoff to avoid exceeding its airspeed limit.

6. IFF/SIF—As required.
7. Zero delay lanyard — Check connected (980 N/C/W).
8. Drogue-gun arming cable—Check connected (980 C/W).

ENGINE CHECK.

See figure 1-10 for exhaust nozzle positions at various throttle settings and figure 5-1 for engine limitations. See figure 5-2 for rpm and EGT schedule at Military and afterburner power. 19

Note 19

Runway temperature should be checked prior to takeoff and figure 5-2 consulted for exhaust gas temperature and engine speed variation with CIT. (Runway temperature may be used in lieu of CIT during static operation).

Takeoff Area Engine Check. 3B 

1. Nosewheel centered—Check.
2. Throttle—Military, check engine acceleration and instruments.

Check as follows:

a. Engine acceleration—10 seconds maximum.
b. RPM—100% (±) 1%.
c. EGT—575°C (±10°C) 3B, 590°C (±10°C) 

During steady state operation the EGT gage may fluctuate ±5°C with peaks up to 10°C. This is normal providing the peaks of 10°C do not occur more often than every 5 seconds.

d. Nozzle position—⅛ to ¼ or 1 to 3.5
e. Fuel flow—Check (see figure 2-3).
f. Oil pressure—Check.

CAUTION

After oil pressure has stabilized, check gage indications against oil pressure record card at 100% rpm. If stabilized oil pressure varies more than 5 psi from that listed on the oil pressure record card, flight should be aborted and engine inspected.

g. Oil quantity–Check.

3. Throttle–Reduce slowly to 80% rpm; check for compressor stall. If compressor stall is encountered, throttle OFF.

4. Throttle–Military.

5. Canopy unsafe (flashing) warning light–Check, (974 C/W).

6. Throttle–Rapidly retard to IDLE. Check for compressor stall, and throttle linkage.

7. Throttle–Military.
Advanced throttle rapidly to Military and check for normal engine acceleration.

8. External fuel quantity indicator–Note quantity.
If external tanks have not stopped feeding, abort (953 N/C/W). C D

Takeoff Area Engine Check. 19

1. Nosewheel centered–Check.

2. Throttle–Advance rapidly to Military stop, and then retard rapidly to IDLE stop when engine speed reaches 93% rpm. Check for compressor stall, and throttle linkage.

3. Throttle–90% rpm.

4. Fuel flow–Check (see figure 2-4).

5. Oil pressure–Check.

CAUTION

After oil pressure has stabilized, check oil pressure corrected to 100% rpm. If corrected pressure is not placard psi ±5 psi, abort the mission.

6. Oil quantity–Check.

TAKEOFF.

The following procedures will produce the results shown in the takeoff charts of the applicable Appendix.

Note

Maximum or Military thrust may be used for takeoff. Check applicable Appendix for differences in takeoff distances. Military thrust takeoffs with external stores will result in abnormally long takeoff runs.

NORMAL TAKEOFF.

(See figure 2-5.)

1. Throttle–Military. 3B 7A

2. Brakes–Release.

3. Throttle–Rapidly to Military, check engine acceleration and instruments 19 . Check during initial takeoff roll as follows 19 :

a. Engine acceleration–10 seconds maximum.

b. RPM–Normal.

c. EGT–Normal.

d. Nozzle position ⅛ to ¼ or 1 to 3.5.

e. Fuel flow–Check.

f. Oil pressure–Check.

4. Throttle–Minimum afterburner (ensure a stabilized afterburner light).

Note

It is recommended that a stabilized afterburner light be obtained prior to advancing throttle to maximum afterburner position.

A stabilized afterburner light will be indicated by the following:

a. RPM may roll back, then return to normal and stabilize.

b. EGT will increase to above 600°C, 3B 7A and 700°C 19 , then decrease and stabilize between 580°C and 600°C. 3B 7A and between 660°C and 688°C 19 .

c. Nozzle position will stabilize between 3.5 and 5 in minimum afterburner, depending on ambient temperature and altitude.

5. Throttle–Maximum thrust.

6. Engine instruments–Check.

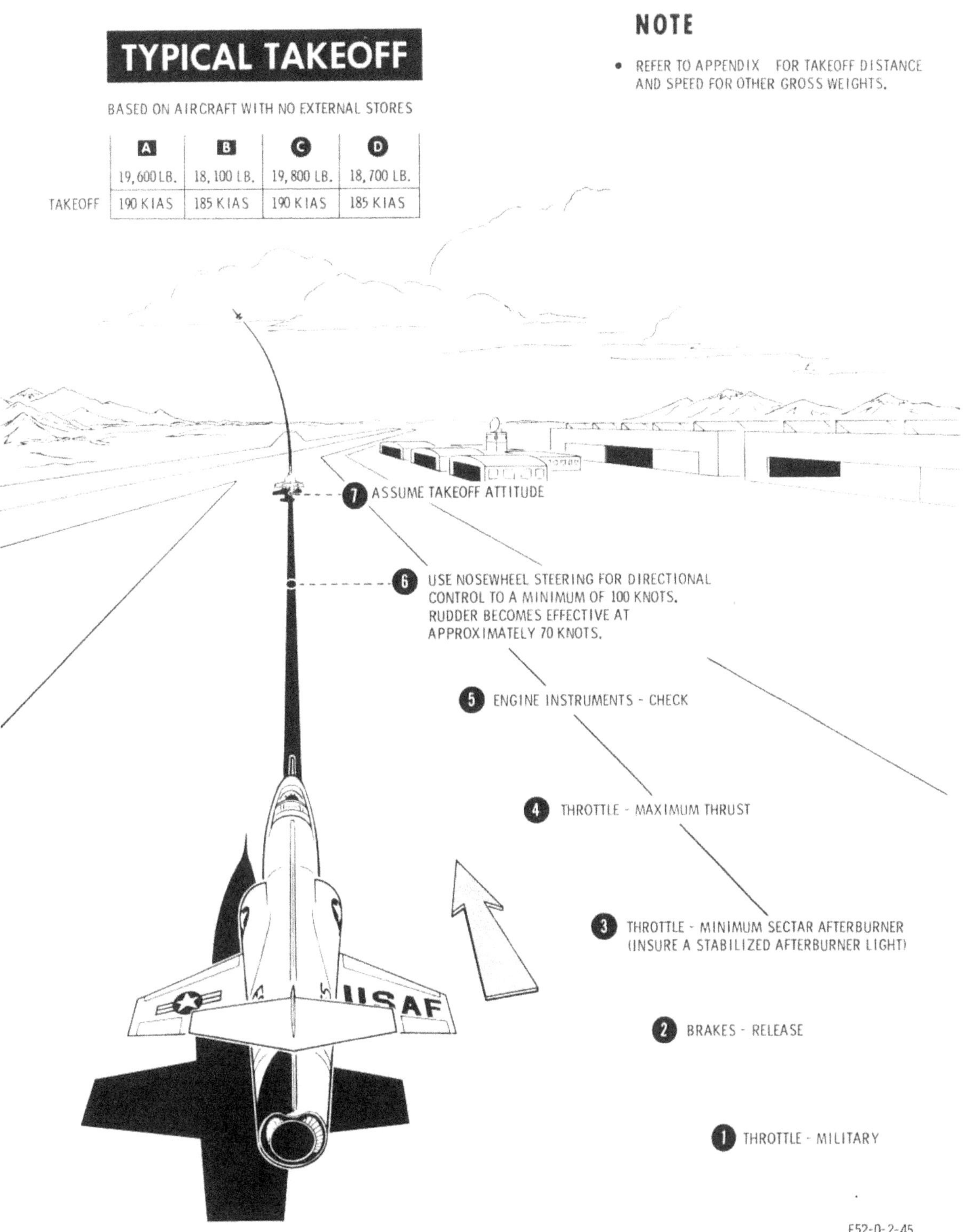
TYPICAL TAKEOFF
BASED ON AIRCRAFT WITH NO EXTERNAL STORES

	A	B	C	D
	19,600 LB.	18,100 LB.	19,800 LB.	18,700 LB.
TAKEOFF	190 KIAS	185 KIAS	190 KIAS	185 KIAS

NOTE
• REFER TO APPENDIX FOR TAKEOFF DISTANCE AND SPEED FOR OTHER GROSS WEIGHTS.
7 ASSUME TAKEOFF ATTITUDE
6 USE NOSEWHEEL STEERING FOR DIRECTIONAL CONTROL TO A MINIMUM OF 100 KNOTS. RUDDER BECOMES EFFECTIVE AT APPROXIMATELY 70 KNOTS.
5 ENGINE INSTRUMENTS - CHECK
4 THROTTLE - MAXIMUM THRUST
3 THROTTLE - MINIMUM SECTAR AFTERBURNER (INSURE A STABILIZED AFTERBURNER LIGHT)
2 BRAKES - RELEASE
1 THROTTLE - MILITARY
USAF
F52-0-2-45

Figure 2-5

WARNING

With throttle at maximum thrust, nozzle position will stabilize between 8.5 and 9.5. With throttle remaining at maximum thrust, afterburner blowout will be indicated by a definite loss of thrust and a nozzle position reading of less than 7 accompanied by an EGT below 500°C 3B 7A and 600°C 19 . If blowout occurs, thrust will be considerably below Military. Thus, takeoff should either be aborted or continued at Military thrust (if Military thrust can be attained) depending on speed and runway remaining.

Avoid moving throttle into the sector range during afterburner takeoffs because there is less protection against a nozzle failure to the closed position. 7A

7. Use nosewheel steering for directional control to a minimum of 100 knots. Rudder becomes effective at approximately 70 knots.

CAUTION

Nosewheel steering should be disengaged prior to nosewheel lift-off to ensure proper steering clutch release.

8. Assume takeoff attitude.

Note

Proper technique is to anticipate aircraft acceleration in order to rotate the nose so that takeoff attitude and speed are reached smoothly and simultaneously. Apply back stick pressure at approximately 20 to 25 knots below the computed takeoff speed. Rotation and nosewheel lift-off will occur 10 to 20 knots below the computed takeoff speed except with a forward center of gravity. With fuselage stores C installed, aircraft rotation and nosewheel lift-off will occur approximately 5 to 10 knots below the computed takeoff speed. Once rotation and nosewheel lift-off occurs, further aft stick is unnecessary. Refer to appendix for takeoff speed. During rapid acceleration/short ground run, rotation technique is not as critical as during slower accelerations and long ground runs. Improper stabilizer trim settings, airplane weight and aircraft center of gravity will affect nosewheel lift-off speed. A lowered or binding nose gear strut will increase the speed at which the nose will begin to rotate, but it will not affect the indicated speed at which the nosewheel leaves the runway.

MINIMUM RUN TAKEOFF.

Maximum performance takeoff speed is 10 knots lower than for normal performance tokeoff.

Note

Do not reduce rotation airspeed, but use more rapid stick application.

OBSTACLE CLEARANCE TAKEOFF.

Takeoff procedure for clearing an obstacle on takeoff is the same as for normal takeoff with afterburner; refer to the applicable Appendix for distances to clear a 50-foot obstacle.

CROSSWIND TAKEOFF.

In addition to the procedures used for normal takeoff, increase nosewheel lift-off and takeoff speeds 5-10 knots to compensate for gusts. Nosewheel steering may be required above 100 knots in strong crosswinds.

AFTER TAKEOFF.

1. Landing gear lever—UP.

When airplane is definitely airborne, retract gear and check red and green landing gear position indicator lights out.

CAUTION

Immediate gear retraction is important when making afterburner takeoffs to prevent exceeding the landing gear transient limit airspeed. The landing gear and doors should be completely up and locked before the placard speed is reached; otherwise, excessive airloads may damage the mechanism or prevent gear retraction.

2. Wing flap lever—UP.

Check indicator.

Note

- Do not retract wing flaps before reaching 260 knots, as buffeting may be experienced.
- Expect an easily controllable nose-up tendency as the flaps retract.

3. Throttle—As desired.

As soon as afterburner thrust is no longer needed, shut down the afterburner by moving throttle aft and inboard. Monitor the nozzle position indicator to check that the nozzles close normally as the throttle is being retarded from maximum afterburning position.

4. Fuel quantity and engine instruments—Check.

5. Zero-delay lanyard – Disconnect (in accordance with zero-delay lanyard connection requirements in Section III).

6. Oxygen diluter lever—Normal.

7. External tanks fuel and air refueling selector switch —TIP or PYLON (as required) after internal fuel quantity has depleted approximately 3500 pounds Ⓒ and 2500 pounds Ⓓ from the initial full indication. (953 N/C/W Ⓒ Ⓓ).

8. External tank fuel and air refueling selector switch—As required (maintain internal fuel from 500 pounds to 2000 pounds below the initial full indication until external tanks are empty. (953 N/C/W Ⓒ Ⓓ).

Note 

If air refueling is accomplished continue to maintain internal fuel quantity between 500 and 2000 pounds below the initial full indication until external tanks are empty. (953 N/C/W).

CLIMB.

The climbing attitude with Maximum thrust is extremely steep and until experience is gained, some difficulty in holding the climb schedule will be experienced. Refer to climb charts in the applicable Appendix for recommended speeds to be used during climb and for rates of climb and fuel consumption.

CRUISE.

Refer to the applicable Appendix for Cruise Operating Data. Operate the windshield and canopy defrosting system throughout the flight at the highest flow possible, consistent with pilot comfort, so that a sufficiently high temperature is maintained to preheat the canopy and windshield areas. It is necessary to preheat because during rapid descents there is insufficient time to heat these areas to temperatures which prevent the formation of frost or fog.

Note

The APC and stick shaker may be checked in flight as follows: While slowly applying back pressure on the stick, note an increase on the APC indicator in relation to angle of attack and increasing G force. This indicates satisfactory system operation and sensing of vane angle. Apply a small rapid stick deflection and note the APC indicator reading increase rapidly in relation to the increasing pitch rate, indicating a satisfactory signal from the pitch rate gyro. The stick deflection should be great enough to induce a pitch rate sufficient to actuate the stick shaker.

FLIGHT CHARACTERISTICS.

(Refer to Section VI for information regarding flight characteristics.)

DESCENT.

Refer to Appendix I for recommended descent technique and accomplish the following steps:

1. Engine anti-ice, defrost and pitot heat—As desired.
2. Armament switches—OFF, Sight caged.
3. Fuel, oil quantity, and engine instruments—Check (determine final approach speed).
4. Zero-delay lanyard—Connect (in accordance with zero-delay lanyard connection requirements in Section III).
5. Oxygen diluter lever—As required.
6. Using latest RCR report, compute stopping distance.

Note

If no RCR is available use 12 for wet runways and 15 for icy runways.

BEFORE LANDING.

The before landing procedures set forth below will produce the results shown in the landing charts in the applicable Appendix. Refer to figure 2-6 for a typical landing pattern.

Note

The airspeeds listed herein are based on a normal landing gross weight of about 14,600 pounds (approximately 1000 pounds fuel remaining and no ammunition). Increase base leg, approach and landing speeds 5 knots for each 1000 pounds of fuel remaining above 1500 pounds and 5 knots for each additional 1000 pounds of external stores.

INITIAL.

1. Wing flap lever—TAKEOFF (check indicators).
2. Airspeed—300 to 350 knots.

DOWNWIND.

1. Landing gear lever—DOWN below 260 knots (check indicators).
2. Wing flap lever—LAND below 240 knots and above 210 knots. (Check indicators.)

Maintain level flight and keep hand on lever until it is determined that the flaps and BLC are functioning normally.

Note

A mild roll transient may be experienced on some aircraft as flaps move from the TAKE-OFF to the LAND position. This is attributed to asymmetric difference in the boundary layer control system and will vary in intensity and direction with individual aircraft. (Maximum lateral stick displacement should not exceed 1 inch.) After the flaps are in the full DOWN position some lateral unbalance may persist, but it can be trimmed out, if desired.

3. Airspeed—210 knots minimum.

WARNING

Under various conditions of high gross weight or high ambient temperatures with flaps in the LAND position, sufficient thrust may not be available at Military to maintain correct rate of descent and airspeed during turn from downwind to final. Refer to Heavyweight Landing paragraph.

BASE LEG TURN.

1. Landing gear down and locked—Check.
2. Airspeed—200 knots minimum.

FINAL.

1. Roll out on final approach, approximately 6000 feet from end of runway, approximately 300 feet above terrain; 190 knots recommended airspeed.
2. Throttle—87-90 percent rpm, 3B 7A and 85-88 percent rpm 19 .
3. Airspeed—170 knots recommended.

WARNING

The recommended final approach speed does not include sufficient margin to allow for air turbulence. Under gusty wind conditions, increase approach speed 5 KIAS for each 10 knots above steady wind velocity.

LANDING.

BOUNDARY LAYER CONTROL.

The installation of boundary layer control (BLC) to effect low landing approach and touchdown speeds has resulted in some new flight characteristics and changes in required piloting technique. The pilot should remember at all times when using LAND flaps that the additional lift afforded by BLC is dependent on engine airflow. This lift, therefore, varies with airspeed, altitude, and engine rpm with the greatest variation occurring at low airspeed, low altitude, and engine speeds above 80 percent (although some effectiveness is still retained at lower rpm). This means that proper use of the throttle is mandatory, especially as touchdown is approached, to accomplish a smooth reduction in engine rpm so that a smooth reduction in the effects of BLC on lift will result.

LANDING TECHNIQUE.

The approach angle which results from using the recommended landing speed and power settings is approximately as flat as a GCA or ILS final and makes for a relatively small flareout rotation angle. Speed should be monitored and rpm varied as necessary to arrive at flareout altitude just short of the runway. Airspeed responds very rapidly to throttle change in this speed and rpm range, making it relatively easy to establish a good approach. Because of the high drag characteristics in the landing configuration, speed brakes are not needed on the final, but may be used during the flareout to adjust the point of touchdown. Approximately 88 percent rpm 3B 7A and 86 percent rpm 19 should be carried through the flareout, after which power should be reduced smoothly to 82-83 percent rpm 3B 7A and 81-82 percent rpm 19 and maintained until touchdown. It may seem unnatural to hold more than idle thrust to touchdown, but this procedure is recommended because the torque effect of rpm reduction induces a right rolloff tendency. An abrupt thrust reduction results in an abrupt rolloff as well as a rapid increase in sink rate. When thrust reduction is smooth the rolloff is not noticeable. The speeds recommended for approach and landing contain a certain margin to offset the effects of turbulence, small weight variations, etc.; however, the margin should not be dissipated unnecessarily, even in ideal conditions, because at lower speeds lateral stability and control deteriorate and wing drop tendencies appear. Furthermore, at the high pitch angle required to maintain flight at low airspeeds, it is possible to drag the tail.

NORMAL LANDING.

(See figure 2-6.)

1. Throttle—Retard to IDLE (after touchdown).
2. Nosewheel—Lower.
3. Nosewheel steering—Engage.

Note

If nosewheel shimmy is encountered, release nosewheel steering and attempt to hold weight off the nosewheel.

4. Drag chute—Deploy.

To obtain maximum aerodynamic braking, deploy drag chute as soon as nosewheel is on the ground.

CAUTION

- To prevent damaging the noesgear, do not deploy the drag chute until all three gears are on the ground. The location of the drag chute causes a nose down pitching moment when deployed.
- The speed brakes should remain out after landing because nosewheel steering may be lost if the two are operated simultaneously. Loss of nosewheel steering while taxiing in a congested area can be a safety hazard. Also, extension of the speed brakes while ground personnel are in this area is hazardous.

TAKEOFF FLAP LANDING.

Under certain circumstances, a takeoff flap landing may be desirable or necessary. In such an event, fly a wider than normal pattern using 230-240 KIAS on downwind and 220-230 KIAS on base leg. Roll out on final approach a minimum of 2 miles from the runway and fly final at not less than 190 KIAS maintaining a normal glide slope. When landing is assured, the throttle may be retarded to idle with no significant increase in sink rate. There may even be a tendency to float during the flare. Touchdown should be accomplished at not less than 160 KIAS. Stick shaker may be experienced as the speed drops to 160 KIAS.

CROSSWIND LANDING.

Wind drift may be compensated for by crabbing or the wing down method or a combination of both for approach and landing. In strong crosswinds the crab method or a combination of the two methods is more suitable. In crosswinds of 15 knots or more, the use of TAKEOFF flaps is recommended. The most important things to remember are to lower the nose immediately after touchdown and engage the nosewheel steering before deploying the drag chute. For dry runway conditions the drag chute may be deployed in 90 degree crosswinds of 20 knots or 45 degree crosswinds of 30 knots provided nosewheel steering is engaged. Landings are not recommended when the crosswind components on the runway exceeds 20 knots because maintaining alignment on the runway is difficult and because such components are greater than recommended for drag chute deployment. The airplane tends to weather-vane but directional control can be maintained with nosewheel steering. After landing, some difficulty may be encountered in releasing the drag chute, however, turning the aircraft directly into the wind, should solve the difficulty. When landing on wet or icy runways in strong crosswinds the weather-vaning effect of the drag chute may be sufficient to cause a skid. Therefore, the pilot should be prepared to jettison the chute, whenever a strong crosswind, slick runway situation exists. The fact that slick runway conditions reduce braking capability make it desirable to obtain the initial braking of the chute even though it may be necessary to jettison it later to retain directional control. Under extreme weather conditions when low visibility prevents the pilot from seeing that directional control is being maintained, the drag chute should be jettisoned.

Note

- Increase touchdown speed 5 knots for each 10 knots of effective crosswind velocity, if landing with LAND flaps.
- Do not actuate the nosewheel steering button unless the nosewheel and rudder pedals are aligned. If the pedals are deflected when the nosewheel steering button is actuated, clutch friction within the steering system may cause an undesired turn as the pedals are moved to aline with the nosewheel.

HEAVYWEIGHT LANDING.

When a heavyweight landing must be made, adjust the approach and touchdown airspeeds for gross weight. Refer to the landing charts in the applicable Appendix for the airspeed at any landing gross weight. Fly a larger than normal pattern or make a straight-in approach. This is especially important on approaches during hot weather and landing at high altitudes. Rate of descent should be monitored closely and not allowed to become excessive.

TYPICAL LANDING PATTERN

BASED ON A LANDING GROSS WEIGHT OF 14,600 LB (1000 LB FUEL REMAINING AND NO AMMUNITION).

NOTE

INCREASE BASE LEG, APPROACH, AND TOUCHDOWN SPEEDS 5 KNOTS FOR EACH 1000 LB OF FUEL REMAINING ABOVE 1500 LB AND 5 KNOTS FOR EACH ADDITIONAL 1000 LB OF EXTERNAL LOAD.

REFER TO LANDING DISTANCE CHARTS IN APPENDIX FOR FINAL APPROACH AND TOUCHDOWN SPEEDS AT OTHER GROSS WEIGHTS.

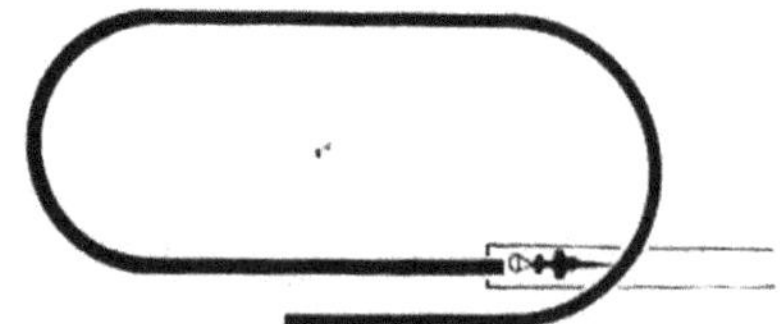

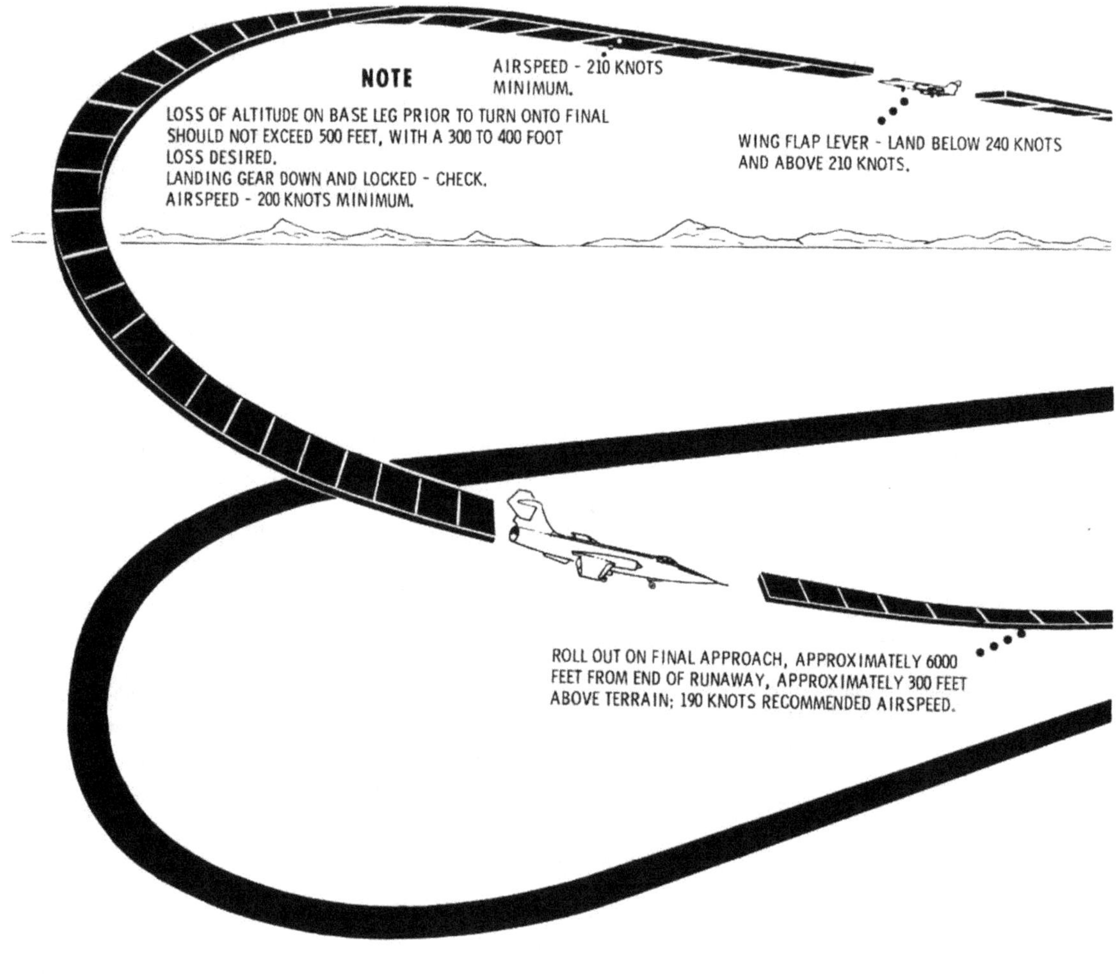

AIRSPEED - 210 KNOTS MINIMUM.

NOTE

LOSS OF ALTITUDE ON BASE LEG PRIOR TO TURN ONTO FINAL SHOULD NOT EXCEED 500 FEET, WITH A 300 TO 400 FOOT LOSS DESIRED.
LANDING GEAR DOWN AND LOCKED - CHECK.
AIRSPEED - 200 KNOTS MINIMUM.

WING FLAP LEVER - LAND BELOW 240 KNOTS AND ABOVE 210 KNOTS.

ROLL OUT ON FINAL APPROACH, APPROXIMATELY 6000 FEET FROM END OF RUNAWAY, APPROXIMATELY 300 FEET ABOVE TERRAIN; 190 KNOTS RECOMMENDED AIRSPEED.

F52-0-3-46(1)

Figure 2-6 (Sheet 1 of 2)

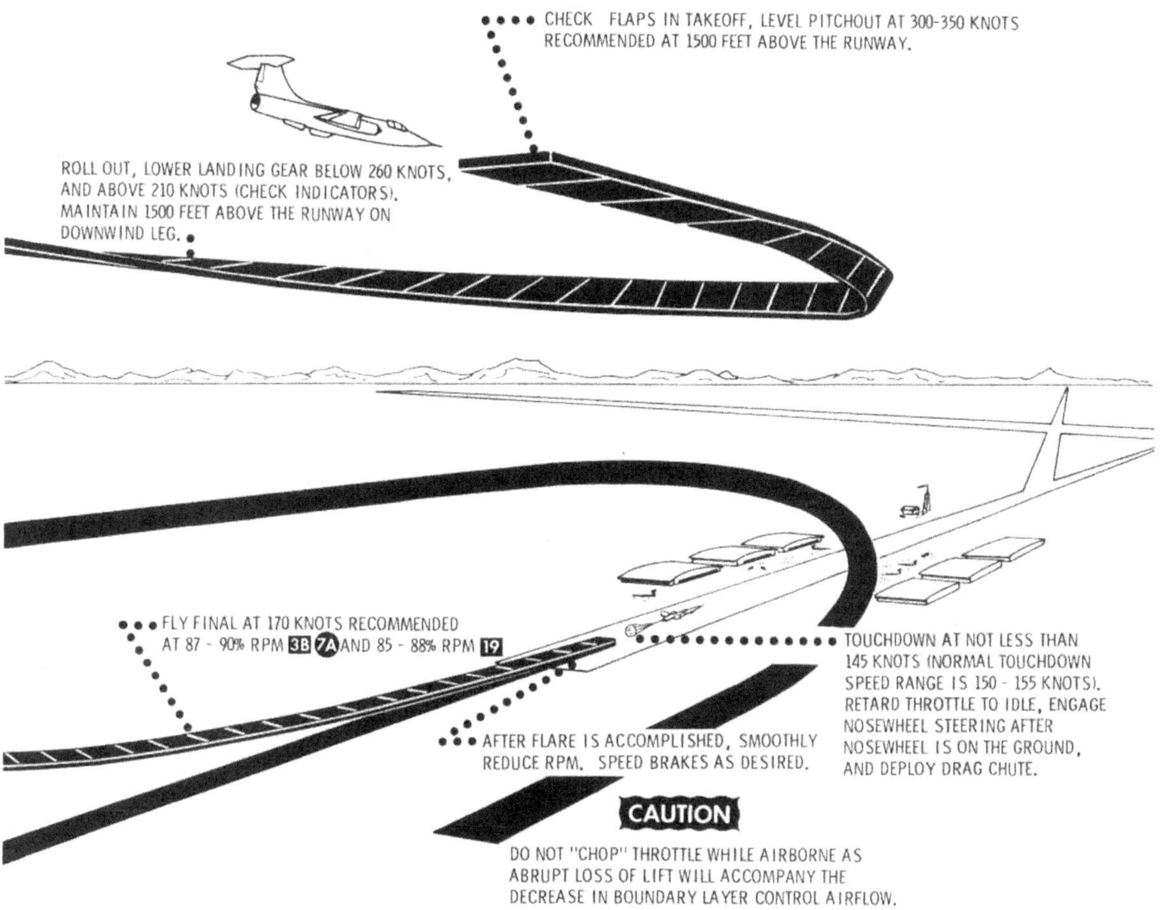

CHECK FLAPS IN TAKEOFF, LEVEL PITCHOUT AT 300-350 KNOTS RECOMMENDED AT 1500 FEET ABOVE THE RUNWAY.
ROLL OUT, LOWER LANDING GEAR BELOW 260 KNOTS, AND ABOVE 210 KNOTS (CHECK INDICATORS). MAINTAIN 1500 FEET ABOVE THE RUNWAY ON DOWNWIND LEG.
FLY FINAL AT 170 KNOTS RECOMMENDED AT 87 - 90% RPM 3B 7A AND 85 - 88% RPM 19
TOUCHDOWN AT NOT LESS THAN 145 KNOTS (NORMAL TOUCHDOWN SPEED RANGE IS 150 - 155 KNOTS). RETARD THROTTLE TO IDLE, ENGAGE NOSEWHEEL STEERING AFTER NOSEWHEEL IS ON THE GROUND, AND DEPLOY DRAG CHUTE.
AFTER FLARE IS ACCOMPLISHED, SMOOTHLY REDUCE RPM. SPEED BRAKES AS DESIRED.
CAUTION
DO NOT "CHOP" THROTTLE WHILE AIRBORNE AS ABRUPT LOSS OF LIFT WILL ACCOMPANY THE DECREASE IN BOUNDARY LAYER CONTROL AIRFLOW.

CAUTION

- STEEP FINAL APPROACHES CAN BE HAZARDOUS IF THE AIRSPEED DROPS BELOW NORMAL, TURNS ARE MADE, OR GUSTY WINDS PREVAIL. THESE FACTORS CAN CAUSE AN EXCESSIVE RATE OF SINK WHICH MAY NOT BE RECOGNIZED AND CORRECTED IN TIME TO PREVENT GROUND CONTACT.
- ALL FINAL APPROACHES SHOULD BE MADE WITH POWER, AND ON A GLIDE SLOPE SIMILAR TO THAT FOR ILS/PAR (700-800 FEET PER MINUTE). THIS SLOPE MAY BE INTERCEPTED AT ANY POINT, BUT SHOULD BE INTERCEPTED AT NOT LESS THAN ONE MILE FROM TOUCHDOWN.

F52-0-2-46(2)

Figure 2-6 (Sheet 2 of 2)

Be prepared to use afterburning thrust if necessary. Refer to Section VI and the applicable Appendix for charts showing the variation of flight performance to expect. Under marginal conditions, a straight-in approach is recommended. In addition, minimize drag by using a TAKEOFF-flap or gear-up configuration for the approach, changing to the final landing configuration when the landing is assured. Under certain conditions of forward center of gravity, TAKEOFF flaps Ⓒ must be used for the landing. (Refer to Landing With Fuselage Stores paragraph in Section VI Ⓒ.) If landing roll distance is a major consideration and center of gravity is not, use LAND flaps to reduce the touchdown speed and delay gear extension until the flare is assured.

WARNING

Under these conditions, afterburner will have to be used if a go-around is attempted after the landing gear has been extended.

MINIMUM RUN LANDING.

For a landing with minimum ground roll, fly the approach so that close control can be exercised over airspeed and touchdown point. Land as near to the end of the runway as possible, touching down at 140 knots for normal landing gross weight. Use the speed brakes to aid in controlling touchdown point and speed as well as for maximum drag during the rollout. Plan the chute deployment so that it blossoms as the nosewheel touches down. Apply heavy braking but do not skid the tires. Hold heavy braking action until the aircraft stops. Be prepared to use nosewheel steering in the event of a blown tire.

Note

- Stick shaker action can be experienced as the airspeed drops to 140 knots.
- Heavy braking is accomplished by applying high brake pedal force as soon as the drag chute deploys. Hold brake pedal force with no pumping action until the aircraft stops. This procedure causes the brakes to heat and is not recommended as normal practice.
- To prevent damaging brakes, tires, or wheels due to heat, sufficient time must be allowed between maximum effort stops for cooling the brakes to handling temperatures.

LANDING ON SLIPPERY RUNWAYS.

Refer to the applicable Appendix for computing ground roll distance when landing on slippery runways.

Wet Runway.

When landing on a wet surface, use the same landing approach as for a minimum-run landing. Leave the flaps at LAND throughout the landing roll for maximum aerodynamic drag. Above 110 knots, use light braking only, to prevent skidding on the wet surface. Normal braking may be used below 100 knots but remain alert for the possibility of skidding. No difficulty in control should be experienced during a wet-runway landing. If a yaw occurs, release both brakes and regain directional control with nosewheel steering and only a light application of brakes.

Icy Runway.

Landings on icy runways are most hazardous and should be attempted only when absolutely necessary to complete operational requirements. Landing on packed snow or icy runways requires a ground roll distance up to 2.3 times that required on a dry runway. Use approach and landing procedures as outlined for wet runways except to avoid wheel braking if possible. When patches of ice are on the runway, avoid braking if possible. If braking is necessary, use short and intermittent applications to avoid skidding.

TOUCH-AND-GO LANDING.

After touchdown proceed as follows:

1. Wing flap lever—TAKEOFF.
2. Throttle—MILITARY.

Note

To avoid BLC rolloff, do not fly aircraft off ground until flaps have reached takeoff position.

3. Speed brakes switch—IN.
4. Trim—Set as required.
5. Use normal takeoff technique.

GO-AROUND.

(See figure 2-7.)

Make decision to go around as soon as possible and use the following procedures.

1. Throttle—Military (Maximum thrust if necessary).

TYPICAL GO-AROUND

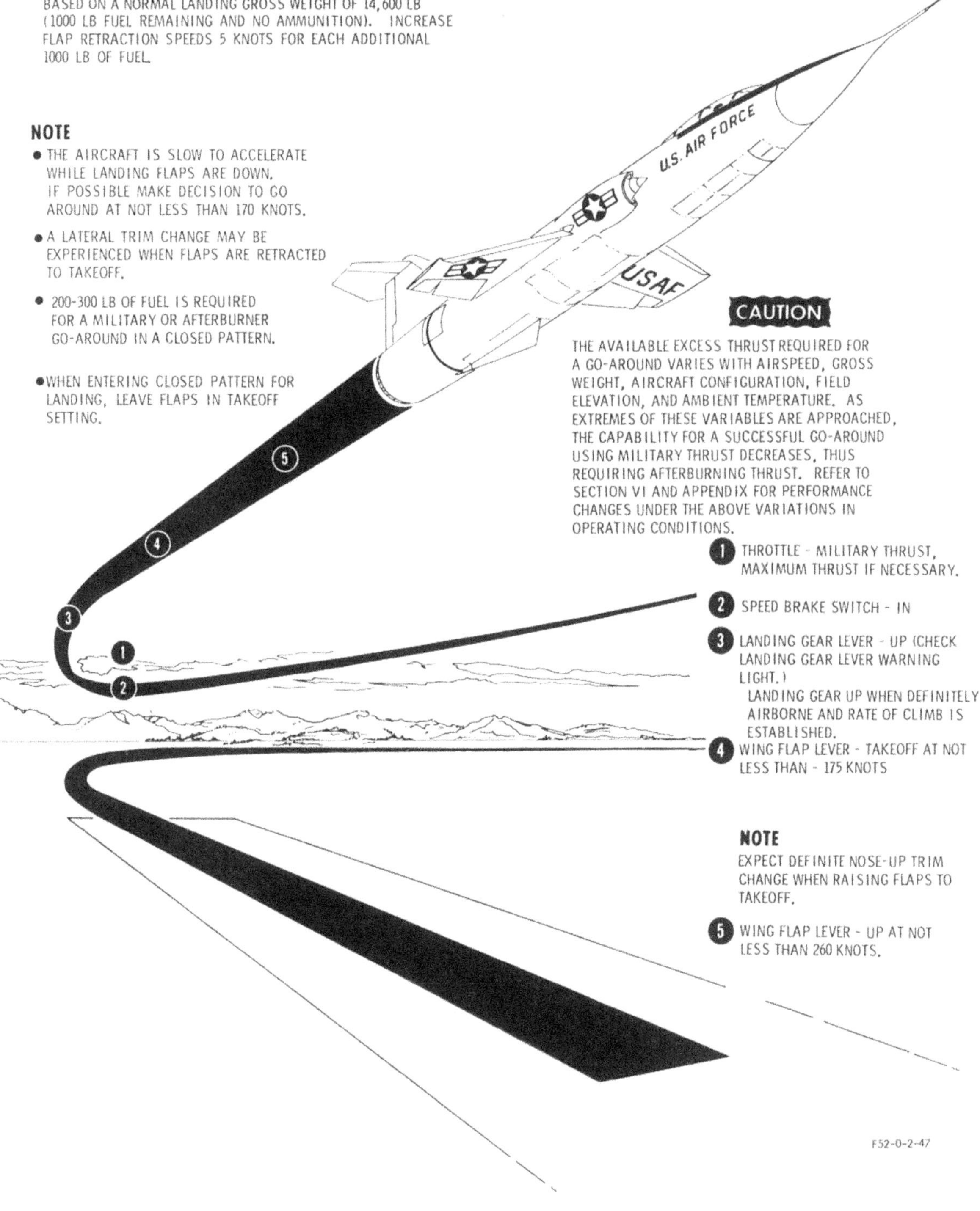

BASED ON A NORMAL LANDING GROSS WEIGHT OF 14,600 LB (1000 LB FUEL REMAINING AND NO AMMUNITION). INCREASE FLAP RETRACTION SPEEDS 5 KNOTS FOR EACH ADDITIONAL 1000 LB OF FUEL.
NOTE
● THE AIRCRAFT IS SLOW TO ACCELERATE WHILE LANDING FLAPS ARE DOWN. IF POSSIBLE MAKE DECISION TO GO AROUND AT NOT LESS THAN 170 KNOTS.
● A LATERAL TRIM CHANGE MAY BE EXPERIENCED WHEN FLAPS ARE RETRACTED TO TAKEOFF.
● 200-300 LB OF FUEL IS REQUIRED FOR A MILITARY OR AFTERBURNER GO-AROUND IN A CLOSED PATTERN.
● WHEN ENTERING CLOSED PATTERN FOR LANDING, LEAVE FLAPS IN TAKEOFF SETTING.
U.S. AIR FORCE
USAF
CAUTION
THE AVAILABLE EXCESS THRUST REQUIRED FOR A GO-AROUND VARIES WITH AIRSPEED, GROSS WEIGHT, AIRCRAFT CONFIGURATION, FIELD ELEVATION, AND AMBIENT TEMPERATURE. AS EXTREMES OF THESE VARIABLES ARE APPROACHED, THE CAPABILITY FOR A SUCCESSFUL GO-AROUND USING MILITARY THRUST DECREASES, THUS REQUIRING AFTERBURNING THRUST. REFER TO SECTION VI AND APPENDIX FOR PERFORMANCE CHANGES UNDER THE ABOVE VARIATIONS IN OPERATING CONDITIONS.
1 THROTTLE - MILITARY THRUST, MAXIMUM THRUST IF NECESSARY.
2 SPEED BRAKE SWITCH - IN
3 LANDING GEAR LEVER - UP (CHECK LANDING GEAR LEVER WARNING LIGHT.)
LANDING GEAR UP WHEN DEFINITELY AIRBORNE AND RATE OF CLIMB IS ESTABLISHED.
4 WING FLAP LEVER - TAKEOFF AT NOT LESS THAN - 175 KNOTS
NOTE
EXPECT DEFINITE NOSE-UP TRIM CHANGE WHEN RAISING FLAPS TO TAKEOFF.
5 WING FLAP LEVER - UP AT NOT LESS THAN 260 KNOTS.
F52-0-2-47

Figure 2-7

CAUTION

- The use of excessive nose-up trim during final approach will appreciably reduce the effect of forward stick. Therefore, as power is advanced, trim the aircraft toward neutral.
- The available excess thrust to perform a go-around varies with airspeed, gross weight, airplane configuration, field elevation, and ambient temperature. As extremes of these variables are approached the ability to perform a successful go-around with Military thrust decreases, thus requiring afterburning thrust. Refer to Section VI and the applicable Appendix for illustrations and charts showing the variation in performance with changes in these operating conditions.

2. Speed brake switch—IN.
3. Landing gear lever—UP. Check landing gear lever warning light.
4. Wing flap lever—TAKEOFF.

Move flap lever to TAKEOFF position at not less than 175 knots.

Note

Expect a definite nose-up trim change when raising the flaps to TAKEOFF.

5. Wing flap lever—UP (as required).

Move flap lever to UP at not less than 260 knots.

AFTER LANDING.

After clearing runway, proceed as follows:

1. Speed brake switch—IN.

CAUTION

If the speed brakes are operated at the same time the nosewheel steering system receives an input, such an initiating a turn off the runway, nosewheel steering may become inoperative momentarily, because of the drop in hydraulic pressure. Reengagement of the steering may become necessary.

2. Wing flap lever—TAKEOFF (check indicator).
3. Drag chute—Jettison in appropriate area.
4. Rain remover switch—OFF.

Note

- If rain remover has not been used, turn switch ON for not more than 30 seconds, then OFF to remove condensation and protect the rain removal shutoff valve from corrosion.
- If visible moisture disappears before 30 seconds, turn switch OFF.
- If the rain remover fails to retract, open the ram air scoop momentarily.

5. Engine anti-ice, pitot heat, and defroster—OFF.
6. Trim-Takeoff.
7. Ejection seat safety pin—Insert from left side.
8. Canopy—As desired.

CAUTION

When unlocking canopy, pilot must have a firm grip on canopy lift handle to prevent loss of or damage to canopy due to high or gusty winds. When opening canopy to full-open position, maintain a firm grip on canopy lift handle until canopy is in full-open lock position.

9. TACAN, VOR/ILS, and IFF/SIF—OFF.

ENGINE SHUTDOWN.

1. Speed brake switch—OUT.
2. BLC ducts—Check.

The BLC and ducts condition should be checked with the wing flaps in takeoff.

3. Wing flap lever—UP.
4. UHF radio—OFF.
5. Fuel boost pumps—Check.

The crew chief will check the output of the individual fuel booster pumps prior to engine shutdown.

6. Twenty-amp transformer-rectifier unit—Check.
   a. The crew chief will turn the dc power circuit off.
   b. The pilot will monitor the warning light panel.

If the DC MONITORED BUS OUT, and the INST ON EMER POWER warning light illuminates, power is coming from the dc emergency bus, and the 20-amp transformer-rectifier unit is operative.

7. IDLE engine for 3 minutes for proper cooling.

Note

Operation during taxi can be considered as part of this time.

8. Throttle—OFF.

9. Speed brakes switch—IN (after electrical power fails).

Note

- Check that engine decelerates freely. Listen for any excessive noise during shutdown.
- Check speed brake closure.

10. Fuel shutoff switch—OFF.

BEFORE LEAVING AIRPLANE.

1. Ejection seat safety pin—Installed (check).
2. Pressure suit oxygen lever—OFF.
3. Wheels—Chocked.
4. Landing gear safety pins and arrestor hook safety lock—Installed.
5. External stores automatic drop system safety pins—Installed.
6. Drogue-gun arming cable—Disconnect (980 C/W Ballistic Parachute).
7. Form 781—Complete.

CAUTION

In addition to established requirements for reporting any system defects, or unusual and excessive operations, the pilot will also make entries in Form 781 to indicate if any limits in the Flight Manual have been exceeded.

STRANGE-FIELD PROCEDURES.

Insure that required inspections are accomplished in accordance with T.O. 00-20A-1. See figure 2-8 for aircraft servicing.

1. Servicing specifications as follows:

   a. Fuel—See figure 2-9 for fuel grades, properties and limits.

   b. Oil—MIL-L-7808, 7808C, or 7808D.

   c. Hydraulic fluid—MIL-H-5606.

   d. Oxygen—Liquid BB-O-925 Type II.

   e. Hydraulic system accumulators—Nitrogen MIL-N-6011, Grade A, Type I (ALTERNATE—air).

   f. Tires—14 ply nose—Stock No. 3900-20060
   —18 ply main—Stock No. 1630-674-6592.

   g. Tire pressures—Refer to aircraft workcards for tire pressure under various weight conditions.

   h. Single point refueling—50 psi (use only when necessary).

2. External air for starting—MA-1 GTC, MA-2 MP, MA-3 MP, GTC-85 (Navy).

STARTING AIR REQUIREMENTS.

Engine starting air requirements at the starter are shown in the following table:

Rated Input	350°F and 45 psia at 110 lb/min.
Maximum Pressure Input	250°F and 70 psia at 110 lb/min.

CAUTION

Do not use Navy RCPP 105A.

3. External Electric Power—MD3-A, MA-2 MP, B-10, MA-1 MP (110 volt, 400 cycle, 3 phase ac).

ALERT COCKING PROCEDURES.

1. External electrical power—ON.
2. Aircraft preflight—Accomplish normal preflight inspection.
3. Engine Start—Accomplish normal engine start.
4. Accomplish all pre-taxi and pilot/crew chief checks except:
   a. Do not remove ejection seat pin.
   b. Do not remove external load safety pins.
5. Engine—Accomplish a normal engine shutdown except:
   a. Fuel shutoff switch—OFF.
   b. Flaps—TAKEOFF.
   c. UHF Radio—ON.
   d. Pitot heat—As required.
   e. Navigation and Taxi Lights—ON (as required).
   f. TACAN—Rec, VOR-ON, IFF—STANDBY.
6. External electrical power—Leave connected.

ALERT SCRAMBLE PROCEDURES.

1. External electrical power—ON (if required).
2. Personal equipment—All required equipment on and secure.
3. Engine start—Accomplish normal engine start.
4. Ejection seat pin—Removed.
5. External load safety pins—Removed.
6. Wheel chocks—Removed.
7. Canopy—Locked, light out.
8. Takeoff—Accomplish normal takeoff for configuration.

SERVICING DIAGRAM

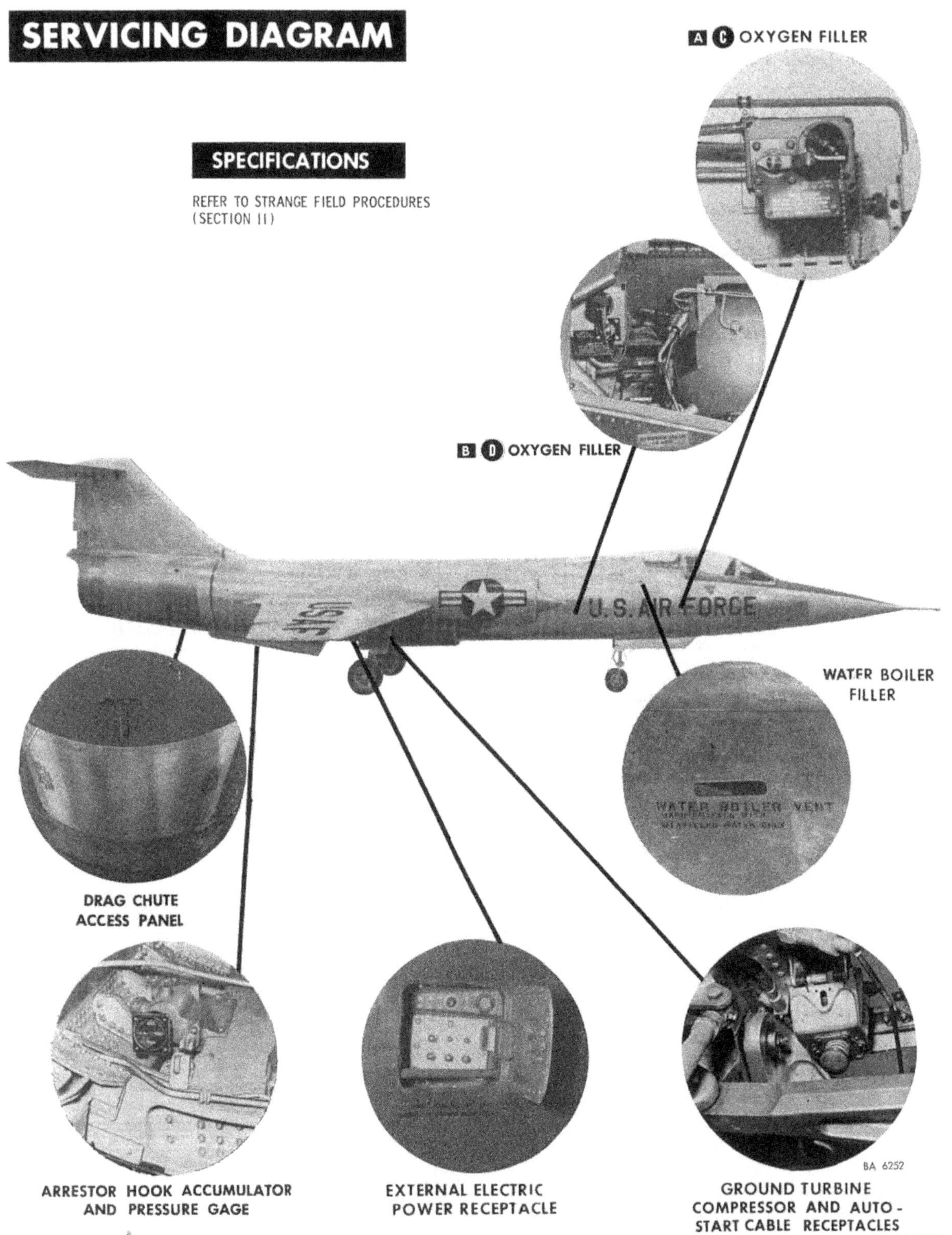

Figure 2-8 (Sheet 1 of 2)

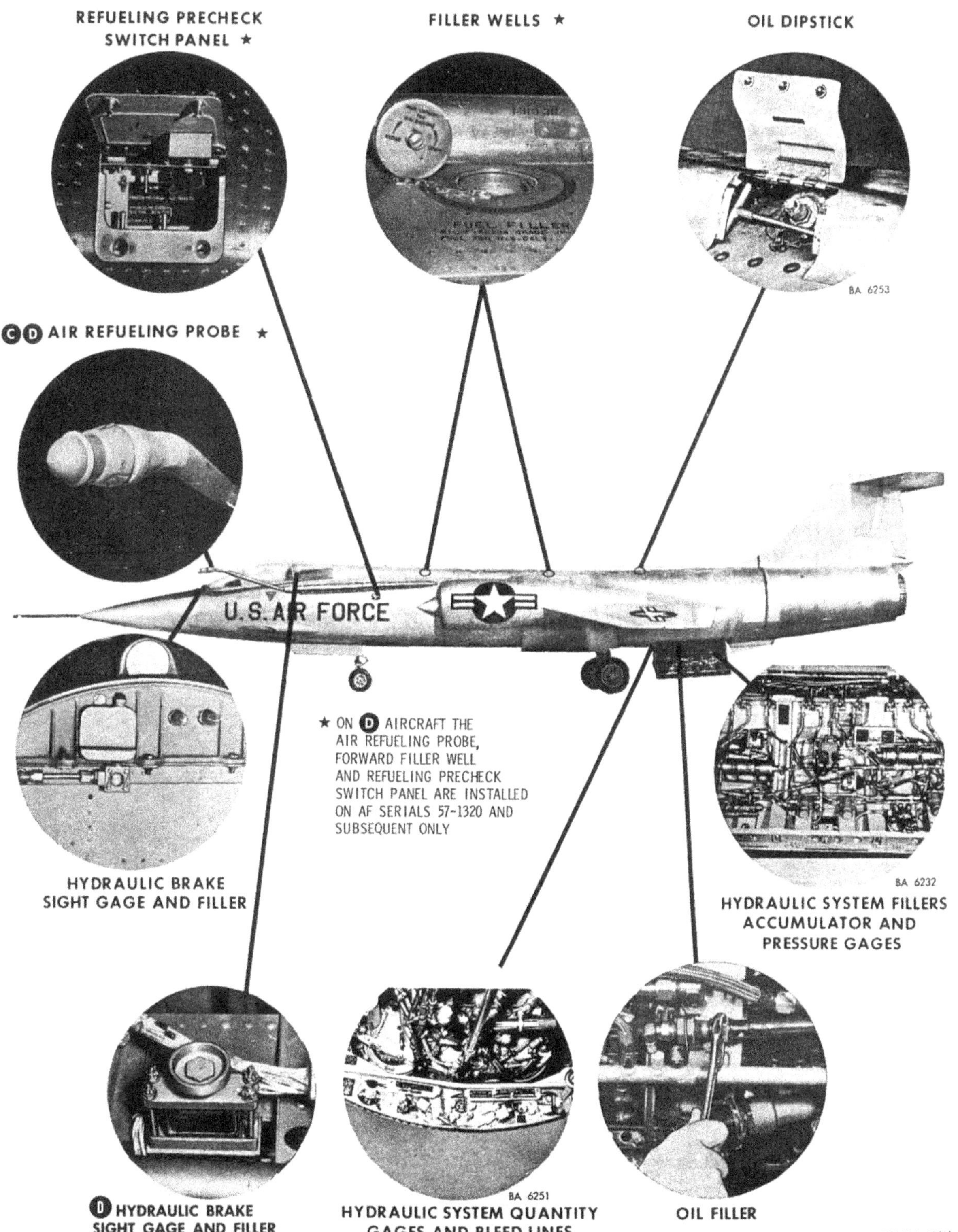
REFUELING PRECHECK SWITCH PANEL ★
FILLER WELLS ★
OIL DIPSTICK
BA 6253
C D AIR REFUELING PROBE ★
U.S. AIR FORCE
★ ON D AIRCRAFT THE AIR REFUELING PROBE, FORWARD FILLER WELL AND REFUELING PRECHECK SWITCH PANEL ARE INSTALLED ON AF SERIALS 57-1320 AND SUBSEQUENT ONLY
HYDRAULIC BRAKE SIGHT GAGE AND FILLER
BA 6232
HYDRAULIC SYSTEM FILLERS ACCUMULATOR AND PRESSURE GAGES
D HYDRAULIC BRAKE SIGHT GAGE AND FILLER FOR AFT COCKPIT
BA 6251
HYDRAULIC SYSTEM QUANTITY GAGES AND BLEED LINES
OIL FILLER
F52-0-1-40(2)

Figure 2-8 (Sheet 2 of 2)

FUEL GRADE PROPERTIES AND LIMITS
(Shown in Order of Preferences)

USE	FUEL TYPE	GRADE	NATO SYMBOL	U.S. MILITARY SPECIFICATION	SPECIFIC GRAVITY	FREEZE POINT °F	LIMITS
Recommended Fuel	Wide Cut Gasoline	JP-4	F-40	MIL-T-5624	.802-.721	−76	
Alternate Fuel	Wide Cut Gasoline	Jet-B	Commercial	None	.802-.751	−60	1, 3, 5
		JP-5	F-44	MIL-T-5624	.845-.775	−55	1
	Kerosene	Jet-A-1	Commercial	None	.829-.775	−58	1, 2, 3
		Jet-A	Commercial	None	.845-.788	−55	1, 2, 3
Emergency	Aviation Gasoline (Avgas) plus 3% grade 1100 oil	80/87	F-12	MIL-G-5572	.706	−76	4
		91/96	F-15	MIL-G-5572	.706	−76	4
		100/130	F-18	MIL-G-5572	.706	−76	4
		115/145	F-22	MIL-G-5572	.706	−76	4

LIMITS

WARNING

Emergency fuel use is limited to five hours of operation and requires adjustment of the main and afterburner fuel controls. These controls should be adjusted whenever any substitute fuel is used by changing the specified gravity adjustment on these controls to correspond with the specific gravity value of the fuel selected. These values can be obtained from the above table. If a specific gravity range is given, the adjustment should be set to correspond with a mid-range value. The alternate fuels listed do not require a time limit on their use, but inconsistent engine starting can be expected at OAT less than 60°F. Theoretical studies indicate that engine can not be started with alternate fuels at OAT below −20°F.

1. Avoid flying at altitudes where indicated OAT is below the freeze point of the fuel.
2. Engine starts may be inconsistent when OAT is 60°F or less.
3. Prior to using commercial fuel obtain freeze point from vendor or airline supplying the fuel then follow the limit. If there is any indication of improper fuel handling procedures, a fuel sample should be taken in a glass container and observed for fogginess, presence of water or rust.
4. Average value limits are not controlled by specification.
5. JET-B-FUEL is an authorized alternate fuel. 7A JET-B-FUEL is an authorized emergency fuel. 3B The five-hour limitation and inspection requirements do not apply to 3B when the use of JET-B-FUEL is required.

Figure 2-9

emergency procedures

SECTION III

TABLE OF CONTENTS

EMERGENCY PROCEDURES (Continued)

TABLE OF CONTENTS (Continued)

APPROACH AND LANDING EMERGENCIES

Note

- Emergency Procedures are divided into critical and non-critical items.

  Critical—Those steps that must be performed immediately without reference to the checklist. These critical steps must be committed to memory and are printed in **BOLDFACE.**

  Non-critical—All other steps wherein there is time available to consult a checklist.

Note

- The meaning of Land As Soon As Possible and Land As Soon As Practicable, as used in this section is as follows:

  Land As Soon As Possible—Emergency conditions are urgent and require an immediate landing at the nearest adequate airfield.

  Land As Soon As Practicable—Emergency conditions are less urgent, and in the pilot's judgment, the degree of emergency may be such that an immediate landing at the nearest airfield is not necessary.

- To assure that a distinction is made between a Flameout Landing Pattern and a Precautionary Landing Pattern the following interpretations will be used in all references:

  Flameout Landing Pattern—An overhead approach designed to land the aircraft with engine failure. A *flameout landing will not be attempted unless escape from the aircraft is impossible.*

  Precautionary Landing Pattern (PLP)—A landing approach in which an emergency exists but for which engine response is still available for a power approach. The object of this pattern is to land the aircraft safely, in the minimum amount of time with the least amount of risk to the pilot. The pattern is normally a straight-in approach but may be modified as necessary by the pilot.

GROUND EMERGENCIES

EMERGENCY ENTRANCE.

The procedure to be used by rescue personnel in assisting the pilot from the aircraft following a crash landing is shown in figure 3-1.

EMERGENCY CANOPY REMOVAL.

In an emergency such as crash landing, the canopy may be opened or removed either by the flight crew or ground personnel as follows:

REMOVAL BY FLIGHT CREW.

The canopy may be removed by pulling the canopy jettison handle or opened by unlocking the canopy and opening it manually.

WARNING

- The canopy should not be jettisoned if fuel fumes are detected in the cockpit, because firing the canopy remover may ignite the fuel fumes.
- If the canopy cannot be jettisoned or opened manually use the canopy breaking tool depicted in figure 3-1 to break the glass and escape from the aircraft.

REMOVAL BY GROUND CREW.

The procedure for removing the canopy by the ground crew is illustrated by figure 3-1.

ENGINE FIRE DURING START.

Illumination of the fire warning lights or other evidence of fire during engine starting is an indication of a broken or disconnected fuel line. If this condition occurs proceed as follows:

1. **THROTTLE—OFF.**
2. Fuel shutoff switch—OFF.
3. Start switches—STOP-START.
4. Abandon aircraft as quickly as possible.

ENGINE FIRE AFTER SHUTDOWN.

1. Throttle OFF—Check.
2. Fuel shutoff switch—OFF.
3. Abandon aircraft as quickly as possible.

GROUND ABANDONMENT.

If rapid abandonment is required, proceed as follows:

1. Survival kit release handle – Pull or remove parachute harness.

Note

Pulling the survival kit release handle will free the pilot of the survival kit (including the lanyard) without inflating the life raft if the survival kit is in the seat bucket.

WARNING

- If it becomes necessary to open the survival kit on the ground, use the manual lid release lock button located aft of the left hand webbing adjuster. Care should be taken to keep all parts of the body away from the lid because the compressible mass of the kit and life raft may cause the lid to spring open, with enough force to cause injury.

2. Lap belt – Open manually.
3. Foot retractors cables – Disconnect.
4. If time is critical or fire exists, the canopy should be jettisoned.

WARNING 

When the forward cockpit internal canopy jettison handle is pulled, the forward canopy jettisons instantaneously. This has no effect on the aft cockpit jettison system. When the aft cockpit internal canopy jettison handle is pulled, the aft canopy jettisons 3 seconds later. This has no effect on the forward canopy jettison system.

5. If time is not of prime importance or no fire exists, the canopy should be opened manually.

EMERGENCY ENTRANCE

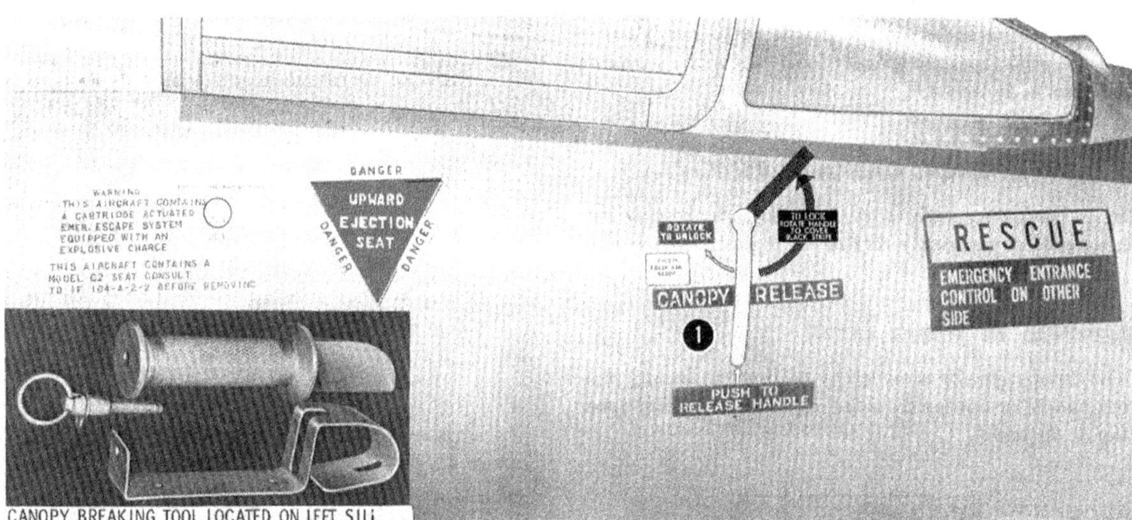
WARNING
THIS AIRCRAFT CONTAINS
A CARTRIDGE ACTUATED
EMER. ESCAPE SYSTEM
EQUIPPED WITH AN
EXPLOSIVE CHARGE
DANGER
UPWARD
EJECTION
SEAT
DANGER
DANGER
ROTATE TO UNLOCK
TO LOCK ROTATE HANDLE TO COVER BLACK STRIPE
CANOPY RELEASE
1
PUSH TO RELEASE HANDLE
RESCUE
EMERGENCY ENTRANCE CONTROL ON OTHER SIDE

CANOPY BREAKING TOOL LOCATED ON LEFT SILL

1 IF CANOPY IS LOCKED, UNLOCK BY ROTATING THE EXTERNAL LOCKING LEVER ❶, AFT AND OPEN CANOPY.

2 IF AIRCRAFT IS ON FIRE, JETTISON CANOPY BY PULLING CANOPY JETTISON "T" HANDLE ❷.

WARNING B D

WHEN THE "T" HANDLE IS PULLED, THE FORWARD CANOPY WILL JETTISON INSTANTANEOUSLY AND THE AFT CANOPY 3-SECONDS LATER.

3 CUT CATAPULT HOSE AND SEAT-MAN SEPARATOR, LOCATED BEHIND HEADREST (USE HEAVY DIAGONALS OR BOLT CUTTER.)

4 OPEN HELMET FACE PLATE BEFORE DISCONNECTING OXYGE LINE TO AVOID POSSIBLE SUFFOCATION OF PILOT.

5 SHUTOFF OXYGEN SUPPLY AT OXYGEN CONTROL PANEL.

6 INSTALL EJECTION RING SAFETY PIN TO PREVENT ACCIDENTAL FIRING OF PYROTECHNIC DEVICES.

7 RELEASE SEAT BELT AND SHOULDER HARNESS.

8 DISCONNECT PILOT'S PERSONAL LEADS.

9 DISCONNECT DROGUE-GUN ARMING CABLE (980 C/W).

10 PULL SURVIVAL KIT RELEASE HANDLE.

11 PULL MANUAL CABLE CUTTER RING.

12 REMOVE PILOT GENTLY TO AVOID AGGRAVATING POSSIBLE INTERNAL INJURIES.

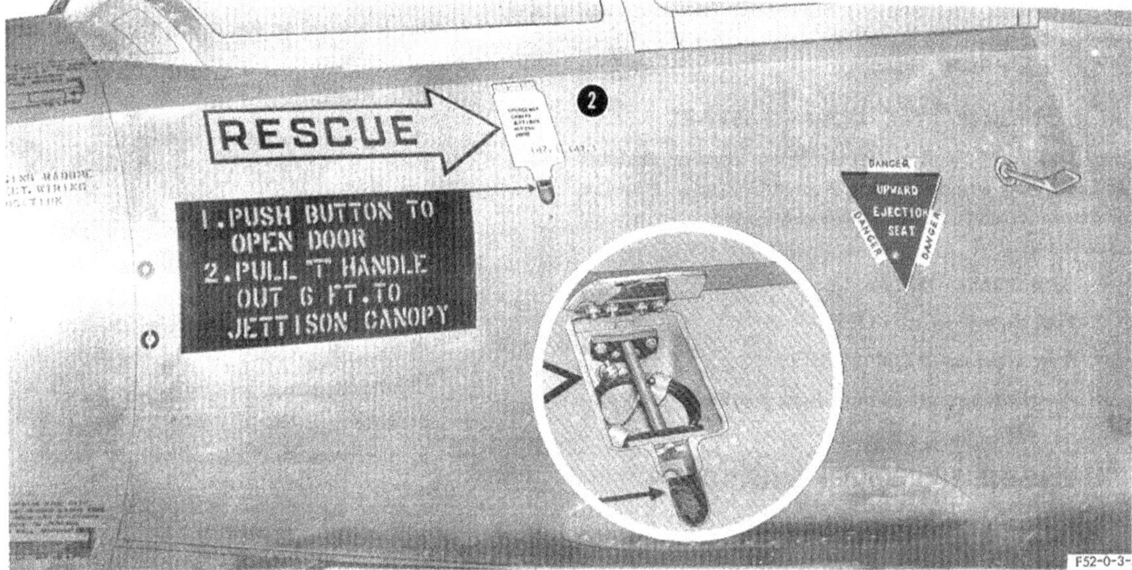
RESCUE
2
1.PUSH BUTTON TO
OPEN DOOR
2.PULL "T" HANDLE
OUT 6 FT.TO
JETTISON CANOPY
DANGER
UPWARD
EJECTION
SEAT
DANGER
DANGER
F52-0-3-

Figure 3-1

TAKEOFF EMERGENCIES

ABORT.

For aborted takeoff or barrier engagement after landing, accomplish those of the following steps necessary to stop aircraft. Refer to Table 1.

1. THROTTLE—IDLE (OFF FOR FIRE).

Note

Throttle off for fire, flat nosewheel tire, extreme nosewheel shimmy, or oil starvation, (conditions permitting). Nosewheel steering becomes inoperative with throttle off.

2. EXTERNAL LOAD—JETTISON (IF NECESSARY).

Retain stores if the aircraft can be safely stopped within the remaining runway. Refer to External Load Emergency Jettison paragraph in this section.

Note

- Jettisoned pylon tanks may strike the adjacent main landing gear but will not alter the course of the aircraft.
- Stores should be jettisoned prior to landing in those cases of a known emergency.
- Retain empty tip tanks if they are the only external store.

3. DRAG CHUTE—DEPLOY.

4. ARRESTING HOOK—EXTEND.

Arresting hook should be lowered at least 2000 feet from barrier if possible.

Note

Hook should be extended when engaging any type of barrier.

Contact barrier as close to a 90-degree angle as possible.

MAXIMUM BARRIER ENGAGEMENT SPEEDS

Design Hook Strength 60,000 Pounds

A/C Weight	*BAK-9*	*A/C G Load*	*BAK-12*	*A/C G Load*
14,000	188K	4.3	181K	4.3
16,000	186K	3.75	179K	3.75
18,000	184K	3.35	177K	3.35
20,000	182K	3.0	175K	3.0
22,000	180K	2.7	173K	2.7
24,000	178K	2.5	171K	2.5
26,000	176K	2.3	169K	2.3
28,000	174K	2.15	167K	2.15

Limiting Factor: Tailhook

Yield Hook Strength 69,000 Pounds

A/C Weight	*BAK-9*	*A/C G Load*	*BAK-12*	*A/C G Load*
14,000	190K*	4.4	190K*	4.85
16,000	190K*	4.0	189K**	4.3
18,000	190K*	3.65	187K**	3.85
20,000	190K*	3.35	185K**	3.45
22,000	190K*	3.15	181K**	3.15
24,000	188K**	2.85	179K**	2.85
26,000	186K**	2.65	177K**	2.65
28,000	184K**	2.45	175K**	2.45

Limiting Factor: *Barrier, **Tailhook

Table 1

TAKEOFF EMERGENCIES (Continued)

CAUTION

- Release brakes prior to engagement. A locked wheel, regardless of tire state, will snag or cut the BAK9 arresting hook cable.
- Throttle off, if engaging net type barrier, to prevent foreign object damage.

5. Throttle—OFF (if required, after fire crew confirms that no fire hazard exists from discharged fuel).

WARNING

- If one-gear engagement is made and aircraft becomes uncontrollable, throttle off and turn off fuel shutoff switch.
- Do not unfasten the lap belt or shoulder harness until the aircraft is stopped.

AFTERBURNER FAILURE DURING TAKEOFF.

Afterburner blowout is indicated by:

a. Nozzle position reading of less than 7.

b. An abnormally low EGT.

c. A definite loss of thrust.

If Decision Is Made To Stop:

1. **ABORT.**

If Takeoff Is Continued:

1. **THROTTLE—MILITARY.**
2. **EXTERNAL LOAD—JETTISON (IF NECESSARY).**
3. Continue takeoff at Military.

WARNING

Do not attempt an afterburner relight until attaining safe airspeed and altitude.

Note

Thrust available at throttle settings above minimum afterburner throttle position is less than Military if afterburner light does not occur.

Afterburner Surge.

Afterburner surge can easily be detected by unstable feel, exhaust gas temperature rise, and nozzle position indicator oscillation. If afterburner surge occurs, proceed as follows:

1. Throttle—Military.

Move throttle out of afterburner range as soon as possible, preferably before more than two cycles of surge.

WARNING

Compressor stall and flameout may occur if throttle is not moved out of afterburner range following afterburner surge.

2. Do not use afterburner unless necessary to maintain safe flight.

Note 

If afterburner is used, it should be recognized that afterburner surge normally occurs near the switchover point. An attempt should be made to select afterburner operation below or above this point.

CANOPY OPEN/LOSS/BROKEN DURING TAKEOFF.

If Decision Is Made To Stop:

1. **ABORT.**

If Takeoff Is Continued:

1. **CANOPY — JETTISON (IF FRAME IS NOT LOCKED).**
2. **THROTTLE—MAINTAIN SETTING.**
3. Climb to a safe ejection altitude leaving flaps at takeoff position.

TAKEOFF EMERGENCIES (Continued)

CAUTION

Do not change power setting. Throttle movement may precipitate an engine stall if engine has sustained foreign object damage. Engine stall may occur due to pressure changes accompanying afterburner throttling or shutdown, as well as in changing rpm.

4. Keep airspeed below 300 knots to minimize windblast and noise, use speed brakes as necessary.

5. External load—Jettison, if necessary.

6. Land as soon as practicable, using a precautionary pattern.

ENGINE FAILURE DURING TAKEOFF.

Engine failure is defined as complete power failure which, in the pilot's judgment, makes a restart impossible or inadvisable. Examples are engine seizure, explosion, etc.

If Decision Is Made To Stop:

1. **ABORT.**

If Takeoff Is Continued:

If conditions permit, eject rather than land on an unprepared surface.

1. **EXTERNAL LOAD—JETTISON.**

Note

Maximum altitude gain can be achieved by jettisoning stores prior to zoom. The later in the zoom the stores are jettisoned, the less additional altitude will be gained.

2. **ZOOM, IF POSSIBLE, AND EJECT.**

Note

If a decision is made to eject, the aircraft should be allowed to climb as far as possible. Eject while the nose of the aircraft is above the horizon, prior to reaching a stall or sink. Do not pull up too rapidly as the aircraft will stall before sufficient altitude has been gained, even though the initial airspeed seems to be adequate. At 240 knots indicated airspeed, it is possible to zoom nearly 400 feet with a dead engine.

ENGINE FIRE DURING TAKEOFF.

Illumination of the fire warning lights during takeoff requires immediate action. The exact procedure to follow varies with each set of circumstances and depends upon altitude, airspeed, length of runway and overrun clearing remaining, location of populated areas, etc. Perform the following procedures if possible:

If Decision Is Made To Stop:

1. **ABORT.**

If Takeoff Is Continued:

1. **THROTTLE—MAINTAIN SETTING TO SAFE EJECTION ALTITUDE.**

Note

At safe altitude, retarding throttle to Military, if appropriate, may be beneficial in eliminating fire.

2. **EXTERNAL LOAD—JETTISON (IF NECESSARY).**

3. **IF ON FIRE—EJECT.**

Confirm fire by any possible means such as report from ground, other aircraft, engine instruments, smoke in cockpit or visible smoke trail behind aircraft.

4. Fire warning lights—Test.

5. If fire cannot be confirmed, make decision to land or eject.

EXTERNAL LOAD EMERGENCY JETTISON.

To jettison the external stores (except the special weapon Ⓒ) during an emergency, use one of the following procedures:

1. External stores jettison button—Press.

Pressing the external stores jettison button jettisons pylon stores, tip stores, and fuselage-mounted AIM-9B missiles.

2. If stores fail to release, external stores release selector switch—As required.

3. External stores release button (bomb/rocket button)—Press.

Note

Refer to Section V for jettisoning airspeed limitations.

TAKEOFF EMERGENCIES (Continued)

SPECIAL WEAPON OR SUU-21 EMERGENCY JETTISON. Ⓒ

1. Special weapon droplock switch at READY—Press special weapon emergency jettison button.

Note

- The arming condition of the special weapon depends on the switch setting of the special weapon control and monitor panel.
- Refer to Section V for jettisoning airspeed limitations. The catamaran is not jettisonable.

LANDING GEAR LEVER DOWNLOCK MALFUNCTION.

Note

During any of the following landing gear procedures, lower flaps to takeoff position prior to reducing speed below 260 KIAS.

If the landing gear lever will not move to the UP position when airborne, proceed as follows:

1. Keep airspeed below 260 KIAS.
2. Landing gear lever override button—Press.
3. Landing gear lever—UP.

LANDING GEAR RETRACTION FAILURE.

If the landing gear warning light in the landing gear lever remains on after the lever has been placed in the UP position, proceed as follows:

1. Keep airspeed below 260 KIAS.
2. Recycle landing gear lever.

If Warning Light Remains On:

3. Recycle gear at lowest practical airspeed.
4. If warning light remains on, lower gear and land as soon as practicable.

NOSEWHEEL SHIMMY.

If Decision Is Made To Stop:

1. Nosewheel steering—Release.
2. Abort.
3. Hold weight off nose gear.
4. Throttle—IDLE or OFF (as necessary). If shimmy is severe, throttle OFF to prevent engine damage from debris if nose gear tire fails.
5. Drag chute—Deploy.
6. Brakes—Apply.

If Takeoff Is Continued:

1. Nosewheel steering—Release.
2. Retract gear immediately.
3. Throttle—Maintain setting to safe altitude.
4. Check for F.O.D. and indications of tripped circuit breakers in AC load center.

NOZZLE CONTROL SYSTEM FAILURE DURING TAKEOFF.

The following procedures are recommended in event of an exhaust nozzle control system failure.

Note

- Under any of the following exhaust nozzle emergency conditions, subsequent landing should be made with flaps at takeoff position. Also, landing gear should not be extended until on final approach and landing is assured.
- The landing roll distance will be increased with the exhaust nozzle closed because of the increased thrust at idle rpm and possible drag chute failure.

Nozzle Fails to Open Position During Afterburner Takeoff.

Indicated by:

a. A slight reduction in thrust.
b. EGT approximately 550°C.
c. An increase in nozzle area to approximately 10.

Failure will probably not be detected by the pilot. Afterburner will continue to operate provided throttle is not retarded. As long as full afterburning is maintained, immediate corrective action is not required.

TAKEOFF EMERGENCIES (Continued)

If Decision Is Made To Stop:

1. ABORT.

If Takeoff Is Continued:

1. MAINTAIN MAXIMUM AFTERBURNER AND ATTAIN SAFE ALTITUDE.

Sufficient thrust will be available with full afterburning to climb to a safe altitude and establish a position from which a safe landing with an open nozzle can be accomplished.

2. Accomplish Nozzle Fails to Open Position During Flight procedures.

Nozzle Fails to Open Position During Military Thrust Takeoff.

Indicated by:

a. Significant thrust decrease.

b. EGT approximately 350°C. Sufficient thrust, probably, is not available to complete takeoff or maintain level flight with any configuration.

c. An increase in nozzle area to approximately 10.

If Decision Is Made To Stop:

1. ABORT.

If Takeoff Is Continued:

1. NOZZLE SWITCH—MANUAL 3B **. NOZZLE HANDLE—PULL** 19 7A **.**

2. EXTERNAL LOAD—JETTISON (IF NECESSARY).

If Nozzle Does Not Close:

3. THROTTLE—MAXIMUM AFTERBURNER (use rapid movement of throttle and if afterburner light is obtained, return nozzle handle to **IN** 19 7A or nozzle switch to **AUTO** 3B).

4. IF NO AFTERBURNER LIGHT IS OBTAINED—EJECT.

WARNING

During afterburner operation with nozzle failed to open position, reducing the throttle below full afterburner will cause afterburner blowout. Throttle should remain in maximum afterburner until landing is assured.

5. Land, using a precautionary pattern or land with maximum afterburner.

TIRE FAILURE DURING TAKEOFF.

The following procedure is recommended when a tire fails during takeoff run. The recommended technique applies to all gross weights and airplane configurations. Directional control of the airplane becomes more difficult as airplane gross weight increases. With main gear tire failure and less than 150 knots, an abort is recommended.

If Decision Is Made To Stop:

1. ABORT.

If Takeoff is Continued:

1. EXTERNAL LOAD—JETTISON (IF NECESSARY).

2. WITH NOSE GEAR TIRE FAILURE—RETRACT GEAR IMMEDIATELY AFTER AIRBORNE AND CLIMB TO SAFE EJECTION ALTITUDE AT MAXIMUM AFTERBURNER.

3. WITH MAIN GEAR TIRE FAILURE—LEAVE GEAR EXTENDED AND CLIMB TO SAFE EJECTION ALTITUDE AT MAXIMUM AFTERBURNER.

WARNING

- With nose gear tire failure, retract gear immediately after airborne as engine may be subjected to foreign object damage. Climb to safe ejection altitude at maximum afterburner. Make subsequent landing in accordance with Nose Gear Flat Tire Landing procedure.
- With main gear tire failure, do not retract gear until failed tire has been checked for fire by another airplane or the tower. If no fire is evident, and the priority of the mission dictates the gear be retracted, apply wheel brakes prior to retracting gear to prevent tire fragment damage to equipment in wheel well. Make subsequent landing in accordance with Main Gear Flat Tire Landing procedure.

IN-FLIGHT EMERGENCIES

AIR START.

If a flameout has occurred, an air start may be made using the following procedure:

1. START SWITCHES — START (hold momentarily to ensure switch contact).

Monitor engine instruments for immediate relight if engine rpm is still high. An increase of EGT is the primary indication of an air start.

2. IF RELIGHT IS NOT OBTAINED OR RPM HANGUP OCCURS, THROTTLE OFF AND RETURN TO MILITARY, START SWITCHES—START.

Note

Establish best glide speed and head aircraft toward nearest suitable landing field.

3. IF NO START OCCURS, RAT HANDLE — PULL, START SWITCHES—START.

Note

- During the second start attempt, do not move throttle to OFF prior to actuating the start switches.
- Do not extend RAT above 35,000 unless electrical or hydraulic power is required. The chances of obtaining normal engine operation are remote and the increased drag will reduce glide speed.
- Allow engine instruments to stabilize and adjust throttle to settings necessary for flight. Engine instruments will give the most reliable indication of a relight.

AUTO-PITCH CONTROL SYSTEM FAILURE.

If the APC system fails (as indicated by illumination of the AUTO PITCH OUT warning light) or malfunctions in any way, such as giving repeated or unreleased kicks under low angle of attack flight conditions, proceed as follows:

1. APC cutout switch—OFF.
2. Observe stick shaker boundary as kicker will be inoperative.

Stick Shaker Failure.

1. Stick shaker circuit breaker—Pull.

If the stick shaker circuit breaker is pulled to deactivate the stick shaker for any reason, the AUTO PITCH OUT warning light will illuminate. Thus, further indication of APC kicker malfunction will be lost. When the stick shaker circuit breaker has been pulled, continue as follows:

2. APC switch—OFF.
3. Exercise extreme care to avoid abrupt maneuvers, low airspeeds, or any maneuver that requires operating at high angles of attack.

BLEED AIR DUCT SEPARATION.

If fire warning lights illuminate during flight and there are no other indications of fire, a possible cause is leakage of hot compressor air from BLC or other bleed air ducts into the engine compartment where it can impinge against the fire warning detectors. One indication of this type of failure is the lights are likely to go out after a minute or two of operation at IDLE rpm, because retarding the throttle reduces the volume and temperature of compressor bleed air. Further indications of this type of failure depend on the location of the leak and may include loss of cockpit pressurization, T_2 reset actuation 3B 7A, rpm reset actuation 19, and a severe rolloff tendency when the flaps are moved to the LAND position. The rolloff tendency is an indication of BLC duct separation on one side resulting in asymmetric BLC airflow; therefore, it affords a means of checking for BLC duct separation at a safe altitude and airspeed (240 KIAS maximum). T_2 reset actuation 3B 7A, may occur if duct failure permits hot compressor air to contact the CIT sensor. In this case, the rpm could increase to 104 percent and remain in the reset range T_2 3B 7A, rpm reset range 19, regardless of throttle position. (During T_2 reset operation 3B 7A, rpm reset operation 19, retarding the throttle below Military will not reduce rpm, but will reduce thrust because the exhaust nozzle will open.) If the fire warning lights illuminate without other indications of fire and BLC or bleed air duct separation is indicated, proceed as follows:

IN-FLIGHT EMERGENCIES (Continued)

WARNING

If a BLC duct separation is indicated, do not place the wing flap lever to the LAND position in the landing pattern because this may result in a severe rolloff due to asymmetric airflow over the flaps.

1. Land as soon as possible, continually checking for fire. Make a takeoff flap landing if BLC duct separation is indicated.

CANOPY OPEN/LOSS/BROKEN DURING FLIGHT.

1. Canopy—JETTISON (if frame is not locked).
2. Attain safe ejection altitude.
3. Slow the aircraft to 300 knots IAS or less to minimize windblast and noise.
4. External load—Jettison (if necessary).
5. Land as soon as practicable, using precautionary pattern.

WARNING

- In any case of loss, opening or broken canopy, the engine may sustain foreign object damage. Therefore, be prepared to follow engine stall clearing procedure.
- Loss of canopy in supersonic flight may cause sufficient pressure change at engine inlet ducts to cause compressor stall or engine flameout. Foreign object damage may not be involved. Therefore, stall clearing or air start procedures should be performed as applicable.

COCKPIT PRESSURIZATION MALFUNCTION.

Separation of the hot air duct at the refrigerator inlet can cause a loss of cockpit pressurization, damage to wiring, and subsequent failure of the electrical system. The electrical system failure can occur within a few minutes from hot compressor air melting the insulation on the wiring in the electrical compartment located behind the cockpit. If the fresh air scoop is opened promptly after the cockpit pressure loss is recognized, the bleed air shutoff valve will shut off the hot air and prevent failure of the electrical system. If cockpit pressurization reduces substantially and the cause is not apparent, proceed as follows:

1. Start immediate descent to 25,000 feet (or lower if circumstances permit).
2. Fresh air scoop lever—OPEN.

Open fresh air scoop as soon as practicable, depending on pressurization and altitude. If complete pressure loss is experienced or if at a safe flight level for depressurization, open fresh air scoop immediately.

3. If using oxygen mask adjust regulator as necessary.

COMPRESSOR STALLS.

Refer to Engine Compressor Stalls in Section I for additional information.

Below 15,000 Feet.

1. **THROTTLE—OFF.**
2. **START SWITCHES—START.**
3. **RPM — 70 PERCENT 19 7A, 60 PERCENT 3B OR BELOW.**
4. **THROTTLE—RAPIDLY TO MILITARY.**
5. Monitor rpm to 100 percent 3B 7A, Military 19. Land as soon as practicable using a precautionary landing pattern. Do not decrease rpm below 97 percent 3B 7A, or Military, 19 until landing is assured.

IN-FLIGHT EMERGENCIES (Continued)

WARNING

If a flameout, engine stall, or substantial power loss occurs in the landing pattern (with either VFR or IFR conditions) after the final landing configuration has been established, immediate ejection is essential. See figure 3-3 for minimum safe ejection altitudes–airspeed versus dive angle.

6. If an rpm hangup occurs, IGV Switch–MAN. 3B or land as soon as practicable adjusting power as necessary 19 7A . With an rpm hangup at 94 percent 3B 7A or 90 percent 19 , a cold shift IGV stall has occurred.

Note 3B

- Positioning the IGV switch to manual will not clear any stall. If the IGV switch has been moved to the MAN position, and the capability of accelerating to 100 percent rpm is no longer required, the throttle may be retarded on final approach to control airspeed. Cold-shift stall will not recur with the IGV switch in MAN.
- Maximum available thrust will be equal to or greater than that obtained at 90 percent 19 , 94 percent 7A under normal conditions. Throttle may be manipulated throughout the entire IDLE to Military range. Afterburner operation may be initiated for emergency use if CIT indicates +38°C or less.

Above 15,000 Feet.

1. Throttle–Military.
2. Throttle–IDLE (check for abnormal EGT and rpm for possible hangup).
3. If stall persists, use procedure for below 15,000 feet.

EJECTION.

The basic ejection procedure is shown in figure 3-2.

WARNING

- Pull ejection ring straight up to preclude binding.
- Under no circumstances should the ejection ring be safety wired.
- Simultaneous ejection should be avoided when possible, to prevent chute entanglement.

Ejection Versus Flameout Landing.

Landing with the engine inoperative will not be attempted unless escape from the aircraft is impossible.

Ejection Altitudes.

Whenever ejection is necessary, the aircraft should be maneuvered to an erect, nose-up, wings level attitude if possible.

The following information should be considered when ejection is imminent.

a. Under level flight conditions, eject at least 2000 feet above the terrain whenever possible.

b. Under spin conditions, if rotation has not stopped, eject at least 15,000 feet above the terrain whenever possible.

WARNING

Do not delay ejection below 2000 feet in a futile attempt to start the engine or for other reasons that may commit you to an unsafe ejection or a dangerous flameout landing. Accident statistics emphatically show a progressive decrease in successful ejections as altitude decreases below 2000 feet.

c. Refer to figure 3-3 for Minimum Safe Ejection Altitudes, Airspeed vs Dive Angle (980 N/C/W).

EJECTION PROCEDURE

BEFORE EJECTION

(IF TIME AND CONDITIONS PERMIT)

WARNING

NEVER OPEN THE SEAT BELT PRIOR TO EJECTION REGARDLESS OF ALTITUDE

1 ADVISE OTHER OCCUPANT OF DECISION TO EJECT B D

WARNING B D

OCCUPANT OF AFT SEAT SHOULD EJECT FIRST TO PREVENT INJURY BY COLLISION WITH FORWARD CANOPY OR BY EFFECTS OF FORWARD SEAT ROCKET BLAST. IF PILOT IN FORWARD SEAT SHOULD EJECT FIRST, DO NOT JETTISON AFT CANOPY UNTIL ROCKET FLAME FROM FORWARD SEAT IS OBSERVED. IF A MINIMUM ALTITUDE EJECTION IS REQUIRED FROM THE AFT SEAT, DO NOT ATTEMPT TO JETTISON CANOPY USING THE CANOPY JETTISON HANDLE BECAUSE OF THE 3 SECOND TIME DELAY BUILT INTO THE AFT CANOPY MANUAL JETTISON SYSTEM

2 REDUCE SPEED AS MUCH AS POSSIBLE

3 HEAD AIRCRAFT TOWARD UNPOPULATED AREA

4 GIVE LOCATION AND INTENTIONS TO NEAREST RADIO FACILITY AND TURN IFF TO EMERGENCY

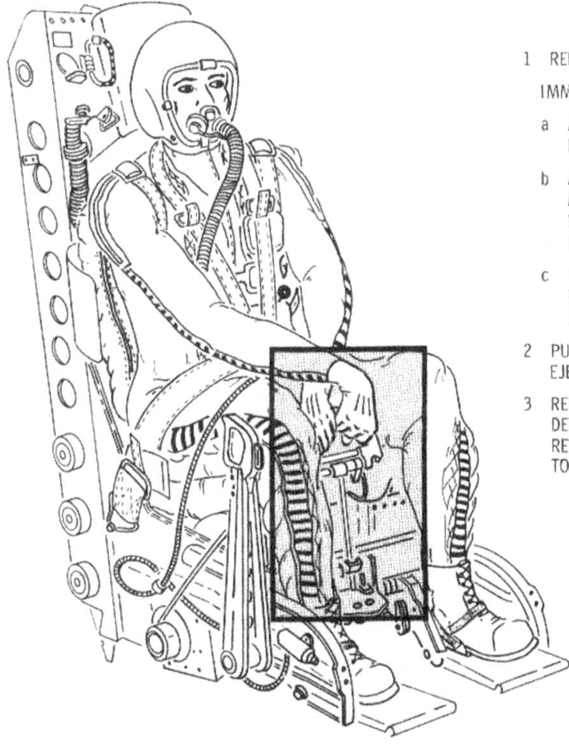

F52-0-3-30

5 EMERGENCY NOZZLE CLOSURE HANDLE IN - CHECK

6 LOWER VISOR

7 ACTUATE BAILOUT BOTTLE IF USING A-13A MASK

8 SIT BACK IN SEAT. CHECK SEAT BELT AND SHOULDER HARNESS - TIGHT

9 OXYGEN MASK - TIGHTEN

10 CHIN STRAP FASTENED - CHECK

11 CANOPY JETTISON HANDLE - PULL

EJECTION

1. ASSUME EJECTION POSITION
2. PULL EJECTION RING WITH BOTH HANDS

- A SLIGHT DELAY WILL BE EXPERIENCED FROM THE TIME THE EJECTION RING IS PULLED UNTIL EJECTION OCCURS
- IN THE EVENT THE CANOPY FAILS TO JETTISON, EITHER MANUALLY OR AUTOMATICALLY, THE PILOT CAN EJECT THROUGH THE CANOPY

FAILURE OF SEAT TO EJECT

1 FEET IN STIRRUPS - CHECK

2 BRING HEAD BACK TO HEADREST

3 EJECTION RING-PULL AGAIN THROUGH MAXIMUM TRAVEL

AFTER EJECTION

1 RELEASE EJECTION RING

IMMEDIATELY AFTER EJECTION

a ATTEMPT TO OPEN THE SEAT BELT. THE AUTOMATIC ACTION WILL HAVE OPERATED IF THE SYSTEM IS FUNCTIONING NORMALLY

b AS SOON AS THE SEAT BELT RELEASES, A DETERMINED EFFORT MUST BE MADE TO SEPARATE FROM THE SEAT TO OBTAIN FULL PARACHUTE DEPLOYMENT AT MAXIMUM TERRAIN CLEARANCE. **THIS IS EXTREMELY IMPORTANT FOR LOW-ALTITUDE EJECTIONS**

c IF THE BELT IS MANUALLY OPENED (ELIMINATING THE AUTOMATIC PARACHUTE FEATURE) PULL PARACHUTE ARMING LANYARD IF ABOVE 14,000 FEET. PULL D-RING FOR ALL EJECTIONS BELOW 14,000 FEET

2 PULL D-RING IMMEDIATELY FOLLOWING SEAT SEPARATION FOR ALL EJECTIONS BELOW 14,000 FEET

3 RELEASE SURVIVAL KIT RELEASE AFTER PARACHUTE IS FULLY DEPLOYED AND HAS STABILIZED, BY GRASPING THE YELLOW RELEASE HANDLE AND PULLING SHARPLY UPWARD AND BACKWARD TO SEPARATE THE HANDLE FROM THE SEAT

WARNING

- RELEASING SURVIVAL KIT DISCONNECTS EMERGENCY OXYGEN. THEREFORE DO NOT RELEASE KIT ABOVE 14,000 FEET
- RELEASE OF THE SURVIVAL KIT PRIOR TO THE TIME THE PARACHUTE STABILIZES MAY CAUSE THE SURVIVAL KIT OR ATTACHING DROP LINE TO FOUL THE PARACHUTE
- THE RELEASE HANDLE MUST BE PULLED RAPIDLY THROUGH THE COMPLETE ARC OF TRAVEL TO ALLOW PROPER FUNCTIONING OF THE SURVIVAL KIT SYSTEM. FAILURE TO FOLLOW THIS PROCEDURE WILL RESULT IN MALFUNCTION OF THE KIT AND COULD PRESENT A SERIOUS HAZARD TO THE PILOT DURING PARACHUTE LANDING

Figure 3-2

IN-FLIGHT EMERGENCIES (Continued)

Low Altitude Ejections.

During any low altitude ejection, the chances for successful ejection can be greatly increased by zooming the aircraft (if airspeed permits) to exchange airspeed for altitude. Zoom should not exceed 20 degrees nose up attitude. Ejection should be accomplished while the aircraft is in a positive climb and airspeed is above 120 knots; this will result in a more nearly vertical trajectory for the seat and crewmember, thus providing more altitude and time for seat separation and parachute deployment.

Emergency minimum ejection altitudes (980 N/C/W) and using the C-2 rocket catapult seat, the B-15 or -18 back pack parachute at 120 knots minimum are as follows:

Zero delay lanyard connected–Zero feet terrain clearance.

Zero delay lanyard not connected using F-1B timer–125 feet terrain clearance.

Aircraft With 980 C/W. When the canopy is jettisoned as a part of the ejection sequence, ground level escape capability requires a minimum speed of 60 knots. When the canopy is jettisoned manually prior to seat ejection, zero-speed, zero-altitude capability is provided.

Ground level escape capability at high speed is limited to approximately 400 KIAS. At speeds greater than 400 KIAS, an altitude of 50 feet or more must be attained to provide the necessary time/altitude required for proper parachute deployment.

WARNING

Emergency minimum ejection altitudes quoted above were determined through extensive flight tests and are based on distance above terrain on initiation of seat ejection (i.e., time seat is fired). These figures do not provide any safety factor for such matters as equipment malfunction, delays in separating from the seat, etc. These figures are quoted only to show the minimum altitude you must *go up to* in the event of such low altitude emergencies as fire on take-off. *They shall not be used as the basis for delaying ejection when above 2000 feet since accident statistics emphatically show a progressive decrease in successful ejections as altitude decreases below 2000 feet.*

ZERO-DELAY LANYARD CONNECTION REQUIREMENT. (980 N/C/W)

The zero-delay parachute lanyard will be connected and disconnected as follows:

a. Connected prior to takeoff.

b. Leave connected at all times below 10,000 feet pressure altitude including flights in which 10,000 feet may be temporarily exceeded.

c. Disconnect when passing through 10,000 feet pressure altitude when this altitude will be exceeded for prolonged periods.

d. Connect prior to initial penetration or at 10,000 feet pressure altitude during en route descent.

Note

If operating above terrain over 8,000 feet in elevation, the zero-delay lanyard should be connected whenever terrain clearance is 2000 feet or less.

When ejecting under completely controlled conditions above 2000 feet AGL, disconnect the Zero Delay Lanyard.

WARNING

Do not attempt to connect Zero Delay Lanyard, if not connected, when ejecting. Time lost in trying to connect may be greater than any time gained by the one second shorter chute opening feature provided with the Zero Delay Lanyard connected.

MINIMUM SAFE EJECTION ALTITUDES

AIRSPEED VS DIVE ANGLE

980 N/C/W

NOTE

CURVES ARE FOR AN ANGLE OF ATTACK OF 2 DEG. 13 MIN.

ALL CURVES ARE PREDICATED UPON NORMAL FUNCTIONING OF ALL COMPONENTS OF THE ESCAPE AND RECOVERY SYSTEMS.

ANY EJECTION AT OVER 550 KNOTS IS IN THE GRAY AREA OF THE SYSTEM, WHERE SUCCESS DEPENDS ON THE USE OF A PARACHUTE SYSTEM CAPABLE OF PROPER FUNCTIONING AT THESE SPEEDS.

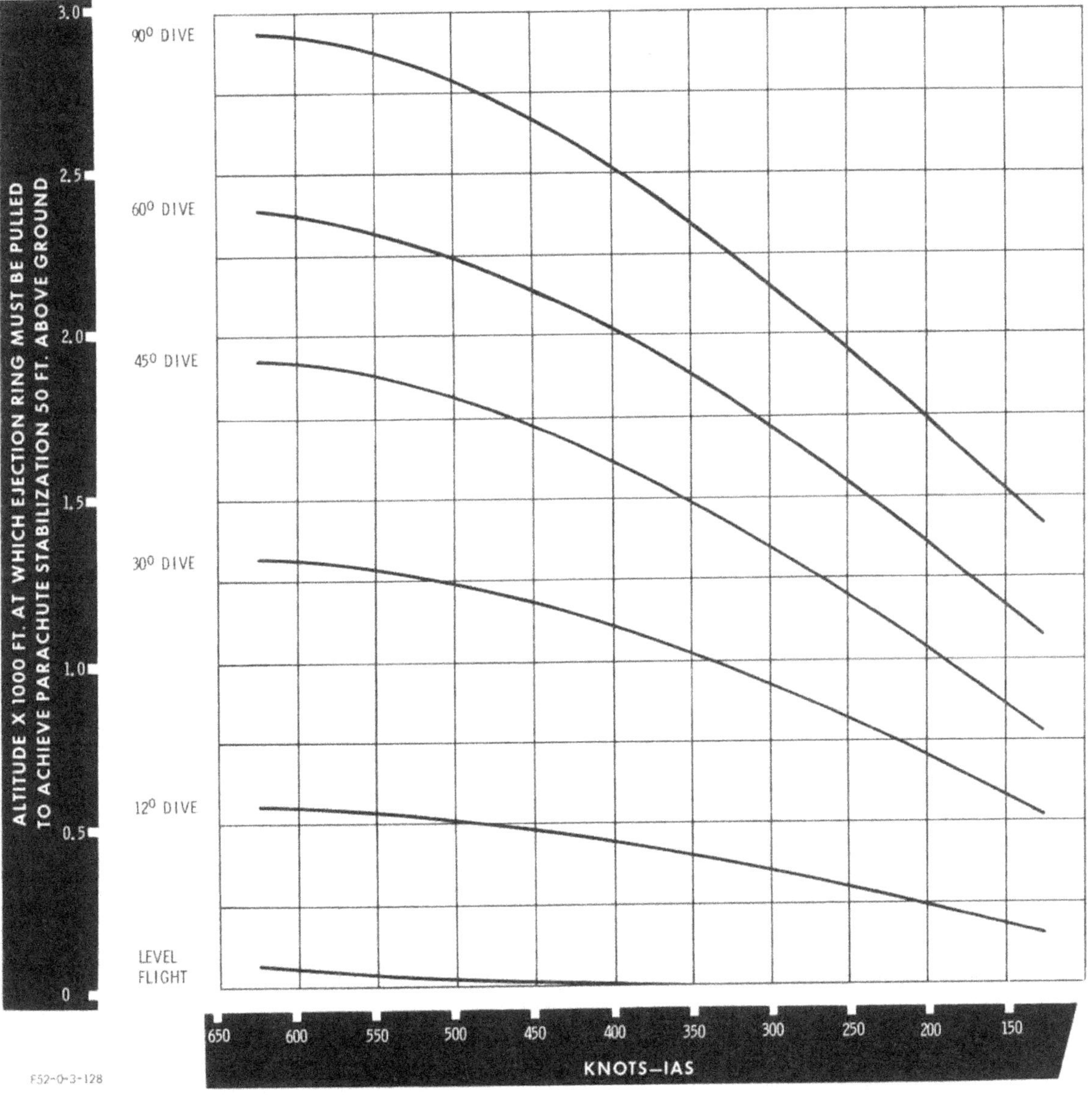

Figure 3-3

IN-FLIGHT EMERGENCIES (Continued)

Ejection Speed.

Eject at the lowest practicable airspeed ("lowest practicable" would be that speed below which level flight cannot be maintained). Below 120 knots IAS, airflow is not sufficient to ensure rapid parachute deployment (980 N/C/W). Therefore, it becomes extremely important during low-altitude ejection to obtain at least minimum required airspeed to ensure complete parachute deployment at the greatest height above the terrain. During high-altitude ejection, observing this minimum airspeed becomes less important since there is adequate time (in the form of altitude) for parachute deployment. The need to be at the lowest possible airspeed prior to ejection is predicated on many factors, such as avoiding bodily injury, avoiding parachute or seat structural failure, and providing adequate tail clearance. Complete coverage of maximum safe airspeeds for ejection would require a complex chart because of the many factors involved and because the limiting airspeeds vary with altitude and Mach number. The chart would be very difficult to commit to memory. Actually, there is no need to quote maximum airspeeds since the ejecting crewmember has no practical use for this information. If the aircraft is controllable, airspeed will be reduced to a minimum. If the aircraft is not controllable, ejection must be accomplished at whatever speed exists at the time since ejection offers the only opportunity for survival. As a matter of general interest, it may be well to point out that at sea level, wind blast will exert only minor forces on the body up to 525 knots IAS, appreciable forces from 525 to 600 knots IAS, and excessive forces above 600 knots IAS. As altitude is increased, these speeds become progressively less. In view of the preceding, a detailed presentation of maximum safe airspeeds for ejection would be purely academic and inclusion in this manual is not warranted.

WARNING

Under no circumstance should a zero altitude ejection be attempted below 120 knots since in all probability parachute deployment will be unsuccessful. On aircraft modified by T.O. 980, ejection should not be attempted at less than 60 knots unless the canopy has been previously jettisoned.

SMOKE OR FUMES IN COCKPIT.

If smoke or fumes enter the cockpit proceed as follows:

1. **OXYGEN DILUTER LEVER—100%.**
2. Descend to 25,000 feet or lower if circumstances permit.
3. Fresh air scoop lever—OPEN.
4. Generator switches—OFF.
5. If smoke persists, land as soon as possible. Jettison canopy if necessary.
6. If it can be determined that the smoke is caused by an electrical fire, use Electrical Fire procedures; otherwise, reset generators.

Note

If oil fumes enter the cockpit, refer to Oil System Malfunction in this section.

ELECTRICAL FIRE.

Circuit breakers and fuses protect most of the circuits and tend to prevent electrical fires; however, if electrical fire does occur, proceed as follows:

1. Oxygen diluter lever—100%.
2. Generator switches—OFF.

Note

Cockpit pressurization will be lost when the generator switches are turned OFF.

3. All electrical accessory switches—OFF.
4. Operate only those units necessary for safe flight and landing by resetting the generators.
5. Return generator switches to OFF position when operation is complete.
6. Land as soon as practicable.

IN-FLIGHT EMERGENCIES (Continued)

ELECTRICAL SYSTEM FAILURE.

COMPLETE ELECTRICAL SYSTEM FAILURE.

If a complete electrical failure occurs, (which includes failure of both engine driven generators and the ram air turbine-driven generator) only those items powered by the battery bus will be operable. Battery power should be available for a minimum of 30 minutes (see figure 1-39). Flight under these conditions is limited, and the following procedure should be applied:

1. Oxygen lever—EMERGENCY.

Note

Without electric power, cockpit pressure is dumped.

2. Land as soon as practicable.
3. Use manual landing gear release handle to lower landing gear.
4. Use Flap Failure procedure. (It will be impossible to lower the wing flaps.)

Note

Under the above conditions of complete electrical failure, all the instruments except the tachometer, exhaust gas temperature gage, airspeed and Mach number indicator, accelerometer, clock, altimeter, cabin altimeter, and vertical velocity indicator, will be inoperative.

GENERATOR FAILURE.

No. 1 or No. 2 Generator Out.

If NO. 1 GENERATOR OUT or NO. 2 GENERATOR OUT warning light illuminates, do the following:

1. Move corresponding generator switch to OFF, then to ON-RESET and release.

This will restore generator to service if failure was caused by momentary overvoltage.

Both Generators Out.

1. Both generators—ON-RESET.
2. If electrical power is not restored, No. 2 Generator switch—OFF.
3. If failure is not remedied No. 2 generator switch—ON-RESET.
4. No. 1 generator switch—OFF.

Note

Leaving one of the two generator switches in the OFF position should activate the bus transfer system and allow the other generator to assume the entire load.

5. If generator operation is not restored and electrical power is required extend RAT.

Note

When using the RAT for electrical power, all units powered from the dc emergency bus will be inoperative during the period of wing flap operation.

DC MONITORED BUS FAILURE.

If the DC MONITORED BUS OUT warning light illuminates, the INST ON EMER POWER light will also illuminate, and the flight should be aborted. See figure 1-39 for a list of systems rendered inoperative with the dc monitored bus out.

Note

Illumination of the DC MONITORED BUS OUT and the INST ON EMER POWER warning lights may also indicate automatic bus transfer failure. In this case the No. 1 generator switch should be moved to OFF to activate the bus transfer system and allow the No. 2 generator to assume the entire load.

ENGINE FAILURE DURING FLIGHT.

Note

Engine failure is defined as a complete power failure which, in the pilot's judgment, makes it impossible or inadvisable to attempt a new start. Examples are engine seizure, explosion, etc. Landing with the engine inoperative will not be attempted unless escape from the aircraft is impossible.

IN-FLIGHT EMERGENCIES (Continued)

If complete loss of thrust occurs, and an airstart is inadvisable or unsuccessful proceed as follows:

1. Throttle—OFF.
2. Rat handle—PULL.
3. Wing flap lever—TAKEOFF.
4. Glide speed—245 knots.
5. IFF—EMERGENCY.
6. Radio—Advise.
7. Eject.

Note

When the decision to eject is made, the pilot should first attempt to head the aircraft toward an area where injury or damage to persons or property on the ground or water is least likely to occur.

WARNING

If a flameout, engine stall, or substantial power loss occurs in the landing pattern (with either VFR or IFR conditions) after the final landing configuration has been established, immediate ejection is essential. See figure 3-3 for minimum safe ejection altitudes—airspeed versus dive angle.

ENGINE FIRE DURING FLIGHT.

1. THROTTLE—MINIMUM PRACTICABLE POWER.

2. IF ON FIRE—EJECT.

Confirm fire by any possible means such as report from other aircraft, engine instruments, smoke in cockpit or visible smoke trail behind aircraft.

3. Fire warning lights—Test.
4. If fire cannot be confirmed—Land as soon as practicable continually checking for fire.

EXTERNAL LOAD EMERGENCY JETTISON.

To jettison the external stores (except the special weapon **C**) during an emergency, use one of the following procedures:

1. External stores jettison button—Press.

Pressing the external stores jettison button jettisons pylon stores, tip stores, and fuselage-mounted AIM-9B missiles.

2. If stores fail to release, external stores release selector switch—As required.
3. External stores release button (bomb/rocket button)—Press.

Note

Refer to Section V for jettisoning airspeed limitations.

SPECIAL WEAPON OR SUU-21A EMERGENCY JETTISON. C

1. Special weapon droplock switch at READY—Press special weapon emergency jettison button.

Note

The arming condition of the special weapon depends on the switch settings of the special weapon control and monitor panel.

Refer to Section V for jettisoning airspeed limitations. The catamaran is not jettisonable.

FUEL SYSTEM FAILURE.

AIRCRAFT FUEL SYSTEM. A B

If the boost pump failure warning light (**A** aircraft prior to AF Serial 56-878) illuminates, avoid steep nose-down attitudes which may starve the aft pumps of fuel. Abort the mission and land.

Note

- Any one of the boost pumps will furnish sufficient fuel pressure for engine operation as long as the pump is submerged in fuel.
- Fuel may be trapped in the auxiliary fuel cell **A** due to failure of the transfer pump. Fuel quantity gage will indicate correctly the total fuel available for flight.

IN-FLIGHT EMERGENCIES (Continued)

Failure of the fuel air shut-off valve in the tip or pylon tanks may result in pressurization of the main fuel cell. This pressurization may cause the flapper valves between the main and aft fuel cells to close. Therefore, fuel rmaining in the aft fuel cells will be trapped and the engine can flame out after main fuel is consumed even though total fuel remaining is indicated to be adequate. If the fuel low-level warning light illuminates and total fuel remaining exceeds 1525 pounds, proceed as follows:

1. Fuel quantity indicator—TEST.

2. External tanks fuel selector switch—OFF.

Switching to the OFF position may relieve the pressure in the main fuel tank.

3. Airspeed—Reduce.

Extend speed brakes and retard throttle.

4. Apply positive G load to aircraft.

5. Fuel low-level warning light—Check.

a. If light goes out, check warning light test circuit. If circuit test is satisfactory, continue mission.

b. If light does not go out or does not test correctly, land immediately.

6. External Tanks – Jettison if immediate landing is impossible.

Jettison external fuel tanks when extended flight will require the use of more than 1000 pounds of fuel from the time low-level warning light illuminates. This action should depressurize the main fuel cell, allowing aft main fuel to flow into main tank.

7. Land as soon as practicable.

EXTERNAL FUEL TRANSFER FAILURE. CD

1. EXT TANK FUEL TRANS circuit breaker—Pull.

2. Reset circuit breaker after affected tanks are empty. When tip and pylon tanks are both installed, it is impossible to transfer fuel from the tip tanks until the pylon tanks are empty. If fuel fails to transfer from the pylon tanks, pulling the EXT TANK FUEL TRANS circuit breaker on the left console deenergizes the circuit to the transfer valves which will allow them to open and fuel to transfer. If this fails to correct the malfunction, it may be necessary to jettison the pylon tanks in order to transfer fuel from the tip tanks. If carrying tip tanks only, and fuel fails to transfer, pulling the EXT TANK FUEL TRANS circuit breaker allows the transfer valves to open and the fuel to transfer. In either case reset the circuit breaker after the fuel has transferred from the affected tanks.

HYDRAULIC SYSTEM FAILURE.

NO. 1 SYSTEM FAILURE.

If the No. 1 hydraulic system fails, as indicated by the HYD SYSTEM OUT and AUTO PITCH OUT warning lights, the stick trim and yaw damper will be inoperative but the stick shaker and auxiliary trim will be operative. If this failure occurs, proceed as follows:

1. Trim selector switch—AUX TRIM.

2. Hydraulic system pressure gage—Monitor No. 2 pressure for remainder of flight.

NO. 2 SYSTEM FAILURE.

WARNING

Close speed brakes if a hydraulic failure is imminent. Without No. 2 hydraulic system pressure the speed brakes cannot be closed.

Failure of the No. 2 system will render the pitch and roll dampers inoperative as well as those items operated by the utility hydraulic system. If a No. 2 system failure is experienced, as indicated by the illumination of the HYD SYSTEM OUT warning light, proceed as follows:

1. Hydraulic system pressure gage—Monitor No. 1 pressure for remainder of flight.

2. Land as soon as practicable. Extend the gear with the manual landing gear release handle.

Note

Nosewheel steering is inoperative with No. 2 system out or when gear is extended by the manual landing gear release handle.

IN-FLIGHT EMERGENCIES (Continued)

NO. 1 AND NO. 2 SYSTEMS FAILURE.

WARNING

Close speed brakes if a hydraulic failure is imminent. Without No. 2 hydraulic system pressure the speed brakes cannot be closed.

1. RAT extension handle—Pull above minimum recommended airspeed.

(Refer to Flight With RAT Extended paragraph.)

2. Hydraulic system pressure gage – Monitor No. 1 pressure.

3. If pressure builds up, land as soon as practicable. Continue to monitor pressure and extend landing gear with manual landing gear release handle.

Note

Maximum hydraulic flow available under these conditions is reduced; however, it is sufficiently high for safe flight and the moderate maneuvers necessary for landing.

4. If pressure fails to increase sufficiently for adequate flight control response—Eject.

Note

Aircraft may be steered toward selected ejection area, using power and rudder.

NOZZLE CONTROL SYSTEM FAILURE.

The following procedures are recommended in event of an exhaust nozzle control system failure.

Note

- Under any of the following exhaust nozzle emergency conditions, subsequent landing should be made with flaps at takeoff position. Also, landing gear should not be extended until on final approach and landing is assured.
- The landing roll distance will be increased with the exhaust nozzle closed because of the increased thrust and possible drag chute failure. Therefore, (if aerodynamic loads permit) the nozzle closure handle should be pushed in 19 7A or the nozzle switch placed in AUTO 3B after touchdown to open the nozzle.

If Nozzle Fails to Open Position During Flight.

Afterburning.

Indicated by:

a. A slight reduction in thrust.

b. EGT approximately 550°C.

c. An increase in nozzle area to approximately 10.

Non-Afterburning.

Indicated by:

a. Significant thrust decrease.

b. EGT approximately 350°C. Sufficient thrust probably, is not available to maintain level flight with any configuration.

c. An increase in nozzle area to approximately 10.

Note

- Failure during afterburning will probably not be detected by the pilot. Afterburner will continue to operate provided throttle is not retarded. As long as full afterburning is maintained, immediate corrective action is not required.
- If afterburner is being used, maintain maximum afterburner setting. Retarding the throttle from this position will probably cause afterburner blowout. Maintain afterburner operation until reaching a position from which a safe landing is assured.

If a landing without afterburner is to be made, proceed as follows:

1. **NOZZLE HANDLE—PULL** 19 7A.

NOZZLE SWITCH—MANUAL 3B.

CAUTION

After nozzle is closed, do not light afterburner. Lighting afterburner will result in an over-temperature condition and may cause excessive rpm drop or engine stall. Monitor EGT for possible over-temperature.

IN-FLIGHT EMERGENCIES (Continued)

If Nozzle Does Not Close:

2. THROTTLE—MAXIMUM AFTERBURNER (USE RAPID MOVEMENT OF THROTTLE).

Note

- A 3 to 5 second delay *may* occur before an afterburner light is obtained. Afterburner lights with the nozzle failed open are not assured, but the probability of successful lights increases as altitude decreases. Best airspeed/altitude combination for afterburner light with an open nozzle is 240 knots below 15,000 feet.
- If an afterburner light is not obtained, leaving the throttle in maximum, afterburner will decrease the fuel load and lighten the aircraft. Best flight capability with an open nozzle failure is realized at 300 knots clean (gear, flaps and speed brakes retracted) or 200 knots with flaps in takeoff position, gear and speed brakes retracted.

3. Nozzle handle—In 19 7A
Nozzle switch—AUTO 3B

WARNING

Level flight with the nozzles failed open is probably not possible in any configuration except under ideal conditions. If the nozzle fails open in the final landing configuration and the above procedures do not correct the situation, push nozzle handle in and eject immediately.

4. Land as soon as possible, using a precautionary pattern.

If Nozzle Fails to the Mechanical Schedule or Severe Nozzle Fluctuations Occur.

Afterburning.

Indicated by:

a. EGT of approximately 700°C.

b. Nozzle indication of 6.5.

Note

Overtemperature will result, but excessive rpm drop or compressor stall should not occur.

Non-Afterburning.

Indicated by:

a. EGT of approximately 700°C.

b. Nozzle indication of 0.5.

CAUTION

Military thrust will be available; however, overtemperature may occur. Do not light afterburner. Lighting afterburner will result in an overtemperature condition and may cause excessive rpm drop or engine stall.

1. AFTERBURNER—OFF (If being used at time of failure).

2. Nozzle handle—Pull 19 7A. Nozzle switch—Manual 3B

3. EGT—Monitor.

4. Nozzle handle—In 19 7A. Nozzle switch—AUTO 3B after touchdown.

OIL SYSTEM MALFUNCTION.

Engine oil is used to lubricate the engine and to operate the exhaust nozzle. Depending on the type or location of the failure, either or both systems may be affected. Malfunctions in the lubrication system, such as failure of the engine lubrication pump, or clogged lines, will only affect engine operation. Failures which occur because of an oil leak will affect the exhaust nozzle system, and may affect engine lubrication, depending on the location of the leak.

If an oil system malfunction has caused prolonged oil starvation of engine bearings, the result will be a progressive engine failure and subsequent engine seizure. The time interval from the moment of oil starvation to complete failure depends on such factors as condition of the bearings prior to oil starvation, operating temperature of bearings, and bearing loads. With a complete interruption of the supply of oil to the engine, the engine will operate for approximately 1 minute without detrimental effects to the bearings. Limited experience has indicated that the

IN-FLIGHT EMERGENCIES (Continued)

engine should operate for a period of approximately 4-5 minutes at 80 to 90 percent rpm before a complete failure occurs.

If an airfield is near enough to glide to a successful landing, the pilot should set rpm at 86-89 percent and position himself for a safe precautionary landing pattern. However, if thrust is required to fly a considerable distance to an airfield, he should immediately attempt a maximum afterburner light. It is important to attempt the afterburner light soon after the oil level low warning light illuminates, since the nozzles do not fail wide open immediately. If an afterburner light is to be successful at altitude, it must be attained before the nozzles fail fully open. If an afterburner light is successful, the pilot must closely monitor the oil quantity and pressure gage. As long as quantity and pressure remain constant, afterburner operation may be continued, limited only by fuel consumption. Afterburner thrust should be used as required until a precautionary landing pattern can be established. If the oil quantity or pressure begins to drop or fluctuate, oil is being lost and will eventually result in zero oil pressure. At this point, reduce rpm to 86-89 percent and perform Oil Pressure Failure procedures.

If symptoms of seizure are noted, it is important to shut down the engine before seizure is complete. If the engine is not shut down, but is allowed to grind to a halt, it is possible for the compressor rotor to shift forward when the No. 2 bearing fails, allowing contact of rotating parts with stationary parts. The resulting damage will be extensive, and the danger of fire due to broken or cracked fuel lines will be extreme. Therefore, always shut down the engine at the first sign of engine roughness, rising EGT and dropping rpm—rather than to wait until seizure occurs.

To best prolong engine life, abrupt aircraft maneuvers should be kept at a minimum in order not to add any unnecessary "G" load to the No. 2 bearing. For the same reason, rpm changes should be avoided since these vary the thrust loading on the No. 2 bearing. If a relatively smooth flight path is maintained, and rpm is kept in the 86-89 percent rpm range, the pilot is doing all he can do to prevent engine seizure.

OIL SYSTEM PRESSURE FAILURE.

CAUTION

An increase or decrease in oil pressure outside of placard limits is an indication of oil system malfunction which may lead eventually to bearing failure and subsequent engine failure. Land as soon as practical anticipating engine seizure.

Note 3B

On aircraft equipped with an exhaust nozzle control switch it is possible to close the exhaust nozzles to the mechanical schedule by placing the switch in MANUAL provided oil level is above 0.8 gallon. If the oil level has decreased to 0.8 gallon level, the exhaust nozzles will fail open regardless of switch position.

In view of aforementioned information, the following guidance is given for oil pressure fluctuations.

1. If a suitable landing field is within glide range using 86-89 percent rpm, set rpm at this value, pull nozzle handle 19 7A and if necessary jettison external stores to maintain safe altitude.

2. If a suitable landing field is outside glide range using 86-89 percent rpm, proceed to a landing field using afterburner thrust. Retain external fuel tanks if they contain fuel and it is needed.

3. Avoid abrupt maneuvers causing high G forces.

4. Throttle changes should be small and smooth and made only when necessary.

5. RAT handle—Pull if engine freezes.

WARNING

During any oil pressure irregularities be constantly alert and ready to pull the RAT handle if the engine freezes.

IN-FLIGHT EMERGENCIES (Continued)

6. Land as soon as possible using a precautionary landing pattern to ensure a safe landing in the event of engine failure.

7. Nozzle handle—In 19 7A after touchdown.

8. Shut down engine as soon as practicable when clear of runway.

LOSS OF ENGINE OIL.

Because of their effect on aircraft operation, oil leaks are categorized into the following three types of malfunctions.

a. Leak in the lubrication system. Complete oil starvation may be expected since oil for engine lubrication is extracted from the bottom of the oil tank. When oil level reaches the 0.8 gallon pendulum inlet the nozzle will fail open. If the emergency nozzle closure handle is pulled, 19 7A, the nozzles will close and remain closed until the oil level falls below the 0.5 gallon standpipe, then as the nozzles begin to open, the nozzle locks will engage the nozle actuators.

Note

Oil pressure may not be affected by oil loss until complete starvation occurs, depending upon the location of the leak. When complete starvation occurs, oil pressure will drop to zero and engine seizure is imminent.

b. Leaks downstream of the nozzle closure transfer value. Loss of oil in actuator lines, nozzle actuators or return lines usually causes a rapid depletion of oil. When the oil level reaches the 0.8 gallon pendulum the nozzles will fail open. If the emergency nozzle closure handle 19 7A, is pulled, the 0.3 gallon emergency nozzle closure oil supply will be lost, however, 0.5 gallons will be reserved for engine lubrication. Depending upon the severity of the leak, using the emergency nozzle closure handle 19 7A, may or may not close the nozzles and allow the nozzle locks to become effective. If the nozzles fail to close, afterburner operation will probably be necessary for level or climbing flight.

Note

With an oil level of 0.5 gallons, oil pressure fluctuations may occur due to oil aeration.

c. Leaks upstream of the nozzle closure transfer valve. A leak in this area is the least serious of the three malfunctions. When oil level reaches the 0.8 gallon pendulum outlet, the nozzles will fail open. If the emergency nozzle closure handle 19 7A is pulled, the nozzles will close and remain closed until oil level drops to 0.5 gallons. The nozzles will then begin to open until the nozzle locks engage the nozzle actuators.

WARNING

- Loss of engine oil as indicated by illumination of engine oil level low warning light and an abnormal decrease in oil quantity will also result in loss of exhaust nozzle control. The consequent loss of thrust with nozzle in open position may be as much as 70 percent at 100 percent rpm. Refer to Engine Oil Level Low Warning Light procedure.
- Increasing vibration is an indication of a bearing failure. Extreme vibration, usually accompanied by a rise in EGT, indicates engine seizure will occur within a few minutes. The throttle should be positioned to OFF to prevent excessive engine damage and possible damage to airplane structure.

Note

High thrust settings should be avoided when possible to keep temperature and bearing loads at a minimum. Upon detection of an oil system malfunction as evidenced by the oil pressure gage and/or the oil quantity indicator, a minimum thrust setting should be established, depending on aircraft configuration, gross weight and altitude. The thrust setting should be sufficient to maintain level flight and to allow safe approach maneuvers. Subsequent throttle movement should be avoided if possible. If the malfunction has passed unnoticed and has progressed to the point where bearing failure has started (as evidenced by vibration), the throttle should not be retarded. If throttle is retarded, engine seizure may be accelerated.

IN-FLIGHT EMERGENCIES (Continued)

In all cases, the first indication of an engine oil loss should be a low indication on the nucleonic oil quantity indicator and/or illumination of the Engine Oil Level Low warning light which is energized when the oil level drops to approximately 14 pints (one mark below ½ on the gage). If an oil loss occurs, proceed as follows:

Without Nozzle Failure:

1. Nozzle handle—Pull 19 7A

2. Land as soon as possible (aircraft with the nozzle switch installed 3B should anticipate nozzle failure).

With Nozzle Failure:

1. Without an oil pressure drop—follow procedures for Exhaust Nozzle Control System Failure this section.

2. With an oil pressure drop—follow procedures for Oil Pressure Failure this section.

ENGINE OIL LEVEL LOW WARNING LIGHT ILLUMINATION.

Illumination of the ENGINE OIL LEVEL LOW warning light indicates the oil has been depleted to 6.4 pints and the nozzle has failed open. (On aircraft incorporating the nucleonic oil quantity indicating system, the oil level low warning light will illuminate when the oil quantity decreases to 14 pints). Actuation of the nozzle handle transfers the nozzle actuation oil supply to a standpipe within the oil tank which prevents any nozzle system oil leak from depleting the lube oil supply below a level of 4 pints. At this point the nozzle will try to drift open; however, it will be held closed by the nozzle locks. If indicated oil pressure drops, follow procedures established for Oil System Failure.

If Light Illuminates in Flight

1. NOZZLE HANDLE—PULL 
NOZZLE SWITCH—MANUAL 3B

Note

The nozzle may not close under certain conditions of airspeed and altitude. If the nozzle does not close, reduce throttle setting to decrease nozzle pressure.

CAUTION

After nozzle is closed, do not light afterburner. Lighting afterburner will result in an overtemperature condition and may cause excessive rpm drop or engine stall.

If Nozzle Does Not Close:

2. THROTTLE — MAXIMUM AFTERBURNER (USE RAPID MOVEMENT OF THROTTLE).

3. NOZZLE HANDLE—IN. 
NOZZLE SWITCH—AUTO 3B

4. Land as soon as possible using a precautionary pattern.

RAT EXTENDED FLIGHT.

The ram air turbine (RAT) is available for emergency electrical and hydraulic power when the engine-driven power sources are lost. Extension of the RAT with the engine running can, under certain conditions, adversely affect engine operation. Because several inadvertent RAT extensions have been experienced, an operating envelope with the engine running and the RAT extended is provided below.

a. The RAT can be extended in level flight without affecting engine operation within the following airspeed limits.

Altitude	*Airspeed Limits (Knots IAS)*	
	Minimum	*Maximum*
Up to 30,000 feet	None	550
Above 30,000 feet	350	

b. Normal air starts with the RAT extended can be made at all altitudes up to 35,000 feet.

c. Maneuverability is satisfactory with the No. 1 and No. 2 hydraulic pumps inoperative and the RAT supplying hydraulic pressure up to 550 knots IAS.

IN-FLIGHT EMERGENCIES (Continued)

d. Spiral climbs and desecents can be made without affecting normal engine operation or airplane maneuverability.

e. Best range with the RAT extended and 3000 pounds of fuel remaining is realized by cruising at 0.82 Mach at 27,000 feet. Range will be approximately 170 nautical miles per 1000 pounds of fuel used.

f. Factors such as G's, yaw, abrupt maneuvers, or rapid throttle movements may induce engine instability, stalls, or flameouts with the RAT extended, especially above 30,000 feet. Below 30,000 feet, 45-degree banks do not affect engine operation.

Deploy the RAT under the following circumstances.

a. Double hydraulic failure.

b. Double generator failure.

c. Flameout landing.

d. Seized engine.

e. Dead engine descent in weather.

Note

If a flameout or engine stall occurs when the RAT is extended, accomplish normal air start or stall-clearing procedures.

When flying with the RAT extended, avoid abrupt or uncoordinated maneuvers and move throttle slowly and only when necessary. Do not attempt afterburner lights unless absolutely necessary. Land as soon as practicable and use thrust as required. If possible, fly a precautionary pattern.

Note

The leading and trailing edge flaps are sequenced to extend separately to the TAKEOFF position only when using ram air turbine-driven generator for electrical power. Therefore, the LAND or UP position should never be selected under this condition as it may stall the generator. Keep airspeed above 200 knots IAS until flaps have reached TAKEOFF position. (The wing flap position indicator will be inoperative.)

WARNING

Flight with RAT extended and wing flaps in LAND position will result in a strong right-roll tendency at speeds below 160 knots IAS. The roll is caused by turbulent airflow from the RAT over the inboard right wing section. Full aileron may be required to stop the roll-off and maintain wings-level flight; therefore, do not extend RAT with LAND flaps extended or extend wing flaps to LAND with RAT extended.

SPEED BRAKE FAILURE.

Operation of the speed brakes is through the priority valve by means of the No. 2 hydraulic system. The priority valve will close and prevent speed brake operation if the No. 2 system pressure drops below 2175 psi. If hydraulic pressure is lost the speed brakes will not retract, due to air load distribution. Because of the decreased range capabilities of the aircraft in this configuration a decision should be made to land as soon as practicable. In the event of electrical power loss or engine flameout with the speed brakes extended, provisions are incorporated for automatically closing the speed brakes. Electrical power from the No. 1 emergency dc bus is only required to open the speed brakes or to hold them open. When the solenoid-operated control valve in the speed brake system is deenergized it moves to the closed position, allowing the speed brakes to close provided normal hydraulic pressure or windmilling engine hydraulic pressure is available. The RAT will furnish electrical power for speed brake control and the windmilling engine at best glide speed will supply sufficient hydraulic pressure to the No. 2 system to operate the speed brakes.

WARNING

If flameout is due to a seized engine, the speed brakes cannot be retracted and the resulting high rate of descent will preclude a safe forced landing.

IN-FLIGHT EMERGENCIES (Continued)

SPIN RECOVERY.

Refer to Section VI, Flight Characteristics for detailed information on pitch-up/spin characteristics, prevention, and use of drag chute.

1. FULL RUDDER OPPOSITE TO ROTATION.

2. FULL FORWARD STICK WITH FULL NOSEDOWN TRIM.

3. FULL AILERON IN DIRECTION OF ROTATION.

4. Throttle—IDLE.

5. Neutralize aileron and rudder controls when rotation stops.

6. If above procedure fails—drag chute deploy.

If aircraft enters an inverted spin or vertical stall:

1. NEUTRALIZE ALL CONTROLS.

STABILITY AUGMENTATION SYSTEM FAILURE.

Failure in any one of the stability augmentation system channels (roll, pitch or yaw) may cause control system oscillation. One or all three of the STABILITY CONT circuits can be disengaged as follows:

1. Roll, pitch, or yaw switches (as required)—OFF.

TRIM FAILURE OR RUNWAY TRIM.

In event of trim failure, proceed as follows:

1. Trim selector switch—AUX. TRIM.

2. Auxiliary trim control switch—Use as necessary.

3. If trim still malfunctions, TRIM CONTROL circuit breaker—Pull.

Note

Maximum nose down stabilizer travel is dependent upon trim setting. In the event of stick trim button failure, resulting in full nose up trim, the auxiliary trim switch will have to be used to decrease the nose up trim in order to gain full nose down capability of the stabilizer.

AIRSPEED INDICATOR SYSTEM FAILURE.

The best procedure for an approach and landing with an inoperable airspeed indicator is to fly formation with another aircraft. However, if another aircraft is unavailable, the APC meter can be used because it indicates equivalent angle of attack which can be used for all conditions of weight and drag. If a chase aircraft is unavailable use the APC meter and accomplish the following:

1. At a safe altitude fly a 1G stall approach to stick shaker action with gear and land flaps extended.

WARNING

Do not fly aircraft below stick shaker actuation speed because kicker protection is not afforded with gear and land flaps extended.

2. Note the APC meter reading at the beginning of the stick shaker action.

3. Subtract 2½ from the APC meter stick shaker value and hold this meter number on final approach.

4. If unable to perform the stall approach to stick shaker action, fly an APC meter reading of 1 on final approach.

APPROACH AND LANDING EMERGENCIES

APPROACH-END ARRESTMENTS.

Approach-end arrestments reduce the exposure time to which the pilot and aircraft are subjected during a landing roll with adverse directional control; therefore, approach-end engagements can be made when landing with one main gear up or unlocked, or whenever a directional control problem after touchdown is anticipated.

Note

Landing with a blown main tire does not present a critical directional control problem; therefore, barrier arrestment is optional under this condition.

Approach-end arrestments are practical only when the barrier has 1000 feet of runway ahead of the barrier and a clear approach. Make sure the MA-1A barrier has been removed prior to landing. If possible, burn excess fuel and jettison external stores to reduce landing gross weight and minimize fire hazard. However, if landing with one main gear up or unlocked, retain the empty tip and pylon tanks to cushion wing drop. In any event, retain emtpy tip tanks if they are the only external store and proceed as follows:

1. Inertia reel—LOCKED.
2. Arresting hook—EXTEND. If time permits, confirm hook extension by other aircraft or tower.
3. Make straight-in flat approach at minimum practicable landing speed. Plan touchdown, on runway or hard surfaced overrun, 500 to 1000 feet short of the BAK-9. Immediately After Touchdown:
4. Throttle—IDLE.
5. Lower nosewheel to runway.

CAUTION

The nosewheel must be on the runway prior to barrier engagement, otherwise the nose gear may fail as it contacts the runway.

6. Nosewheel steering—Engage. Contact barrier as close as possible to 90° angle. Attempt to maintain directional control for centerline engagement. Be prepared to correct for yaw after engagement.

Note

The cockpit canopy provides protection from flash fire; therefore, do not jettison the canopy.

CAUTION

Do not use the brakes. A locked wheel may snag or cut the cable. The wheel should be rolling when passing over the cable.

7. Throttle—Off. (If required, after fire crew confirms that no fire hazard exists from discharged fuel.)

ASYMMETRIC EXTERNAL TANK FUEL LOAD.

Adequate control is available for landing with one external tank full and one external tank empty under smooth air conditions. Lateral control can be improved by using TAKEOFF flaps. Consideration should be given to the added aileron requirements under strong or gusty crosswind conditions before attempting a landing with an asymmetric fuel load. A crosswind from the side with the light tank increases the aileron requirements in the same direction as used to balance the heavy tank. Low speed control should be tested prior to entering the landing pattern. If lateral control appears marginal for the landing condition, the tanks should be jettisoned.

BARRIER ENGAGEMENT.

Refer to ABORT procedures under Takeoff Emergencies.

BELLY LANDING DITCHING.

Abandon the aircraft rather than attempt a belly landing or ditching.

APPROACH AND LANDING EMERGENCIES (Continued)

BOUNDARY LAYER CONTROL MALFUNCTION.

WARNING

All the following speeds are based on a landing gross weight of 14,600 pounds (approximately 1000 pounds of fuel remaining and no ammunition). Increase approach and touchdown speeds 5 knots for each additional 1000 pounds of aircraft weight.

If a boundary layer control system malfunction is experienced as manifested by a strong rolling tendency as the wing flaps travel to the LAND position, return flap lever to TAKEOFF and continue with Takeoff Flap Landing procedure.

FLAMEOUT LANDING PATTERN.

The recommended procedures for a flameout landing pattern are illustrated in figure 3-4. The overhead pattern offers the most accurate control of the touchdown point and should be utilized when possible. Since it may not be possible to enter the pattern at the High Key point in all cases, conditions should be practiced with pattern entry at any point down to the Low Key position to develop technique and proficiency for these cases as well as the ideal situation. The most important elements of a successful flameout landing are simulated flameout landing practice, close control of glide speed, and a carefully executed flare. The pilot must take into consideration aircraft weight, field elevation, and wind conditions to determine if the recommended glide speed requires adjustment. The glide speed recommended for a flameout approach is 245 knots, based on no external stores (except tip stores), 1500 pounds of fuel or less, the RAT extended, and flaps in the TAKEOFF position. The 245-knot recommended speed is adequate for the pattern, provided it is maintained to the flare. To allow maneuvering speed, a 260-knot glide speed (attained prior to final approach) can be used. Under no circumstances should glide speed be less than 245 knots prior to flaring for landing.

Various glide speed allowances for weight, field elevation, and wind are as follows:

a. If the fuel weight is greater than 1500 pounds, increase glide speed 5 knots per 1000 pounds. If the remaining fuel weight is less than 1500 pounds, no speed correction is necessary.

b. If the pattern is entered at minimum altitude, a 245-knot speed throughout the approach may be required to reach the field.

WARNING

Do not extend the landing gear until after the flare is assured to avoid excessive sink rates from which a flare may not be possible.

Note

Successful flameout landings can be made carrying external stores. However, glide distance and flare capabilities are substantially improved without external stores. Stores should be jettisoned whenever possible. If unable to jettison external stores, increase pattern airspeed 5 knots for each 1000 pounds of external stores. Empty tip tanks should be returned.

AIR START ATTEMPTS DURING FLAMEOUT LANDING PATTERN.

These instructions in no way alter previously established requirements for ejection versus flameout landing. *Landing with the engine inoperative will not be attempted unless escape from the aircraft is impossible.*

In the event of a flameout, attempt to complete all air start efforts before High Key is reached so that full attention may be devoted to accomplishing a successful flameout landing. If the circumstances of flameout have prevented conclusive air start attempts prior to High Key, further air starts may be attempted but primary attention should be devoted to proper execution of the flameout landing.

Do not attempt air starts after Low Key is reached unless the flameout occurred below the Low Key position altitude.

APPROACH AND LANDING EMERGENCIES (Continued)

SIMULATED FLAMEOUT LANDING.

Simulated flameout landings may be accomplished in the following configuration:

1. Throttle—82 percent rpm. 3B 7A, 81 percent rpm 19
2. Speed brakes—OUT.
3. Landing gear—UP.
4. Flaps—TAKEOFF.
5. Indicated airspeed—260 knots minimum.
6. Landing gear lever—DOWN, when flare is assured.

This landing configuration results in drag approximating that which occurs during a dead-engine descent with TAKEOFF flaps, RAT extended, and gear retracted. It is recommended that practice flameout patterns be made using the above configuration, so that landing gear will be extended during the landing flare. If it is desired to simulate a glide to the flameout pattern with flaps up, gear up, and RAT retracted, glide at 275 knots and 87 percent rpm 3B 7A, 85 percent rpm 19 with the speed brakes fully extended.

PRECAUTIONARY LANDING PATTERN. (PLP)

A landing approach that simulates the presence of some emergency, or in which an emergency actually does exist, other than a flamed-out engine, and where the objective is to land the aircraft safely in the minimum amount of time and with the least amount of risk to the pilot. This will be a straight-in approach, when possible, maintaining 260 knots until landing is assured, to provide zoom capability. Acceptable minimum safe altitude for ejection will be maintained as long as possible and during the final approach and the 260 knots airspeed will give the pilot a zoom ejection capability down to the flare.

FLAP FAILURE.

Because of high approach and touchdown speeds required to accomplish a no-flap or trailing-edge-flap-failure landing, the following procedure is recommended.

WARNING

All of the following speeds are based on a normal landing gross weight of 14,600 pounds. These weights include approximately 1000 pounds fuel remaining and no ammunition. Increase approach and touchdown speeds 5 knots for each additional 1000 pounds of aircraft weight.

TRAILING EDGE FLAP FAILURE.

If the trailing edge flaps fail to extend, regardless of the position of the leading edge flaps, a straight in approach is recommended using the following procedure.

1. Aileron limiter circuit breaker—Pull.

Pulling the AILERON LIMITER circuit breaker A C or the RUD/AIL LIMITER circuit breaker B D will remove aileron (and rudder B D) travel limits.

WARNING

The use of full unlimited aileron or rudder travel in maneuvers at speeds above 300 KIAS can result in structural damage and possible loss of the aircraft.

2. APC switch—OFF (monitor APC gage)
3. Recommended runway length—10,000 feet.

Note

A runway length of 10,000 feet is recommended as an added safety precaution in the event of brake or drag chute failure.

4. Final approach speed—230 knots minimum.
5. Make flat approach.

A flat approach decreases required rotation for flare.

Note

Airframe buffeting will be experienced as speed is reduced or G-load is increased.

6. Touchdown speed—190 knots minimum.
7. Lower nose and deploy drag chute immediately.

LEADING EDGE FLAP FAILURE.

1. If only the leading edge flaps fail and the trailing edge flaps can be lowered to the LAND position (thereby making boundary layer control available) normal pattern and touchdown speeds can be used.

2. If trailing edge flaps can be extended only to the TAKEOFF position, fly final approach at not less than 190 knots and touch down at not less than 160 knots.

TYPICAL FLAMEOUT LANDING PATTERN

BASED ON NO EXTERNAL STORES (EXCEPT TIP STORES), 1500 POUNDS OF FUEL OR LESS, THE RAM AIR TURBINE EXTENDED, AND FLAPS IN THE TAKEOFF POSITION. INCREASE PATTERN AIRSPEED 5 KNOTS FOR EACH 1000 POUNDS OF FUEL IN EXCESS OF 1500 POUNDS.

NOTE

- WINDMILLING OR FROZEN ENGINE GLIDE CHARACTERISTICS ARE THE SAME.
- ALTITUDES SHOWN ARE ABOVE TERRAIN.

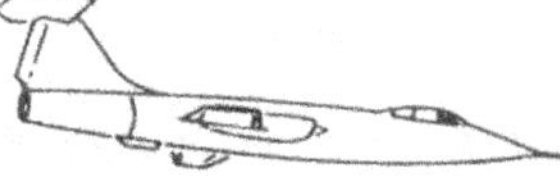

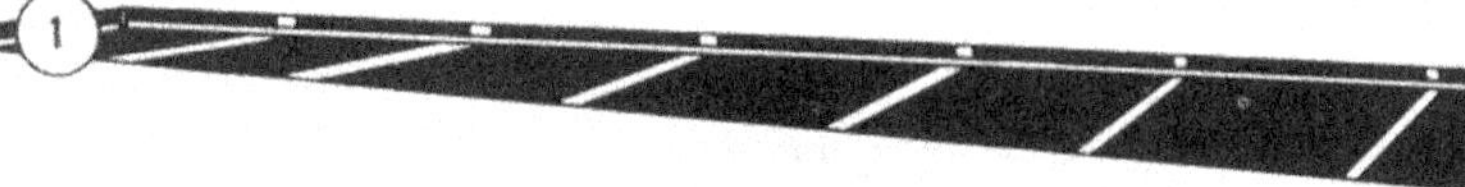

INITIAL

A. GLIDE - 245-260 KNOTS

B. RAM AIR TURBINE - EXTENDED

C. WING FLAPS - TAKEOFF

LOW KEY

A. 6000 FEET MINIMUM, 8000 FEET DESIRED

B. AIRSPEED - 245-260 KNOTS

3

FINAL TURN

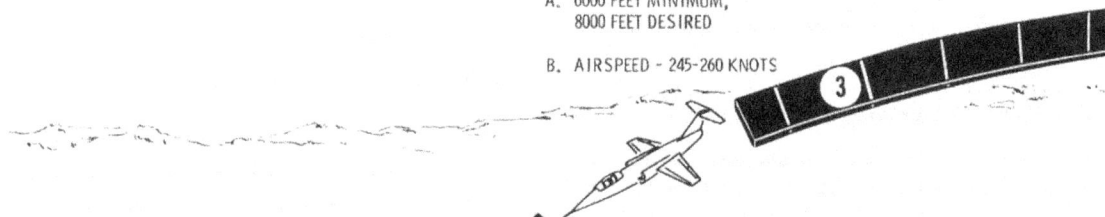

A. FLY TURN TO ROLL OUT ON FINAL APPROACH NOT LESS THAN 1,000 FEET ABOVE AND 3/4 MILE FROM THE END OF THE RUNWAY.

B. AIRSPEED - 260 KNOTS

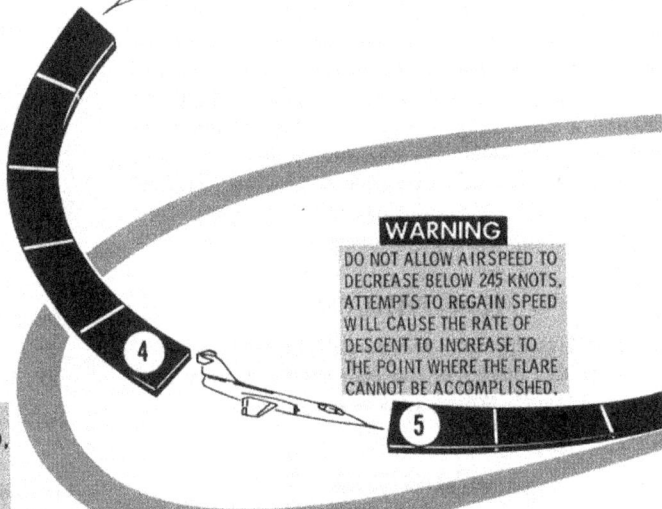

WARNING

DO NOT ALLOW AIRSPEED TO DECREASE BELOW 245 KNOTS. ATTEMPTS TO REGAIN SPEED WILL CAUSE THE RATE OF DESCENT TO INCREASE TO THE POINT WHERE THE FLARE CANNOT BE ACCOMPLISHED.

4

5

WARNING

IT IS IMPERATIVE THAT THE LANDING GEAR REMAIN RETRACTED UNTIL AFTER THE FLARE HAS BEEN ASSURED, OTHERWISE THE RATE OF DESCENT WILL BE INCREASED FROM APPROXIMATELY 7,000 FEET TO APPROXIMATELY 11,000 FEET PER MINUTE AND THE ALTITUDE AND SPEED LOSS REQUIRED FOR FLARE WILL BE INCREASED TO THE POINT THAT A SAFE DEAD-STICK LANDING WILL BE EXTREMELY DIFFICULT TO PERFORM. IT HAS BEEN FOUND THAT AFTER LEAVING THE LOW-KEY POINT THE AIRSPEED SHOULD BE MONITORED CLOSELY AND INCREASED AS NECESSARY TO THE RECOMMENDED 260 KNOTS.

FLARE

A. START FLARE 300-500 FEET ABOVE GROUND

B. WHEN FLARE IS ASSURED, PULL THE MANUAL LANDING GEAR RELEASE HANDLE

F52-0-3-49( )

Figure 3-4 (Sheet 1 of 2)

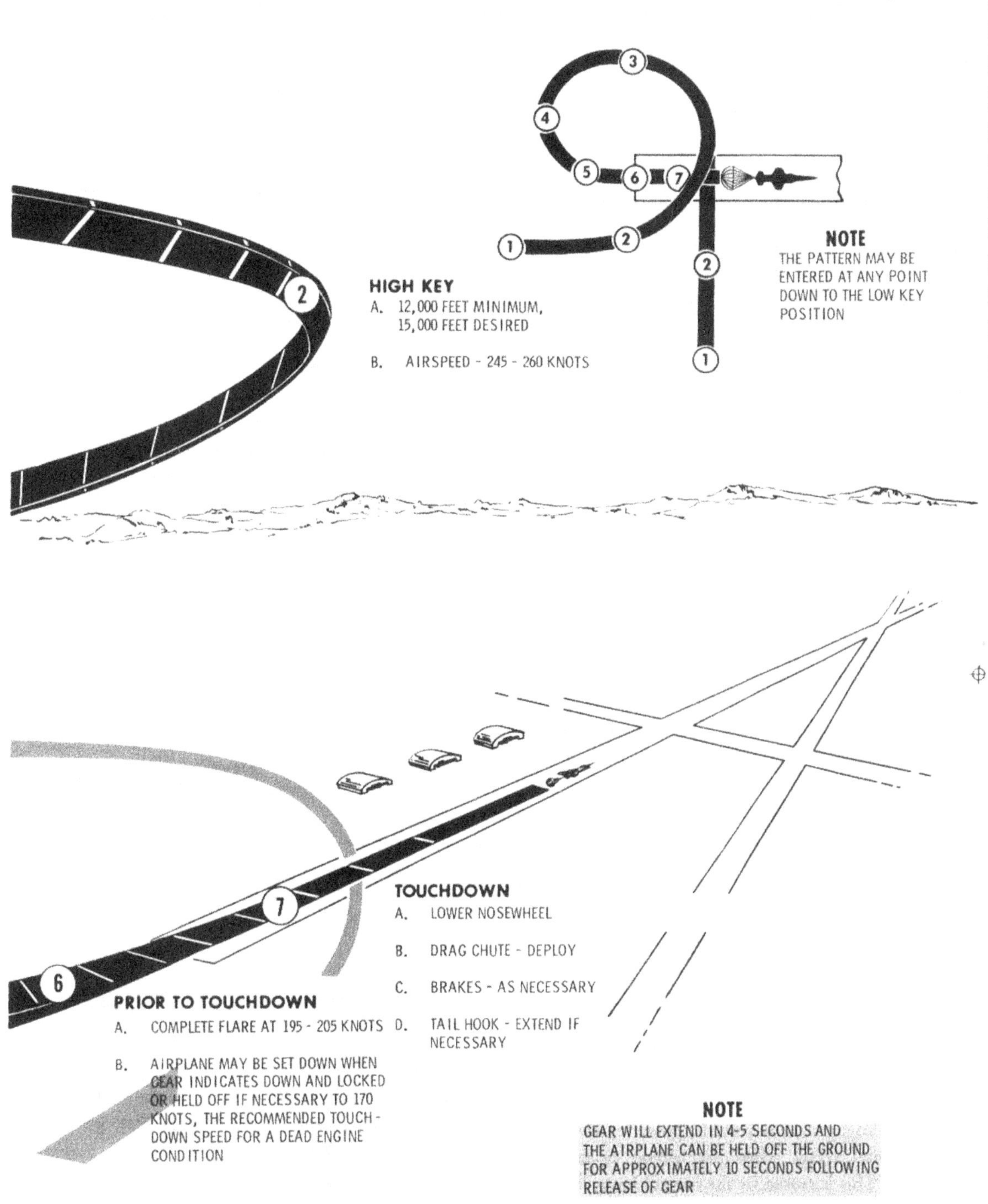

1
2
3
4
5
6
7
NOTE
THE PATTERN MAY BE ENTERED AT ANY POINT DOWN TO THE LOW KEY POSITION
HIGH KEY
A. 12,000 FEET MINIMUM, 15,000 FEET DESIRED
B. AIRSPEED - 245 - 260 KNOTS
TOUCHDOWN
A. LOWER NOSEWHEEL
B. DRAG CHUTE - DEPLOY
C. BRAKES - AS NECESSARY
D. TAIL HOOK - EXTEND IF NECESSARY
PRIOR TO TOUCHDOWN
A. COMPLETE FLARE AT 195 - 205 KNOTS
B. AIRPLANE MAY BE SET DOWN WHEN GEAR INDICATES DOWN AND LOCKED OR HELD OFF IF NECESSARY TO 170 KNOTS, THE RECOMMENDED TOUCH-DOWN SPEED FOR A DEAD ENGINE CONDITION
NOTE
GEAR WILL EXTEND IN 4-5 SECONDS AND THE AIRPLANE CAN BE HELD OFF THE GROUND FOR APPROXIMATELY 10 SECONDS FOLLOWING RELEASE OF GEAR
F52-0-3-49(2)

Figure 3-4 (Sheet 2 of 2)

APPROACH AND LANDING EMERGENCIES (Continued)

ASYMMETRICAL FLAPS.

It is possible to obtain an asymmetrical wing flap condition any time the flap configuration is changed. In the event of asymmetrical flap travel in excess of 5 degrees, the flap asymmetry detector will open the trailing edge flap control circuit stopping the flap movement and prevent further operation of the trailing edge flaps. Operation of the flap asymmetry detector will deactivate the aileron limiters and full aileron travel will be available. Under most conditions, lateral control will be sufficient to maintain level flight and to land. The most critical time for flap asymmetry will be when an asymmetry occurs during the landing pattern. During asymmetric conditions wherein the lowest trailing edge flap has extended 30 to 36 degrees (2/3 from TAKEOFF to LAND position), full aileron travel may not be sufficient to retain lateral control. If an asymmetric wing flap condition should occur proceed as follows:

1. Immediately return flap handle to previous position.

Note

- Immediately returning the flap lever to the previous position may stop the asymmetry before the detector operates.
- Once the detection system has been activated power is no longer available to the trailing edge flaps; consequently the landing must be accomplished in whatever flap configuration existed at the time the asymmetry occurred.

2. Aileron limiter circuit breaker—PULL. Pulling the AILERON LIMITER circuit breaker **A** **C** or the RUD/AIL LIMITER circuit breaker **B** **D** will remove aileron and (rudder **B** **D**) travel limits.

Note

- Pulling the circuit breaker will assure full aileron travel in case the asymmetry detector did not operate.
- If full surface travel has been applied with limiter engaged, it may not be possible to attain additional travel when the limiter is disengaged. This is caused by the control input interfering with the limiter stop which will hold it in the limited position. Therefore it may be necessary to relax the control input toward neutral slightly so that the limiter will retract.
- Jettison external stores if aileron control is marginal.

WARNING

The use of full unlimited aileron or rudder travel in maneuvers at speeds above 300 KIAS can result in structural damage and possible loss of the aircraft.

3. Make a straight-in approach at 230 knots.

4. Touchdown at not less than 190 knots.

FULL OR PARTIALLY FULL PYLON TANK LANDING.

With fuel in the pylon tanks, the pylon strength may be exceeded during a landing; therefore, if a landing must be made with more than 1000 pounds total fuel in the pylon tanks, adhere to the recommended landing speeds and exercise close control over sink rate at touchdown.

LANDING WITH BOTH MAIN GEAR UP.

It is advisable to abandon the aircraft rather than attempt a landing with both main landing gear up or partially extended.

LANDING GEAR EMERGENCY EXTENSION.

If the landing gear indicators do not show gear down and locked after lever is moved to the DOWN position, keep speed below the transient landing gear structural limit and proceed as follows:

1. Recycle gear.

2. If gear does not lock down, move landing gear lever UP.

3. Manual landing gear release handle—Pull.

4. Landing gear lever—DOWN.

APPROACH AND LANDING EMERGENCIES (Continued)

Note

- A force of up to 50 pounds may be required to pull the manual landing gear release handle for manual landing gear extension.
- It is recommended that a ground or air check be made to determine landing gear position before landing.
- The landing gear cannot be retracted in flight after being lowered by means of the manual landing gear release handle.
- Nosewheel steering will be inoperative if the gear is lowered by this method.
- Airspeed must be below 225 knots before the nose gear will lock down. B D
- Pulling G's and yawing the aircraft will help to lock the gear in the down position.

MAIN GEAR FLAT TIRE LANDING.

1. Touch down on good tire.

Touch down on the side of the runway away from the flat tire.

2. Nosewheel–Lower.
3. Nosewheel steering–Engage.
4. Drag chute–Deploy.

MAXIMUM GLIDE.

WINDMILLING OR FROZEN ENGINE.

Figure 3-5 shows the glide distance obtainable with a windmilling or frozen engine. The recommended configuration is TAKEOFF flaps extended, gliding at 245 knots. The same distance can be obtained by gliding with flaps up at 275 knots; however, the rate of descent with TAKEOFF flaps is approximately 1000 feet per minute less due to the lower speed for the same glide ratio. In addition, no change in configuration or speed is required when the flameout landing pattern is entered. The data shown in Figure 3-5 are for the RAT extended because this is the highest drag configuration, and because the RAT is needed for hydraulic power with a frozen engine and for electrical power to extend the flaps whenever the engine is inoperative. Gliding without the RAT extended would increase these distances approximately 2 nautical miles per 10,000 feet of altitude.

Note

Unless the engine is damaged, the windmilling engine speed will produce sufficient hydraulic pressure to operate the flight control system.

NOSE GEAR FLAT TIRE LANDING.

1. Nose gear–Hold off.

Hold the nose gear wheel off as long as practicable, then lower gently to the runway.

2. Throttle–off after touchdown.
3. Drag chute–Deploy after nosewheel is lowered.

Do not deploy the drag chute until nosewheel is on the ground because of the nose-down pitching moment which occurs when the drag chute inflates.

CAUTION

Use caution during braking because even application of braking is difficult due to rudder pedal vibration.

NOSE GEAR UP LANDING.

1. Inertia reel lock lever–LOCKED.
2. Survival kit release handle–Pull.
3. Make normal landing.
4. Throttle–off after touchdown.
5. Lower nose at minimum of 135 knots.

Note

If necessary, light braking action may be used with nose held off.

6. Drag chute–Deploy after nose contacts runway.
7. Apply brakes, using differential braking to maintain directional control.

MAXIMUM GLIDE DISTANCE

ZERO WIND STRAIGHT-LINE GLIDE
ENGINE WINDMILLING OR FROZEN
EXTERNAL STORES - NONE OR TIP STORES INSTALLED
GEAR UP RAT EXTENDED
FLAPS - TAKEOFF

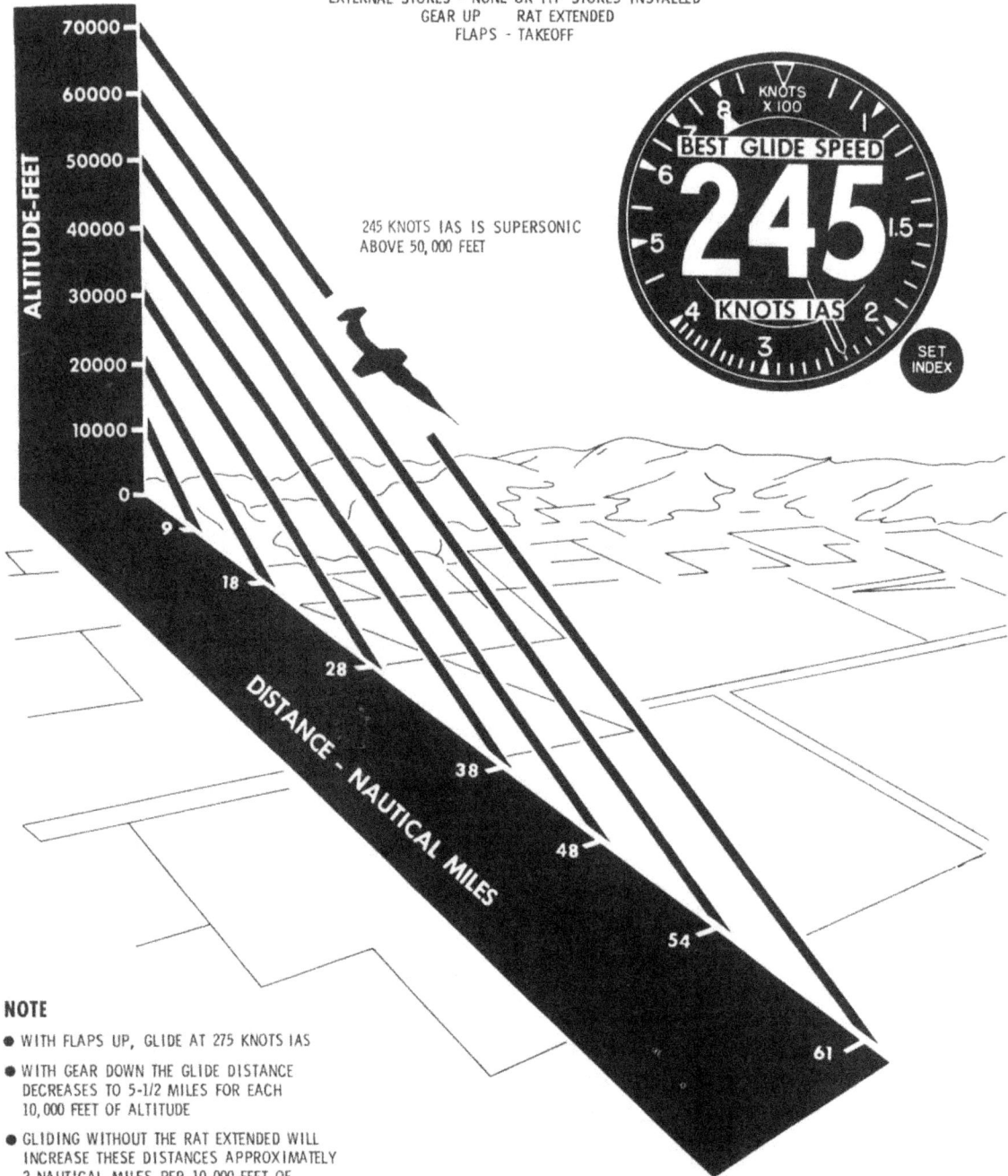

NOTE

- WITH FLAPS UP, GLIDE AT 275 KNOTS IAS
- WITH GEAR DOWN THE GLIDE DISTANCE DECREASES TO 5-1/2 MILES FOR EACH 10,000 FEET OF ALTITUDE
- GLIDING WITHOUT THE RAT EXTENDED WILL INCREASE THESE DISTANCES APPROXIMATELY 2 NAUTICAL MILES PER 10,000 FEET OF ALTITUDE

F52-0-3-48

Figure 3-5

APPROACH AND LANDING EMERGENCIES (Continued)

ONE MAIN GEAR UP OR UNLOCKED LANDING.

If one main gear remains up or in an intermediate position after all procedures to extend have failed, elect to eject or land. (Refer to Landing Gear Emergency Extension procedure.) A decision to land should include consideration of the availability of a long, wide, runway with an adjoining unobstructed runout area; the condition of the surface and area adjacent to the runway, and the weather conditions. Also, an approach-end arrestment may be made with the BAK-9/12 cable (Refer to Approach-end Arrestment). To land, proceed as follows:

1. External stores—Jettison (if required).

Retain empty tip and pylon tanks to absorb initial shock.

Note

If time and conditions permit, fire all amunition and burn excess fuel to lighten airplane and minimize fire hazard.

2. Inertia reel lock lever—LOCKED.

Ascertain that seat belt and harness are tight.

3. Helmet visor—Down.
4. Rudder limit control circuit breaker—Pull. **B** **D**
5. Survival kit release handle—Pull.
6. Make normal approach and landing.

Touch down on side of runway opposite faulty gear.

7. Throttle—IDLE.
8. Nosewheel steering—Engage after nosewheel is on ground.
9. Drag chute—Deploy.
10. Hold faulty gear off runway as long as possible.
11. Brakes—As required.

Use differential braking for directional control.

WARNING

- Nosewheel steering is not available after the manual landing gear release handle has been pulled.
- Do not hesitate to move the throttle OFF and turn off fuel switch if it appears the landing gear is collapsing.

12. Throttle—OFF.
13. Fuel shutoff switch—OFF.

STUCK THROTTLE LANDING.

If all efforts to reduce thrust fail as a result of a throttle stuck at a high thrust setting proceed as follows:

1. Burn fuel down to normal landing weight, if practicable.
2. Reduce speed (using speed brakes, G forces, and climb as necessary) to permit extension of flaps and landing gear.

Note

With speed brakes out, flaps in TAKEOFF, and gear down, speed may be reduced to 240 knots for land flap extension by pulling 2-3 G's, by turning and/or climbing.

3. Establish a flat final approach. A flat final approach will result in a slower airspeed. With speed brakes, land flaps, and gear down at Military power, 190 to 200 knots is typical (230 to 240 knots is typical with afterburner). Speed and glide slope may be controlled somewhat by modulation of speed brakes.

Note

If fuel is shut off prior to touchdown, a right rolloff will be experienced as engine torque is lost, but this rolloff is easily controlled. Sufficient hydraulic pressure will be available for the flight controls to control touchdown.

4. Fuel shutoff switch—OFF (after touchdown).
5. Drag chute—Deploy.

Note

Nosewheel steering will be inoperative. Directional control must be maintained by use of the brakes.

6. Hook—Extend, if barrier engagement is to be made.

APPROACH AND LANDING EMERGENCIES (Continued)

T_2/RPM RESET LANDING.

If a landing with the engine operating in T_2 reset 3B 7A or rpm reset 19, is necessary, accomplish the following:

1. Burn fuel down to normal landing weight if practicable.
2. Reduce airspeed (using speed brakes, G forces or climb as necessary) to permit extension of flaps.

Note

- With speed brakes out, flaps in TAKEOFF and gear down, speed may be reduced to 240 knots for land flap extension by pulling 2-3 G's and by turning and/or climbing. If rolloff occurs during land flap extension, BLC duct separation has occurred; therefore, landing must be made using TAKEOFF flaps.

- Retarding the throttle will result in a reduction in thrust even though rpm remains at 103.5 percent. This is due to exhaust nozzle modulation with throttle position.

WARNING

If a BLC duct separation is indicated, do not place the wing flap lever to the LAND position in the landing pattern because this may result in a severe rolloff due to asymmetric airflow over the flaps.

3. Establish a flat final approach.

A flat final approach will result in a slow airspeed. With speed brakes, land flaps, and gear down at Military power, 190 to 200 knots is typical (230 to 240 knots is typical with afterburner). Speed and glide slope may be controlled somewhat by modulation of speed brakes.

4. Throttle—OFF, after touchdown.
5. Fuel shutoff switch—OFF.
6. Drag chute—Deploy.

Note

Nosewheel steering will be inoperative. Directional control must be maintained by use of the brakes.

7. Hook—Extend, if barrier engagement is to be made

auxiliary equipment

SECTION IV

TABLE OF CONTENTS

AIR CONDITIONING AND PRESSURIZATION SYSTEM.

COCKPIT AIR CONDITIONING.

Heated, compressed air for cockpit air conditioning and pressurization is obtained by bleeding air from the 17th stage of the engine compressor (figure 4-1.) After passing through a primary heat exchanger, a small part of the air is directed to the fuel tank pressurization system. The main flow of air passes through a shutoff valve, after which a portion goes to the rain removal duct, canopy, electronic compartment, anti-G suit, and radar pressurization systems. The remainder then passes through or around a refrigeration unit (figure 4-1), depending upon the positions of the bypass valves. The compressor air which goes through the bypass valves is directed to an air mixing chamber where it mixes with the air which has gone through the refrigeration unit. This mixture is directed through a water separator, and enters the cockpit through shoulder outlets and foot warmers. The temperature of the air entering the cockpit depends upon the position of the bypass valves. For maximum heating, the bypass valves will be fully opened and most of the air entering the cockpit will bypass the refrigeration unit. For maximum cooling, the bypass valves will be completely closed and all the air entering the cockpit will pass through the refrigeration unit which includes a secondary heat exchanger, a water boiler and a cooling turbine. The water boiler operates in such a manner that if the inlet temperature is above the boiling temperature of water, the water will boil and the air will be cooled through an evaporation process. The temperature of the air entering the cockpit can be varied by the cockpit heat rheostat which controls the position of the bypass valves. In normal operation, air temperature is maintained between 40° and 100°F automatically by means of a thermostatic control. This senses cockpit temperature, compares this temperature with the cockpit heat rheostat selection, and sends electrical signals to the bypass valves to change their positions as necessary to make cockpit air temperature correspond with rheostat selection. The pilot can also control the temperature manually by means of the cockpit heat rheostat. When this is done, the thermostat control is bypassed, and the bypass valves are directly positioned in accordance with rheostat selections.

AIR CONDITIONING AND PRESSURIZATION SYSTEM

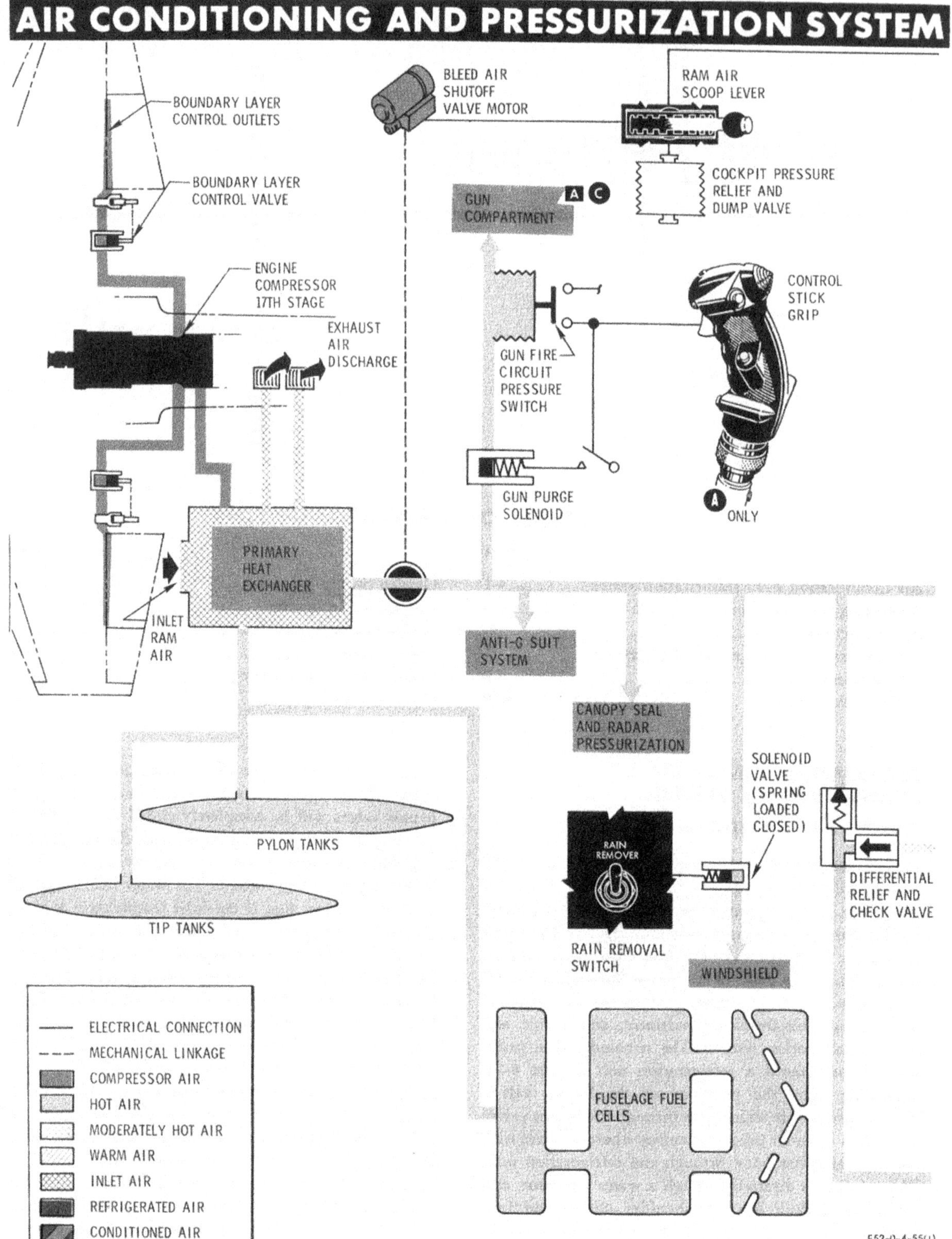
BOUNDARY LAYER CONTROL OUTLETS
BLEED AIR SHUTOFF VALVE MOTOR
RAM AIR SCOOP LEVER
BOUNDARY LAYER CONTROL VALVE
GUN COMPARTMENT
A C
COCKPIT PRESSURE RELIEF AND DUMP VALVE
ENGINE COMPRESSOR 17TH STAGE
EXHAUST AIR DISCHARGE
CONTROL STICK GRIP
GUN FIRE CIRCUIT PRESSURE SWITCH
GUN PURGE SOLENOID
A ONLY
PRIMARY HEAT EXCHANGER
INLET RAM AIR
ANTI-G SUIT SYSTEM
CANOPY SEAL AND RADAR PRESSURIZATION
SOLENOID VALVE (SPRING LOADED CLOSED)
PYLON TANKS
RAIN REMOVER
DIFFERENTIAL RELIEF AND CHECK VALVE
TIP TANKS
RAIN REMOVAL SWITCH
WINDSHIELD
ELECTRICAL CONNECTION
MECHANICAL LINKAGE
COMPRESSOR AIR
HOT AIR
MODERATELY HOT AIR
WARM AIR
INLET AIR
REFRIGERATED AIR
CONDITIONED AIR
FUSELAGE FUEL CELLS
F52-0-4-55(1)

Figure 4-1 (Sheet 1 of 2)

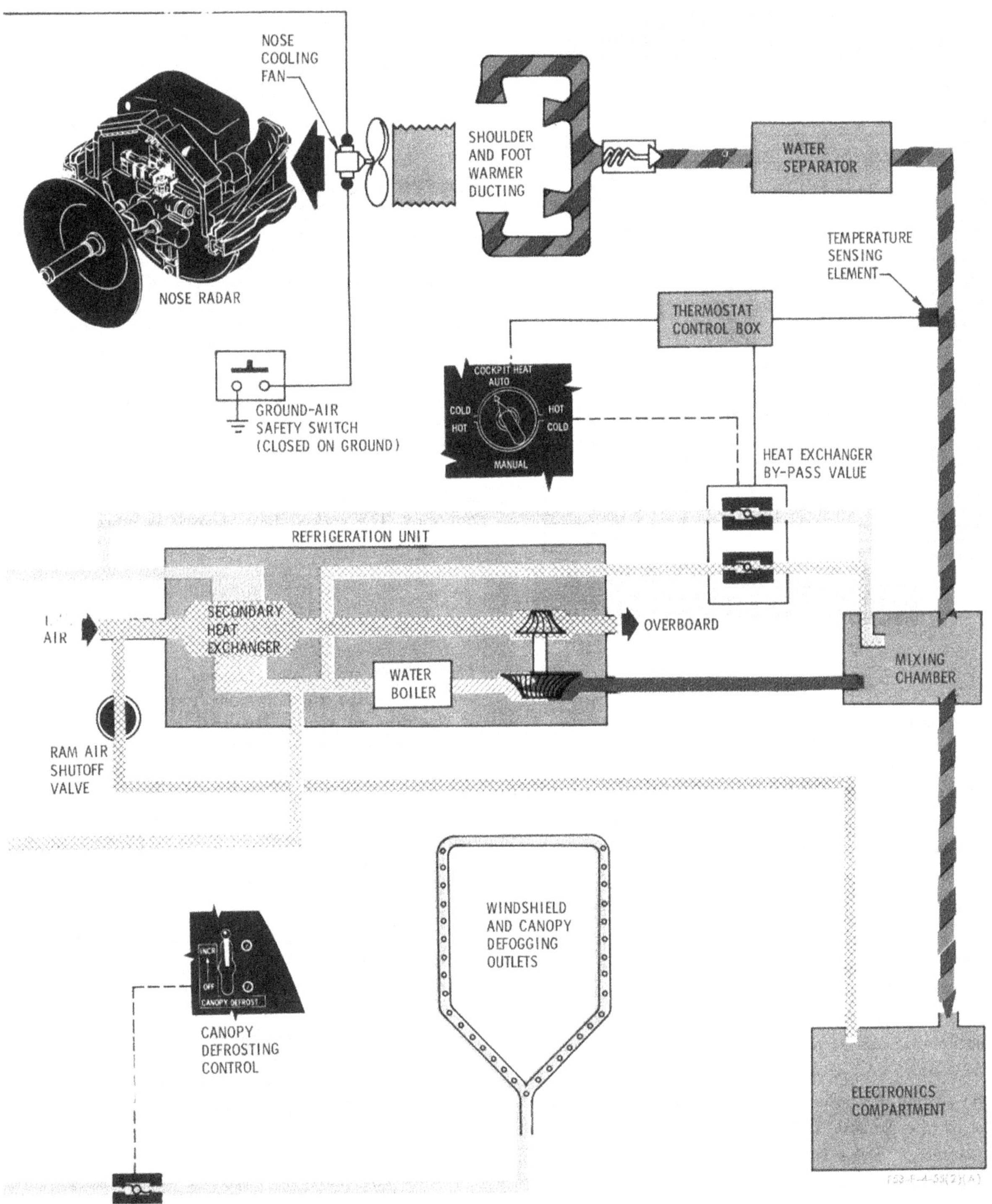
NOSE COOLING FAN
NOSE RADAR
SHOULDER AND FOOT WARMER DUCTING
WATER SEPARATOR
TEMPERATURE SENSING ELEMENT
THERMOSTAT CONTROL BOX
COCKPIT HEAT
AUTO
COLD
HOT
HOT
COLD
MANUAL
GROUND-AIR SAFETY SWITCH (CLOSED ON GROUND)
HEAT EXCHANGER BY-PASS VALUE
REFRIGERATION UNIT
AIR
SECONDARY HEAT EXCHANGER
OVERBOARD
WATER BOILER
MIXING CHAMBER
RAM AIR SHUTOFF VALVE
WINDSHIELD AND CANOPY DEFOGGING OUTLETS
INCR
OFF
CANOPY DEFROST
CANOPY DEFROSTING CONTROL
ELECTRONICS COMPARTMENT

Figure 4-1 (Sheet 2 of 2)

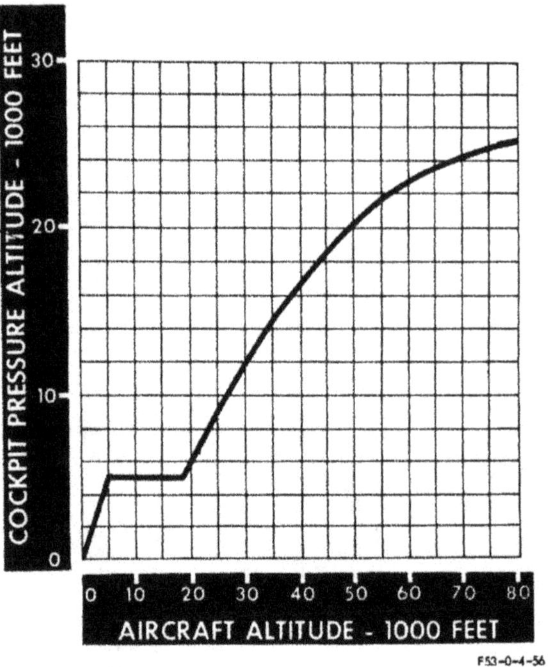

Figure 4-2

COCKPIT PRESSURIZATION.

Cockpit pressurization is maintained at the proper level by an automatic cockpit pressure regulator located in the left forward cockpit area. There is no pressurization in the cockpit below 5000 feet. Between 5000 and 18,500 feet, the cockpit altitude will be constant (figure 4-2), while the differential pressure will vary from 0 to 5.0 psi. Above 18,500 feet, cockpit pressure is maintained at 5.0 psi differential regardless of aircraft altitude. Exhaust air from the cockpit pressure regulator is ducted through the radar compartment forward of the cockpit for cooling purposes. The cockpit pressure regulator unit incorporates a cooling fan which forces cockpit air into the radar compartment whenever the aircraft is on the ground. This fan is also actuated whenever the ram-air scoop is opened. If the pressure regulator malfunctions, excessive cockpit pressure will be relieved through the cockpit pressure relief and dump valve. If cockpit air becomes contaminated, the pilot can alleviate the condition by opening the ram air scoop. Opening the ram air scoop allows fresh air to enter the cockpit, shuts off compressor air to the cockpit, and opens the cockpit pressure relief and dump valve to discharge the contaminated air. Pressurization may be checked on the ground with the canopy locked by pulling the landing gear (IND) circuit breaker and noting a slight pressure rise (aft cockpit **B** **D**).

COCKPIT HEAT RHEOSTAT.

The cockpit heat rheostat (figure 4-3) located on the right console (forward cockpit **B** **D**) is used to control cockpit temperature. Under normal conditions the rheostat is used in the AUTO range of operation and may be set at any point between COLD and HOT. Cockpit temperature will then be maintained automatically through the thermostat control unit which uses emergency ac bus power to control the pneumatically operated bypass valves. With the rheostat in the MANUAL mode of operation, the thermostat does not function and the bypass valves are positioned directly in response to movement of the rheostat between the COLD and HOT positions. The cockpit heat rheostat is powered from emergency ac bus.

RAM AIR SCOOP LEVER.

The ram air scoop lever (figures 1-16, 1-26) located outboard of the right console, controls the position of the ram air scoop. Depressing a button on the handle of the lever allows forward movement which opens the scoop. Aft movement of the lever, which closes the ram air scoop, does not require depressing the button, however, the button must be depressed before the lever can be placed in the CLOSED (last aft detent) position. Initial movement of the lever out of the last aft detent actuates a switch which causes emergency dc bus power to close the hot air shutoff valve, open the cockpit relief and dump valve, and energize the nose cooling fan. Full forward movement of the lever will move the scoop to an open position.

CAUTION

On the ground, with the engine operating and the ram air scoop open, the supply of cooling air to the electronic compartment is shut off. This can cause the electronic equipment to reach overtemperature limits. For this reason make certain that the ram air scoop handle is in the last aft detent so that cooling air for the electronic compartment and cockpit pressurization is available.

ELECTRONICS COMPARTMENT COOLING. 

The electronics compartment is cooled by cold air from the cooling turbine. At low engine rpm an electronics compartment cooling control valve, located downstream of the water separator, moves toward the closed position, decreasing the airflow through shoulder and foot warmer outlets and venting a greater proportion of cooling air to the electronics compartment. In the event bleed air is lost (engine flameout, seizure, etc.) or shut off when the ram air scoop is opened, a ram air shutoff valve automatically opens, diverting outside cooling air to the electronics compartment.

ELECTRONICS COMPARTMENT COOLING. 

Electronics compartment cooling is controlled by a cooling air selector valve on the air-conditioning package. At aircraft altitudes below 25,000 feet the electronics compartment cooling air selector valve allows air at the same temperature as that provided to the cockpit to pass into the electronics compartment. At aircraft altitudes above 25,000 feet, the valve allows cold air to pass into the electronics equipment. A ground cooling air control valve, located in the ram air duct, ensures a supply of cooling air to the electronic equipment during taxi or low engine rpm.

CABIN ALTIMETER.

The cabin altimeter (figures 1-12, 1-22) located on the right side of the lower instrument panel, is vented to the inside of the cockpit only. This instrument gives an accurate indication of cockpit pressure altitude.

NORMAL OPERATION OF COCKPIT AIR-CONDITIONING AND PRESSURIZATION SYSTEM.

1. Ram air scoop lever—CLOSED.

2. Cockpit heat rheostat—AUTO, and positioned as desired.

EMERGENCY OPERATION OF COCKPIT AIR CONDITIONING SYSTEM.

Pressure surging may be encountered when operating on MANUAL. The surging is caused by the thermal switch, which is installed in the system as a high temperature safeguard to shut off the hot air to the mixing chamber when the air in the duct reaches 210°F. Shutting off this air increases the airflow to the turbine, which causes a pressure drop in the air to the cockpit. When the cold air from the turbine reaches the thermal switch, it opens and allows hot air to flow again. This cycle may occur at from 80 to 40 times per minute depending on the temperature of the bleed air and the setting of the control. At slow aircraft speeds, where bleed air temperature is below 200°F, no surging will occur even on full HOT. At higher aircraft speeds, where bleed air temperature may exceed 400°F, surging will occur at one-quarter MANUAL HOT setting, and if setting is increased the surge cycle will increase to a higher rate. If cockpit temperature is not maintained automatically at the desired level, accomplish the following:

1. Cockpit heat rheostat—MANUAL, and position as desired.

Note

- If airflow surge occurs, move cockpit heat rheostat toward COLD.
- If cockpit temperature is excessive and cannot be decreased automatically or manually, open the ram air scoop.

CAUTION

Manual control is provided as a backup feature only and should not be used except in case of automatic control failure. There is danger of fogging up the cockpit during takeoff if manual control is used. This will not happen on automatic.

COCKPIT PRESSURIZATION MALFUNCTION.

Separation of the hot air duct at the refrigerator inlet will cause loss of cockpit pressurization, and may damage wiring with subsequent failure of the electrical systems within a few minutes. Electrical system failure occurs when hot compressor air melts the wiring insulation in the electrical compartment located behind the cockpit. If the fresh air scoop is opened when cockpit pressure loss is recognized, the bleed air shutoff valve will then keep hot air from entering the electrical system. If air in the cockpit becomes contaminated, or if the cockpit pressurization reduces substantially and the cause is not apparent, accomplish the following:

1. If using an MA-13A oxygen mask, diluter level—100%.

2. Ram air scoop lever—OPEN.

Open ram air scoop as soon as practicable, depending on pressurization and altitude. If complete pressure loss is experienced or if at a safe flight level for depressurization, open ram air scoop immediately.

DEFROSTING AND RAIN REMOVAL SYSTEM.

DEFROSTING SYSTEM.

The defrosting system consists of a number of small air jets directed parallel to the canopy and windshield surfaces. These jets attract cockpit air and cause it to flow over the inside surfaces, thereby raising the surface temperatures. As long as the surface temperatures are above the cockpit dew point, no fog or frost will form. Air for the defrosting system is normally routed from the secondary heat exchanger through a check valve and the defrost flow control and shutoff valve (figure 4-1) to the defrosting outlets located along the inside base of the windshield canopy. This airflow in itself is not sufficient to meet all the requirements of the system so to supplement this flow a bleed line is provided which directs air from a point just downstream of the hot air shutoff valve to a differential relief and check valve. When pressure in the normal flow line drops because of large demands on the system (defrost flow control valve open), the differential relief valve will open and furnish the additional air necessary for effective defrosting under all conditions.

CANOPY DEFROSTING LEVER.

The amount of air directed to the windshield and canopy defrost outlets is determined by the position of the canopy defrosting lever (figures 1-20, 1-21) located on the right forward panel. Upward movement of the lever increases the amount of defrost air to the outlets by actuating the pneumatically operated shutoff valve. With the lever in the INCR position, the valve will be opened fully, while in the OFF position, the valve will be closed and no defrosting air will be available.

Note

> The windshield and canopy defrosting system should be operated throughout the flight at the highest flow possible consistent with pilot comfort so that sufficiently high temperature is maintained to preheat the canopy and windshield areas. It is necessary to preheat because there is insufficient time during rapid descents to heat these areas to temperatures that prevent the formation of frost or fog.

ELECTRICALLY HEATED WINDSHIELD.

The left windshield panel is electrically heated on all modified aircraft. Glass temperature is controlled by a thermal switch (no manual switch is installed). This switch will provide electrical power to the heating element whenever the glass temperature falls below 95° (±5°)F. When the glass is heated to 105° (±5°) F, the electrical power will be automatically disconnected. The windshield obtains power from the emergency ac bus. A circuit breaker located on the right console A C forward cockpit B D, labeled WINDSHIELD DEFOG (see figures 1-40 and 1-41) may be pulled to deactivate the system in case of a malfunction.

FACE PLATE HEAT SYSTEM.

Heating elements are incorporated in the pilot's face plate to prevent or remove any accumulation of moisture on the face plate which would hinder the pilot's vision. This system becomes especially important at high altitudes in the event of any malfunction which may cause rapid decrease in cockpit temperature and pressure. To ensure that face-plate heating will be available under all operating conditions (except during complete electrical failure), electrical power for the heating elements is taken from the No. 1 battery bus for A and forward cockpit B D. The aft cockpit heating element B D receives power from the No. 2 ac bus through the 115-to-28-volt auto-transformer.

Face Plate Heat Rheostat.

DC electrical power from the battery bus to the face-plate heating elements is controlled by the face-plate rheostat (figures 1-16, 1-22) located on the right console A B and on the lower right instrument panel C D. Heat may be applied to the face plate in varying degrees by moving the rheostat clockwise from OFF to any desired position. Heating intensity will be maximum with the rheostat in the ON (extreme clockwise) position.

Note

- Prior to takeoff, check face plate heat for proper operation.
- Use the minimum required heat to prevent or remove any accumulation of moisture on the face plate.
- The face plate heat rheostat should be at maximum heat just long enough to remove moisture, then returned to the minimum heat required to prevent moisture accumulation.

HEATING CONTROL PANEL

NOTE B D
PANEL IN FOWARD
COCKPIT ONLY

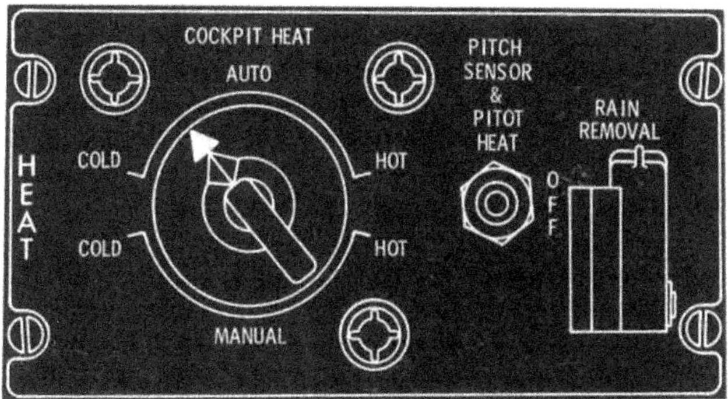

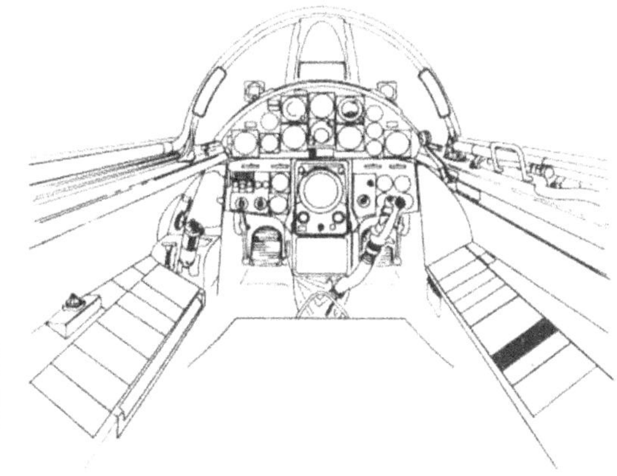

F52-0-4-57

Figure 4-3

RAIN REMOVAL SYSTEM.

The rain removal system receives compressor air from the same line that furnishes pressure for the canopy seal, radar system, and anti-G suit valve (figure 4-1). Rain-removal air passes through a pilot-controlled shutoff valve to a nozzle at the outside base of the left windshield panel. This high-velocity hot air flows over the panel to remove rain and to prevent windshield icing.

CAUTION

Rain removal air is ducted through the left side of the cockpit. If a leak should develop in this duct line, air at very high temperature will enter the cockpit, in which case the ram air scoop should be opened. This will shut off all compressor air to the duct line and direct cold ram air into the cockpit.

Rain Removal Switch. The guarded rain removal switch (figure 4-3) located on the right console outboard of the cockpit heat rheostat, controls the flow of compressor air to the rain removal outlets. Moving the switch forward from OFF to the RAIN REMOVAL position closes a 28-volt dc monitored bus circuit to the rain removal shutoff valve, opening the valve and allowing hot, pressurized air to pass through the valve to the outlets.

CAUTION

- Do not turn on the rain removal system above its limit airspeed, or the rain removal nozzle may be damaged.
- Do not leave on for more than 30 seconds except in flight.

NORMAL OPERATION OF DEFROSTING AND RAIN REMOVAL SYSTEMS.

If any portion of the windshield or canopy becomes obscured by moisture do the following:

1. Canopy defrosting lever—INCR.
2. Cockpit heat rheostat—AUTO-HOT.
3. Rain removal switch—RAIN REMOVAL. If precipitation is obscuring forward visibility.

Note

Canopy defrosting air should be operated at all times at the highest temperature consistent with pilot comfort. This will minimize the possibility of windshield and canopy fogging caused by extreme temperature differentials accompanying an engine failure or a rapid descent from high altitude.

EMERGENCY OPERATION OF DEFROSTING AND RAIN REMOVAL SYSTEMS.

If the windshield cannot be cleared by normal procedures and it is necessary to land without delay, proceed as follows:

1. Canopy defrosting lever—Check (INCR position).
2. Cockpit heat rheostat—MANUAL—HOT.
3. Rain removal switch—RAIN REMOVAL.
4. Engine rpm—Maximum, if fuel and time permit.

The above procedure will direct compressor air to the windshield outlets at its maximum available temperature and pressure.

Note

If excessive fog, vapor, or visible moisture of any kind enters the cockpit and restricts visibility on takeoff, open the ram air scoop.

ANTI-ICING SYSTEMS.

ENGINE ANTI-ICING SYSTEM.

The engine anti-icing system is designed to prevent ice formation in the compressor inlet. Icing of the inlet guide vanes reduces airflow through the engine and causes a loss of power possibly accompanied by an increase in nozzle area and fuel flow. Hot, seventeenth-stage compressor air flows through a port in the compressor rear frame to the inlet of the solenoid-operated anti-ice valve. The anti-ice valve regulates pressure and airflow to the horizontal struts of the engine front frame. Air is ported through the struts into a manifold in the hub of the frame. Air in the manifold enters the top vertical strut and inlet guide vanes. Holes in the outer end of the vanes and top strut allow air to discharge into the inlet airstream. The bottom strut is anti-iced continuously by scavenge oil flowing through it.

Engine Anti-Ice Switch.

The engine anti-ice switch (figures 1-20, 1-21) located on the left forward panel, controls the flow of compressor air to the engine front frame and inlet guide vanes by actuating the solenoid-operated engine anti-ice valve. When the switch is in the ON position power from the No. 2 ac bus energizes the circuit which opens the valve and permits compressor air to be directed to the engine front frame and inlet guide vanes. Moving the switch to the OFF position deenergizes the circuit, permitting the valve to close.

Engine Anti-Icing On Warning Light.  

The engine anti-icing ON warning light (figures 1-20, 1-21) is provided as a visual indication that the anti-icing system is operating. The light is operated by a temperature-sensing device mounted in the air duct between the anti-icing valve and the compressor front frame. This temperature-sensing device will cause the warning light to illuminate whenever anti-icing air temperature reaches approximately 163°C. The light normally remains on for approximately ½ minute after the anti-icing valve has closed, because of hot air remaining in the duct.

Engine Anti-Icing On Warning Light. 

A light on the warning light panel (figures 1-20, 1-21) is provided as a visual indication that the anti-icing system is operating. A differential pressure-operated switch which responds instantly to changes in pressure within the anti-icing system causes the ENG ANTI-ICING ON light to illuminate when the anti-ice switch is operated.

Note

- Due to the extreme sensitivity of the warning light pressure sensing switch, the warning light may illuminate momentarily during rapid throttle bursts.
- The placard normally extinguishes immediately after the engine anti-icing switch is placed in the OFF position.

OPERATION OF THE ENGINE ANTI-ICING SYSTEM.

Icing will occur on the inlet ducts and engine compressor front frame at subsonic speeds only. Ram air temperature rise at supersonic speeds is sufficient to prevent icing. If the engine is operated above 82 percent rpm, the anti-icing air temperature is sufficient to prevent rapid ice buildup on the engine front frame and inlet guide vanes. The engine can safely ingest aircraft inlet duct ice at engine speeds less than 85 percent rpm 3B 7A or 88 percent rpm 19. At higher engine speeds, the inlet guide vanes may be damaged. Engine operation is still possible with limited inlet guide vane damage. The requirement for engine anti-icing is a direct function of indicated compressor inlet temperature (CIT). Operation of the anti-icing system above a CIT of 10° centigrade compromises the service life expectancy of the magnesium front frame. If weather conditions indicate a need for anti-icing, the system should be used only at a CIT indication of 10° centigrade, or below.

Ground Check Prior to Flight Under Icing Conditions.

1. Engine Idle rpm.
2. Engine anti-ice switch—ON.

Note 

- Advance throttle until ENG ANTI-ICING ON warning light illuminates. The light should illuminate between idle and 85 percent rpm depending on ambient temperature. Do not exceed 85 percent rpm.
- ENG ANTI-ICING ON warning light 19 should illuminate within 5 seconds. If light does not illuminate, advance throttle to 80 percent rpm.

3. Engine anti-ice switch—OFF (after light illuminates).

WARNING

- Monitor warning light and maintain rpm.

  Abort the flight if light stays on more than 2 minutes after switch is deactivated; make appropriate entry on Form 781.

- Engine anti-ice warning light must extinguish within 5 seconds. 19

  Abort flight if warning light does not illuminate or remains illuminated more than 5 seconds after engine anti-ice switch is placed in OFF position. Make appropriate entry in Form 781.

In-Flight Procedure.

1. If flight is anticipated through known or suspected icing conditions, activate the anti-icing system when at subsonic speed and when the indicated CIT is 10° centigrade or below. Do not exceed a maximum speed of 350 knots or Mach 1.0, whichever is lower, with the anti-icing valve open.

2. After flying in moderate to heavy icing for 2 minutes or more, reduce thrust (where practical) to 85 percent 3B 7A or 88 percent 19 to minimize inlet duct ice ingestion damage to the engine.

3. Should it be necessary to fly in known icing conditions at low altitude and low thrust settings (80 to 85 percent rpm), engine power should be increased to 100 percent rpm every 5 minutes to ensure that adequate anti-icing air circulation is available at the engine compressor front frame. This thrust increase should be maintained for approximately 30 seconds.

PITCH SENSORS AND PITOT HEAT SWITCH.

The APC vanes, stick shaker pitch sensor vanes, and pitot-static head are heated electrically by power from the No. 2 ac bus. Heating elements within the pitch sensor vanes and the pitot-head receive this power whenever the heating circuit is closed. This is done by placing the pitch sensor and pitot heat switch (figure 4-3) on the cockpit right console from OFF to the PITCH SENSOR & PITOT HEAT position. Heat should be applied whenever instrument flying conditions are encountered in order to prevent the formation of ice on these units.

COMMUNICATIONS AND ASSOCIATED ELECTRONIC EQUIPMENT.

The communications and associated electronic equipment installed in the aircraft is listed in figure 4-4.

MICROPHONE AND HEADSET CONNECTIONS.  

The microphone and headset connections are a complement of the oxygen supply hose and plug into the pilot's personal headgear equipment.

MICROPHONE SWITCH.

The microphone switch consists of a button (figure 1-9) located on the throttle grip. It is used for transmitting with the UHF command radio and for manual interphone communications on B D aircraft.

AN/AIC-10 INTERCOMMUNICATION SET. B D

The AN/AIC-10 intercommunication set provides high intelligibility of speech and communications at all altitudes. It gives simplified control over the radio receivers and transmitters and permits maximum flexibility of communication facilities: communication between cockpits, communication with ground stations and other aircraft, monitoring received radio signals including simultaneous monitoring of three radio receivers, and a call facility for use in establishing interphone communication between the cockpits. The set incorporates two AN/AIC-10 control panels and a relay assembly for "hot-mike" operation. "Hot-mike" operation provides continuous operation on interphone without the necessity of manual operation of the microphone button. This equipment is powered by the dc emergency bus and is protected by a circuit breaker located on the aft cockpit left side panel.

TABLE OF COMMUNICATIONS AND ASSOCIATED ELECTRONIC EQUIPMENT

TYPE	DESIGNATION	FUNCTION	PRIMARY OPERATOR	RANGE	LOCATION OF CONTROLS
B D INTERPHONE	AN/AIC-10	Communication Between Cockpits and to Ground Crew	Either Crew Member	Between Cockpits	Right Console
UHF COMMAND	AN/ARC-66	Two-Way Communications (and Interphone A C)	Either Crew Member	Line of Sight	Left Console (Interphone Button on Right Console A C)
VHF NAVIGATION	AN/ARN-56	VOR Navigation Voice and Localizer Reception	Either Crew Member	Line of Sight	Right Console
	AN/ARN-55	Glide Slope Reception	Either Crew Member	Line of Sight	Right Console
		Marker Beacon Reception	Automatic	Any Distance Over Marker Beacon	None
IFF	AN/APX-35	Aircraft Identification	Forward Cockpit Only	Line of Sight	Right Console (Forward Cockpit B D)
TACAN	AN/ARN-21	Distance Measuring and Station Bearing	Forward Cockpit Only	Line of Sight up to 195 Nautical Miles	Left Console (Forward Cockpit B D)

F52-0-4-109

Figure 4-4

AN/AIC-10 INTERPHONE CONTROL PANEL. B D

An interphone control panel (figure 4-5) is located on the right console in each cockpit. It acts as a master control box for the associated electronic equipment, radios, and intercommunication equipment. The panel does not contain an on-off switch: the equipment is on whenever the dc emergency bus is energized. The system utilizes the "hot-microphone" arrangement for communication between both cockpits and the ground crew. If the emergency dc bus fails, the interphone will be powered from the battery bus; however, when the landing gear is extended, the left gear uplock switch will deenergize the interphone circuit. The panel contains a volume control, monitoring switches, selector knobs, and auxiliary listening switch.

Note

The interphone power source will automatically transfer from the dc emergency bus to the battery bus when engine rpm falls below 63 percent; however, the gear must be retracted for interphone communication.

Volume Control. B D

The volume control is provided for the adjustment of aural signal intensity.

Monitoring Switches. B D

The five monitoring switches provide individual or simultaneous reception of audio signals with the rotary selector knob in either the INTER or COMM INTER position, as follows:

INTER. For interphone reception only.
COMM. For AN/ARC-66 reception.
MARKER. For AN/ARN-55 visual reception only.
VHF NAV. For AN/ARN-56 reception.

Rotary Selector Knob. B D

The rotary selector knob permits selection of individual transmission and reception in accordance with the following four functions placarded on the rotary base.

CALL. For intercommunication; permits the user in an emergency to interrupt or override any signals being received by the other pilot if the other pilot is operating his interphone with the rotary selector knob set on any position other than INTER or COMM INTER.

COMM INTER. For transmission or reception with the AN/ARC-66 radio; two way "hot mike" intercommunication; and the reception of other signals as selected by the monitoring switches.

INTER. For manual transmission and reception of intercommunication signals using the MIC button, on the throttle and the reception of other signals as selected by the monitoring switches.

COMM. For transmission or reception with the AN/ARC-66 radio only.

NORMAL, AUX LISTEN Switch. B D

A toggle switch, placarded NORMAL and AUX LISTEN, is used to control the audio signal path. The NORMAL position allows all audio signals to pass through the AN/AIC-10 amplifier, thus allowing the volume control knob on the AN/AIC-10 panel to adjust audio signal intensity. The switch in the AUX LISTEN position bypasses the amplifier, in case it fails, and audio signal intensity must be adjusted with the individual receiver volume control.

VHF AND UHF CONTROL TRANSFER PANEL. B D

The VHF and UHF control transfer panel (figure 4-6) is located on the left console of both cockpits. The panel contains two switches and two green indicator lights. The inboard switch, placarded COMM, is the command radio control transfer switch. It transfers control of channel selection between cockpits for the AN/ARC-66 command radio. The outboard switch, placarded NAV, is the navigation receiver control transfer switch. It transfers control of channel selection between cockpits for the AN/ARN-56 VHF-NAV receiver. The green indicator light associated with each switch illuminates only in the cockpit having control. The operator in the cockpit that does not have control can transmit and receive but cannot control frequency selection.

INTERPHONE CONTROL PANEL B D

Figure 4-5

UHF COMMAND RADIO AN/ARC-66.

Note

> Make no transmission on emergency (distress) frequency channels except for actual emergency purposes. For test, demonstration, or drill purposes, the radio equipment must be operated in a shielded room to prevent transmission of messages that could be construed as emergency messages.

The AN/ARC-66 UHF command radio which is installed in the aircraft provides two-way radio communications (air-to-air and air-to-ground) on 1750 different frequencies in a range extending from 225.0 through 399.9 megacycles. Any of these frequencies may be selected manually; however, the radio is preset on the ground to select only the 20 most commonly used frequencies (channels) during normal operation.

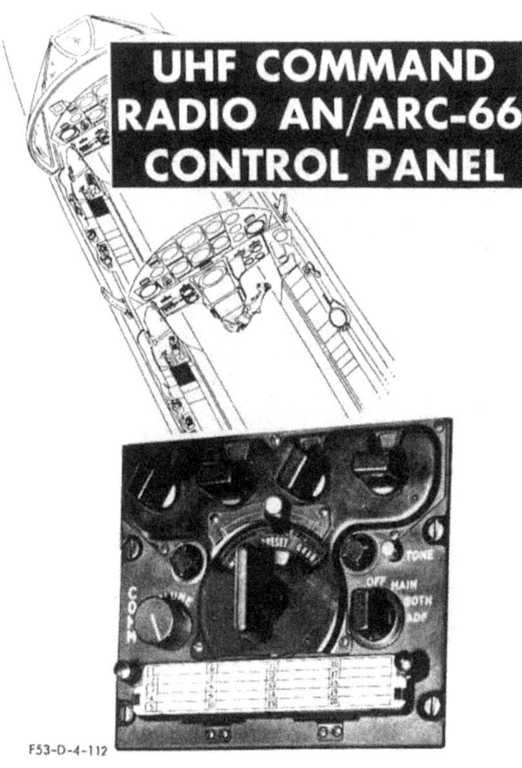

Figure 4-6

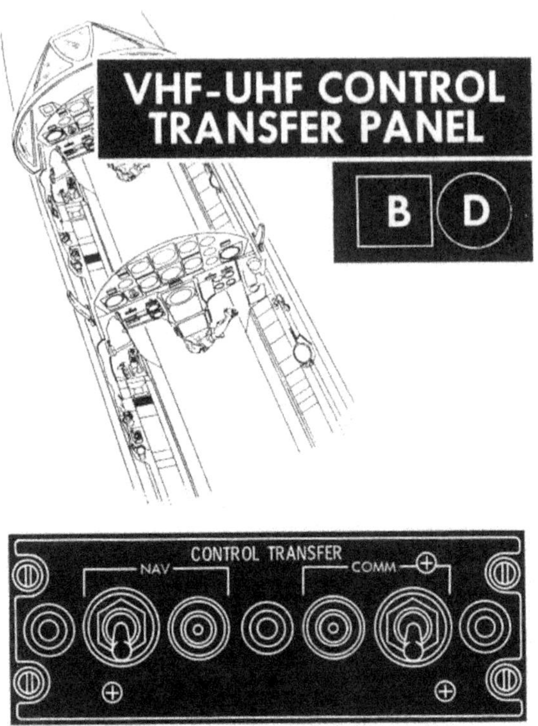

Figure 4-7

In addition to the main receiver, the set utilizes a guard receiver which can cover a frequency range between 238.0 and 248.0 megacycles, but which must be pretuned on the ground, to provide an emergency channel which is constantly altered. The control panel for the set is located on the left console and includes a function switch, a selector switch, a volume rheostat, a tone button, and four manual tuning knobs (see figure 4-7). The function switch in the OFF position disconnects the set from its power source (dc emergency bus and ac emergency bus). With the switch in the MAIN position, the transmitter and main receiver both operate on the selected frequency, but the guard receiver is inoperative. With the function switch at BOTH, the transmitter and main receiver operate as indicated above, and the guard receiver functions simultaneously to provide reception on guard channel. The ADF position is inoperative. The selector switch determines frequency selection and has three positions, MANUAL, PRESET, and GUARD. Normally, the PRESET position is used, and permits the pilot to choose any of the 20 preset frequencies (channels) by operating the channel selector knob at the center of the selector switch. A numerical indication of the selected channel is provided in a window directly above the channel selector knob. When the selector switch is in MANUAL, any of the 1750 frequencies in the 225.0 to 399.9 megacycles range may be selected by moving the four manual tuning knobs to the desired positions. An indication of the frequency selected is provided in the windows adjacent to and forward of each tuning knob. On modified aircraft a remote channel indicator is installed on the instrument panel (figures 1-12, 1-22) to facilitate ease of interpretation during tuning. The GUARD mode of selector switch operation places the main receiver and transmitter on the fixed guard frequency, permitting the pilot to transmit, as well as receive, on guard channel. Depressing the tone button cuts out radio reception and transmits a continuous tone which aids ground stations in obtaining a bearing on the aircraft during direction-finding procedures.

UHF COMMAND RADIO INTERPHONE. A C

The AN/ARC-66 UHF command radio package also contains the interphone system which is powered by the dc emergency bus. The interphone system provides communication between the pilot and ground crew during starting and pre-taxi procedures. The interphone is connected to the aircraft through a jack in the external electrical power receptacle. The pilot can receive transmissions from the ground crew whenever the AN/ARC-66 UHF radio is operating and his headset is connected. In order to transmit to the ground crew, the pilot must first depress the interphone button (figures 1-16, 1-26) on the right console. The landing gear warning signal is also connected through the interphone system.

Operation of UHF Command Radio.

1. Set interphone panel as desired. B D
2. Obtain control with the command radio control transfer switch and check indicator light. B D
3. Selector switch—PRESET.
4. Function switch—BOTH and allow 2 minutes for warmup.
5. Channel selector knob—As desired.

Note

In order to obtain maximum transmitting and receiving effectiveness, some channel other than the one desired should be selected first. Allow the tuning cycle to be completed and then select the desired channel. Because of an inherent characteristic of the set, full power will not be available unless this procedure is followed.

6. Volume rheostat—As desired.
7. To select a frequency other than one of the pre-set channels do the following:
   a. Function switch—MAIN or BOTH (if in BOTH, guard channel will be stronger).
   b. Selector switch—MANUAL.
   c. Manual tuning knobs—Position as required to obtain the desired frequency. (A numerical indication of the selected frequency will be presented by the digits appearing in the indicator windows at the top of the control panel.)
8. To transmit as well as receive on guard channel, move the selector switch to GUARD.

Note

The channeling drive motor cuts out automatically after 50 to 125 seconds of continuous operation. If this should occur, move the function switch to OFF, allow 30 seconds for cool-in, then place the switch to BOTH and select the desired channel.

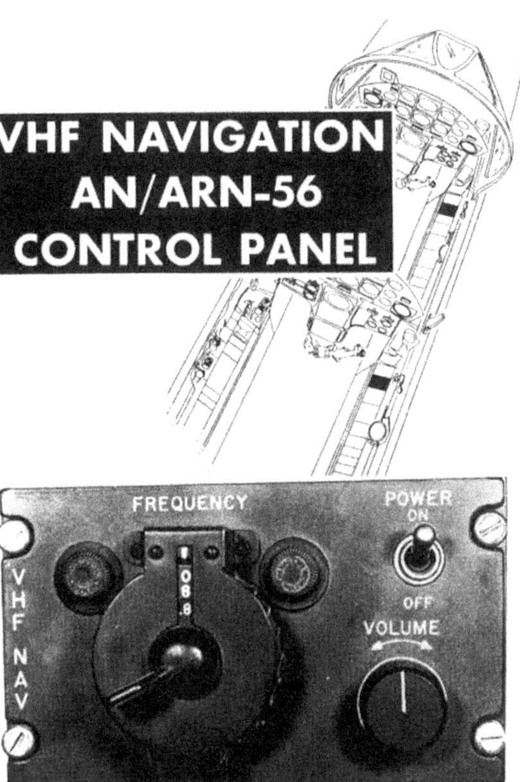

Figure 4-8

VHF NAVIGATION EQUIPMENT AN/ARN-56.

The VHF navigation set can receive transmissions in a frequency range of 108.0 to 135.9 megacycles. Visual information and aural station identification are provided by this equipment to assist the pilot in determining the position of the aircraft in relation to VOR stations on the ground. The receiver components utilize 28-volt dc from the emergency bus, and 200/115 volts from the No. 2 ac bus, while the indicators operate on 26-volt ac from the instrument autotransformer.

Note

The set can be tuned to the proper frequency for receiving weather broadcasts, tower instructions, and general information.

AN/ARN-56 CONTROL PANEL.

The VHF navigation control panel (figure 4-8) has a power switch, a frequency selector, and a volume rheostat. The power switch, when moved forward from OFF to POWER ON, puts the set into operation. Frequency selection is made by rotating the concentric knobs until the desired frequency appears in the vertical indicator window. Starting at the top, the numbers in the

ID-250 RADIO MAGNETIC INDICATOR

BA-1880 F53-E2-4-115

Figure 4-9

ID-526 BEARING DISTANCE HEADING INDICATOR

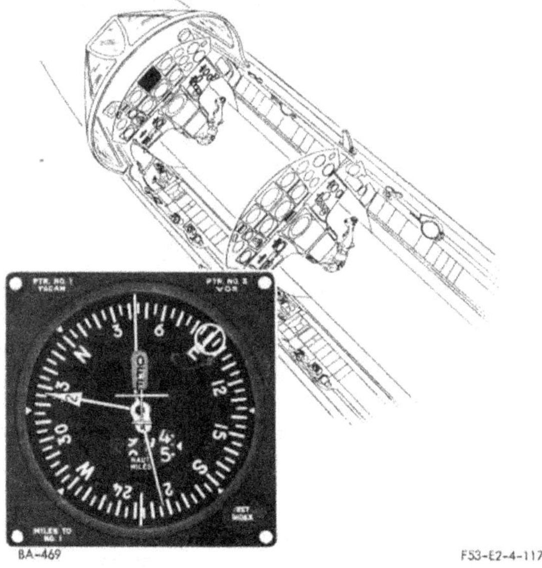

Figure 4-10

window represent hundreds, tens, units, and tenths of megacycles, respectively. Volume can be adjusted as desired by rotating the volume control knob. On B D aircraft the receiver may be monitored aurally through the AIC-10 interphone panel by placing the VHF-NAV monitoring switch in the VHF-NAV position.

RADIO MAGNETIC INDICATOR, ID-250.

The radio magnetic indicator (RMI) ID-250 (figure 4-9) provides directional gyro heading or slaved gyro magnetic heading information and magnetic bearing indications. The outer ring of the instrument has a fixed triangular index at the top of the dial under which aircraft heading is indicated. Seven smaller fixed triangular indices are spaced 45 degrees apart on the periphery of the dial to facilitate instrument interpretation. The compass card is coupled to the J-4 heading indicator system so that the aircraft heading is always indicated under the top index.

Bearing Pointers. A B

Two bearing pointers No. 1 and No. 2 provide magnetic bearing to either or both TACAN and VOR transmitter. The RMI receives power from the instrument ac bus and the dc emergency bus. Failure of either source of electrical energy will render the RMI inoperative.

On aircraft equipped with TACAN only or VOR only, pointers No. 1 and No. 2 on A aircraft are electrically tied together and move as one. On B aircraft pointer No. 1 is electrically locked in the vertical position and pointer No. 2 moves.

In the aft cockpit of B aircraft that are equipped with both TACAN and VOR, the No. 1 pointer is connected to the TACAN receiver and pointer No. 2 is connected to the VOR receiver.

Bearing Pointers. 

Two bearing pointer indicators are provided. On aircraft not modified to incorporate TACAN the pointers are connected and operate as one to indicate magnetic bearing to the selected VOR/ILS station. On aircraft incorporating both TACAN and VOR/ILS, pointer No. 1 indicates magnetic bearing to the selected TACAN station and pointer No. 2 indicates magnetic bearing to the selected VOR/ILS station. The RMI receives power from the instrument ac bus and the dc emergency bus. Failure of either source of electrical energy will render the RMI inoperative.

Radio Magnetic Indicator, ID-250 A B
Location.

On aircraft not incorporating TACAN equipment, the ID-250 RMI is located on the left side of the instrument panel A and in the same place both cockpits B. On aircraft incorporating TACAN in place of VOR, the ID-250 RMI is located on the top center of the instrument panel A and in the same place in both cockpits B. On aircraft having both TACAN and VOR, the ID-250 RMI is located in the aft cockpit of B aircraft only. (See figure 4-9.) The forward cockpit B and A aircraft instrument panels incorporate the ID-526 BDHI in place of the ID-250 RMI.

Radio Magnetic Indicator, ID-250 C D
Location.

On aircraft not incorporating TACAN, the ID-250 RMI is located on the center of the instrument panel C and in the same place both cockpits D. On aircraft incorporating TACAN, the ID-250 RMI is located on the center of the aft cockpit instrument panel D aircraft only. On C aircraft and front cockpit D aircraft the ID-250 RMI is replaced with the ID-526 BDHI.

Bearing Distance Heading Indicator, ID-526 BDHI.

The ID-526 bearing distance heading indicator (BDHI), figure 4-10, displays aircraft heading simultaneously with bearing from a TACAN or VOR/ILS station and distance to the TACAN station. It is powered by the instrument inverter through the 26-volt instrument power transformer. The indicator provides the display functions and operating controls listed in the following paragraphs.

Rotating Azimuth Card. The rotating azimuth card is calibrated in units of 5 degrees from 0 through 360 degrees. The card provides an azimuth ring against which aircraft heading, VOR/ILS station bearing, and TACAN station bearing are read.

Fiducial Marker. The fiducial marker indicates aircraft magnetic heading on the rotating azimuth card.

Bearing Pointers. The No. 1 pointer indicates bearing from the selected TACAN station. The No. 2 pointer indicates bearing from the selected VOR/ILS station.

Range Counter. The range counter window indicates slant range distance in nautical miles from the aircraft to the selected TACAN station.

Note A B

A red warning band instead of the distance indication appears in the range counter window whenever unreliable distance information is being transmitted to the BDHI.

OFF/LIM Flag. When the OFF flag appears, C D range information is unreliable. When the LIM flag is displayed range information can be relied upon.

Set Index Knob. The set index knob positions the request heading marker index against a desired heading on the rotating azimuth card. The engage position (knob pulled out) provides automatic interception of a predetermined heading when an automatic pilot is installed. This position is not applicable in this aircraft. The request-heading marker index tracks the heading on the rotating azimuth card as positioned by the set index knob. This facilitates navigation by providing a method of selecting a predetermined heading.

DISTANCE INDICATOR, ID-310. A B

On aircraft with 747 C/W, the ID-310 distance indicator (figure 4-11) is installed on the instrument panels in both A and B aircraft to indicate slant range distance in nautical miles from a TACAN station. If the TACAN equipment is turned OFF or is searching for a station, or the aircraft is too far away from the station, a red warning band appears across the window of the instrument to warn the pilot that range indication is incorrect.

Note B

The ID-310 distance indicator will furnish range information in the cockpit which has control of the TACAN equipment. The indicator in the other cockpit will display the red warning band.

COURSE INDICATOR, ID-249 OR ID-351.

The aircraft may be equipped with either an ID-249 or ID-351 course indicator, (figure 4-12) mounted on the center instrument panels. There is no electrical, functional, or physical difference between the ID-249 and ID-351 course indicators. Signals are directed into the indicator from the VOR or TACAN receiver to operate the course deviation needle for course guidance. On modified aircraft the position of the CDI selector switch determines which signal (TACAN or VOR/ILS) controls the operation of the course deviation needle. A

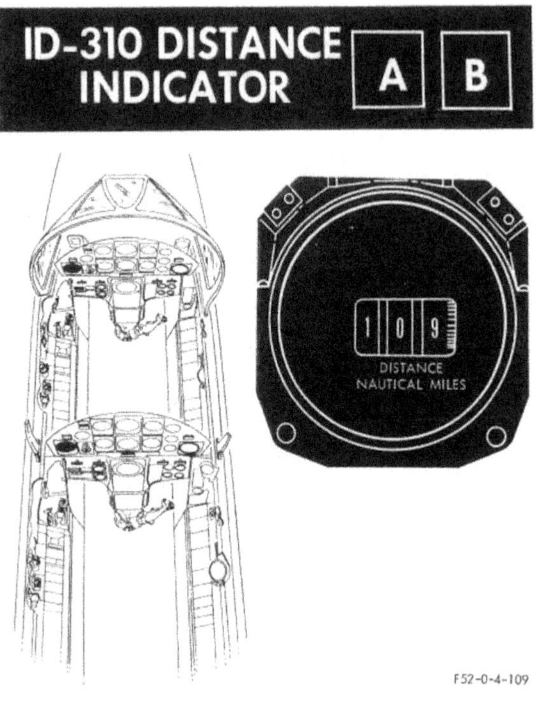

Figure 4-11

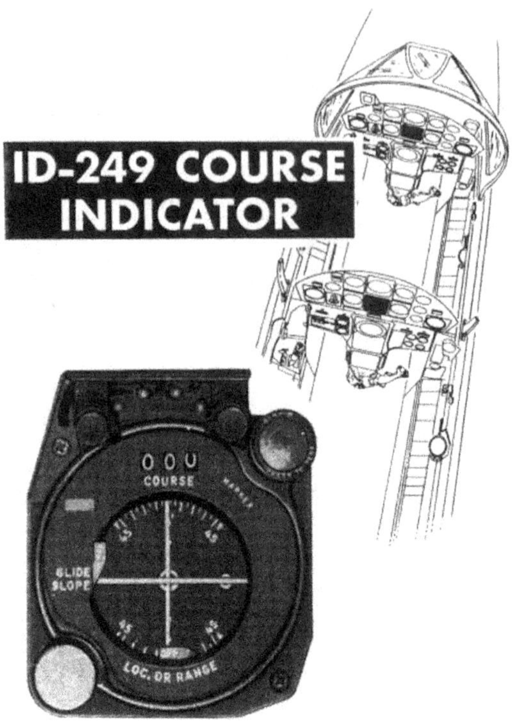

Figure 4-12

course SET knob in the lower left corner of the instrument is used to select the desired inbound or outbound magnetic course in the course selector window at the top of the instrument. The glide slope indicator is operated by the AN/ARN-55 glide slope receiver during ILS operations. TO and FROM indications are shown in a window in the upper left corner of the instrument. This instrument is provided with two warning flags (one for course and one for glide slope), which operate any time a signal is unreliable, weak or nonexistent. The instrument uses ac power from the instrument ac bus and dc power from the dc emergency bus. Failure of the dc source of electrical energy will render both indicators inoperative. Failure of the ac source of electrical energy will render the glide slope indicator inoperative.

Note

Navigation is still possible on VOR or ILS after ac power failure. The TO-FROM indicator and the course deviation indicator operate on dc power.

CDI SELECTOR SWITCH.

The CDI selector switch (figure 4-13) is provided to select either TACAN or VOR/ILS operation of the course deviation indicator (CDI) on the course indicator. The switch is labeled INST SELECT and has two placarded positions, TACAN and VOR/ILS.

TACAN-VOR/ILS INDICATOR LIGHT.

On aircraft with 923 C/W, indicator lights (figures 1-12, 1-22) are provided for the pilot to positively identify which system, TACAN or VOR/ILS, is being displayed on the course indicator (figure 4-12). The indicator lights consist of two panels located on the forward instrument panel below the glare shield.

WARNING

Prior to initiating an ILS approach, make sure the CDI selector switch is in the VOR/ILS position. If the station has both TACAN and ILS, it is possible to make an approach using ILS glide slope indications, and TACAN course indications, but the aircraft may not be aligned with the center of the runway.

TACAN CONTROL PANELS

C-1763/ARN-21

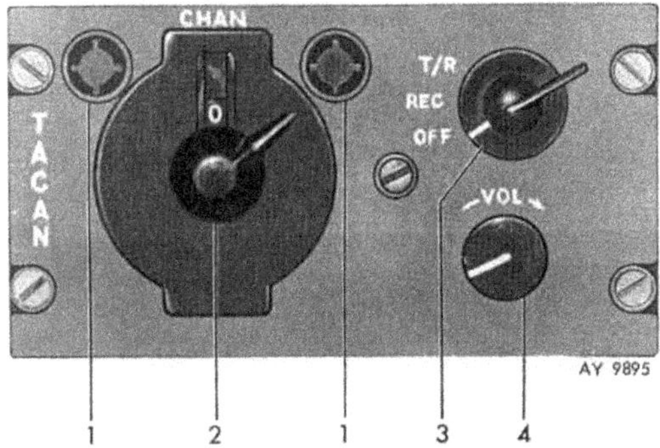

1 PANEL LIGHTS
2 CHANNEL SELECTOR
3 POWER SWITCH
4 VOLUME CONTROL

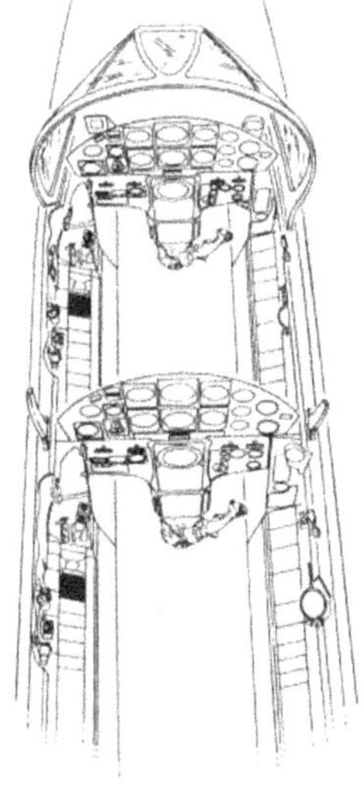

ID-249 CDI SELECTOR SWITCH

F53-E2-4-118

Figure 4-13

GLIDE SLOPE AND MARKER BEACON RECEIVER, AN/ARN-57. A B, AN/ARN-55 C D.

A glide slope receiver is provided for instrument landings. Selection of proper frequencies for an indication on the GSI of the course indicator (figure 4-12) is automatic and needs no further action on the part of the pilot other than selection of a frequency authorized for the place of landing. The GSI will indicate to the pilot whether the airplane is above, below, or on the glide-slope during an ILS approach to landing. The CDI will indicate whether the airplane is to the left, right, or on course during an ILS approach. The AN/ARN-56 is used for localizer frequency selection. The marker beacon receiver is automatically turned on when power is supplied to the aircraft electrical system. A marker beacon indicator light is located on the upper right corner of the ID-249 course indicator. The marker beacon receiver is powered from the emergency ac bus.

TACAN, AN/ARN-21 (MODIFIED AIRCRAFT).

The tactical air navigation (TACAN) system consists of a receiver and transmitter installed in the electronics compartment; control panels and indicators in the cockpits, and an antenna system. TACAN provides the pilot with continuous visual indication of bearing and distance information to a selected TACAN beacon. The system operates in the 1000-mc band. One hundred and twenty-six 2-way operating channels, spaced 1 mc apart, are available. The equipment will provide bearing and distance information to any selected surface TACAN installation within a line of sight distance up to 195 nautical miles or less, depending on aircraft altitude and station location. Variable-frequency ac power is provided by the No. 2 ac bus, fixed-frequency ac power is from the TACAN inverter, and dc power is provided by the dc emergency bus. The TACAN controls and indicators are as follows:

Control Panel, C-1763/ARN-21.

On aircraft with 747 C/W, the C-1763/ARN-21 control panel is located on the right console of A aircraft and on the right console in both cockpits B aircraft in place of the VHF navigation control panel. On aircraft with 731 C/W, the C-1763/ARN-21 control panel is located on the left console A C aircraft and on the left console forward cockpit B D aircraft (figures 1-14, 1-24, 1-15, 1-25). The panels are placarded TACAN on the inboard edge. Each panel contains two lamps for illumination and the controls listed in the following paragraphs.

Function Selector Switch. The function selector is a three-position, rotary switch placarded clockwise as follows:

OFF—Deenergizes the set.

REC—Selects bearing information to the station as presented by the No. 1 pointer of the ID-526 BDHI or ID-250 RMI, and course information on the ID-249 course indicator.

T/R—Set functions the same as in the REC position and in addition, slant range line-of-sight distance information up to 195 nautical miles is presented on the ID-526A BDHI.

Volume Control Knob. Ground beacon indentification audio level may be adjusted by rotating the knob placarded VOL to the right or left.

Channel Selector. The channel selector contain two concentric knobs. The outer knob selects hundreds and tens (digits 100-120) and the inner knob selects units (digits 0-9); thus, 126 channels may be selected.

TACAN Operation.

1. CDI selector switch—TACAN. (Verify indicator light agrees with switch position).
2. Power switch—REC (allow a 90-second warmup period).
3. Channel selector—Desired channel.
4. Volume control—As desired.
5. Verify station identification.
6. Observe the bearing to the station on the azimuth scale opposite the No. 1 pointer of the ID-526 BDHI or ID-250 RMI.
7. Observe deviation of the CDI and a TO and FROM indication on the course indicator.
8. Power switch—T/R.
9. Observe distance to the station on the ID-526 BDHI.
10. Power switch—OFF to deenergize the set.

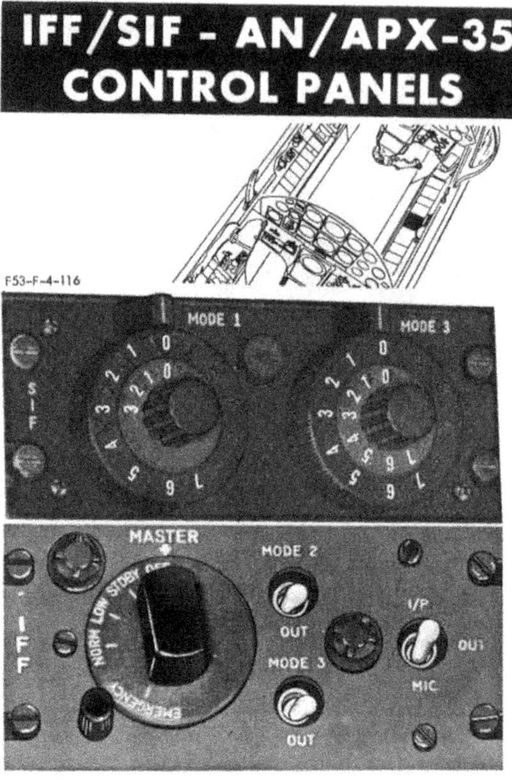

Figure 4-14

TACAN, False Lockon Procedure.

Occasionally TACAN equipment will lock on to a false bearing which will be 40 degrees, or a multiple of 40 degrees, in error. The error can be either side of the correct bearing. When using TACAN, cross check for false lockon with ground radar, airborne radar, dead reckoning, or other available means. These cross checks are especially important when switching channels or when turning set on. If a false lockon is suspected, proceed as follows:

1. Switch to another channel, check it for correct bearing, and then switch back to the desired channel.
2. Check for correct lockon.
3. If false lockon is still suspected, turn set OFF and then on.
4. Recheck for correct lockon.
5. If false lockon persists, utilize the other equipment or aids available.

Note

- TACAN still can be utilized during an emergency if the size and direction of bearing error can be determined and compensated for.
- The range information provided by TACAN is not affected.

IFF/SIF SYSTEM—AN/APX-35.

An AN/APX-35-IFF/SIF set is installed to automatically identify the aircraft as friendly whenever it is properly challenged by suitably equipped friendly air or surface equipment. The control panels (figure 4-14) are in the cockpit on the right console A C and forward cockpit B D. The IFF is powered by the emergency ac bus and the emergency dc bus.

On A B aircraft with 924 C/W, the ejection system will automatically activate the IFF system to military and civilian (FAA) emergency coding upon ejection from the aircraft. The emergency code transmitted by the IFF will provide ground radar stations with a tracking signal from point of ejection to impact of the aircraft.

Operation of AN/APX-35 IFF/SIF System.

1. IFF master switch—STBY. Allow 3 to 4 minutes for equipment to warm up.
2. IFF master switch—NORM.
3. Set mode 2 and mode 3 switches as required.
4. Set I/P—MIC switch as required.
5. On SIF control panel, set mode 1 and mode 3 knobs as required.
6. To turn equipment off, rotate IFF master switch to OFF.

LIGHTING EQUIPMENT.

Landing and Taxi Lights.

Two landing lights are provided, one on each main gear aft door. The lights are in position for use any time the landing gear is extended. On A C aircraft a taxi light is installed on the nose gear shock strut and is also available whenever the gear is extended. The switch has three positions, LANDING LT, OFF, and TAXI LT. However, either the LANDING LT position or the TAXI LT position will energize the taxi light and the landing lights. The lights are automatically shut off when the gear is retracted.

LIGHTING CONTROL PANELS

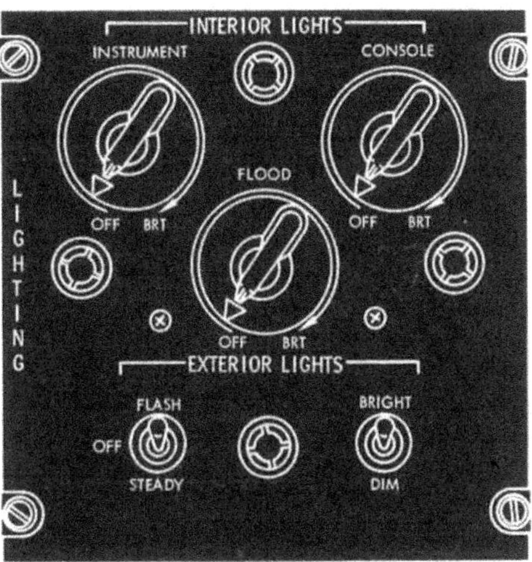

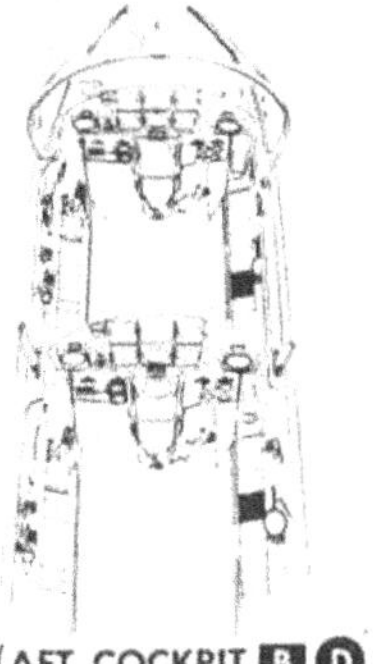

(AFT COCKPIT B D)

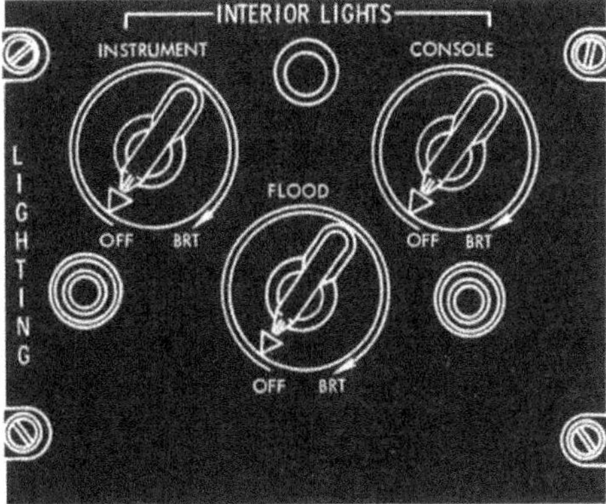

HG 08063
F52-0-4-59

Figure 4-15

Navigation Lights and Switches.

The navigation lights include two yellow upper tail lights, two white lower tail lights, a green and a red fuselage light, and white top and bottom fuselage lights. On aircraft with 960 C/W, the upper tail lights are white flood lights which illuminate the tail section. All navigation and formation lights are energized by 6 volt ac. The lights are controlled by a selector switch and a dimming switch (figure 4-15) located on a panel on the right console. The lights are energized by 28-volt ac from the No. 2 ac bus autotransformer when the selector switch is moved from OFF to STEADY or FLASH. Intensity of the navigation lights depends upon the position (BRIGHT or DIM) of the dimming switch. With the selector switch in the STEADY position, all of the navigation lights are energized continuously. In the FLASH position, the top and bottom fuselage lights still burn steadily while the remaining navigation lights are energized intermittently through a flasher unit at a rate of 40 flashes per minute. Formation lights are installed on the missile launchers and tip tanks. Also formation lights are installed on the wing tips. These lights automatically illuminate if the tip tanks are jettisoned, provided the selector switch is in the STEADY or FLASH position.

Cockpit Lighting System.

The cockpit lighting system includes instrument lights, console panel lights, console floodlights, thunderstorm lights, utility spotlights, and associated wiring, circuit breakers, and controls. The spotlights and floodlights receive power from the No. 2 ac bus through the autotransformer while the remainder of the cockpit lighting system is powered directly from the emergency ac bus. The instruments are individually illuminated by lights placed in shields above each instrument on the panel. The consoles are lighted by recessed lamps so that all of the controls and decals on each panel are readily discernible. The console floodlights are provided to light the left and right consoles directly. The thunderstorm lights are located on the left and right consoles and direct light forward onto the instrument panels to avoid blindness caused by lightning. A C-4A type utility spotlight is mounted on each side of the cockpit above the right and left consoles. These spotlights are detachable and may be moved about the cockpit to take care of special lighting situations. A rheostat on the aft end of each spotlight is used to vary the light intensity. Red or white light may be selected by rotating the lens. In addition to this, a push-button switch enables the pilot to bypass the rheostat and obtain maximum spotlight brilliance instantaneously. The instrument lights, console panel lights, and floodlights are controlled by three dimming rheostats, (figure 4-15) located on the right console. These rheostats, labeled INSTRUMENT, CONSOLE, and FLOOD, may be rotated clockwise from OFF to BRT as desired to vary the intensity of the associated lights. When starting the engine at night the cockpit light will be at maximum brilliance and the rheostat must be repositioned to dim the lights. The thunderstorm lights are controlled by a single ON-OFF switch (figures 1-16, 1-17, 1-26, 1-27, 1-29) on the right console.

On aircraft with 992 C/W, fuse panels (16, figures 1-16, 1-17, 1-19, and 12, figures 1-26, 1-27, 1-29) are installed for instrument, console and flood light circuits. The fuse panels incorporate four fuse holders which are identified on the panels with SPARE 3A, INSTR Lts 3A, CONSOLE Lts 3A, and FLOOD Lts 3A.

Emergency Cockpit Light Switch (Some Airplanes).

The emergency cockpit light switch (figures 1-14, 1-15), located on the left console, provides battery power to the cockpit spotlight when the spotlight rheostat is ON. The switch has two positions, NORMAL and EMERGENCY, and is connected in series with the spotlight rheostat control.

Note

If the spotlight rheostat is in the OFF position, the emergency cockpit light switch will not light the spotlight.

It is recommended that the emergency cockpit light switch be used only when light is required to accomplish emergency procedures. When not in use the switch should be in the NORMAL position.

CAUTION

Continued use of the emergency cockpit light switch EMERGENCY position will discharge the aircraft battery.

OXYGEN SYSTEM.

A liquid oxygen system (figure 4-16) is used to provide the normal oxygen supply requirements. The liquid oxygen is converted to a gaseous state in a converter container tank having a capacity of 5 litters (1.3 gallons) A C, 10 liters (2.6 gallons) B D. The oxygen is made suitable for breathing by passing through a heat exchanger which keeps the oxygen within a few degrees of cockpit ambient temperature. Oxygen is delivered to the oxygen control panel at a pressure of approximately 70 psi B C. On B D aircraft oxygen is delivered to a reducer valve at the control panel where pressure is reduced from approximately 300 psi to 70 psi.

OXYGEN SUPPLY SYSTEM

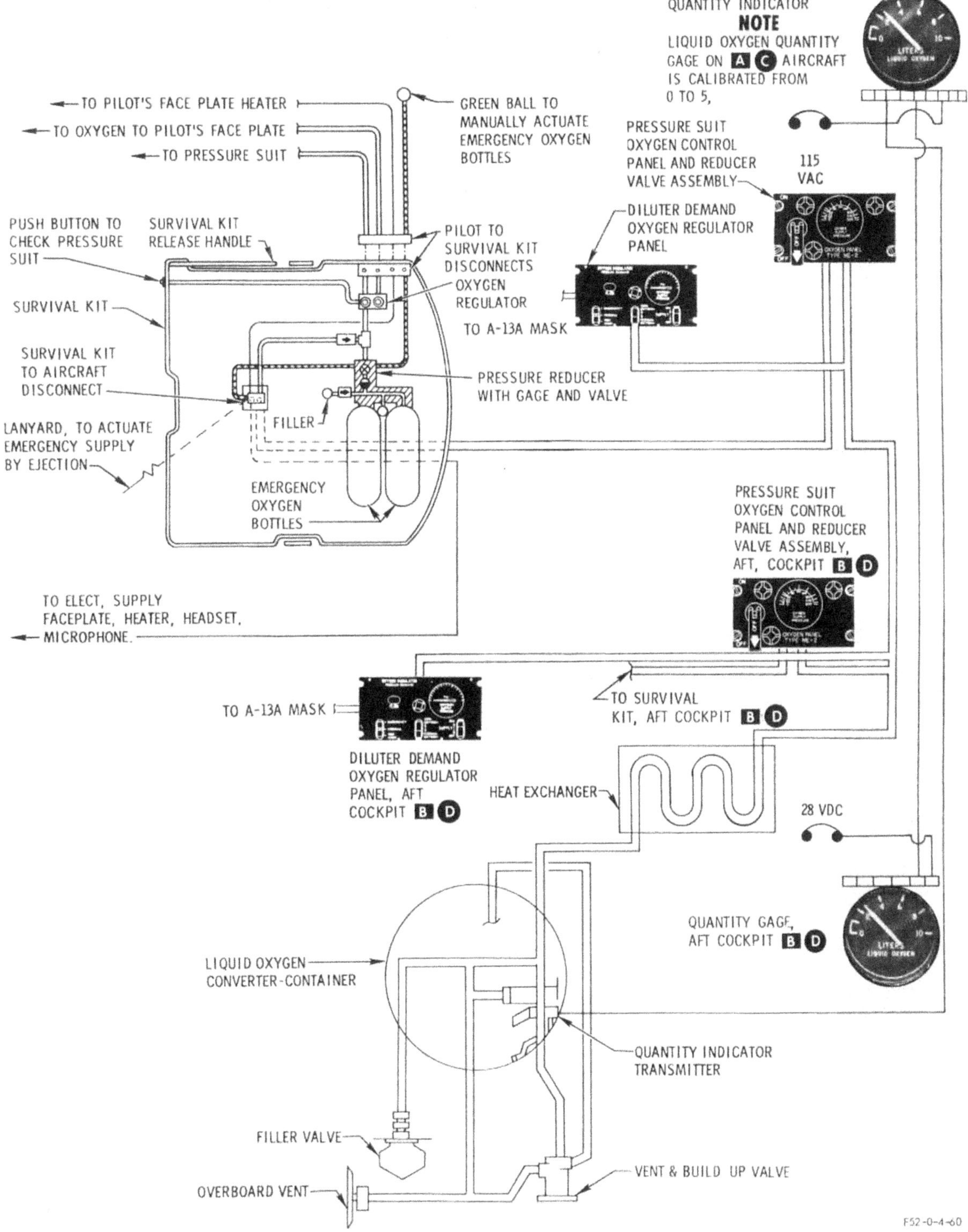

QUANTITY INDICATOR
NOTE
LIQUID OXYGEN QUANTITY GAGE ON A C AIRCRAFT IS CALIBRATED FROM 0 TO 5.
TO PILOT'S FACE PLATE HEATER
TO OXYGEN TO PILOT'S FACE PLATE
TO PRESSURE SUIT
GREEN BALL TO MANUALLY ACTUATE EMERGENCY OXYGEN BOTTLES
PRESSURE SUIT OXYGEN CONTROL PANEL AND REDUCER VALVE ASSEMBLY
115 VAC
DILUTER DEMAND OXYGEN REGULATOR PANEL
PUSH BUTTON TO CHECK PRESSURE SUIT
SURVIVAL KIT RELEASE HANDLE
PILOT TO SURVIVAL KIT DISCONNECTS
OXYGEN REGULATOR
SURVIVAL KIT
TO A-13A MASK
SURVIVAL KIT TO AIRCRAFT DISCONNECT
PRESSURE REDUCER WITH GAGE AND VALVE
FILLER
LANYARD, TO ACTUATE EMERGENCY SUPPLY BY EJECTION
EMERGENCY OXYGEN BOTTLES
PRESSURE SUIT OXYGEN CONTROL PANEL AND REDUCER VALVE ASSEMBLY, AFT, COCKPIT B D
TO ELECT, SUPPLY FACEPLATE, HEATER, HEADSET, MICROPHONE.
TO A-13A MASK
TO SURVIVAL KIT, AFT COCKPIT B D
DILUTER DEMAND OXYGEN REGULATOR PANEL, AFT COCKPIT B D
HEAT EXCHANGER
28 VDC
QUANTITY GAGE, AFT COCKPIT B D
LIQUID OXYGEN CONVERTER-CONTAINER
QUANTITY INDICATOR TRANSMITTER
FILLER VALVE
VENT & BUILD UP VALVE
OVERBOARD VENT
F52-0-4-60

Figure 4-16

DILUTER DEMAND OXYGEN DURATION - HOURS A C

COCKPIT ALTITUDE (FEET)	GAGE QUANTITY—LITERS 5.0	4.5	4.0	3.5	3.0	2.5	2.0	1.5	1.0	.5	BELOW .5
35,000 & UP	31.4 31.4	28.3 28.3	25.1 25.1	22.0 22.0	18.9 18.9	15.7 15.7	12.6 12.6	9.4 9.4	6.3 6.3	3.1 3.1	EMERGENCY DESCEND TO ALTITUDE NOT REQUIRING OXYGEN
30,000	22.6 23.3	20.4 21.0	18.1 18.6	15.9 16.3	13.6 14.0	11.3 11.6	9.1 9.3	6.8 7.0	4.5 4.7	2.3 2.3	
25,000	17.5 22.0	15.7 19.8	14.0 17.6	12.2 15.4	10.5 13.2	8.7 11.0	7.0 8.8	5.2 6.6	3.5 4.4	1.8 2.2	
20,000	13.3 24.9	12.0 22.4	10.6 19.9	9.3 17.4	8.0 14.9	6.7 12.4	5.3 10.0	4.0 7.5	2.7 5.0	1.3 2.5	
15,000	10.7 30.2	9.6 27.2	8.5 24.1	7.5 21.1	6.4 18.1	5.3 15.1	4.3 12.1	3.2 9.1	2.1 6.0	1.1 3.0	
10,000	8.6 30.2	7.7 27.2	6.9 24.1	6.0 21.1	5.1 18.1	4.3 15.1	3.4 12.1	2.6 9.1	1.7 6.0	.9 3.0	
5,000	6.7 30.2	6.3 27.2	5.6 24.1	4.9 21.1	4.2 18.1	3.5 15.1	2.8 12.1	2.1 9.1	1.4 6.0	.7 3.0	
SEA LEVEL	5.7 30.2	5.1 27.2	4.6 24.1	4.0 21.1	3.4 18.1	2.9 15.1	2.3 12.1	1.7 9.1	1.1 6.0	.6 3.0	

UPPER FIGURES INDICATE DILUTER LEVER 100% OXYGEN
LOWER FIGURES INDICATE DILUTER LEVER NORMAL OXYGEN

BREATHING RATES FOR A-13A PRESSURE DEMAND MASK

5 LITER LIQUID OXYGEN CONVERTER

PRESSURE SUIT OXYGEN DURATION - HOURS A C

COCKPIT ALTITUDE (FEET)	GAGE QUANTITY—LITERS 5.0	4.5	4.0	3.5	3.0	2.5	2.0	1.5	1.0	.5	BELOW .5
35,000 & UP	16.6	14.9	13.3	11.6	10.0	8.3	6.6	5.0	3.3	1.7	EMERGENCY DESCEND TO ALTITUDE NOT REQUIRING OXYGEN
30,000	12.6	11.3	10.1	8.8	7.6	6.3	5.0	3.8	2.5	1.3	
25,000	9.6	8.7	7.7	6.7	5.8	4.8	3.9	2.9	1.9	1.0	
20,000	7.5	6.7	6.0	5.2	4.5	3.7	3.0	2.3	1.5	.8	
15,000	5.9	5.3	4.7	4.1	3.5	3.0	2.4	1.8	1.2	.6	
10,000	4.7	4.3	3.8	3.3	2.8	2.4	1.9	1.4	.9	.5	
5,000	3.9	3.5	3.1	2.7	2.3	1.9	1.5	1.2	.8	.4	
SEA LEVEL	3.2	2.8	2.5	2.2	1.9	1.6	1.3	1.0	.6	.3	

5 LITER LIQUID OXYGEN CONVERTER

BREATHING RATES USING SURVIVAL KIT OXYGEN REGULATOR AND PRESSURE SUIT

F52-0-4-64

Figure 4-17

DILUTER DEMAND OXYGEN DURATION - HOURS B D

COCKPIT ALTITUDE (FEET)	QUANTITY - LITERS																		
	10.0	9.5	9.0	8.5	8.0	7.5	7.0	6.5	6.0	5.5	5.0	4.5	4.0	3.5	3.0	2.5	2.0	1.5	1.0	BELOW 1.0
35,000 & UP	31.4 31.4	29.9 29.9	28.3 28.3	26.7 26.7	25.1 25.1	23.6 23.6	22.0 22.0	20.4 20.4	18.9 18.9	17.3 17.3	15.7 15.7	14.1 14.1	12.6 12.6	11.0 11.0	9.4 9.4	7.9 7.9	6.3 6.3	4.7 4.7	3.1 3.1	EMERGENCY DESCEND TO ALTITUDE NOT REQUIRING OXYGEN
30,000	22.6 23.3	21.5 22.1	20.4 21.0	19.3 19.8	18.1 18.6	17.0 17.5	15.9 16.3	14.7 15.1	13.6 14.0	12.5 12.8	11.3 11.6	10.2 10.5	9.1 9.3	7.9 8.2	6.8 7.0	5.7 5.8	4.5 4.7	3.4 3.5	2.3 2.3	
25,000	17.5 22.0	16.6 20.9	15.7 19.8	14.9 18.7	14.0 17.6	13.1 16.5	12.2 15.4	11.4 14.3	10.5 13.2	9.6 12.1	8.7 11.0	7.9 9.9	7.0 8.8	6.1 7.7	5.2 6.6	4.4 5.5	3.5 4.4	2.6 3.3	1.8 2.2	
20,000	13.3 24.9	12.6 23.7	12.0 22.4	11.3 21.2	10.6 19.9	10.0 18.7	9.3 17.4	8.7 16.2	8.0 14.9	7.3 13.7	6.7 12.4	6.0 11.2	5.3 10.0	4.7 8.7	4.0 7.5	3.3 6.2	2.7 5.0	2.0 3.7	1.3 2.5	
15,000	10.7 30.2	10.1 28.7	9.6 27.2	9.1 25.6	8.5 24.1	8.0 22.6	7.5 21.1	6.9 19.6	6.4 18.1	5.9 16.6	5.3 15.1	4.8 13.6	4.3 12.1	3.7 10.6	3.2 9.1	2.7 7.5	2.1 6.0	1.6 4.5	1.1 3.0	
10,000	8.6 30.2	8.1 28.7	7.7 27.2	7.3 25.6	6.9 24.1	6.4 22.6	6.0 21.1	5.6 19.6	5.1 18.1	4.7 16.6	4.3 15.1	3.9 13.6	3.4 12.1	3.0 10.6	2.6 9.1	2.1 7.5	1.7 6.0	1.3 4.5	.9 3.0	
5,000	7.0 30.2	6.6 28.7	6.3 27.2	5.9 25.6	5.2 22.6	4.9 21.1	4.5 19.6	4.2 18.1	3.8 16.6	3.5 15.1	3.1 13.6	2.8 12.1	2.4 10.6	5.6 24.1	2.1 9.1	1.7 7.5	1.4 6.0	1.1 4.5	.7 3.0	
SEA LEVEL	5.7 30.2	5.4 28.7	5.1 27.2	4.9 25.6	4.6 24.1	4.3 22.6	4.0 21.1	3.7 19.6	3.4 18.1	3.1 16.6	2.9 15.1	2.6 13.6	2.3 12.1	2.0 10.6	1.7 9.1	1.4 7.5	1.1 6.0	.9 4.5	.6 3.0	

UPPER FIGURE IN EACH BLOCK INDICATES "100"% OXYGEN.
LOWER FIGURE IN EACH BLOCK INDICATES NORMAL OXYGEN.

ONE TEN LITER LIQUID OXYGEN CONVERTER
BREATHING RATES FOR A-13A PRESSURE DEMAND MASK
TWO CREW MEMBERS

PRESSURE SUIT OXYGEN DURATION - HOURS B D

COCKPIT ALTITUDE (FEET)	QUANTITY - LITERS																		
	10.0	9.5	9.0	8.5	8.0	7.5	7.0	6.5	6.0	5.5	5.0	4.5	4.0	3.5	3.0	2.5	2.0	1.5	1.0	BELOW 1.0
35,000 & UP	16.3	15.5	14.6	13.8	13.0	12.2	11.4	10.6	9.8	9.0	8.1	7.3	6.5	5.7	4.9	4.1	3.3	2.4	1.6	EMERGENCY DESCEND TO ALTITUDE NOT REQUIRING OXYGEN
30,000	12.8	12.1	11.5	10.8	10.2	9.6	8.9	8.3	7.7	7.0	6.4	5.7	5.1	4.5	3.8	3.2	2.6	1.9	1.3	
25,000	9.7	9.3	8.8	8.3	7.8	7.3	6.8	6.3	5.8	5.4	4.9	4.4	3.9	3.4	2.9	2.4	1.9	1.5	1.0	
20,000	7.6	7.2	6.8	6.4	6.1	5.7	5.3	4.9	4.5	4.2	3.8	3.4	3.0	2.6	2.3	1.9	1.5	1.1	.8	
15,000	6.0	5.7	5.4	5.1	4.8	4.5	4.2	3.9	3.6	3.3	3.0	2.7	2.4	2.1	1.8	1.5	1.2	.9	.6	
10,000	4.8	4.6	4.3	4.1	3.8	3.6	3.4	3.1	2.9	2.6	2.4	2.2	1.9	1.7	1.4	1.2	1.0	.7	.5	
5,000	3.9	3.7	3.5	3.3.	3.1	2.9	2.7	2.5	2.3	2.1	2.0	1.8	1.6	1.4	1.2	1.0	.8	.6	.4	
SEA LEVEL	3.1	2.9	2.7	2.6	2.4	2.3	2.1	2.0	1.8	1.7	1.5	1.4	1.2	1.1	.9	.8	.6	.5	.3	

BREATHING RATES FOR MC-3 OR MC-4 PRESSURE SUIT AND HELMET

TWO CREW MEMBERS. HG 07386 F52-0-4-61

Figure 4-18

OXYGEN CONTROL PANELS

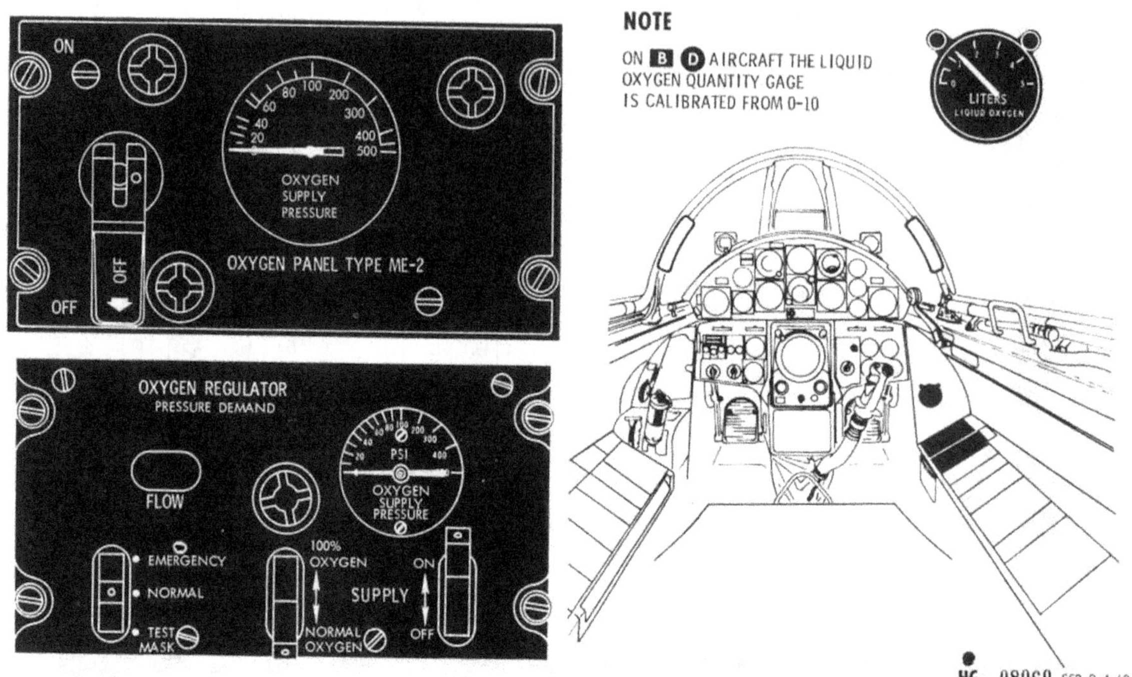

Figure 4-19

SURVIVAL KIT CONNECTION.

From the oxygen control panel, oxygen flows through a disconnect on the bottom of the pilot's seat to a manifold assembly in the rear section of the survival kit (figure 4-16). This section of the survival kit also contains two emergency oxygen bottles, connected to the manifold assembly, and a regulator unit. The manifold assembly includes a pressure gage, relief valve, check valve and filler valve. Either normal aircraft oxygen or emergency oxygen can be directed from the manifold assembly to the regulator unit which sends oxygen pressure to the pilot's pressure suit as well as delivering the correct amount of breathing oxygen to the pilot's faceplate hose from sea level up to the maximum operational altitude of the aircraft. The hoses from the regulator to the pilot leave the survival kit at the right rear corner. These hoses are designed for use with pressure suits. A press-to-test button is located on the right front of the survival kit to test operation of the oxygen supply system. If there is no malfunction, oxygen will flow through the pressure suit and faceplate hoses when the button is depressed.

PRESSURE SUIT OXYGEN CONTROL PANEL.

An oxygen pressure gage and supply lever are located on the oxygen system control panel (figure 4-19) on the right console. The supply lever has two positions, ON and OFF. Placing the lever in the ON position opens the supply valve and allows oxygen to flow through the panel into the system. Moving the lever to OFF closes the supply valve, shutting off the oxygen supply. The gage indicates gaseous oxygen pressure at the panel and should read approximately 70 psi for A C aircraft and approximately 300 psi for B D aircraft. The gage is calibrated from 0 to 150 psi on A C aircraft and from 0 to 500 psi on B D aircraft.

Liquid Oxygen Quantity Gage.

The liquid oxygen quantity gage (figure 4-19) measures liquid content of the oxygen converter and is calibrated in liters from 0 to 5 on A C aircraft and 0 to 10 on B D aircraft. Electrical power for the gage is from the emergency ac bus. The aft cockpit gage of B D aircraft also requires dc power which is furnished by the dc emergency bus.

DILUTER DEMAND OXYGEN REGULATOR PANEL.

All aircraft incorporate a type MD-1 combination pressure-breathing, diluter demand oxygen regulator (figure 4-19) on the right console. This regulator is provided for use with the A-13A oxygen mask when the pressure suit is not worn. The panel has three levers, the supply lever, the diluter lever, and the emergency lever. When the diluter lever is at NORMAL and the supply lever ON, the regulator mixes air with oxygen in varying amounts according to altitude and makes available a quantity of the mixture each time the pilot inhales. At high altitudes, the regulator supplies oxygen at continuous positive pressure to the pilot. The delivery pressure automatically changes with cockpit altitude. Also on the regulator panel are an oxygen pressure gage and flow indicator.

Diluter Lever. The (black) diluter lever (figure 4-19), is on the oxygen regulator control panel. The lever should be set at NORMAL for normal oxygen use, and at 100% for emergency oxygen use.

Emergency Lever. The (red) emergency lever (figure 4-19), on the oxygen regulator panel should be in the center NORMAL position at all times unless an unscheduled oxygen pressure increase is required. Moving the lever to EMERGENCY provides continuous positive pressure to the mask for emergency use. When the lever is held at TEST, oxygen at positive pressure is provided to test the mask for leaks.

CAUTION

When positive pressures are required, it is mandatory that the oxygen mask be well fitted to the face. Unless special precautions are taken to prevent leakage, continued use of positive pressure will result in rapid depletion of the oxygen supply. This rapid depletion could result in extremely cold oxygen flowing to the mask.

Supply Lever. The (green) supply lever (figure 4-19), on the oxygen regulator panel, has two positions (ON and OFF), and is used to turn on or shut off the supply of oxygen at the panel.

Pressure Gage and Flow Indicator. The pressure gage and flow indicator (figure 4-19) are on the oxygen regulator control panel. The pressure gage shows oxygen system pressure. The flow indicator (blinker) consists of an oblong opening in the face of the regulator panel which alternates black and white during the breathing cycle.

EMERGENCY OXYGEN SUPPLY.

An emergency supply of oxygen for use in the event of failure of the normal supply system or for high altitude ejection is stored in two bottles (cylinders) in the survival kit. The emergency supply system is actuated automatically during ejection, or manually whenever desired. (Oxygen passes through the manifold assembly, which incorporates a pressure reducer.) Upon ejection, movement of the seat creates a force which triggers the disconnect mechanism, separating the seat, survival kit, and associated oxygen equipment from the normal oxygen supply line. Simultaneously, the emergency oxygen pressure-reducer valve in the manifold assembly is opened, allowing the emergency oxygen supply to flow through this reducer valve (where pressure is reduced from 1800 psi to 70 psi), and into the regulator. If the emergency bottles are fully serviced (1800 psi), they will provide the pilot with a regulated supply of oxygen for the pressure suit, as well as breathing, for a minimum of 10 minutes. The emergency oxygen supply may be actuated manually by pulling a green ball handle connected to the right aft corner of the survival kit. The emergency pressure-reducer valve is then opened by a cable attached to the ball handle. Oxygen pressure in the emergency bottles can be determined by means of a pressure gage attached to the manifold assembly in the survival kit. This is accessible through a hinged door on top of the rear section of the kit.

Note

When using the diluter-demand system and A-13A oxygen mask, the only emergency oxygen supply available is from the bailout bottle attached to the parachute.

Oxygen Hose Attachment.

The proper attachment of the oxygen mask connector is extremely important to ensure the following:

a. The oxygen hose does not become accidentally disconnected during flight, resulting in loss of oxygen supply to the pilot.

b. The oxygen hose does not prevent quick separation from the seat during ejection.

c. The oxygen hose does not flail during ejection, causing pilot injury.

When the oxygen mask to regulator connector, is employed, the following procedure should be followed to properly attach the personal oxygen leads:

1. Insert connector into the mounting plate attached to the parachute harness. Check that the connector is firmly attached and that the lockpin is locked.

2. Couple the aircraft-oxygen-supply-hose to the lower port of the connector.

3. Insert the male bayonet connector on the end of the oxygen mask tube into the female receiving port of the connector and turn the bayonet connector to lock its prongs into the recesses in the lip of the receiving port.

4. Attach the coupling on the end of the emergency oxygen supply hose (from the bailout bottle) to the swiveling port of the connector by exerting, respectively, a downward and clockwise force against the spring-loaded collar so as to depress and lock it in position.

WARNING

If a stowage strap is installed on the seat oxygen hose, the strap shall not be attached to the connector. Connecting the strap may retard proper seat/man separation during ejection.

Personal Leads Routing and Connection.

The proper routing and connection of the pilots personal leads is very important for increasing chance of survival during low altitude ejection. Improper routing of personal leads, especially the anti-G suit hose, can open the manual side of the lapbelt during ejection, thereby preventing automatic operation of the parachute. Consequently, it is imperative that the personal leads be attached as follows:

1. Route the pilot's anti-G suit hose under the lapbelt.

2. Route the aircraft's anti-G suit hose over the lapbelt and connect to the pilot's hose.

Note

A satisfactory connection may not be maintained if both anti-G suit hoses are routed under the lapbelt.

3. If the aircraft anti-G suit hose is not used, it must be routed to lie under the lapbelt and along the pilot's thigh.

4. Other personal leads (radio, oxygen, and vent suit) must be routed under the lapbelt when there is a possibility they may fall over the lapbelt and to the left of the lapbelt release handle.

Note

- Care must be taken to ensure that flight clothing, such as sleeves, will not catch and release the lapbelt during separation.
- The zero-second lanyard may be of such length as to hang down and to the left of the lapbelt release. Care must be taken to ensure this does not happen.

OXYGEN SYSTEM PREFLIGHT CHECK.

Note A C

- Normal oxygen pressure is 65—75 psi as indicated on the control panel and regulator gages when oxygen is being used (in-flight condition). Normal oxygen pressure when the aircraft is on standby or preflight condition can vary from 70 to 120 psi, depending on the time span between the filling of the converter and the reading of the gages. For example, if the gage is read approximately 10 minutes after filling, the gage reads approximately 70 psi. However, if the gage is read several hours after filling, it reads between 100 and 120 psi. The difference in pressure is due to temperature effect.

A C

- If an oxygen pressure reading of over 120 psi is observed, an unsatisfactory condition exists and the system should be inspected prior to flight.

B D

- Normal oxygen pressure when oxygen is being used (flight conditions) is 295-315 psi. In a preflight status the pressure may vary from 300 to 370 psi depending on the time span between filling of the converter and reading the gage. For example, if the gages are read 10 minutes after filling the converter, they would read about 300 psi. If another reading is taken several hours later the gages would read between 320 and 370 psi. (Low-pressure relief valve setting). This difference is due to temperature effect.

B D

- If system pressure reads over 370 psi during the preflight inspection, an unsatisfactory condition exists and the system should be checked before the aircraft is flown.

Pressure Suit.

1. Diluter demand oxygen supply lever—OFF (both cockpits B D).

WARNING

- If the diluter demand oxygen system is not to be used, the supply lever on the oxygen regulator panel must be placed in the OFF position. If left in the ON position, the regulator will automatically allow positive pressure oxygen flow above 25,000 feet cockpit altitude, which would rapidly exhaust the oxygen supply. B D
- Before solo flights, both the diluter demand supply lever and the survival kit oxygen supply lever in the aft cockpit should be OFF.

2. Oxygen pressure approximately 70 psi A C, approximately 300 psi B D.
3. Liquid oxygen quantity gage—2 liters minimum A C, 4 liters B D.
4. Quick-disconnect on bottom of survival kit—Secure.
5. Survival kit emergency oxygen pressure 1800 psi—Check through window in aft section of kit.
6. Check that survival kit cover and straps are connected to lower part of kit.
7. Check security and connection of fitting and hoses at right aft corner of kit.
8. Check between sides of seat and kit for obstructions.
9. Connect and lock kit straps to parachute harness.
10. Connect and lock oxygen and radio connections.
11. Pressure suit oxygen supply lever—ON.
12. Press-to-test button—Depress and note positive pressure to suit and face plate.

Diluter Demand.

1. Pressure suit oxygen supply lever, OFF—Check (both cockpits B D).
2. Oxygen pressure—Approximately 75 psi A C, approximately 300 psi B D.
3. Liquid oxygen quantity gage—2 liters minimum A C, 4 liters minimum B D.
4. Check oxygen regulator with diluter lever first at NORMAL and then at 100% as follows: Blow gently into end of oxygen regulator hose as during normal exhalation. There should be resistance to blowing. Little or no resistance to blowing indicates a leak or faulty regulator operation.
5. With diluter demand oxygen supply lever ON, oxygen mask connected to regulator, and diluter lever at 100%, breathe normally into mask and conduct following checks:
   a. Observe flow indicator for proper operation.
   b. Move emergency lever to EMERGENCY. A positive pressure should be supplied to the mask. Hold breath to determine whether there is leakage around mask. Return emergency lever to NORMAL position. Positive pressure should cease.

Note

All connections and checks should be made with the assistance of a personal equipment man or someone qualified to perform the function.

NORMAL OPERATION OF THE OXYGEN SYSTEM.

Pressure Suit.

1. Oxygen pressure gage – Approximately 70 psi A C, approximately 300 psi B D.
2. Liquid oxygen quantity gage—3 liters minimum A C, 6 liters minimum B D.
3. Pressure suit oxygen supply lever—ON (occupied cockpit only B D).
4. Diluter-demand supply lever—OFF (both cockpits B D).

Diluter Demand.

1. Oxygen pressure gage – Approximately 70 psi A C, approximately 300 psi B D.
2. Liquid oxygen quantity gage—2 liters minimum A C, 4 liters minimum B D.
3. Diluter demand oxygen supply lever—ON occupied cockpit only B D).
4. Diluter lever—NORMAL.
5. Emergency lever—NORMAL.
6. Pressure suit oxygen supply lever—OFF (both cockpits B D).

EMERGENCY OPERATION OF THE OXYGEN SYSTEM.

Pressure Suit.

Any time that symptoms of hypoxia are noted, or if it is known that the normal oxygen system has failed, proceed as follows:

1. Manual emergency oxygen supply actuator (green ball)—PULL.

J-4 HEADING INDICATOR PANEL

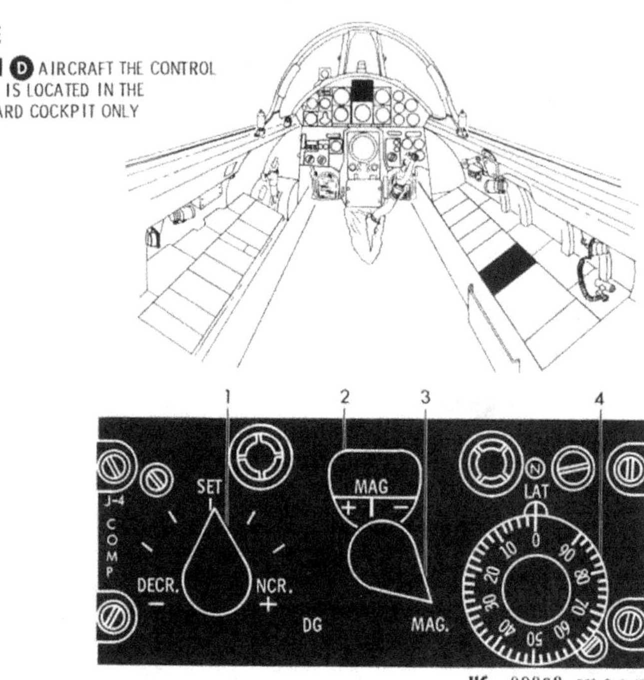

Figure 4-20

Note

When pulling green ball, disconnect the normal oxygen connection as normal oxygen may be contaminated.

2. Descend to an altitude where oxygen is not required.

Diluter Demand.

1. Diluter lever—100%.
2. Emergency lever—EMERGENCY.
3. If oxygen regulator becomes inoperative, pull the green ball handle on bailout bottle to actuate the emergency oxygen supply.
4. Disconnect oxygen hose from normal system.
5. Descend to an altitude where oxygen is not required.

NAVIGATION EQUIPMENT.

J-4 HEADING INDICATOR SYSTEM.

The J-4 heading indicator system provides the pilot with a heading reference by operating either as a heading gyro or a slaved gyro magnetic compass. The system is coupled to the compass card of the RMI. The control panel (figure 4-20) contains all of the controls necessary for proper operation of the system under all conditions. The system requires 28 volts dc from the emergency bus, as well as instrument ac bus power, for normal operation.

Function Selector Switch.

A function selector switch (3, figure 4-20) is provided to select the mode of operation of the heading indicator system. When this switch is in the MAG. position the system operates as a normal slaved gyro magnetic compass and the ID-526 BDHI heading index will indicate magnetic heading. Moving the function selector switch to the DG position causes the compass to operate as a directional gyro. This mode of operation is designed for use in the polar regions where the earth's magnetic field is such that the slaved gyro magnetic compass is very unreliable. If deemed necessary, the system can be sent into a fast slaving cycle by moving the function selector switch from MAG. to DG and back to MAG. The gyro will then be erected, and any large errors in the system eliminated very rapidly.

Indicator Set Switch.

The indicator set switch (1, figure 4-20) is used during the magnetic compass mode of operation to effect synchronization of the compass system and the transmitter which feeds heading information to the heading indicator. This control is used during directional gyro or slaved gyro magnetic compass MAG. operation to position the transmitter to any desired reference.

Synchronizing Indicator.

A synchronizing indicator (2, figure 4-20) is provided to indicate synchronization to within ±¼ degree between the compass system and the transmitter in the magnetic mode of operation. When the system is not synchronized, the synchronizing indicator will show the direction in which the indicator set switch must be turned to achieve the necessary correction. The set switch must be turned clockwise when the indicator is in the (+) region and counterclockwise when a (−) appears.

Latitude Correction Controller.

The latitude correction controller (4, figure 4-20) is used in the DG mode of compass operation to correct for the apparent drift of the directional gyro due to the earth's rotation. Latitude corrections are made in a clockwise direction in the northern hemisphere and counterclockwise in the southern hemisphere.

Directional Indicator and Course Selector Knob. (Aircraft Not Incorporating TACAN). A B

The directional indicator located on the instrument panel (replaced by the ID-250 or ID-526 on modified airplanes) receives heading information from the compass system and gives the pilot visual indication of compass heading by means of an indicator pointer and a compass card. Any desired course may be placed under the index at the top of the indicator by turning the course selector knob at the lower left of the indicator.

ARMAMENT EQUIPMENT

Note C D

The description and operational capabilities for delivery of nonnuclear weapons are contained in T.O. 1F-104C-34-1-1 AIRCREW NON-NUCLEAR WEAPONS DELIVERY MANUAL. All information on armament equipment description or operational capabilities contained herein is in addition to or is a duplication of that contained in the Weapons Delivery Manual and is included for clarity and continuity only.

The armament consists of AIM-9B missiles. (Modified A aircraft also have a 20-mm gun installed.) The missiles are fired by the camera–armament trigger switch on the control stick grip which also actuates an N-9 camera to record firing accuracy. Target searching and tracking information is provided by the AN/ASG-14T1 fire control system. This system includes a lightweight radar set which is effective to an altitude of 70,000 feet and is used in conjunction with an optical infrared sight system.

AN/ASG-14T1 FIRE CONTROL SYSTEM.

The radar system, optical sight, and infrared sight combine to form a well integrated fire control system with a high kill potential. Although these systems complement each other, neither system is wholly dependent on any other for operation. This means a mission can be successfully completed with one or more of the systems inoperative. For instance, during the day a target could possibly be acquired visually without the use of the radar system and the attack completed. At night either the radar system or the infrared sight can be used alone for detecting and tracking the target to complete an intercept, although the latter system will have considerably less search capability. In an extreme case, the AIM-9B missile alone can be used to complete a mission. During the initial phase of the attack, the target will normally be detected by the radar in search mode. The target presentation will appear on the radar indicator in the form of an arc indicating target range and position relative to the interceptor. The aircraft should then be flown toward the target until within visual range, at which time the optical sight may be utilized to direct the remainder of the attack. An infrared sight may be used in conjunction with the optical sight to augment the night attack capabilities of the fire control system.

RADAR SYSTEM.

The AN/ASG-14T1 radar system is a lightweight search and track radar system. Its primary function is to provide the pilot with steering and range information for tracking an airborne target after the interceptor has been directed to the target area and radar contact established. It is inherent in this radar system (antenna scan and indicator display method) that a tail-on pursuit will be established as the interceptor pilot steers to obtain a target boresight presentation on the radar indicator. This is the most advantageous position for effecting a missile launch. The target tail-on aspect is optimum for infrared seeking devices (IR sight and AIM-9B missile); thus, the fire control and armament components are highly compatible and make up an efficient and effective system.

ARMAMENT CONTROL PANEL A B AND UNMODIFIED C D

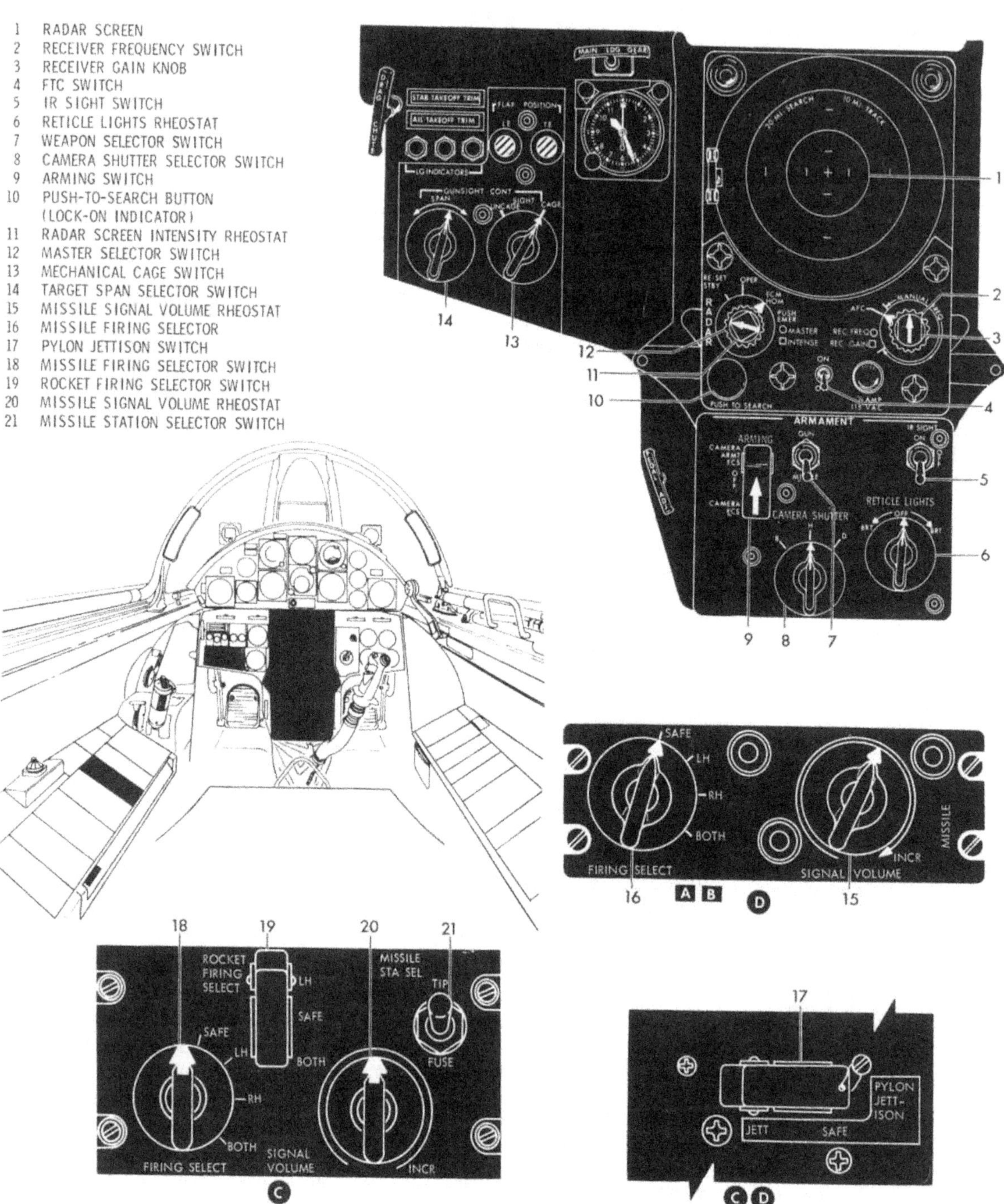
1 RADAR SCREEN
2 RECEIVER FREQUENCY SWITCH
3 RECEIVER GAIN KNOB
4 FTC SWITCH
5 IR SIGHT SWITCH
6 RETICLE LIGHTS RHEOSTAT
7 WEAPON SELECTOR SWITCH
8 CAMERA SHUTTER SELECTOR SWITCH
9 ARMING SWITCH
10 PUSH-TO-SEARCH BUTTON (LOCK-ON INDICATOR)
11 RADAR SCREEN INTENSITY RHEOSTAT
12 MASTER SELECTOR SWITCH
13 MECHANICAL CAGE SWITCH
14 TARGET SPAN SELECTOR SWITCH
15 MISSILE SIGNAL VOLUME RHEOSTAT
16 MISSILE FIRING SELECTOR
17 PYLON JETTISON SWITCH
18 MISSILE FIRING SELECTOR SWITCH
19 ROCKET FIRING SELECTOR SWITCH
20 MISSILE SIGNAL VOLUME RHEOSTAT
21 MISSILE STATION SELECTOR SWITCH
ARMAMENT
RETICLE LIGHTS
CAMERA SHUTTER
PUSH TO SEARCH
FIRING SELECT
SAFE
LH
RH
BOTH
SIGNAL VOLUME
INCR
MISSILE
ROCKET FIRING SELECT
MISSILE STA SEL
TIP
FUSE
PYLON JETT-ISON
JETT
F52-0-4-68

Figure 4-21

AFT RADAR CONTROL PANELS B D

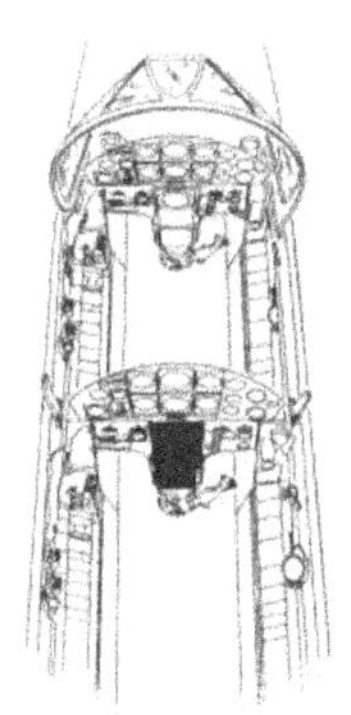

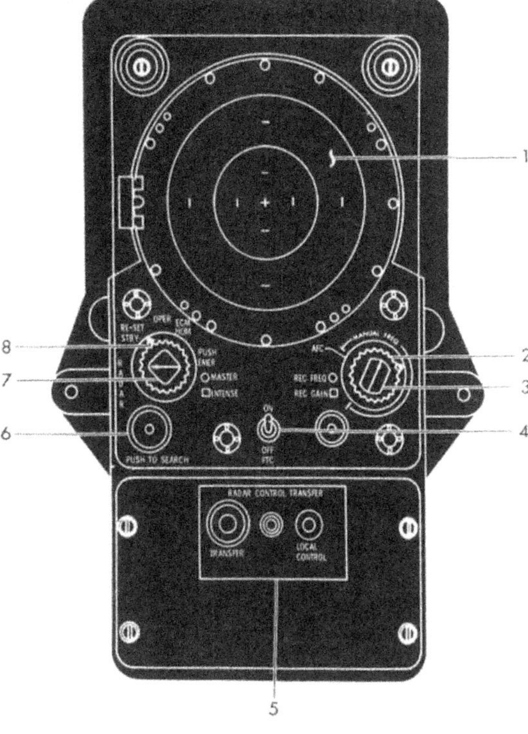

B AND UNMODIFIED D - (MOD I INSTALLATION)

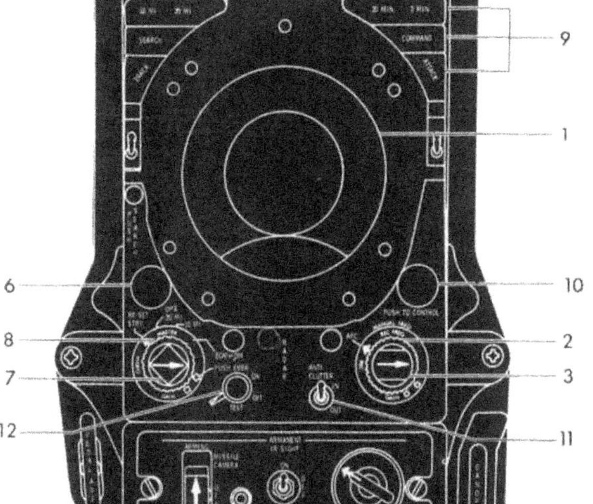

MODIFIED D -(MOD II INSTALLATION)

1 RADAR SCOPE
2 RECEIVER FREQUENCY SWITCH
3 RECEIVER GAIN KNOB
4 FTC SWITCH
5 RADAR CONTROL TRANSFER AND INDICATOR LIGHT PANEL
6 PUSH TO SEARCH SWITCH (LOCK-ON INDICATOR)
7 RADAR SCOPE INTENSITY RHEOSTAT
8 MASTER SELECTOR SWITCH
9 INACTIVE
10 RADAR CONTROL TRANSFER BUTTON AND INDICATOR LIGHT
11 ANTI-CLUTTER SWITCH
12 INDICATOR LIGHTS TEST SWITCH

F52-0-4-73

Figure 4-22

ARMAMENT CONTROL PANEL MODIFIED (C)

(MOD II INSTALLATION)

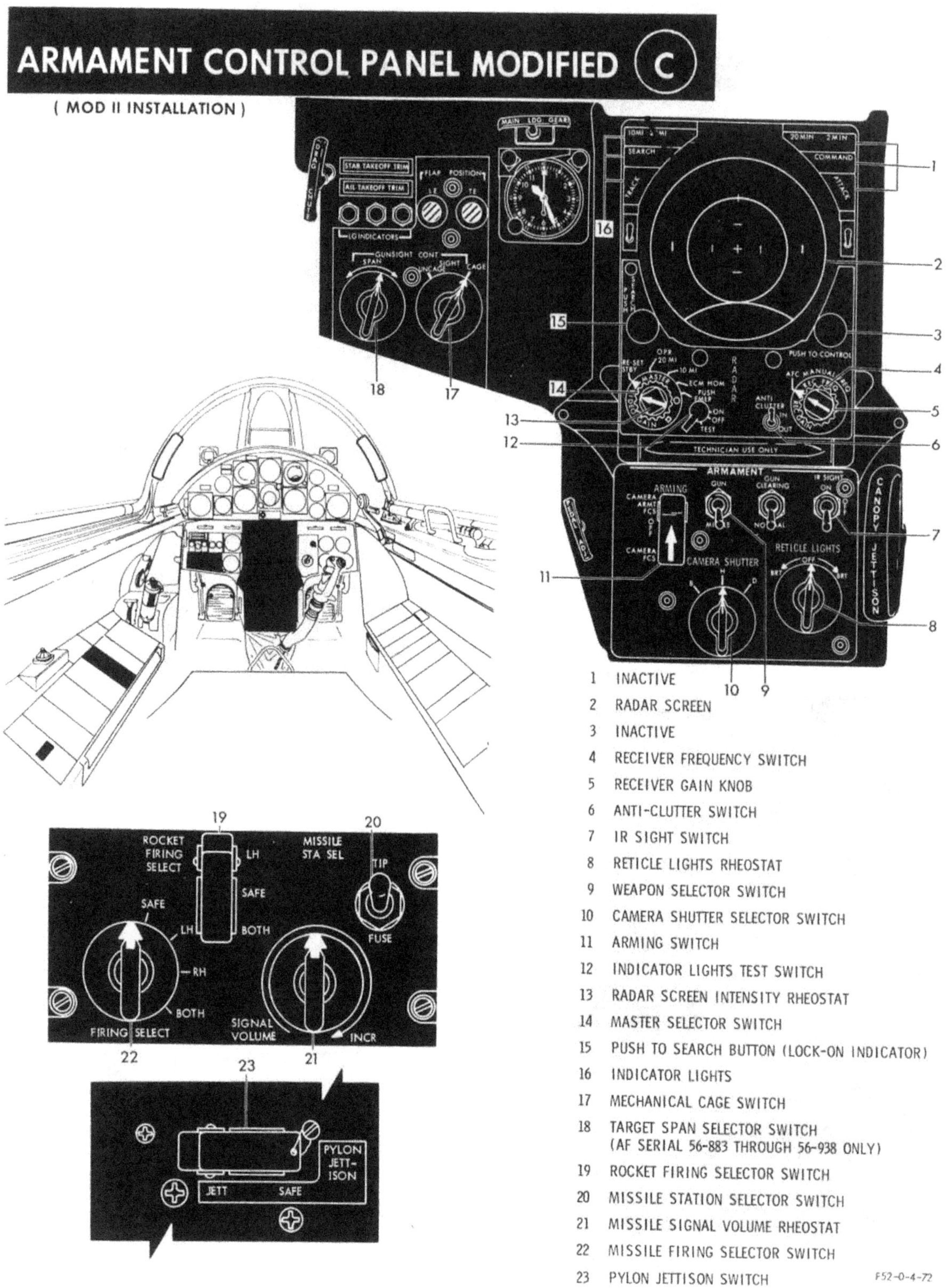
ROCKET FIRING SELECT
LH
SAFE
BOTH
RH
FIRING SELECT
MISSILE STA SEL
TIP
FUSE
SIGNAL VOLUME
INCR
PYLON JETT-ISON
JETT
SAFE
ARMAMENT
ARMING
CAMERA SHUTTER
RETICLE LIGHTS
TECHNICIAN USE ONLY
PUSH TO CONTROL
1 INACTIVE
2 RADAR SCREEN
3 INACTIVE
4 RECEIVER FREQUENCY SWITCH
5 RECEIVER GAIN KNOB
6 ANTI-CLUTTER SWITCH
7 IR SIGHT SWITCH
8 RETICLE LIGHTS RHEOSTAT
9 WEAPON SELECTOR SWITCH
10 CAMERA SHUTTER SELECTOR SWITCH
11 ARMING SWITCH
12 INDICATOR LIGHTS TEST SWITCH
13 RADAR SCREEN INTENSITY RHEOSTAT
14 MASTER SELECTOR SWITCH
15 PUSH TO SEARCH BUTTON (LOCK-ON INDICATOR)
16 INDICATOR LIGHTS
17 MECHANICAL CAGE SWITCH
18 TARGET SPAN SELECTOR SWITCH (AF SERIAL 56-883 THROUGH 56-938 ONLY)
19 ROCKET FIRING SELECTOR SWITCH
20 MISSILE STATION SELECTOR SWITCH
21 MISSILE SIGNAL VOLUME RHEOSTAT
22 MISSILE FIRING SELECTOR SWITCH
23 PYLON JETTISON SWITCH
F52-0-4-72

Figure 4-23

FORWARD ARMAMENT CONTROL PANEL MODIFIED (D)

(MOD II INSTALLATION)

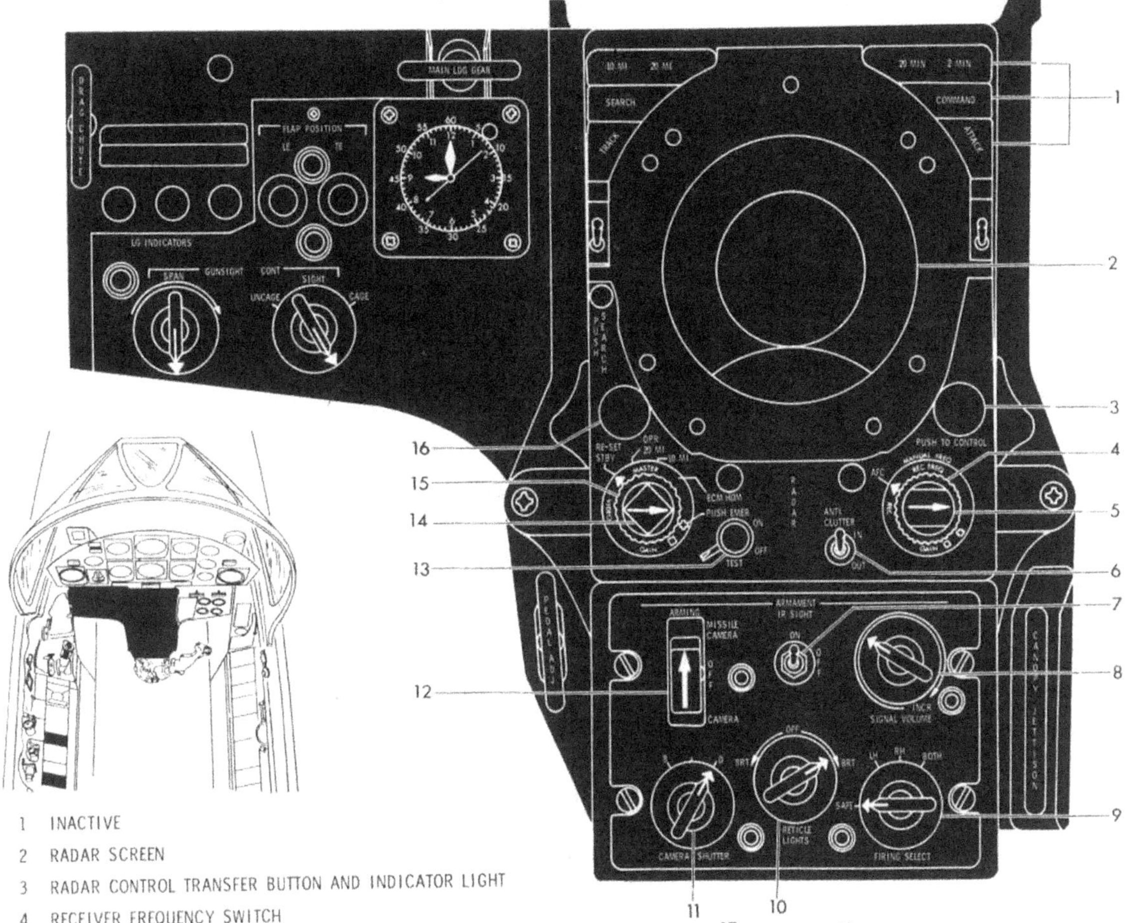

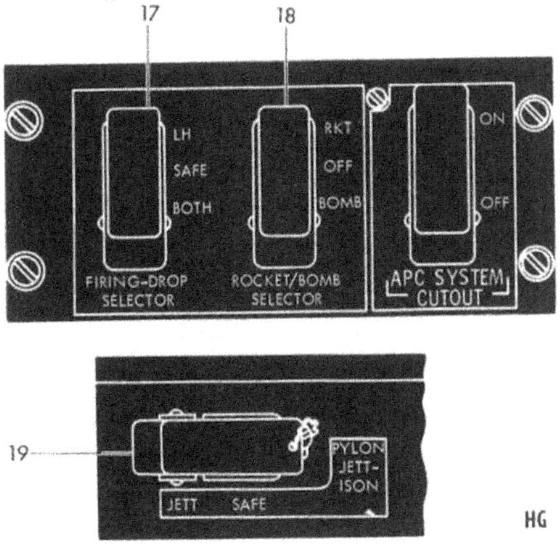

1 INACTIVE
2 RADAR SCREEN
3 RADAR CONTROL TRANSFER BUTTON AND INDICATOR LIGHT
4 RECEIVER FREQUENCY SWITCH
5 RECEIVER GAIN KNOB
6 ANTI-CLUTTER SWITCH
7 IR SIGHT SWITCH
8 MISSILE SIGNAL VOLUME CONTROL
9 MISSILE FIRING SELECTOR SWITCH
10 RETICLE LIGHTS RHEOSTAT
11 CAMERA SHUTTER SELECTOR SWITCH
12 ARMING SWITCH
13 INDICATOR LIGHTS TEST SWITCH
14 RADAR SCREEN INTENSITY RHEOSTAT
15 MASTER SELECTOR SWITCH
16 PUSH TO SEARCH BUTTON (LOCK ON INDICATOR)
17 FIRING-DROP SELECTOR SWITCH
18 ROCKET-BOMB SELECTOR SWITCH
19 PYLON JETTISON SWITCH

HG 08064
F52-0-4-2

Figure 4-24

There are three pilot-selected modes of operation, search, track, and ECM HOM (electronic countermeasures and homing). The search mode provides recurrent radar coverage of a 90-degree conical area forward at a 3-second scan rate, and a 20-nautical mile range scale on the indicator. The track mode provides recurrent radar coverage of a 20-degree conical area forward, at a 0.1-second scan rate and a 10-nautical mile range scale on the indicator; it presents a display of relative opening or closure rate to the target and provides target lockon capability for automatic range tracking. The ECM HOM mode provides capability of homing on jamming signals. The radar system is passive in this mode and therefore offers no range information. AC power for operation of the radar system is furnished by the No. 2 ac bus, while the dc requirements are received from the dc monitored bus.

Radar Control Transfer Panels. B D

Forward cockpit radar controls are duplicated in the aft cockpit. Radar control transfer between cockpits is accomplished by use of a switch (5, figure 4-22) located in the aft cockpit on the center console pedestal. A light adjacent to the switch will illuminate when aft cockpit radar control is selected. On modified aircraft, a radar control transfer button and light are located on both forward and aft radar control panels. A light in the center of the button illuminates in the cockpit having radar control. Radar control transfer between cockpits is made by use of either radar control switch.

Fire Control Master Switch (FCS).

The fire control master switch (FCS) (figures 1-20, 1-21) supplies 28 volt dc to the radar and sight power relays, allowing these relays to close and send 3 phase ac power to the complete fire control system.

Master Selector Switch. The main radar system control is a four-position, rotary master selector switch (figures 4-21, 4-22, 4-23, 4-24). This switch, (placarded RE-SET STBY, OPER, ECM HOM, and PUSH EMER) in conjunction with the radar track action button on the control stick grip enables the pilot to select the desired mode of operation. With the master selector switch in the OPER (operate) position, the transmitter is activated and the antenna scans a search or track pattern (figure 4-25), depending upon the mode of operation. The radar system begins to warm up as soon as power is supplied to the aircraft. To allow a warmup period for the rest of the radar system before the transmitter is turned on, a time delay of approximately 3 minutes is incorporated between the time at which the engine is started and that at which the transmitter can be used. If the master selector switch is in the OPER position when the engine is started, the antenna and transmitter will be turned on automatically after the time delay, thus putting the radar system in operational status. If the master selector switch is in RE-SET STBY when the engine is started, both the transmitter and the antenna are inoperative, and both will remain so until the end of the warmup period, even if the switch is turned to the OPER position during warmup. While the engine is operating, the radar system may be disabled temporarily by turning the master selector switch to the RE-SET STBY position, thereby deactivating the transmitter and antenna. Since the time delay is effective only from a cold start, the radar system will be immediately operative when the master selector switch is turned to OPER or ECM HOM. The ECM HOM position enables the pilot to home on jamming transmissions, since the radar transmitter is turned off (thus removing the normal radar responses from the radar indicator), while the antenna continues to scan as it does in the regular modes. The only indications on the radar indicator will be those due to the source of the interference or some other source with roughly the same frequency. The final position on the master selector switch is the PUSH EMER (push for emergency operation) setting. Operation of the master selector switch to this position allows the radar system to be made fully operational immediately after the engine is started, without waiting for the expiration of the time-delay period.

Note

The aircraft is delivered with the PUSH EMER position inoperative.

Radar Screen Intensity Rheostat Knob. The intensity (INTENS) rheostat (figures 4-21, 4-22, 4-23, 4-24) is controlled by a square knob mounted concentrically with the master selector switch. Radar indicator presentation brilliance is adjusted by rotating this knob.

Receiver Frequency Switch. Both automatic and manual frequency control is incorporated in the radar system. When the receiver frequency (REC FREQ) switch (figures 4-21, 4-22, 4-23, 4-24) is turned to the extreme counterclockwise (AFC) position, an in-out switch is operated and the receiver is automatically tuned for maximum response to the echoes from the transmitter with which it is associated. When the receiver frequency switch

ANTENNA PATTERNS

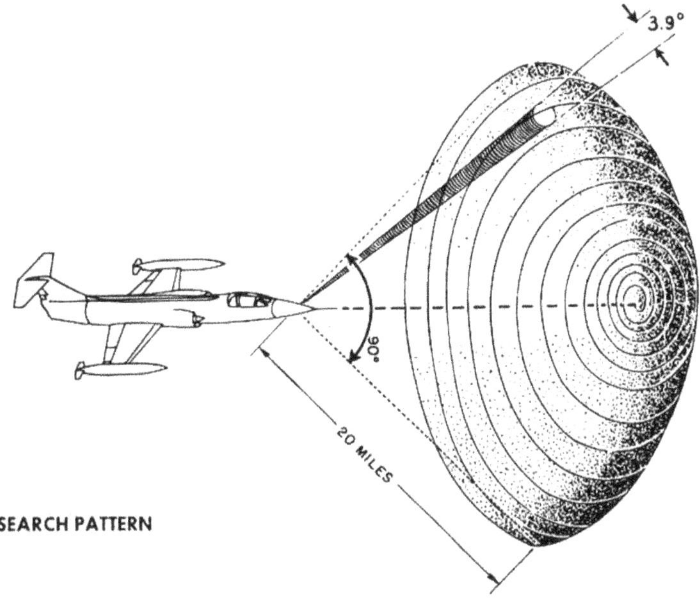

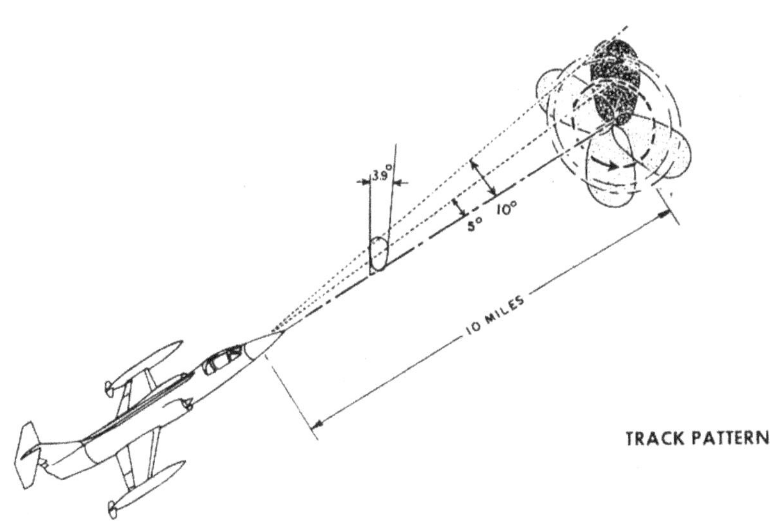

HG 07374
F52-0-4-71

Figure 4-25

is turned clockwise out of detent, manual frequency operation is set up, allowing the pilot to tune the receiver manually. This manual operation is critical in its tuning and should be used only when automatic frequency control fails or during ECM HOM mode operation.

Receiver Gain Knob. The receiver gain (REC GAIN) knob (figures 4-21, 4-22, 4-23, 4-24), mounted concentrically with the receiver frequency switch, determines the sensitivity of the radar system to the echoes picked up by the antenna. The knob should be kept in its maximum clockwise position. Gain adjustment is a preflight position and should not be changed during flight except to overcome jamming.

Push-To-Search Button and Lock-on Indicator. The function of the push-to-search button (figures 4-21, 4-22, 4-23, 4-24) is to return the radar system to the search mode after the track mode has been used. A red lockon indicator is mechanically integrated with the push-to-search button. This indicator will light when tracking has been successfully initiated and the radar system is locked onto a target. There is an additional amber lockon light adjacent to the optical sight combining glass.

Lock-on Sensitivity (LOCK-ON-SENS) Rheostat Knob (1024 C/W). A lock-on sensitivity knob (figures 1-12, 1-22) provides the pilot with a means of increasing lock-on sensitivity to track targets with lower return signal strength, i.e. the DART. Normal position of the knob is full counterclockwise, and is rotated in the clockwise direction only when, and no more than, is necessary to maintain lock-on. Excessive clockwise rotation will result in a sustained lock-on-noise condition.

FTC Switch. Fast time constant (FTC) circuitry has been incorporated as an anti-jamming measure, and to eliminate long formless trains of cloud, ground, or sea return echoes. This switch (figures 4-21, 4-22, 4-23, 4-24) should be left on unless it is felt the target is being degraded or weakened.

Radar Track Action Button. Changing the radar system from search mode to track mode is accomplished by means of the pushbutton-type track action button (4, figure 1-44) on the control stick grip. This button also slews the range strobe out and in.

Radar Test Panel. A test panel (figure 4-26), located on the left console (aft cockpit **B**), is provided primarily for preflight test of the system by ground crew personnel. An 11-position rotary selector switch enables a quick check of various circuits under operating conditions, a good–bad indication being obtained from a monitor meter located just above the switch. Each position of the switch is designated both by nomenclature which shows the circuit selected for test, and by color code

RADAR TEST PANEL

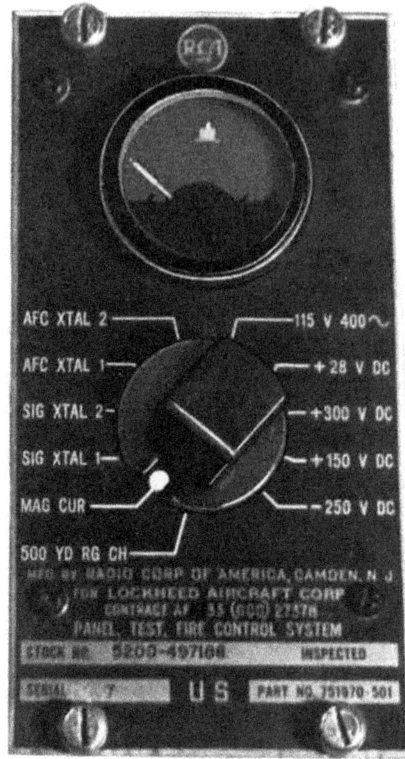

F53-0-4-66

Figure 4-26

which shows on which of the three meter scales (correspondingly color-coded) the indication is to be checked. An on-scale reading indicates that the circuit is functioning normally while an off-scale reading indicates the circuit requires adjustment.

Radar DC Power Switch (Some Airplanes). The radar dc power switch located on the automatic pitch control cutoff panel has been deactivated.

Radar Indicator. The radar indicator (figures 4-21, 4-22, 4-23, 4-24) is located on the radar and armament control panel. Two different clamp-on filters are used to cover the indicator screen. A light-green polaroid filter is used for daytime flying. Its primary function is to minimize sun glare and bright ambient lighting interference with the indicator presentation. The second filter is a deep-red adjustable one used for night flying to reduce glare and brightness emanating from the indicator itself. Ground personnel will install the proper filter for the mission.

Range Rate Indicator. (Rate of closure.) A range rate indicator is integrated with the radar indicator to show, in the track mode, relative range rates of the target and interceptor from 100 knots opening to 400 knots closing.

RADAR SCREEN PRESENTATIONS

Search Mode.

To operate in the search mode, turn the master selector switch to OPER. Check the following control positions: receiver gain knob full clockwise, receiver frequency switch in AFC detent, FTC switch on. Adjust the radar screen intensity rheostat until background (in clutter-free area) is just discernible. Setting the rheostat too high can result in a display which might obscure a target (figure 4-27). Slight readjustment may be desirable at times during the flight. In search mode the maximum displayed range is 20 nautical miles; hence, the engraved markers on the radar scope represent 15, 10, and 5 miles. The antenna beam scans a 90-degree conical area (figure 4-25) ahead of the aircraft once each 3 seconds (approximately). Complete coverage of this area is accomplished by the antenna spiraling about the radar boresight axis in a spiral of decreasing diameter, from the maximum off-boresight angle (46 degrees) to boresight. Since it takes the antenna approximately 3 seconds to spiral from its maximum angle to the center (one frame time) a target will be scanned only once each 3 seconds. This causes a search mode target to "paint" on the radar indicator at a 3-second rate.

The radar boresight (also optical sight and IR sight) is 2¼ degrees below the longitudinal axis of the aircraft, but nearly 3 degrees above the IG flight path (see figure 4-28). Therefore, a target alined with the boresight axis of the interceptor will be above it. This altitude differential is of the order of 300 feet per mile. A boresighted target at 5 miles will be 1500 feet above the aircraft; at 10 miles it will be 3000 feet above, etc. The search mode target range versus off-boresight angle envelope (figure 4-29) should be thoroughly studied so that optimum radar usage can be obtained. The shape of the radar detection envelope will remain essentially the same for any target. Ranges at all angles will increase or decrease in proportion to the target size. The example shown in figure 4-29 illustrates a maximum usable boresight range of 18 miles for a given target. Therefore, the maximum usable ranges against this same target were decreased as the target angle off-boresight increased, as shown, to where 9 miles would be maximum at off angles

RADAR SCOPE PRESENTATIONS

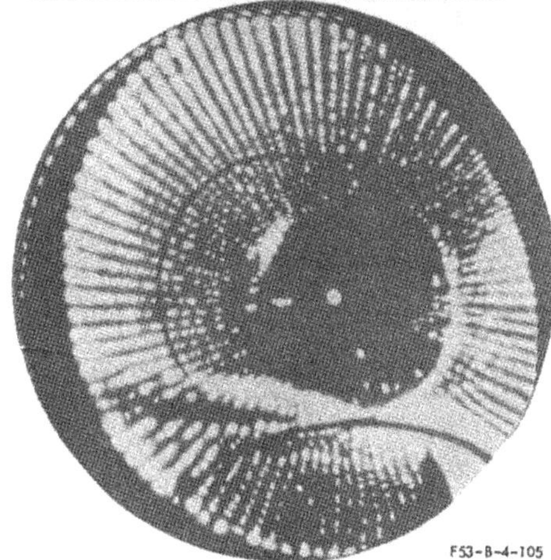

Figure 4-27

greater than 15 degrees. This particular example is typical of a large jet bomber. Because of this search mode detection envelope, the relationship of airplane angle of attack, fire control system, and missile boresight must be fully understood so that the airplane nose-up attitude can be used to best radar advantage. This is accomplished by allowing for altitude separation between target and interceptor. Flying at the same altitude as the target is a disadvantage to the interceptor because the control target detection is then in the 6-o'clock indicator position where the horizon clutter paints. Target recognition is naturally more difficult in this area. Target information displayed on the radar indicator will immediately show the clock position of the target relative to the interceptor radar boresight axis (A, figure 4-30) and range to the target. Commencing with A, figure 4-30, consider the interceptor as the center point position of the radar indicator and interpret this presentation to determine the target's position and range relative to you. The target displayed is a small arc at the 9-o'clock position, thus the target is to your left (at an angle not greater than 45 degrees) and at a range of 7 to 8 miles (denoted by the distance from the center of the radar indicator to the arc). The interceptor should then be steered in the direction of the target arc (left) with a resulting increase of target arc length (B, figure 4-30). Continuing to steer in the direction of the arc will result in corresponding presentations (C and D, figure 4-30). A complete circle indicates that the target is boresighted (in line with the radar boresight axis). The length of the target arc is an indication of the target's angle off-boresight. (Figure 4-29 illustrates the relationship.)

FIRE CONTROL SYSTEM BORESIGHT

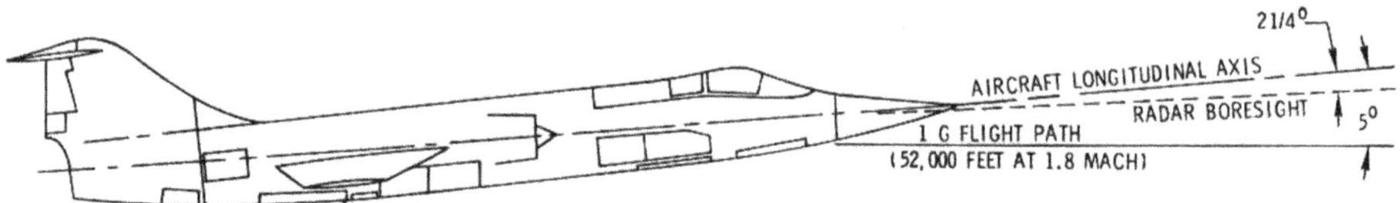

NOTE ANGLES ARE EXAGGERATED IN THIS DRAWING FOR PURPOSES OF ILLUSTRATION

F53-8-4-107

Figure 4-28

Return signals from the ground are also displayed on the radar indicator in search mode due to the wide angle of antenna scan. In straight-and-level flight and with the FTC switch off (which disables anti-clutter circuit), the ground return (hereafter referred to as clutter) appears as in E, figure 4-30. Targets could not be distinguished within this area but the clutter display is useful as a horizon reference; thus, this clutter is referred to as horizon clutter. F, figure 4-30 reveals the effect of the anti-clutter circuit when the FTC switch is on. It is now possible to distinguish a target in this clutter area, while the broken-up horizon clutter still serves as a horizon reference. The position of the horizon clutter in F, figure 4-30 indicates that the interceptor is in a left bank and also shows another ground clutter display which is a normal occurrence when the interceptor banks. It is the crescent-shaped clutter appearing at the 12-o'clock position and is referred to as altitude clutter since its range on the radar indicator does correspond to the interceptor's altitude above the terrain. Its clock position must be disregarded since it is not a true relative position indication. The example is shown here for purposes of recognition so as not to confuse the altitude clutter presentation with a target arc. The radar indicator is normally void of altitude clutter in straight-and-level flight unless the terrain below is particularly irregular.

Track Mode.

Track mode is initiated by momentarily depressing the track action button. At this time the antenna reverses its spin direction and counterweights pull back one half of the antenna reflector (disk) slightly. This forms a fan-shaped beam of approximately 4 degrees by 10 degrees (see figure 4-25). The antenna does not spiral in track mode but spins about a fixed point (offset slightly from the boresight axis) and a 20-degree conical volume is scanned. Therefore, the track mode envelope provides a constant range versus angle off boresight (±10 degrees). In the track mode the maximum range on the radar indicator is 10 nautical miles and the engraved markers represent 7.5, 5, and 2.5 miles. The track mode should not be used until the search mode display indicates target range to be less than 10 miles and arc length 90 degrees or greater. This will ensure that the target is within the track cone. Readjustment of the radar screen intensity rheostat may be required when switching modes. Track mode target presentation is interpreted in the same manner as in search mode. There is the addition of the range strobe in track operation. The strobe appears as a circle and slews out and in with successive actuation of the track action button and remains stationary when the button is released.

An automatic slew feature of the radar will continuously slew the strobe from 200 yards to 3000 yards whenever it is manually slewed into this range. The strobe will then automatically lock onto the closest target it sees within this range. Manual lockon of targets beyond 1.5 miles is accomplished by holding the track action button down and slewing the strobe to the target. Release the button when the strobe coincides with the target to establish lockon. If desired, the range strobe

RADAR DETECTION ENVELOPE

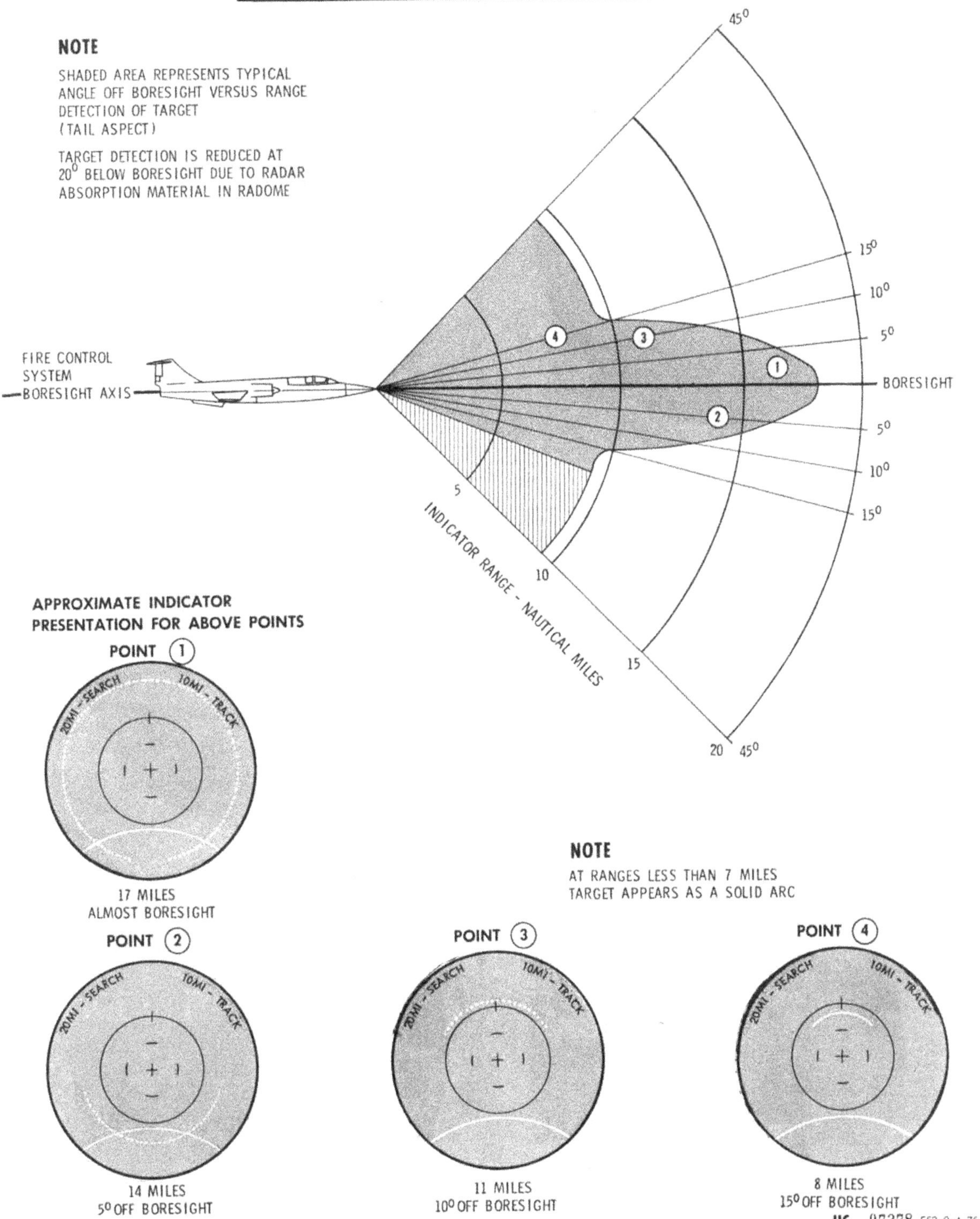
NOTE
SHADED AREA REPRESENTS TYPICAL ANGLE OFF BORESIGHT VERSUS RANGE DETECTION OF TARGET (TAIL ASPECT)
TARGET DETECTION IS REDUCED AT 20° BELOW BORESIGHT DUE TO RADAR ABSORPTION MATERIAL IN RADOME
FIRE CONTROL SYSTEM BORESIGHT AXIS
BORESIGHT
45°
15°
10°
5°
INDICATOR RANGE - NAUTICAL MILES
5
10
15
20
APPROXIMATE INDICATOR PRESENTATION FOR ABOVE POINTS
POINT 1
20MI - SEARCH
10MI - TRACK
17 MILES
ALMOST BORESIGHT
POINT 2
14 MILES
5° OFF BORESIGHT
NOTE
AT RANGES LESS THAN 7 MILES TARGET APPEARS AS A SOLID ARC
POINT 3
11 MILES
10° OFF BORESIGHT
POINT 4
8 MILES
15° OFF BORESIGHT
HG 07378 F52-0-4-75

Figure 4-29

RADAR SCOPE PRESENTATIONS

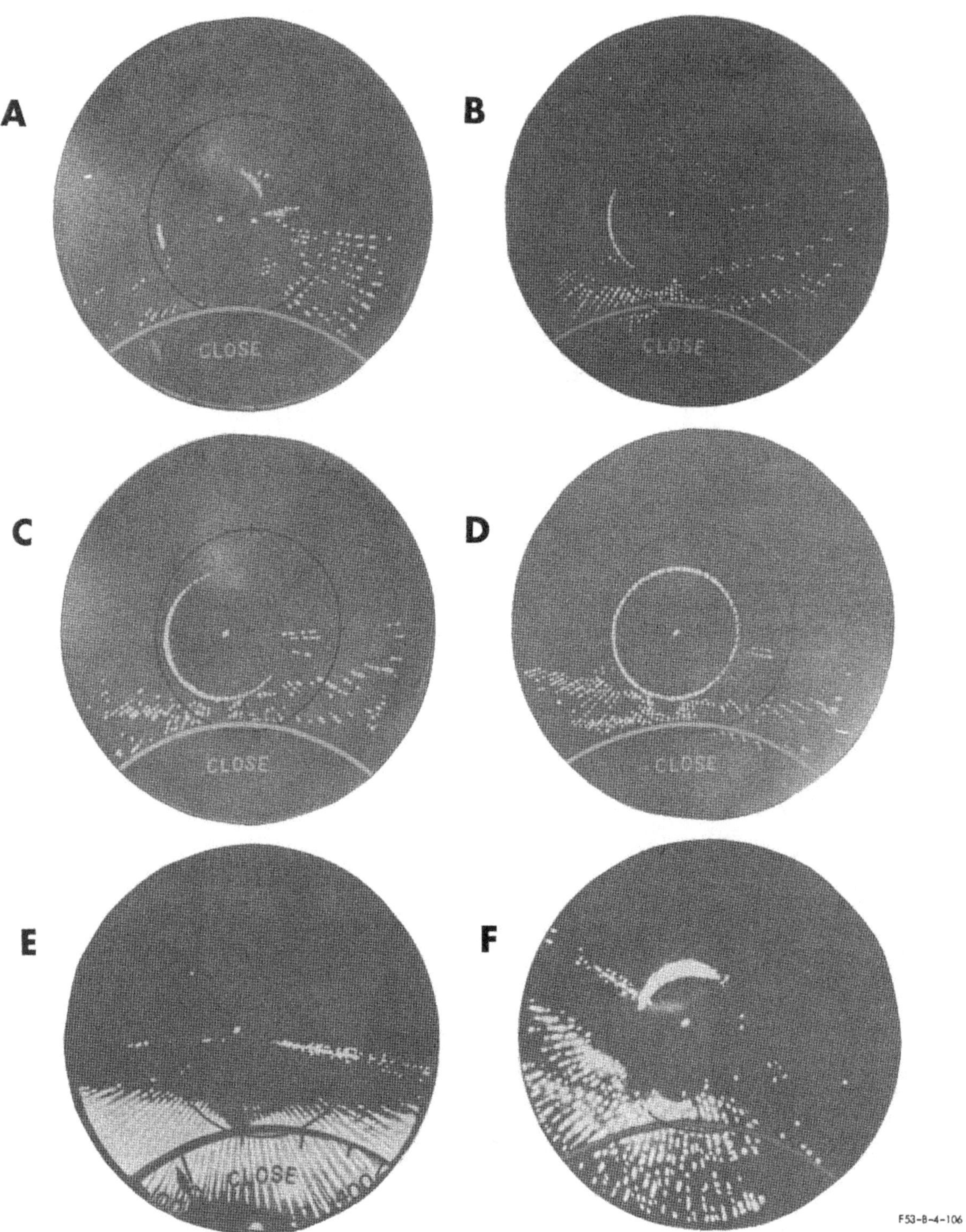

Figure 4-30

RADAR SCOPE PRESENTATIONS

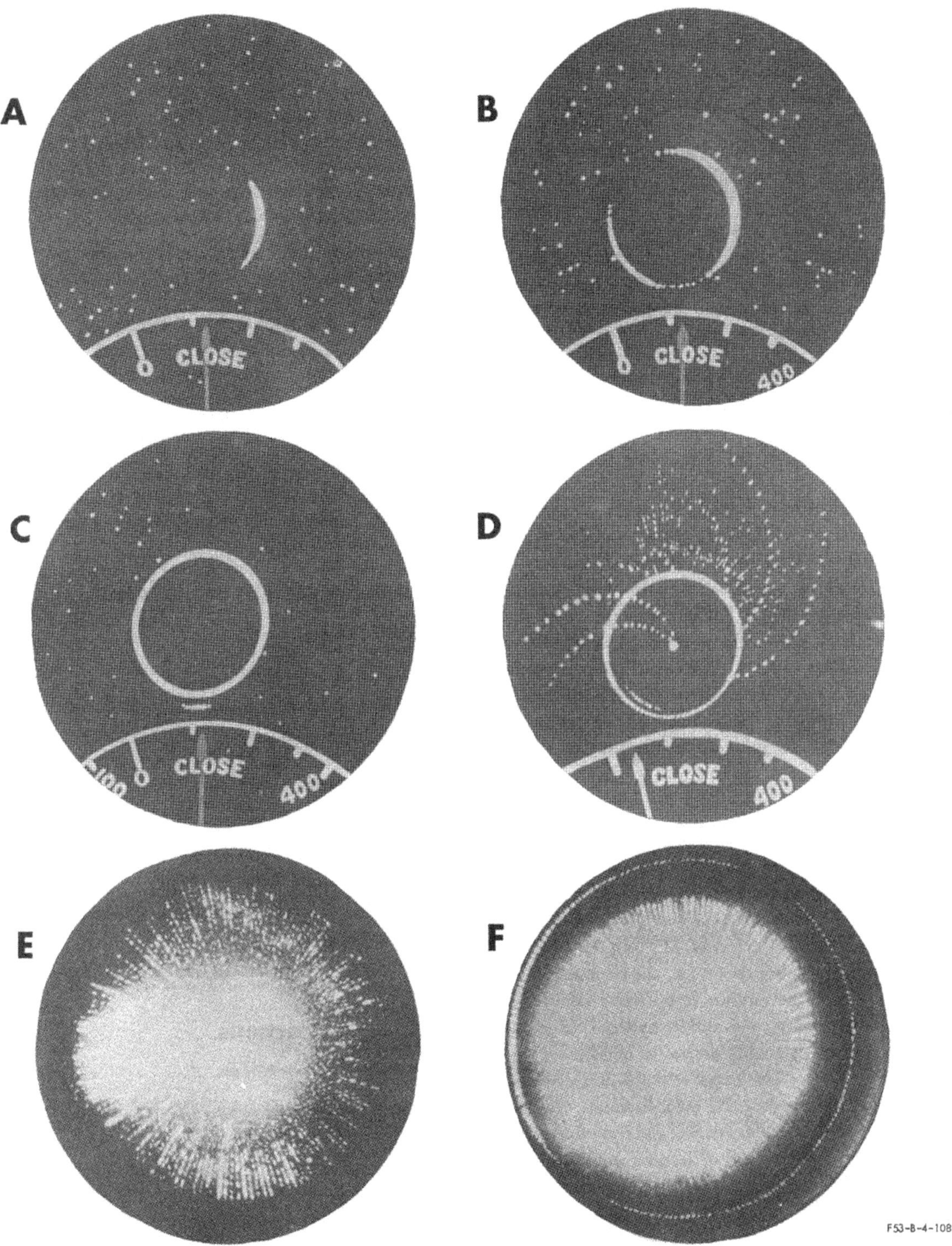

Figure 4-31

can be slewed toward the target just short of the target range. As target range decreases, lockon will occur when the target and strobe coincide. The radar lockon indicator as well as the one adjacent to the left side of the optical sight combining glass display will illuminate to indicate lockon and the range strobe disappears from the display. When lockon is accomplished, the range rate meter on the radar indicator will show the opening or closing rate in knots (true speed), and provide range information to the optical sight. Typical track target presentations are shown in A, B, and C, figure 4-31. Commencing with A, a target to your right at 3 miles is displayed. Steering right in the direction of the arc results in a near boresight (B) and then boresight (C). A range strobe is not present in these photographs as lockon exists.

The track presentation is normally entirely free of any ground clutter. Altitude clutter may appear during interceptor bank angles of 45 degrees or greater or when flying over water. In the latter case, it takes on the appearance of a boresighted target, but is recognizable as altitude clutter by remaining at a range corresponding to the interceptor altitude. A classic example of interference from other radars is illustrated in D, figure 4-31 This would appear the same in search mode also. Since the antenna scans only a 20-degree volume ahead of the aircraft in track mode, at a 0.1-second scan or spin rate, the target display appears continuously (does not pulsate as in search mode). This allows the pilot to track the target with greater precision and maintain target boresight which will assure a satisfactory overlap with the missile boresight cone.

Electronic Countermeasures Homing Mode.

The electronic countermeasures homing mode is selected by rotating the master selector switch to ECM HOM position. In this mode the radar sweep is noticeably shortened for positive indication of ECM HOM mode. The radar system becomes passive; i.e., the transmitter is disabled, and only the receiver is operative allowing the system to be used as a direction finder. During radar system operation, jamming devices or other radar equipment may interfere with target selection and acquisition. The display presented on the radar indicator may take a variety of forms, both symmetrical and irregular, depending on the particular type of interference encountered. When ECM HOM mode is selected, the receiver gain knob must be in the full clockwise position, and the receiver frequency switch must be turned out of AFC detent position and rotated until the interference is tuned in. The reciever gain knob may then be adjusted along with the radar screen intensity rheostat, to produce a nonblooming, nicely defined presentation on the radar indicator. Frequent readjustment of the receiver frequency switch may be necessary. E, figure 4-31 shows an off-boresight source of continuous-wave jamming tuned in ECM HOM mode. The pilot would steer toward the center of this splash of interference just as he would turn toward an off-boresight target arc. When the interference becomes a circular pattern (F, figure 4-31), the source is boresighted. No range information is available from the radar system in ECM HOM mode.

Chaff released from an aircraft within the zone of radar detection results in indications on the display that resemble targets when the radar system is in search or track modes. These indications are readily detected. Since chaff has little or no horizontal velocity, it will always appear as the innermost target or targets on the radar indicator. ECM HOM mode usually will be selected only when jamming totally obliterates the target and renders search and track modes useless. There are many different forms of radar jamming that are clever and almost impossible to counteract. Therefore, the successful tracking of a target through jamming will depend largely upon the pilot's experience and skill.

NORMAL OPERATION OF THE RADAR

Before Takeoff.

1. FCS switch—ON.
2. Transfer radar control—As desired.
3. Master selector switch—RE-SET STBY.

After Takeoff.

1. Master selector switch—OPER.
2. Receiver frequency switch—AFC.
3. FTC switch—ON.
4. Receiver gain knob—Extreme clockwise (maximum gain) position.
5. Radar screen intensity rheostat—Desired brilliance.

RADAR MALFUNCTIONS.

No Radar Presentation.

If the display on the radar indicator disappears entirely, use the following procedure:

1. Check the circuit breakers on the left console (forward cockpit B D) to determine if one of them has popped out. Reset the circuit breakers. If the power failure was due to a temporary overload the breaker will hold.

2. If display is still absent, remove the fuse on the radar control panel and replace it with the spare which is mounted on clips at the top of the indicator. On **C D** aircraft with the MOD II installation there are no provisions for fuse replacement.

3. If the previous steps are ineffective, turn the master selector switch to the RE-SET STBY position and return to the OPER position.

Erratic Radar Presentation.

If presentations on the radar indicator are erratic, the radar test panel may be used to check certain circuits in the radar system as follows:

1. Rotate the 11-position rotary selector switch to each position in turn, checking that the indication lies within the range of the scale corresponding to the color-coded dot revealed by the cutout in the flange of the selector knob.

2. Since the circuits checked are all within the radar nose package, the pilot can do nothing about an abnormal indication except when the indication is obtained in the AFC XTAL positions. With defective automatic frequency control the radar receiver will be detuned. By operating the receiver frequency switch to the MANUAL FREQ range and adjusting for an optimum presentation, the pilot will be able to complete the mission. (The receiver frequency switch may require periodic readjustment.)

Note

An abnormal reading does not necessarily indicate that the radar system cannot be used at least to some extent, although its performance will not be up to standard.

Erratic in Search Mode Only.

If the radar system becomes defective only when operated in the search mode, it is possible to initiate and complete an attack in the track mode. The following procedure may be used to locate and acquire a target:

1. With the master selector switch in the OPER position, press and hold the radar track action button until the strobe has run out to the edge off the radar screen.

2. Using the normal operating procedure previously outlined, adjust the display and pick out a target.

3. Again depress the radar track action button and hold it down until the strobe coincides with the target.

Failure To Lock-On Target.

If lock-on does not occur when the target and range strobe coincide, turn the LOCK-ON SENS control knob clockwise (slowly) until lock-on occurs. If lock-on does not occur by the time full clockwise position is reached, nothing more can be done by the pilot to effect it.

Operation Without Proper Warmup.

When it is necessary to use the radar immediately after engine start and before the customary 3-minute warmup period has terminated, use the following procedure:

1. Rotate the master selector switch on the armament control panel to the ECM HOM position, then depress the knob and rotate it to the PUSH EMER position.

Note

The master selector switch is so constructed that the PUSH EMER position cannot be selected inadvertently. The switch must be depressed before this position can be reached. The switch may be returned to one of the other positions in the normal manner.

CAUTION

Do not use the PUSH EMER position of the master selector switch except in an emergency. Indiscriminate use of this feature may damage the equipment.

2. To locate and track a target, operate the set as though it were in the OPER position.

Jamming.

During radar operation, jamming devices or other radar equipment may interfere with target selection and acquisition. The display presented on the indicator screen may take a variety of forms, symmetrical or irregular depending upon the particular type of interference encountered. Interference may be reduced or even eliminated by applying the following procedure:

1. Operate the master selector switch to the ECM HOM position and check the display to see if the interference is being caused by the target. If it is, leave the master selector switch in the ECM HOM position and vary the intensity and receiver gain knob settings to attempt to isolate the target from the jamming. Locate the target from the resulting display.

Note

The FTC circuit is inoperative in the ECM HOM mode.

2. Countermeasures personnel may be able to supply additional procedures to combat jamming.

Chaff released from an aircraft within the zone of radar detection produces indications on the display that resemble targets. These indications are readily detected since chaff has little or no horizontal velocity. Consequently, the range rate will be considerably different from that of an airborne target. During automatic track, the equipment discriminates against all echoes that do not occur at the same range or have the same range rate as the target being tracked.

OPTICAL SIGHT SYSTEM. A B

The optical sight is a gyro computing sight which automatically computes proper lead angle for aerial gunnery attacks. During the missile mode attack the optical sight is mechanically caged. The mechanically caged sight presents to the pilot a zero lead angle which is 1 degree below the physical boresight of the AIM-9B missile. The AIM-9B missile has a search cone of 4 degrees, thereby being completely compatible in tracking with the fixed AN/ASG-14T1 optical sight. Electrical power for the optical sight is derived from the No. 1 ac bus and the dc monitored bus.

Reticle Lights Rheostat. A B

The reticle lights rheostat (figure 4-21) controls the intensity of the reticle on the optical sight combining glass display. The reticle brightness can be adjusted by turning the rheostat from OFF toward BRT in either direction. The reticle lamp is a dual-filament lamp; the second filament (counterclockwise rotation) is used as a standby. Use the first filament (clockwise rotation) for optimum reticle brightness. Power is derived from the dc monitored bus.

Mechanical Cage Switch. A B

The rotary mechanical cage switch (figure 4-21) is provided to cage the sight gyro. The gyro may be caged by turning the switch clockwise to the CAGE position and may be uncaged by moving the switch counterclockwise to the UNCAGE position.

CAUTION

The gyro should be mechanically caged for all takeoffs and landings to avoid damaging the sight.

Target Span Selector Switch. A B

The target span selector switch, placarded SPAN (figure 4-21), enables the pilot to adjust the sight reticle size to some definite dimension on the target by turning the switch. Any desired span setting from 12 to 60 feet can be set into the sight. The selected span numbers will appear on the lower right side of the optical sight combining glass whenever the range numerals indicate 3000 feet or over. In aircraft using amplifier P/N 167D30702, when the sight is mechanically caged and the radar and manual range grip in detent position, a fixed 1200-foot range signal is fed to the optical sight. In aircraft using amplifier P/N 167D30703 a maximum range of 5 miles is presented with a decreasing range as the aircraft closes in on the target. When the sight is mechanically caged and the radar and manual range grip is in detent position, a fixed 1200-foot range signal is fed to the optical sight.

Electrical Cage Switch. A B

The sight reticle image may be electrically stabilized at approximately zero lead angle by pressing the electrical cage button on the throttle (figure 1-9). The sight will be uncaged and operable when the electrical cage button is released. The mechanical caging of the optical sight will override this feature and will hold the sight gyro at zero lead angle, regardless of the position of the electrical cage button. Electrically caging the optical sight during level flight with the sight mechanically uncaged will cause the sight gyro to stabilize at approximately 1–2 mills of the zero lead angle and will not alter target range numerals in the sight presentation.

Radar and Manual Range Grip. A B

Both radar ranging and manual ranging controls are installed on the throttle. Turning the radar and manual range grip (figure 1-9) to the full counterclockwise position until the detent is engaged allows radar range to be supplied to the sight head from the radar system unless the optical sight is mechanically caged. In aircraft using amplifier P/N 167D30702 when the optical sight is in the radar mode (detent position) and mechanically caged, a fixed range signal of 1200-feet is fed into the optical sight. When the optical sight is in radar mode (detent position) and mechanically caged, a fixed-range signal of 1200 feet is fed into the optical sight. Manual ranging of the sight (control clockwise out of detent position) will interrupt this signal and verify range information. The manual range feature of the optical sight is not used in a missile mode attack.

SIGHT COMBINING GLASS DISPLAY

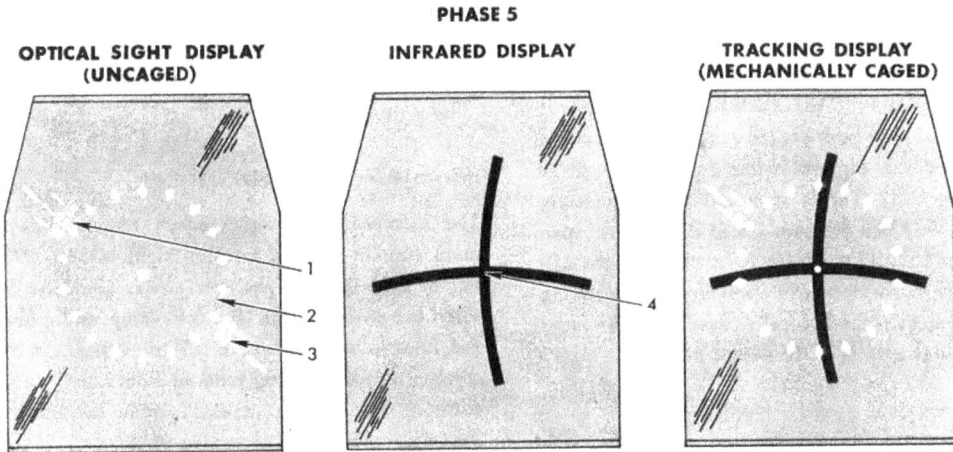

PHASE 5

OPTICAL SIGHT DISPLAY (UNCAGED)

INFRARED DISPLAY

TRACKING DISPLAY (MECHANICALLY CAGED)

1 RANGE NUMERALS (HUNDREDS OF FEET)
2 RETICLE IMAGE
3 TARGET SPAN NUMERALS (FEET)
4 TARGET LOCATION INDICATED BY INTERSECTION OF TWO ARCS

PHASE 7
OPTICAL SIGHT DISPLAY
C D

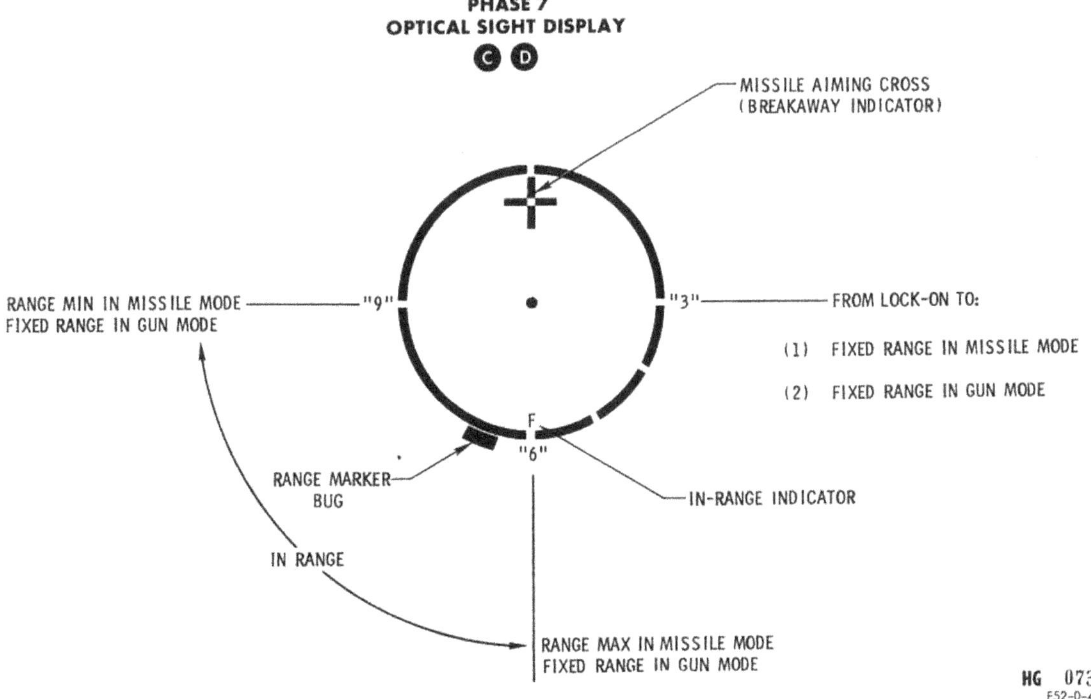

HG 07382
F52-0-4-52

Figure 4-32

Sight Combining Glass Display. A B

The sight combining glass display (figure 4-32) is composed of a variable-diameter reticle image, target range, and target span numerals. The range numerals at the 10-o'clock position are in hundreds of feet except in aircraft using amplifier P/N 167D30703, when the sight is in the mechanical cage position the range is presented in miles (0 to 5 miles). Figures visible are 10 through 50 (1000 to 5000 feet). Target span numerals which are located at the 4-o'clock position are in actual feet. Span numerals range from 12 to 60 feet. The optical sight will present a 50-mil diameter reticle when target span setting is 60 feet, the sight is mechanically caged, and the radar and manual range grip is in the detent position.

Armament Ground Test Panel. A B

A sight head and firing override test panel (figures 1-14, 1-15) is located on the left console. This panel is used by ground maintenance personnel.

INFRARED SIGHT SYSTEM. A B

With the use of the infrared (IR) sight, attacks can be made when the pilot is unable to see the target visually. The infrared radiation emitted by the target is scanned by a disc having two pairs of slits and a field of view of approximately ±7 degrees from zero lead angle. The energy passing through a certain portion of the slits is detected by an infrared sensitive photocell and converted to electrical energy. The electrical energy is amplified and actuates a neon lamp. A disc similar to the scanning disc rotates in front of this lamp. Whenever the lamp is lighted, an illuminated arc will be projected onto the combining glass of the optical sight (figure 4-32). Since there are two pairs of slits and the arcs in each pair are effectively perpendicular, the lines will form a cross. With the optical sight mechanically caged (missile mode), the pilot merely superimposes the fixed optical sight "pipper" over the infrared cross. Maximum range of the infrared unit is dependent on atmospheric conditions, type of target aircraft, exhaust gas temperature, and area of relatively hot skin surfaces near the engine. A large four-engine jet bomber target at 14–15 miles range will appear as a single cross. As target range decreases, the IR sight will paint two targets (two-engine clusters). If the target range is decreased more, the IR sight may actually define each engine by a thick horizontal arc and as many properly spaced vertical arcs as there are engines. The main intersection of the various arcs defines each engine or each aircraft as in the case when chasing a close-flying formation. If the IR sight views no definite target, the general background return appears as an infinite number of small targets. The IR sight then paints many targets or intersections which appear like a basketweave pattern.

Infrared Sight Switch. A B

The infrared (IR) sight switch (figure 4-21) is the main control for the infrared sight system. When the switch is in the ON position, power from the dc monitored bus energizes the IR strobe lamp, and a number of red lines in a basketweave pattern appear on the sight combining glass. These random lines break up into the form of a cross (figure 4-32) when the infrared unit senses a target. The intersection of this cross is the target position.

GUNNERY SYSTEM (Modified aircraft). A C

The 20-mm gun, installed in the lower left side of the forward fuselage, is capable of firing electrically primed cartridges at rates in excess of 4000 rounds per minute. The gun is operated by a double-wound motor, one winding being energized by the No. 1 ac bus while the other receives its power from the No. 2 ac bus. When the gun is fired the cases are stored and links ejected overboard. A supply of 725 rounds of ammunition may be carried in the ammunition compartment.

CAUTION

- When the aircraft is configured to retain both the links and expended casings aboard the aircraft, the amount of ammunition carried must be restricted to 400 rounds due to limited capacity of the gun debris compartment. A
- Whenever the aircraft is configured to eject ammunition links overboard, the centerline store must be released prior to firing the M-61 gun. C
- When the aircraft is configured to retain both the links and expended casings aboard the aircraft, the M-61 gun and centerline store may be used in any sequence. In this case, however, the amount of ammunition carried must be restricted to 450 rounds due to the limited capacity of the gun debris compartment. C

Gun Firing. A C

Firing the gun above 47,500 feet may result in afterburner blowout and/or compressor stall, especially when gun firing is accompanied by high G forces and maneuvering. However, during gun firing tests, no actual engine flameouts were experienced, even above 50,000 feet. Afterburner blowouts and compressor stalls can be corrected in most instances by reducing speed or altitude or, in more severe cases, by engine shutdown and restart.

Note

- Vibration may cause the tachometer needle to fluctuate during gun firing. Normal operation will resume after gun firing has ceased.
- During forward firing of armament, the inlet guide vanes close 5 degrees to minimize inlet distortion effect on the engine. This causes reduction in fuel flow.

Arming Switch. The guarded arming switch (figure 4-21) controls power from the dc monitored bus for operating the gun, missiles, and camera. The arming switch positions are ARMT & CAMERA (up), OFF (guarded), and CAMERA (down). When the switch is in the CAMERA position, the camera may be operated by pressing the trigger. The gun and camera or missile and camera may be actuated by placing the switch in the ARMT & CAMERA position and pressing the trigger.

Camera—Armament Trigger Switch. The gun firing missile firing, and camera circuits are energized by pressing the trigger (figure 1-44) on the control stick. Electrical power for the trigger is from the dc monitored bus. The trigger has two detent positions. With the arming switch in the CAMERA position, the camera will operate when the trigger is pressed to either detent position. With the arming switch in the ARMT & CAMERA position, the first detent position of the trigger completes the camera circuit, and the second fires the missile or energizes the gun purge valve and fires the gun. Opening the gun purge valve allows compressor bleed air from the engine to operate a jet pump which removes gun gases. Ram air from the refrigerator unit is also diverted to the gun compartment. When the trigger is released from the fully pressed position, the gun fires the remaining round as it stops and a time-delay unit keeps the purge valve open for an additional 10 seconds.

Note

- If the ram air scoop is open or if the gun A C purge valve fails to open, the gun firing circuit will not be closed, and the gun will not fire.
- A delay feature on the camera system A C permits ground-setting the camera to continue running for up to 3 seconds after the trigger is released. To extend the camera overrun time it is necessary to hold the trigger in the first detent position.

Gun Firing Power Circuit Breaker. The FIRE A C PWR circuit breaker on the left console (see figures 1-39, 1-40) may be pulled prior to landing as an added precaution against inadvertent firing of the gun.

AIM-9B MISSILE SYSTEM.

The AIM-9B is a passive infrared-homing air-to-air guided missile. It homes on infrared energy radiated by heated parts of the target. Since the missile is a passive homing device, it does not need to transmit a signal for guidance and is therefore relatively impervious to jamming. Launch conditions are a function of range, altitude, missile seeker tone, and G load at launch time. When launched, the AIM-9B missile turns into a pursuit course to the target. If the target maneuvers, the missile turns at about four times the turning rate of the target to maintain the required course. After launching, the aircraft is free to maneuver since all further course corrections originate within the missile.

The missile is 5 inches in diameter, 9 feet long, and weighs 155 pounds. It consists of four sections, guidance and control section, warhead, influence fuse, and rocket motor. The guidance and control section contains the optical system for tracking, a hot gas-operated control servo with aerodynamic fins to control the flight of the missile to the target, the electronic components to convert target signals into missile control signals, a hot gas-driven generator to supply electrical power during missile flight, and the contact fuse. While the missile is attached to the aircraft, standby electrical power is furnished by the aircraft's No. 2 ac bus and dc monitored bus through an umbilical connection to the launcher.

The warhead, a 25-pound controlled fragmentation type, is detonated by the action of either the contact or the influence fuse. When exploded, it puts out approximately 1500 metal fragments that travel 6000 feet per second and are capable of penetrating 1 inch aluminum or 3/8 inch steel plate at 30 feet. The influence fuse converts near misses into kills. If the missile passes within 30 feet of the target, this fuse detonates the warhead. The motor is a standard 5-inch HVAR rocket motor which accelerates the missile to Mach 1.7 above the speed of the launching aircraft. This section also carries the fixed aft-stabilizing fins and suspension lugs.

Arming Switch.

Refer to Gunnery System this Section.

Weapon Selector Switch.

The weapon selector switch (figures 4-21, 4-23, 4-24) is a two-position switch. The switch is labeled GUN and MISSILE. When placed in the MISSILE position, the missile firing selector switch is energized.

Missile Selector Switch.

The missile firing selector switch (figures 4-21, 4-23, 4-24) is used to select either or both missiles for firing. The switch has four positions labeled SAFE, LH, RH, and BOTH. With missiles installed and the aircraft electrical system energized, closing the missile power breakers will operate the missile seeker heads regardless of the position of the missile firing selector switch or other firing circuits. The missiles cannot be launched if the missile firing selector switch is in the SAFE position. To launch either or both missiles the missile firing selector switch must be placed in LH, RH, or BOTH, the weapon selector switch must be in MISSILE, the guarded arming switch must be in the ARMT CAMERA position, and the camera and armament trigger switch depressed to the second detent.

Note

There is no automatic firing sequence from one missile to the other. The pilot must manually select the remaining missile. On modified aircraft, an automatic sequencing circuit has been incorporated so that when the missile firing selector switch is in the BOTH position, the left missile is fired first when the trigger switch is pressed, and the right missile second when the trigger switch is pressed the second time.

Missile Signal Volume Rheostat.

The missile signal volume rheostat (figures 4-21, 4-23, 4-24) is used to adjust the ratio of the target signal versus background signal of the missile selected by the missile firing selector switch. The missile signal from the right-hand missile is heard in the pilot's earphones when the missile firing selector switch is set to the BOTH position. The missile seeker audio tone may be checked on the ground by passing a flashlight across the seeker head at a distance of approximately 10 feet.

Camera—Armament Trigger Switch

Refer to Gunnery System in this section.

Missile Jettison Controls.

The external stores release or jettison controls may be used to jettison the missiles and launchers. (Refer to External Stores Release Selector Switch External Stores Release Button, and External Stores Jettison Button in Section I.)

Note

Only missile and launcher combinations may be jettisoned. The launchers cannot be jettisoned separately.

NORMAL OPERATION OF MISSILE LAUNCHING SYSTEM.

Switch Sequence and Firing Procedure.

After the pilot is in the cockpit and normal prestart operations have been completed, check the missiles. With external power on, the seeker heads are in operation and the pilot is able to make an audio check to ascertain satisfactory missile seeker operation. When the missiles are installed on the launchers, protective covers are in place over the missile heads. As the pilot first listens to the audio signal on the selected missile, a very faint signal will be received. When ground crewmen remove the covers prior to taxiing, a louder signal will be heard as the seeker system picks up the infrared radiations from the surrounding area. A light should be directed into the seeker head with a corresponding signal increase in the earphones; this will provide a satisfactory check of seeker operation. On climbout each missile should be checked on another aircraft in the flight. This check will help ascertain that the missile is still in operation, give the pilot an indication of relative signal strength as the target changes position in the seeker view, and most important, give the pilot a chance to check correct boresight and maximum signal strength from the missile with the mechanically caged "pipper."

CAUTION

To avoid objects being blown against glass seeker head, do not taxi too closely behind other aircraft.

The missile seeker head has a null area of approximately 70 mils at its center (very similar to human night vision), and best detects radiation slightly off center. Each aircraft should have a fairly constant boresight versus maximum signal discrepancy which should be placarded in the cockpit.

WARNING

Make certain missile firing circuit is unarmed before checking mssile signal volume and bore sight.

Note

The missile seeker system derives power from the aircraft electrical system and operates throughout the flight.

Missile Firing.

The missile must not be considered infallible. Basically, there are two areas or envelopes in which the aircraft must be before launching the missile, the radiation envelope of the target and the performance envelope of the missile. The radiation envelope of the target is dependent upon its configuration; that is, prop or jet, number of engines, and altitude. The performance envelope of this missile is determined by the maximum and minimum guidance range of the missile and the maximum G that the missile can pull at a given altitude. When the attacking aircraft is in firing position the pilot should hear a missile tone due to proximity of the target. The boresight of the gunsight pipper and the missile differ by approximately 1 degree therefore, if missile tone is not heard, the pipper should be depresed 1 degree below the target. The pilot should maintain no more than the required G's on his aircraft before pressing the trigger on the control stick. The trigger must be held for a period of about 1 second, or until the missile has released, in order to prevent possible missile hang-fire. (There is a short delay occasioned by the time necessary to ignite servo grains in the missile power generator.) Once the missile has been fired the pilot may maneuver to avoid contact, press the attack with another missile, or close to gunfire range. Due to the fact that the missile will maneuver itself into collision course with the target with no more action from the attacking aircraft, the pilot is free for further action. The accuracy and reliability of the missile are sufficent to ensure target destruction. When the accompanying procedures are followed, it will seldom be necessary to salvo both missiles.

Note

- In order to obtain missile tone on centerline missiles at minimum range it may be necessary to use a slightly higher than normal aiming point.
- In less than 1G flight, expect an engine chug when firing fuselage-mounted missiles. At high altitude, a compressor stall may result even during 1G flight.

CAUTION

If spent links are jettisoned overboard, they will collide with and damage the right fuselage missile. Consequently, this missile should be fired before firing the gun.

GUN/MISSILE FIRING PROCEDURES.  

Before Takeoff.

1. Arming switch—OFF.
2. Firing circuit breaker—Out.
3. Weapon selector switch as desired.
4. Trigger pin—In.
5. Reticle lights rheostat—On
6. Missile firing selector switch—SAFE, then alternate between LH and RH for audio check.

In-flight.

1. Arming switch—ARMT CAMERA.
2. Firing circuit breaker—In.
3. Weapon selector switch—MISSILE/GUN (as required).
4. Missile firing selector switch—LH, RH, or BOTH.
5. Trigger pin—Out.
6. Mechanical cage switch—CAGE (Missile)
UNCAGED (Gun)
7. Fly "pipper" on target. (Check G's for missile firing).
8. Listen for audio tone for missile.
9. Depress trigger when in range.

Note

Use the same procedure for night attacks, except that the infrared sight should be used in conjunction with the optical sight. (Refer to Infrared Sight System, this section).

Note

When firing missiles the trigger must be held in the second detent position until the missile has left the launcher.

Before Landing.

1. Arming switch—OFF.
2. Firing circuit breaker—Out.
3. Missile firing selector switch—SAFE.
4. Trigger pin—In.
5. Gun sight—Caged.
6. Master selector switch—ECM HOM.

Note

Damage can occur to the antenna if it is not in motion when the aircraft lands.

SPECIAL WEAPONS CONTROL PANELS (C)

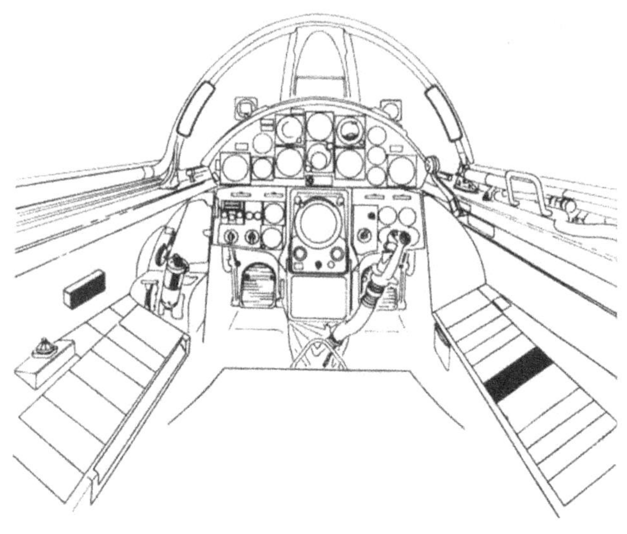

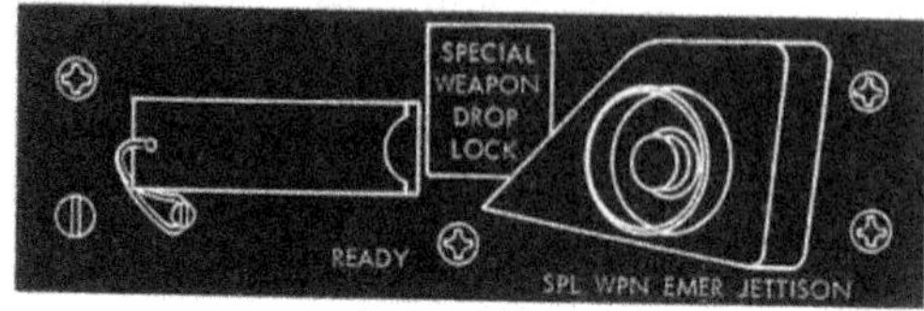

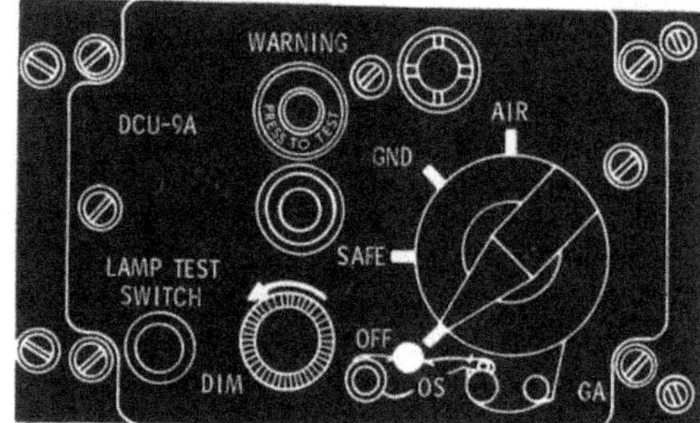

F52-0-4-98

Figure 4-33

SPECIAL WEAPON SYSTEM (C)

A special weapon may be carried on an externally mounted ejector rack located on the lower fuselage surface between the nose and main gear wheel wells. A fairing encases the rack and two sway braces provide stability to the weapon during flight. Special weapon control panels necessary for both normal and emergency release of the weapon are located on the left and right consoles. The external stores release button (bomb/rocket button) on the control stick is used for normal release of the weapon in flight. Refer to T.O. 1F-104C-16 for loading information pertaining to the special weapon. Refer to T.O. 1F-104C-25-1 and T.O. 1F-104C-25-10 for specific information relative to special weapons delivery procedures, delivery techniques, and pertinent safety precautions.

Special Store and Monitor Panel DCU-9/A. (C)

A special weapon control panel (figure 4-33) is installed on the pilot's right console to control and monitor the weapon in flight. The switches and warning light are all powered from the dc emergency bus. The panel contains the following controls and indicators:

Selector Switch. The mechanically locked selector switch is placarded OFF, SAFE, GND, and AIR. When the switch is in a position other than OFF, emergency dc bus power is supplied to the special store. When released the special store detonates in the air, upon ground contact, or is dropped safe, depending on the selected position. When the SUU-21A practice bomb dispenser is carried, selecting the GND or AIR position will open the dispenser doors. The dispenser is set to drop one bomblet at a time, consequently the doors will close and the selector switch must be moved to SAFE and back to GND or AIR to open the doors for another drop. The selector switch may be operated between the AIR, GND, and SAFE positions only with the lock in the SGA position; with the lock in the OS position, the selector switch may be operated between the OFF and SAFE positions. Lock position may be changed only with the selector switch in the SAFE position.

Lamp Test Switch. The lamp test switch is used to switch the filament in the WARNING light. If the filament is intact, the WARNING light glows when the switch is depressed, provided the selector switch is not in the OFF position.

WARNING Light. The WARNING light glows when there is a malfunction in the internal mechanism of the special store. If the malfunction-detection circuitry is in order, depressing the WARNING light will cause it to glow. When the SUU-21A practice bomb dispenser is carried, illumination of the light indicates doors open.

DIM Control Knob. Not connected.

Special Weapon Droplock Panel. C

A panel (figure 4-33) located above the left console contains the special weapon droplock switch and emergency jettison button.

Special Weapon Droplock Switch. The guarded, safety-wired, special weapon droplock switch has two positions, SAFE and READY. When the switch is in the SAFE position, the external stores release button on the control stick is inoperative. When the guard is raised and the switch is moved forward to the READY position, the weapon may be released by depressing the external stores release button (bomb/rocket button) or the special weapon emergency jettison button. The external stores release selector switch on the fuel control panel must also be in SPL WPN position before the special weapon can be released.

Special Weapon Emergency Jettison Button. C The special weapon emergency jettison button is used to jettison the special weapon in an emergency. The switch is inoperative unless the special weapon droplock switch is in the READY position. The weapon can be jettisoned, armed or safe, depending on the switch settings on the special weapon control and monitor panel.

Special Weapon Release Selector Switch. C A switch labeled BOMB RELEASE SELECTOR, with positions LABS and DIRECT, is located on the right console. The LABS position is used when the special weapon release is to be governed by the DUAL timers. The DIRECT position is used when the special weapon is to be released without a time delay.

Special Weapon Rack Safety Lock Mechanism Monitor Light. A special weapon rack safety lock mechanism monitor light may be installed on the main instrument panel to the right of the radar indicator. The light will illuminate when the special weapon rack safety lock is in the unlocked position. The lock is unlocked when the rotary selector switch on the fuel control panel is in the SPL WPN position and the special weapon droplock switch is in the READY position. After the special weapon has been released the light will flash for a period of approximately 30 seconds.

Note

Upon initial application or interruption of electrical power, the light will flash for a period of approximately 30 seconds.

Dual Timer System. C

A dual timer system is incorporated to compute the programmed release of droppable weapons. A control panel containing the timers is located on the left console. (See figure 1-24). Refer to T.O. 1F-104C-25-1 and T.O. 1F-104C-25-10 for weapons delivery procedures, delivery techniques, and safety precautions.

Ladd Indicator Light. C On modified aircraft, after bomb release the LADD indicator light (figure 1-22) will stay on until the special stores droplock switch is returned to the SAFE position. Refer to T.O. 1F-104C-25-10 for additional information.

Normal Operation of Special Weapon System Before Takeoff. C

Refer to T.O. 1F-104C-25-10 and -27 for operational procedures.

TOW TARGETS.

DART TOW PROCEDURES.

For use the A/A 37U-15 tow target system and TDU-10B dart target.

WARNING

Do not move the external stores release selector switch from the OFF position unless it is intended to jettison the entire dart tow rig.

Preflight.

1. Condition and security of target—Check.
2. Tow assembly—Securely mounted.
3. Tow reel—No side play, check cable.
4. Cable secured to target harness and rope. Rope and harness safety wired to the target wing—Check.
5. Proper routing and security of the rope—Check.
6. Dart target sway braces tight (locked). No cracks or breaks—Check.
7. Dart wings not warped by excessive pressure from sway brace adjustment—Check.

8. Nose pin in guide rail and guide rail securely bolted —Check.

9. Cable cutter cannon plug connected—Check.

10. Intake air duct on pod, clear and free of obstructions—Check.

Interior Check.

1. Flap restrictor guard—Installed.
2. Rudder trim—
   With balancing pylon tank—Neutral.
   No pylon tank—Full right (3 o'clock).
3. External stores release selector switch—OFF.

WARNING

Do not move the external store release selector switch from the OFF position unless it is intended to jettison the entire dart tow rig.

4. Rocket firing selector—SAFE. Ⓒ Ⓓ
   TPV-10 B cable cutter circuit breaker—Out. [A] [B]
5. External tank fuel and air refueling selector switch —OFF or TIP if pylon tank installed Ⓒ Ⓓ.
   External tank fuel selector switch—TIP, if pylon tank is installed. [A] [B] and unmodified Ⓓ.

Takeoff and Cruise. (Maximum crosswind component—15 knots).

When carrying a full pylon tank for balance, pylon fuel may be used after takeoff.

1. Increase normal takeoff speed 10 KIAS.

Note

Increased takeoff speed alleviate dragging the target on the runway during rotation to takeoff attitude.

Note

- With a balancing pylon tank, left control stick application should be initiated approximately 30 knots prior to the anticipated lift-off speed. At lift-off, left control stick application for ¼ to ½ aileron will be required to hold the wings level when carrying a full pylon tank.
- Without the balancing pylon tank, right control stick application for ¼ to ½ aileron will be required.

2. Climb and cruise—325 KIAS.
3. External fuel selector switch—As desired.
4. Maximum speed—325 KIAS.
5. Maximum G—1.5 positive.

Dart Launch.

1. Flaps—Takeoff.
2. Airspeed—230 KIAS, level 1G flight.
3. Rocket firing selector switch—LH. Ⓒ Ⓓ
   TPV-10B cable cutter circuit breaker—IN. [A] [B]
4. External stores release button (bomb/rocket button)—Depress. Ⓒ Ⓓ
   Tow target release switch—Actuate. [A] [B]
5. Rocket firing selector switch—Safe, after target is completely reeled out. Ⓒ Ⓓ
6. Accelerate to 350 KIAS and climb to altitude.

Towing Limits (dart deployed).

1. Airspeed—400 KIAS maximum.
2. Acceleration limit—2G positive.

Dart Drop

1. Airspeed—250 KIAS without drag chute.—210 KIAS with drag chute.
2. Altitude—1,000 feet AGL minimum.
3. Rocket firing selector switch—Both. Ⓒ Ⓓ
4. External stores release button (bomb/rocket button)—Depress. Ⓒ Ⓓ
   Tow target release switch—Activate a second time.

Note

This step activates the cable cutter.

5. Rocket firing selector switch—SAFE. Ⓒ Ⓓ

Landing (Maximum crosswind component — 15 knots).

1. Accomplish a normal takeoff flap landing.

Landing with dart stowed (Maximum crosswind component—15 knots).

1. Flaps—Takeoff.
2. Increase normal takeoff flap approach and touchdown speed—10 KIAS.

Note

A straight in approach landing should be accomplished.

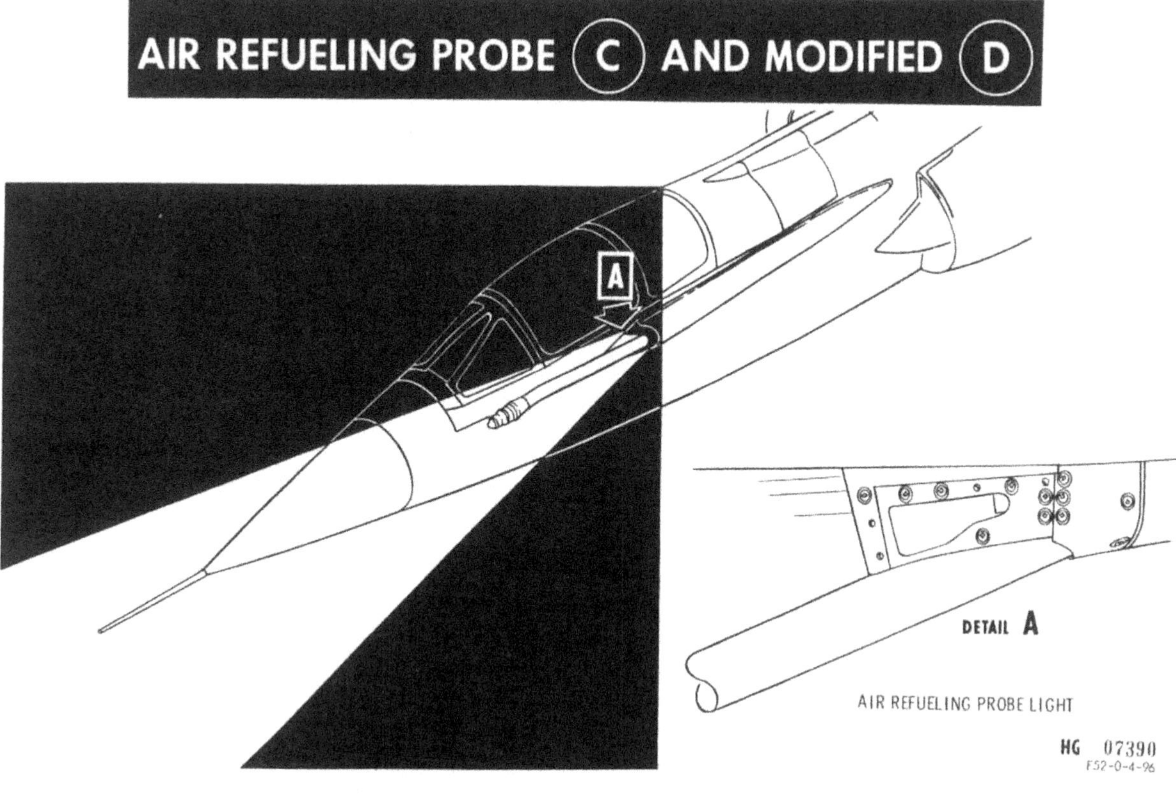

Figure 4-34

EMERGENCY JETTISON PROCEDURES.

WARNING

The tow pod may be jettisoned when the dart is stowed or being towed. The tow pod only should not be jettisoned because it is unstable and most likely will strike the trailing edge flap.

1. Flaps—Up.
2. Airspeed—325 KIAS.
3. External stores jettison button (panic button)—Depress (Tip stores will also jettison).

Alternate Method.

1. External stores release (rotary C) selector switch—
   LH or BOTH. C
   PYLON. A B D
2. External stores release button (bomb/rocket button)—Depress.

PRESSURE REFUELING SYSTEM. C D

(AF Serial 57-1320 and subsequent D). The pressure refueling system makes it possible to fill all internal fuel cells and external fuel tanks on the ground by single-point refueling and in flight by probe-and-drogue refueling.

GROUND REFUELING.

Single-Point Refueling.

The internal fuel cells and external fuel tanks are normally filled by using the single-point refueling system. The internal fuel cells can be filled in about 3 minutes, the internal fuel cells and external fuel tanks in about 5 minutes. The single-point refueling receptacle is located on the left side of the fuselage, forward of the intake ducts. When the air-refueling probe is installed, a special fitting must be used to adapt the ground refueling hose to the probe nozzle. Cell-mounted, dual fuel level control valves automatically shut off fuel to the internal fuel cells as they become full. Precheck test switches are provided to ensure proper operation of these valves. An electrical external power source should be connected, and the external tank fuel and air refueling selector switch placed in the REFUEL position. A refueling valve is provided for each set of external fuel tanks. Float switches, located in each tank, close the respective refueling valve as soon as either tip tank or pylon tank becomes full.

Fuel Level Control Valve Selector Switches and External Tanks Refuel Selector Switch. A refueling precheck switch panel (figure 2-8) located forward and below the single-point refueling receptacle, contains three switches used to check the internal cells dual fuel level control valves for proper operation. These switches are powered by the dc monitored bus. The external tanks refuel selector switch located on the right console (figures 1-26, 1-27) is labeled TIP, PYLON, and BOTH and is guarded to the BOTH position. The auxiliary cell and forward main cell precheck switches are for maintenance personnel use only. The master precheck switch is labeled PRIMARY and SECONDARY and is used to test the primary and secondary operation of the dual fuel level control valves. This switch is spring loaded to the center OFF position. During the first few seconds of refueling the master precheck switch should be placed first to the PRIMARY and then to the SECONDARY position to check that the dual fuel level control valves close. Satisfactory valve operation is indicated by the shutoff of fuel flow, causing gradual stiffening of the refueling hose after the switch is moved to each position. A more positive indication of fuel shutoff, however, can be obtained by checking the counter on the ground refueling equipment. There is approximately a 10-second delay between the time the switch is activated and the shutoff of fuel. If fuel flow continues, pressure refueling must be stopped immediately to prevent possible fuel cell rupture or airframe damage, and this fact entered in Form 781. If necessary, the aircraft can then be refueled by the alternate refueling method. A switch, labeled GRD REFUEL PWR is installed on the refueling precheck switch panel. It has two positions, placarded BATTERY and NORMAL. With the switch in the NORMAL position, an auxiliary electrical power source must be connected to the aircraft for ground refueling. With the switch in the BATTERY position, the electrical components of the refueling system receive power directly from the battery bus. The coverplate for the refueling precheck switch panel, when in place, assures that the GRD REFUEL PWR switch is in the NORMAL position.

WARNING

If the pressure refueling system is not operating properly, air refueling should not be attempted.

Alternate Refueling Method.

When single-point refueling cannot be used, the aircraft can be refueled in the conventional manner. Two filler wells (figure 2-8) are provided for refueling the internal fuel cells, individual filled wells are provided for refueling the pylon tanks. Two filler wells are provided for each tip tank. Both must be used to fully refuel both compartments of each tip tank.

AIR REFUELING.

Air refueling permits all internal fuel cells and external fuel tanks to be filled from a tanker aircraft by means of probe-and-drogue type refueling equipment. The probe, which consists of a boom and nozzle, is a detachable unit mounted on the left side of the fuselage and connected through an adapter elbow to the single-point refueling receptacle. A light at the probe fairing shines forward to light the probe and the tanker drogue for night refueling operations. (See figure 4-34).

External Tank Fuel and Air Refueling Selector Switch. The external tank fuel and air refueling selector switch is a four position switch on all Ⓒ and on air refuelable Ⓓ aircraft. The switch is placarded PYLON, OFF, TIP and REFUEL and controls the fail-open solenoid-operated tip and pylon tank refueling valves, and pressurization of the external fuel tanks. The switch in the OFF position closes the refueling valves, allowing the external tanks to pressurize. The TIP or PYLON position also closes the refueling valves and allows the external tanks to pressurize and feed as selected. The PYLON or TIP position also energizes the auxiliary cell transfer pump. The switch in the REFUEL position causes the refueling valves to open and shuts off and dumps external tank air pressure, allowing the tanks to be refueled. If external tanks are to be air-refueled, the switch must be moved to REFUEL position prior to hookup. The switch need not be used to air-refuel internal fuel cells only.

The switch in the REFUEL position causes the refueling valves to open and shuts off and dumps external tank air pressure, allowing the tanks to be refueled. If external tanks are to be air-refueled, the air-refueling switch must be moved to REFUEL prior to hookup. The switch need not be used to air-refuel internal fuel cells only.

CAUTION

Since positioning the external tank fuel and air refueling selector switch to the REFUEL position dumps external tank air pressure and prevents the external tanks from feeding, return the selector switch to the desired external tanks position as soon as possible after breakaway from the drogue.

Note

In the event of dc monitored bus failure, the fail-open tip and pylon tank refueling valves will allow the external tanks to be air refueled. However, external tank air pressure will not be shut off or dumped, and refueling time will be increased considerably.

Air Refueling Probe Light Switch. The light on the refueling probe fairing is controlled by a rheostat-type switch on the right console (forward cockpit D). See figures 1-26 and 1-27. The switch is powered by the No. 2 ac bus and increases the intensity of the air refueling probe light as it is rotated clockwise.

Note

The landing gear indicator circuit breaker must be pulled in order to ground check the refueling probe light.

Air Refueling Procedure.

Experience has shown that there is a possibility of engine stall or flameout during air refueling. As a result, the following recommendations are made:

a. During air refueling, the pilot should keep out of the tanker jet wake as much as possible.

b. Pilots should refrain from engaging drogues that appear to be damaged.

c. If hookups are performed at lower than recommended speeds, some stick-shaker action may be encountered. This shaker action is usually a function of rate input and occurs just when contacting the drogue.

MISCELLANEOUS EQUIPMENT.

ANTI-G SUIT EQUIPMENT.

The anti-G suit equipment consists of a pressure regulating valve and valve control (figures 1-14, 1-15, 1-18, 1-24, 1-25, 1-28) on the left console and a pressure hose leading from the valve outlet, through the quick-disconnect on the left rear of the seat, to the pilot's anti-G suit tube. When this tube is connected to the pressure hose, air from the engine compressor flows into the pilot's anti-G suit under pressures which vary in accordance with valve control setting and aircraft G forces. When the valve control is in the LOW position, the valve opens at 1.7 G, and suit pressurization increases at a rate of 1.0 psi for each additional G. With the valve control in the HI position, suit pressurization begins at 1.5 G and increases at a rate of 1.5 psi per G. A button on top of the valve control can be depressed manually to inflate the anti-G suit when desired. This feature may be used to produce a massaging effect which will help lessen fatigue during prolonged flight.

VENTILATED SUIT BLOWER.

The blower supplies cooling air to the pilot's ventilated suit. Flexible ducting carries the cool air from the blower, through a quick-disconnect on the left side of the seat, to the suit. The blower receives its electrical power from the No. 2 ac bus.

Ventilated Suit Blower Switch.

A two-position switch (figures 1-16, 1-17, 1-26, 1-27), located on the right console forward cockpit B D and powered by the No. 2 ac bus may be used to energize the ventilated suit blower. The switch positions are labeled ON and OFF.

REAR-VIEW MIRROR.

Three adjustable rear-view mirrors are installed in the cockpit, one on each side of the aft edge of the windshield and one top center of the windshield.

COMPUTER. C D

A manually operated computer located above the right console is provided to aid the pilot in solving navigational problems. The computer is mounted on a swivel arm so that it may be used whenever necessary and stowed underneath the canopy sill when not in use. Both sides of the computer face may be used to solve problems, and the computer itself is constructed in such a manner as to be completely operable with one hand.

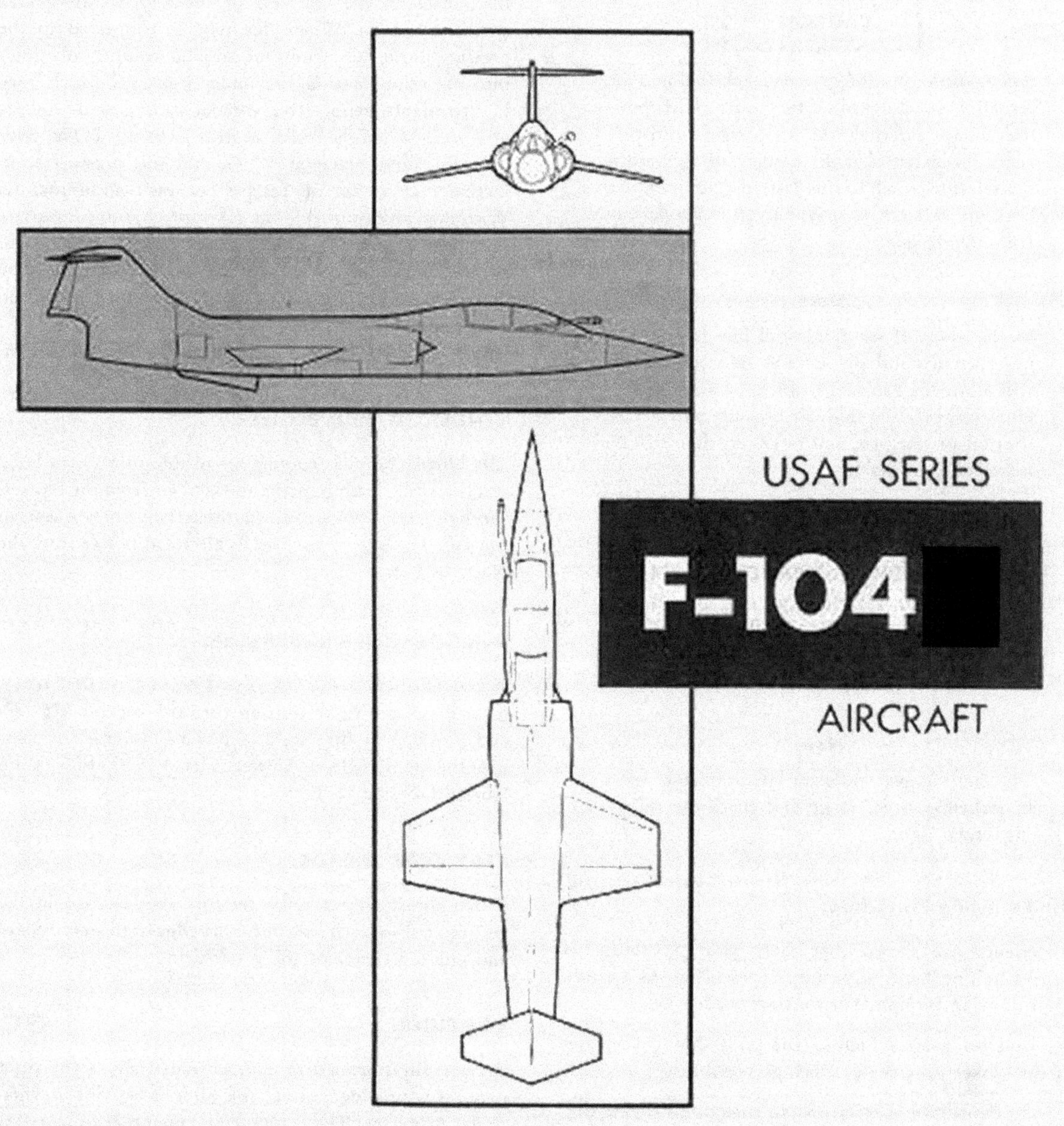

This page intentionally left blank.

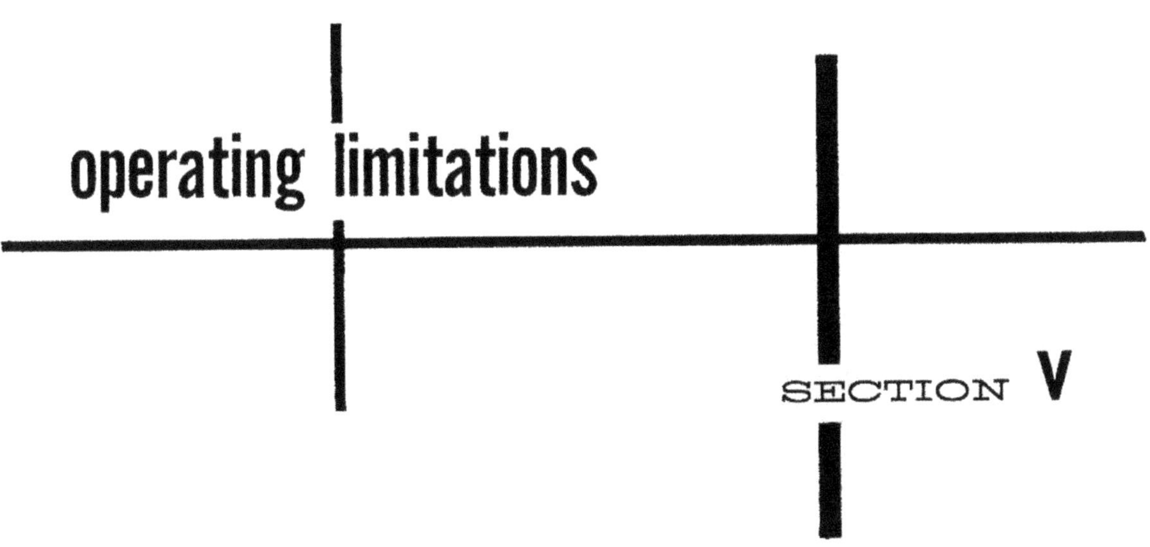

TABLE OF CONTENTS

INTRODUCTION.

This section includes the engine and aircraft limitations that must be observed during normal operation. Attention must be given to the instrument markings, figure 5-1, since they represent limitations that are not necessarily repeated in the text. Further explanation of the markings will be covered in the text under appropriate paragraph headings.

ENGINE LIMITATIONS.

See figures 5-1, 5-2, 5-4 for the engine limitations.

THRUST DEFINITIONS AND TIME LIMITS.

Military Thrust.

Military thrust is obtained with a full (100% rpm and maximum allowable EGT 3B 7A) non-afterburning throttle setting 19 , (see figure 5-2). There are no time limits for inflight operation at this throttle setting. Ground operation is limited to 45 seconds 3B 19 and 90 seconds 7A at Military thrust or above to prevent excessive air-frame/engine overtemperature conditions.

Note

Limit ground operation time at Military thrust or above can be repeated after retarding the throttle to IDLE, then advancing to 80–82 percent rpm for a 2-minute cooling run.

INSTRUMENT MARKINGS

BASED ON JP-4 FUEL

AIRSPEED

240 KNOTS IAS MAXIMUM WITH FLAPS IN LAND POSITION

ENGINE AIR INLET TEMPERATURE

100°C MAXIMUM
-70° to 100°C OPERATING RANGE

ACCELEROMETER SYMMETRICAL MANEUVER LIMITS

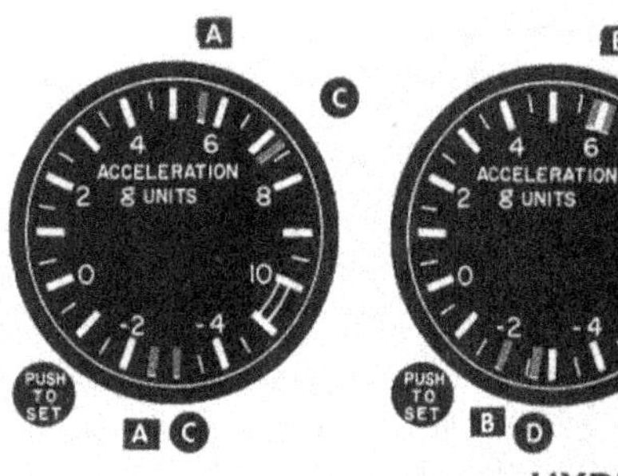

+5.6G MAXIMUM WITH 4000 LB OR LESS FUEL REMAINING AND NO EXTERNAL STORES [A]
+7.33G MAXIMUM WITH NO EXTERNAL STORES AND 1000 POUNDS OR LESS FUEL REMAINING [C]
-2.5G MAXIMUM WITH FLAPS UP [A]
-3.0G MAXIMUM WITH NO EXTERNAL STORES AND 1000 POUNDS OR LESS FUEL REMAINING [C]
+5.9G MAXIMUM WITH NO EXTERNAL STORES [B]
+6.1G MAXIMUM WITH NO EXTERNAL STORES [D]
-2.0G MAXIMUM WITH FLAPS UP [B]
-2.6G MAXIMUM WITH NO EXTERNAL STORES [D]

WARNING

ACCELERATION LIMITS VARY WITH FUEL LOADING AND EXTERNAL STORES CONFIGURATION. REFER TO FIGURES 5-8 THROUGH 5-13 FOR COMPLETE LIMITS

HYDRAULIC SYSTEMS PRESSURE

NOTE

GAGE MARKINGS ARE THE SAME FOR ALL MODELS AND FOR BOTH SYSTEMS.

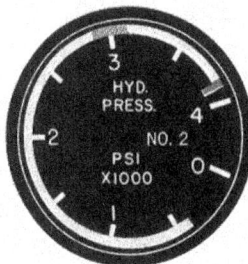

	NO. 1 SYSTEM	NO. 2 SYSTEM
400-2800 PSI	PERMISSIBLE WITH HIGH FLOW DEMANDS ON SYSTEM	
		400-2300 PSI FLIGHT CONTROLS HAVE PRIORITY OVER UTILITY SYSTEM
	SHOWS MALFUNCTION WITH NO FLOW DEMANDS ON SYSTEM	
2800-3100 PSI	NORMAL	
3100-3850 PSI	PERMISSIBLE SURGE DURING RAPID CONTROL SURFACE MOVEMENT	
	SHOWS MALFUNCTION WITH CONTROL SURFACE STATIC	
3850 PSI	MAXIMUM	

F52-0-5-70(1)

Figure 5-1 (Sheet 1 of 2)

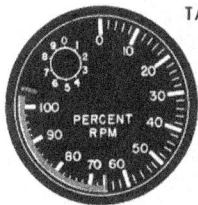

TACHOMETER 3B 7A

66% IDLE
66-101% NORMAL OPERATING RANGE (WITHOUT T_2 RESET)
103.5±1% WITH T_2 RESET
93.5 MINIMUM WITH T_2 CUTBACK
107% MAXIMUM PERMISSIBLE OVERSPEED
105-107%-5 SECOND MAXIMUM

TACHOMETER 19

66% MINIMUM
66%-103.5 NORMAL OPERATING RANGE
103.5 MAXIMUM
MAXIMUM ENGINE SPEED VARIES WITH CIT UP TO 45°C
MAXIMUM ENGINE SPEED AT 45°C AND ABOVE IS 103.5% RPM.
REFER TO FIGURE 5-2

CAUTION

EXCLUDING NORMAL TRANSIENT OVERSPEED PEAKS, ANY OPERATION ABOVE THE MAXIMUM ALLOWABLE SPEED IS CONSIDERED AN OVERSPEED AND MUST BE REPORTED FOR CORRECTIVE ACTION PRIOR TO THE NEXT FLIGHT

OIL PRESSURE 19

12 PSI MINIMUM IDLE
12 PSI TO PLACARD PSI+8 PSI CONTINUOUS OPERATION
PLACARD PSI+8 PSI WITH MAXIMUM ENGINE RPM OF 103.5%

NOTE

THE GAGE MARKINGS SHOWN ARE FOR THE PURPOSE OF ILLUSTRATION ONLY. THIS EXAMPLE SHOWS MARKINGS FOR AN ENGINE/AIRFRAME COMBINATION WITH A PLACARD OIL PRESSURE OF 50 PSI. THIS MEANS THAT THE OIL PRESSURE WILL BE WITHIN LIMITS WITH AN INDICATION OF 45 TO 55 PSI AT 100% RPM OR A MAXIMUM OF 58 PSI WITH AN ENGINE SPEED OF 103.5% RPM. OIL PRESSURE GAGE MARKINGS VARY WITH EACH ENGINE/AIRFRAME INSTALLATION. REFER TO ENGINE OIL PRESSURE SECTION I.

OIL PRESSURE 3B 7A

12 PSI MININUM IDLE
12 PSI TO PLACARD PSI + 5 PSI CONTINUOUS OPERATION
PLACARD PSI ± 5 PSI MAXIMUM RPM
PLACARD PSI + 11-5 PSI PERMISSIBLE RANGE WITH T_2 RESET
PLACARD PSI + 11 PSI MAXIMUM WITH FULL T_2 RESET

NOTE

PLACARD PSI IS THAT INDICATED ON THE OIL PRESSURE RECORD CARD. REFER TO SECTION 1 FOR SPECIFIC OIL PRESSURE RECORD CARD APPLICATION

FUEL FLOW

400 LB/HR MINIMUM 3B 7A 250 LB/HR MINIMUM 19
400-12,000 LB/HR NORMAL OPERATING RANGE 3B 7A
250-12,000 LB/HR NORMAL OPERATING RANGE 19

EXHAUST GAS TEMPERATURE 3B

100°C MINIMUM
100°-585°C NORMAL OPERATING RANGE
585°C MAXIMUM STEADY STATE
585°-1000°C TIME-LIMITED

ACCELERATION OR AFTERBURNER OPERATION:
615°C, 5 MINUTES MAXIMUM
635°C, 6 SECONDS MAXIMUM
735°C, 3 SECONDS MAXIMUM

START:
705°C, 30 SECONDS MAXIMUM
725°C, 20 SECONDS MAXIMUM
750°C, 10 SECONDS MAXIMUM

1000°C MAXIMUM ALLOWABLE OVERTEMPERATURE (REQUIRES TURBINE REPLACEMENT IF EXCEEDED)

EXHAUST GAS TEMPERATURE 7A

50°C MINIMUM
50°-600°C NORMAL OPERATION
600°C MAXIMUM STEADY STATE
600°-1000°C TIME LIMITED

START:
705°C 20 SECOND MAXIMUM
725°C 13 SECOND MAXIMUM
750°C 8 SECOND MAXIMUM
980°C 4 SECOND MAXIMUM

ACCELERATION OR AFTERBURNER OPERATION:
615°C 5 MINUTES MAXIMUM
635°C 40 SECOND MAXIMUM
735°C 3 SECOND MAXIMUM

1000°C MAXIMUM ALLOWABLE OVER TEMPERATURE (REQUIRES TURBINE REPLACEMENT IF EXCEEDED)

EXHAUST GAS TEMPERATURE 19

50°C MINIMUM
50°C TO 688°C NORMAL OPERATING RANGE
688°C MAXIMUM STEADY STATE
688°C TO 1000°C TIME-LIMITED
ACCELERATION OR AFTERBURNER OPERATION:
750°C , 60 SECONDS MAXIMUM

START:
900°C, 80 SECONDS MAXIMUM
975°C, 12 SECONDS MAXIMUM
1000°C 3 SECONDS MAXIMUM

CAUTION

ANY OPERATION IN EXCESS OF THE ABOVE LIMITS REQUIRES THE ENGINE BE RETURNED TO MAINTENANCE FOR CORRECTIVE ACTION. REFER TO FIGURE 5-4

F52-0-5-70(2)

Figure 5-1 (Sheet 2 of 2)

RPM AND EGT SCHEDULE FOR MILITARY AND AFTERBURNER POWER 19

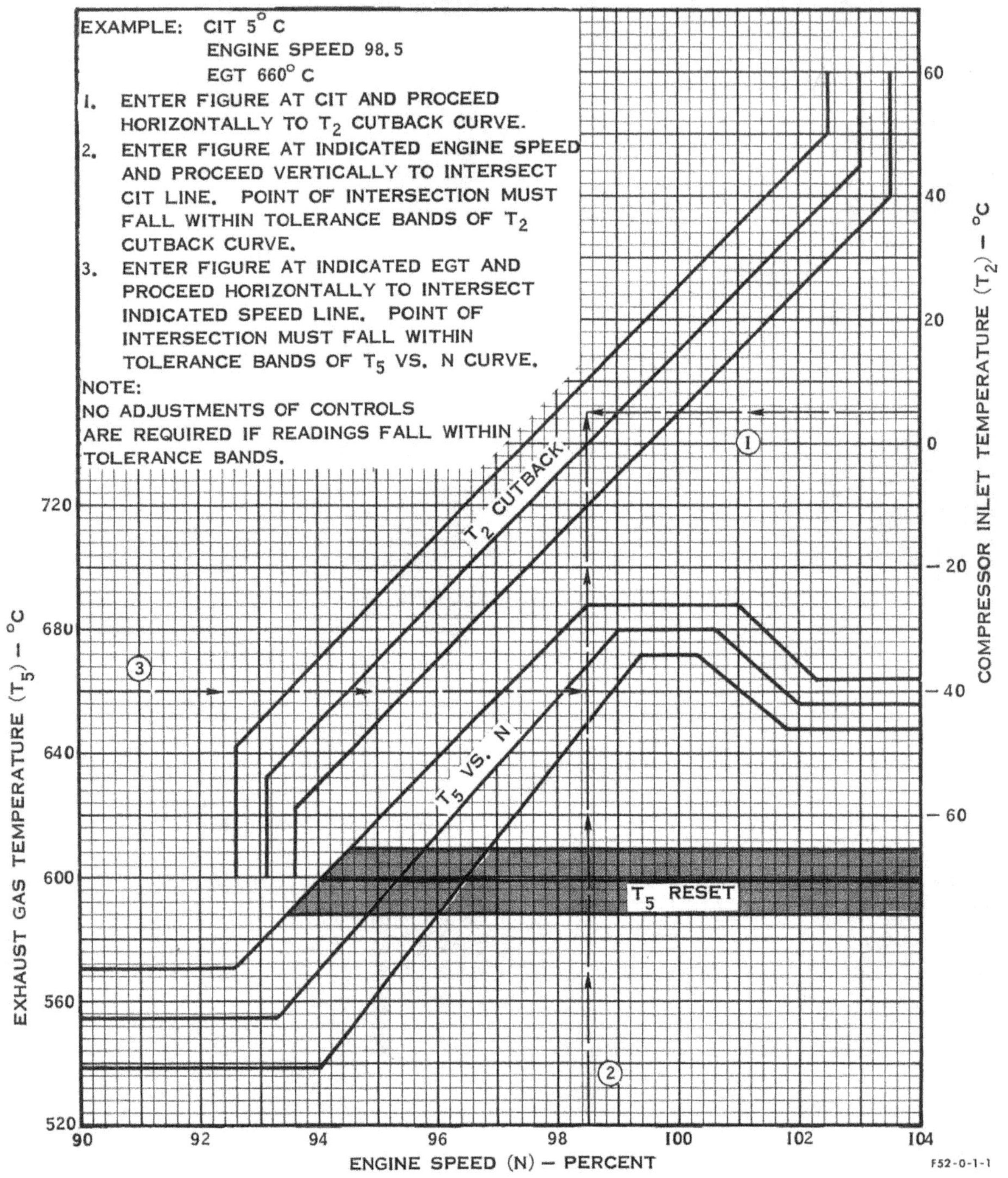
EXAMPLE: CIT 5° C
ENGINE SPEED 98.5
EGT 660° C
1. ENTER FIGURE AT CIT AND PROCEED HORIZONTALLY TO T_2 CUTBACK CURVE.
2. ENTER FIGURE AT INDICATED ENGINE SPEED AND PROCEED VERTICALLY TO INTERSECT CIT LINE. POINT OF INTERSECTION MUST FALL WITHIN TOLERANCE BANDS OF T_2 CUTBACK CURVE.
3. ENTER FIGURE AT INDICATED EGT AND PROCEED HORIZONTALLY TO INTERSECT INDICATED SPEED LINE. POINT OF INTERSECTION MUST FALL WITHIN TOLERANCE BANDS OF T_5 VS. N CURVE.
NOTE:
NO ADJUSTMENTS OF CONTROLS ARE REQUIRED IF READINGS FALL WITHIN TOLERANCE BANDS.
T_2 CUTBACK
T_5 VS. N
T_5 RESET
EXHAUST GAS TEMPERATURE (T_5) — °C
720
680
640
600
560
520
COMPRESSOR INLET TEMPERATURE (T_2) — °C
60
40
20
0
– 20
– 40
– 60
90
92
94
96
98
100
102
104
ENGINE SPEED (N) — PERCENT
F52-0-1-1

Figure 5-2

MAXIMUM AIRSPEED LIMITATIONS

NO EXTERNAL STORES

SEE FIGURES 5-5 THROUGH 5-7 FOR AIRSPEED LIMITS WITH AIRCRAFT IN OTHER CONFIGURATIONS

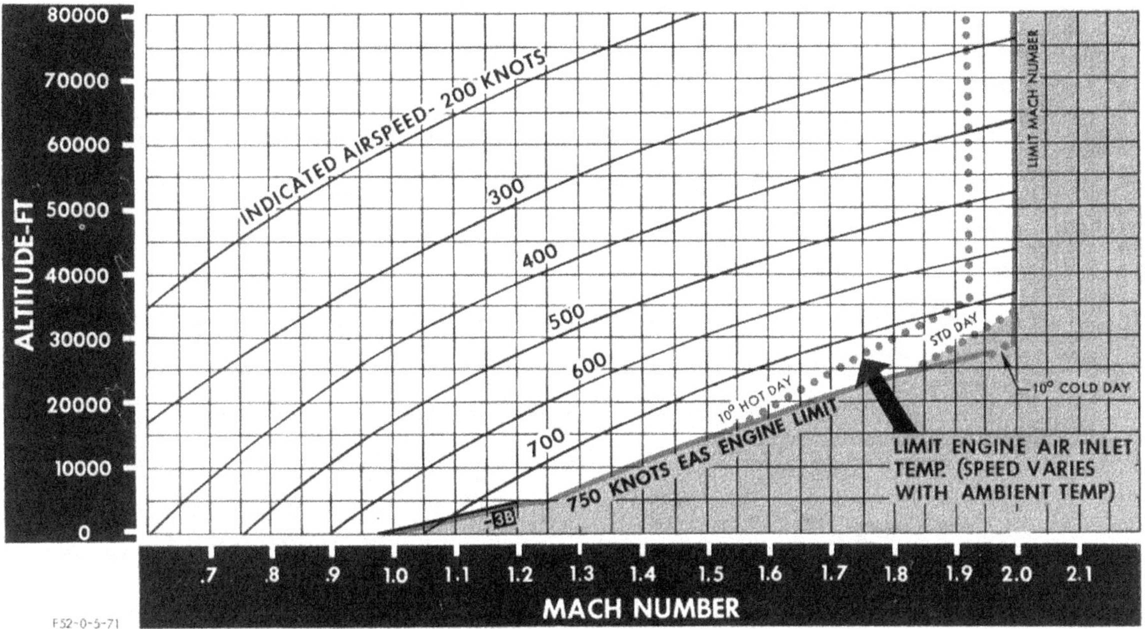

Figure 5-3

Maximum Thrust.

Maximum thrust is obtained with a full afterburning throttle setting and has the same time limits as Military thrust.

COMPRESSOR INLET TEMPERATURE.

The compressor inlet temperature limit is a function of the outside air temperature and flight Mach number. Therefore, the speed at which the limit temperature is reached varies with altitude, and from day to day at a given altitude. Note on figure 5-3 that above approximately 16,000 feet, when the ambient temperature is 10°C higher than standard, CIT is the factor which restricts the maximum permissible speed rather than Mach number or airspeed limits. This may also be indicated by illumination of the SLOW LIGHT.

T_2 RESET LIMITATION. 3B 7A

Reset may occur at CIT as low as 70°C on the cockpit indicator during full afterburner accelerations. After reset occurs, rpm should be between 102.5 and 104.5 percent.

ROLL STABILITY AUGMENTER LIMITATIONS.

The roll stability augmenter should be turned off before reaching 575 knots with wing tip stores installed. With tip stores installed and the roll stability augmenter operating, wing torsional oscillations sufficient to cause structural damage may be experienced at high indicated airspeeds. Missile launchers are not considered tip stores; therefore, the roll stability augmenter should be left on when carrying bare launchers.

STARTING EGT LIMITS 19

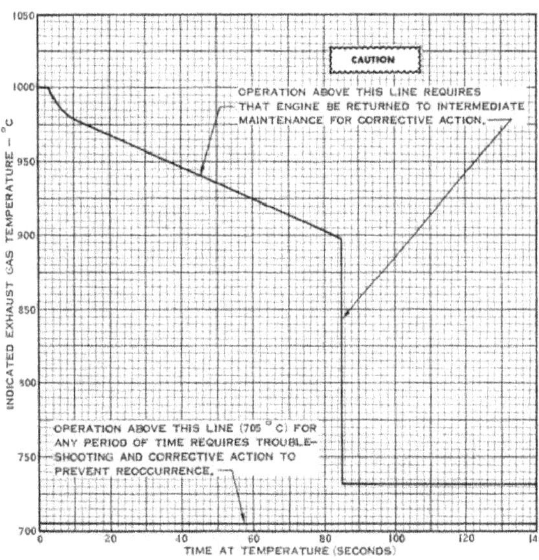

EGT LIMITS 19

(All conditions except starting)

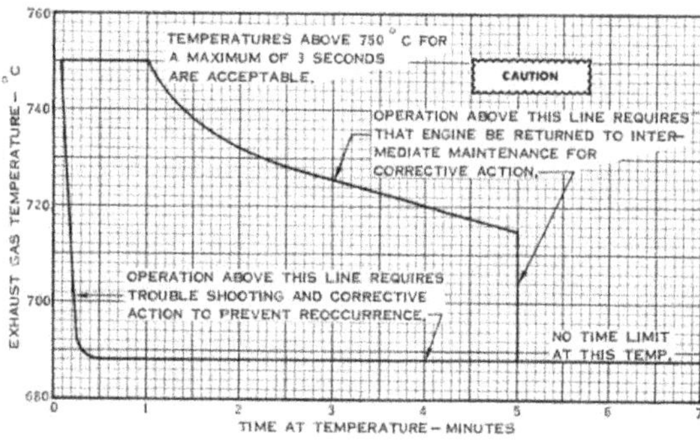

Figure 5-4

AIRSPEED LIMITATIONS.

Landing gear:

Emergency transient operation B D .... 225 knots

B D

Airspeed for landing gear emergency transient operation must be below 225 knots or the nose gear will not lock down.

Landing gear (cont.)

Transient operation .... 260 knots

Down and locked .... 295 knots

Wing flaps:

LAND setting .... 240 knots

TAKEOFF setting .... (See figures 5-8 and 5-9 A B and 5-10 and 5-11 C D)

Pylon racks .... Mach 1.75

Aerial refueling probe C D .... Mach 1.75

Drag chute operation .... 185 knots

Note

The drag chute may be deployed in excess of 185 knots in any emergency.

Winshield rain remover operation .... 295 knots

Full speed brakes .... Mach 1.6

CAUTION

- The aircraft may be taxied with the canopy in the full-open position; however, care must be exercised to avoid fast taxiing over bumpy strips because high vertical loads can damage the canopy mechanism. In strong crosswinds it is possible for the canopy to slam shut.
- Do not unlock the canopy in flight.

RAT EXTENSION LIMITS.

The RAT can be extended in level flight without affecting engine operation within the following airspeed limits:

ALTITUDE (FEET)	AIRSPEED LIMITS (KNOTS)	
	MINIMUM	MAXIMUM
Up to 30,000	None	550
Above 30,000	350	

MAXIMUM ALLOWABLE AIRSPEED.

The maximum allowable airspeed for any external stores configuration is presented in figures 5-8 through 5-13. In addition, the limits for the no-external-stores configuration are presented in figure 5-3.

EXTERNAL STORES JETTISON LIMITS

External Store	*Maximum Allowable Airspeed*
Wing Tip AIM-9B Missile-Launcher Combination	Mach 1.4
Pylon Tanks	Mach 1.5
Wing Pylons	Mach 0.9
Bombs (C)	Refer to figure 5-7
SUU-21 Dispenser (C)	Mach 1.4 But Not Exceeding 500 Knots
Empty or Full MA-2 Rocket Launchers (C)	450 Knots
Empty LAU-3/A Rocket Pods (C)	575 Knots
Full LAU-3/A Rocket Pods (C)	Mach 0.8 But Not Exceeding 400 Knots
Fuselage AIM-9B Missiles (C)	Mach 0.95
Tip Tanks	Mach 0.9 **Note** In an emergency, empty tip tanks may be jettisoned at supersonic speeds. If possible, however, jettison tip tanks at less than Mach 1.5.

Note

- When possible, jettison external stores in 1G flight.
- Any external store may be jettisoned up to Mach 0.8, or 350 knots except wing tip missile launchers.

Figure 5-5

EXTERNAL STORES JETTISON

See figure 5-5 for external stores jettison limits.

BOMB RELEASE LIMITS.

Figures 5-6 presents the maximum allowable airspeed and load factors at which bombs may be released from the airplane.

PROHIBITED MANEUVERS.

PITCHUP AND SPINS.

Intentional pitchup and spins are prohibited because of the high loads imposed on the aircraft. These loads can be of sufficient magnitude to cause structural damage to the aircraft.

CAUTION

Exercise extreme care to avoid abrupt maneuvers or low indicated airspeeds when the APC warning light is on or there are other indications that the APC system is inoperative.

FORMATION TAKEOFF.

Formation takeoffs involving any aircraft in an asymmetrical load configuration is prohibited.

RESTRICTED MANEUVERS.

INVERTED FLIGHT.

Prolonged inverted flight or any maneuvers resulting in prolonged negative load factor will result in engine flameout as a result of fuel starvation. Do not fly inverted for longer than 20 seconds.

AILERON ROLL LIMITATIONS.

In order to avoid coupling and high structural loads approaching limit values, aileron rolls are subject to the following restrictions.

WING FLAPS RETRACTED.

Entry Load Factor of 0.5G and Above.

Full-deflection rolls are limited to 360 degrees. Below 1G with pitch or yaw stability augmenters inoperative, full-deflection, 360 degree rolls are prohibited.

BOMB RELEASE LIMITS ⊖

Configuration		Maximum Allowable Speed: Airspeed Knots	Maximum Allowable Speed: Mach Number	Maximum Allowable Load Factor At Release
Fuselage Mounted Bombs	Without tip stores	750 EAS	Below 1.7	4G
			1.7 to 1.9	2G
	More than 4000 lb internal fuel or fuel in tip tanks	575 IAS	1.7	3G
	4000 lb or less fuel and empty tip tanks			4G
Pylon Mounted M117A Bombs	With or without Tip tanks	450 IAS Takeoff Flaps Extended	0.80	4G
SUU-21A Dispenser	Without tip tanks	650 IAS	1.5	4G
	Tip tanks	575 IAS	1.5	4G
M116-A2 Bomb BLU-1/B, BLU-27/B (finned or unfinned)	With or without Tip tanks	450 IAS	1.0	1G

Figure 5-6

ENTRY LOAD FACTOR BELOW 0.5 G.

Full-deflection rolls are limited to 180 degrees and must have either the pitch or the yaw stability augmenter operative. Recovery must be initiated at approximately 90 degrees. With pitch and yaw stability augmenters inoperative, aileron rolls are prohibited.

ENTRY LOAD FACTOR BELOW ZERO G.

All rolls below zero G entry load factor must be executed with extreme caution and should be avoided whenever possible.

Note

Application of some back stick pressure in rolls entered at or below 1 G helps to more rapidly terminate the roll maneuver and make a smoother transition to normal flight.

TAKEOFF (MANEUVERING) FLAPS EXTENDED.

1. Rolls are limited to 360 degrees. High roll rates can develop from moderate aileron application.

2. Either the pitch or yaw stability augmenter must be operative for all rolling maneuvers.

3. Aileron rolls are prohibited for entry load factors less than 1G.

Note

Regardless of flap position, application of some back stick pressure during rolls helps to terminate the roll more rapidly and make a smoother transition to normal flight.

OPERATING FLIGHT LIMITS A C

FOR SYMMETRICAL FLIGHT END SMOOTH AIR GEAR AND FLAPS UP
NO EXTERNAL LOAD AND LESS THAN 1000 LBS FUEL REMAINING

REFER TO FIGURES 5-8 THROUGH 5-13 FOR ACCELERATION LIMITS AT OTHER LOADINGS

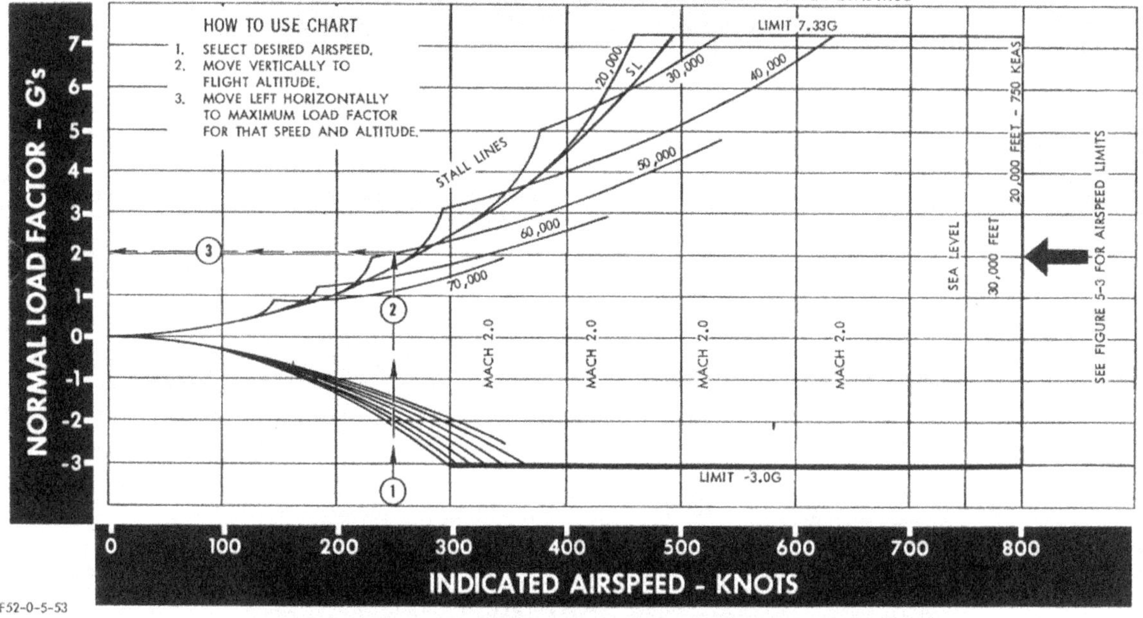

OPERATING FLIGHT LIMITS B D

FOR SYMMETRICAL FLIGHT IN SMOOTH AIR
NO EXTERNAL LOAD GEAR AND FLAPS UP

B FULL INTERNAL FUEL D 4000 POUNDS FUEL

SEE FIGURES 5-8 THROUGH 5-13 FOR ACCELERATION LIMITS AT OTHER LOADINGS

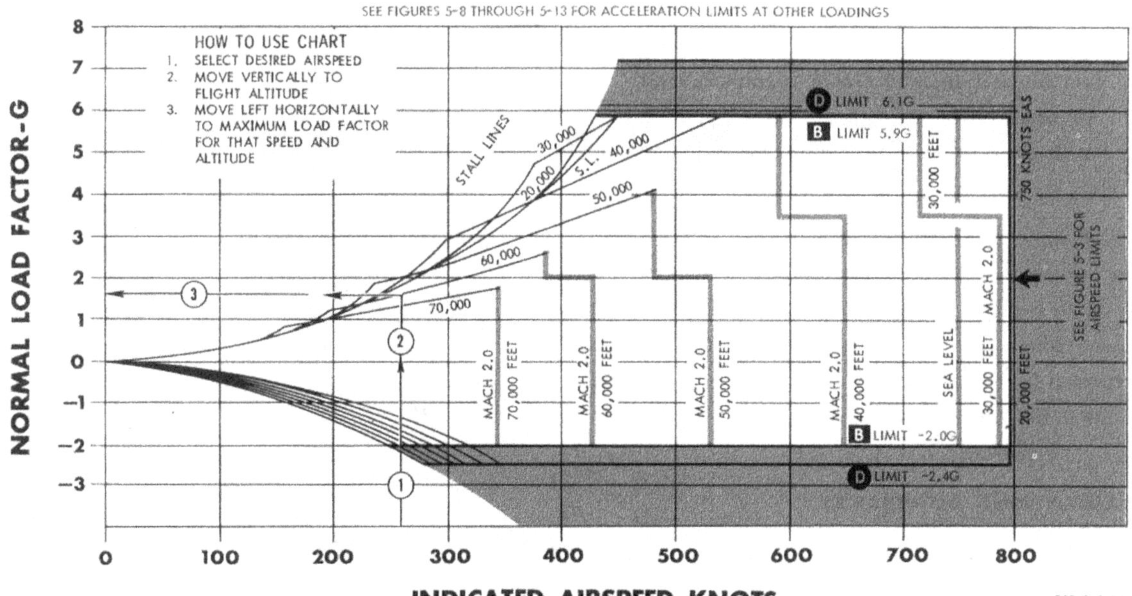

INDICATED AIRSPEED-KNOTS

F52-0-5-54

Figure 5-7

ACCELERATION LIMITATIONS.

One of the primary factors determining the acceleration limitations on an aircraft is the center-of-gravity position. As external fuel tanks are located close to the aircraft center of gravity, there is minor movement of the center of gravity as fuel is used. However, all of the internal fuel is located in the fuselage, which results in a significant movement of the center-of-gravity position from forward to aft as fuel is used. This movement of the CG with internal fuel expenditure results in a fairly wide variation of permissible load factor. This information is too complex to permit instrument markings which would cover all operating conditions; therefore, a tabular listing of the limits for the various airplane loadings is included in figures 5-8 through 5-13.

WARNING B D

Two Place aircraft are restricted to 2G above Mach 1.6 with yaw stability augmenter off or inoperative.

CAUTION

The instrument markings of figure 5-1 are for maximum load factor that can be utilized without external stores; therefore, cognizance must be taken of the chart limits when operating with external stores or higher fuel loadings.

The G-limits shown in the upper portion of the tables are for symmetrical maneuvering such as straight pullups or steady turns. In rolling pullouts or rolling pushovers, lower G-limits must be observed because of the higher structural loads imposed on the aircraft. These limits are noted in the lower portion of the charts.

MANEUVERING BOUNDARIES.

Operating flight limits are shown in figure 5-7. These diagrams show the maximum maneuvering load factors over the operating range of speeds and altitudes. They include the load factor and airspeed combination at which stalls (Refer to Stalls in Section VI) occur as well as the maximum allowable structural G-limits for a clean configuration. Also, it will be noted that the upper right corner of the envelopes for B D aircraft are limited for altitudes of 30,000 feet and above. These additional limits are to prevent flight into areas where the vertical tail structure may be overloaded. Use of the diagrams is illustrated. Since the maximum allowable airspeed depends on different limiting factors in various altitude ranges, the diagram for any particular altitude is cut off at the airspeed at which the applicable limit is encountered. For example, this is indicated at the higher altitudes shown on the figures by the vertical lines labeled Mach 2.0. The diagrams do not include the engine air inlet temperature airspeed limitation; therefore, reference should be made to the airspeed limitations of figure 5-3. A study of figure 5-3 will also permit the determination of the corresponding Mach number for any airspeed and altitude combination if the maximum load factor for a particular Mach is desired.

CENTER OF GRAVITY LIMITATIONS.

With any combination of standard external load items such as AIM-9B missiles, pylon tanks or tip tanks, the center of gravity remains within the accepted range.

CAUTION

Wing tip stores approved for use on this aircraft meet certain requirements as to balance and aerodynamic stability. Pilots should make certain that standard wing tip stores are used or that replacement components conform to the standard aerodynamic configuration and center of gravity.

WEIGHT LIMITATIONS.

There are no weight limitations for takeoff or landing as long as standard external load items are used.

MAXIMUM ALLOWABLE AIRSPEED AND ACCELERATION LIMITS A

SYMMETRICAL MANEUVERS*

AIRPLANE CONFIGURATION		AIRSPEED LIMITS Observe EAS, IAS, Mach Number, Engine Air Inlet Temperature Limit or Slow light, whichever occurs first.	ACCELERATION LIMITS (G) More than 4000 lb internal fuel or fuel in external fuel tanks	ACCELERATION LIMITS (G) 4000 lb or less fuel remaining and empty external fuel tanks
No External Stores		• Above 5000 feet** 750 knots EAS, Mach 2.0. • Below 5000 feet, 650 knots at sea level varying linearly to 750 knots at 5000 feet.	4.4	5.6†
AIM-9B Missiles			4.4	5.6
Missile Launchers			4.4	5.6†
Tip Tanks		• Above 25,000 feet** 750 knots, Mach 1.9. • Below 25,000 feet, 575 knots.	4.0	5.0
Pylon Tanks and AIM-9B Missiles		575 knots or Mach 1.5.	4.0	5.0
Pylon Tanks and Missile Launchers				
Pylon Tanks				
Pylon Tanks and Tip Tanks		• 575 knots or Mach 1.5. • Do not exceed 500 knots with empty tip tanks and more than residual fuel in pylon tanks.	3.8	5.0
TAKE OFF Flaps	During Extension	450 knots or indicated Mach 0.80. There is no Mach limitation if 330 knots is not exceeded.	See applicable external configuration above	
	Extended or During Retraction	450 knots or indicated Mach 0.80. There is no Mach limitation if 330 knots is not exceeded.		

THE MINIMUM SYMMETRICAL G LIMITS ARE:

(a) −2.5 G with flaps UP.†
(b) −1.0 G with TAKE OFF flaps.
(c) 0.0 G with LAND flaps.

ROLLING PULLOUTS

AIM-9B MISSILES OR NO EXTERNAL STORES	Flaps UP	Below Mach 1.9	3.3	4.0
		Mach 1.9 to 2.0	3.0	3.5
	TAKE OFF Flaps	Same as symmetrical limits	3.0	3.4
Any external tank configuration	Flaps UP	Same as symmetrical limits	2.6	3.3
	TAKE OFF Flaps	Same as symmetrical limits		

ROLLING PUSHOVERS

See aileron roll limitations.

*Refer to text for definition.

**Aircraft not modified with steel tail are limited to:

(a) Above 20,000 feet, 700 knots or Mach 2.0.
(b) Below 20,000 feet, 575 knots.

† For no external stores or missile launchers and 2000 lb or less internal fuel, the symmetrical limits are 7.33 G and −3.0 G.

Figure 5-8

MAXIMUM ALLOWABLE AIRSPEED AND ACCELERATION LIMITS B

SYMMETRICAL MANEUVERS*

CONFIGURATION		AIRSPEED LIMITS Observe EAS, IAS, Mach Number, Engine Air Inlet Temperature Limit, or Slow Light, whichever occurs first.	ACCELERATION LIMITS (G)		
			MACH	UP TO 40,000 FT.	ABOVE 40,000 FT.
Missile Launchers or No External Stores		● Above 5000 feet, 750 knots EAS, Mach 2.0. ● Below 5000 feet, 650 knots at sea level varying linearly to 750 knots at 5000 feet.	Below 1.8	5.9	5.9
			1.8 to 2.0	3.5	2.0
AIM-9B Missiles			Below 1.8	5.2	5.2
			1.8 to 2.0	3.5	2.0
Tip Tanks		● Above 25,000 feet, 750 knots, Mach 1.8. ● Below 25,000 feet, 575 knots.	Below 1.6	4.9	4.9
			1.6 to 1.8	3.0	2.0
All pylon Tank Configurations		● 575 knots or Mach 1.5. ● Do not exceed 500 knots with empty Tip Tanks and more than residual fuel in Pylon Tanks.	–	4.5	4.5
TAKE OFF Flaps	During Extension	450 knots or indicated Mach 0.80. There is no Mach limitation if 330 knots is not exceeded.	See applicable external stores configuration above.		
	Extended or During Retraction	450 knots or indicated Mach 0.80. There is no Mach limitation if 330 knots is not exceeded.			

THE MINIMUM SYMMETRICAL G LIMITS ARE:

(a) −2.0 with flaps UP.
(b) −1.0 G with TAKE OFF flaps.
(c) 0.0 G with LAND flaps.

ROLLING PULLOUTS

CONFIGURATION	AIRSPEED LIMITS	ACCELERATION LIMITS		
		MACH	FLAPS UP	TAKE OFF FLAPS
AIM-9B Missiles or No External Stores	Same as for symmetrical maneuvers.	Below 1.6	3.5	3.3
		1.6 to 2.0	2.0	–
Tip Tanks		Below 1.6	3.3	2.7
		1.6 to 1.8	2.0	–
All Pylon Tank Configurations		–	3.0	2.5

ROLLING PUSHOVERS

See aileron roll limitations.

*Refer to text for definition.

Figure 5-9

MAXIMUM ALLOWABLE ACCELERATION AND AIRSPEED LIMITS Ⓒ INTERCEPTOR CONFIGURATIONS

SYMMETRICAL MANEUVERS

AIRPLANE CONFIGURATION			ACCELERATION LIMITS (G)		
External Stores Location			More Than 4000 Lb Internal Fuel and/or Fuel in External Tanks, When Installed	4000 Lb or Less Internal Fuel and Empty External Tanks, When Installed	AIRSPEED LIMITS OBSERVE EAS, IAS, MACH NUMBER, ENGINE AIR INLET TEMPERATURE LIMIT, OR SLOW LIGHT, WHICHEVER OCCURS FIRST.
WING TIP	PYLON	FUSELAGE			
NONE	NONE	NONE	5.0 —2.0	6.0* —2.4	750 KNOTS EAS, MACH 2.0, OR ENGINE AIR INLET TEMPERATURE.
MISSILE LAUNCHERS			4.9 —1.9	6.0 —2.4	
AIM-9B MISSILES			4.6 —1.8	5.3 —2.1	
NONE	NONE	AIM-9B MISSILES** OR LAUNCHERS	DO NOT EXCEED +2.0G ABOVE MACH 1.7 4.7 —1.9	5.6 —2.2	750 KNOTS EAS OR MACH 1.9.
MISSILE LAUNCHERS			DO NOT EXCEED +2.0G ABOVE MACH 1.7 4.7 —2.0	5.5 —2.2	
AIM-9B MISSILES			DO NOT EXCEED +2.0G ABOVE MACH 1.7 4.4 —1.7	5.1 —2.0	
TANKS	NONE	NONE	4.3 —1.7	5.0 —2.0	ABOVE 25,000 FEET — 750 KNOTS OR MACH 1.9. BELOW 25,000 FEET — 575 KNOTS.
TANKS	NONE	AIM-9B MISSILES** OR LAUNCHERS	4.1 —1.6	4.8 —1.9	ABOVE 25,000 FEET — 750 KNOTS MACH 1.7. BELOW 25,000 FEET — 575 KNOTS.
WITH OR WITHOUT MISSILE LAUNCHERS	TANKS	NONE	4.6 —1.8	5.0 —2.0	750 KNOTS EAS OR MACH 1.5.
NONE		AIM-9B MISSILES** OR LAUNCHERS	4.3 —1.7	5.0 —2.0	
MISSILE LAUNCHERS		AIM-9B MISSILES** OR LAUNCHERS	4.3 —1.7	5.0 —2.0	
AIM-9B MISSILES		NONE	4.0 —1.6	5.0 —2.0	
AIM-9B MISSILES		AIM-9B MISSILES** OR LAUNCHERS	3.8 —1.5	5.0 —2.0	
TANKS	TANKS	NONE	4.2 —1.7	5.0 —2.0	575 KNOTS OR MACH 1.5.
		AIM-9B MISSILES** OR LAUNCHERS	3.9 —1.5	4.8 —1.9	
TAKEOFF FLAPS	DURING FLAP EXTENSION		FOR POSITIVE ACCELERATION LIMITS SEE APPLICABLE EXTERNAL STORE CONFIGURATION ABOVE. THE MINIMUM NEGATIVE-G LIMIT IS —1.0G		450 KNOTS OR MACH 0.80. THERE IS NO MACH LIMIT IF 330 KNOTS IS NOT EXCEEDED.
	FLAPS EXTENDED OR RETACTING				450 KNOTS OR MACH 0.80. THERE IS NO MACH LIMIT IF 350 KNOTS IS NOT EXCEEDED.
LAND FLAPS	THE MINIMUM SYMMETRICAL LIMIT WITH LAND FLAPS IS 0.0G				

UNSYMMETRICAL (ROLLING) MANEUVERS

WING TIP	PYLON	FUSELAGE	More Than 4000 Lb	4000 Lb or Less	AIRSPEED LIMITS
NONE	NONE	NONE	3.2	3.5	MACH 1.9 TO 2.0
			⅓ SYMMETRICAL LIMITS		BELOW MACH 1.9
ANY EXTERNAL STORES CONFIGURATION			⅔ SYMMETRICAL LIMITS		SAME AS SYMMETRICAL MANEUVERS
TAKEOFF FLAPS WITH ANY EXTERNAL STORES CONFIGURATION			½ SYMMETRICAL LIMITS		

FOR ROLLING PUSHOVERS SEE AILERON ROLL LIMITATIONS

NOTES

*1. For no external stores and 1000 lb or less internal fuel, the symmetrical acceleration limits are 7.33G and —3G.

**2. Estimated limits not verified by Contractor's Flight Tests.

3. Do not exceed 500 knots with empty tip tanks and more than residual fuel in pylon tanks.

Figure 5-10

MAXIMUM ALLOWABLE ACCELERATION AND AIRSPEED LIMITS, FIGHTER-BOMBER CONFIGURATIONS ©

SYMMETRICAL MANEUVERS

AIRPLANE CONFIGURATION			ACCELERATION LIMITS (G)		AIRSPEED LIMITS
External Stores Location			More Than 4000 Lb Internal Fuel and/or Fuel in External Tanks When Installed	4000 Lb or Less Internal Fuel and Empty External Tanks When Installed	OBSERVE EAS, IAS, MACH NUMBER, ENGINE AIR INLET TEMPERATURE LIMIT OR SLOW LIGHT, WHICHEVER OCCURS FIRST.
WING TIP	PYLON	FUSELAGE			
NONE	NONE	NONE	5.0 −2.0	6.0* −2.4	750 KNOTS EAS OR MACH 2.0.
NONE	NONE	MD-6, OR BDU/8B	DO NOT EXCEED +2.0G ABOVE MACH 1.7 4.2 −1.7	5.0 −2.0	750 KNOTS EAS OR MACH 1.9.
NONE	TANKS	NONE	4.6 −1.8	5.0 −2.0	750 KNOTS EAS OR MACH 1.5.
	TANKS	MD-6, OR BDU/8B	3.9 −1.5	4.8 −2.0	
TANKS	NONE	NONE	4.3 −1.7	5.0 −2.0	ABOVE 25,000 FEET — 750 KNOTS OR MACH 1.9. BELOW 25,000 FEET — 575 KNOTS.
TANKS	NONE	MD-6, OR BDU/8B	3.7 −1.5	4.5 −1.8	ABOVE 25,000 FEET — MACH 1.7. BELOW 25,000 FEET — 575 KNOTS.
NONE	NONE	SUU-21	4.7 −1.9	5.6 −2.2	650 KNOTS OR MACH 1.5.
	TANKS	SUU-21	4.3 −1.7	5.0 −2.0	
NONE	BLU-1/B, BLU-27/B FINNED OR UNFINNED	NONE	4.0 −1.9	4.0 −2.0	600 KNOTS OR MACH 1.5
		MD-6, SUU-21, OR BDU/8B	4.0 −1.7	4.0 −2.0	
TANKS	BLU-1/B, BLU-27/B FINNED OR UNFINNED	NONE	4.0 −1.6	4.0 −1.8	575 KNOTS OR MACH 1.5.
		MD-6, SUU-21, OR BDU/8B	3.6 −1.4	4.0 −1.7	
TANKS	TANKS	NONE	4.2 −1.7	5.0 −2.0	
		MD-6, OR BDU/8B	3.6 −1.4	4.5 −1.8	
NONE	LAU-3/A ROCKET PODS	WITH OR WITHOUT MD-6, SUU-21 OR BDU/8B	4.0 −1.6	4.0 −1.6	
TANKS	LAU-3/A ROCKET PODS	WITH OR WITHOUT SUU-21	3.8 −1.5	4.0 −1.6	
	LAU-3/A ROCKET PODS	MD-6, OR BDU/8B	3.6 −1.4	4.0 −1.6	
	TANKS	SUU-21	3.8 −1.5	4.8 −1.9	
	NONE	SUU-21	4.1 −1.6	4.8 −1.9	
NONE	MA-2 ROCKET LAUNCHERS**	NONE	4.8 −1.9	6.0* −2.4	575 KNOTS OR MACH 1.2.
		MD-6, SUU-21, OR BDU/8B	4.2 −1.7	5.0 −2.0	
TANKS	MA-2 ROCKET LAUNCHERS**	WITH OR WITHOUT SUU-21	3.9 −1.5	4.3 −1.7	
		MD-6, OR BDU/8B	3.6 −1.4	4.0 −1.6	

Figure 5-11 (Sheet 1 of 2)

NONE	M117A BOMB**	NONE	4.8	—1.9	6.0*	—2.4	575 KNOTS OR MACH 1.0.
		MD-6, SUU-21, OR BDU/88	4.2	—1.7	5.0	—2.0	
TANKS	M117A BOMB**	NONE	4.1	—1.6	4.7	—1.8	
		MD-6, SUU-21, OR BDU/88	3.6	—1.4	4.2	—1.7	
NONE	M116-A2 NAPALM	NONE	4.0	—1.9	4.0	—2.0	500 KNOTS OR MACH 1.0.
		MD-6, SUU-21, OR BDU/88	4.0	—1.7	4.0	—2.0	
TANKS	M116-A2 NAPALM	NONE	4.0	—1.6	4.0	—1.8	
		MD-6, SUU-21, OR BDU/88	3.6	—1.4	4.0	—1.7	
TAKEOFF	DURING FLAP EXTENSION		FOR POSITIVE ACCELERATION LIMITS, SEE APPLICABLE EXTERNAL STORE CONFIGURATION ABOVE.				450 KNOTS OR INDICATED MACH 0.80. NO MACH LIMITATION IF 330 KNOTS IS NOT EXCEEDED.
FLAPS	FLAPS EXTENDED OR RETRACTING		THE MINIMUM NEGATIVE-G LIMIT IS —1.0G.				450 KNOTS OR INDICATED MACH 0.80. NO MACH LIMITATION IF 350 KNOTS IS NOT EXCEEDED.
LAND FLAPS	THE MINIMUM SYMMETRICAL LIMIT WITH LAND FLAPS IS 0.0G						

UNSYMMETRICAL (ROLLING) MANEUVERS

NONE	NONE	NONE	3.4	3.7	MACH 1.9 TO 2.0
			⅔ OF SYMMETRICAL LIMITS		BELOW MACH 1.9
WITH OR WITHOUT TANKS	ANY SYMMETRICAL LOADING	WITH OR WITHOUT CENTERLINE STORES	⅔ OF SYMMETRICAL LIMITS		SAME AS SYMMETRICAL MANEUVERS
	1 LAU-3/A ROCKET POD MA-2 ROCKET LAUNCHER** M116-A2 NAPALM M117A** OR LAU-10/A ROCKET POD BOMB BLU-1/B**, BLU-27/B** (finned or unfinned)	WITH OR WITHOUT CENTERLINE STORES	2.5	2.7	
			2.5	2.7	
TAKEOFF FLAPS WITH ANY EXTERNAL STORE CONFIGURATION			½ OF SYMMTERICAL LIMITS		

FOR ROLLING PUSHOVERS SEE AILERON ROLL LIMITATIONS

NOTES

*1. For no external stores and 1000 lb or less internal fuel, the symmetrical acceleration limits are 7.33G and —3.0G.

**2. Estimated limits not verified by Contractor's Flight Tests.

3. Do not exceed 500 knots with empty tip tanks and more than residual fuel in pylon tanks.

4. Symmetrical G limits for pylon-mounted armament are applicable for one or two pylon stores.

Figure 5-11 (Sheet 2 of 2)

MAXIMUM ALLOWABLE ACCELERATION AND AIRSPEED LIMITS Ⓓ

AIRPLANE CONFIGURATION		ACCELERATION LIMITS (G)			AIRSPEED LIMITS
External Store Location		MACH	UP TO 40,000 FEET	ABOVE 40,000 FEET	OBSERVE EAS, IAS, MACH NUMBER, ENGINE AIR INLET TEMPERATURE LIMIT OR SLOW LIGHT, WHICHEVER OCCURS FIRST.
WING TIP	PYLON				
SYMMETRICAL MANEUVERS					
WITH OR WITHOUT AIM-9B LAUNCHERS	NONE	BELOW 1.8	6.1* —2.4	6.1* —2.4	ABOVE 5000 FEET — 750 KNOTS EAS, OR MACH 2.0.
		1.8 TO 2.0	3.5 —2.4	2.0 —2.4	
AIM-9B MISSILES	NONE	BELOW 1.8	5.2 —2.1	5.2 —2.1	
		1.8 TO 2.0	3.5 —2.1	2.0 —2.1	
TANKS	NONE	BELOW 1.6	4.9 —1.9	4.9 —1.9	ABOVE 25,000 FEET — 750 KNOTS OR MACH 1.8. BELOW 25,000 FEET — 575 KNOTS.
		1.6 TO 1.8	2.5* —1.9	2.0 —1.9	
WITH OR WITHOUT AIM-9B LAUNCHERS	TANKS	TO 1.5	5.0 —2.0	5.0 —2.0	750 KNOTS, EAS OR MACH 1.5.
AIM-9B MISSILES			4.4 —1.7	4.4 —1.7	
TANKS	TANKS	TO 1.5	4.9 —1.9	4.9 —1.9	575 KNOTS OR MACH 1.5.
WITH OR WITHOUT TANKS	LAU-3/A ROCKET PODS		4.0 —1.6	4.0 —1.6	
NONE	MA-2 ROCKET** LAUNCHERS	TO 1.2	5.7 —2.3	5.1 —2.3	575 KNOTS OR MACH 1.2.
TANKS			4.3 —1.7	4.3 —1.7	
NONE	M-117 BOMBS**	TO 1.0	5.9 —2.3	5.9 —2.3	575 KNOTS OR MACH 1.0.
TANKS			4.4 —1.7	4.4 —1.7	
NONE	M116-A2 NAPALM*** BOMBS	TO 1.0	4.0 —2.0	4.0 —2.0	500 KNOTS OR MACH 1.0.
TANKS			4.0 —1.7	4.0 —1.7	
TAKEOFF FLAPS	DURING FLAP EXTENSION		FOR POSITIVE ACCELERATION LIMITS SEE APPLICABLE EXTERNAL STORES CONFIGURATION ABOVE. THE MINIMUM NEGATIVE G LIMIT IS —1.0G.		450 KNOTS OR INDICATED MACH 0.80. THERE IS NO MACH LIMITATION IF 330 KNOTS IS NOT EXCEEDED.
	FLAPS EXTENDED OR RETRACTING				450 KNOTS OR INDICATED MACH 0.80. THERE IS NO MACH LIMITATION IF 350 KNOTS IS NOT EXCEEDED.
LAND FLAPS	THE MINIMUM SYMMETRICAL LIMIT WITH LAND FLAPS IS 0.0G				
UNSYMMETRICAL (ROLLING) MANEUVERS					
WITH OR WITHOUT LAUNCHERS	NONE	BELOW 1.6	3.9		SAME AS SYMMETRICAL MANEUVERS
		1.6 TO 2.0	2.0		
AIM-9B MISSILES	NONE	BELOW 1.6	3.5		
		1.6 TO 2.0	2.0		
TANKS	NONE	BELOW 1.6	3.3		
		1.6 TO 1.8	2.0		
WITH OR WITHOUT LAUNCHERS OR AIM-9/B MISSILES	TANKS	TO 1.5	⅔ OF SYMMETRICAL LIMITS		
TANKS	ANY SYMMETRICAL LOADING	———	⅔ OF SYMMETRICAL LIMITS		
ANY OR NONE	1 LAU-3/A ROCKET POD OR M116-A2 NAPALM***	———	2.5		
ANY OR NONE	1 MA-2** ROCKET LAUNCHER	———	3.0		
NONE	M-117 BOMB** MK-83 BOMB OR LAU-10/A ROCKET POD	———	3.0		
TANKS		———	2.9		
TAKEOFF FLAPS WITH ANY EXTERNAL STORE CONFIGURATION		———	⅓ OF SYMMETRICAL LIMITS		

FOR ROLLING PUSHOVERS SEE AILERON ROLL LIMITATIONS

NOTES

*1. For airplanes without gun bay fuel provisions (AF serial numbers prior to 57-1320) increase load factor 0.5G.
**2. Estimated limits not verified by Contractor's Flight Tests.
3. Do not exceed 500 knots with empty tip tanks and more than residual fuel in pylon tanks.
4. Symmetrical G limits for pylon-mounted armament are applicable for one or two pylon stores.
***5. BLU-1/B, BLU-27/B (finned or unfinned) BLU-32/B Aircraft limits the same when carried.

MAXIMUM ALLOWABLE ACCELERATION & AIRSPEED LIMITS A/A 37U-15 TOW TARGET SYSTEM INSTALLED ON LEFT WING PYLON

Configuration	Symmetrical Maneuver Acceleration Limits G		Airspeed Limits	
			Knots	Mach
Stowed Target	1.5	−.5	325	1.1
During Target Launch (Take-off Flaps must be extended)	1.0		230	—
Towing Target	2.0	−1.0	400	1.1
Target Drop (Take-off Flaps must be extended)	1.0		250	—
Target Reel Pod only	3.0	−1.2	450	1.3

1. Estimated limits not verified by Contractor's Flight tests.
2. Limits apply with or without tip tanks.
3. Unsymmetrical (rolling) maneuvers using abrupt full aileron travel are prohibited.

Figure 5-13

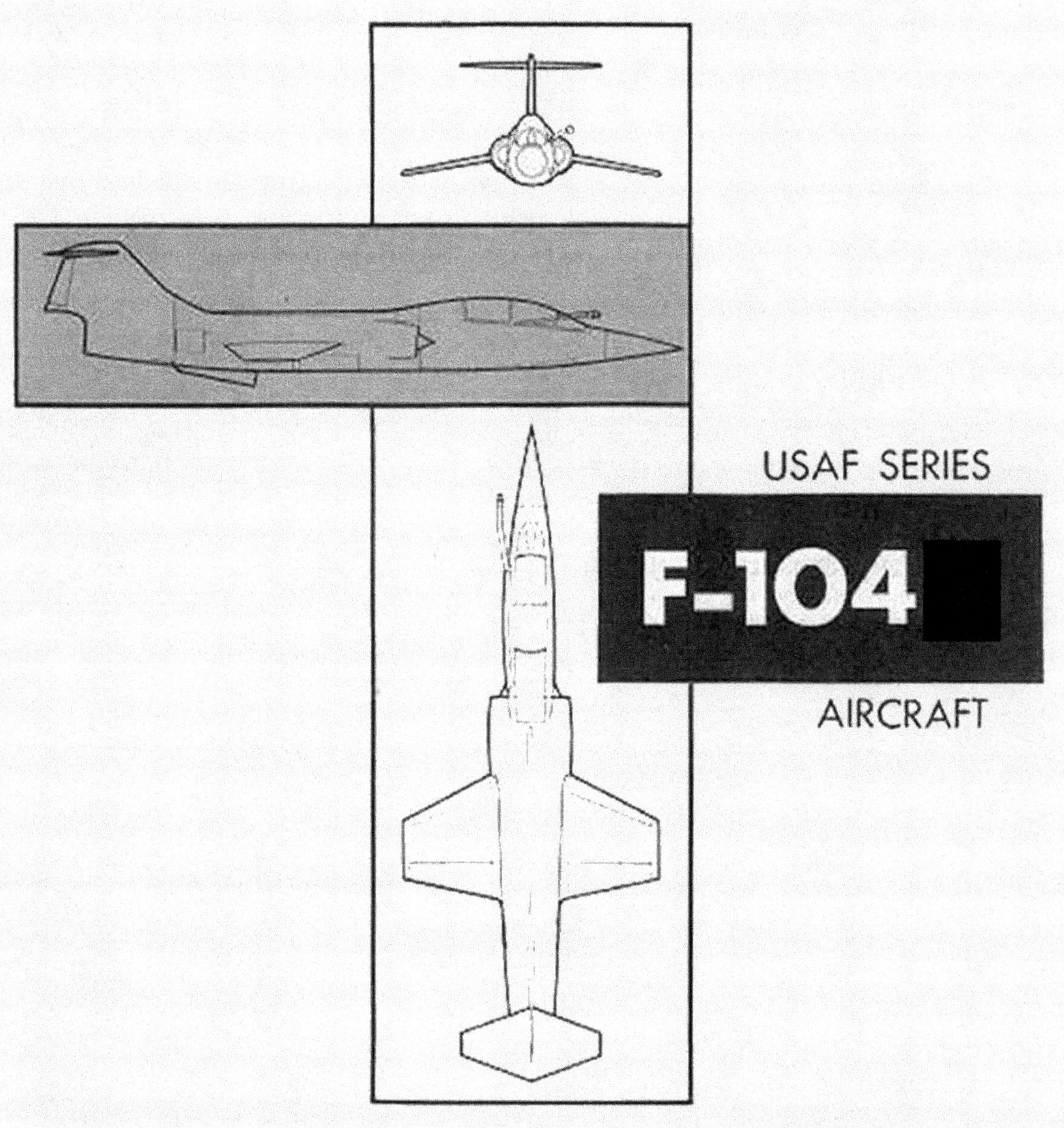

This page intentionally left blank.

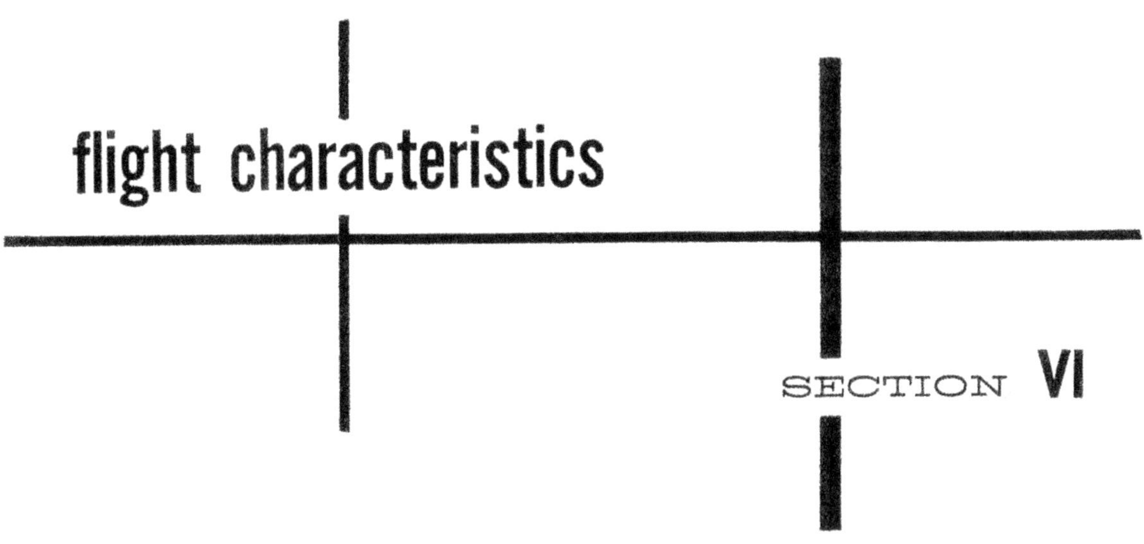

TABLE OF CONTENTS

INTRODUCTION.

The operational speed and altitude capabilities of this aircraft are considerably greater than previous fighter types. These capabilities include level flight and climb speeds of Mach 2.0 and altitudes in excess of 90,000 feet. Flight characteristics and handling qualities of the aircraft are excellent over the entire operating range.

MACH NUMBER.

Except for possibly the low-speed stall, flight characteristics are generally a function of Mach number rather than indicated airspeed. Flight characteristics are therefore more easily associated with Mach number than IAS. Increasing altitude at a constant indicated airspeed results in increasing Mach number; therefore, for each altitude there is a different indicated airspeed for the same Mach number. The effect of airspeed at a given Mach number is simply to vary the magnitude of a particular flight characteristic. At high indicated airspeeds, a given flight characteristic generally is more pronounced. For these reasons, reference to flight speed generally will be made in terms of Mach number rather than airspeed. The airspeed for a desired Mach number at any altitude may be determined by referring to figure 5-3. Enter the bottom of the chart with Mach number, move vertically to the flight altitude (using the scale on the left), and read IAS from the curved airspeed lines. Interpolation is necessary between the airplane lines.

AIRSPEED AND ALTITUDE ERRORS.

Stall speeds and minimum operating speeds shown in this section are indicated values with the compensating airspeed head. The compensated airspeed head system minimizes altimeter error at low altitude throughout the airspeed range. In flight calibration of the system established the existence of small error affected by airplane attitude at the subsonic speeds. The error is sufficiently small to be disregarded during takeoff and landing and normal flight at low altitudes. In 1G level flight at cruise speed the altimeter indicates an altitude higher than the true pressure altitude. On entering a level turn at low altitude the altimeter will indicate a loss of altitude of 200-300 feet depending on the airplane load factor used. In level turns at high altitude during supersonic flight the altimeter will also indicate a loss of altitude of about 300 feet. In order to provide altitude corrections insuring terrain clearance during low altitude operation, calibrations are included in the Appendix.

AIRCRAFT CONFIGURATION.

The over-all configuration of the aircraft was chosen with an emphasis on high Mach number flight while maintaining conventional landing and takeoff characteristics. Since the appearance of this aircraft is somewhat unique, a brief discussion of some of the aerodynamic aspects of its configuration is given before describing the flight characteristics.

NEGATIVE DIHEDRAL.

With the exception of the short span of the thin, straight wing, the configuration item arousing the most interest on the aircraft is the 10 degree negative wing dihedral. The negative dihedral actually resulted from the solution to the problem of providing satisfactory longitudinal flight characteristics over a wide speed range; therefore, the empennage and wing will be discussed first and then the dihedral effect.

EMPENNAGE.

The empennage of the aircraft, aside from its very high effectiveness, is conventional in most respects. The unconventional aspect of the empennage is the location of the horizontal stabilizer on top of the vertical fin. This location of the horizontal stabilizer was determined from extensive wind tunnel tests of the tail located in many positions, from below the fuselage to its present position. These tests showed that the high position gave the best stability and control characteristics about the pitch axis over the wide operating range of the aircraft. This tail configuration gives a minimum of transonic trim changes and provides high stabilizer effectiveness throughout the speed range. In addition, the high location results in minimum drag at supersonic speeds.

WING.

The wing is of basically straight planform in order to minimize drag at very high Mach numbers. The full span leading edge flap is deflected for landing and takeoff in order to delay flow separation over the sharp leading edge at the higher angles of attack. Inboard trailing edge flaps incorporating boundary layer control and conventional outboard ailerons are provided. The boundary layer control system blows high energy air over the trailing edge flap in the land position, thereby delaying flow separation on the flap. This permits the use of larger flap deflections than normally would be possible with a resulting increase in lift at high angles of attack. The combination of leading and trailing edge flaps results in normal approach and landing touchdown speeds, while maintaining the capability of very high speed flight with the basic wing.

DIHEDRAL EFFECT.

The position of the stabilizer atop the fin makes it act as an end plate to the vertical fin. The effective aspect ratio of the fin is thus greatly increased raising the center of pressure of the side load on the fin higher than would be the case for a low horizontal-stabilizer position. This high-side center-of-pressure location on the fin results in a relatively large rolling moment in a sideslip condition. Comparison of the fin height to the wing semispan shows that the fin is almost as important in producing roll as the wing. Thus, the high center of pressure resulting from the stabilizer location provides the equivalent dihedral effect of 15 to 20 degrees of positive wing dihedral angle. Negative dihedral of the wing is then introduced to reduce the net positive dihedral effect to that equivalent to 5 to 10 degrees of dihedral. It is to be emphasized that despite the negative wing dihedral, the airplane possesses a normal positive dihedral effect, as you will immediately detect from the position of the stick in maintaining a steady sideslip at low speeds.

MANEUVERING FLAPS.

Maneuvering capabilities of the aircraft may be improved by the use of "maneuvering flaps." "Maneuvering flaps" are defined as lowering the wing flaps to TAKEOFF position with the gear retracted. This permits an increase of approximately 1G in the available load factor over that with the flaps up, thereby improving the turn radius.

STABILIZER.

The fully powered horizontal stabilizer is an extremely powerful longitudinal control and provides excellent maneuvering characteristics at all flight speeds. Due to the high response rates possible with this type of control, caution should be used in rapid maneuvering, especially at high indicated subsonic airspeeds, until you are familiar with its effectiveness. The artificial feel system provides satisfactory stick forces under all conditions with good centering and excellent incremental control qualities.

WARNING

> The design of the stabilizer control trim system results in a reduction of available aircraft nose-down stabilizer with large amounts of aircraft nose-up trim; therefore, to ensure adequate nose down pitch control, avoid unnecessary trimming in practice stall approaches.

AILERONS.

The ailerons are fully powered and have stick forces supplied by feel springs. This results in essentially constant stick forces for a given amount of deflection regardless of airspeed. When the wing flaps are retracted, the ailerons, which are capable of developing extremely high roll rates, have decreased travel to reduce their effectiveness and thus avoid inertial coupling tendencies in rolls over the wide operating range of the aircraft.

RUDDER.  

Operation and effectiveness of the rudder are conventional at low speeds except for the relatively high breakout force of the rudder lock at neutral. The rudder is effective above approximately 70 knots. Above flaps-up speed there is little need for rudder control because the aircraft is coordinated in normal maneuvering without its use. Use of the rudder at high Mach numbers is not recommended. Because the rudder system is unboosted, very little control is available if operated at high indicated airspeeds and its use merely trips the rudder lock and results in aerodynamic interaction from the yaw damper. Initial rudder inputs forces will cause damper action to oppose the input. However, if rudder force is held constant, damper action will washout and allow execution of the maneuver.

RUDDER.  

This aircraft incorporates a fully powered irreversible rudder control system and 25 per cent greater vertical fin area than single place aircraft. Without the increased tail size, the directional stability would be less than that of the single place aircraft due to the larger two-place canopy and cockpit area. The fully powered rudder system allows the incorporation of yaw damping into the rudder surface, thereby eliminating the necessity for an auxiliary surface and the mechanical neutral rudder lock. Rudder pedal feel forces are provided by feel springs up to the power limit of the system. In order to maintain tail loads (due to rudder deflection) below structural limit values, the rudder system incorporates two deflection limits. With gear extended, the rudder travel is ±20 degrees. On retracting the gear, rudder travel is automatically limited to ±6 degrees. The rudder limiter is actuated by microswitches located on the left main gear door. Directional trim is provided through the rudder with ±2.8 degrees of rudder deflection for trim purposes. There is little need for rudder at speeds above 300 knots as the aircraft is coordinated in normal maneuvering.

STABILITY AUGMENTERS.

The dynamic response and handling characteristics of the aircraft are greatly improved through the use of stability augmenters about all three aircraft axes. The yaw and roll augmenters provide effective damping of "dutch roll" motion and the pitch augmenter provides longitudinal damping, resulting in a steady and effective gun platform. To obtain optimum handling characteristics, the yaw and pitch augmenters should be in use at all times and the roll augmenter should be ON at all

EFFECT OF STABILITY AUGMENTERS ON ROLL AND YAW DYNAMIC FLIGHT CHARACTERISTICS

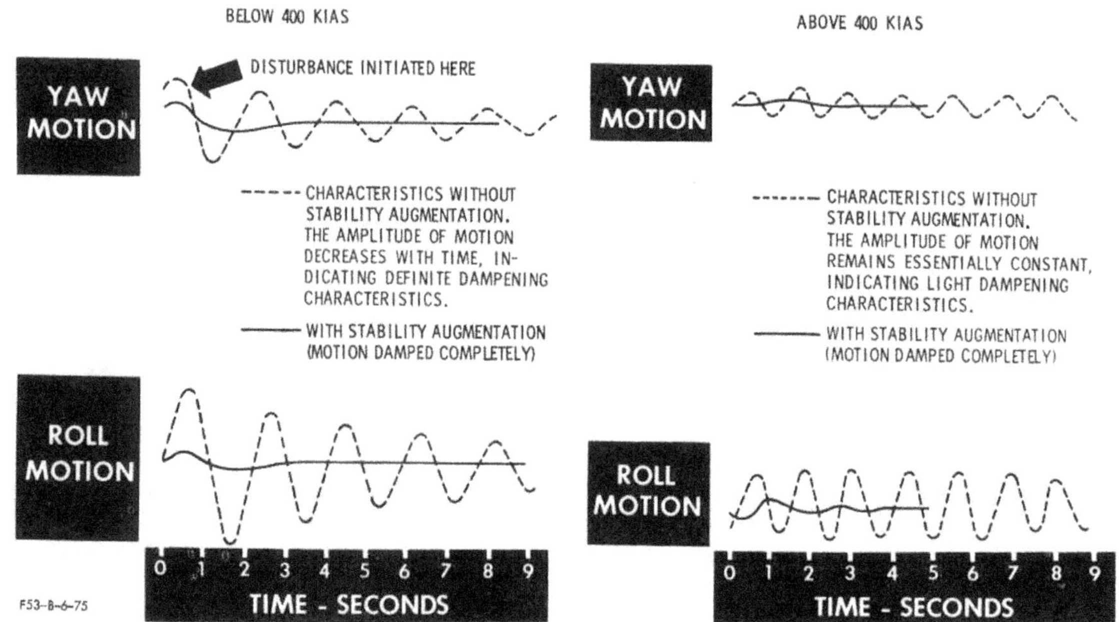

Figure 6-1

times except as limited with tip stores installed. (Refer to Section V.) Figures 6-1 and 6-2 graphically illustrate the effect of these augmenters, showing typical characteristics with and without the augmenters in operation. Should failure occur in the A C yaw augmenter system, the surface will remain stationary or drift slowly to any position within its operating range. With trim lost A C aircraft will be yawed slightly and yaw damping will be noticeably reduced. Should failure occur in the B D yaw augmenter system, yaw damping will be noticeably reduced and directional trim will be lost; however, pilot control of the rudder surface will still be available. At speeds below 400 knots, a low level of positive damping will be present and oscillation characteristics will be the same as illustrated in figure 6-1 for the yaw-damper-OFF case for speeds below 400 knots. Above 400 knots, damping of the oscillation will occur for disturbances in excess of ±1.0 degree sideslip; however, a residual oscillation of ±1.0 degree or less sideslip will be encountered. Although the oscillations will be uncomfortable, they present no hazard to safe flight. These high-speed oscillatory characteristics will be the same as illustrated for the yaw-damper-OFF case for speeds above 400 knots in figure 6-1. The damping of the oscillation is improved in accelerated flight, resulting in a reduction in oscillation amplitude, even though the initial pilot impression is the opposite because of the increase in oscillation frequency that also occurs. No attempt should be made to dampen oscillation with the flight controls as the frequency of the oscillation is too high for adequate pilot response and oscillation will become worse. Successful AIM-9B missile firings may be accomplished, even though the yaw augmenter has failed, because the oscillation amplitudes are within the cone of the infrared target seeker. Failure of the roll augmenter system does not reduce the effectiveness of the aircraft, but the aircraft is more sensitive to roll disturbances in turbulent air. Flight may be continued, and in smooth air, little or no effect will be noticed. This is because the yaw augmenter is sufficient to effectively dampen the "dutch roll" even though the roll augmenter

EFFECT OF PITCH STABILITY AUGMENTER ON DYNAMIC LONGITUDINAL CHARACTERISTICS

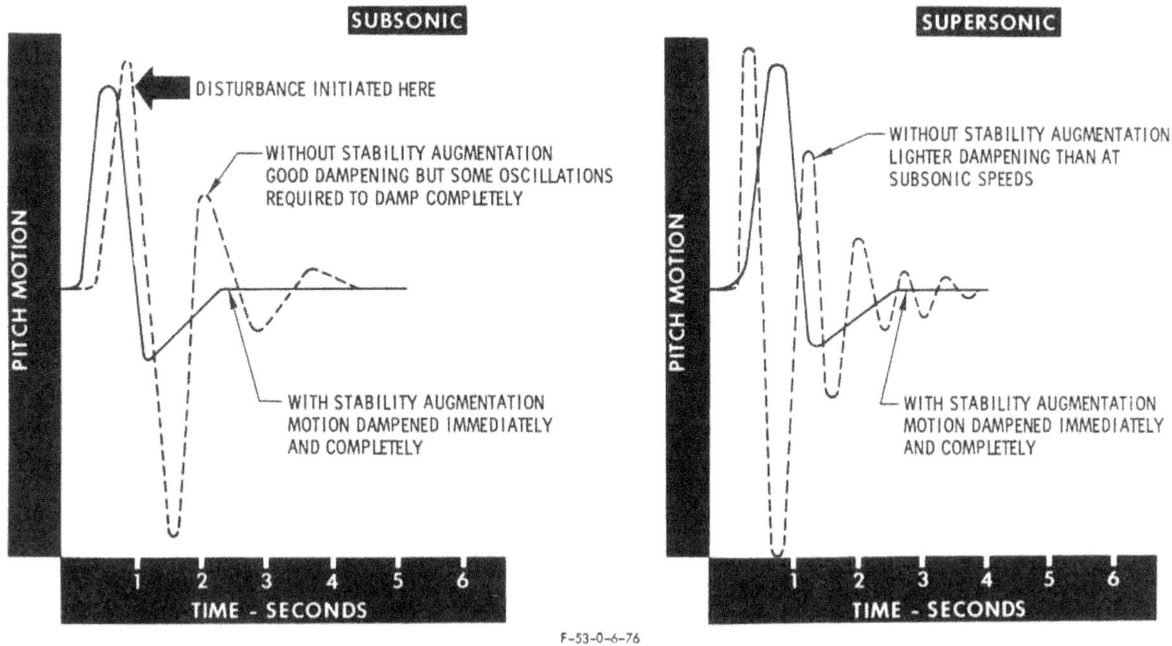

Figure 6-2

is inoperative. Loss of the pitch stability augmenter will be evident primarily in tracking maneuvers in that effective pitch control is impaired.

SPEED BRAKES.

Speed brake effectiveness is proportional to airspeed. At high speeds (within the limitations specified in Section V) they produce tremendous drag without objectionable buffeting and only a mild nose-up trim change. Combined with engine power reduction they provide exceptionally rapid deceleration particularly at the lower altitudes.

AIR INTAKE SCOOPS.

The air intake scoops are of the high-supersonic type. The conical ramps leading up to the inlet cause oblique or slanting, shock waves at high supersonic speeds rather than vertical or normal shocks. These oblique shocks decelerate the airflow before it enters the inlet, thereby reducing the intensity and resultant pressure losses through the normal shock at the inlet. These scoops combined with the internal characteristics of the ducts accomplish efficient compression of the air and maintain a high level of pressure at the engine inlet over the wide operating range of the aircraft.

TAKEOFF CHARACTERISTICS.

Airplane handling qualities and response during takeoff are excellent. Upon aft stick application the nose will initially raise until the nose strut is fully extended and the the aircraft will rotate to the takeoff attitude. The minimum speed at which the airplane will begin to rotate and assume the takeoff attitude is dependent on the stabilizer deflection, the rate at which back stick is applied, aircraft gross weight and the airplane center of gravity. In general, the speed at which rotation and subsequent nose-wheel lift-off occur will increase as the aircraft weight is increased and as the center of gravity is moved forward. The most forward center of gravity condition occurs with fuselage mounted stores Ⓒ. The addition of external fuel tanks or wing pylon armament will result in an increase in takeoff weight but will result in a more aft center of gravity than without external stores.

The amount of stabilizer deflection and the rate at which the stick is moved aft can have a large effect on rotation and nosewheel lift-off. Flight tests have shown that a dynamic stabilizer input results in a more nose up moment on the airplane than if the stabilizer were at full travel in a static condition. Therefore, in high rate back stick application instances, it is possible to achieve rotation and nosewheel lift-off with less stabilizer deflection than would be required at a slower rate of back stick application. If a high rate stick input is made too early in the takeoff, i.e., too low an airspeed, this dynamic effect can cause the nose to raise slightly due to full or partial nose strut extension and then seem to fall back again once the inertial (dynamic) effect bleeds off. This will give the sensation of an ineffective stabilizer or "light stick." Because of this, it is important that back stick be initiated at the speed at which the stabilizer will develop sufficient lift to raise the nose and achieve takeoff attitude. The speed at which the nosewheel leaves the runway should always be less than or equal to the computed takeoff speed.

The recommended technique is to anticipate the aircraft acceleration in order to rotate the nose so that takeoff attitude and speed are reached smoothly and simultaneously. Rotation should be initiated approximately 20 to 25 knots below the computed takeoff speed. Rotation and nosewheel lift-off will occur 10 to 20 knots below the computed takeoff speed except for forward center of gravity configurations. At forward centers of gravity Ⓒ rotation and nosewheel lift-off will occur approximately 50 to 10 knots below the computed takeoff speed. Once rotation and nosewheel lift-off occurs, further aft stick is unnecessary.

Additional factors that can affect take-off characteristics are stabilizer trim setting and a lowered or binding nose gear strut. The maximum amount of aircraft nose up stabilizer travel of 17 degrees leading edge down can be obtained only when the stabilizer is trimmed between 1 degree and 11 degrees leading edge down. The take-off trim setting is 5 degrees leading edge down. If the trim is set at less than 1 degree leading edge down, full back stick will not provide the full 17 degrees of travel. A lowered or binding nose gear strut will affect and increase the speed at which the nose will begin to rotate, however, it will not affect the indicated speed at which the nose wheel leaves the runway.

STALLS.

The airflow characteristics associated with the high fineness ratio fuselage and the sharp leading edge, low aspect ratio wing at high angles of attack, combined with the high horizontal tail position, result in a pronounced pitchup characteristic in the fully stalled condition. Beyond a certain point, this pitchup is uncontrollable and results in severe gyration of the aircraft and a considerable loss in altitude before recovery to level flight. At high indicated airspeeds, structural failure of the aircraft will result under the excessive airloads at the large angles of pitch and yaw encountered in such a maneuver. In addition to this type of characteristics at the stall, it is possible to develop stall angles of attack very readily and rapidly in abrupt maneuvering such as quick pullups, even though relatively small amounts of stabilizer are used. This is the result of the combination of high stabilizer effectiveness and the high inertia in pitch of the modern supersonic aircraft. The usual stall warnings are inadequate under these conditions to prevent assuming an excessive angle of attack. Because of these characteristics, this aircraft incorporates an automatic pitch control system which provides adequate warning by initiating corrective action at the proper time to prevent assuming of a high enough angle of attack to encounter pitch-up under any operating condition.

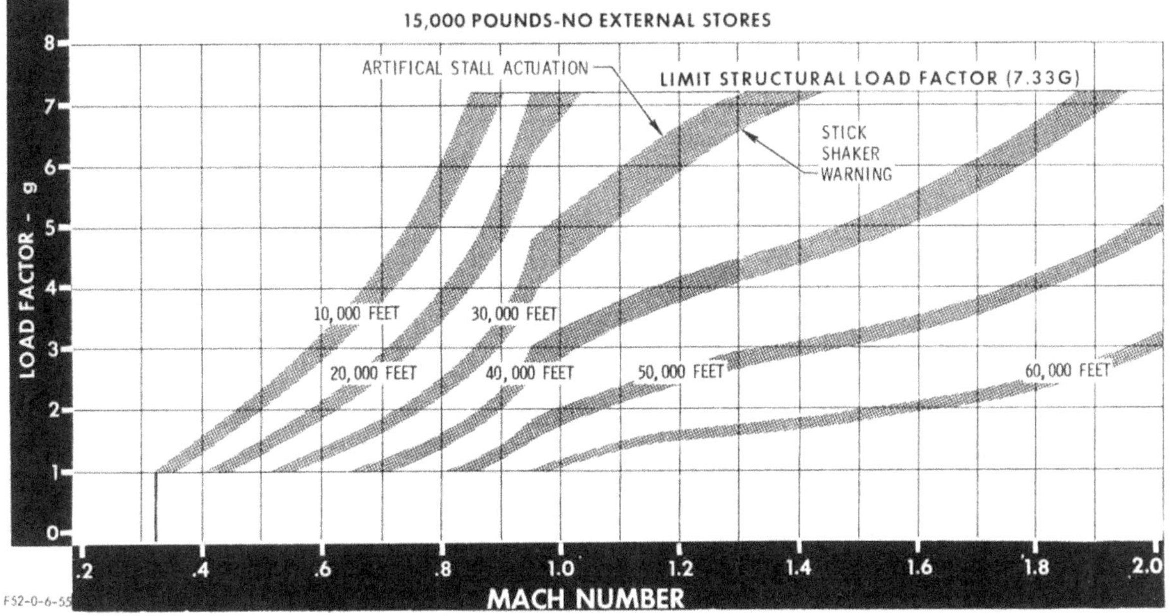

Figure 6-3

AUTOMATIC PITCH CONTROL (APC).

The APC system provides stall warning in the form of a stick shaker followed by kicking the stick forward abruptly. This action provides pilot warning and automatically applies airplane nose down stabilizer to initiate pilot follow-through. It is, in effect, both a built-in buffet warning and an artificial stall that occurs ahead of the aerodynamic stall. The APC operational boundaries are actuated by two stick shaker channels, and a single kicker channel which also drives the APC meter in the cockpit. One stick shaker channel responds to angle-of-attack only, sensed by the vane located on the forward left side of the fuselage. The second stick shaker channel provides similar response utilizing the vane on the forward right side of the fuselage. The third response channel provides kicker operation signals, also sensed by the vane on the right forward fuselage. In addition, pitch rate is used in combination with the right forward fuselage vane shaker and kicker channels to provide an anticipatory function during maneuvering flight.

The left and right vanes provide shaker operation sufficiently before kicker operation to warn of the impending stall. The left vane actuates the stick shaker from low speed to approximately 1.3 Mach number. The right vane actuates the stick shaker at high Mach numbers. The angle at which the angle of attack sensing vanes energize the stick shaker or kicker is the same at all flap settings.

In maneuvering flight such as a turn or dive pullout, the airplane experiences a pitch rate about its pitch axis. This is necessary in order to change the flight direction. Under steady-state turn or pull-up conditions, the pitch rate will be constant; and there will be no change in airplane angle-of-attack. However, when such a maneuver is initiated, there is a change in angle-of-attack and an angular pitch acceleration. Under these conditions the airplane moment of inertia and the angular rate of pitch change will result in momentum to continue pitching. The desired G will be overshot unless it is anticipated and back stick is relaxed prior to reaching the desired G. The amount of overshoot will depend on the magnitude of the rate of change of angle-of-attack generated; consequently, the higher the rate – the more overshoot. This means that, when back stick is applied abruptly to initiate a pullup, the stick must be moved forward much

MANEUVERING BOUNDARIES OF AUTOMATIC PITCH CONTROL SYSTEM B D

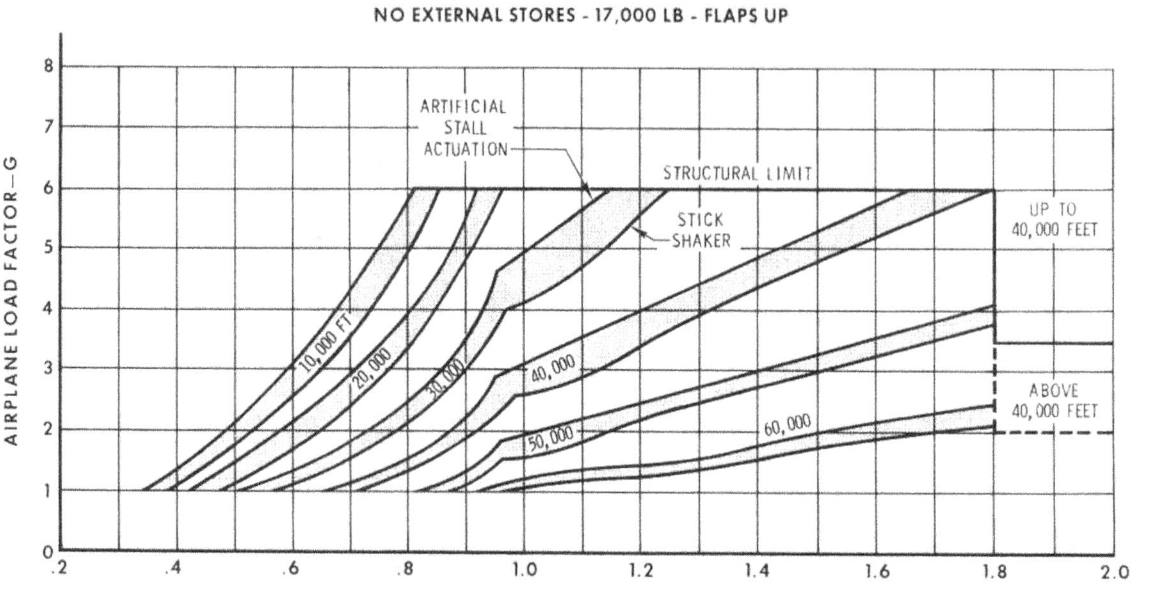

Figure 6-4

earlier to stop the nose up pitching than in a slow entry pullup. When this characteristic is related to the APC system, it may be seen that the shaker and kicker also must anticipate in order to prevent the airplane overshooting into the pitch-up flight regime. The shaker and kicker are set to operate as a function of airplane pitch rate as well as angle-of-attack to provide this anticipatory function. Under steady-state turning or pullup conditions, the airplane will have a pitch rate but the rate of angle-of-attack change will be zero. Under these conditions, there will be no overshoot into pitch up; therefore, the anticipatory function of the pitch rate input would penalize the airplane maneuverability.

In order to avoid this loss of maneuverability due to the pitch rate input to the APC, the pitch rate signal is "washed out" prior to summing with the angle-of-attack vane. Washout is accomplished such that any given constant airplane pitch rate signal into the APC will be reduced to 1/3 of the airplane pitching rate in 1/2 second. Therefore, the APC provides pitch-up protection by anticipating the overshoot in any type of maneuver entry such that the angle-of-attack never exceeds the maximum safe value.

As long as the aircraft is operated beyond the safe maneuvering range, the kicker will continue to operate and continue to force the stick forward. The kicker moves the stick forward to slightly ahead of neutral. The amount of airplane nose-down stabilizer that is applied is therefore dependent on the stabilizer trim setting. Under normal operating conditions, this amount of stabilizer ensures adequate nose down corrective action. If the aircraft is trimmed close to a high angle-of-attack condition, additional pilot follow through corrective action is necessary. The kicker is operative with takeoff flaps if the gear is up and locked. The kicker is inoperative with takeoff flaps if the gear is extended or the land flaps are extended. Thus the kicker feature is available for high speed maneuvering with takeoff flaps, but is inoperative when the gear is down to prevent undesirable kicker operation during takeoff and landing.

Figures 6-3 and 6-4 show the maneuvering boundary of the kicker and stick shaker in terms of Mach number, and figure 5-7 presents the kicker boundary in terms of indicated airspeed.

MINIMUM OPERATING SPEEDS—KNOTS

AND MINIMUM CONTROL SPEEDS (VALUES IN PARENTHESIS) COMPENSATING AIRSPEED HEAD

ALTITUDE SEA LEVEL TO 10000 FEET		GEAR AND FLAPS UP POWER ON OR OFF			TAKE OFF FLAPS GEAR UP OR DOWN POWER ON OR OFF			GEAR AND LANDING FLAPS DOWN POWER ON		
EXTERNAL CONFIGURATION (WITH OR WITHOUT FUSELAGE STORE)	BANK ANGLE	0°	40°	60°	0°	40°	60°	0°	40°	60°
	LOAD FACTOR	1.0G	1.3G	2.0G	1.0G	1.3G	2.0G	1.0G	1.3G	2.0G
NO EXTERNAL STORES OR PYLON TANKS	23500 POUNDS	245 (220)	280 (250)	345 (310)	225 (205)	255 (230)	320 (290)	180 (170)	205 (195)	255 (240)
	21500 POUNDS	235 (210)	270 (240)	330 (295)	215 (195)	245 (220)	305 (275)	175 (165)	195 (185)	245 (230)
	19500 POUNDS	225 (200)	260 (230)	315 (280)	205 (185)	235 (210)	290 (260)	165 (155)	190 (180)	235 (220)
	14500 POUNDS	190 (170)	220 (195)	270 (240)	180 (160)	205 (185)	250 (225)	140 (135)	160 (155)	200 (190)
MISSILES OR MISSILES PLUS PYLON TANKS	25000 POUNDS	245 (220)	280 (250)	345 (310)	225 (205)	255 (235)	315 (290)	180 (170)	205 (195)	255 (245)
	23000 POUNDS	235 (210)	270 (240)	330 (295)	215 (200)	245 (225)	305 (280)	175 (165)	200 (190)	245 (235)
	19500 POUNDS	215 (195)	250 (225)	305 (275)	200 (185)	225 (210)	280 (260)	160 (155)	185 (175)	225 (215)
	14500 POUNDS	185 (165)	215 (195)	260 (235)	170 (160)	195 (180)	240 (220)	140 (135)	160 (150)	195 (185)
TIP TANKS OR TIP TANKS PLUS PYLON TANKS	27000 POUNDS	245 (225)	280 (255)	340 (315)	225 (210)	260 (235)	320 (295)	185 (175)	210 (200)	265 (250)
	25000 POUNDS	235 (215)	270 (245)	330 (305)	215 (200)	245 (225)	305 (285)	180 (170)	205 (195)	255 (240)
	23000 POUNDS	225 (205)	260 (235)	315 (290)	210 (195)	235 (220)	295 (275)	170 (165)	195 (185)	240 (230)
	19500 POUNDS	205 (190)	240 (220)	290 (265)	195 (180)	220 (205)	270 (250)	155 (150)	180 (170)	220 (210)
	14500 POUNDS	180 (165)	205 (185)	250 (230)	165 (155)	190 (175)	235 (215)	135 (130)	155 (150)	195 (185)

NOTE
1. MINIMUM OPERATING SPEED ARE THE SPEEDS AT WHICH AUTOMATIC STICK SHAKER ACTION IS EXPERIENCED.
2. MINIMUM CONTROL SPEEDS ARE THE SPEEDS AT WHICH:
   a) KICKER IS EXPERIENCED - FLAPS UP AND TAKE OFF (MANEUVERING) FLAPS.
   b) NOTICEABLE STABILITY REDUCTION IS EXPERIENCED-TAKE-OFF FLAPS AND GEAR DOWN AND LAND FLAPS.
3. FULL STALL WILL BE ENCOUNTERED IF THERE IS FURTHER REDUCTION OF SPEED.
4. SPEEDS IN EXCESS OF LIMITS SHOWN FOR INTERPOLATION PURPOSES ONLY.

F52-0-6-74

Figure 6-5

WARNING

Avoid rapid maneuvers during pull-outs or turns which induce high pitch rates with the APC system de-activated. Stay out of the stick shaker boundary as there is no way of knowing how far the boundary has been penetrated until pitch-up occurs. If the stick shaker boundary is penetrated inadvertently, reduce the G-load and increase power if necessary.

UNACCELERATED STALLS.

Since APC actuation is, in effect, a built-in stall, the word *stall* is used in the following discussions to define the point of APC operation. The low-speed *stall* is preceded by a rather wide speed band of heavy airframe buffet. This buffeting builds up from mild to heavy and then remains heavy with further reduction in airspeed. Speeds below the onset of heavy buffeting do not represent a useful operating range of the aircraft. With further reduction in speed, the aircraft becomes laterally unstable. This lateral instability may increase in intensity or reflect a definite wing drop tendency just prior to the *stall*. The stick shaker action will be noticeable under the airframe buffeting condition, indicating that further reduction in speed will result in *stall*.

WARNING

Stall approaches in aircraft configurations where the kicker is inoperative should be terminated at stick shaker action, lateral instability, or wing drop. In addition, without the kicker operating, the stall warnings in abrupt high-pitch-rate maneuvers are inadequate. Therefore, this type of maneuvering must also be avoided. The kicker is inoperative whenever the gear is down with takeoff flaps extended or when the land flaps are extended.

ACCELERATED STALLS.

In the subsonic region, stall characteristics are similar to those described under unaccelerated stalls in that a band of natural airframe buffet and lateral instability warning precedes the *stall*. In the transonic region, the speed or G band of natural buffet and lateral instability warning gradually reduces and is indicated to be non-existent above approximately Mach 0.9. In this subsonic range and at all supersonic speeds the stick shaker warning preceding the *stall* in normal maneuvering flight provides the only warning prior to the *stall*.

PRACTICE STALLS.

WARNING

The design of the stabilizer control trim system results in a reduction of available aircraft nose-down stabilizer with large amounts of aircraft nose-up trim; therefore, to ensure adequate nose-down pitch control avoid unnecessary trimming in practice stall approaches.

Practice stalls to stick shaker warning or the minimum control speeds of figure 6-5 may be executed at any reasonable altitude; however, it is recommended that 25,000 feet be used for general familiarization with aircraft characteristics. The airspeeds at which the various low-speed flight characteristics occur vary with gross weight, altitude, and load factor; however, typical unaccelerated stall approaches for an aircraft with no external stores and a gross weight of 14,600 pounds (normal landing weight with 1000 pounds of fuel remaining) are described in the following paragraphs. Speeds are shown for operation with the compensating airspeed head installed. With the SUU-21A airspeed head, the values will generally be 5 knots lower than shown. The addition of wing-tip stores will lower the typical speeds. (See figure 6-5 for magnitude.) Increase speeds approximately 5 knots for each additional 1000 pounds of fuel remaining.

Gear and Flaps Up.

In the clean configuration, the aircraft starts buffeting at approximately 225 knots, becoming heavy at 215 knots. The stick shaker operates below approximately 200 knots. Lateral instability is experienced at approximately 190 knots, increasing in intensity to kicker operation at 170 knots.

TAKEOFF Flaps, Gear Up or Down.

With takeoff flaps extended, the stick shaker action is the initial stall warning at 180 knots. Moderate airframe buffet is experienced at 165 knots with lateral instability at 165 knots, the minimum control speed with gear up. The kicker will operate at 160 knots with gear up.

WARNING

With takeoff flaps extended and a gear unsafe indication, the pilot must assume that the kicker is inoperative.

Gear Down and LAND Flaps.

In this configuration and with sufficient engine rpm for boundary layer control operation, there is no airframe buffet or significant lateral instability. At 25,000 feet with Military Power, the stick shaker action is felt at 150 knots with some wing drop and a general lowering of overall stability occurring at the minimum control speed of 142 knots. Under landing conditions, these characteristics occur approximately 10 knots lower due to the increased boundary layer control effectiveness at the lower altitude.

WARNING

Stall approaches in aircraft configurations where the kicker is inoperative should be terminated at stick shaker action, lateral instability, or wing drop. In addition, the stall warnings in abrupt high-pitch-rate maneuvers are inadequate, therefore, this type of maneuvering must also be avoided. The kicker is inoperative whenever the gear is down with takeoff flaps extended or when the land flaps are extended.

Ground Effect.

Due to the ground effect during takeoff and landing, buffet and lateral instability characteristics will not be experienced if the recommended operating speeds are used; however, if the aircraft is lifted off or held off to speeds below the recommended speeds, lateral stability and control will deteriorate and wing drop tendencies will be experienced. In addition, the high pitch angles required for flight at these low speeds will be execssive and can result in tail dragging.

PITCHUP.

SUBSONIC 1-G FLIGHT.

Pitchups are preceded by stick shaker operation, heavy buffet, lateral instability and APC kicker operation. If the airplane is permitted to progress beyond the APC kicker operation, airplane angle of attack will increase out of proportion to stick application. The airplane may begin to oscillate in roll and yaw and also there may be a sensation of "digging in." Immediate recovery must be initiated by applying full forward stick and full nose down trim.

SPINS.

SUBSONIC 1-G FLIGHT.

If pitchup occurs and the previously described characteristics are not recognized, hence no corrective action has been taken, the airplane may pitch to extreme attitudes of about 50 to 60 degrees. During this period, the oscillations in roll and yaw will diverge in magnitude. At forward center of gravity locations (more than 2,000 pounds of fuel remaining) the aircraft is considered spin resistant and will generally oscillate out of control about all three axes until a nose down attitude is attained. At fuel loadings of less than 2,000 pounds (aft c.g.), the airplane will probably enter a spin following any pitchup. If the engine is running, the spin will probably be to the right due to a large gyroscopic inertia moment causing a right yaw during the pitchup. With engine out the spin may be to either the left or right. The spin is characterized by pronounced oscillations in pitch, roll and yaw which may develop into a stable flat spin if recovery is not effected in the early stages. A spin revolution will result in a loss of about 1800 to 2000 feet with each revolution taking 5 to 6 seconds and producing rates of descent of approximately 18,000 feet per minute. Flight tests evaluating pitchups and spins with external stores have not been conducted.

SUBSONIC ACCELERATED FLIGHT.

The same stall warnings are present when entered from accelerated flight; however, the airplane will progress through buffet and lateral instability more rapidly and pitchup will be more abrupt.

SUPERSONIC FLIGHT.

Supersonic pitchup and spins have not been investigated. Slow rate approaches have been carried into the neutral stability region but not allowed to develop into the uncontrollable region. Natural stall warnings such as buffet or lateral instability are non-existent; therefore, the stick shaker and the APC kicker provide the only supersonic stall warning.

PITCHUP/SPIN RECOVERY.

The spin Flight Test program was limited in scope and did not include full investigation of all spin modes nor spins in the very high altitude regime, nor spins with the engine off. Subsequent operational experience has proven that the airplane does have a flat spin mode from which recovery may not be effected using the flight controls. In the event the airplane enters a pitch-up and spin:

1. Apply full rudder opposite the direction of rotation.
2. Apply full forward stick with full nosedown trim.
3. Apply full aileron in direction of rotation.
4. Retard throttle to idle to minimize engine temperature in case of compressor stall.

Note

Retract gear, flaps and speed brakes if they are extended.

5. Neutralize aileron and rudder controls as soon as rotation stops. Begin gradual pullout, activate start switches and apply power.

Note

- It is important that recovery procedures be accomplished promptly to prevent the early oscillatory spin from developing into a stable spin. This is because recovery capability from a stable spin has not been established. After spin rotation has been stopped, altitude required for dive recovery can be as much as 12,000 feet due to low initial airspeed. The dive recovery must be gradual to avoid excessive angles of attack. It may not be possible to rely on the APC system because it will be inoperative if rpm has dropped below 65%.
- It is recommended that attention not be diverted from spin recovery to attempt an airstart.

6. If normal recovery technique fails or a stable spin has developed, deploy the drag chute. As soon as rotation stops, stabilize the airplane in a vertical nose-down attitude. If there are persistent pitching oscillations, jettison the drag chute as the nose swings down. Application of forward stick as the chute is jettisoned may be required to prevent abrupt nose-up pitching. Use slight aft stick pressure to recover without exceeding the shaker boundary. If the APC system is inoperative, control attitude by avoiding excessive airplane buffet.

Note

- If the chute is used, it should be deployed above 25,000 feet. This is to provide recovery by 5000 feet, since an altitude loss of 6000 to 8000 feet may occur from the time of deployment to jettison and a loss of 12,000 feet during dive recovery.
- There is no maximum altitude limit for chute deployment. Deployment of the drag chute at or above 40,000 feet is recommended in spins entered at high altitude.

WARNING

The aircraft should be abandoned if rotation has not stopped by 15,000 feet above ground level.

INVERTED SPINS.

Inverted spins have not been investigated; however, standard recovery procedure for inverted spins is to neutralize all controls.

VERTICAL STALL RECOVERY.

In the event extremely steep or vertical climb paths are maintained beyond the point where normal recovery appears questionable, the recommended procedure is to neutralize the controls and allow the maneuver to "peak out." In most cases, the aircraft will arc over the top of its zoom and normal dive recovery can be effected when sufficient airspeed has been regained. In the extreme case of a vertical zoom, a mild "hammerhead" type maneuver will probably be executed at the apex of the flight path as the aircraft reverses direction of flight and heads back toward the ground. Altitude required for complete recovery to level flight can be as much as 15,000 to 20,000 feet. In all probability, a pitchup will not be encountered; however, the possibility should not be ignored. In such cases, follow the proper recovery procedure.

PERFORMANCE CAPABILITIES.

THRUST AND DRAG.

The relatively low drag and the high thrust-to-weight ratio of this aircraft results in high performance capabilities. This relationship of thrust and drag results in supersonic level flight speeds over a wide range of altitude. An understanding of the thrust and drag relationship will permit optimum utilization of these capabilities. Figure 6-6 shows typical thrust and drag variations over the flight range of speed and altitude. At a given speed, the difference between the thrust and the drag represents the excess thrust that is available to climb, to accelerate the aircraft from one speed to another, or to maneuver without losing speed. The intersections of the thrust and drag lines are the points where the thrust and drag are equal, and therefore represent the stabilized level flight conditions. The thrust lines shown are for Maximum thrust operation. Obviously, at lower power settings the entire level of thrust is lowered, resulting in less excess thrust and lower stabilized level-flight speeds. Near sea level level-flight speeds are only slightly supersonic, even at maximum afterburning thrust. Maximum rate of climb under these conditions occurs at high subsonic speed. At intermediate altitudes the thrust and drag curves do not intersect within the permissible speed range, and maximum level-flight speed is limited only by engine and airframe design limitations. In this altitude range, sufficient excess thrust is available at all flight speeds for climb, acceleration, or maneuvering flight without loss of speed. As altitude is increased, due to the relative shape of the two curves, the drag exceeds the thrust at subsonic speed at a lower altitude than at supersonic speed. This results in a considerable variance in the power-limited ceiling with flight speed. Near the subsonic ceiling the thrust exceeds the drag in two regions, a subsonic and a supersonic region. This means that in order to be supersonic at this altitude the proper climb schedule must be used. For example, if you climbed to this altitude at a subsonic speed the aircraft would not accelerate past the transonic drag rise. The only way to reach supersonic speed in this case would be to lose altitude, accelerate, and make a supersonic climb to the desired altitude. In the supersonic speed range, the excess power (excess thrust × velocity) increases with flight speed, resulting in the most excess power at Mach 2.0. At high Mach number, dependent on ambient temperature, an increase in engine rpm (due to T_2 reset) occurs resulting in an increase in thrust available 3B 7A . This is also illustrated in figure 6-6. At this speed maximum supersonic rate of climb and constant speed maneuvering load factor are obtainable. The maximum level-flight altitude will be obtained also at this speed as it is the last point at which the thrust and drag curves touch.

THRUST AND DRAG

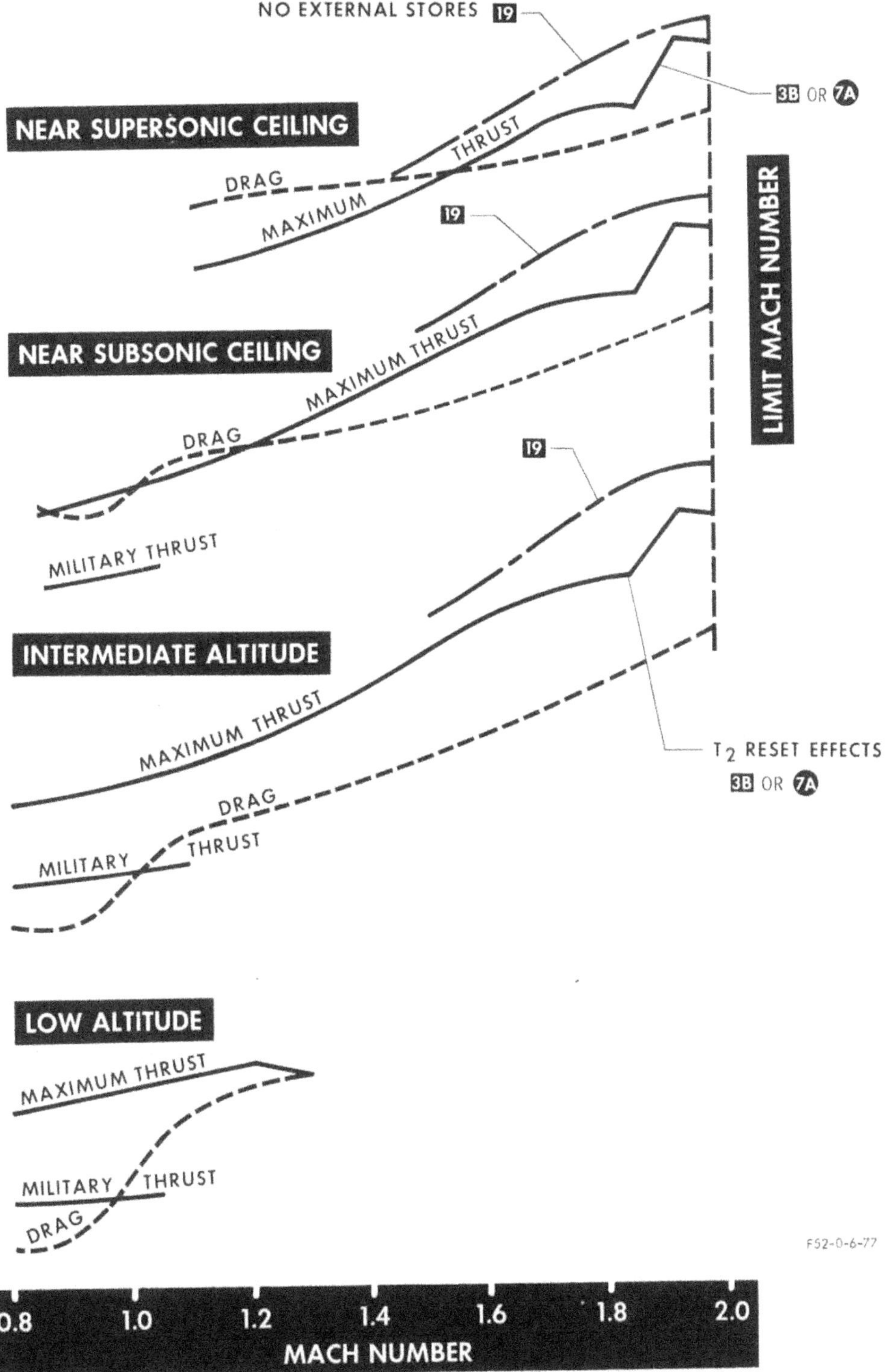
NO EXTERNAL STORES 19
3B OR 7A
NEAR SUPERSONIC CEILING
DRAG
MAXIMUM THRUST
19
LIMIT MACH NUMBER
NEAR SUBSONIC CEILING
MAXIMUM THRUST
DRAG
MILITARY THRUST
19
INTERMEDIATE ALTITUDE
MAXIMUM THRUST
T2 RESET EFFECTS
3B OR 7A
DRAG
MILITARY THRUST
LOW ALTITUDE
MAXIMUM THRUST
MILITARY THRUST
DRAG
F52-0-6-77
0.8
1.0
1.2
1.4
1.6
1.8
2.0
MACH NUMBER

Figure 6-6

NO EXTERNAL STORES EXCEPT AS NOTED
GROSS WEIGHT - 16000 LB

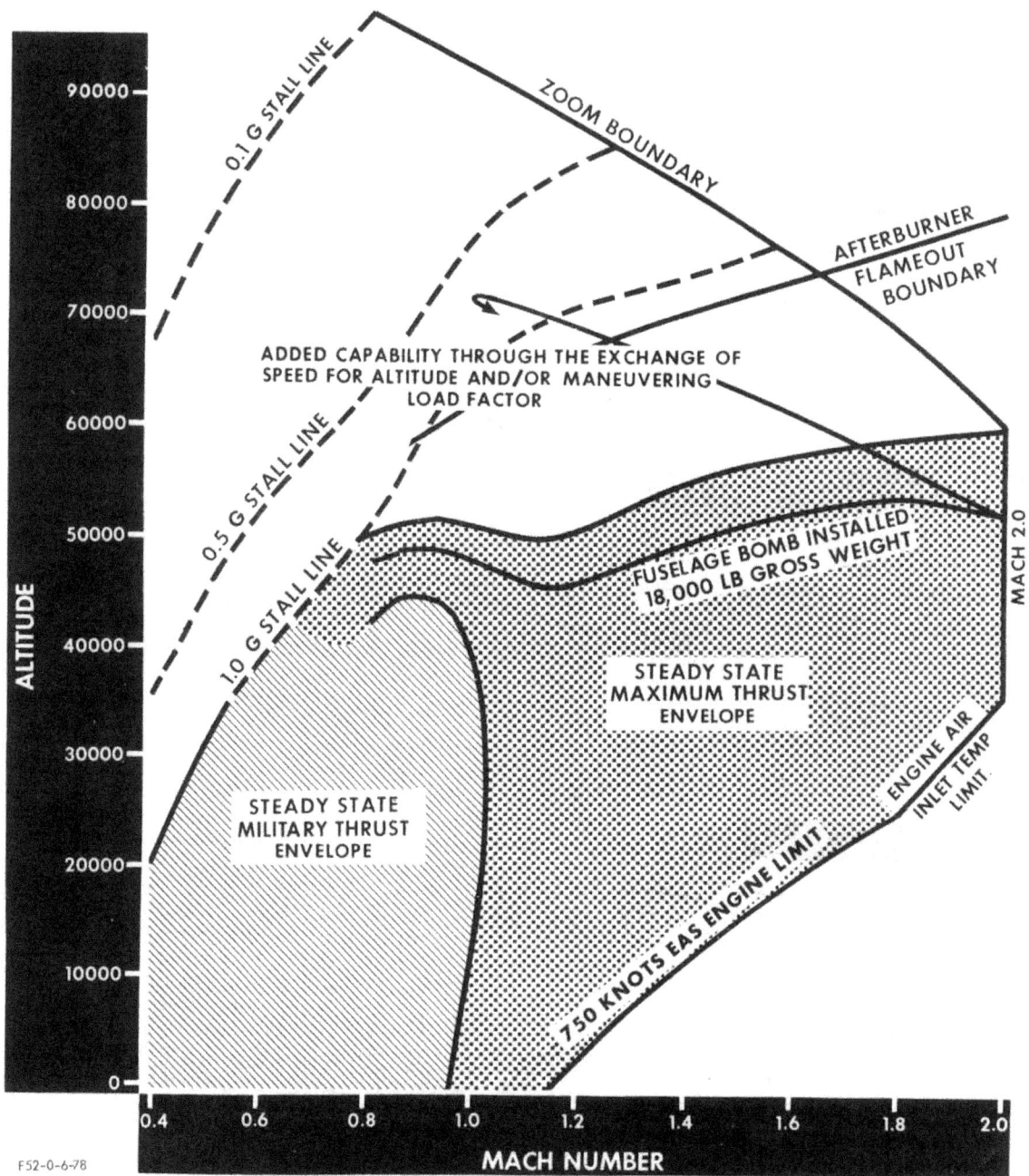

Figure 6-7

FLIGHT ENVELOPE 19

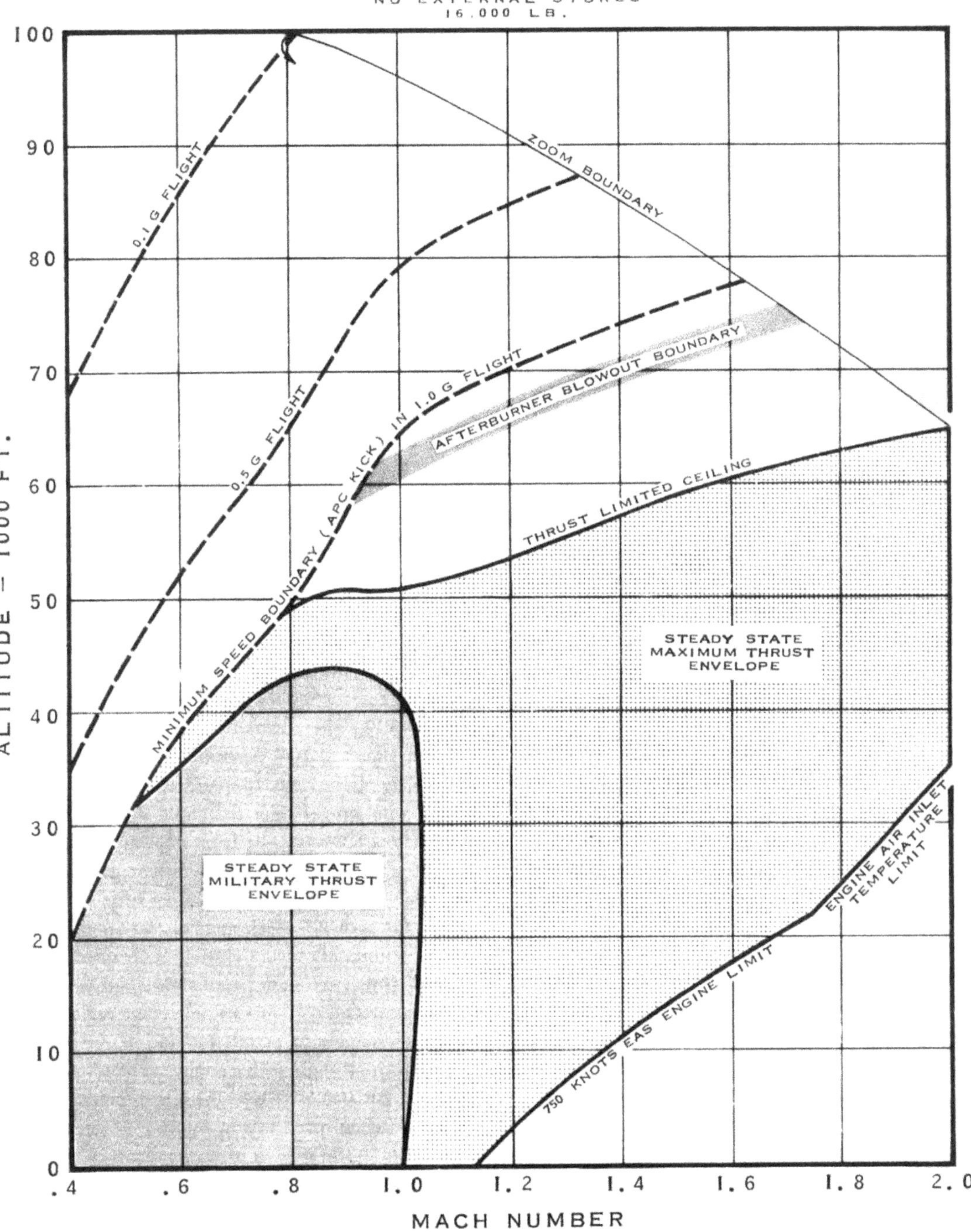

Figure 6-8

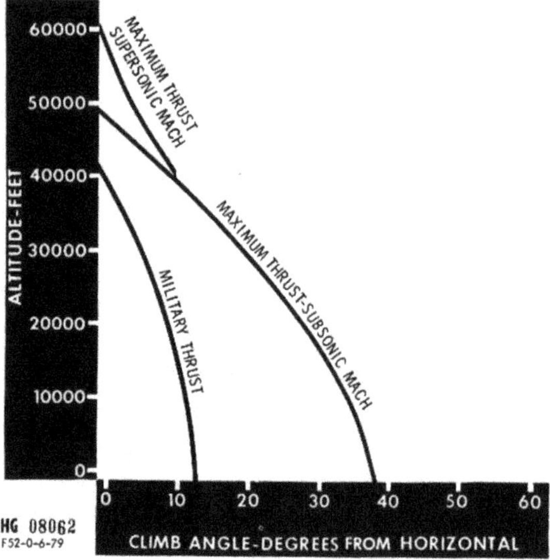

Figure 6-9

PERFORMANCE ENVELOPE.

The performance envelope, the speed and altitude capability of this aircraft, contains three separate and distinct regions. These are illustrated in figures 6-7 and 6-8. The Military thrust region is limited in speed and altitude by the available thrust and by the low speed stall. The right-hand boundary is the maximum level-flight speed without afterburning. This boundary can be extended in dives to about Mach 1.4. The Maximum thrust region represents the level-flight speed versus altitude capability with full afterburning thrust. Level-flight speeds are limited under standard atmospheric temperature conditions only by engine compressor restrictions from altitudes above 10,000 feet to altitudes well over 50,000 feet. Note the increase in ceiling of approximately 10,000 feet obtainable at high supersonic speeds. This ceiling is also dependent upon aircraft gross weight and ambient temperature and will therefore vary slightly from day to day. The upper, or zoom path, region is where the aircraft is trading airspeed for altitude. The aircraft possesses a high level of energy at high speed and can greatly increase its altitude capability by zooming to altitudes as great as 30,000 feet above the power-limited ceiling. In this region the drag exceeds the thrust available from the engine and steady speeds cannot be maintained without loss of altitude. Therefore, careful flight planning is necessary for optimum utilization of zoom capabilities.

CLIMB.

At Maximum thrust, the high rate of climb at best climb Mach number results in a steep flight patch angle. Care should be exercised following takeoff to anticipate the high forward acceleration of the aircraft as climb speed is approached and to assume the proper climb attitude to ensure maximum performance. Figure 6-8 shows the relative angles for the various climb configurations.

ZOOM CLIMBS.

CAUTION

The maximum performance zoom climb is a hazardous maneuver which can result in a spin and should be performed only if the operational requirement warrants.

A zoom climb forms an important aspect of the performance capability of the aircraft. It is the quickest way to reach a higher altitude once an adequate level of total energy has been achieved. The high speed capability of the aircraft permits a wide flexibility in changing altitude in zooming flight in relatively short distances and permits zooming to altitudes far in excess of the thrust-limited ceiling. Zoom climbs can be initiated from any point within the thrust envelope of the aircraft. The altitude reached and the final speed are dependent upon the speed and altitude at the start of the zoom. Generally speaking, the higher the initial speed and altitude, the higher will be the airspeed upon reaching a given altitude. In zooms started from 40,000 to 45,000 feet, and a Mach number of 2.0, approximately 4000 feet may be gained with proper pilot technique, for each 0.1 Mach number loss. Zooms made from a lower speed or higher altitude give a smaller ratio of height gained to speed lost. This ratio may decrease to as little as 2000 feet gained for each 0.1 Mach number lost from the thrust-limited ceiling. Maximum altitude is obtained in a zoom initiated from maximum permissible speed in the 40,000 foot altitude range. In this altitude range sufficient excess thrust is available to permit rotation of the flight path to a steep climb angle with a minimum bleed-off in speed. In zooms initiated at or near the thrust-limited ceiling of the aircraft, the speed loss in rotating to steep angles is greater due to the absence of excess thrust to hold speed. Practice is required to perfect pilot technique. Zooms to intercept a target should be preplanned as much as possible since the intercept altitude, desired intercept speed, etc., will dictate the technique required. It is essential to position the aircraft correctly before the zoom is started because further maneuvering after the zoom is initiated will decrease the energy available for the zoom. Therefore, the approximate time and distance required must be known to conserve energy and assure closure on the target. In tactical situations, zoom climbs will probably not be initiated until target detection has been obtained on the radar indicator. A pullup to boresight will be accomplished with a boresighted flight path followed from that point on to firing range. In this case, the technique to be used is automatic since the flight path is dictated by the boresight requirements. In practice zooms from the Mach 2.0 thrust ceiling to a preselected altitude, it is best to make a pullup of approximately 1.5g, attaining a maximum climb angle of approximately 20 degrees. The pushover to the preselected altitude should be started after approximately one half the desired altitude gain. In zooms to above 65,000 feet, afterburner blowout will occur as the minimum operating pressure level of the afterburner is crossed. The speed and altitude combination for this boundary is approximated in figures 6-7 and 6-8. Actually, the boundary is a fairly wide band because the blowout point is affected by individual afterburner performance and is also sensitive to pullup or pushover technique. Also, if the flight path is leveled prior to afterburner blowout, the afterburner will blowout as speed bleeds to the blowout boundary. As the zoom continues above the afterburner blowout boundary, the minimum fuel flow that can be supplied by the fuel control will become greater than required to maintain maximum engine speed. When this happens the nozzle will open and EGT and rpm will increase. To avoid exceeding limit EGT the throttle may have to be retarded to OFF.

CAUTION

Throttle reduction to IDLE or possible engine shutdown may be necessary in order to control EGT. If a shutdown is necessary a restart can be accomplished during the descent following the zoom.

Note

At very high altitudes following high Mach or sustained afterburner operation, cooling airflow is reduced due to low airspeeds, it is possible for the aft section temperature to increase enough to cause illumination of the fire warning lights.

If the throttle is retarded to OFF, the engine will be windmilling. Should the windmill rpm drop below approximately 65% rpm, the under frequency relays will cut the generators off the buses. Under this condition all electrically operated equipment except the number 2 boost pump and the battery bus will be inoperative. Of particular importance is the fact that the APC system will be off and stabilizer trim system will be inoperative. Therefore, airplane buffet (subsonic flight) and possibly attitude will be the only indications of a high angle of attack condition. Zooms accomplished to attain maximum altitude are initiated, as stated previously, from 40,000 feet or wherever in this altitude range maximum Mach number is permissible. An initial pullup of 2.0g to 2.5g should be used to increase climb angle. As the climb progresses, increasing back stick will be required to hold the nose up; however, at no time should the stick shaker stall warning be exceeded. A maximum climb attitude of 45 degrees will be reached at about 50,000 feet. Greater climb attitudes should not be used because indicated airspeed may drop to too low a value at the apogee. Beginning no later than 60,000 feet a small nose down pitch rate must be established to maintain airplane attitude in a safe relation to the ballistic flight path. This is done by maintaining angle of attack well below the shaker boundary. Although indicated airspeed over the top may fall below normal 1g stall speed, the aircraft load factor will be less than 1; and consequently airplane angle of attack will be well below stall attitude. Zoom climbs initiated from 40,000 feet might reach 80,000 feet if unchecked.

Note

The APC system will not be available if the generators have dropped off the line. Therefore, with APC off, airplane buffet (in subsonic flight) and possibly attitude will be the only indication of a high angle of attack.

Because of the pressure lag in the airspeed system, the indicated readings will lag the actual flight path. This becomes obvious when the peak of the zoom has been passed as indicated by the airspeed increasing while the altimeter still shows a climb. Altimeter range limitations are exceeded in maximum altitude zooms, resulting in a maximum reading of 85,000 to 87,000 feet. Prior to making a high altitude zoom, a pressure check on the

CHANGE IN GO-AROUND CAPABILITY WITH AIRSPEED, ALTITUDE, TEMPERATURE AND WEIGHT

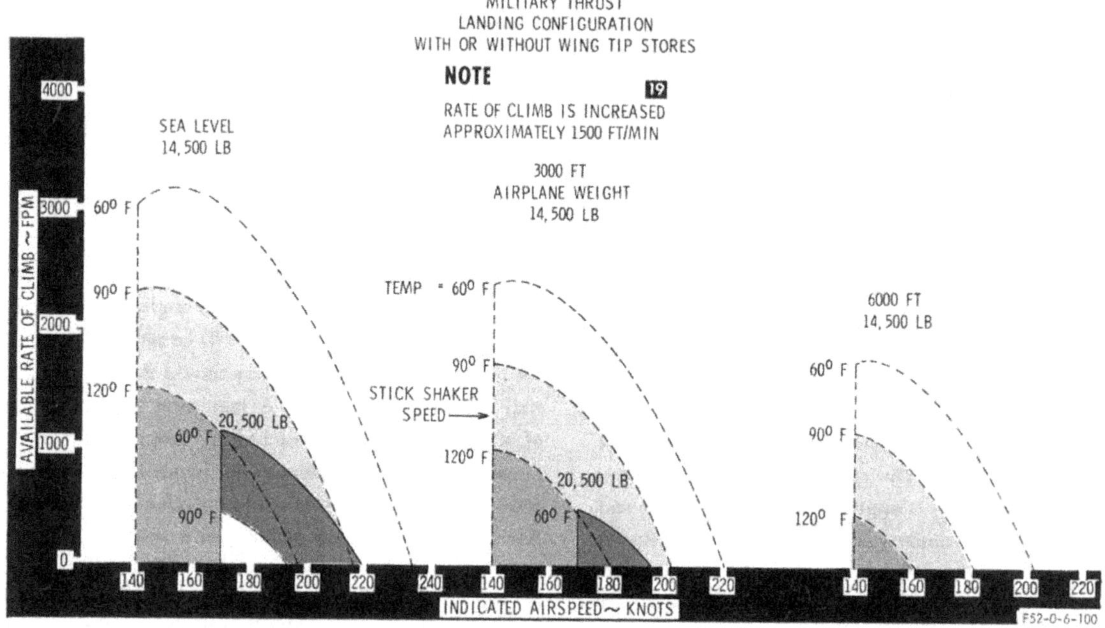

Figure 6-10

high altitude suit should be made as well as cinching down the helmet because cockpit pressurization can be expected to decrease, causing suit inflation if engine stall is encountered above the afterburner blowout point. The natural descent angle from a zoom can be expected to be approximately as steep as the climb angle.

GO-AROUND.

The excess thrust available for go-around varies with aircraft configuration, airspeed, gross weight, attitude, and ambient temperature. In the landing configuration, Military thrust may be inadequate for go-around (or even approach) as extremes of these variables are approached; afterburning thrust will then be necessary. Figure 6-10 shows the effect of temperature, altitude, and weight on go-around capability in terms of maximum speed and rate of climb available with Military thrust. However, before a rate of climb can be attained, several seconds may be required to make the transition from the downward flight path. Altitude lost during this time may exceed 100 feet depending upon the steepness of the glide slope. Therefore, flat approaches are essential and the pilot should be ready to apply immediate power under marginal conditions. In addition, under marginal conditions, a straight-in approach with take-off flaps, or gear-up configuration, is recommended. Change to final landing configuration only after the landing is assured. Determination of marginal conditions can be made readily before flight from the Rate-of-Climb for Go-Around Chart in Appendix I.

LEVEL FLIGHT CHARACTERISTICS.

LOW SPEEDS.

Low speed handling characteristics are good. Longitudinal and lateral control are positive and effective down to the minimum usable speeds. Sideslips may be used as desired.

The rudder should not be used to pick up a low wing, because it tends to lower the wing further.

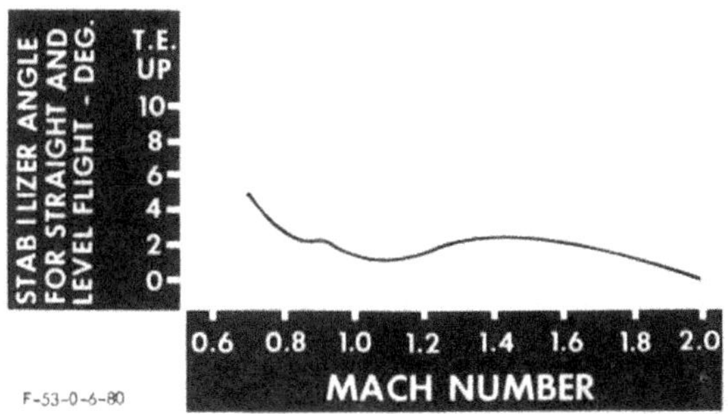

Figure 6-11

CRUISE AND TRANSONIC SPEEDS.

At cruise speeds and in the transonic speed range, excellent stability and control characteristics are exhibited. There are no tendencies for wing drop or any significant attitude changes when operating in or passing through this speed range. Longitudinal stability is positive except for a mild nose-down attitude change experienced around Mach 0.88 to 0.90. This is so slight that it will be barely perceptible. In the 450 to 550 knot speed region, at medium and low altitudes, small amplitude residual yaw oscillations may be experienced on some aircraft. This characteristic is considered normal although it is evidence of less than optimum operation of the yaw stability augmenter in the individual airplane.

SUPERSONIC FLIGHT.

A slight nose-down attitude change will be noticed as speed is increased from Mach 1.05 to approximately Mach 1.5. The normal nose-up attitude change is experienced with further increase in speed. Although there is this change in attitude over the supersonic speed range the magnitude of the change is very small, as indicated in figure 6-11. In addition, at any speed in this range positive maneuvering stability will be evident in that a back pressure on the stick control is always necessary to increase the normal acceleration and vice versa (figure 6-14). A directional attitude change that requires increasing trim with increasing Mach number may be experienced or detected on some aircraft. Generally, the attitude change is a sideslip to the left, giving left ball displacement. In most cases, the directional trim is adequate; however, some cases may be experienced in which a small ball displacement will persist near design speed with full trim applied.

LEVEL FLIGHT SPEED ACCELERATION.

Operation of this aircraft in the supersonic region requires an acceleration from subsonic speed to the desired supersonic speed. This acceleration is a component of any mission utilizing the high-speed and high-altitude capabilities of this aircraft. Figure 6-12 shows the difference in time, fuel, and distance requirements to accelerate at various altitudes. The change with altitude is emphasized in figure 6-13 which shows that the

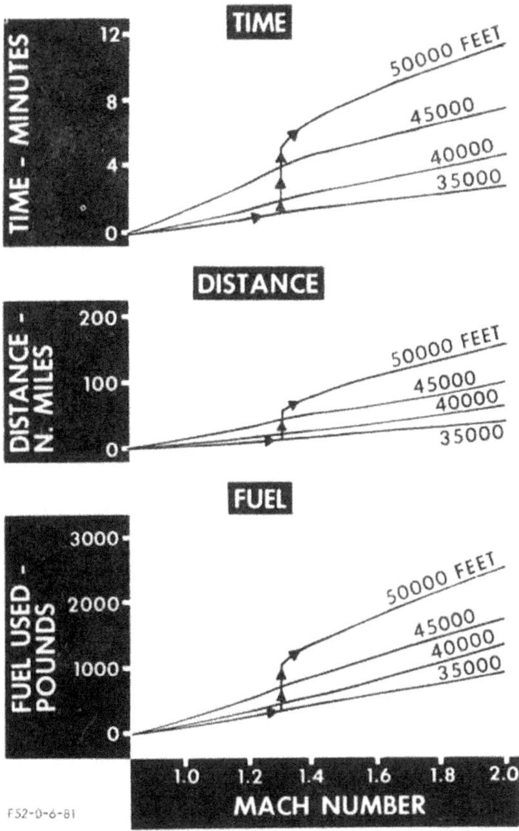

Figure 6-12

BEST ACCELERATING ALTITUDE

NO EXTERNAL STORES

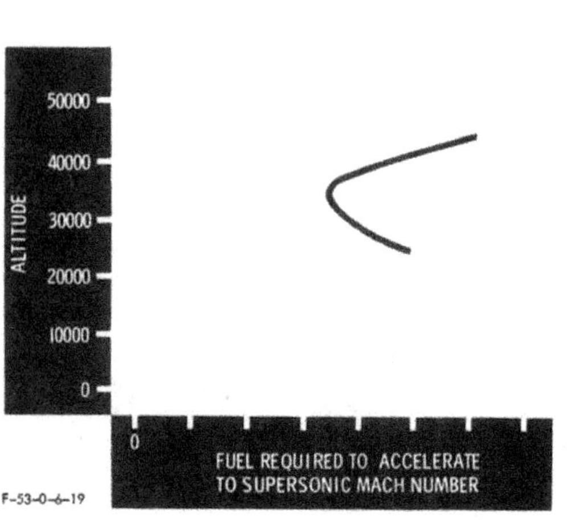

Figure 6-13

MANEUVERING STICK FORCES

NO EXTERNAL STORES
COMBAT GROSS WEIGHT - 15860 LB

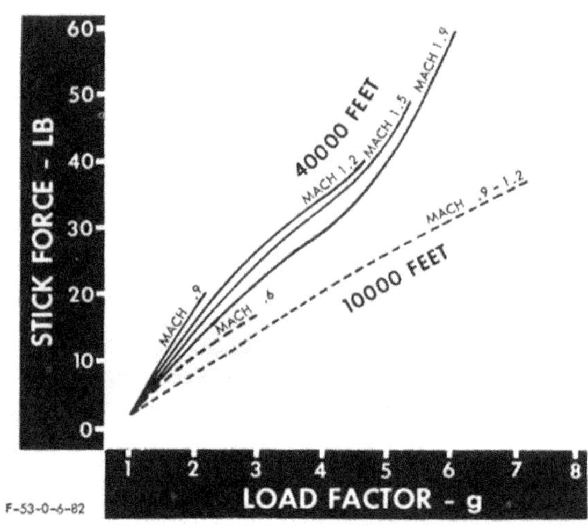

Figure 6-14

optimum altitude for minimum fuel is 35,000 feet. This will vary somewhat with the existing atmospheric temperature but usually occurs in the 35,000 to 40,000-foot altitude range. This is not intended to imply that this range is the only possible acceleration altitude, but to emphasize that the best time, fuel, and distance capabilities are available in this range.

MANEUVERING FLIGHT.

Maneuvering stick forces are moderate and generally unaffected by Mach number at a given altitude. (See figure 6-14). However, forces will vary with altitude, increasing as altitude is increased. This is because forces vary with the amount of stabilizer deflection and bobweight effect, and are not dependent upon airloads at the control surface as is the case in unboosted or semiboosted control systems. As a result, the aircraft will feel more stable and be more comfortable in maneuvers at altitude where greater stabilizer deflection is required. In turning flight, adverse sideslip is not experienced, therefore, it is not necessary to use the rudder above flaps-up speed.

TURNING PERFORMANCE.

This aircraft has an unusually large amount of excess thrust under normal operating conditions which gives it excellent constant-speed maneuverability. This maneuverability is somewhat disguised by the relatively large turn radius incurred in high speed flight. Figure 6-15 shows this normal increase in turn radius due to Mach number. Figures 6-16 and 6-18 show the maneuvering capabilities of this aircraft without a speed loss for various altitudes in terms of both load factor and turn radius. Notice that at any altitude the available constant-speed G's increase with Mach number and are maximum at Mach 2.0, where excess thrust is greatest. Minimum turn radius, however, is the result of the combined effect of speed and available constant-speed load factor and varies considerably, therefore, with flight condition. Figure 6-16 also illustrates the constant Mach number and constant load factor capability in a climbing turn. For example, it can be seen that ample constant speed is available to permit a 1.5G turn with sufficient excess thrust remaining to climb quite readily to approximately 50,000 feet, at which altitude there is only enough excess thrust to maintain the 1.5G turn. Load factors

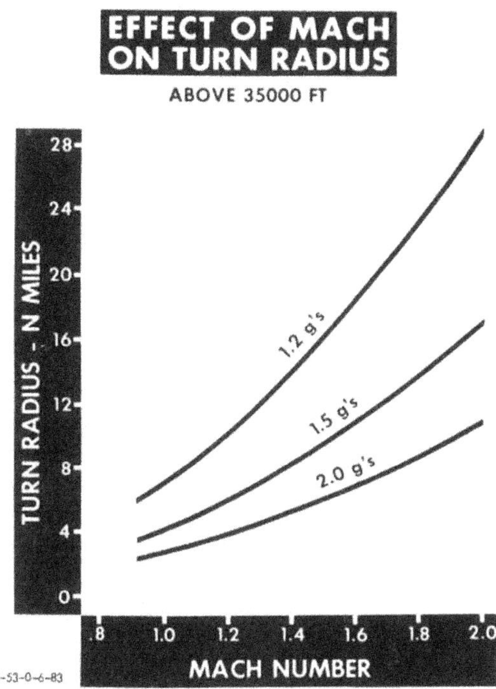

Figure 6-15

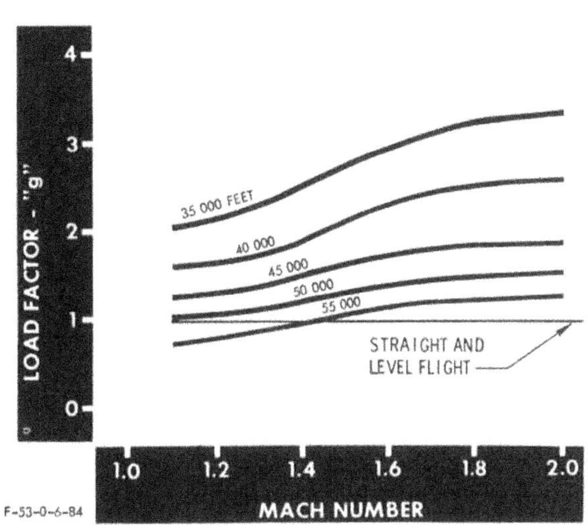

Figure 6-16

higher than shown on these figures can be utilized to accomplish the desired maneuvering in decelerating flight.

DIVING.

As the maximum allowable Mach number in dive and level flight are the same, all of the foregoing comments on stability and control cover the speed range encountered in dives. This means that flight characteristics during dives at all speeds are excellent and no new or different trim changes will be experienced. The stick forces remain at comfortable levels and the airplane is easily controlled. Due to the high rates of descent that are possible, steep dives should be executed with caution.

ALTITUDE LOSS IN DIVE RECOVERY.

Altitude loss in dive recovery is shown in figure 6-17 for any combination of speed, dive angle, and pull-out load factor. The altitude loss in recovery is the same for this aircraft for the same conditions of speed, G, dive angle and altitude as for other aircraft; however, cognizance must be taken of the higher permissible speeds of this aircraft. Because the maximum permissible speeds can be reached in level flight over a large portion of the altitude range, limit speeds can be reached quite readily; therefore, care should be exercised in diving flight to prevent exceeding speed limits.

FLIGHT WITH EXTERNAL STORES.

Flight characteristics with external stores installed are essentially the same as without external stores; and, performance is decreased in proportion to the increased weight and drag of the individual stores. In rough air, it is normal for the pitching motion of the tip tanks to be large enough to be both seen and felt. During takeoffs with the fuselage stores, nosewheel lift-off speed will be nearly the same as takeoff speed, due to the forward center-of-gravity location.

ALTITUDE LOSS IN DIVE RECOVERY

SEA LEVEL TO 20,000 FEET

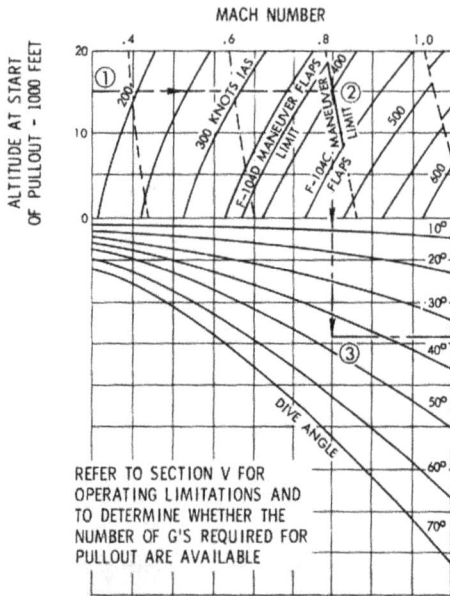

NOTE: REFER TO V-G DIAGRAM, FIGURE 5-3, TO DETERMINE WHETHER THE NUMBER OF G'S REQUIRED FOR PULLOUT ARE AVAILABLE.

EXAMPLE:

1. ENTER CHART AT ALTITUDE AT START OF PULLOUT (15,000 FEET).
2. MOVE RIGHT AT CONSTANT ALTITUDE TO AIRSPEED AT WHICH PULLOUT IS STARTED (MACH 0.8, 400 KNOTS IAS).
3. MOVE VERTICALLY DOWN TO DIVE ANGLE (45°).
4. MOVE TO RIGHT TO PULLOUT LOAD FACTOR (4G).
5. READ ALTITUDE LOST DURING PULLOUT (3400 FEET).

MACH NUMBER

.4 .6 .8 1.0

ALTITUDE AT START OF PULLOUT - 1000 FEET

20 10 0

200 300 KNOTS IAS 500 600

F-104D MANEUVER FLAPS LIMIT

F-104C MANEUVER FLAPS LIMIT

400

10° 20° 30° 40° 50° 60° 70°

DIVE ANGLE

REFER TO SECTION V FOR OPERATING LIMITATIONS AND TO DETERMINE WHETHER THE NUMBER OF G'S REQUIRED FOR PULLOUT ARE AVAILABLE

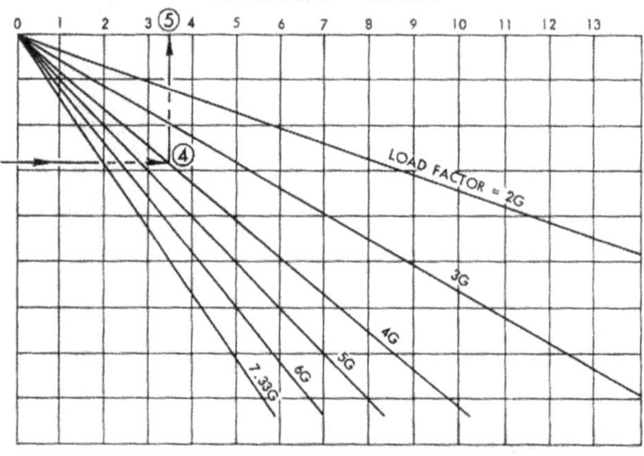

SEA LEVEL TO 70,000 FEET

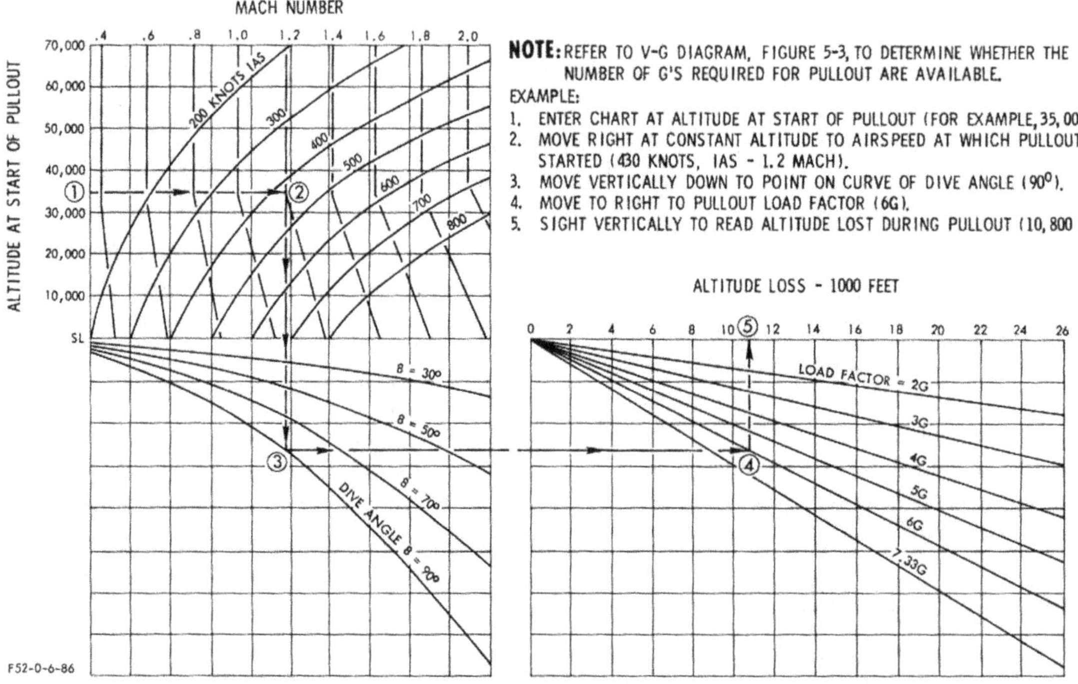

NOTE: REFER TO V-G DIAGRAM, FIGURE 5-3, TO DETERMINE WHETHER THE NUMBER OF G'S REQUIRED FOR PULLOUT ARE AVAILABLE.

EXAMPLE:

1. ENTER CHART AT ALTITUDE AT START OF PULLOUT (FOR EXAMPLE, 35,000 FEET).
2. MOVE RIGHT AT CONSTANT ALTITUDE TO AIRSPEED AT WHICH PULLOUT IS STARTED (430 KNOTS, IAS - 1.2 MACH).
3. MOVE VERTICALLY DOWN TO POINT ON CURVE OF DIVE ANGLE (90°).
4. MOVE TO RIGHT TO PULLOUT LOAD FACTOR (6G).
5. SIGHT VERTICALLY TO READ ALTITUDE LOST DURING PULLOUT (10,800 FEET).

F52-0-6-86

Figure 6-17

MINIMUM TURNING RADIUS AT CONSTANT SPEED

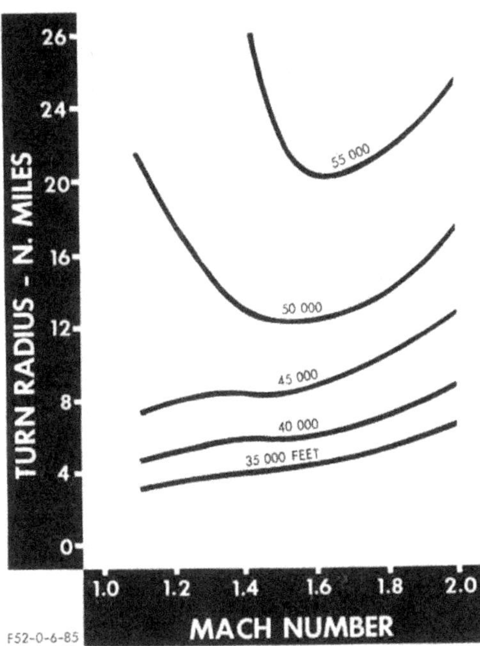

Figure 6-18

WARNING

- Do not fly with modified tip stores unless they meet the requirements of standard tip stores as to configuration and center of gravity. For example, if the power package is removed from the missile launcher, it must be replaced by an equivalent ballast properly secured in the same location.

- With external tip stores and roll damper operative, wing torsional oscillations may be experienced at high indicated airspeed, resulting in structural damage. With tip stores installed, turn roll damper off before reaching 575 knots.

TIP TANK OSCILLATIONS.

Flight tests and operational experience have shown that, under certain conditions, a steady and continued oscillation of the tip tanks can be encountered. This characteristic is usually the result of a high yaw damper setting, but it may also occur if there is a malfunction in the or roll damper. Therefore, if an oscillation occurs, both the yaw and roll damper should be deactivated to assure elimination of the condition. Deactivating the pitch damper has no significant effect. The oscillation is most likely to be encountered below 5000 feet at approximately 0.80 Mach number with 400–800 pounds of fuel in each tip tank. It can be mild or severe; however, it is not of sufficient magnitude to cause structural failure. The nose of the tip tank moves up and down at about 4 cycles per second. The airplane response is noted as a lateral-directional oscillation at the same frequency and is most predominant in yaw. For severe cases, cockpit lateral accelerations may approach ½ G. Once the oscillation has started, the intensity can be aggravated by aileron inputs. These inputs can be pilot induced or the result of a defective roll damper. Pilot inputs are inadvertent and result from the cockpit side motion experience during the oscillation. They can be minimized by attempting to hold the stick in a fixed position to prevent lateral stick movement. Aileron inputs resulting from a defective roll damper can be considerably larger than those induced by the pilot. Accordingly, the intensity of the oscillation will be more severe.

Generally, oscillation initially encountered in 1G flight will not be aggravated by increasing load factor. Also, if an oscillation is encountered in accelerated flight, the severity will probably be reduced by decreasing load factor. Speed reduction may also be helpful in eliminating a tip tank oscillation. This may be accomplished through the use of throttle and speed brakes.

LANDING WITH FUSELAGE STORE. (C)

Heavyweight landings with the fuselage store installed are critical due to the forward center-of-gravity position. At forward center-of-gravity positions and landing flaps extended, there is danger of insufficient stabilizer travel to land. Inasmuch as TAKEOFF flaps require less stabilizer travel for trim, it is recommended that for landings in the extreme forward CG range TAKEOFF flaps be used. The typical landing pattern described in Section II is satisfactory except that final approach and touchdown speeds should be increased to compensate for use of TAKEOFF flaps and heavier weight. Recommended final approach speeds are tabulated in figure 6-19 for airplane loadings where extreme forward center-of-gravity positions are encountered.

LANDING CONDITIONS REQUIRING USE OF TAKEOFF FLAPS (C)

AIRPLANE CONFIGURATION	FUEL ON BOARD FOR FORWARD CG	RECOMMENDED* FINAL APPROACH SPEED
FUSELAGE STORE ONLY	2800 LB OR MORE FUEL REMAINING	215 KNOTS (AT 2800-LB FUEL)
FUSELAGE STORE WITH TIP TANKS OR PYLON TANKS	3300 LB OR MORE FUEL REMAINING	215 KNOTS (AT 3300-LB FUEL)
FUSELAGE STORE WITH PYLON TANKS AND TIP TANKS	4000 LB OR MORE FUEL REMAINING	220 KNOTS (AT 4000-LB FUEL)

* FOR HEAVIER FUEL LOADINGS, ADD 5 KNOTS FOR 1000 LB ADDITIONAL WEIGHT

F52-0-6-2

Figure 6-19

FUSELAGE STORE RELEASE. (C)

Release of a store from the fuselage rack results in a nose up attitude change due to the bomb ejection force, the abrupt decrease in airplane weight, and an aft movement of the center of gravity. Since the weight of the store determines both the change in airplane weight and CG, the attitude change will increase as the weight of the store increases. For example, the attitude change in a 4 G release of a 2000 pound bomb will result in an actual load factor increase of 1.5 before corrective action can be taken; therefore, the maximum load factors at which bombs may be released are lower than the maximum load factor at which the bomb may be carried. During release, the cockpit accelerometer may register vertical accelerations in excess of the limits of Section V. These high values are due to the low damping of the accelerometer and do not represent the actual load factor experienced by the aircraft. If bombs are released within the limits of figure 5-6 of Section V, the load factor increase due to release will not result in load factors in excess of airplane limits. There is a possibility of stick kicker operation immediately following a release under accelerated flight release conditions. Due to the nose up trim change, the kicker action can result in longitudinal oscillations of large amplitude, caused by repeated kicker firings resulting from out-of-phase pilot control. To avoid this oscillation, it is recommended that the kicker be deactivated just prior to fuselage store release by placing the APC cutout switch in the OFF position. Stick shaker warning will still be available. The AUTO-PITCH OUT and MASTER CAUTION lights will be illuminated until the APC system is reactivated.

PYLON BOMB RELEASE.

Release of one or two pylon bombs results in a small nose-down attitude change that is easily controlled. During release of a bomb from the left wing, the airplane will roll to the right and release of a bomb from the right wing will result in a roll to the left. The magnitude of the rolloff increases with airplane load factor. During subsonic releases of the M-117 750-pound bomb, lateral control is not sufficient to maintain control in releases above 1G. Because of the higher lateral control requirements necessary in releasing the 750-pound bomb, flight with or release of one bomb is restricted to a subsonic speed. (See figure 5-6.)

FUSELAGE-MOUNTED WING TIP AIM-9B MISSILE FIRING OR JETTISON.

During firing or jettisoning of the fuselage AIM-9B missiles, a barely perceptible nose-up attitude change will be experienced due to slight aft movement of center of gravity.

PYLON-MOUNTED ROCKET PODS—FIRING OR JETTISON.

Firing of rockets from the LAU-3/A, or MA-2 launchers or jettison of the launchers results in a barely perceptible nose down attitude change. When rockets are fired from one launcher only or one launcher is jettisoned, the heavy wing will drop and opposite aileron will be necessary to balance the asymmetrical loading. A wing drop of approximately 5 to 15 degrees in the heavy wing direction may occur before corrective action arrests the wing drop.

FLIGHT WITH ASYMMETRICAL LOAD.

WING TIP AIM-9B MISSILES.

Installation of wing tip stores increases the efficiency of the wing and produces additional lift. Installation of a single missile results, therefore, in more lift on one wing than the other, creating a rolling moment. The rolling moment is easily controllable under all flight conditions; it is most pronounced under high-lift conditions, such as low airspeed, or in accelerated flight. On takeoff, the wing which has the missile installed will roll up immediately after the aircraft is airborne. During negative-load-factor maneuvers the wing with the missile will roll down. This characteristic is also noticeable during longitudinal acceleration and deceleration. The former produces a wing-up rolling tendency, whereas during deceleration the missile wing rolls down. When firing missiles, a slight wing drop will be noticeable to the side of the fired missile, due to the reduced lift on that side when the missile leaves the wing tip.

WARNING

Formation takeoffs involving any aircraft in a one-missile configuration is prohibited. When flight in a one-missile configuration is required, caution should be exercised during takeoff and during low airspeed, negative-G maneuvers.

ASYMMETRIC TIP TANK FUEL LOAD.

Adequate control is available for landing with one tip tank full and one tank empty under smooth air conditions; however, consideration should be given to the added aileron requirements under strong or gusty cross-wind conditions before attempting a landing with an asymmetric fuel load. A crosswind from the side with the light tank increases the aileron requirements in the same direction as used to balance the heavy tank. It is recommended that low-speed control be evaluated prior to entering the landing pattern. If the lateral control appears marginal for the existing landing condition, the tanks should be jettisoned.

PYLON ARMAMENT.

In asymmetric loadings of the wing pylons the airplane will tend to roll to the heavy side. During a takeoff under these conditions the airplane will tend to turn into the heavy wing due to the weight outboard of the aircraft center of gravity. Nosewheel steering will be necessary at higher than normal speeds to correct this tendency. At nosewheel lift-off the heavy wing will drop but is easily picked up with aileron. For this reason formation takeoffs have been prohibited. During flight, lateral trim will be required to maintain wings-level flight. Trim requirements are largest at speeds near APC kicker operation, decreasing as speed is increased up to Mach 1.0. In accelerated flight the aileron trim necessary to balance the asymmetric load increases with airplane load factor. Maneuvering characteristics with a 750-pound bomb have not been evaluated above Mach 1.0; consequently, flight with this bomb is limited to Mach 1.0. The yawing moment due to asymmetric wing pylon load is negligible at all allowable speeds. Use of directional trim is not recommended because it will increase aileron trim requirements. Adequate lateral control is available for landing with an asymmetric load; however, a wider than normal pattern should be used and final approach and touchdown speeds should be increased 10 knots.

A/A-37U-15 TOW TARGET.

The A/A-37U-15 tow target on the left wing pylon will result in an airplane tendency to roll and yaw to the left, due to the asymmetric wing loading. During takeoff, without a counter balancing pylon tank on the right wing, the airplane will tend to turn to the left due to the weight outboard of the aircraft center of gravity. Nosewheel steering will be required to higher than normal speeds and full right rudder trim should be used in correcting this tendency. At nosewheel liftoff, the heavier left wing will drop, but can be picked up with opposing aileron. The roll off should be anticipated by applying right stick at start of rotation so 1/4 to 1/2 aileron will have been applied at liftoff. Optimum handling characteristics are experienced when a pylon tank is carried on the right wing to counter balance the tow target. In this configuration, rudder trim should be neutral and the pylon tank should be full of fuel. With a full pylon tank, a slight overbalance exists and a right roll tendency will occur at takeoff. The proper technique is to anticipate this roll by applying left stick at start of rotation so that 1/4 to 1/2 aileron will have been applied at liftoff.

Normal takeoff speeds should be increased 10 knots to provide better lateral control at liftoff and to minimize dragging the Dart on the runway. Pylon tank fuel, if carried, may be used after takeoff. During flight, small amounts of aileron may be required. Trim requirements are highest at low airspeed. Although lateral control is adequate for landing with the Dart. Final approach and touchdown speeds should be increased 10KIAS to provide better lateral control and minimize dragging the Dart.

Landings without the Dart may be accomplished using the normal takeoff flap landing speed schedules.

Jettison of the Dart system may be accomplished with the Dart either in the stowed position or while being towed. The tow pod alone should not be jettisoned, because it is unstable and most likely will strike the trailing edge flap.

FORMATION FLYING.

Close and combat formation characteristics of the aircraft are good throughout the entire speed range of the aircraft. Because of the rapid airplane acceleration characteristics and the segmented burning characteristics of the afterburner, a pilot of low proficiency may find himself quite busy while flying afterburner formation; however, after a learning period of two or three flights, a good close formation takeoff and flight can be made.

AFTERBURNER FORMATION TAKEOFFS.

Due to the rapid acceleration of the aircraft, it is necessary for the leader to use a power setting somewhat less than full uniform to allow the wingman to maintain his position. This should be an indicated nozzle position approximately 8.0. Large variations in thrust with relatively small throttle movement are obtained when operating with the afterburner, particularly when the afterburner shifts from sector to uniform buring. If the wingman modulates through this point during takeoff, he will fall behind and then overtake the leader rapidly as maximum power is attained. It is preferable to remain in uniform burning throughout the takeoff roll. Because of the short time involved in a takeoff, the wingman may find some difficulty in stabilizing his position. The wingman should become airborne with the leader; gear and takeoff flaps should be retracted on a signal from the leader. After gear and flap retraction, the leader may advance power to almost full uniform. If afterburner light is accomplished simultaneously between two aircraft and power adjustments made immediately, the wingman will be able to maintain a satisfactory position throughout takeoff with small power changes.

AFTERBURNER FORMATION CLIMB.

If the wingman is in formation at takeoff he can easily maintain position throughout an afterburner climb to subsonic ceiling. The leader must select a power setting less than full throttle to allow the wingman to make power adjustments. Formation join-up from single ship takeoffs can be made if the leader turns after takeoff and retards his throttle to minimum afterburning. A leader who maintains an excessively high power setting probably will reach cruise altitude before his wingman can reach formation climb position.

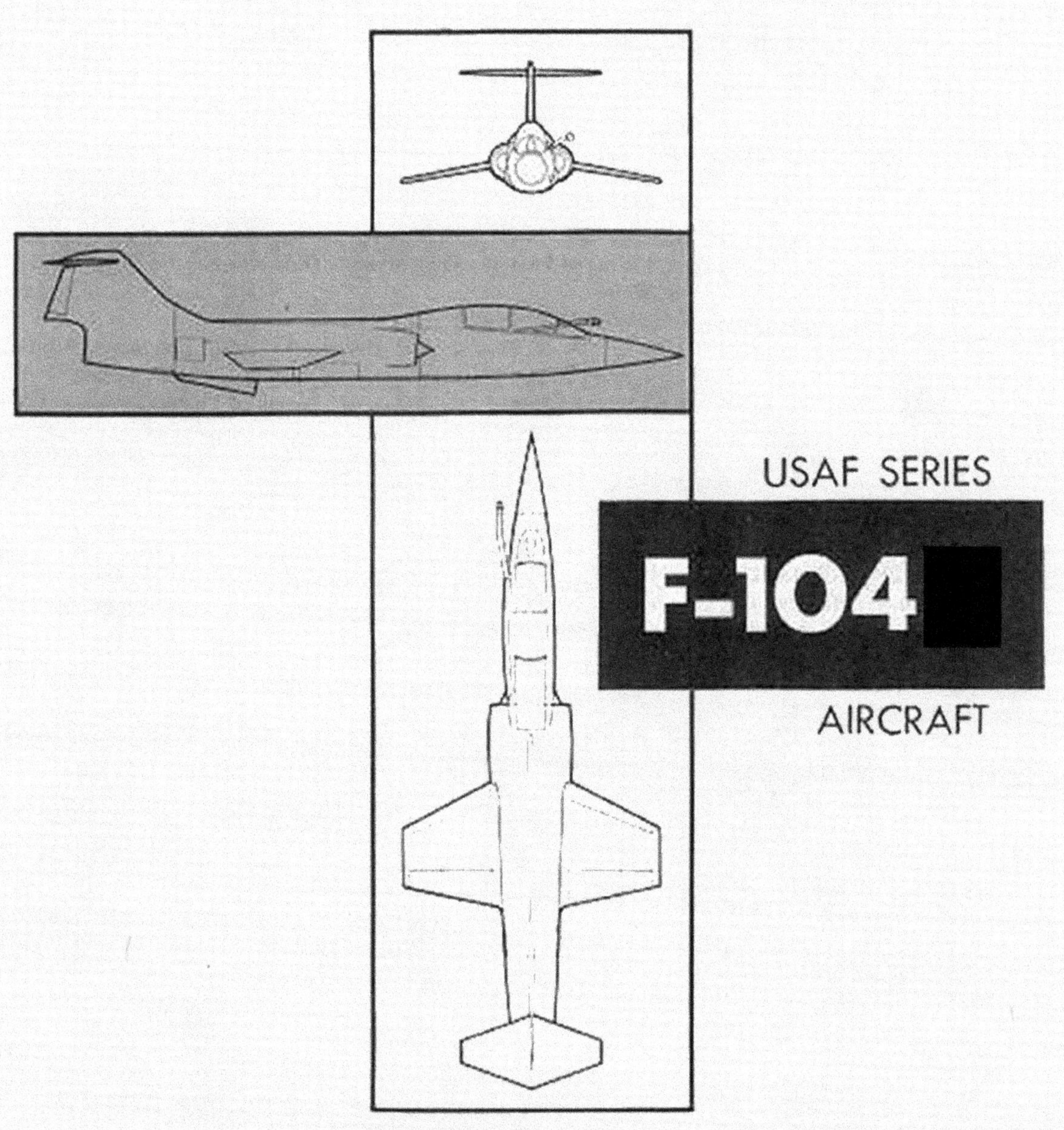

This page intentionally left blank.

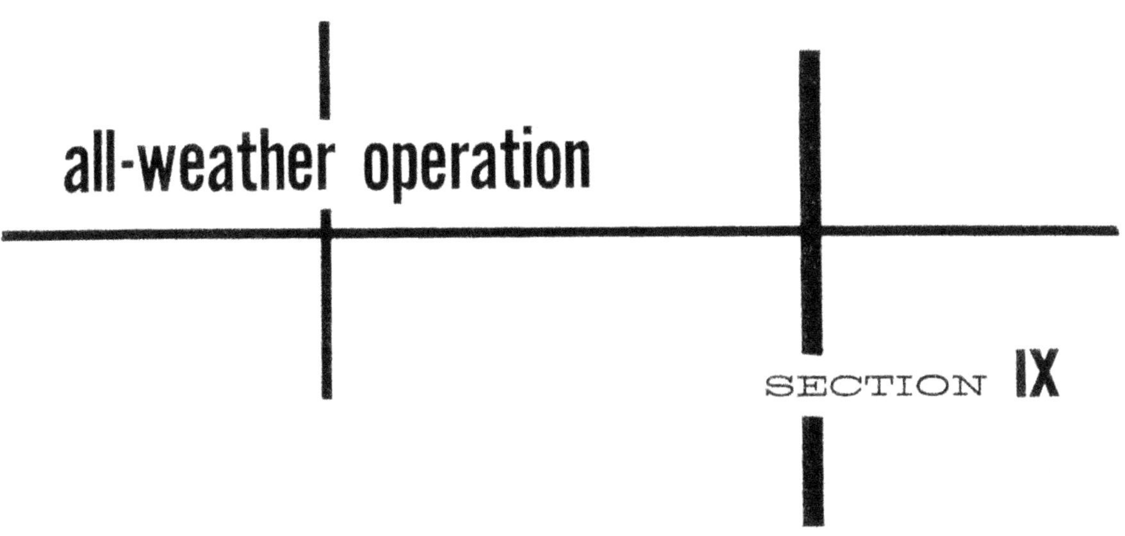

TABLE OF CONTENTS

INSTRUMENT FLIGHT PROCEDURES.

These procedures and techniques pertain primarily to instrument flight conditions and are in addition to normal procedures. The data are based on aircraft normal gross weight. Because navigation facilities and terrain features are different at each base, this information is intended to serve only as a guide to commanders in establishing instrument flight procedures.

INSTRUMENT TAKEOFF.

An instrument takeoff is essentially the same as a normal VFR takeoff, and may be made using either Military or Maximum thrust.

INSTRUMENT CLIMB.

1. Hold a nose-high attitude of 8 degrees until climb airspeed is attained.

2. Adjust aircraft pitch attitude to maintain desired climb speed. Afterburner climb pitch angle indications will vary between 35 and 50 degrees nose-up on the attitude indicator.

3. Landing gear lever -- UP, when defintiely airborne.

Note

If the landing gear lever is not moved to the UP position until a climb is indicated on the altimeter and vertical velocity indicator, transient gear speed limit will be exeeceded.

WARNING

When turns are made during afterburner climb, the nose of the aircraft tends to describe an arc, not parallel to the horizon, but increasing in pitch attitude. This inclination is conducive to vertigo. Therefore, turns during an afterburner instrument climb should be made only as necessary.

INSTRUMENT CRUISING FLIGHT.

Aircraft handling qualities make supersonic instrument cruise flight possible. Refer to Section VI for level flight characteristics at high speeds.

Note

> Upon initiating a turn, expect a momentary instrument indication opposite to the direction of bank. During transition from subsonic to supersonic flight, all pitot static instruments will be unreliable due to the aircraft shock wave. The attitude indicator will erroneously indicate a climb due to acceleration.

HOLDING.

The following configuration results in minimum fuel consumption and provides optimum stability for formation flying.

1. Flaps—Takeoff.
2. Airspeed—260 knots.

Note

> For ease and precision of flight, limit bank angles to 30 degrees. Add power as necessary during turns to maintain desired airspeed.

JET PENETRATION.

Both engine and airframe must be considered during descents. Inlet guide vanes icing is most probable at 82 percent rpm or below, because of inadequate airflow for anti-icing. If icing is anticipated, maintain a minimum of 85 percent rpm during descent.

Approaching the Fix (See figure 9-1).

1. Throttle—As required.
2. Wing flap lever—Takeoff.
3. Pitot heat switch—ON.
4. Engine anti-ice switch ON whenever CIT gage indicates within ±10° C and moisture is visible.
5. Canopy defrost lever—INCR.

Initial Penetration Altitude.

1. Throttle—85 percent rpm, 3B 7A and 83 percent rpm 19
2. Speed brakes switch—OUT.
3. Pitch attitude—Lower nose 10-15 degrees, and maintain 275 knots.

At 1000 Feet Above Desired Level-off Altitude.

1. Speed brakes switch—IN.

Note

- The average rate of descent will be 4200 fpm. With takeoff flaps and 85 percent rpm 3B 7A and 83 percent rpm 19 , the aircraft will stabilize in level flight at approximately 250 knots inbound to the station.
- Engine airflow should be adequate for anti-icing in light-to-moderate icing conditions. This procedure requires 7 to 8 minutes to return to the radio fix from 20,000 feet. Distance is about 19 miles from station. Fuel required is approximately 350 pounds. (See figure 9-1.)

GCI RECOVERY (See figure 9-2).

When a radar or ILS approach is required, descent from the inbound cruising altitude should be initiated at a sufficient distance to permit a straight-in descent at jet penetration airspeed. Five to seven miles should be allowed for decelerating and changing to approach configuration before reaching the turn-on point (gate) to final approach. Aircraft configuration will be the same as that used during a jet penetration.

ENROUTE DESCENT.

If an enroute descent is desired, use the following configuration:

Flaps—UP, Speed brakes—IN, 85 percent rpm 3B 7A and 83 percent rpm 19, .80 indicated Mach until 300 knots is reached, hold until 5-7 miles from hand-off point.

RADAR APPROACH (See figure 9-2).

When approaching the radar pickup point, adjust throttle to 85 percent rpm 3B 7A and 83 percent rpm 19, and check flap lever in TAKEOFF position. Airspeed will stabilize at approximately 250 knots. Limit all bank angles to 30 degrees. Lower landing gear on base leg, or 10 miles out if making a straight-in approach. Airspeed will bleed off to approximately 220 knots. During turn to final approach, maintain 220 knots, move flap lever to LAND position 1 mile prior to entering the glide path and advance throttle to approximately 89 percent rpm 3B 7A and 87 percent rpm 19. Let airspeed decrease to 175 knots and maintain this airspeed on glide path. Rate of descent will be approximately 750 feet per minute.

Note

When making a takeoff flap landing, retard throttle to approximately 83 percent rpm 3B 7A and 82 percent rpm 19 as glide slope is intercepted. Airspeed will be 195 knots and rate of descent approximately 850 feet per minute.

ILS APPROACH (See figure 9-3).

During an ILS approach, maintain aircraft attitude with the basic flight instruments and monitor the course indicator for reference to the localizer and glide slope. If localizer interception is from a radio fix or by GCI, and is at an angle of 90 degrees or less, allow sufficient distance for final cockpit check, slow to approach speed and intercept the localizer course.

WARNING

Prior to making an ILS approach be sure the CDI selector switch is in the VOR/ILS position. If the station has both TACAN and ILS, it is possible to make an approach with ILS glide slope and TACAN course indications, but the aircraft may not be aligned with the runway. Check TACAN-ILS/VOR indicator lights to identify correct CDI switch position.

MISSED APPROACHES.

In case of a missed approach, follow the procedure given in Section II for go-around. Adjust throttle to 85 percent rpm 3B 7A and 83 percent rpm 19 if you are to remain in the pattern; this will maintain approximately 250 knots.

ICE AND RAIN.

Although this airplane does not have anti-icing systems for the wing, empennage, or inlet ducts, flight under icing conditions can be made. Defrosting, rain removal, inlet guide vane anti-icing, and pitch sensor and pitot heat should be turned on prior to entering an area where icing conditions prevail or are suspected. Flight tests have shown that, although engine flameout did not occur, the inlet guide vanes and variable stator blades were damaged and compressor stalls did occur when heavy ice was ingested at 98 percent rpm. The compressor stalls resulted in a reduction of thrust to idle rpm and prevented obtaining higher than idle rpm. Heavy ice was ingested at 88 percent rpm and below, without encountering engine damage or compressor stall. With pitot heat on, ice formed over the static port of the pitot head during heavy icing, resulting in a loss of proper indications on the airspeed and altimeter indicators. The pitot heat was sufficient to clear this ice off the pitot head within 1 to 2 minutes after leaving the icing area. Continued use of the rain removal system may result in discoloration and eventual failure of the windshield adjacent to the rain removal nozzle. Successive flights through rain at high speeds may cause erosion of the radome. In view of the above, the following procedures should be followed:

1. Whenever possible, avoid flight in conditions conducive to a rapid buildup of ice.

2. Inspect windshield for discoloration after any flight in which the rain remover was used, and have windshield replaced if discoloration is noted.

3. After flying in moderate-to-heavy icing for 2 minutes or more do not use more than 88 percent rpm and land as soon as practicable.

When an instrument takeoff or approach is to be made and rain is anticipated the windshield rain removal system should be placed in operation to maintain forward visibility through the left windshield panel.

Note

The cleared area of the windshield will be slightly smaller in heavy rain than in moderate rain. If very heavy rain is encountered, some visibility will be retained but it will be substantially impaired.

Refer to Sections IV and V for operating procedures and limitations of the anti-icing and rain removal equipment.

TURBULENCE AND THUNDERSTORMS.

Flight through turbulence and thunderstorms can result in engine flameout or structural damage to the aircraft. Hail can cause rapid deterioration of the radome or shatter the infrared sight cover, causing cockpit depressurization. Engine flameouts have been experienced in jet aircraft which incorporate through-flow inlet systems, due singly or in combination to such factors as the following:

1. Penetration of cumulus buildups with associated high liquid content.

2. Icing of duct inlet or engine inlet guide vanes.

3. High concentration of ice crystals associated with tops of cumulus clouds.

4. Changes in engine inlet pressure associated with turbulent air penetration.

5. Operating above 40,000 feet where engine surge margin is reduced.

The last two factors are significant primarily at low indicated airspeed. Operating in the sector range of afterburning also increases the possibility of flameout (7A) This is due to the greater sensitivity of the afterburner in this range to flow disturbances. The rapid closure of the exhaust nozzle when the afterburner blows out can in turn cause engine flameout when operating under the marginal conditions mentioned above.

CAUTION

Flying in turbulence or hail may increase inlet distortion. At high altitudes, this distortion can result in engine surge and possible flameout. However, normal air restarts may be accomplished as outlined in Section III.

Areas of turbulent air, hailstorms, or thunderstorms should be avoided whenever possible because of the increased danger of engine flameout. If these areas cannot be avoided, the following should be performed:

1. Turn on engine anti-icing, pitch sensor and pitot heat.

2. Establish a penetration airspeed of 350 knots for a clean aircraft, or 275 knots if takeoff flaps are extended. At altitudes where 350 knots is higher than normal cruise speed, thus penalizing range performance, use the best operating speed instead. If a climb over the top is attempted, use the recommended climb Mach number to obtain best performance. Above 40,000 feet, modify the climb schedule to maintain a minimum of 275 knots and use full afterburning in order to ensure adequate engine surge margin.

CAUTION

- When the instrument lights are turned on, the warning panel lights are dimmed automatically, and special care should be exercised to detect any warning light illumination.
- Monitor all engine instruments continuously to ensure timely corrective action.

Refer to Ice and Rain paragraph and to Section IV for operating procedures of the anti-icing and rain removal systems.

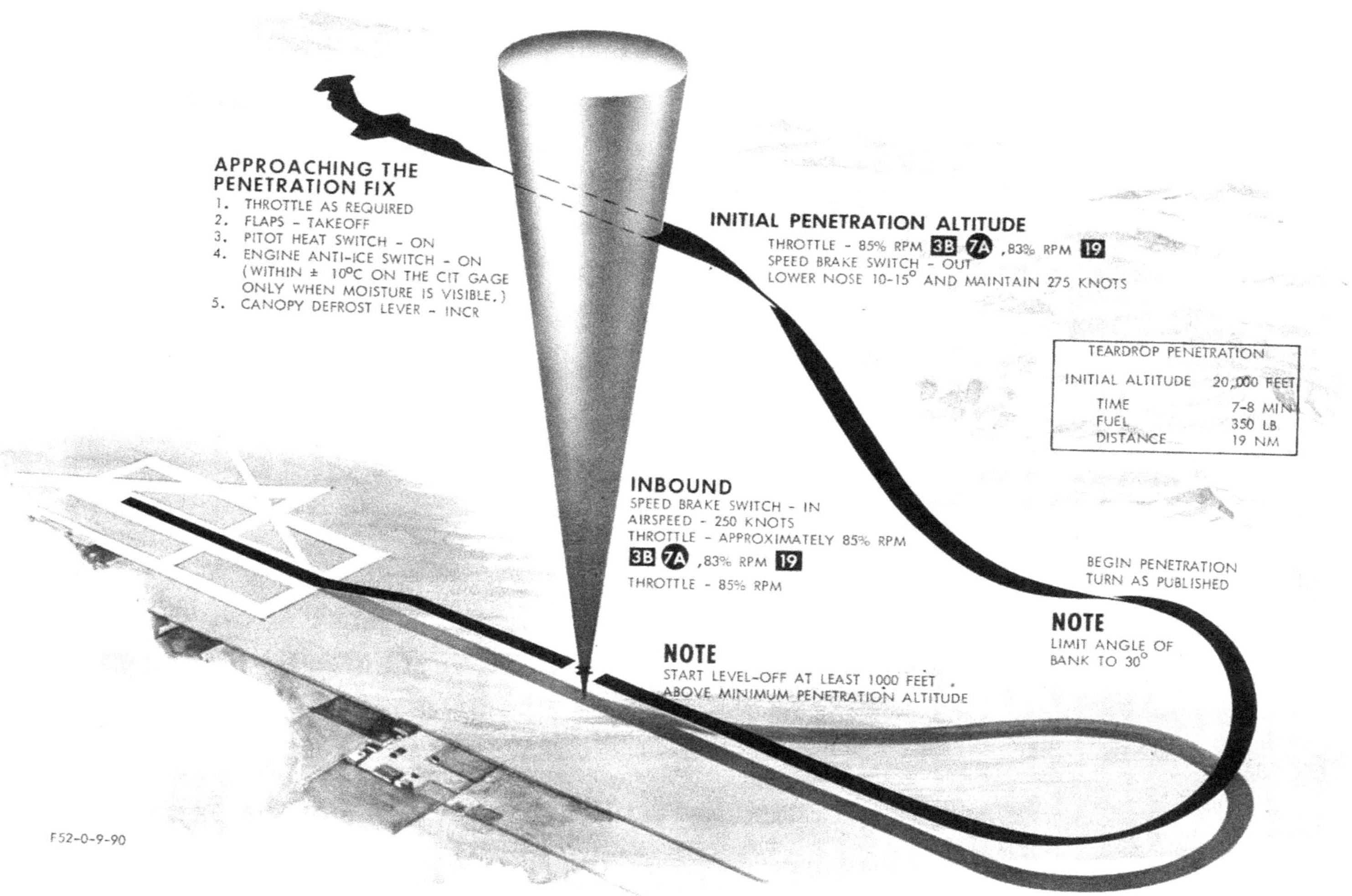
TYPICAL PENETRATION VOR/TACAN
APPROACHING THE
PENETRATION FIX
1. THROTTLE AS REQUIRED
2. FLAPS - TAKEOFF
3. PITOT HEAT SWITCH - ON
4. ENGINE ANTI-ICE SWITCH - ON
(WITHIN ± 10°C ON THE CIT GAGE
ONLY WHEN MOISTURE IS VISIBLE.)
5. CANOPY DEFROST LEVER - INCR
INITIAL PENETRATION ALTITUDE
THROTTLE - 85% RPM 3B 7A ,83% RPM 19
SPEED BRAKE SWITCH - OUT
LOWER NOSE 10-15° AND MAINTAIN 275 KNOTS
TEARDROP PENETRATION
INITIAL ALTITUDE 20,000 FEET
TIME 7-8 MIN
FUEL 350 LB
DISTANCE 19 NM
INBOUND
SPEED BRAKE SWITCH - IN
AIRSPEED - 250 KNOTS
THROTTLE - APPROXIMATELY 85% RPM
3B 7A ,83% RPM 19
THROTTLE - 85% RPM
BEGIN PENETRATION
TURN AS PUBLISHED
NOTE
LIMIT ANGLE OF
BANK TO 30°
NOTE
START LEVEL-OFF AT LEAST 1000 FEET
ABOVE MINIMUM PENETRATION ALTITUDE
F52-0-9-90

Figure 9-1

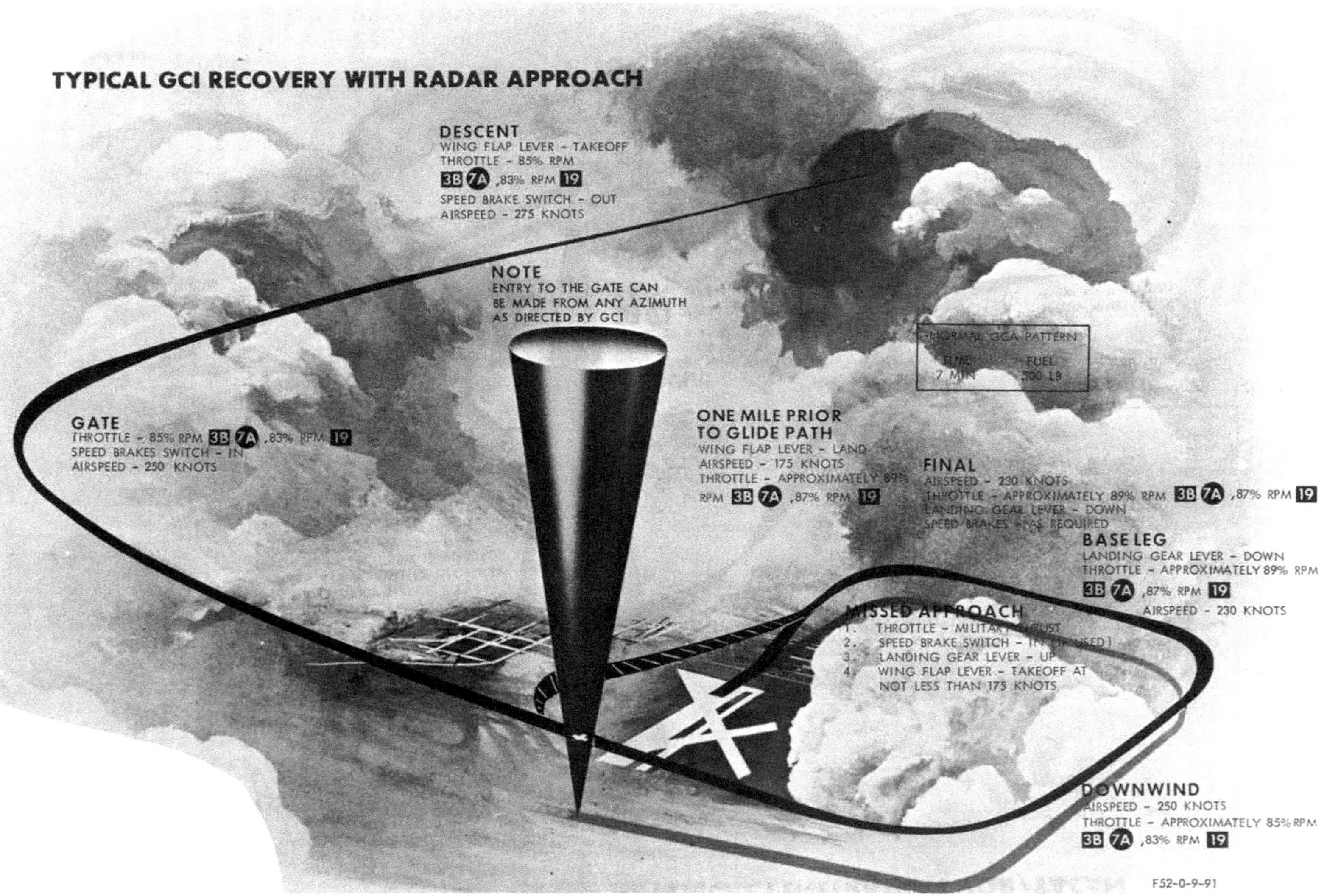
TYPICAL GCI RECOVERY WITH RADAR APPROACH
DESCENT
WING FLAP LEVER - TAKEOFF
THROTTLE - 85% RPM
3B 7A ,83% RPM 19
SPEED BRAKE SWITCH - OUT
AIRSPEED - 275 KNOTS
NOTE
ENTRY TO THE GATE CAN
BE MADE FROM ANY AZIMUTH
AS DIRECTED BY GCI
GATE
THROTTLE - 85% RPM 3B 7A ,83% RPM 19
SPEED BRAKES SWITCH - IN
AIRSPEED - 250 KNOTS
NORMAL GCA PATTERN
7 MIN
FUEL
ONE MILE PRIOR
TO GLIDE PATH
WING FLAP LEVER - LAND
AIRSPEED - 175 KNOTS
THROTTLE - APPROXIMATELY 89%
RPM 3B 7A ,87% RPM 19
FINAL
AIRSPEED - 230 KNOTS
THROTTLE - APPROXIMATELY 89% RPM 3B 7A ,87% RPM 19
LANDING GEAR LEVER - DOWN
SPEED BRAKES - AS REQUIRED
BASE LEG
LANDING GEAR LEVER - DOWN
THROTTLE - APPROXIMATELY 89% RPM
3B 7A ,87% RPM 19
AIRSPEED - 230 KNOTS
MISSED APPROACH
3. LANDING GEAR LEVER - UP
4. WING FLAP LEVER - TAKEOFF AT
NOT LESS THAN 175 KNOTS
DOWNWIND
AIRSPEED - 250 KNOTS
THROTTLE - APPROXIMATELY 85% RPM
3B 7A ,83% RPM 19
F52-0-9-91

Figure 9-2

TYPICAL ILS APPROACH

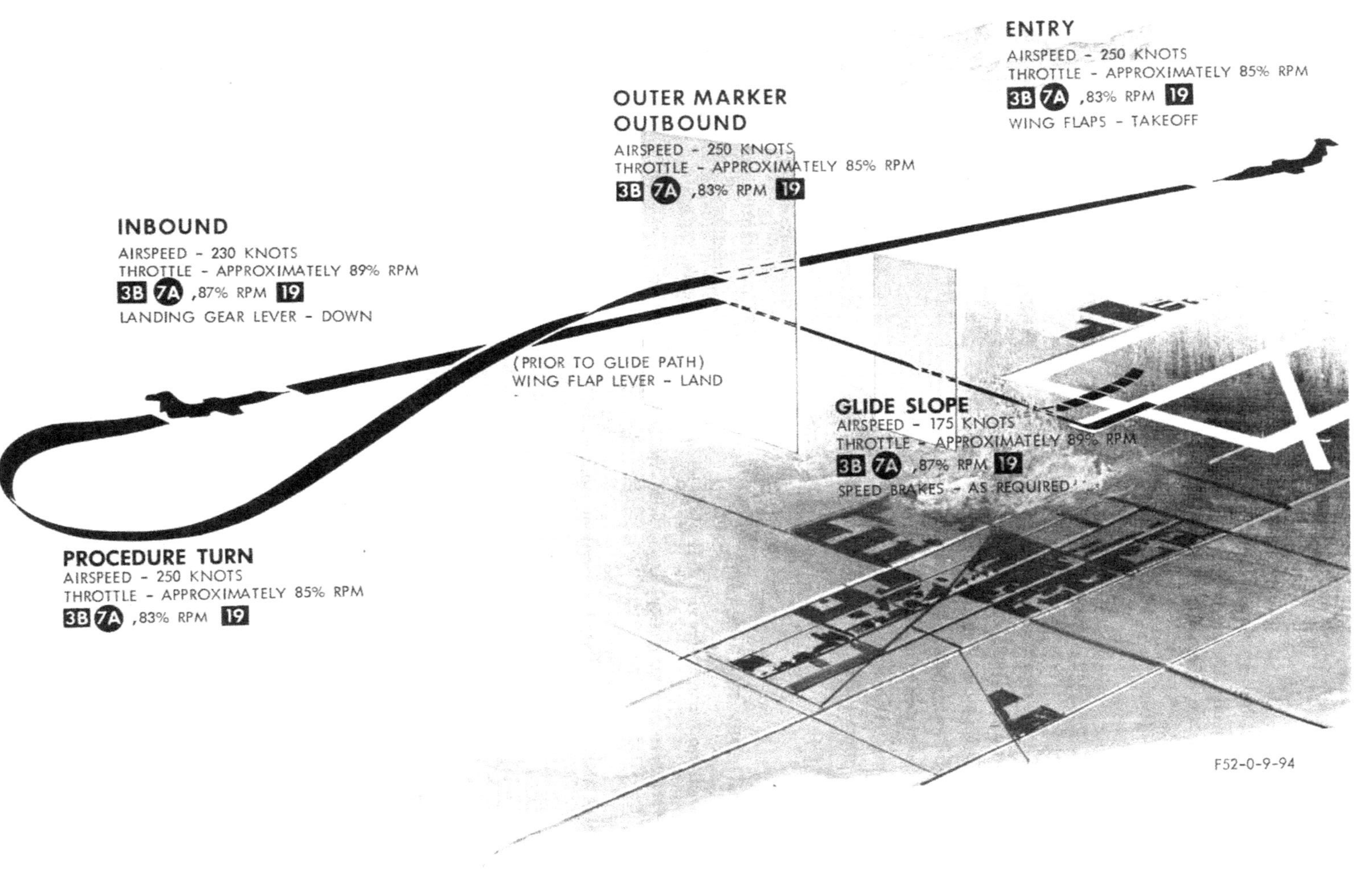
ENTRY
AIRSPEED - 250 KNOTS
THROTTLE - APPROXIMATELY 85% RPM
3B 7A ,83% RPM 19
WING FLAPS - TAKEOFF
OUTER MARKER OUTBOUND
AIRSPEED - 250 KNOTS
THROTTLE - APPROXIMATELY 85% RPM
3B 7A ,83% RPM 19
INBOUND
AIRSPEED - 230 KNOTS
THROTTLE - APPROXIMATELY 89% RPM
3B 7A ,87% RPM 19
LANDING GEAR LEVER - DOWN
(PRIOR TO GLIDE PATH)
WING FLAP LEVER - LAND
GLIDE SLOPE
AIRSPEED - 175 KNOTS
THROTTLE - APPROXIMATELY 89% RPM
3B 7A ,87% RPM 19
SPEED BRAKES - AS REQUIRED
PROCEDURE TURN
AIRSPEED - 250 KNOTS
THROTTLE - APPROXIMATELY 85% RPM
3B 7A ,83% RPM 19
F52-0-9-94

Figure 9-3

NIGHT FLYING.

During night flights this aircraft does not present any special problems or require unusual techniques except during landing. During final approach at night, the runway lights are reflected in the windshield panels and disorientation can easily occur. This condition is especially noticeable from the aft cockpit. Utilize all possible clues to attitude and flight path, ignoring runway light reflection in the windshield.

COLD WEATHER OPERATIONS.

The success of low-temperature operation depends primarily upon the preparations made during the postflight inspection in anticipation of the requirements for operation on the following day. The procedures outlined should be followed during outdoor operation to expedite the preflight inspection and to ensure satisfactory operation of the aircraft and its systems during the next flight.

BEFORE ENTERING THE AIRCRAFT.

1. Have all protective covers and duct plugs removed.
2. Perform exterior inspection as outlined in Section II.
3. Check the entire aircraft for freedom from snow and ice.

WARNING

Loss of lift and stalls may result if the aircraft is not adequately cleaned of all snow, frost, and ice. Do not attempt to take off if there is any ice, frost, or snow on the aircraft.

4. Place heater duct in cockpit for 5 minutes when temperature is below −30°F.
5. The pressure of both hydraulic accumulators will drop with temperature. A pressure as low as 700 psi can be expected at −65°F.
6. Inspect plastic airspeed and altitude pitot lines for cracking at temperatures of −30°F and below.

BEFORE STARTING ENGINE.

Make normal checks as outlined in Section II.

STARTING ENGINE.

Make normal start as outlined in Section II except use both start switches.

Note

- During low ambient temperature engine starts, excessive engine oil pressure for a short period of time is a normal condition and will not of itself cause engine damage.
- Consistently successful starts cannot be expected with fuel temperatures of 10°F or below.

CAUTION

The aircraft will slide forward on ice with the brakes locked at approximately 84-88 percent rpm 3B 7A and 83-87 percent rpm 19. Make certain the area ahead of the aircraft is clear before advancing the throttle.

WARMUP AND GROUND CHECK.

Use normal procedures.

Note

It will require 2-4 minutes to obtain warm air from the defroster. If immediate defrosting or deicing is required, turn rain remover ON until the left windscreen and canopy have cleared, then turn rain remover OFF.

1. Check hydraulic pressure, oil pressure, and engine instruments. Allow oil pressure to decrease within limits before taxiing.
2. Check flight instruments.

WARNING

Make sure all instruments have warmed up sufficiently to ensure normal operation. Check for sluggish instrument indications during taxiing.

TAXI INSTRUCTIONS.

1. Taxi at slow speed over rough snow-packed surfaces.

2. Allow more distance than allowed on a cleared surface to bring the aircraft to a stop.

3. Successful taxiing can be accomplished in snow up to 6 inches deep.

Note

Only nosewheel steering should be used in deep snow. Braking will cause the snow to melt and moisture to form which may later freeze on the wheels.

BEFORE TAKEOFF.

Make normal before-takeoff check as outlined in Section II.

Note

Canopy defrosting air should be operated at highest temperature consistent with pilot comfort at all times. This will minimize the possibility of windshield and canopy fogging caused by extreme temperature differentials accompanying an engine failure or rapid descent from altitude.

TAKEOFF.

Be prepared for an increase in takeoff distance if runway is covered with water, soft snow or slush.

CAUTION

Acceleration is very rapid in cold weather. Make certain the aircraft is rolling straight down the runway before selecting afterburner.

AFTER TAKEOFF.

Follow after-takeoff procedure as outlined in Section II. Climb performance will be improved during cold weather operation at lower altitudes. Follow recommended climb speeds as given in the climb charts in Appendix I.

ENGINE OPERATION IN FLIGHT.

Use normal procedures for engine operation during flight in cold weather.

LANDING.

Use normal landing procedures. Refer to Landing on Slippery Runways in Section II.

STOPPING THE ENGINE.

The engine is shut down in the normal manner.

BEFORE LEAVING THE AIRCRAFT.

Use normal procedures to secure the aircraft.

HOT WEATHER AND DESERT OPERATIONS.

Hot weather and desert procedures differ from normal procedures mainly in that additional precautions must be taken to protect the airplane from damage due to high temperature and dust. Particular care should be taken to prevent the entrance of sand into the various airplane components and systems; engine, fuel system, pitot—static systems, etc. All filters should be checked more frequently than under normal conditions. Units incorporating plastic and rubber parts should be protected as much as possible from wind-blown sand and excessive temperatures. The canopy and electronic compartment should be protected from the sun by use of a canopy-electronic compartment sun shade. Tires should be checked frequently for signs of blistering, etc.

TAKEOFF.

Takeoff distances will be increased during high ambient temperatures. Check takeoff distances required for existing conditions by referring to takeoff charts in the Appendix I.

CAUTION

It is imperative that takeoff be made at the recommended speed. More than the usual takeoff distance will be required to obtain takeoff speed during high ambient air temperature. Therefore, exercise caution against lifting off the runway too soon.

APPROACH AND LANDING.

Monitor rate of descent closely on approach. Do not allow rate of descent to exceed the 700-800 feet per minute recommended during the final portion of the approach. Be prepared to use afterburner if necessary. Refer to discussions in Section VI and the charts in Appendix I pertaining to variations in performance for changes in temperature, weight, and altitude.

Warships DVD Series

WARSHIPS DVD SERIES

WARSHIPS: LEYTE GULF TO TOKYO BAY

LEYTE GULF TO TOKYO BAY

THE AIRCRAFT CARRIER WAR 1944-1945

WARSHIPS DVD VOL. 6

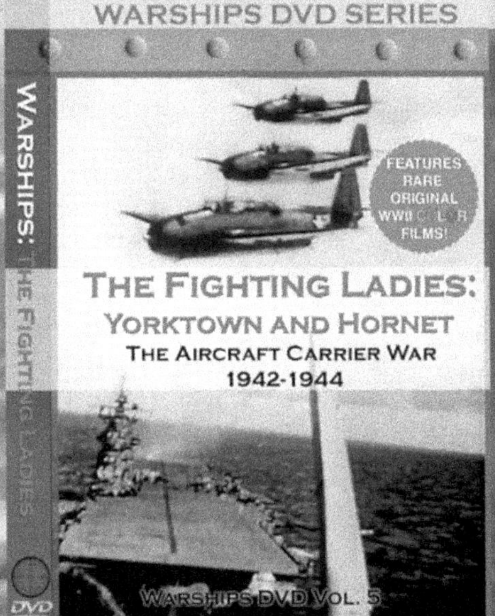

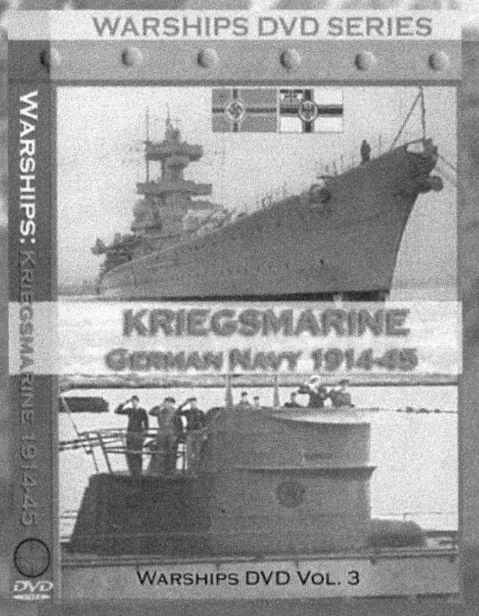

Now Available!

AIRCRAFT AT WAR DVD SERIES

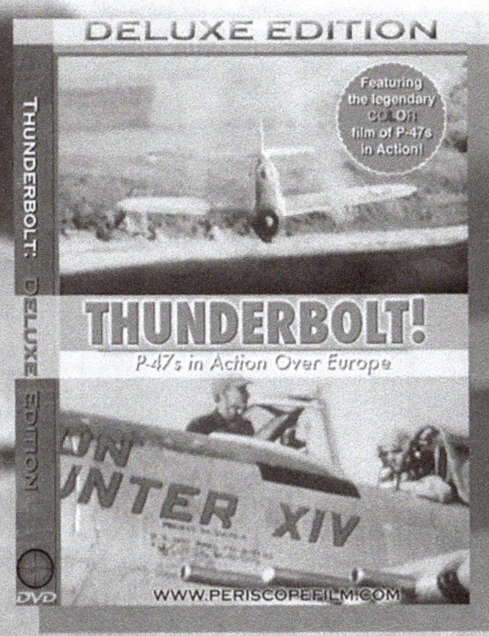

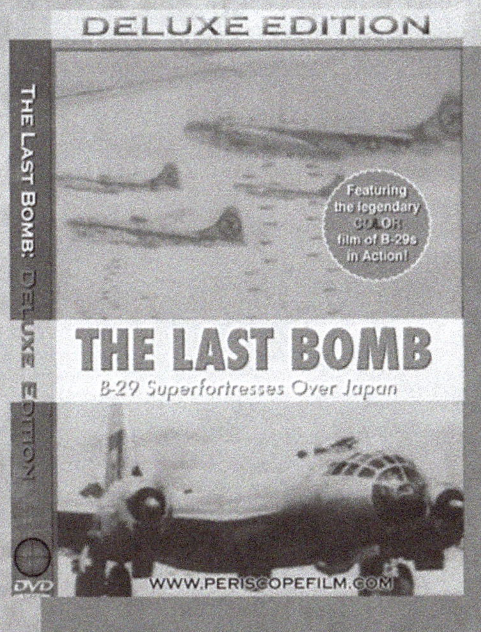

NOW AVAILABLE!

ISBN 978-1-935700-47-0
WWW.PERISCOPEFILM.COM

www.ingramcontent.com/pod-product-compliance
Lightning Source LLC
Chambersburg PA
CBHW050405110426
42812CB00006BA/1807

* 9 7 8 1 9 4 0 4 5 3 4 2 2 *